D0490295

Engineer's Handbook of Management Techniques

Editor: DENNIS LOCK

Foreword by
Sir Arnold Lindley DSc, CGIA, CEng,
Chairman, Engineering Industry Training Board
Former Chairman, Council of Engineering Institutions

A Gower Press Handbook

First published in Great Britain by Gower Press Limited, Epping, Essex

ISBN 0 7161 0152 1

Set in eleven on thirteen Times and printed by
Lowe & Brydone (Printers) Ltd,
Thetford, Norfolk

Contents

Foreword by Sir Arnold Lindley, DSc, CGIA, CEng.

PART ONE: FINANCIAL MANAGEMENT 1

1 Management of Working Capital
Martin S Grass 3
Control of liquidity 4
Control of cash 8
Sources of short-term finance 13
Short-term investments 17

2 Evaluating Capital Expenditure
Balint Bodroghy 19
Need for evaluation 20
Context of evaluation 21
Techniques of evaluation 25
Risk and return 36
Presentation of the results 41
Summary 43

3 Interpreting Company Financial Reports
W P Ridley 45
Coverage of the published accounts 45
Management performance standards 51
Summary 55

4 Cost Accounting
Ernest Laidler 56
Costing methods and techniques 57
Classification of costs 60

Cost units and cost centres 63
Material costs 63
Labour costs 65
Overheads 67
Factory job costing 69
Process costing 71
Work in progress 71
Marginal costing 72
Standard costing and variance analysis 76

5 Budgetary Planning and Control
M J Wright 81
Planning 82
Control 83
Budgets 86
Budget preparation 89
Performance reporting 97
Project cost control 102
Long-term profit planning 105

PART TWO: MARKETING MANAGEMENT 107

6 Techniques of Industrial Market Research
E P Danger 109
Marketing for the engineering industry 111
The basic marketing problem 114
New products 117
Improving sales 119
Improving profits 120
Some general problems 123
The essentials of industrial market research 125
How industrial market research works 127

7 Market Economics and Pricing
Leon Simons 130
Standard and non-standard products 131
Market price 132
Conventional pricing 134
Finding the market price 138
Summary 141

8	**Selling Industrial Products**	
	D W Newill	143
	Establishing a sales policy and budget	143
	Selling outlets	146
	Publicity and advertising	150
	Organising and managing the technical sales force	154
	Screening customer inquiries	157
	Preparation of proposals and quotations	160
	Useful check-lists	161
9	**Sales Engineering**	
	John Fenton	165
	The sales engineer as a person	167
	Planning sales engineering activities	172
	Reports and customer records	178
	Inquiries from advertising	186
	Quotations and proposals	188
	After-sales service	193
PART THREE: ADMINISTRATION		195
10	**Company Law and Patents**	
	F W Rose	197
	Legal status of a public limited company	197
	Formation of a public limited company	198
	Capital and shares	201
	Directors	204
	Meetings	207
	Dividends	207
	Patents	208
11	**Contracts between Companies**	
	F W Rose	214
	Offer and acceptance	214
	Consideration	217
	Form of a contract	218
	Capacity to make a contract	219
	Mistakes in the contract	220
	Misrepresentation	222

Damages for breach of contract 223
Specific performance 226

12 Organisation and Methods
H W Mount 227
Contribution of organisation and methods studies 228
Conduct of organisation and methods work 230
Use of clerial work measurement 237
Document control 241
Selection of office equipment 245

13 Planning Office Space
P Lebus 248
Information 249
Analysis 250
Solution 258
Implementation 261
Government legislation 261

14 Data Processing Applications
D A Barrett 267
What is a computer? 267
Computers in management 270
Applications 273
The management of computers 277

PART FOUR: PERSONNEL, HUMAN RELATIONS AND TRAINING 285

15 Manpower Planning
E S M Chadwick 287
Role and content of manpower planning 288
Time-scale 291
Limitations of manpower planning 292
Analysis and forecasting 295
Control and evaluation 305
Conclusion 306

16 Recruitment and Selection
F A Sneath 308
Main steps 308
Identifying job requirements through job analysis 310
Reaching candidates 312
Assessing candidates 314
The use of consultants 319

17 Payment Structures and Incentives
G L Buckingham 321
Principles of payment 322
Design of the payment system 325
Relating wages and performance 329
Relating salaries and performance 333
Implementing a new pay system 335

18 Legal Aspects of the Employer/Employee Relationship
F W Rose 341
Contracts of employment 342
Payment of wages and salaries 344
Termination of employment 349
Damages for wrongful dismissal 353
Provision of references 355
Restraining employees from disclosing trade secrets 357
Redundancy payments 359

19 The Industrial Relations Act 1971
Darek Celinski 363
General principles 364
Main elements 365
Institutions 366
Protection for the community in emergency situations 371
Rights of employees 372
Concept of unfair industrial practice 375
Collective bargaining 376
Code of Industrial Relations Practice 378

20 Management by Objectives
Frederick A Rose 391

The management by objectives system 393
Business strategies and plans 394
Setting unit and functional objectives 398
Unit action plans 406
The individual manager's contribution 410
Management development 419
Characterisics of successful MBO 423

21 Training within Companies
Darek Celinski 427
Induction training 428
Apprentice training 432
Non-apprentice training 435
Operator training 435
Training to maximise yield from changes 441
Training to bring about improvements 444
Supervisor training and development 447
Management training and development 451
Questions 456

22 Speaking, Reports and Meetings
Gordon Bell 460
Speaking 460
Preparing an effective talk 462
Speaking style 467
Speaking for a special occasion 471
Some thoughts 473
Reports 473
Circulation and distribution 474
Physical layout 476
Information by numbers 478
Visual aids 478
Language in reports 478
Report writing check-list 483
Meetings 485
Preparation for the meeting 487
Conduct of the meeting 488
Chairmanship – reminders 490

PART FIVE: PRODUCTION MANAGEMENT 493

23 Value Engineering
John F A Gibson and Richard Dick-Larkam 495
Definition 496
What is value? 496
Unnecessary cost 497
Involvement 499
The team 499
The job plan 500
Organising a value programme 508
Results 511

24 Planning New Production Facilities
Alan J Clarke 512
Production objectives 513
Information 513
Layout 520
Installation and commissioning 526
Evaluating the results 530

25 Project Scheduling
Dennis Lock 532
Project objectives 532
Seven steps for practical scheduling 534

26 Production Control
H Beddard 550
Definition 550
Formulating the production programme 553
Scheduling 553
Shop loading 555
Aids to the quantitative aspects of production control 566
Controlling: batch-production versus flow-production 569

27 Materials Management
Peter Baily and David Farmer 570
Purchasing and cost reduction 571
Sourcing 575

Stock control and ABC analysis 580
Expediting 583
Materials handling equipment and techniques 587

28 Work Study
B D Speed 589
Purpose of work study 589
Work study techniques – method study 590
Work study techniques – work measurement 596
Industrial relations and the introduction of change 606
Conducting work study in an engineering company 609

29 Quality Control
R M McRobb 614
Management attitudes and expectations 615
Establishing standards and specifications 619
Development and testing 623
Process control and inspection 626
Supplier evaluation 632

30 Planned Maintenance
Adrian F Stedman 637
Breakdown maintenance 637
Planned maintenance 638
Control of scheduled maintenance routines 645
Planned rectification and shop loading 650
Summary 655

Illustrations

1:1 Cash budget 10
1:2 Sources and uses of funds 12
2:1 Typical cash flow transient of a capital investment project 27
2:2 Table of discount factors 31
2:3 Calculation of DCF rate by reiteration 33
2:4 Equivalent mean investment period 36
2:5 Subjective assessment of probability 39
2:6 Decision-branches 42
3:1 Abbreviated balance sheet 47
3:2 Abbreviated profit and loss account 49
3:3 Standard ratios of company performance 52
4:1 Costing methods and techniques 58
4:2 Cost and profit sructure 61
4:3 Form of job card 70
5:1 Budget preparation 90
5:2 Direct labour-hours analysis 94
5:3 Profit budget performance report – summary 99
5:4 Profit budget performance report – variance analysis 100
5:5 Profit budget performance report – capital employed 101
5:6 Project status report 104
5:7 Project completion report 105
6:1 Home deliveries of UK machine tools 110
6:2 Deliveries of numerically-controlled metalworking machine tools 111
6:3 Construction materials of boats exhibited at the International Boat Show 113
6:4 Manufacture of locomotives 114

6:5	British Rail stock of locomotives	115
6:6	Product life-cycle	117
6:7	UK production of cars, commercial vehicles and agricultural tractors	122
7:1	Example of a table ranking sample product quotations	140
8:1	Controls for selling techniques	148
9:1	Table determining frequency of sales calls	174
9:2	Weekly call plan – SCRS system	179
9:3	Customer record file, yearly call plan, salesman's weekly work case and sales forecasting sheet	180
9:4	Weekly call analysis visit report and personal performance record – SCRS system	181
9:5	Monthly prospect list – SCRS system	184
9:6	Example of a typical quotation and proposal	188
9:7	The selling proposal	190
12:1	Flow diagram	232
13:1	Creation of a block layout	252
13:2	Relationship diagram	253
13:3	Typical open-space or landscaped office	254
13:4	Open-plan office	256
13:5	Characteristics of layouts	258
13:6	Landscaped layout	260
14:1	Basic arrangement of a computer	268
15:1	A procedure for manpower planning	290
15:2	Manpower planning check-list	293
15:3	Age analysis	296
15:4	Manpower forecast sheet	298
15:5	Derivation of the quantitative five-year forecast for a function	299
15:6	Recruitment Targets 1972, 1973	301
15:7	Forward projections of the working population of the UK, 1967–1981	302
15:8	Index approach for assessing trends in contribution made by manpower	306
17:1	Form of job sample ranking by paired comparison	327
17:2	Analysis of staff salaries	336
17:3	Analysis of wages	338
19:1	The Industrial Relations Act 1971	367
19:2	The system of expert and judicial institutions	369

19:3	The Code of Industrial Relations Practice	381
20:1	Management by objectives as a dynamic system	394
20:2	Approach to determining business strategies	395
20:3	The tactical planning stage	397
20:4	Search and analysis process	401
20:5	Decision tree	404
20:6	Unit action plan	408
20:7	Planning framework	409
20:8	Results influence analysis	411
20:9	Typical results guide format	412
20:10	Typical results guide entries	413
20:11	Individual action plan	416
20:12	Basic review cycle	417
20:13	Management training process	421
20:14	Improving management performance	422
21:1	Induction training programme in outline	431
21:2	Typical learning curve	438
21:3	Typical systematic learning curve	438
21:4	Typical gain through systematic training	439
21:5	Outline plan of methods for management training and development	454
21:6	Estimated relative effectiveness of learning various instructional techniques	456
22:1	Value/time axes	468
22:2	Value and interest versus time	469
22:3	Four ways of presenting numerical results	479
23:1	Function/cost analysis chart	504
24:1	Information phase	515
24:2	Sales forecast	516
24:3	Gopertz curve	517
24:4	Production method related to quantity	519
24:5	Product quantity/variety relationship	523
24:6	Block layout	524
24:7	Detailed layout of jobbing machine shop, using standard symbols	527
25:1	Check-list for an effective project schedule	535
25:2	Some factors to be considered in project schedule preparation	536
25:3	The seven steps	538

25:4	Comparison between bar chart and network diagram	541
25:5	Concept of time-limited and resource-limited schedules	545
25:6	Comparison between resource aggregation, resource-limited and time-limited schedules	547
25:7	Contribution of scheduling to project control	549
26:1	Production control procedure	552
26:2	Master schedule	554
26:3	Part of shop loading chart	557
26:4	Works documentation – route card	558
26:5	Works documentation – job card	559
26:6	Works documentation – material requisition (stores)	560
26:7	Works documentation – material requisition (costs)	561
26:8	Works documentation – stores receipt	562
26:9	Works documentation – loading and progress advice	563
26:10	Progress chart	565
26:11	Economic batch quantity	568
27:1	The 80/20 law: simplified pattern of purchase expenditure	573
27:2	Typical food industry usage value curves	574
27:3	Supplier evaluation	577
27:4	Usage value classification of stock items	581
27:5	EOQ table	584
28:1	Process charting symbols	592
28:2	Flow process chart	593
28:3	Multiple activity chart	595
28:4	String diagram	596
28:5	Typical time study observation sheet	598
28:6	Simplified PMTS	602
28:7	Basic work data (BWD)	605
28:8	Example of measurement technique identification	611
29:1	Economics of quality of design	616
29:2	Costs of quality of conformance	617
29:3	Real cost of quality	627
30:1	Plant maintenance analysis sheet – mechanical plant	643
30:2	Plant maintenance analysis sheet – building	644

30:3 Economic planned maintenance and frequency curve 646
30:4 Standard electrical inspection sheet layout 647
30:5 Standard mechanical inspection sheet layout 648
30:6 Standard grouped inspection sheet layout 649
30:7 Labour control 651
30:8 Cost control 653
30:9 Planned maintenance stabilisation curve 654

Notes on Contributors

D A Barrett (Data Processing Applications) is Manager of Systems Development, K and H Business Consultants Limited. He graduated from London University and spent six years working for IBM Limited, firstly in general computer programming and then in the inventory management group. He became their principal United Kingdom specialist in inventory management techniques. After leaving IBM in 1967. Mr Barrett joined K and H Business Consultants in London, where he is responsible for the development of computer software packages. He has also worked in America, France, Israel and South Africa.

Peter Baily (Materials management) is a lecturer in Business Studies at Glamorgan Polytechnic and Senior Associate of David Farmer and Associates. Mr Baily has extensive experience of purchasing and supply work and is co-author, with David Farmer, of *Managing Materials in Industry*, Gower Press, 1972, and *Purchasing and Supply Management*, Chapman and Hall, 1969. He has a B Sc (Econ) degree and is a Member of the Institute of Purchasing and Supply.

H Beddard (Production control) is Chairman and Managing Director of A.I.M. Consultants Limited. Before entering consultancy Mr Beddard served an engineering apprenticeship, followed by production engineering and management appointments in light engineering, aircraft, motor manufacture and machine tool industries. He was Director of a large production management school and has extensive lecturing experience. Mr Beddard has a B Sc and is a Chartered Engineer; he is a Member of the Institution of Production Engineers, a Member of the Institute of Works Managers, a Fellow of the Institute of Materials Handling, a fellow of the Institute of Work Study Practitioners, a Fellow of the Institute of Production Control and a Fellow of the Institute of Directors.

Gordon Bell (Speaking, reports and meetings) is the senior partner of Gordon Bell and Partners, a group of specialists who teach communications. Gordon Bell began as a scientist and a writer and developed his teaching methods after intensive study of the needs of people in industry. His own experience ranges from floor sweeper to Company Chairman. Gordon Bell and Partners conduct successful courses not only in the United Kingdom but also in many countries abroad.

B G Bodroghy (Evaluating capital expenditure) is an industrial marketing and planning consultant and director of Peter Ward Associates (Interplan) Limited and associated companies. After graduating in mechanical engineering at the University of Toronto he did research in nuclear engineering at Imperial College, London and then became assistant editor of *Engineering*. He then worked for the Canadian company, Air Liquide where he was project engineer and was later responsible for creating subsidiaries, negotiation of licences and acquisitions, and expanding the company's activities outside existing lines of business. Mr Bodroghy entered consultancy in 1964, applying financial, econometric and operational research methods to corporate and regional planning.

G L Buckingham (Payment structures and incentives) is General Manager, Personnel, with Gallaher Limited and a director of North, Paul & Associates Limited. Mr Buckingham obtained an honours degree at Corpus Christi College, Cambridge and the Diploma in Personnel Management Studies of the London School of Economics. He has run national seminars on wage systems and productivity bargaining and is co-author of the successful *Productivity Bargaining and Wage Systems* (Gower Press, 1969).

Darek Celinski (The Industrial Relations Act 1971 and Training within companies) is Personnel Manager of Herbert-Ingersoll Limited. Before his present appointment Mr Celinski was a member of the academic staff at Llangattock Park, the Conference and Training Centre of the British Steel Corporation, South Wales Group. Prior to that he was a training officer in the Aviation Division of Smiths Industries Limited where he initiated and developed a succession of training schemes for experienced designers, technical specialists, operator training instructors, supervisors and managers. Mr Celinski is a Member of the Institute of Personnel Management.

E S M Chadwick (Manpower planning) is a director of Technical and Management Consultants Limited. He is a Fellow of the Chartered Institute of Secretaries, a member of the British Institute of Management and a Member of the Institute of Personnel Management. Mr Chadwick has had a varied experience in industrial and personnel management at home and abroad; as Manager, Manpower Reserch and Planning for the British Petroleum Group he was involved with pioneering the development of manpower planning in companies.

Alan J Clarke (Planning new production facilities) is the Projects Manager, Productivity Services Group, Honeywell Limited. The projects section provides an internal consultancy service for Honeywell Scottish Factories, specialising in the implementation of production and management techniques. Previously he was Manager of the Medical Division and subsequently, Factory Manager at Honeywell's Hemel Hempstead plant. An engineer by training, following a technical apprenticeship, he commenced his career as a contracts engineer handling instrument and automatic control contracts for power stations and process plant.

E P Danger (Techniques of industrial market research) is the Managing Director of Technical Market Research Limited, specialising in industrial market research in the engineering industry. Mr Danger began his career in selling and marketing insurance and after war service he joined an export marketing organisation handling industrial products and capital goods. In the early 1950s he became involved in industrial market research during its early growth period and in 1959 set up his own market research business. Mr Danger has recently been elected the first Fellow of the British Industrial Marketing Association; he is also a member of the Industrial Marketing Research Association and the British Institute of Management and the author of *Using Colour to Sell* (Gower Press) as well as various articles on selling and marketing.

Richard Dick-Larkam (Value engineering) is Project Manager Central Productivity Services, The British Oxygen Company Limited. He graduated from London University with an honours B Sc (Eng) and served as an Engineer Officer in the Royal Air Force Volunteer Reserve. Mr Dick-Larkam has been a works manager in several companies and his experience includes that of Development, Quality Control and Site Manager in the British Oxygen Company Limited. He is a Fellow of the Institute of Mechanical Engineers, a Fellow of the Welding Institute, a past Chairman of the North West London Productivity Association, Vice-President and Director of the West London Productivity Association Limited, and a Member of the Institute of Value Management.

David Farmer (Materials management) is Principal of David Farmer and Associates and specialises in training consultancy in the purchasing and management of materials. He was formerly Senior Lecturer in Purchasing at Slough College and has an M Sc degree. He has many years' experience in his specialist field and is co-author, with Peter Baily, of *Managing Materials in Industry*, (Gower Press, 1971), and *Purchasing Principles and Techniques,* (the Institute of Purchasing and Supply).

John Fenton (Sales engineering) is Director-General of the Institution of Sales Engineers. Apart from being a Fellow of the Institution he is also a member of the Institute of Marketing and the Institute of Materials Handling. Mr Fenton is a director of Structured Training Limited and writes and lectures on his subject.

John F A Gibson (Value engineering) is a member of the staff of the Production Director of Osram (GEC) Limited. After graduating from Southampton University, with a B Sc and a B Sc (Eng), Mr Gibson worked in commercial engineering with the BTH Company Limited before working in management services, including value analysis. He was a consultant in value analysis with AEI Limited before his present appointment. Mr Gibson is a Member of the Institution of Electrical Engineers.

Martin S Grass (Management of working capital) has spent most of his working life in journalism and was for several years chief accountant of a major industrial research organisation. Apart from his management experience, he gained first-hand knowledge of the internal organisation of the accountancy profession during his employment in the Institute of Cost and Management Accountants where he was editor of the ICMA monthly journal, *Management Accounting*. He is now editor of *Accountants Weekly* and has edited the book *Control of Working Capital*, (Gower Press).

Ernest Laidler (Cost accounting) is a Lecturer in cost and management accountancy at Liverpool Polytechnic. He recently retired from industry after more than forty years' experience in a variety of costing and accountancy functions and is a Fellow of the Institute of Cost and Management Accountants. Mr Laidler is an Examiner for the Society of Commercial Accountants and the Institute of Purchasing and Supply, and a Moderator in costing for the London Chamber of Commerce. He is a member of the ICMA's Terminology Committee and the author of *Suggested Answers* to the Institute's examination questions on cost and management accountancy.

Peter Lebus (Planning office space) was for six years responsible for the daily operations of Space Planning Services Limited, and for the development of new office planning techniques. He also lectures and writes on office space planning. Previously, he had spent ten years in US and British industry working in production, O & M and computer studies. His BA is in Mechanical Sciences from Cambridge

University. Mr Lebus has recently become Managing Director of C E Planning Limited, a subsidiary of Design Research Unit.

Dennis Lock (Editor and author of chapter on project scheduling) is internal adviser on project management systems to the Engineering Division of Selection Trust Limited, the international mining finance company. Previously he was for five years Contracts Control Manager in the Medical Division of Honeywell Controls Limited, followed by three years as Manager, Engineering Administrative Services, Herbert–Ingersoll Limited. After training as a physicist Mr Lock joined the Applied Electronic Laboratories of the General Electric Company Limited. He has a very wide industrial experience embracing sub-miniature electronics, giant machine tools and mining engineering, and he has undertaken consultancy work in Europe and the United States. He is the author of *Project Management* and *Industrial Scheduling Techniques* (Gower Press, 1968 and 1971), and has also edited the successful *Director's Guide to Management Techniques*.

R M McRobb (Quality control) is a management consultant specialising in quality assurance and training. He has over thirty years of experience in all aspects of inspection and quality control in various industries and lectures widely in his field. He is a Member of the Institution of Mechanical Engineers, a Fellow of the Institute of Quality Assurance (lately a Council Member), and a Senior Member of the American Society for Quality Control.

H W Mount (Organisation and methods) is a management consultant. Mr Mount has carried out and managed consultancy assignments over a wide cross-section of industry and commerce over the past sixteen years, prior to which he worked in senior line-management positions. Much of Mr Mount's consultancy work is in the field of organisation and administrative procedures. He is a Fellow of the Chartered Institute of Secretaries, a Member of the British Institute of Management and a Member of the Institute of Management Consultants.

D W Newill (Selling industrial products) held sales management positions in the Dunlop group of companies in the United Kingdom and overseas from 1953 to 1961 when he became market research and development manager and later marketing manager for a Dunlop division. In 1968 he joined Inplan Limited, marketing and management consultants, and was also appointed European Vice-President for a leading American research company. In 1970 he became a director of European Operations for the GFM-Chemie Institut of West Germany. Mr Newill was the founder chairman of the Industrial Marketing Research Association from 1963 to 1966 and of the Industrial Marketing Council from 1964 to 1968, and was a council member of the National Marketing Council from 1965 to 1971. He was also the president of the European Association for Industrial Marketing Research from 1965 to 1968, during which time he founded the European Technological Forecasting Association. In 1969 he was appointed research and industrial sales adviser to the European College of Marketing and Marketing Research.

W P Ridley (Interpreting company financial reports) is a consultant with Merrett Cyriax Associates, specialising in the financial appraisal of companies. He read law at Oxford and qualified as an accountant in 1961. He became a Fellow of the Institute of Chartered Accountants in 1972. He taught in Uganda and at Hendon Technical College before joining the Economic and Investment Research Department of the Bank of London and South America. Between 1965 and 1968 Mr Ridley worked for the Commonwealth Development Corporation.

Frederick A Rose (Management by objectives) is a director of Urwick International Limited with responsibility for operations outside Europe; he is also Chairman and President of Urwick International Incorporated, New York. After fifteen years experience with the Urwick Group as a professional consultant he has a particular knowledge of the steel, oil, engineering, transportation and retailing industries and his special interests and experience are in long-range planning, organisation studies, management development and training and the management of technology. He has worked in the United Kingdom, the United States, East Africa, South Africa, Australia,

South America and the Middle East and has presented seminars on management by objectives to business audiences in many parts of the world.

F W Rose (Company law and patents. Contracts between companies. Legal aspects of the employer/employee relationship) is Principal Lecturer in Law at the City of Birmingham Polytechnic where he is tutor for the University of London external LlB course. Mr Rose has an LlB from Birmingham University and an LlM from King's College, London. From 1960 to 1962 he was Assistant to the Secretary of Associated Iliffe Press Limited before spending a year at the Institute of Actuaries in a similar function. Mr Rose is an Associate of the Chartered Institute of Secretaries and he was called to the bar at Gray's Inn in 1958. His publications include *Personnel Management Law* (Gower Press) and the chapter on Employment Law in *Company Administration Handbook* (Gower Press), in addition to articles in *Secretaries Chronicle* and *Legal Executive*.

Leon Simons (Market economics and pricing) is a director of Foulks Lynch (Management Services) Limited. He is a graduate of Glasgow University and a chartered accountant with experience in the accountancy profession and industry as a company secretary, financial adviser and industrial consultant. Mr Simons specialises as a management consultant in finance and pricing and he lectures extensively on these subjects both in the United Kingdom and abroad.

F A Sneath (Recruitment and selection) is on the staff of the Department of Occupational psychology in Birkbeck College, London. After working in personnel selection in the Royal Air Force, Dr Sneath spent thirteen years in the Ministry of Labour as a psychologist. He joined Birkbeck College in 1964.

B D Speed (Work study) is a Management Consultant in the Management Economics Division of PERA. After studying engineering and graduating in commerce, Mr Speed spent several years in the electronics, textile and general engineering industries before becoming a consultant specialising in the practical application of work study in both production and service departments.

Adrian F Stedman (Planned maintenance) is a consulting engineer specialising in works engineering and plant maintenance. Before commencing in practice as a consultant Mr Stedman trained as an aeronautical engineer, transferring to production and plant engineering in 1950, after which he worked with PERA, Petfoods Limited, Brown and Polson Limited and the Plessey Company Limited. He lectures extensively and is a Fellow of the Institute of Plant Engineers and a Member of the Institution of Works Engineers.

M J Wright (Budgetary planning and control) is the finance director and company secretary of a company manufacturing special purpose machine tools. After graduating with Honours in Industrial Economics from Nottingham University in 1959, he served articles in accountancy for a period of three years. In 1965 he joined a large engineering company where he carried out special projects on standard costing and marginal costing, followed by periods as a Trading Unit Accountant and Financial Planning Manager at divisional level. Prior to his present position he was Financial Planning Manager for a company manufacturing large special-purpose machine tools. Mr Wright is an Associate of the Institute of Chartered Accountants and an Associate of the Institute of Cost and Management Accountants.

Foreword

by Sir Arnold Lindley, DSc, CGIA, CEng

Chairman, Engineering Industry Training Board
Former Chairman, Council of Engineering Institutions

This publication draws together the carefully written words of many authors on the subject of management techniques especially for the engineer. There is hardly an aspect of management, whether it concerns marketing, industrial relations or the use of money as distinct from accounting, which is not touched upon in one form or another.

It has been traditional that the various training courses for engineers have been more concerned with such subjects as design, factors of safety, use of materials and the more technical aspects of their work, but this handbook brings together these factors in their relationship to management in the sense that to be a successful engineer one simply also has to understand and practise the art of management. There is a wealth of information for the engineer to absorb and the various authors have presented their contributions in such a way as to provide interesting reading. To be a good manager as well as an engineer one needs to have the ability to manage as well as the possession of knowledge, and the handbook also provides a valuable help in this direction.

Every engineer who is in a progressive post should have a copy of this handbook readily available and he will find many answers to questions which will frequently arise in his career.

PART ONE

Financial Management

Chapter 1

Management of Working Capital

Martin S Grass, Editor, Accountants Weekly

In recent years insolvencies have begun to happen even in the best regulated businesses. The combination of world-wide shortages of liquidity, economic stagnation and growing interference of central governments in industry and commerce have revealed a number of hitherto unrecognised weaknesses in the managerial and financial structure of business organisations. The financial plight of some well-known and respected companies has shown very clearly that neither size nor past record can offer any long-term protection against failure.

The post-mortem of a bankrupt organisation will inevitably reveal that the victim perished as a result of a sudden and incurable deficiency of liquid resources. Such a diagnosis, however, is only a superficial description of the most obvious and visible symptoms of corporate death.

The real causes of the disease may lie hidden in the past history of weak management, inefficiency, and lack of basic controls combined with poor planning and wrong decision, often aggravated by successive periods of internal and external difficulties. Inflation, credit squeeze, punitive taxation, labour unrest and rapid changes in the industrial and social environment inevitably affect every business enterprise. But a well-managed, financially strong company has a better chance to survive these strains and stresses than a weak and inefficient firm.

While there is no cure for bad management (except instant dismissal of the bungling executives) many hazards of operating in a risk-prone environment can be avoided or, at least, minimised by efficient control of the company's liquid resources.

Cash is the only common denominator in all industries and in every type of business organisation. The management of cash is, therefore, the most convenient and generally applicable test of efficiency for executives at all levels. The cumulative impact of their decisions and actions on the company's liquidity will determine whether or not the enterprise can survive and grow in our complex and hazardous universe.

Control of liquidity

The notion of liquidity and the concept of working capital are closely related and the two terms are often used interchangeably.

Broadly speaking, liquidity is the company's ability to meet its short-term obligations when they fall due. This ability is a dynamic property which is largely conditioned by the following factors:

1 The actual amount of cash in the company's bank account.
2 Availability of negotiable instruments and short-term investments which can be converted into cash at short notice.
3 Availability and extent of bank overdraft facilities or ready access to other sources of temporary finance.
4 The inflow of receipts from customers as they settle their debts arising from the purchase of goods.
5 Willingness of suppliers to sell goods and services to the company on credit terms.
6 The proportion of funds invested in stocks of raw materials, work-in-progress and finished goods.

These six basic elements of liquidity also represent the main component parts of working capital, which can be described as the amount of money required for the financing of the firm's daily operations, provided partly by the company's owners (shareholders) and partly by its trading partners (creditors).

The accountant's definition of working capital as 'the excess of current assets over current liabilities' or 'net current assets' emphasises the *net* aspect of the concept, which means that the company is not expected to finance its operations entirely with its own funds.

Current assets consist partly of cash and near-cash (items 1 and 2) and partly of physical goods, services and claims which can be reasonably expected to be converted into cash within a year (items 4 and 6).

Current liabilities, which are claims against the company to be discharged within a year, consist of bank overdrafts, short-term loans (item 3) and trade creditors (item 5).

Liquidity and the operating cycle

The need for working capital arises primarily from the fact that the whole process of purchasing raw materials or goods, converting them through various production stages into finished products, selling the merchandise and collecting the revenue will normally take many weeks or months to complete. During that time, as each operating unit and department incurs various costs, the company must have enough cash in hand to pay for services received and goods purchased in order to maintain its day-to-day operations.

As mentioned before, some of these operations may be financed by willing suppliers who agree to the company's obtaining goods and services immediately in exchange for a promise to pay at a later date. When these obligations mature, the company can meet them by asking its bankers to provide overdraft facilities or temporary loans.

A proportion of expenditure incurred during the cycle of cash investment to cash receipt will have to be met from the company's own resources. Obviously, the longer the company can delay the outflow of its own funds and the more cash it can obtain from outside sources, the less of its own capital it will need. The time-delay factor is the main feature in the concept of operating cycle, which has been defined as the length of time which must elapse from the moment an expenditure for the purchase of raw material is made to the moment in which payments are received for the sale of the finished product.

The amount of working capital committed to investment in short-term assets depends to a large extent on the length of the operating cycle. The longer it takes to convert stocks and products into cash, the more capital will be needed during the whole 'waiting' period.

The length of the operating cycle varies from industry to industry and there can be significant differences between individual firms in the same sector of industry. The level of sales, the available production capacity, the turnover of stocks and the terms of credit granted and received will determine the rate at which cash flows in and out of the company. By manipulating these variables, management can effectively shorten the operating cycle, accelerate the inflow of cash and thus improve the company's liquid position.

Liquidity ratios

Management's primary task is to take all measures necessary to maintain and improve the company's profitability. Although in the short run liquid resources may produce higher revenue than capital assets, profitability is generally associated with long term investment in buildings, plant and machinery. The manipulation of liquidity is an expedient rather than a long-term objective.

A typical example of the expediency of manipulating liquid assets is the well-known practice of 'window dressing', in which many publicly quoted companies indulge every year. By accelerating the collection of debts and by repaying a temporary loan, the company can present a reassuring picture of financial health in its balance sheet. The fact that the loan will be re-activated immediately after the date of the balance sheet may escape the notice of an unsophisticated user of company accounts.

Uninformative and, in some cases, unintentionally misleading financial statements published by companies are currently the subject of lively discussion and it is almost certain that various steps will be taken to improve the quality of financial reporting for outsiders. In the meantime, users of company reports must exercise a great deal of caution in judging a company on the basis of information published for external consumption. In spite of their shortcomings, however, the balance sheets and other statutory accounts are extensively used in the calculation of various financial ratios.

Financial ratios are diagnostic tools, popular with management as well as investment analysts, bankers and shareholders in assessing the company's past performance and future prospects.

Interpretation of company financial reports, including the employment of ratio analysis, is discussed in Chapter 3. Briefly, any two figures found in a set of financial statements can be expressed as a ratio. Such an exercise, however, would not necessarily yield much information unless the results were obtained for a particular reason and the message conveyed by them fully understood by the user.

Information about the company's liquidity is usually obtained from its balance sheet. There are two ratios which measure the firm's ability to meet its short-term obligations: the ratio of current assets to current liabilities (the current ratio) and the ratio of 'quick' assets, that is, current assets less stocks, to current liabilities (the liquidity ratio).

Current ratio. The current ratio indicates the size of the company's short-term resources which are available for the payment of its current debts. Although broadly speaking this is a correct assumption, there are two limitations which should be taken into account when interpreting the current ratio.

Firstly, the ratio is valid only if the figures on which it is based do not appreciably change after the date of the balance sheet. While management can easily ascertain every significant variation in this ratio at frequent intervals, the position of outsiders who have no access to the company's internal information is less favourable. Normally, they have to wait for the next financial statement before they can discover whether any major changes in the current ratio have taken place. By that time management could have made temporary adjustments to any deterioration in the company liquid position by selling some of its investments, adjusting stock levels or accelerating the payment of debts.

Secondly, a current ratio that exceeds 1:1 implies, at first sight, that the company's debts are fully covered. It means that the value of current assets shown in the balance sheet represents funds available for the discharge of current liabilities. But such an assumption is not necessarily true. In a going concern the value of assets is subject to continual change in a situation that is dynamic through the operation of the business. A static relationship between current liabilities and current assets, which the balance sheet represents, may, therefore, be totally misleading. The static relationship will only hold good when a company is in liquidation at the date of the balance sheet, with its operations stopped, and its assets being sold to satisfy the demands of creditors.

One must also remember that the comparative liquidity of various assets depends on their nature and purpose. Stocks, for example, can be converted into cash in an emergency, but such a step could seriously disrupt production, cause delays in deliveries and make the financial situation worse than before. As stock values are often based on cost or estimates of their market price, their inclusion in the calculation of the current ratio also tends to distort its significance as the true measure of corporate liquidity.

Liquidity ratio. A somewhat sharper focus on the company's debt-paying ability can be achieved with the 'liquidity ratio' which is calculated in the same way as the current ratio, except that the stock figure is excluded. Debtors, short-term investments and cash are thought to represent those resources which are more directly relevant to the payment of current liabilities, assuming that the amounts owed to the company will be paid in full at their maturity date. A large, defaulting customer can make an appreciable difference to the company's debt-paying ability.

The ratio of cash to current liabilities gives the ultimate test of the company's ability to pay its debts on demand.

Ratio analysis should be based on as much information as it is possible to extract from financial data and even then it should be remembered that ratios are only symptoms of certain conditions. In order to interpret the language of symptoms, one must first learn the art of correct diagnosis.

Comparisons with the typical or average ratios for various industries or with pre-established targets should be used in such interpretation if the object of the exercise is to arrive at some valid conclusions about the company's past, present or future performance.

Control of cash

In a situation where the company has to meet its obligations but finds that its cash resources are insufficient, management must either resort to expensive borrowing or face the consequence of technical insolvency. Living dangerously with a chronic overdraft and large debts puts a severe strain on management and prevents a steady and healthy growth. On the other hand, playing safe by retaining large cash balances in the bank in the anticipation of future payments would be both inefficient and incompatible with the objective of profitable employment of the company's funds. The cost of unused cash is the cost of lost opportunities. The company which adopts such a policy must eventually end up on the scrap heap of corporate failures.

Cash budgets

The problem of reconciling the need for adequate liquidity with the objective of profitable use of resources can be solved only by systematic planning, control and frequent evaluation of the company's flow of funds. Corporate plans expressed in terms of future activities, costs and revenues are known as budgets. Their aim is to provide management with information which is the basis of their decisions relating to the achievement of the company's objectives. While operating budgets deal mainly with the expected costs of planned operations and the revenue which should result from them, cash budgets are designed to show whether the company will have enough money to carry out its plans.

Figure 1:1 shows a monthly cash budget for a company in which a seasonal pattern of sales is strongly marked. Most businesses have a distinctive rhythm of activities which fluctuate in sympathy with larger trade cycles, seasonal changes, fashions and other periodical increases and decreases in demand. The main result of these swings is an uneven, and often unpredictable, flow of cash in and out of business enterprise. The function of cash budgets is to anticipate these fluctuations and, if possible, achieve a more even spread of payments and receipts.

In Figure 1:1 a seasonal rise in activity is reflected in the estimated receipts and payments. The figures indicate that there are two peaks of activity: the company's disbursements are at their highest in March, while the flow of receipts reaches its peak in July. The cash budget takes into account the delays which will inevitably occur in the collection of revenues and in the payment of outstanding debts.

The operational peaks of activity will be shown in the production and sales budgets and, again, these two will not necessarily coincide. In fact, there will be probably a long period of stock build-up pre-

							£000
RECEIPTS	Jan	Feb	Mar	Apr	May	Jun	Jul
Opening balance	300	200	(50)	(325)	(450)	(225)	200
Receipts from debtors	-	-	100	175	350	600	400
Other income	50	-	50	100	150	125	100
TOTAL INFLOW OF FUNDS	350	200	100	(50)	50	500	700
PAYMENTS							
Payments to creditors	-	150	250	250	150	150	150
Wages, salaries	50	50	75	100	50	50	45
Other expenses	100	50	100	50	75	100	105
TOTAL OUTFLOW OF FUNDS	150	250	425	400	275	300	300
CASH SURPLUS (DEFICIT)	200	(50)	(325)	(450)	(225)	200	400

Deficit financed by bank overdraft

Excess cash to be invested in short term securities

FIGURE 1:1 CASH BUDGET

Monthly forecasts of cash receipts and payments are an essential element in the management control of working capital

ceding the seasonal rise in sales. In such a case the outflow of cash may not occur on any large scale until the beginning of the sales period, assuming that suppliers are prepared to wait for their money.

One major difficulty which many companies with a highly seasonal variation in activity encounter is the unavoidable shortage of liquidity due to the imbalance between payments and receipts. There are various courses of action open to the company that finds itself in such a situation.

One of these is to accelerate the process of debt collection by the most economical and advantageous means available. Higher discounts and price incentives, factoring, invoice discounting or tighter control measures, coupled with the pruning out of unreliable debtors, could lead to a faster inflow of cash.

Delaying payment to suppliers beyond the agreed period of credit does not recommend itself as the best policy although this is what often happens, especially when the debtor company is a large and important customer and can presumably afford the risk of damaging its relationship with a smaller trading partner. The goodwill of suppliers, whatever their size, is an important asset and should not be jeopardised unless the company has exhausted all other possibilities of meeting its debts.

The extent of management control over direct costs, such as raw materials and labour, can also affect the company's liquid position. Efficient stock control often means that there are no wasteful safety margins which, unless strictly defined, could well reflect the stock controller's subjective view of what is 'safe'. Wage payment systems can often be redesigned and improved so that any unfavourable variances are quickly spotted and steps taken to improve the cost-efficiency of labour.

In addition to cash budgets, management also needs information about the sources and uses of the company's liquid resources. This supplementary data can be obtained from a specially prepared financial statement which is occasionally published in the annual accounts of United Kingdom companies. Its use is more widespread in the United States. There is no standard form for this 'Source and Application of Funds' statement and companies use a confusing variety of 'funds flow' or 'cash flow' statements whose purpose or meaning is not always very clear. Figure 1:2 illustrates an attempt to present a 'liquidity movement' type of statement containing details of the cash receipts and the manner of their disposition.

In this example, the main sources of the company's cash are divided into external and internal cash flows, while the uses of funds show how cash was spent on fixed assets and other long-term investments and how the increases or decreases in working capital affected the company's liquid position.

As depreciation, which is originally deducted from gross profit, is not an actual outflow of cash (being only an allocation of past

SOURCE OF FUNDS	Current period		£000
External cash flow:			
Loan from merchant bank	660		
Issue of share capital	15	675	
Internal cash flow:			
Profits retained	153		
Add: depreciation	173		
	326		
Disposal of fixed assets	15		
Taxation provisions	32		
		373	
TOTAL SOURCES		1048	
USE OF FUNDS			
Fixed assets:			
Capital expenditure on plant, etc.	376		
Purchase of a subsidiary	665		
Amounts written off investment	46		
		1087	
Increase (decrease) in working capital:			
Increase in stocks	83		
Increase in debtors	141		
Decrease in bank balances and cash	(198)		
	26		
deduct			
Increase in creditors and liabilities	65		
		(39)	
TOTAL USES		1048	

FIGURE 1:2 SOURCES AND USES OF FUNDS

This type of financial statement enables management to identify the main sources of liquid funds and ascertain the manner of their disposition

expenditure to current periods), it must be added back to net profits retained.

It should be noted that increases (or decreases) in current liabilities are usually shown as a deduction from the total changes in current assets rather than as a source of funds. Their function is to enable the company to postpone the outflow of cash, but they do not result in any inflow of cash.

In the absence of any definite recommendations on the preparation of these statements, their correct interpretation is open to misunderstanding and a great deal of caution is advisable in drawing conclusions from the published specimens. But when full information is available, these statements can be prepared in some detail and can then serve as a useful guide to management. In the opinion of some writers, cash flow statements are more informative than balance sheets and provide investors and managers with a more meaningful tool of analysis.

Sources of short-term finance

Self-financing may be an ideal way of running a business, but in practice most firms rely heavily on external sources of short-term capital. Internally generated funds can be often more profitably invested in long-term assets and it can be argued that short-term borrowing is, in fact, a much cheaper way of financing day-to-day operations, especially in a period of rapid inflation.

In the majority of cases, companies make use of external sources of finance to provide additional working capital or to improve their liquid position, which may have deteriorated owing to rapid growth or unforeseen delays in the inflow of cash. Occasionally, the need to take advantage of some profitable opportunities or to finance special transactions in the overseas markets may induce the company to seek short-term loans.

A brief survey of the main sources of short-term finance must necessarily exclude a growing number of financial services and facilities which are nowadays offered to businesses by banks, finance houses and many firms and agencies specialising in the supply of various types of capital. All these channels provide a continuous flow of funds into industry and commerce.

Trade credit

Trade credit is one of the firmly established and popular methods of obtaining short-term finance. Most companies give credit to their customers as a matter of policy or because it is a normal trade practice in their sector of industry. Trade credit is, of course, a two-way traffic and the company which sells its goods on credit can usually expect similar facilities from its suppliers.

Theoretically, it should be possible to match credit sales with credit purchases. In practice these two items fluctuate all the time as credit received rises during a period of stock purchases in anticipation of sales which, in turn, induce the company to give credit to its customers in order to sell more goods.

Thus, most companies become net debtors during one part of their operating cycle and net creditors when the sales reach their peak. In order to maintain its liquidity at a reasonable level the company should attempt to control the ratio of debtors to creditors, although like all other ratios this one should not be interpreted in isolation from other significant factors. For example, a large number of outstanding debts may be simply the result of poor credit control or overtrading, while a small amount of credit taken may indicate that the company is unwilling or unable to make use of this important source of short-term finance.

Trade credit is by no means the cheapest source of finance, although its true cost is not always very obvious. Where the suppliers do not offer discounts, the company gains by delaying the outflow of cash which may be profitably employed elsewhere. But even if the cost of taking trade credit exceeds the expense involved in arranging a bank overdraft, the former course of action may be more convenient because of its informality and lack of serious sanctions if the credit is taken for longer than the agreed period.

The main problem in using trade credit is the need to increase sales turnover without corresponding increase in debtors so that the company does not become a net grantor of credit to other firms. Strict credit control should ensure that this does not happen permanently.

Bank overdrafts

Banks regard themselves as the primary suppliers of short-term finance, which is invariably given in the form of overdraft facilities. The procedure is fairly simple and easy: provided the bank is satisfied with the customer's credit standing and the upper limit of the overdraft has been agreed, the company can draw cheques in excess of its current bank balance knowing that the bank will honour them. The cost to the company will be the interest charged on amounts overdrawn on a day-to-day basis. This means that the company can, to some extent, control the cost of overdraft by reducing it when it is no longer required or when there is an adequate inflow of cash and by taking advantage of the facilities when the cash outflow justifies this course of action.

Interest rates charged on overdrafts fluctuate in sympathy with the general changes in the money market and are usually linked to the Bank Rate, although recent evidence suggests that the latter is no longer a dominant influence in the banks' decision to fix a particular rate for overdrafts.

One major disadvantage of this form of finance is that it may be suddenly withdrawn or drastically curtailed if the clearing banks are forced by the government's monetary policy to restrict their lending to the private sector.

It is, of course, advisable for the company to have permanent standing arrangements with the bank regarding its overdraft so that it can be used at a short notice in case of need.

Normally, the bank will not attempt to inquire into the actual use of the money provided by overdraft, but it is usually assumed that the borrower will not divert these funds into the purchase of long-term assets.

Bills of exchange

Bills of exchange are negotiable instruments which represent sums of money payable on demand or at a fixed and determinable future time. The most important aspect of this type of finance is the credit-worthiness of the person or institution accepting the bill. 'Acceptance' is the process of signing the bill, and thereby acknowledging the existence of the debt and promising to pay the sum stated according to the terms of the bill.

Bills of exchange can be discounted in the money market and, because of the reputation they enjoy in the City, only 'bank bills' are easily negotiable. These are bills of exchange which have been accepted by a well-known financial institution. Trade bills which are exchanged between firms are, for the reasons stated above, more difficult to negotiate and their use is limited.

The most usual form of bill finance is the acceptance credit which can be obtained from accepting and discount houses. At the request of the borrower (who is probably recommended by his bank) the accepting house provides him with a letter of credit which allows him to draw bills of exchange on the banker. The letter of credit may be given for only one transaction or extended over a period of time for a specified number of transactions. Acceptance credit is usually more difficult to arrange than a bank overdraft and the purpose for which this type of finance is available must be disclosed. Self-liquidating transactions and overseas export/import operations are frequently financed by acceptance credit.

The accepting houses charge a commission for their services and, in addition, the costs involve discount rates which vary in relation to the credit standing of the borrower and general conditions in the money market. The acceptor of the bill guarantees its payment on maturity, but if he fails to do so, the current holder of the bill has the right to claim the amount due from every person who endorsed the bill as well as from the original drawer.

Factoring and invoice discounting

Factoring provides a combination of short-term finance and accounting and administrative services. Confidential invoice discounting is only a source of temporary finance. Both forms of financing involve the purchase of the company's book debts, but the principles and procedures involved differ in each case.

Factoring is basically a method of overcoming some of the disadvantages of credit sales. Debtors are a necessary evil, but if the company decides to employ a factor it can at least improve its liquidity by releasing the funds represented by debit balances. The usual procedure is for the company to agree with the factor the credit limits which will be given to approved customers over a period of time (either a year or on a revolving basis). From then on, the factor will buy from the company all the book debts arising from its transaction and falling within the terms of the agreement. The package deal normally includes other services to be performed by the factor, such as credit investigations, the sending out of monthly statements and actual collection of debts.

While there are some undeniable advantages in such a complete service arrangement, the charges for this type of package are fairly high. Some companies, however, may find the cost of installing their own accounting department and credit control procedures even more expensive. There is no convincing evidence that factoring has any negative effect on the company's relations with its customers, although it is sometimes claimed that they resent the loss of the more direct and flexible contact with the firm.

If the company does not wish to surrender its control of debtors to the factor it can use confidential invoice discounting. This arrangement enables the company to sell any proportion of its book debts at a discount and reimburse the finance company as and when the debts are settled by the customers.

Short-term investments

Cash must be put to some use before its revenue-earning capacity is released. Large sums of money deposited on current account may look impressive on paper, but they make no contribution to the company's profits. In fact, the purchasing power of such idle deposits is decreasing all the time, especially in a period of rapidly changing money values. Retention of large cash balances as a buffer against unforeseen expenses is both wasteful and inefficient.

The amount of cash on current account which management regards as a necessary safety margin is a matter of judgment, based on careful budgeting and related to past experience. This margin will obviously vary from company to company but its main purpose should be to prevent expensive short-term borrowing to finance day-to-day transactions. Any cash that is in excess of this margin should be diverted into temporary investments.

If the cash budget is based on realistic assumptions and the actual cash flow conforms to the predicted pattern, the company has a much easier task in deciding how to use its excess cash balances. As many outgoings occur regularly, it is possible to ascertain in advance when cash will be needed. The exact timing of payments is an important factor in the company's planning of short-term investments.

Income from these investments will depend on the rates of interest obtainable in the money market and these will be determined by Bank Rate, the amount available for investment and the required time of repayment. Investments which can be withdrawn on demand, or which have a short life, will normally carry a low rate of interest. The degree of risk inherent in a particular type of investment will also influence the rates, although other factors – such as negotiability – should be taken into account when choosing the most profitable and the least risky outlet for the excess cash.

Among the main outlets for the company's excess cash are clearing banks' deposits, Treasury bills, deposits with merchant bankers and finance houses, local authority deposits and loans, inter-company loans and sterling certificates of deposit. In a number of cases the borrower specifies the minimum amount acceptable for investment and this factor will, naturally, restrict the choice of smaller companies to those borrowers who are willing to accept any amount.

Apart from the task of releasing the earning potential of the company's unused cash resources, management should also make sure that the actual flow of cash is fully accounted for and that there are no idle balances 'in transit' between various collection points (branches, salesmen, etc.) and the headquarters, or between the company and its suppliers.

In the first case delays in transit can be very costly and the company should ensure that cash transfer procedures operate smoothly. Increasing the frequency of branch returns or centralising the collection of cash can often make an appreciable difference to the company's disposable cash balances.

The transfer of money from the company to its creditors should be carried out as economically as possible. The number of separate branch bank accounts should be kept to a minimum and, if necessary, the whole payment system should be centralised. It is often possible to take full advantage of the usual period of delay between the posting of the cheques and the actual transfer of cash from the company's account to the banks of the suppliers.

Speedy identification of any unused cash balances is a key factor in the efficient management of liquid resources.

Chapter 2

Evaluating Capital Expenditure

Balint Bodroghy, Peter Ward Associates, (Interplan) Ltd

As the professional career of an engineer unfolds, his involvement in the financial evaluation of projects inevitably deepens. At the pinnacle of his career, an engineer will be pre-occupied with financial matters almost to the exclusion of design and technology. The transition from matters professional to matters financial, typical of many careers, is easy for engineers compared with other professionals, such as doctors or scientists, because an engineer is taught from the outset to seek solutions to problems that take account of limitations on resources.

The techniques of financial evaluation were first articulated by non-engineers. As a result there is now an apparent division between the two disciplines when, in fact, engineering and financial evaluation are merely different aspects of a continuous spectrum of activity. Stripped of jargon, this could be called making purposeful use of resources, or getting things done in an effective manner. To bridge the gap, the basic concepts of financial evaluation are here re-introduced in engineering terms, and the practices (they can be called design practices) of evaluation explained.

Need for evaluation

A product of engineering, no matter what its background, is conceived and created in a competitive environment. Competition arises from two entirely different sources, substitutes and alternatives, and the purpose of evaluation is to permit a rational choice between them. It is implied that at the end of the evaluation someone will make a choice – a decision – and that the decision will concern the allocation of resources, be they time, effort, machinery, or money.

Engineers are familiar with competition from substitutes. Nylon 6/6 could be made from butadiene using the old chlorine process, or one of the newer cyanide processes. Which is preferred? A gearbox selector lever could be made by forging, casting or powder metallurgy. Which is better? The composition of plant effluent could be monitored by gas chromatography or wet chemical analysis. Which is appropriate? Such judgements over substitutes are made by engineers daily, as a matter of routine, and it could be argued that it is the essence of their job. In contrast, the choice between alternatives is less familiar to them, and yet it is the essence of management.

The choice between alternatives can be illustrated with similar examples. Should one build a new nylon plant, or spend money on the development of a new yarn texturising process? Is it time to design a new gearbox, or should engineering effort now be concentrated on enhanced passenger safety? Is it wise to spend money on effluent monitoring, when changes in the market-place may soon necessitate a fundamental change in the process itself?

The above examples illustrate a deliberately narrow range of choices. In practice, it is in the nature of alternatives that their number is infinite. Thus the alternatives to building a nylon plant might include the following totally unrelated options:

1 Raise the company dividend
2 Reduce corporate debt
3 Cancel plans to issue shares
4 Move the head office to new premises
5 Buy a company making plastic cups
6 Expand in Argentina

The list is obviously infinite, and limited in practice only by the ability of decision-makers to accumulate, assimilate and evaluate information needed for making a reasoned choice in a very limited time. Thus an important secondary purpose of financial evaluation is to save time for the decision-maker and, hopefully, to improve his choice.

Responsibility

The choice between substitutes and alternatives is broadly similar: therefore engineers familiar with one should be able to cope with the other. There is one very important difference, however, which affects the manner of presentation more than the method of evaluation: in the case of substitutes, the choice is usually made by the person responsible for the analysis (the engineer), or someone almost equally familiar with the problem (his superior). In the case of alternatives, the choice is almost invariably made by someone other than the analyst. The decision-maker (typically the managing director) may not possess the technical skills, or may not have the time to perform the analysis. Hence, engineers in a junior capacity are often involved in preparing and analysing background information needed by others in decisions concerning alternatives.

If an evaluation is to be used by decision-makers not fully familiar with the background, it is obvious that a report must be prepared; that the report must be comparable with other reports dealing with alternatives; and that it must articulate information that might otherwise be taken for granted. Apart from these differences in form, the evaluation of substitutes (with which all engineers are familiar) and the evaluation of alternatives (which is less well known in engineering circles) is identical. It is also true that experience with one is of use in the other, and any advance made in handling the problem in one area will benefit the other. Engineers therefore approach the problems of project evaluation with a stock of advantages over, say, accountants. All they need for proficiency is to acquire a minimum of financial vocabulary and to assimilate the methods of presentation accepted as good practice by management.

Context of evaluation

The purpose of evaluating projects is to decide how to allocate scarce resources. To make use of this simple statement, it is necessary to arrive at some understanding of the decision-maker's purpose in allocating resources, and the nature of the resources at his disposal.

Purpose

Much philosophical speculation is possible about the decision-maker's purpose in allocating resources. Involved are considerations of personal and corporate objectives, and obligations to stakeholders in the organisation (shareholders, employees, and the public at large in the case of a business enterprise; or members of the administration, supporters of the party, or citizens of the nation in the case of a public body). For the present purposes it is sufficient to state that, in allocating resources, the decision-maker's purpose is to get things done in accordance with certain priorities.

The existence of priorities implies ranking, and ranking requires measurement, both of effect and effectiveness. Since each decision involves simultaneously a choice between alternatives and substitutes (even though this may not be stated explicitly in each case), the measures must be universally applicable.

Resources, assets and capital

Measures used in an evaluation must in some way be related to the resources to be allocated. For instance, in a primitive society where the only effective resource might be labour, the problem of decision-making concerns the optimisation of its use. In contrast, in a space station on an extended mission, the scarce resource dominating the decision problem might be the quantity of propellant carried on board for making attitude corrections, and the decision-maker's problem might be to optimise its use.

In a technological society such as our's the resources at the disposal of the decision-makers are much more diverse. They include manpower, but manpower today comes in many grades of differing scarcity. It includes engineers of particular qualifications, management, and the great variety of skilled trades involved in running a modern economy. Resources also include access to natural resources or particularly attractive locations, and the scarcity value of these varies from case to case or context to context. Resources also include established facilities such as roads and public works, buildings and machinery and plant of various types, as well as the services provided by a civilised society for the execution of a variety of tasks.

Some of the resources are under the control of the decision-maker. In that case they are often called assets, and if expressed in terms of a sum of money, may be called capital. Even within this limited context, the diversity of assets can be great, and the allocation of scarce assets a task of almost unimaginable complication. Yet, in most situations, we manage to cope, almost without making a special effort.

Common measure

In order to manipulate an allocation process involving resources of such diversity, it is necessary to have a common measure, reflecting in some way both magnitude and scarcity. The measure commonly used for this purpose is money: through the mechanism of market forces it can provide a measure both of quantity and relative scarcity.

In summary, resources are simply what a management concerned with getting things done controls, be it in a national, corporate, or private capacity. Money is a convenient, though imperfect, measure of resources. It is convenient because it permits comparison between resources as disparate as land and information, and because it can reflect relative scarcity through the mechanism of a pricing system. Money is an imperfect measure of resources for a good many reasons which need not be of concern here. In general the inconvenience arises from the fact that money is used for many other purposes besides measuring the scarcity of resources, and as a consequence it is subject to arbitary change (such as inflation or devaluation).

Money itself is often regarded as a resource, and in evaluations of capital expenditure one tends to think merely in terms of decisions involving sums of money. Money is, of course, not a resource, only an expression of its control, and those who have lived through periods of catastrophic inflation will realise how tenuous that can be. It is an indication of the convenience of the money concept that, for most practical purposes, the distinction can be ignored and capital can be regarded as a sum of money, to be used for the purpose of getting things done.

Assets in transformation

It was stated above that capital is the sum (expressed in terms of units of money) of assets (that is, or resources) under the control of a decision-maker. The resources themselves are indestructible, in the sense that energy is indestructible in the universe, but management can lose or gain control over resources, and there are variations in the effectiveness of their use. Thus management is concerned mainly with the transformation of resources (for instance converting money into manpower, which, in turn, is converted into finished works), a situation analogous to the transformation of energy in engineering.

If resources are put to use to get things done, the net result may be a gain in the quantity of resources under the control of the decision-maker. If capital is used to sink a mineshaft to a rich seam, that particular transformation can increase the quantity of resources under the control of the decision-maker. In contrast, if the seams turn out to be barren, or the resources are used in a design exercise for an advanced supersonic fighter which is subsequently declared valueless, the quantity of resources under the management's control is diminished, possibly to the vanishing point.

The rate at which assets deployed in various activities increase varies from industry to industry, time to time, and situation to situation. Even though it is a highly variable quantity, certain average or typical figures have become established and these are well known in financial circles. The reasons for variation will be discussed later: they are related to the concept of risk. Here it is merely stated that different norms prevail in different areas of activity. Thus a manager's liking for a particular resource under his control will be determined by the rate at which that resource contributes to the increase of assets under his control, and whether this rate falls below or above his expectations. In an exchange of resources, that is, where one decision-maker transfers (sells) some assets to another, the resource's ability to increase wealth is the determinant of price.

The differing rates (positive or negative) at which particular assets contribute to the sum of resources under a manager's control are analogous to differences in the availability of energy in its various forms. The value of energy in engineering depends on its availability and the ease with which it can be transformed to more available forms. Similarly, the value of an asset in business and economics depends on the rate at which it can contribute to growth, and the ease with which it can be transformed to other, more promising forms.

Time-value of money

Since assets can contribute to the growth of capital it follows that the timing of their acquisition and transformation is of considerable importance. This is the concept of the time-value of returns on investment, or, more simply, the time-value of money (since returns are invariably counted in terms of money). It is best illustrated with an example.

A certain asset (say an insurance policy) provides a return of £1,000 per annum throughout its life of twenty years. Another asset (say a winning combination on the pools) provides a return of £20,000 instantly, and nothing thereafter. Both assets provide the same total return (£20,000). The value of the pools combination is obviously £20,000; while the value of the insurance policy is much less. Why?

The answer is of course that the pools winnings can be transformed immediately into an asset providing a return, and thus increase further the resources under the owner's control. In contrast, the policy yields only £1,000 per annum and therefore provides far less scope for growth. In other words, money earned today is worth more than money earned at some future date. Expressed in engineering terms, the dimensions of money include time, probably to a power greater than one. The implications of this almost childishly simple observation were not fully realised by management accountants until the middle-'fifties. The realisation of the time-value of returns (or money) then brought about a fundamental change in the methods of evaluating capital expenditure. They are described below.

Techniques of evaluation

The context within which projects are evaluated, or decisions concerning capital expenditure are made, varies a great deal, and therefore the decision-maker's objectives may vary over a broad spectrum. Engineers are usually involved in situations where projects are evaluated on the assumption that the ultimate objective is to increase the totality of resources under the management's control. Thus a businessman might simply wish to increase his personal wealth, while a politician concerned with the allocation of national resources might wish to increase national wealth.

Ranking of alternatives

From this concept, it is possible to derive a measure of the effectiveness with which resources are deployed. The measure is the rate at which wealth under the decision-maker's control increases as a consequence of its transformation. Since all resources are expressed in money terms, it is convenient to express this rate also in money terms: it is the familiar rate of return on capital invested, or return on investment (ROI). It is the rate at which resources at the decision-maker's disposal increase as a consequence of his decision. Implicit is the assumption that management's objective is to maximise the returns.

Cash balance, capital and expense

For the purposes of evaluation, a project of capital expenditure can be regarded as a system. An engineer's approach to system evaluation is to draw a boundary around the system, regarding it as a black box. The same approach is used when constructing mass and energy balances of a chemical process or a current balance of electrical circuitry. The only difference is that in financial evaluation the balance involves not mass or energy, but the transfer of resources across the boundary expressed in terms of their cash value. Since time is an important dimension the problem must be treated as a transient, taking note not only of the magnitude of the transfers but also of their exact timing. Using this method, it is possible to obtain a two dimensional oscilloscope trace of the project as shown in Figure 2:1. This is a typical transient describing the behaviour of a project of capital expenditure and it's financial consequences.

It is noted that in creating a resource balance around a project it is necessary to account for the transfer of any resource, whatever its nature, across its boundaries. For historical reasons, accountants tend to draw a distinction between capital expenditure, that is expenditure somehow related to original investment, and running expenses which are incurred during the lifetime of a project.

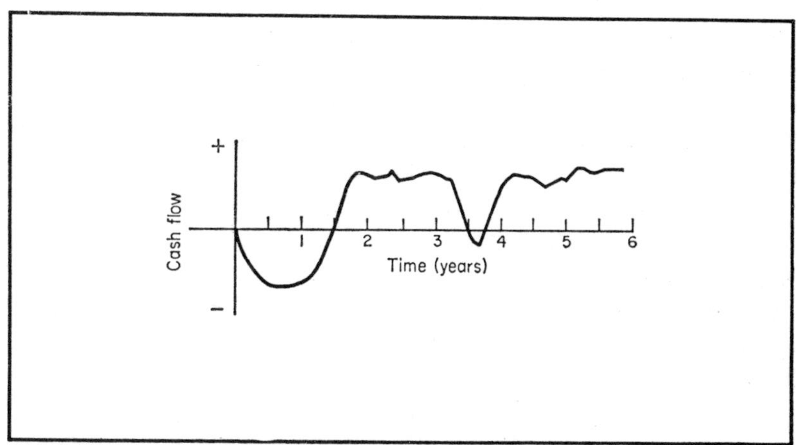

FIGURE 2:1 TYPICAL CASH FLOW TRANSIENT OF A CAPITAL INVESTMENT PROJECT

This shows the period in initial investment and a major replacement project several years later

From the point of view of project evaluation, there is absolutely no basis for making a distinction between 'capital' and 'expense'. The absurdity of the distinction is exemplified by the common practice in coal-mining of considering the cost of sinking a mineshaft as capital, but the cost of digging tunnels as expense, although coal may be produced by both operations (or neither). Similarly, the purchase of plant is always treated as capital and maintenance as expense, but the two are so interrelated as to make distinction senseless: by investing in stainless steel plant of over-conservative design (capital), it is possible to eliminate virtually all maintenance (expense). In fact, capital expenditure and expense differ only with respect to time, otherwise they are identical and a distinction between the two is artificial, unnecessary, and in some instances harmful.

Unfortunately, since tax laws and capital grants tend to be formulated by people trained in accountancy rather than in engineering, these misconceptions are perpetuated in the way company financial statements are drawn up and tax is assessed on them. As a consequence, there is today some scope for minimising taxes by the judicious juggling of sums between capital investment and running expense, and for a truly sensitive evaluation of projects, this must be taken into account.

Ideally, projects should always be evaluated after tax. In many instances tax could be the largest single item of expenditure connected with the project following the initial investment, and for that reason a calculation to minimise taxes is desirable. However, for the purposes of the evaluation, no distinction need or can be made between expenditure that the tax man would regard as capital, and expenditure he would regard as expense; they are both resources being optimised.

The above notions provide a sufficient basis for evaluating capital expenditure. They permit a choice between substitutes as well as alternatives, using money as a universal measure of magnitude as well as relative scarcity of resources, and using the notion of the rate at which resources increase as a universal measure of the relative attractiveness of alternative ways of transforming resources. Since the various options being compared in the decision can vary in terms of size and timing, methods have been developed for reducing these to a common basis of comparison, that is, to an index of performance.

Payback period

Considerable progress has been made within the lifetime of engineers practising today in the methods used for comparing projects. Historically the simplest, and for many purposes a completely inadequate index, is the payback period. In this method the time required to recover the initial investment in terms of the returns is arbitrarily selected as the index of performance in transforming resources. It is independent of the magnitude of the venture and therefore permits comparison between ventures of differing order.

The method was a favourite tool of engineers until about a decade ago and is still used, quite legitimately where:

1 There is no need for great sentitivity
2 Quick results are important
3 The underlying assumptions themselves are so uncertain that a more sophisticated analysis is not warranted
4 Funds are committed over a short period of time, say one year

Two projects of different financial performance are compared by this method in the example below.

	Year 0	*Year 1*	*Year 2*	*Year 3*	*Year 4*	*Year 5*	*Payback Period*
Project A	–12,000	4,000	4,000	4,000	3,000	1,000	3 years
Project B	–500	–	–	500	2,000		3 years

The examples were deliberately chosen to illustrate some of the very obvious shortcomings of payback period as an index of performance. No engineer is likely to fall into such a trap.

Present value

Where greater discrimination between projects is required than afforded by simple payback calculation it is now customary to resort to calculations of discounted cash flow. The concept of discounting is very simple if approached from the point of view of the time value of resources. A project that contributes at a very early stage to the totality of resources under the decision-maker's control is preferable to one that would contribute the same amount over its lifetime, but commences to make contributions at a much later stage. Projects A and B provide the example.

	Year 0	Year 1	Year 2	Year 3	Year 4	Year 5	Present value
Project A							
Cash flow	–12,000	4,000	4,000	4,000	3,000	1,000	
Discounted @ 15%		3,500	3,000	2,600	1,600	500	12,200
Discounted @ 50%		2,700	1,800	1,200	600	130	6,430
Project B							
Cash flow	–500	–	–	500	2,000	–	
Discounted @ 15%		–	–	330	1,150	–	1,480
Discounted @ 50%		–	–	150	400	–	550

To compare project A with project B, whose overall performance in terms of payback is identical, it is desirable to provide some time-related weighting to the returns. This weighting is called discounting, which is the converse of compounding, and is described by the mathematical relationship below:

$$A=R\,(1+r)^{-n}$$

where R is the return earned in year n, A is the present value of R, and r is the rate of discounting (or compounding). Using this formula, or tables based on it as in Figure 2:2, it is possible to calculate an alternative measure of the effectiveness with which resources are deployed. This is called the present value of the project, which is a dimensional term, not suitable for comparison between dissimilar projects. In its normalised form, present value would be expressed as a ratio of the discounted present value and the capital expenditure:

Project A	
Discounted @ 15%	1
Discounted @ 50%	½
Project B	
Discounted @ 15%	3
Discounted @ 50%	1

Prsent value, or its normalised form, is an improvement over the concept of a payback period, and should be used where a slightly greater sensitivity is desired, and where the initial investment is concentrated in a short period of time, that is one year. There are instances, however, where projects are compared where the rate of making the initial investments differs significantly. Such cases are illustrated as projects C and D.

	Year –3	Year - 2	Year –1	Year 0	Years 1 to 20
Project C	–	–	–	–12,000	+3,000
Project D	–1,000	–5,000	–5,000	– 1,000	+3,000

YEAR/RATE	2.5%	3%	5%	7%	7.5%	10%	15%	20%	25%	30%	35%	40%	50%
—3	107.7	109.3	115.8	122.5	124.2	133.1	152.1	172.8	195.3	219.7	246	274.4	337.5
—2	105.1	106.1	110.2	114.5	115.6	121	132.2	144	156.2	169	182.2	196	225
—1	102.5	103	105	107	107.5	110	115	120	125	130	135	140	150
0	100	100	100	100	100	100	100	100	100	100	100	100	100
1	97.6	97.1	95.2	93.5	93	90.9	87	83.3	80	76.9	74.1	71.4	66.7
2	95.2	94.3	90.7	87.3	86.5	82.6	75.6	69.4	64	59.2	54.9	51	44.4
3	92.9	91.5	86.4	81.6	80.5	75.1	65.8	57.9	51	45.5	40.6	36.4	29.6
4	90.6	88.8	82.3	76.3	74.9	68.3	57.2	48.2	41	35	30.1	26	19.8
5	88.4	86.3	78.4	71.3	69.7	62.1	49.7	40.2	32.8	26.9	22.3	18.6	13.2
6	86.2	83.7	74.6	66.6	64.8	56.4	43.2	33.5	26.2	20.7	16.5	13.3	8.8
7	84.1	81.3	71.1	62.3	60.3	51.3	37.6	27.9	21	15.9	12.2	9.5	5.9
8	82.1	78.9	67.7	58.2	56.1	46.7	32.7	23.3	16.8	12.3	9.1	6.8	3.9
9	80.1	76.6	64.5	54.4	52.2	42.4	28.4	19.4	13.4	9.4	6.7	4.8	2.6
10	78.1	74.4	61.4	50.8	48.5	38.6	24.7	16.2	10.7	7.3	5	3.5	1.7
11	76.2	72.2	58.5	47.5	45.1	35	21.5	13.5	8.6	5.6	3.7	2.5	1.2
12	74.4	70.1	55.7	44.4	42	31.9	18.7	11.2	6.9	4.3	2.7	1.8	0.8
13	72.6	68.1	53	41.5	39.1	29	16.3	9.3	5.5	3.3	2	1.3	0.5
14	70.8	66.1	50.5	38.8	36.3	26.3	14.1	7.8	4.4	2.5	1.5	0.9	0.3
15	69	64.2	48.1	36.2	33.8	23.9	12.3	6.5	3.5	2	1.1	0.6	0.2
16	67.4	62.3	45.8	33.9	31.4	21.8	10.7	5.4	2.8	1.5	0.8	0.5	0.2
17	65.7	60.5	43.6	31.7	29.2	19.8	9.3	4.5	2.3	1.2	0.6	0.3	0.1
18	64.1	58.7	41.6	29.6	27.2	18	8.1	3.8	1.8	0.9	0.4	0.2	
19	62.6	57	39.6	27.6	25.3	16.4	7	3.1	1.4	0.7	0.3	0.2	
20	61	55.4	37.7	25.8	23.5	14.9	6.1	2.6	1.2	0.5	0.2	0.1	

FIGURE 2:2 TABLE OF DISCOUNT FACTORS

Useful range of discount factors. The discounted cash flow (DCF) is found by using the appropriate values of cash flow (CF) and discount factor (f) in the formula: $DCF = \frac{CF \times f}{100}$

In the case of project C the entire initial commitment is required during the first year. In the other case the commitment is spread out over a number of years. This might also be the case in a situation where a long lease with option to purchase at the end of the lease is negotiated. The difficulty, of course, could be overcome by discounting both money flowing across the boundary into the project and returns from the project, and calculating the present value on that basis, but the method becomes increasingly unsatisfactory the greater the difference between the cash flow patterns of projects being compared. Calculation of a DCF rate, discussed below, is then preferred.

Nothing has been indicated so far about the magnitude of the discount rate that should be used in calculating present value. In fact, it is an arbitrary figure, loosely based on experience. For any well-defined area of activity there is a representative value of return. Its magnitude is determined, rather imperfectly, by market forces, and is just sufficient to attract investment in amounts commensurate with the available opportunities. The representative discount rate is not the same, or not necessarily the same, as the return on investment (ROI), often employed in discussions of capital investment. The choice of appropriate discount rate must be related to the method of appraisal employed, and will vary, depending on whether the calculation includes considerations of tax, the contribution of grants, and other factors which can vary from case to case, or custom to custom.

DCF calculations

The use of a discount rate appropriate for one industry is obviously legitimate only if the project under consideration is representative in activities of greatly differing character. For instance, they might be considering, as alternative propositions, a scheme to buy a disused coal-mine in the United Kingdom for storing industrial waste, and a project for manufacturing electronic components using low cost female labour in Malaya. Comparing the present value of such projects using identical discount rates is obviously inappropriate, and managements have sought alternative methods of comparison. One that is now widely employed is the calculation of the DCF (discounted cash flow) rate. It is derived by reversing the process of calculating the present value of a project, by making the discount rate the unknown. In this method, a discount rate is calculated that will just exactly equalise the present value of returns flowing out of the project and the present cost of investment flowing into the project. The result is an arbitrary index number of the effectiveness with which resources are transformed. The DCF return has no meaning except in a comparison of projects assessed on the same basis.

The arithmetic of a DCF calculation involves some tedious reiteration, but is, in principle, quite simple. Normally, tables of discount factors as shown in Figure 2:2 are employed to simplify the work. Various discount rates are tried until the correct value is either bracketed or approximated. A calculation is shown in Figure 2:3. A more accurate figure can then be determined by graphical interpolation, although this is a refinement rarely warranted by confidence in the underlying data.

Year	0	1	2	3	4	5	6	Total
Cash flow	(300)	100	100	100	100	100	10	510
Discounted at 10%	(300)	90	83	75	68	62	6	384
Discounted at 20%	(300)	83	69	58	48	40	3	301
Discounted at 30%	(300)	77	59	45	35	27	2	245

FIGURE 2:3 CALCULATION OF DCF RATE BY REITERATION

In this example the present value of a project has been taken as 300 and then cash flows have been calculated at different discounting rates to obtain the approximate rate appropriate to the period under review. Here, a rate of twenty per cent has been found to provide approximately the assumed present value

A variety of computer programmes are available for performing such calculations and this can save a great deal of time. An instance is CAPRI, a programme by Metra incorporating a number of additional refinements. In practice, computers are rarely worth considering in discounting exercises. The need for such calculations occurs infrequently in the work of a single engineer, and it would take him longer to set up a few runs on the computer than to perform the calculations manually. In the rare cases where many alternatives need to be evaluated and where a computer terminal is readily available it may be useful to employ one or another of the ready made programmes that any computer manufacturer includes in his standard package of management programmes.

The discount rate that equalises the negative and positive components of cash flow provides a direct comparison between the financial performance of projects of totally different background and character. It must be emphasised that the choice of measure is purely arbitrary, although it happens to be convenient. DCF has no valid theoretical basis, and, in fact, situations only slightly artificial can be constructed that produce anomalous results. For instance, projects can be conceived where there is no cash inflow, only outflow, access to resources having been obtained through leasing. The appropriate discount rate is then infinite and the DCF method no longer affords a rational comparison with an alternative that involves heavy initial investment in resources. DCF is thus inappropriate for this particular decision.

Although the DCF rate is obtained by the simple manipulation of numbers, considerable judgment is involved in compiling the underlying data. All the figures refer to future events of varying certainty. Thus, the correctness of the DCF assessment depends on the correctness with which future costs and prices have been estimated, the size of the market has been measured, the cost of starting up a plant has been estimated, and a host of other imponderables. The uncertainty associated with such assumptions is implicit in the analysis, but there is no explicit provision for taking it into account. A particularly dangerous situation arises if management is called upon to compare two highly dissimilar projects where the analytical work was performed by different analysts, in isolation from each other, and without providing a full explanation of the implicit assumptions. Thus, DCF is merely a guide, a quite sophisticated guide, in making reasoned judgments about uncertain future outcomes. However, attempts have been made to incorporate an assessment of risk into the technique.

Equivalent mean investment period

A further refinement of project evaluation originated at Nottingham University and has been applied at the National Research Development Corporation. Although less widely used, it is mentioned here for its particular appeal to engineers, and particularly those concerned with development work. The modification is called the equivalent mean investment period (EMIP) method, and bears a striking similarity to the concept of break mean effective pressure (BMEP) familiar to internal combustion engineers.

The EMIP method does the following:

1 Makes projects of widely differing magnitude and cash flow pattern directly comparable.
2 Accentuates the importance of the early part of the cash flow pattern.
3 Reduces the tedium of calculation.

(1) The cash outflow figures are normalised by dividing the cumulative cash flow figure by the arithmetic value of the maximum to afford direct comparisons. (2) The equivalent mean investment period is then calculated as the sum of the normalised cash flow figures from the start of the project to the break-even point (where the cumulative cash flow is zero) ignoring all subsequent events. (3) The EMIP values, and a plot of the normalised cash flow patterns as show in Figure 2:4, are then examined for significance, without discounting. The mean equivalent investment period is, in fact, the area under the cash flow curve, and represents the time during which the maximum cash commitment (total capital investment in accounting terms) would have to be outstanding to produce the same effect.

The main appeal of the EMIP method is its simplicity, and the insight provided by the graphic display of the cash flow patterns. Although claims are made that EMIP is an absolute measure of effectiveness in transforming resources, these are tenuous. EMIP is best

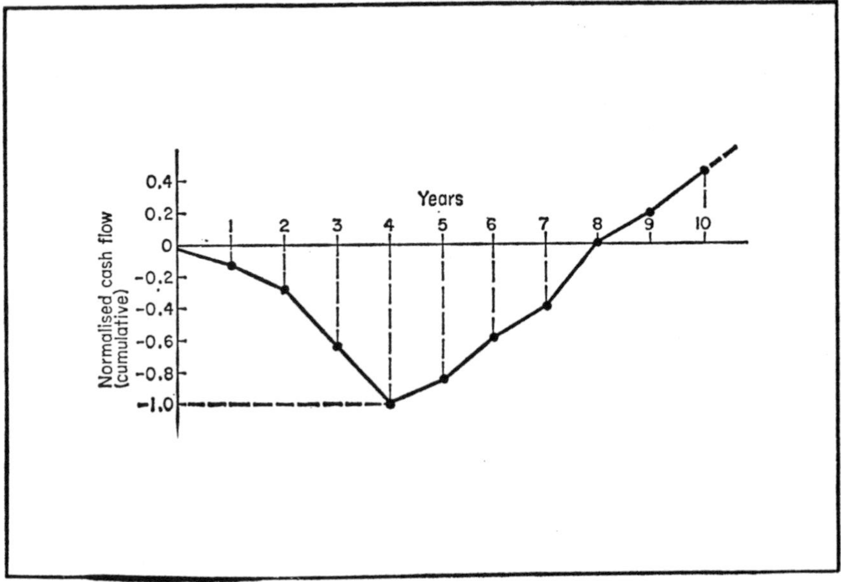

FIGURE 2:4 EQUIVALENT MEAN INVESTMENT PERIOD

Here is a typical graph of the equivalent mean investment period for the assessment of high-risk development projects

regarded as an index number of performance, suitable mainly for comparing speculative ventures, such as research and development.

Risk and return

Using the sophistication of discounting, a decision-maker may find himself contemplating a choice between three alternative courses of action, all involving roughly the same order of investment. They were assessed, using identical methods of discounting, as follows:

Project E	10 per cent	DCF rate
Project F	15 per cent	DCF rate
Project G	20 per cent	DCF rate

On what basis can a choice be made? Would the project with the highest discount rate be automatically and invariably chosen? The answer is, of course, that it would be chosen only if all other circumstances are equal. Unfortunately, it is in the nature of things that projects with a dissimilar rate of return are generally not equal, the inequality showing itself in the differences in risk attached to each.

It was emphasised before that, although the mechanics of a DCF calculation suggest sophistication and accuracy, it is in fact only a very elaborate way of handling relatively crude forecasts. A short reflection about the equalising effect of market forces will show that if all future events could be forecast with the same degree of confidence, the return from investing in all projects would be expected to be the same: risk and return are intimately connected, the magnitude of return being a function of the magnitude of risk, which, in turn, depends exclusively on our ability for forecast, or, more correctly, our belief in our ability to forecast.

The intimate relationship of risk and return is reflected in the rules of every game of chance. In roulette the payoff for a successful bet against a single number is much higher than the payoff on a bet against black or red. Similarly, in the elaborate game of chance called business, higher returns are attached to ventures associated with higher risk. This relationship was amply demonstrated in a detailed study reported in the *Harvard Business Review*[4]. This examined the rate of return from a large cross-section of American companies, and analysed the statistical variance, that is, the upredictability of the return, from year to year. It found a very strong correlation between the two.

The nature of uncertainty is sometimes misunderstood by analysts. Some suggest that risks arise from the particular circumstances of the venture. They say that a proposal to establish a narcotics ring in Marseille is inherently more risky than, for instance, investment in a public utility. But it could be argued, without resort to sophistry, that the difference lies not in inherent risk, but merely in the decision-maker's ability to anticipate the outcome. In the case of the public utility, he can forecast with a measure of confidence that the utility will still be in existence a year from now, and that it will be earning a commercial return on money invested in it. In contrast, the ability to forecast almost anything related to a narcotics ring is much more limited. If the outcome could be forecast with confidence, the risk would be nil.

From the point of view of a project analyst, it is far more useful to think that risk is a result of his inability to forecast, than to assume that it is some quality inherent in a project. Admittedly, the argument could be turned either way. But putting the burden of responsibility on the analyst has certain advantages: it focuses attention on the need to minimise risk by paying attention to detail, and to assessing its magnitude by understanding the limitations of the forecasts.

Coping with risk

Management scientists during the last decade have been preoccupied with attempts to find better methods for coping with risk. An early effort was to introduce some refinements into a DCF calculation to take account of risk. A decision-maker might, for instance, set standards of returns for investment in businesses with which he is fully familiar at a certain level, say thirteen per cent (after tax). When venturing outside his own established lines of business, he might arbitrarily (or following some method) increase the expectations of DCF return.

Some organisations have developed a quite elaborate method for coping with this problem. They might allow one extra percentage point for dealing with a business of similar characteristics to their own but with which they are not fully familiar. They might allow an extra percentage point on top of that for business conducted in a foreign country. They might require two or three extra points if the foreign country is one of questionable political stability. If partners whose background is not fully known are involved in the venture, another point may be added. In this way, the process of allowing for risk (that is, for uncertainty) can be elaborated at will. It serves a useful purpose only as long as it is realised that the elaboration is purely arbitrary and is based on judgment, and that the reliability with which DCF returns can be established on the basis of forecast performance often does not warrant such elaborate precautions.

More elaborate methods for evaluating risk have been developed. The basis of all such methods is to introduce an assessment of the probability of an expected outcome into the calculations, and then to compare competing projects, not only on the basis of expected financial performance, but also on the assessment of the probability of attaining it.

'Probability' is, in fact, a complete misnomer: as used in these calculations it is merely the analyst's expectations of an outcome. It is sometimes called a subjective probability, to distinguish it from objective probabilities of the type determined mathematically, using the fiction of a random event (for instance the probability of withdrawing a black ball from a 'perfectly' mixed bag of black and white balls). Subjective probability is most conveniently expressed as 'chances out of ten', as in the statement that there are 'two chances out of ten that the price of *X* will be £50 per ton in five years time'. A typical probability distribution is shown in Figure 2:5.

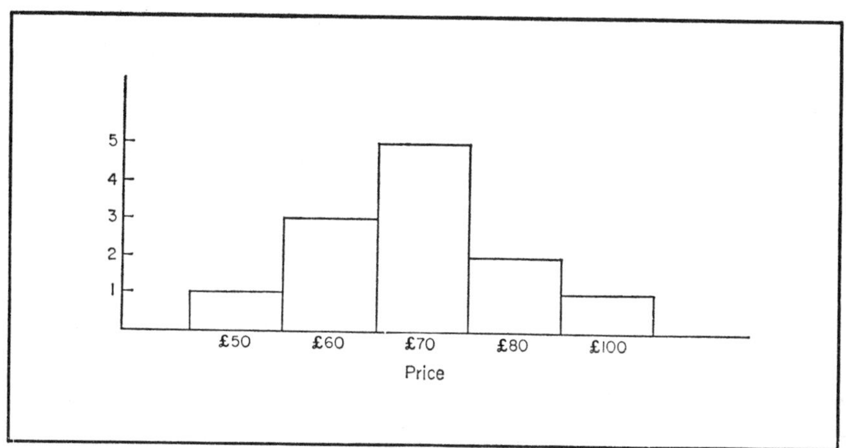

FIGURE 2:5 SUBJECTIVE ASSESSMENT OF PROBABILITY

This is a typical distribution of an assessment of subjective probability regarding a future outcome. In this case, the subject chosen is the price of a commodity in five year's time

In order to make a probabilistic evaluation of a project, such distributions have to be estimated for each variable of the outcome. As a bare minimum, this includes the following:

cost of plant	rate of reaching full output
time of completion	operating costs
cost of start-up	yield
price of raw materials	market size
price of product(s)	market penetration

It is obvious that the list provides a mere skeleton of the problem: each item is itself dependent on a host of other items, and an attempt could be made to assess the variation and its likelihood separately for each. To do that, it would be necessary to construct a deterministic model of the universe, a feat not within our capabilities.

A probabilistic assessment is thus based on individual calculations of the index of performance (be it present value, DCF rate, or EMIP) for each possible combination of outcomes. The end result is a desired distribution of subjective probability for the index of performance.

The execution of such a calculation is tedious in the extreme, and unimaginable without the aid of a computer. Package programs are available for the calculation of the final probability distribution, but the assessment of individual probabilities and checking of incompatibility in the assumptions still represents an enormous workload.

Obviously, such detail would only be considered for the assessment of major projects. Equally obviously, on such projects the detailed work of assessment would be performed by junior staff, and the final decisions made by senior executives. Therein lies one of the problems of the idea: not having been involved in the work, the executive mistrusts the results and is unable to benefit from it.

As a consequence, such assessments tend to be carried out to justify decisions already made by executives using the intuition of an experienced businessman, not to help make better decisions; and the results are 'cooked' until they accord with intuition. The purpose is usually to convince colleagues by blinding them with science, and to demonstrate competence and thoroughness to superiors.

So far, no convincing (or other) proof has been offered that intuition or guesswork applied to the details of a problem, which are then manipulated scientifically, is any better than intuition (or guesswork) applied to the whole. On the contrary, the failure of some of the most over-researched decisions (from Edsel to Corfam, with the

TFX/F-111 fighter providing an interesting sidechain) suggests that the appearance of pseudo-science in decision-making may facilitate the displacement of sound and experienced managers by people speaking the jargon with fluency but unable to make sound decisions, an outcome unfortunate and certainly unexpected by its advocates.

Convincing proof may be offered one day that elaborate methods for incorporating expectations of probability piecemeal into the assessment of capital investment projects can improve decision-making compared with the results achieved by experienced managers using detailed knowledge of the background, and the resolving power of their subconscious. Until then, risk analysis is best kept very simple, confining the work to an exploration of the effect on the apparent viability (that is the chosen index of viability) of the project of changes in a few of the most obvious variables listed above. But that would hardly deserve the name 'risk analysis' because it deals only with a carefully limited range of risks, leaves out of consideration the effect of those risks on competitors, and ignores competitive interactions in the market. An experienced decision-maker, however, would contrive somehow to take such matters into account in making up his mind, generally without articulating the details of his reasoning.

Presentation of the results

In the evaluation of capital investment projects it is more important to choose a method that suits the recipient (the decision-maker) and his, sometimes devious, purposes than to choose one that suits the project. In general, the present generation of senior corporate managers is not equipped to cope with elaborate mathematical analyses and may be uncomfortable if faced with a presentation couched in computer-oriented phraseology.

If the purpose of the analysis is to help clarify a decision problem, the results should be presented in clear plain English, following the practices of good report writing. This implies that the details of derivation should be kept in the background, and that the author should concentrate in his presentation on deviations from the expected. On the other hand, the purpose of the analysis may be to impress rather than clarify, and this has obvious implications for authors of reports on capital investment appraisal.

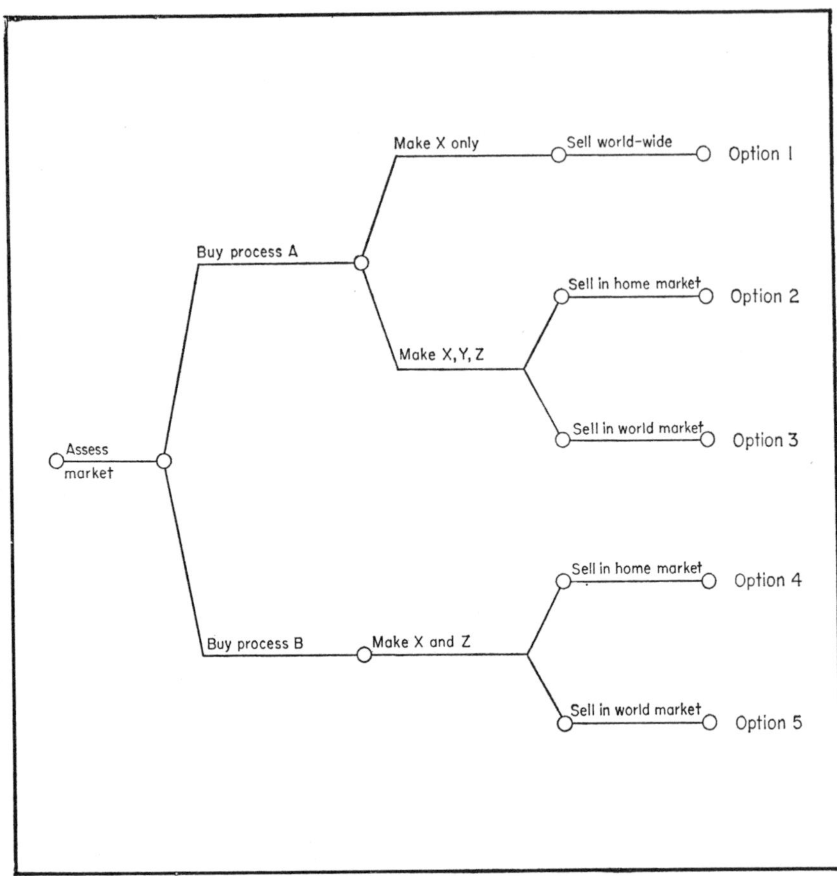

FIGURE 2:6 DECISION-BRANCHES

A useful and simple presentation of a decision problem

Managers make decisions by reference to experience. If presented with an entirely new form of analysis, involving unfamiliar index numbers of performance, they cannot relate it to experience, and will not make use of the analysis. It is up to the analyst to perceive the level and form of the decision-maker's experience, and to draft the results of his work accordingly.

A presentation stripped of jargon and kept as simple as possible is likely to be helpful. A few diagrams showing the branching of the main alternatives, as shown in Figure 2:6, together with simplified tables free from detail, enhance the effectiveness of the presentation. Elaboration, in contrast, requires careful study, and tends to confuse the recipient instead of informing him.

Summary

Capital investment projects are assessed formally in order to provide a sensitive comparison with other projects or alternatives in decision-making. The basis provided for comparison is a normalised index number. Over the years these have evolved from the simple payback period to more sensitive discounted and similar indices. The advantage of discounted indices is that they reflect the time-value of money, a concept fundamental to the effective use of resources.

An assessment is, of necessity, based on a set of assumptions concerning future events, which are uncertain to varying degrees. Thus, confidence in the validity of index numbers derived through the use of various techniques of assessment should be limited to the confidence the decision-maker places on the analyst's forecasts. No amount of sophistication in manipulating the forecasts can improve on their underlying reliability.

Risk is a consequence of the inability to forecast the outcome of decisions with confidence. Probabilistic techniques have been developed to incorporate a view of the confidence placed by the decision-maker in each element of his forecasts. In practice, the value of a probabilistic assessment is limited, and to date there is no evidence to suggest that the results are any better than those achieved by experienced decision-makers using the powers of their intellect in assessing the aggregate risks of a venture.

Whatever techniques are employed, the results of analysis must be communicated to a decision-maker in a form enabling him to relate it to past experience. This demands the use of a common (universal) discipline and limits the scope for experimentation and innovation.

Further reading

1 B G Bodroghy, 'Risk, Return and DCF', *The Director*, July 1966.
2 G L E Spier, 'Project Assessment', *The Director*, October 1966.

3 E P Ward and B G Bodroghy Planning in Conditions of Uncertainty, European Conference on Technological Forecasting, Strathclyde University, 1968.

4 G C Conrad and I H Plotkin, 'Risk/Return: US Industry Pattern', *Harvard Business Review*, (March-April 1968).

5 Derek Allen, Decision Theory, *The Director's Handbook*, McGraw-Hill, 1969.

Chapter 3

Interpreting Company Financial Reports

W P Ridley, Consultant, Merrett Cyriax Associates

In the previous two chapters, the application of internal management systems has been examined; this chapter considers the significance of those accounts which companies are obliged to publish under company legislation. These accounts only offer a broad overall view of the company's financial position, but it is from the information they provide that those outside the company (including banks offering overdraft facilities and prospective shareholders), have to make their assessment of the financial standing of the company. It is therefore advisable to consider carefully what company accounts do (and do not) show; and to examine the implications that are likely to be drawn from the published profit and loss account and the balance sheet, since they will form the basis of an outside judgment on the company's financial and management competence on which its ability to attract funds depends.

Coverage of the published accounts

The central features of published accounts are the statement of profit (or loss) which has been incurred in the preceding trading period, (normally this trading period is for a year) and the balance sheet, which shows that breakdown of assets and liabilities at the end of the trading period. For this purpose the company is considered as a whole (although sometimes two company accounts are shown: one for the holding company and a consolidated one for the holding company with all its subsidiaries). As a result, only limited information is available from these accounts on individual activities within the company; so, on the trading side, exceptionally good profits from one sector of the business may be disguised by poor results from other divisions. Similarly, in terms of assets, no clear indication is given on the valuation of individual buildings or plant owned by the company, since only an aggregated figure for each category of asset is provided.

Thus, the published accounts do not give direct guidance to management efficiency or profitability in individual divisions within the company. Nevertheless, from the profit and loss account it is possible to assess the overall performance of the company, while the balance sheet gives an important indication of the company's basic financial strength.

Balance sheet

The balance sheet can be considered in two parts; the assets employed in the business on the one hand and the method of funding those assets on the other. Thus, in the example of Figure 3:1, the sources of finance are shown at £100m of which shareholders' funds, contribute £60m. Of this total £20m comes from the issued capital of 20 million £1 shares and £40m from profits that have been retained in the business (after payment of tax and dividends). Debt finance contributes the remaining £50m; this amount is split between £30m long-term finance in the form of a debenture not repayable until 1977, and £20m of bank overdraft—requiring negotiations with the bank manager on a continuing basis, to ensure that the facilities can be maintained.

Certain companies retain the practice of adding creditors to the source of funds; in such cases the appropriate set off against assets has to be made in order to distinguish between source of funds and net assets employed.

Sources of finance		£m
Share capital 20m ord shares of £1		20
Retained profits		40
Shareholders' funds		60
Debt finance:	£m	
7% Debenture 1977	30	
Bank overdraft	20	50
Total funds employed		110
Assets employed		£m
Fixed assets		
Property	50	
Machinery	10	
Vehicles	10	70
Net current assets		40
Total assets		110

FIGURE 3:1 ABBREVIATED BALANCE SHEET

The balance sheet compares a firm's assets against the methods used for funding them

The financial pressures on the company therefore depend not only on the level of profitability within the company, but also on the ability of management to ensure adequate funds for the business. This consideration is particularly important in activities such as engineering, where there can be a substantial build-up of stocks (including work in progress and finished goods) and debtors, as the business expands. By contrast, in a retailing business, higher turnover may lead to a reduction of funds employed. The retailer normally receives cash for his goods before he has to pay for them, since suppliers typically offer four to six weeks credit, while goods may well be sold within two weeks.

A satisfactory long-term funding policy must, therefore, be considered in the context of the activity of the business concerned. In the example given, the contribution of £60m from shareholders' funds is relatively small, representing little over half the total funds required. Moreover, of the debt finance, a very large proportion is by way of overdraft which the company may be asked to repay at short notice. Such a financing policy could imperil the continuation of the business and is only likely to be justified if the company holds substantial assets which are easily realisable (for example, quoted investments) or if the assets are substantially under-valued. Full consideration must, therefore, be given to the asset breakdown.

An analysis of the £110m of assets employed in the business shows that £70m is by way of fixed assets and £40m for net current assets – stock, work in progress, finished goods and debtors, less creditors. Of the fixed assets, the property element is of greatest importance, not only because it contributes £50m to the total figure, but also because of the scope for under-valuation. Since revaluations of property are comparatively rare, the basis for the figure given in the balance sheet must be examined in the context of the notes which statutorily have to be included in the annual report. These notes show whether the property is held freehold or leasehold and the basis adopted for valuation. Where these notes indicate the figures given in the balance sheet are based on cost or some out-of-date valuation, it may well be that the company's financial assets – and its ability to raise funds – are, in fact, considerably stronger than is apparent at first.

Another key element in the balance sheet is the level of net current assets. While a substantial figure (as the £40m shown in Figure 3:1) might at first indicate that the company has considerable resources available to meet short-term liabilities, great care must be exercised in analysing the assets included in this figure. An abnormal level of stock and debtors may well indicate that current business is unsatisfactory; for example, that stocks are unsaleable or that debtors, even if solvent, could contest the amounts that they owe to the company. In particular, engineering companies often supply customers with very specialised equipment leading to stock build-up if the customers subsequently find they cannot accept delivery. In other cases. customers may require their suppliers to make considerable modifications of design, especially for new products; while this may lead to higher prices being agreed, such modifications can result in delay in delivery and so increasing stock levels; moreover, even after delivery, payment may be delayed on argument about the cost of the modifications thus adding further strain to the funds of the company.

The £40m of current assets should, therefore, be compared with that required by the business in previous years. However, such a comparison must take into account any changes in the trend of activity in the business since clearly the level of stocks may be expected to vary in line with sales revenue; it is, therefore, necessary to consider the stock figure in relation to the trading amount given.

Profit and loss account

The profit and loss account starts with the sales of the company and leads through to the earnings attributable to the ordinary share of the company. While only certain data is published, the key figures required for assessing the company's financial performance have to be incorporated, either directly or by way of note. In the example (Figure 3:2) an abbreviated profit and loss account is shown which illustrates the information that can be obtained under current company legislation.

Third party sales	£130m
Trading profit before depreciation Depreciation	£11m (£2m)
Pre-interest profit Interest payable	£9m (£4m)
Pre-tax profit Tax	£5m (£2m)
Attributable to ordinary shares	£3m

FIGURE 3:2 ABBREVIATED PROFIT AND LOSS ACCOUNT

Shows the profit (or loss) resulting from company's activities during a specific accounting period

The third party sales of £130m exclude inter-company transfers since the company cannot take credit for purely internal transactions. As a result, it is reasonable to expect sales to bear a consistent relationship between stock and debtors on the one hand, and profits on the other. As can be seen, profit is shown at several levels. Firstly, trading profit is examined before depreciation. Since depreciation is a notional charge based on the spreading of the cost of fixed assets over their expected life; it has to be considered separately from other charges against profit. Moreover, there are a variety of methods for calculating depreciation and, by specifically stating the amount charged, outsiders can assess whether they consider a reasonable deduction has been made. (In particular, a useful guide is to compare the level of depreciation with current annual capital outlays.)

The next item in the profit and loss account above is the £9m pre-interest profit. This represents an important figure for two reasons. Firstly, those lending the company money will look it as the amount out of which their loans can be serviced. Secondly, as is shown in the next section of the chapter, pre-interest profits are used as a base for assessing management's efficiency in the use of its funds. In this example interest at £4m absorbs almost half of the pre-interest profit, reflecting the company's heavy dependence on debt finance, indicated in the analysis of the balance sheet.

Next is shown the tax figure, which in this case at £2m is forty per cent of the £5m pre-tax profit – a rate close to the average for that year. In certain cases, however, the rate may be very much lower, since considerable tax incentives are given for capital investment programmes, particularly in areas scheduled by the government for development. Where the tax rate is low, additional funds are available to the company for payment of dividends or retention in the business, and this can offer a significant, if short-term, support to the company's financial position.

The shareholders of the company are primarily concerned with the after-tax profits. Where there are preference shareholders, they receive priority in payment of their dividend at the rate fixed in the company's articles. In this case, there are only ordinary shareholders and the £3m is therefore attributable equally to the 20m shares of £1. This allows for earnings per share of 15p per share (of which part will be paid out in dividend and part retained in the business). It is this figure of earnings per share that forms the basis for the value of the share, for the share price is normally considered in terms of a multiple of earnings per share; the multiple that the stock market assesses as appropriate typically varies between ten and twenty-five depending on the expected level of company performance (and the degree of risk involved in the type of operations carried on by the company).

Thus, in the engineering industry, a share price might typically be fifteen times the earnings per share figure (such a multiple would give a share value of £2.25 in the example shown). The multiple share price would vary widely around this level moreover for individual companies reflecting the respective sectors of the market which they serve and the capability of the management concerned.

Management performance standards

By selecting certain information from the balance sheet and profit and loss account, it is possible to rate the performance of the company—at least within the industry in which the company is operating. Since the characteristics of each industry tend to vary – in terms of risk, funding requirements and returns. In Figure 3:3, the key standards adopted in such a company assessment are listed.

If these six standard ratios are applied to a company's published financial statements, they allow for its performance to be judged from a variety of standpoints. The first three ratios highlight the company's trading performance, and, therefore, allow direct comparison with others in the same industry. We start with margins (pre-interest profits on sales) where each industry has a clear norm from which such margins can be compared. Thus, in the retailing industry, margins are likely to fluctuate between two and ten per cent, with the grocers typically recording returns of between two and four per cent; and other stores up to ten per cent. Again, in construction, margins are normally low at two and three per cent while in contrast, engineering companies commonly achieve margins of ten per cent. The margins recorded in the example given of 6.9 per cent must therefore be considered against the appropriate industrial pattern.

The major reason for the variance in industrial margins is the differing proportion of capital required to generate turnover. In the retailing industry, as has been noted, suppliers provide a considerable amount of the credit required. In the construction industry, capital requirements are normally limited by the receipt of payments throughout each contract. In the engineering industry, however, the greater

Standard ratios		Application based on company example	Per cent or multiple
Margin	= Pre-interest profit / Sales	£9m / £130m =	6.9%
Capital utilisation	= Sales / Funds employed	£130m / £110m =	1.2
Return on capital	= Pre-interest profit / Funds employed	£9m / £110m =	8.2%
Return to shareholders = Growth in earnings per share		15p against say 10p five years before =	9% per annum
Gearing	= 1 Pre-interest profit / Interest payable	£9m / £4m =	2.25
	= 2 Funds employed / Debt finance	£110m / £50m =	2.2

FIGURE 3:3 STANDARD RATIOS OF COMPANY PERFORMANCE

Financial ratios provide one means for comparing the performance of a particular company against others operating in the same industry. The figures used are taken from the balance sheet and profit and loss account in Figures 3:1 and 3:2

part of the funding requirements for stock and work in progress have to be financed by the company itself; moreover, because of the time required to process each product through the factory, it is likely that the turnover of stock is relatively slow. As a result, while in the retailing industry and construction annual sales are typically four or five times funds employed, in the engineering industry annual sales are only just likely to exceed capital employed (similar to the one to two ratio shown in the example).

The broad figure of capital utilisation is further broken-down in inter-firm comparisons to show sales against the various classes of assets; thus sales can be related to land and buildings; to plant; to stock; to debtors and creditors. While in the past attention has been concentrated on improving utilisation by raising sales, an increasing amount of consideration is now being given to methods of reducing the capital employed; this may be achieved by, for instance, strict control of the level of stocks in the factories; by speedier payment from debtors; and by securing maximum credit terms from suppliers. Management is therefore judged by the amount of capital used to generate each £1 of sales.

The overall efficiency of use of capital is obtained from the return on capital ratio; this ratio merely brings together the first two which have been illustrated so that:

$$\text{return on capital} = \frac{\text{pre-interest profit}}{\text{sales}} \times \frac{\text{sales}}{\text{funds employed}}$$

The return achieved (8.2 per cent in the example given) must be checked against other returns within the same industry to judge the relative performance of the company. Moreover, the return on capital must be measured against the cost of finance – in particular of long-term loans and bank overdrafts. For management can only justify the commitment of funds to a business where there is a prospect of returns substantially in excess of the commercial rate of interest. If there is no such prospect, it is better to use any available funds to reduce debt finance. In the example given, the return on capital is clearly low and new investment would have to offer considerably higher returns to justify any addition to funds employed. For it is the growth in earnings per share, with its impact on the share price, which is of key importance to shareholders. In the example in Figure 3:3, earnings were shown to rise from 10p to 15p per share over a period of years, or nine per cent per annum. This represents a significant improvement and could, therefore, be expected to lead to the shareholders approving of the management.

Earnings growth would not alone, however, give sufficient assurance to prospective lenders to the company. Lenders have to consider the risk element in the financial structure of the company. In particular, lenders look for cover interest payment (offered by current trading profits) and for cover of the amount borrowed (offered by overall funds employed).

The first consideration is tested by checking the total interest payable against the pre-interest profit, and in the example it can be seen that the interest charge of £4m compares with £9m of pre-interest profits giving a two and a quarter times cover.

A very similar cover is available for the total debt, with the £110m of funds employed in the business equivalent to just over those of £50m overall borrowings. While the extent of the cover which lenders require depends on which industry is involved, it is likely that such a cover would be considered relatively low, unless backed by substantial property interests. Even with a satisfactory profit record, therefore, the company might find difficulty in raising additional debt finance, particularly where existing lenders hold preference on the security offered.

In many businesses, for example, in the construction industry, profits fluctuate very widely and a twofold cover for interest charges may disappear rapidly; while, since certain assets may yield considerably less than their book value in a break-up situation, attention has to be paid to a company's liquidity.

As a result, the funds generated by a company form an important consideration in an analysis of company accounts. These self-generated funds consist of retentions of profits (that is, those profits left after payment of tax and dividends) and the depreciation charge. However, the first call on these funds must be the essential replacement of fixed assets and any rise in working capital (such as stock and debtors), resulting from their higher level of turnover. A guide to the funding required can be obtained from the recent record of capital expenditure and trend of working capital. Secondly, companies will have forward commitments for capital expansion programmes; the published accounts have to note the total of legal commitments and the amount which has been authorised by the board.

From the balance between estimated cash requirements and cash generation, an assessment can be made of the likely future pattern of calls on outside finance; by looking at the balance sheet and profit and loss account it is then possible to gauge the company's ability to raise the necessary funds, whether by equity or debt finance. On this judgment will depend the degree of confidence that can be expressed in the future of the business.

Summary

The information published in the profit and loss account and balance sheet therefore offers a broad view of the company's financial position and a guide to the capability of the management. Management performance can be assessed, both at the operating level – by comparing turnover trends, margins and return on capital with others in the industry – and at the financial level through an analysis of the funding structure. It is on such information that those providing funds for the company will make their financial assessment of the company. The judgement that is made is likely to decide the potential for continuing development of the company.

Chapter 4

Cost Accounting

Ernest Laidler, Lecturer, Liverpool Polytechnic

From earlier reading in this book it will have been appreciated that 'financial accounts' are produced as a statutory requirement and that, in the main, they concern the company's relationships with persons and organisations outside the company (for example, debtors, creditors, shareholders and taxation authorities). Whilst financial profit and loss accounts and balance sheets are certainly of interest to internal management, they are not sufficiently detailed to be helpful in the performance of the management function.

Modern industry is complex and those charged with the responsibilities of management must exercise considerable skill and vigilance if their efforts are to be effective. The right products must be produced, not only of the right kind, of the right quality and at the right time, but also at the right cost. It is the main purpose of cost accounting to provide management with up-to-date and meaningful cost information to enable them to function effectively.

A secondary purpose of cost accounting is to provide a sound basis for the valuation of stocks and work in progress, without which company profit and loss accounts and balance sheets would usually be very inaccurate.

Costing methods and techniques

Were the reader to find himself in a position to visit a number of unconnected factories and to make a study of the costing systems in operation he would most probably be surprised and confused by the variety he would find. Basic costing methods are devised to suit the kind of activity which is carried on, that is, the nature of the products and the methods of manufacture. Costing methods may be classified broadly into two groups of three (see Figure 4:1) but it should be noted that each of these six is subject to considerable variety in detail to suit background conditions.

Whilst one single method must be devised to suit the form of activity, it should be noted that, within an undertaking, there may be more than one type of activity; for example, in an iron foundry *process costing* may be used in respect of melting, *job costing* applied to the moulding and finishing of castings and *operating costing* applied to the space heating service provided by the boiler room.

In addition to basic methods, there are certain techniques which may be superimposed or 'grafted' on to whatever basic method has been adopted. These techniques are selected according to the manner in which cost information can best be presented to management for purposes of control. They are illustrated in Figure 4:1. Two techniques may be combined with the basic method, for example, standard-marginal-process costing.

To install a costing system, the cost accountant must have a sound theoretical knowledge of the methods and techniques available, must make an intensive study of the background conditions of the undertaking and the special needs of the management and must then apply common-sense in devising a suitable system.

Figure 4:1 illustrates that the basic methods fall into two main categories:

1 Where the work is varied and intermittent, consisting of specific orders or contracts. Usually it is carried out to the specific requirements of individual customers, although batch production to meet internal requirements may be included in this category.
2 Where standardised products are mass-produced continuously for stock or a standardised service is provided to meet anticipated demands.

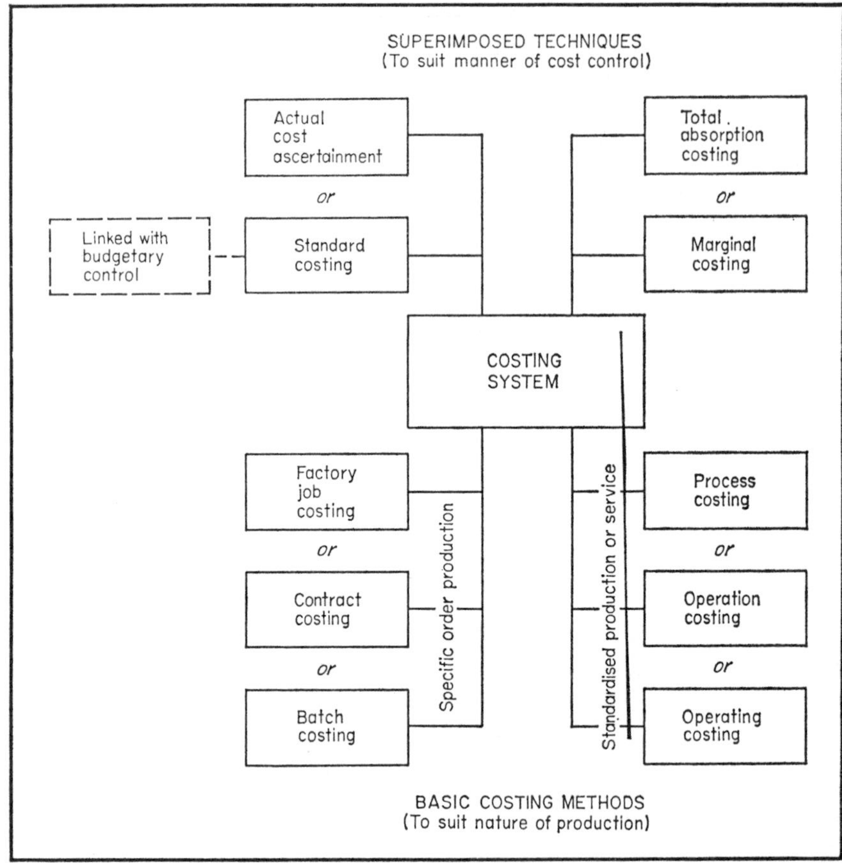

FIGURE 4:1 COSTING METHODS AND TECHNIQUES

The diagram illustrates the basic costing methods which are devised to suit manufacturing and/or operating conditions, also the special techniques which determine the manner of presentation of cost information.

Factory job costing

This applies where each job is carried out to the specific requirements of an individual customer, for example, printing, repair service and metal castings. The method is described in greater detail later in the chapter.

Contract costing

This applies where the work consists of large contracts of lengthy duration, for example, shipbuilding and civil engineering. The costing method closely resembles that of factory job costing. A special feature is that a large proportion of total cost can be clearly identified with individual contracts and there is less need to apply arbitrary apportionments than in other types of activity.

Batch costing

This method is appropriate in two cases: where batches of components are manufactured on the authority of internal orders, being intended for stock and for subsequent use in assemblies; or in certain industries where all, or a large proportion of the total production is of a kind which is most conveniently manufactured in batches, for example, small electrical fittings such as plugs, switches, etc. The costing method is virtually the same as that of factory job costing although a special feature is the determination of unit costs, that is, batch cost divided by the number of units in the batch.

The three methods mentioned above belong to the specific order group. Three different methods apply to the mass-production and service industries. The products or services are uniform and standardised and are produced more or less continuously in anticipation of demand. The costing approach is fundamentally different from that which is applied to the specific order category. A job is terminal, so when it is completed it is possible to ascertain how much it has cost. Mass-production is continuous, yet management still requires cost information at regular short intervals.

The problem is solved by fixing an arbitrary period of time ('costing period') which may be a week but is more usually four weeks or a calendar month. The cost incurred during the selected period is related to the number of units produced during the period. By division, the average unit cost for the period can be calculated. This description is, of course, simplified and by-passes the many intricacies, but it indicates the general approach.

Process costing

This applies where standardised products are manufactured by means of a series of processes, for example, chemicals, food products and paints. This method will be described in some detail later.

Operation costing

This is similar to process costing but the term is used where the costing is applied to an operation, rather than the larger sphere of activity designated as a process, for example, component parts for machines.

Operating costing

Again, this method is similar to process costing but the term applies where a service is rendered instead of the production of tangible goods. The service may be sold or used within the undertaking. Examples are passenger transport, haulage, laundering, catering and internal heating.

Classification of costs

Costs may be classified in several ways for different purposes. These are detailed below. Some of these classifications are also illustrated in Figure 4:2.

Primary elements

Any cost, whether it is that of a product, a process, a department or some other centre of activity, consists of one, two or three elements: namely, material cost, wages and expense. These are the *primary elements*.

Direct and indirect costs

In the ascertainment of product costs, those items of cost which can be identified with and allocated to a specific product are said to be direct. In the manufacture of furniture, the timber, upholstery and other materials which are embodied in the product are *direct materials*, whilst the wages of the carpenters and other craftsmen

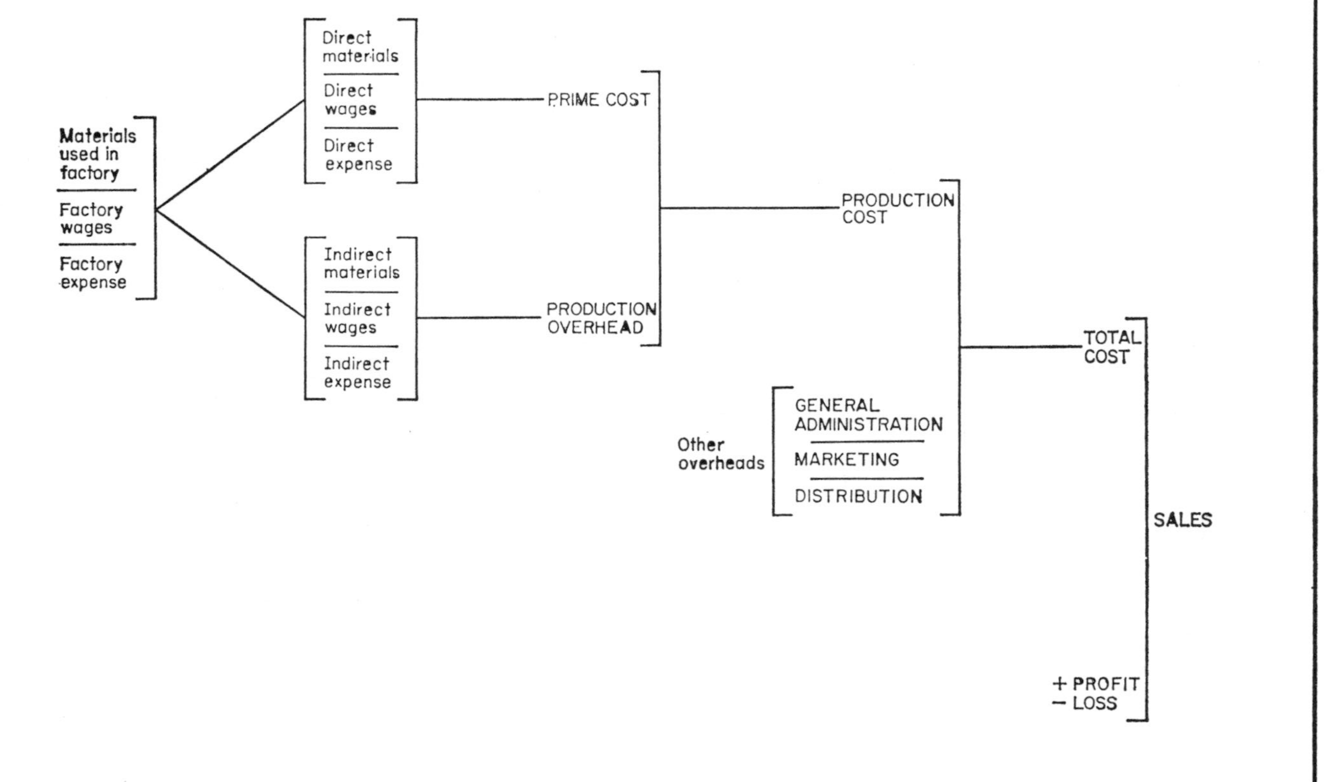

FIGURE 4:2 COST AND PROFIT STRUCTURE

The diagram shows (a) the three elements of cost, (b) the functional classification of costs and (c) the analysis of the sales value

actually working on the product are *direct wages*.

Costs which are too general to be identified with specific products are regarded as *indirect*. Remuneration of supervisors, timekeepers and general labourers would be treated as *indirect wages*, whilst lubricants, abrasives and consumable tools would be classed as *indirect materials*.

A royalty related to a feature of a specific product could be charged directly to that product as could some hired equipment used exclusively on a product and these costs would be classed as *direct expense*.

Whilst this category is common in the case of contract costing it is very rare in factory production where expense is nearly always indirect. Typical items are rates, rent, insurance and depreciation. If it is desired to include such expense in product costs, this must be done by means of some arbitrary method or methods.

Functional classification

Costs are classified according to functions. These may be:

1 *Production*. All costs arising in the areas where work is carried on for productive purposes.
2 *Marketing*. All costs arising in connection with marketing, including advertising and selling.
3 *Distribution*. All costs incurred in warehousing finished products and in conveying them to customers.
4 *General administration*. All other costs incurred in the general running of the undertaking, for example general management, accounting, legal and secretarial.

Classification by time

Costs may be related to those periods of time in which they are incurred. Exceptionally, payments *in advance* or *in arrears* are charged to the periods to which they relate.

Classification by behaviour (in relation to fluctuations in activity)

This is dealt with under the heading of 'Marginal Costing'.

Cost units and cost centres

Cost units

Where a standardised product or service is costed there must be established a quantitative unit of measurement in relation to which average costs can be calculated. Examples are: a ton of steel, 1,000 cubic feet of gas, a gallon of paint, a passenger-mile for trains and buses, a ton-mile for haulage, a pound of butter, 1,000 cigarettes. In the case of specific order costing, the cost unit is, of course, the job, contract or batch.

Cost centres

Management is interested in the costs of running each section of the enterprise as well as the costs of products. Any section of an undertaking in respect of which costs can be ascertained is a cost centre. This may be a large department, a section of a department, a process, a group of similar machines or vehicles or even a single machine or vehicle.

Material costs

Stores ledgers

Records of receipts and issues of materials and daily balances on hand are kept in the form of a stores ledger. It may consist of removable cards or sheets housed in cabinets or binders. The card or sheet, of which there is one for each item of material, is ruled with columns in which are entered quantities and values of receipts, issues and balances.

The stores ledger is not only a key accounting record providing values of stores on hand for periodical balance sheets; it is also an important part of the costing systems providing costs of materials used.

Pricing stores issues

Purchasing and storage procedures are dealt with elsewhere in this book but the costing aspect is relevant here. Purchase prices seldom remain constant for long. Consider the situation where 30 identical bought-out parts are required by the assembly shop and there are 100 in stock, 20 of which were bought at £1 each and 80 at £1.20 each. What value should be placed on the 30 now being issued? This would depend on the particular pricing method adopted. Limitations of space will only allow four to be mentioned. This is not a serious restriction because many of those described in text books are more academic than practical in application.

First in, first out. Adoption of this principle would price 20 at the earlier price of £1 and the next 10 at the later price of £1.20, a total value of £32.

Last in, first out. This assumes that the 30 now issued would be taken from the latest purchase and the issue would be purchased at £1.20 each, that is, a total of £36.

Weighted average. Each time a new purchase is made, the quantity and value are added to the quantity and book value of the current stock balance and a weighted average price calculated. All subsequent issues are valued at this price until another purchase is made, when a new average must be found. In the example, assuming that 20 were in stock when the latest 80 were bought, the weighted average would be £116÷100=£1.16 each. The 30 issued would be given a total value of £34.80.

Standard price. This method would certainly be adopted within a system which incorporates the standard costing technique, but it can also be used without standard costing. For each type of material, an estimated average price is fixed in relation to a specified future period of time (which usually does not exceed one year). All receipts are charged to stock at the standard price. All money differences are transferred to a price variance account, the balance of which is written off against overall profits. It follows that, for each type of material, no question arises as to how issues should be priced as the standard price is used in all cases. It is very economical in clerical work as day-by-day entries in the stores ledgers need only be in terms of quantity.

Charging material costs

As stores are issued, the quantities and values are entered in the issued section of the stores ledger sheet and the figures in the balance columns are accordingly reduced. At the same time, the value of the issue is entered on the stores requisition. Each requisition bears the code symbol of the product or cost centre to be charged. Periodically, the priced requisitions are sorted into sequences of code symbols and a listing is made showing the amount chargeable to each job, product or cost centre. It then remains for the cost clerks to enter the amounts on the appropriate cost records.

Procedures should always be governed by common-sense and short-cuts used wherever possible. Such an instance is where certain materials are used more or less continuously, for example, fuel fed to a boiler. Instead of writing out hundreds of formal requisitions weekly, each requiring separate pricing and other clerical work, it is quite sufficient to assess the quantity in the bin or bunker at the end of each week or month and to find the approximate usage by subtracting the closing stock from the commencing stock, not forgetting, of course, to add any quantities received during the period. Where a basic material is fed continuously into a process, a more precise measurement of quantity may be required than in the previous example, but it is a simple matter to devise a procedure whereby numerous separate weighings are accumulated by listing, then covered by a weekly requisition.

Labour costs

Payroll analysis

Not only is the payroll an essential part of the remuneration procedure but it is also a key document in the costing system. It shows, for each employee and in total, the gross wages earned, the deductions for national insurance, tax, etc., and the net wages payable. It also shows the amounts of the company's additional commitments in respect of national insurance, pension fund, etc.

The gross wages, together with the company's contributions, represent expenditure so far as the company is concerned and must be accounted for. In some systems, only the gross wages are designated *wages* and the company's contributions are classed as *indirect expense*, whereas in other cases the combined amount is treated as *wages*. For the purpose of illustration, it is assumed that the former concept applies and the problem is to analyse gross wages. Each task, whether directly concerned with production or of an ancillary nature, will have been given a distinctive code symbol.

Time recording and analysis

In the case of those employees whose remuneration is based on personal or group productivity, job cards, or similar records showing times and work quantities will be used. These provide the data for payroll purposes, and also for analysis by code symbols.

Where employees who are paid at an hourly rate for time worked are engaged on two or more tasks during the same week, an analysis of their time will be required. Daily or weekly time sheets are used for this purpose. It may be the procedure for employees to enter times on the sheets themselves, but much greater accuracy can be achieved if this is done by time clerks. Wages analysis clerks then have the task of pricing out the times recorded against each code symbol, making sure that:

1 The total clock card time is fully accounted for.
2 The sums of money spread over the different tasks agree, in total, with the employee's gross wages as shown on the payroll.

Many employees, such as timekeepers, are engaged on tasks to which a constant code symbol can be applied. In such cases, the employee's total gross wage can be booked to the relevant symbol, and no analysis is required.

Charging labour costs

The end product of this clerical work is the wages analysis, which will agree with the total gross wages shown on the payroll. From this, the cost clerks can enter the amounts in the costing records.

Overheads

Allocation, apportionment and absorption

Allocation is charging to a cost centre the whole amount of an item of cost which relates exclusively to that cost centre.
Apportionment is the distribution of an item of cost over two or more cost centres, using some logical basis to determine the proportion to be charged to each.
Absorption is charging portions of overheads to jobs or other cost units by means of pre-established rates.

Factory overheads

It will be seen from Figure 4:2 that factory overheads are the sum of indirect materials, indirect wages and indirect expense relating to the factory.

In costing the products of an undertaking, the traditional requirement is to ascertain the cost of each product inclusive of a fair share of overhead. This concept is referred to as *total absorption costing* and it is in contradistinction to *marginal costing*, a technique which is dealt with in a separate section of this chapter.

Accuracy

It is, perhaps, opportune at this point to explain that expressed costs of products or activities *can never be exactly correct*. Inevitably there will be some degree of approximation. It is the duty of the cost accountant to ensure that his figures are sufficiently accurate to give reliable impressions of tendencies within the business, without incurring unnecessarily high expenditure in pursuing additional precision which adds little to the value of the information produced.

Methods of absorption

Because of limited space only the three most commonly used methods of absorption will be described. It will be noted that all three are related to the work of the labour force. This is because close study of the items concerned shows that most of the cost is so related.

Percentage on direct wages. The amounts of direct wages and overhead respectively are estimated for a future period (say one year) and the latter is expressed as a percentage of the former. This percentage is applied throughout the period.

Rate per direct labour hour. In this case the number of direct labour hours to be worked in the projected period is estimated and this is divided into the estimated overheads to give an hourly charging rate. This is suitable for use in cost centres where the work is predominantly manual.

Rate per machine hour. This is similar to the preceding method except that it is based on the running hours of a machine or group of similar machines. It is suitable for use in a mechanised cost centre.

It is very bad practice to use a single absorption rate for an entire factory. In setting up cost centres due regard can be paid to differences in the incidence of overheads, for example, the hourly charging rate for heavy and expensive machines should be higher than for light and inexpensive machines, and if there are various classes of machines in one department and they are grouped according to class, then it is in the interests of good costing to establish each group as a separate cost centre, each having its own machine-hour rate.

Overheads over- and under-absorbed

If, in the January costing period, 12,500 machine hours were worked in the machine cost centre, 10,000 direct labour hours were worked in the assembly cost centre and the absorption rates were £1.25 and £0.60 respectively, the amounts of overheads absorbed would be £15,625 and £6,000 respectively. If the actual overhead costs for the month were £15,900 and £5,850 respectively, the position would be as follows:

	£
Machine cost centre – *under-absorbed*	275
Assembly cost centre – *over-absorbed*	150
Net – *under-absorbed*	125

Product costs would include the *absorbed* overhead and no attempt would be made to adjust them in respect of the above differences, which would merely be written off against the profit for the period.

Factory job costing

Estimating and price fixing

It is a feature of this type of work that the manufacturing company is usually asked to quote a price before the order is placed. Direct materials and labour are estimated, then factory overheads are allowed for at current absorption rates, separately for each cost centre. Further allowances are made for administration and for selling, usually by means of a pre-determinded percentage on production cost. Delivery may be allowed for on a similar basis or, if likely to be comparatively expensive, by means of a separate estimate taking into account the weight, the distance and the means of transport involved.

It is quite common to make a further allowance for contingencies and, finally, there would be added a profit margin calculated in accordance with company policy.

Manufacturing order

If a quotation is accepted, resulting in a a customer's order, then details will be set out on internal, printed forms that are passed to the production departments concerned as authority to carry out the work. These internal forms are variously described: manufacturing order and works order are two examples. Each manufacturing order will be given a job number, against which costs can be booked for purposes of subsequent analysis. A job card will usually be opened for each job; a typical example is given in Figure 4:3.

Preparation of a job cost

The total cost of each job is found by carrying out the following series of steps, using the job card:

1 Direct costs are entered by the cost clerk, in the appropriate columns.

2 Production overheads are applied at the established absorption rates.
3 Uncompleted work at the end of a costing period must be valued at the accumulated factory cost to date.
4 When the job is completed, further cost absorption is effected by the addition of administration, marketing and distribution overheads. (Sometimes, distribution costs may be added separately as ascertained costs rather than absorbed cost.)
5 The total amount on the job card will be the total cost, and the difference between this and the selling price is the profit (or loss).

JOB CARD

Description__________ Job number__________

Drawing number__________ Order date__________

Customer__________

Direct materials		Direct wages			Factory overheads				Direct expenses		Production cost
Date	Cost	Date	Cost centre	Cost	Date	Hours	Rate	Cost	Date	Cost	

Notes:		
	Production cost (as above)	______
	General administration (_____%)	______
	Marketing (_____%)	______
	Delivery	______
		______
	Profit	______
	Selling price	______

FIGURE 4:3 FORM OF JOB CARD

This is an example of the type of record used for collecting the costs of a specific factory job

Process costing

Unlike a 'job', which has a definite start and finish, process work tends to be continuous, and this calls for a quite different costing approach.

Where there is a separate chain of processes for each product, ascertained costs of processes are automatically ascribed to products. In some industries, however, (for example, tobacco), different brands pass through common processes and so it is necessary, firstly, to ascertain the cost of a process, and then to apportion it over the different brands. Taking as the first example a process in which each of three brands receives similar treatment, straight proportion would be satisfactory:

Brand	Weight ex process lbs	Total cost (pence)	Apportioned (pence)
A	15,000	195,000	48,750
B	25,000	=3.25p	81,250
C	20,000	per lb	65,000
	60,000		195,000

Alternatively, it is now assumed that brand A requires double treatment in the process. The apportionment would then be on the following lines:

Brand	Actual lbs	Weighting factor	Points	Total cost (pence)	Apportioned (pence)
A	15,000	×2	30,000	195,000	78,000
B	25,000	–	25,000	=2.60p	65,000
C	20,000	–	20,000	per point	52,000
	60,000		75,000		195,000

Work in progress

Since the work tends to flow continuously it is necessary to cost the work done during a certain *period of time*, that is, the costing period.

By entering on the cost sheet actual materials and wages costs and absorbing overheads at the predetermined rates, the cost clerk ascertains the cost of operating a process during the period. By dividing the cost by the number of units produced he arrives at the cost *per unit* for each process.

The uncompleted product at the end of a period is valued at the average accumulated cost at the particular stage which it has reached. If scrap arises in the course of processing, the actual or estimated recovery value is credited to the process, thereby reducing the cost of that process.

Marginal costing

Theory

If it has cost £20,000 to manufacture 10,000 identical units, how much would it cost to make 12,000? The correct reply is not '£24,000', but: 'It depends upon how the cost of £20,000 is made up'. It is now assumed that, of the £20,000, £15,000 is the direct cost of material and labour, whilst the remainder represents indirect costs such as rent, management salaries, etc. One would expect the aggregate direct or 'variable' cost to increase in the same proportion as the number of units made, that is, £18,000 for 12,000 units. On the other hand, there is no reason why the indirect or 'fixed' costs should alter, so long as the volume of manufacture remained within the usual limits. £5,000 would be constant for either 10,000 or 12,000 units and the total cost of 12,000 units would be £23,000. This, in very simple terms, explains what is meant by marginal theory.

The theory of marginal costing then is that, in relation to a specified volume of output, additional output can normally be obtained at less than proportionate cost because, within limits, the aggregate of certain items of cost will tend to remain fixed and only the aggregate of the remainder will tend to rise proportionately with the increase in output.

Definitions

Marginal costing. A superimposed principle whereby marginal costs are ascertained by differentiating between fixed and variable costs. It is primarily concerned with the provision of information to management on the effects on profit of changes in the volume of sales.

Marginal cost. The variable cost incurred in producing each unit. (Note: the marginal cost is essentially a unit cost. The aggregate of the marginal costs would usually be termed the 'variable cost').

Fixed cost. A cost which, within certain limits, tends to be unaffected in the aggregate by fluctuations in volume of output or turnover. Such costs are incurred in relation to time rather than to production.

Semi-variable cost. A cost which, in the aggregate, is affected by fluctuations in volume of output but changes to a lesser degree than the latter.

Assessment of cost variability

The distinction between variable and fixed costs is fundamental to marginal costing yet, in practice, the segregation of costs into these two categories is far from simple because so many items are neither wholly fixed nor wholly variable, hence the semi-variable category.

In theory, *prime costs* (explained in Figure 4:2) are invariably regarded as variable, although the gradual transition from yesterday's flexible labour force to tomorrow's salaried factory staff is giving direct labour a more fixed characteristic.

Most overheads can be regarded as fixed within the limits of normal activity in the comparatively short term, typical examples being rent and rates, fire insurance and management salaries. Of course, drastic changes in output levels can make it necessary for these so-called fixed costs to change. Few items of overhead are strictly variable. Power may possibly be so classified if it can be separated from lighting. A great many items are classed initially as semi-variable and these have to be apportioned to the fixed and variable categories. Arithmetical and graphical methods of effecting this apportionment are available but they have their shortcomings and it is probably more usual to apportion by the exercise of common sense and judgment.

Marginal costing in practice

The marginal costing principle has sprung from a particular conception and expression of the way in which different costs behave when production volume fluctuates. It assumes that the difference between the variable cost and the selling value of each product *contributes* towards a *fund* to meet the fixed costs and the profit of the undertaking. The following table illustrates this concept:

Product	Total sales value	Variable cost	Contribution	Fund	
	£	£	£	£	
A	20,000	14,000	6,000	18,000	Fixed cost £13,000
B	30,000	20,000	10,000		
C	10,000	9,000	1,000		Profit £5,000
D	5,000	4,000	1,000		

It will be noted that no attempt is made to absorb the fixed cost in product costs.

The following example assumes that a component which is used in assembly is made in the company's own machine shop and the production manager has been informed that the cost is as follows:

	£
Direct material	5.10
Direct wages	3.30
Overheads	4.10
	12.50

The production manager finds that an outside manufacturer is prepared to supply the component at a price of £11 and a recommendation is put forward that the component be purchased in future in order to save £1.50 on each.

The cost accountant investigates the cost and finds that, of the £4.10 overheads, £3.50 is *fixed*. This means that, by ceasing to manufacture the component, the cost actually *avoided* would be £9, so buying out would involve a *loss* of £2 per unit.

Management has to make a variety of policy decisions of which the above *make or buy* decision is but one. Figures presented on *marginal costing* lines are usually essential if management is not to be mislead. It is, of course, vitally important that the cost accountant presenting the figures should be fully aware of the purposes for which they are to be used so that he can ensure that they are presented in the most appropriate form.

Marginal costing is one of the most controversial concepts of cost accounting. It has many supporters and many opponents. Opponents object to the inference that fixed overheads have nothing to do with production and they contend that such costs are incurred because of the products and should be included in the costs of individual products. This contention is more firmly based in some undertakings than in others. If one considers the case of a company manufacturing a wide range of products which differ substantially in nature from each other, some having their own exclusive processes or departments, one must realise that the plant, equipment, expertise and other facilities which result in fixed overhead costs are not utilised evenly by all products, and to fail to analyse these costs against the products for which they are incurred would be faulty costing. Whilst selling prices of standardised products are not usually determined by cost, nevertheless it is a responsibility of management to know the profitability of each product and to ensure that each is, at least, 'paying its way'.

On the other hand, one may find patterns of manufacture where the different products or 'brands' are merely variations on the main theme, passing through common processes and differing only as regards the raw material ingredients. In such cases there is no really strong case for full absorption of overheads in product costs and, therefore, no reason why the marginal principle should not be incorporated in the routine costing procedure.

Two alternatives are open to the cost accountant:

1 *To carry out the routine procedures in accordance with the marginal concept.* Absorption of overhead into product costs would be in respect of variable overhead only. Fixed costs would be collected in a special account then written off in total at the end of the costing period in which they were incurred.
2 *To absorb both fixed and variable overheads into product costs* and to arrive at a net profit for each product in accordance with the concept of full absorption costing, thus informing management as to product profitability. The cost accountant would, however,

still have to be in a position to present figures on which policy decisions such as 'make or buy' could be based. These, he would have to compile on an ad hoc basis, having regard to the special purpose for which they were required.

Standard costing and variance analysis

Relationship with budgetary control

Standard costing, like budgetary control, is a special technique devised to facilitate control by management. Both of these techniques have in common the establishment of planned measures of performance, against which actual results are compared.

In general terms, budgetary control is broader in its conception and application, covering the major activities of the undertaking, advertising, sales production, departmental overheads, cash flow, etc., whilst standard costing is concerned mainly with the standardisation and detailed control of direct costs.

Whilst budgetary control and standard costing are recognisable as two distinct techniques, they are really complementary, and the effectiveness of each is improved by being closely linked with the other. When budgetary control is operated on its own, budgeted production costs can only be based on rough estimates but, joined with standard costing, they are derived from scientifically measured details in which 'work study' plays an important part. Reciprocally, the budgets provide the data from which overhead absorption rates can be established and incorporated into the standard costs.

Standard costing compared with actual cost ascertainment

Actual cost ascertainment (sometimes referred to as 'historical costing') is the ascertainment of costs of commodities or services which *have been* produced. Job costs are compared with the original estimates whilst the costs of mass-produced goods or services are compared with the costs of earlier periods, any adverse tendencies being investigated. Such investigations are not easy, particularly where the *cumulative* principle applies, as in processing. One authority has likened the exercise to 'unscrambling an omelette'; he could have said 'two omelettes' because one is usually comparing two figures. If last month's cost was 25p per unit and this month's 23p per unit, a satisfactory result is indicated on the surface. What is missing is a *standard*. If it were known reasonably efficient working would result in a cost of 21p, one would realise that neither of the actual costs is satisfactory.

The standard costing technique aims at the establishment of figures representing what costs *should be* for each product and at each stage of production.

Performance standards

It is important to be quite clear as to what level of performance is reflected in the standards set. It may be based on:

1 Past average performance
2 Ideal performance
3 Good attainable performance

The first two bases mentioned have now been generally discarded in favour of the third. Standards based on good attainable performance make reasonable allowances for unavoidable wastage, breakdowns and other inevitable lapses from perfection. Nevertheless, a satisfactory level of efficiency is aimed at and managers are presented with targets which are fair and so provide a stimulus to either achieve or surpass them.

Factors

A standard cost is made up of two factors, *quantity* and *rate*. For example, a unit of product may require 4 lb of material 'Z' which costs 50p per lb, or 10 hours of an operative's time at 80p per hour, or overheads charged for 6 machine hours at £1 per machine hour.

Setting standard material costs

1 Standard specifications must be established.
2 Usage quantities must be decided upon, with due allowances for off-cuts, evaporation and other wastage.

3 Prices must be forecast, allowances being made for quantity discounts and for carriage where the latter is not included in the price. Essentially it is a forecast of the *average* price for each material in respect of the period for which the standards will remain in force, usually one year.

Setting standard wages costs

1 The labour grades to be employed on the different classes of work must be decided upon.
2 Standard labour times must be established for each task by the work study department. Usually these times are expressed in standard hours or standard minutes.
3 Standard wage rates must be predetermined. This involves a forecast of the rates relevant to the established grades over the future period. Bonuses, if payable, would be allowed for.

Setting standard variable overhead costs

The most usual way of allowing for variable overheads in standard product costs is by means of an absorption rate *per direct labour hour*. This involves determination of:

1 The number of direct labour hours as already decided upon for the standard wages cost.
2 The absorption rate derived from the *budget* relative to the cost centre, the formula being:

$$\frac{\text{Variable overhead}}{\text{Direct labour hours}}$$

Setting standard fixed overhead costs

These may be allowed for in the same way as the standard variable overhead costs, except that it is the budgeted *fixed* overhead for the cost centre which is divided by the budgeted direct labour hours.

Alternatively, the rate may be based on machine running hours instead of man hours.

Setting standard costs for other overheads

General administration, marketing and distribution are usually included in standard product costs, although methods of doing so vary considerably. The simplest way of providing for these costs is to arrive at absorption rates from budgeted data, the rate being applied as a percentage on the standard production cost.

In certain circumstances, more sophisticated means would be employed. *Distribution costs*, which include warehousing and the making up of packages for customers, as well as delivery costs may vary as between products, and a detailed study of types of packages, packing time, method of delivery, etc., may be called for. Advertising and other marketing costs may require analysis by products if they are not entirely general in character.

Standard cost cards

The standard cost card is a key document in a system of standard costing. One is prepared for each product manufactured and forms a complete record of all details of the cost of that unit.

Variance analysis

The effectiveness of standard costing as a control technique derives from variance analysis. Costs are entered against operations, processes and products, as in 'actual product costing', but, at each stage, where necessary, actuals are converted to standard by clerical adjustment, for example, if an entered cost is £120 but, according to the standard cost card, it should be £110, a *credit* entry of £10 is made by way of adjustment. At the same time the £10 is *debited* to a specific *variance account*. This means, of course, that all work in progress and all complete work is given a *standard* valuation, all the differences having been extracted and transferred to variance accounts. Variances in selling prices are similarly dealt with.

At the end of the cost accounting period, management is presented with a statement on these lines:

	£	
Sales (at *standard* prices)	200,000	Analysed by products
less Cost of Sales (*at standard*)	170,000	
Standard net profit on actual Sales	30,000	
plus or minus Variances (*detailed*)	−4,000	
Actual net profit:	26,000	

The detailed variances, which are designated either *favourable* or *adverse*, include such items as material price, material usage, direct wage rate, direct labour efficiency, idle time, process loss and fixed overhead volume. The number of separate variances may be considerable, particularly when operating variances are detailed by cost centres. This gives management a clear picture of what profit should have been made, and a clear analysis of the difference by *causes*.

Chapter 5

Budgetary Planning and Control

M J Wright, Finance Director and Company Secretary, Stuart Davis Machines Ltd

---

There are four elements of management – planning, control, co-ordination and motivation. Budgetary control is a management technique which combines the two elements of planning and control in one procedure. It is, moreover, a technique which is dependent for success upon the presence of co-ordination. The aim of profit maximisation requires co-ordination of plans and budgets and the definition of limiting factors.

The processes of management to which the technique of budgetary control contributes are:

1 Setting of objectives
2 Preparation of plans
3 Co-ordination of plans
4 Evaluation of plans (preparation of budgets)
5 Control
6 Corrective action

This is a logical progression of activities. Unfortunately, managements do not always think or act in a logical way.

Planning

Planning and control are essentially interrelated, control being the obverse of planning. Planning is the process of deciding what the organisation is going to achieve and the way it will do so. Control is the process of watching to see that the programme of action and the prescribed standards are adhered to, or of highlighting the reasons why this has not been done.

Objectives

As a pre-requisite of planning, top management must establish the objectives of the organisation. The objectives may relate to many things, for example, return on capital employed, expansion of markets, development of new products, improvement of manufacturing facilities. In all cases, however, they must be precise, ambitious and realistic.

The requirement of precision means not only precision in defining the results to be achieved, but also precision in defining factors affecting the organisation and precision in defining actions to be taken. Management must appreciate the need for precision in its approach to planning and control. It must not neglect its basic responsibility for planning and merely content itself with forecasting.

The requirements of being ambitious and realistic can be regarded as one. In effect they mean that objectives must not be too conservative or, yet, too extreme. The objectives must impose a demand on the skills of management but they must also be achievable.

Planning period

The length of the planning period has an important influence on the definition of objectives. A distinction must be made between short-term and long-term plans.

In most organisations the short-term planning period is defined as one year. During this period the objective will be to improve current operating performance and profits and to implement steps in the long-term plans.

The long-term planning cycle must be sufficiently long to allow management to recognise the need for action and to allow for that action to be effective. The plans will tend to be concerned with individual projects such as the development of new products or the improvement of operating efficiency by the provision of new facilities.

Whatever the planning period, each plan must comprise an evaluation of all factors, both internal and external, affecting performance, an objective, a programme of action and an evaluation of the financial effect of the plan. Once more, the logical progression of activities is emphasised.

Definition of responsibilities

The definition of responsibilities is of the utmost importance and requires a sound organisation structure. In the first instance, top management is responsible for defining objectives and the primary objective must be to achieve a specified return on capital employed.

Once the organisation's overall objectives have been established objectives must be developed downwards for all levels of management. Each manager must know precisely what is expected of him and top management must know who is accountable for each part of the plan. This is essential for the proper control of performance.

Control

The objectives of control are:

1 General financial and cost control – requiring the use of budgets and accounts to relate income and expenditure to planned performance.
2 Performance control – requiring the use of standards and costs to disclose technical inefficiencies and the advantages or disadvantages of alternative methods, or alternative courses of action.
3 The establishment of data for future plans.

Preparation of control information and its use

It is important to distinguish between the preparation of control information and its use. The control activity, comprising accounting, costing and management reporting, does not have any right of control over other activities of the organisation. The purpose of control records is to provide information which can be used as a basis for making decisions or taking action. However, the decisions must be made and the action taken by each individual manager in relation to his clearly-defined responsibilities. In brief, accounting, costing and management reporting are not control but a means for control. A similar distinction between the role of management and that of the finance function will be drawn in the section dealing with budgets.

It has been stated many times that management information is not a substitute for management action. The best of management information does not guarantee effective management. Unfortunately, it is sometimes the case that management does not possess the judgment and ability to take action upon management information. To hide this lack of ability criticism is too often made of the control activity.

The control activity

Responsibility for the control activity, defined above as the preparation of control information, ultimately rests with an individual – the chief accountant (or whatever title he may have). The method of organisation for the preparation of control information, however, is a matter of choice. The degree of centralisation or decentralisation adopted will depend on a multitude of factors, for example, the size of the company, the number and size of separate establishments, geographical locations and the methods of manufacture.

Whatever the method of organisation, however, the two sections of the control activity, namely accounting and costing, should come under one head. Costing is sometimes regarded as being separate and distinct from accounting. This is incorrect; costing is dependent upon accounting and must be integrated into the accounting records. Costing is merely an analysis of expenditure recorded in accounts whereby such expenditure is related to units of production or to service provided.

Budgets

A budget is the financial evaluation of management plans. The aim of all management plans is, ultimately, the maximisation of profits in relation to capital employed. Thus, money is the medium through which the success or failure of an organisation and its management will be judged. The medium of the budget is money and this is where its significance lies.

Maximisation of the return on capital employed is a long-term objective. A high return on capital employed can be earned in the short-term to the detriment of the future well-being of the organisation. For instance, a policy of not investing in plant or research and development will restrict capital employed but will probably mean that in the long-term the organisation will become uncompetitive by virtue of obsolete methods or products.

Benefits from budgets

The benefits arising from the introduction of budgets have been well defined in *The Principles and Practice of Management*, edited by E F L Brech. These may be divided into four categories:

1 The co-ordination of objectives, plans and action. Budgets enable:
   (*a*) 'Policies to be expressed with reference to defined objectives and plans'.
   (*b*) 'Co-ordination in the execution of policies to be improbec by imposing an objective which has been accepted, that is, a common objective'.

2 The introduction of control. In a dynamic organisation there will not only be control; there will also be a positive striving for improvements on targets and cost. Budgets enable:
   (*a*) 'Measurement to be applied to the operations of a business by means of comparison between budget and actual results'.
   (*b*) 'Minimum net revenue and expense limits to be fixed with confidence'.
   (*c*) 'Financial requirements to be planned by showing what funds will be required, when they will be required and towards what ends they are to be applied'.
   (*d*) 'Policies and practices to be changed in order that the objective may be achieved altogether or as nearly as possible'.

3 Improvement in the organisation structure. Budgets enable: 'a greater degree of delegation to be exercised, and more freedom in the use of initiative and judgment within the framework and scope of the budgets. Men can direct their efforts to known ends, and because the ends are known, can be given greater freedom in their actions'.

4 Future planning. Budgets enable 'an improved factual basis to be adapted for planning future operations, experience is not only recorded, it is recorded in relation to a plan'.

Budget requirements

The basic budget requirements may be deduced from what has already been said about planning and control. Budgets are the evaluation of management plans. They require, therefore, clearly established and definitive policies. Management cannot fulfil its responsibility for setting objectives and establishing plans by merely instructing the financial function to budget for higher sales and larger profits than the previous year.

Top management must know who is accountable for each part of the plan. Therefore, budgets require a defined and logical organisation structure.

The classification of accounts must cover not only expense headings but must also be relative to the organisation structure and the control activity must be capable of producing information for prompt and meaningful comparison with budgets and standards.

Responsibilities for budgets

The responsibility for planning the profitable conduct of an organisation rests with the management. The control activity, that is, accounting and costing staff, should assist management by:

1 Planning and co-ordinating the timing, development, review and approval of budgets.

2 Establishing cost and profit objectives which will ensure that the budget is compatible with the long-term planning of the organisation.

3 Providing financial data for evaluating alternative policies during the development of budgets.
4 Critically analysing proposed budgets and recommending alternative policies.
5 Ensuring that adequate detail is included in budgets to facilitate subsequent control by the manager responsible.

Cost centres

The budget for an organisation is the sum of the budgets for each of the main functions of the organisation. In turn the budgets for the main functions are supported by subsidiary budgets.

The basic principle to be applied is that costs should be controlled at the point at which they are incurred. As a result costs should be built up on a pyramid system. The base of the pyramid is comprised of *cost centres* – these are areas of responsibility. The cost centre budgets are then consolidated into functional budgets, for example, production, engineering, selling and distribution, administration. The functional budgets are consolidated to form the master budget.

The following is an example of the cost centre classification of the manufacturing function of a machine tool manufacturer:

Code	Cost centre
10	Machine Shop Management and Supervision
11	Direct Machine Shop – Light machining A
12	Direct Machine Shop – Light machining B
13	Direct Machine Shop – Medium machining
14	Direct Machine Shop – Heavy machining
21	Indirect Machine Shop – Fettle, paint and deburr
22	Indirect Machine Shop – Mark out
23	Indirect Machine Shop – Heat treatment
30	Assembly Shop Management and Supervision
31	Direct Assembly Shop – Fixture
32	Direct Assembly shop – Piping
33	Direct Assembly Shop – Main assembly
34	Direct assembly shop – Head
35	Direct Assembly Shop – shop wiring

40 Director of Manufacturing
41 Purchasing
42 Material handling
43 Tool grinding
44 Maintenance
45 Production control

The budget period

It is normal business practice to divide activity into yearly periods and it is natural, therefore, that budgets are prepared for a year or a division or multiple thereof.

The budget period is dependent upon the planning period. The factors which determine this period are:

External economic conditions. The greater the degree of economic uncertainty, the shorter must be the budget period. For example, the demand for an organisation's product may be dictated by changes in fashion. The unpredictability of demand may make a budget of less than one year an absolute necessity.

Internal circumstances. The level of capital investment required may necessitate a long-term budget period. In practice the phrase long-term budget means a budget period of one year supported by a long-term forecast.

The purpose of budgeting is the exercise of control, and therefore the budget period is normally divided into control periods, the length of which may be:

1 Calendar months
2 Four-weekly periods
3 Total number of working days in the year divided by twelve

The basis of control is comparison of results and true comparisons are not achieved with periods 1 and 2. Calendar months do not have the same number of days and the comparison of four-weekly periods is vitiated to some extent by the incidence of holidays.

In addition to the basic control period of one-twelth or one-thirteenth of a year, certain costs will require to be controlled daily or weekly, for example, direct labour performance.

Fixed and flexible budgets

There are two types of budget:

1 Fixed – relating costs to one volume of output
2 Flexible – defining cost structures for various levels of output

The flexible budget is the one which enables costs to be controlled must effectively. It is most unlikely that the level of activity determined upon in a fixed budget will be the one obtained in practice. However, the budgeted level of operation assumed in the plan will have to act as the foundation of the budgetary control system.

Flexible budgeting is the only practical way of controlling factory overheads. The major difficulty, however, is to classify overheads into fixed and variable categories. In practice many costs are of a semi-variable nature.

Budget preparation

The preparation of budgets represents the evaluation of plans and is merely one of the processes of management referred to in the introduction. Budget preparation depends on satisfactory completion of the following processes:

1 Setting the objectives.
2 Preparing the plans – involving the consideration of alternatives.
3 Co-ordinating the plans – involving the definition of limiting factors and the selection of the plan best achieving the main objective, namely, the maximisation of the return on capital employed while securing the long-term well-being of the company.

The evaluation of the plan must proceed in a logical way and the flow of work is shown in Figure 5:1. It is not within the scope of this chapter to describe in detail the preparation of particular types of budget. Procedures will be outlined, and illustrated when appropriate.

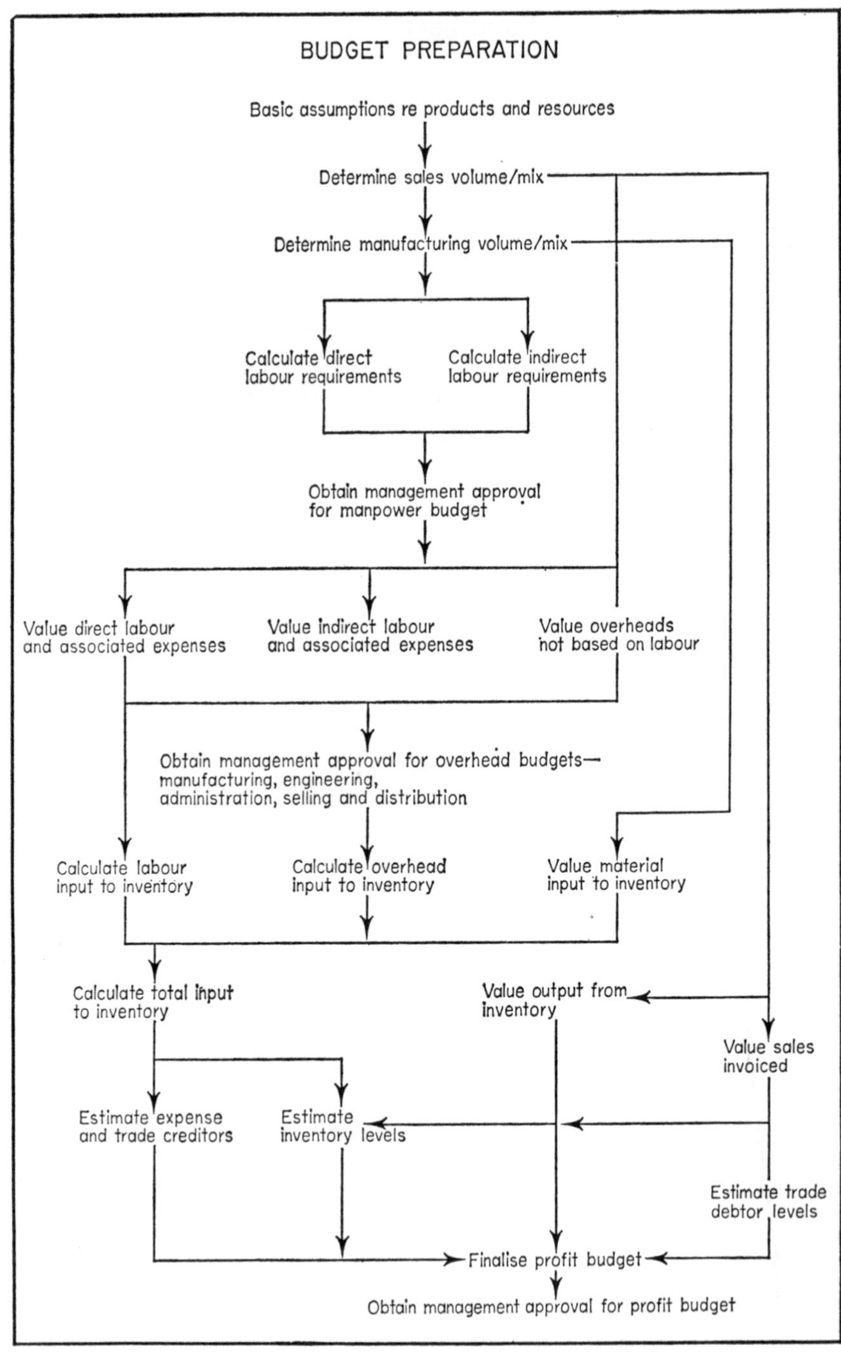

FIGURE 5:1 BUDGET PREPARATION

This chart shows the flow of work involved in the preparation of the profit budget

Budget assumptions

All budgets must be based on assumptions published to managers of cost centres so that, when all aspects of the budget are consolidated, the result will be a coherent evaluation of the plan of the organisation. The assumptions will normally deal with such matters as:

Markets and product sales. These include firm orders in hand, with the latest known delivery dates or terms of sale for each group of products which relate to the budget year; orders expected to be received, with the value of firm orders expected for each product in home and export markets analysed as to year of delivery; new products, their introduction and the build-up of stocks and sales in each market.

Pricing. Including existing products, planned or estimated price changes (to each product group) in home and export markets; new products' pricing plans for each market; changes in discounts and commissions planned for each product group, market or major customer.

Product design and specification changes. The timing of changes made to improve the performance of a product, facilitate manufacture, facilitate marketing or reduce costs.

Make or buy decisions. This includes proposed changes from outside purchase of supplies and services and manufacturing or providing own services, the timing of proposed changes and an estimate of quantities and costs.

Manufacturing assumptions. This involves any proposed transfers of location, and timing thereof, of manufacture between factories showing the products, plant and equipment, floor space, manpower and other manufacturing facilities involved. It also concerns any changes in the method of manufacture, the timing of such changes, and the products and manufacturing facilities involved.

Organisation changes. Changes in departmental responsibility and structure, their timing and the manpower and facilities involved, come into this category; so also do changes in work load responsibility, including the transfer of work responsibility between departments, its timing and the manpower and facilities involved.

Accounting classification changes. This involves any proposed changes in account or cost centre classifications.

Working days. The number of working days in each accounting period.

Economics. This embraces such items as the prices of major materials to be used in production; labour costs, basic working hours, paid holidays, wage rates and overtime and shift premiums to be used in the evaluation of hourly paid and salaried labour costs; employee fringe benefits, such as company pensions, national insurance and graduated pension contributions, etc.

Determination of sales volume/mix

The sales budget will be based upon an analysis of firm orders in hand and orders expected to be received as contained in the budget assumptions. At that stage the degree of product detail, market analysis and customer analysis will have been determined. The degree of analysis determines the layout of the budget schedule and, what is more important, the degree of analysis of profit variance which can be carried out in the budget year.

Determination of manufacturing volume/mix

It has already been stated that limiting factors have been defined and plans co-ordinated. Thus, it is known that manufacturing capacity is or will be sufficient to meet the budgeted sales. The three steps set out below are necessary:

Determine inventory policy and the degree of analysis of inventory and cost of sales. The basic analysis of cost of sales will be direct materials, direct labour and factory overheads but may also include 'engineering costs', for example, special development or design costs.

Determine the basis of evaluation of cost of sales. This will depend upon the product and the method of costing. One of the following bases will probably apply:

Standard products. Standard costs based on budgeted designs and specifications, material prices, labour rates and overhead recovery rates based on budgeted manufacturing volumes and expenses; where no standards or estimates exist and product costing is based on actual costs, the latest known actual cost adjusted to conditions included in the budget assumptions.

Contracts, that is, special products. Cost estimates which formed the basis of the accepted quotation adjusted for changes made at the customer's request; or cost estimates based on a detailed design: any difference between the quotation estimate and the detailed design estimate may be segregated and budgeted as a completed order adjustment.

Evaluate the cost of sales.

At this stage the budget covers the following items: sales (orders in hand and orders anticipated; sales analysis (that is, product analysis); total sales invoiced; the cost of sales (standard or estimated), divided into direct material, direct labour, factory overheads and engineering; the total manufacturing cost and the gross margin.

Calculation of direct labour requirements

Inventory policy and the direct labour content of sales has already been determined. The computation of direct manpower relates the number of productive hours per direct worker available per annum to the budgeted labour input to inventory. For example, if input to inventory (sales value) is £200,000 (that, is sales±movement in work in progress is £200,000), and the labour content is known to be 15 per cent of sales value,=£30,000; direct man-hours available per annum are as follows:

Total hours – 52 weeks at 40 hours per week		2080
Less: Annual holidays 15 days	120	
Statutory holidays 6 days	48	168
		1912
Less: Sickness 2 per cent		38
		1874
Less: Indirect time (waiting time, training, etc.)		153
		1721
Add: Overtime – 10 per cent of attended time		187
Total direct man-hours available per man per annum		1908

DIRECT LABOUR HOURS ANALYSIS													
Direct labour work-load	Number of hours												
	Total	Jan	Feb	Mar	Apr	May	Jun	Jul	Aug	Sep	Oct	Nov	Dec
Working days													
Manpower plan—Direct labour men													
Direct labour—Normal hours													
Direct labour—Overtime hours													
Total direct labour man hours													
Work-in-progress													
Capital projects													
Revenue projects													
Total direct man hours required													
Indirect time:–													
Plant maintenance													
Waiting time													
Training etc													
Lost time ie sickness													
Total direct labour man hours													
Budget overhead recovery (£)													
Direct man hours at standard labour rate:—													
Work-in-progress													
Capital projects													
Revenue projects													
Budget overhead recovery (% of DL)													
Work-in-progress													
Capital projects													
Revenue projects													
Total budget overhead recovery													
Total budget overhead expense													
Budget over/(under) recovery													

FIGURE 5:2 DIRECT LABOUR-HOURS ANALYSIS

This form translates the direct manpower budget into working hours and determines the overtime plan. The basis of overhead recovery is units of direct labour and provision is made for the evaluation of direct man hours at a

If the standard labour rate per hour is £1.05 then the total direct labour-hours required amount to:

$$\frac{30{,}000}{1.05} = 28571 \text{ hours}$$

The average direct manpower required during the year is:

$$\frac{28{,}571}{1{,}908} = 15 \text{ men}$$

A 'direct labour-hours analysis' schedule translates the manpower budget into working hours and also determines the overtime plan (Figure 5:2). It should be completed for each cost centre where labour is charged to work in progress or where an overhead recovery rate is required.

Calculation of indirect manpower requirements

The indirect manpower budget is developed by means of a detailed analysis of current staff levels in the light of future plans and objectives. The procedures are to establish the planned work-load for each cost centre, to develop the work-load criteria where possible, and to list each job performed by an individual or group in the cost centre.

The manpower budget provides the basis for building up the labour section of the overhead budgets.

Calculation of overhead expenses

Expenses budgets are prepared for four main purposes:

1 To establish a minimum level of expense compatible with the planned future work-load of a department.
2 To identify the responsibility for authorising expenses during the budget year.
3 To relate operating expenses to the product.
4 To provide management at all levels with a detailed basis for control of all expenses.

Expense budgets must therefore be prepared for the cost centre originating the cost and related to the product by means of recovery rates. A schedule of operating expenditure is completed for each cost centre with reference to staff requirements calculated in the manpower budget and to the budget assumptions. All expenses are built up by control periods.

Individual cost centre budgets are summarised by major function, that is manufacturing, engineering, service, marketing, and administration.

Calculation of working capital and capital employed

The structure of the working capital budget is a follows:

1 Cash. A detailed cash forecast should be prepared, not only for the budget year, but also for the remainder of the current financial year.
2 Inventories, that is, raw materials, components and sub-assemblies, work in progress, finished products and non-production inventories, less inventory adjustments and provisions relating to obsolescence, revaluation, physical losses, etc.
3 Debtors, less provision for bad debts.
4 Creditors.
5 Progress payments.
6 Deposits received.

Preparation of budget summary

The budget summary presents the key management financial information to top management. It may show:

1 Profit before tax
2 Net trading profit
3 Sales invoiced
4 Capital employed
5 Number of employees
6 Net trading profit as a percentage of sales invoiced
7 Net trading profit as a percentage of capital employed
8 Sales invoiced as a percentage of capital employed
9 Working capital as a percentage of sales invoiced
10 Ratio of current assets to current liabilities

An example of a budget performance report summary is given in the next section.

Performance reporting

Control reports are part of the process of ensuring that approved objectives are achieved. Their purpose is to ensure that the objectives are achieved in spite of deviations from planning assumptions or from planned management action.

A system of performance reporting must provide management at all levels with a financial analysis of actual achievements and future plans compared with the approved budget. The three areas on which reports should concentrate are: measuring performance; highlighting areas where action is required; providing forecasts which express the plans for the remainder of the year. Of these, the highlighting of the need for action is the most important. Control reports must indicate a need for action and show whether the course of action recommended is likely to bring results back in line with the original objectives.

Clear indication of the need for action is preferable to the detailed examination of the causes of variances. Moreover, clear indication of the responsibility for the results of action now necessary is preferable to the assessment of credit or blame for past variances.

Requirements for performance reporting

The basic requirements for performance reporting, set out below, are obviously similar to budget requirements, since control is achieved by reporting actual performance against the approved budget.

Classification. There must be a sound organisation structure and the control information must be classified in accordance with responsibility.

Uniformity. Results must be presented on a consistent basis. Inconsistent or unusual data must always be identified and an explanation provided.

Detail. The amount of detail required is dependent upon the level of management using the control information. Management time and effort is saved by reporting exceptions to the plan.

Timing. The information must relate to a time period appropriate to the objects of the organisation. Moreover, it must be available at a time which enables management to take decisions which will influence the factors represented by the control information.

Detail and timing are, perhaps, the two factors in which control information is most deficient.

Form of reports

Upon the introduction of a budgetary control system reporting procedures should be implemented as quickly as possible. A comprehensive set of reports should be drawn up, the purpose of each report and the degree of detail to be contained therein being clearly established. With regard to detail, the basic principle, as already stated, is that the higher the level of management the less the amount of detail reported.

Reports for top management

The prime requirement is a document summarising the key management financial information of the organisation. It should show:

1 Profit performance
2 Orders and invoicing
3 Capital employed
4 Manpower
5 Return on capital employed

Actual results should be compared with budget and forecasts for the remainder of the budget year may also be compared with budget.

The reporting of the return on capital can only be shown as a year to date average. This means multiplying the net trading profit for the year to date by twelve and dividing by the number of months elapsed. Capital employed is the average of the month-end capital totals in the year to date.

An example of a budget performance report summary is shown in Figure 5:3. This summary may be supported by schedules of variance analysis, (Figure 5:4) trading results, capital employed (Figure 5:5) and manpower.

PROFIT BUDGET PERFORMANCE.REPORT SUMMARY

	Jan	Feb	Mar	Apr	May	June	July	Aug	Sep	Oct	Nov	Dec
	Actual					Forecast						
Profit before tax (cumulative)												
Actual £ 000												
Budget £ 000												
Better/(worse) than budget												
Net trading profit (cumulative)												
Actual £ 000												
Budget £ 000												
Better/(worse) than budget												
Sales invoiced (cumulative)												
Actual £ 000												
Budget £ 000												
Better/(worse) than budget												
Orders received (cumulative) and in hand												
Received-actual £ 000												
Better/(worse) than budget												
In hand												
Capital employed												
Actual £ 000												
Better/(worse) than budget												
Total manpower												
Actual £ 000												
Better/(worse) than budget												
% net trading profit on sales (cumulative)												
Actual %												
Budget %												
% return on capital employed (year to date average)												
Actual %												
Budget %												

FIGURE 5:3 PROFIT BUDGET PERFORMANCE REPORT—SUMMARY
This is a report for top management and summarises the key management financial information

	This month			Year to date			Full-year forecast		
	Actual	Budget	Variance	Actual	Budget	Variance	Actual	Budget	Variance
Profit / (Loss) before tax									
Reasons for variance: Better / (Worse) than budget:									
Sales volume, mix and selling prices:									
Sales volume									
Changes in market mix									
Changes in product mix									
Selling prices									
Product cost changes:									
Material usage									
Material prices									
Labour usage									
Labour rates									
Overheads									
Carriage, freight and insurance									
GROSS MARGIN									
Cost adjustments:									
Factory overheads: Activity									
Expenditure									
Inventory adjustments									
Engineering overheads: Activity									
Expenditure									
GROSS TRADING PROFIT									
Overhead expenses									
Administration									
Selling and distribution									
NET TRADING PROFIT									
Non-trading variances									
Discount allowed									
Agents commission									
Interest									
PROFIT BEFORE TAX									

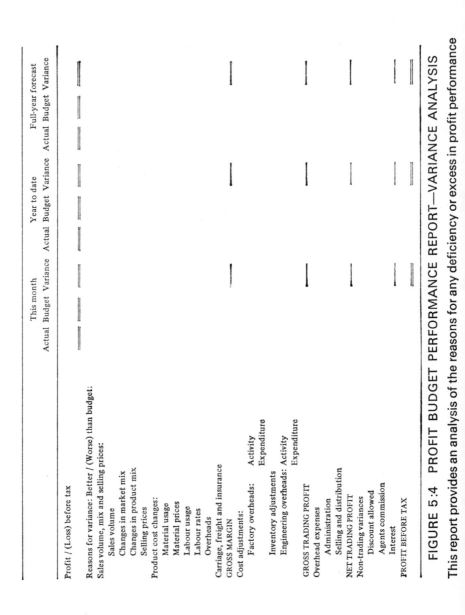

FIGURE 5:4 PROFIT BUDGET PERFORMANCE REPORT—VARIANCE ANALYSIS

This report provides an analysis of the reasons for any deficiency or excess in profit performance

PROFIT BUDGET PERFORMANCE REPORT
Capital employed

Balances at the end of financial period	End of last year	End of last month	This month		Forecast					
			Actual	Better/ (worse) than budget	Next three months			Subsequent three quarters		
Trade debtors: Home										
Overseas										
Non-trade debtors										
Less: Provision for bad debts										
Total debtors										
Raw materials										
Work in progress										
Components and sub-assemblies										
Finished products										
Non-production inventories										
Less: Adjustments and provisions										
Total inventories										
Progress payments										
Advance collections										
Net total inventories										
Trade creditors: Home										
Overseas										
Non-trade creditors										
Accrued liabilities										
Total creditors										
Total working capital										
Total cash at bank and in hand										
Fixed assets at net book value										
Provisions										
Total capital employed										
Average capital employed										

FIGURE 5:5 PROFIT BUDGET PERFORMANCE REPORT—CAPITAL EMPLOYED

This report supports the summary of profit budget performance provided for top management and shows the composition of total capital employed

Reports for subordinate managers

The supporting detail given to top management should be the summary control reports for its immediate subordinates and these, in turn, would be supported by further detail. This process would be repeated right down the management scale, thus ensuring that each level of management has the complete picture of its sphere of operations.

Project cost control

Capital expenditure budgets and plans are an integral part of the planning and budgetary control system. Capital expenditure budget procedures therefore follow the same general principles and involve the same objectives and responsibilities that have already been expounded. The main objective is to direct investment and related actions towards maximum profitability. The achievement of this objective is aided by requiring proposals to be developed on a timely, detailed and well planned basis, all alternative courses of action to be considered, together with their various implications, and full financial analyses and evalutions to be prepred. There should also be adequate control over expenditure and timely implementation of projects and their subsequent operating results. The proposals should be fully integrated into the master budget or profit plan.

Method of preparation of capital expenditure budgets

In broad outline the method of budget preparation is to prepare a proposal for each project showing:

Purpose. This must be consistent with the objectives of the organisation regarding the provision of new capacity and reduction in operating expenses.

Description. This should cover the assets to be acquired, the capacity and utilisation of assets, product and market considerations, other physical factors, other relevant business considerations, and any non-financial benefits.

Cost. The various elements of cost should be analysed, namely: fixed assets and related expenses, that is, the non-capitalised costs of making new assets ready for operation, launching costs (the excess operating costs of bringing new assets into full operation), working capital and total investment, that is, the total non-recurring cash outlays required to implement a project.

Timing. The timing of budget expenditures has an important effect on the cash forecast.

Physical and financial justification. The financial justification will include the financial worth of the proposal; its estimated effects on profit, the risks affecting the planned return, any tax benefits and other allowances, and a discounted cash flow analysis.

In making a financial appraisal of project proposals two fundamental principles should be observed: all reasonable alternative courses of action must be carefully defined, and where they possess genuine profit potential, they must be impartially evaluated against the original proposal; in making comparisons of the alternative courses of action only the financial effects which are attributable to differences between the two should be taken into account.

Control: project status reports

The timely reporting on the progress, completion and control of approved projects requires two basic reports.

Project status report (Figure 5:6). This shows the commitments, latest estimates of total costs, physical progress, estimated completion dates, and actual expenditure to date. The report will compare these costs and dates with those planned and approved in the appropriate project requests. Where the estimated total cost is in excess of the amount authorised, an explanation should be provided and a proposed course of action stated. If the estimated completion date varies from that planned, a statement explaining the circumstances should be provided. *Project Completion Report* (Figure 5:7). Providing a comparison of planned expenditure with actual achieved, together with a commentary on significant variances. Superficial or otherwise inadequate explanations for variances must be avoided. One of the major reasons for reviewing actual expenditure against the original estimate is to improve the quality of estimating. It is, therefore, important to explain variances in a way which will be helpful in analysing the accuracy of the project estimates.

PROJECT STATUS REPORT

Date________

Project number	Project title or category	Total authorised	Committed to date			Forecast cost		Forecast (over)/ under	% complete	Completion date		Expenditure	
			Authorised	Committed	(over)/ under	Uncommitted	Total			Estimated	Original	This month	Total

FIGURE 5 : 6 PROJECT STATUS REPORT

The purpose of this report is to provide a means of controlling both the cost and progress of approved capital projects

PROJECT COMPLETION REPORT

Project number and title ______________________ Date ______________________

	Total cost	Land and buildings	Plant and machinery	Special tools	Installation costs	Related expenses	Completion date
Planned/authorised							
Actual							
(Over)/under authorisation							

Explanations of variance

FIGURE 5:7 PROJECT COMPLETION REPORT

This report is a follow-up of the project status report and provides an analysis of variances, both as regards costs and completion dates, of approved capital projects

Long-term profit planning

In addition to its short-term plans as evaluated in the budget, an organisation will normally develop a detailed long-term plan, say for a period of five years. This plan will embrace all aspects of sales, cost of sales, working capital, manpower and productive capacity.

The general principles to be observed in preparing the long-term plan are as follows:

1 Established objectives, planning assumptions and policy must be properly reflected.
2 The base period for the plan will be the budget year.
3 The long-term plan should be developed simultaneously with the budget and the two must be consistent. All financial and statistical data should be developed on a year-to-year basis and all variances between the years must be explainable.
4 The implications of the capital expenditure budget should be reflected in the forecast levels of fixed assets, working capital, revenues, costs and profits.
5 Responsibility for planning the long-term profitable conduct of an organisation rests with the general management. The responsibilities of the control activity have been dealt with in the section dealing with responsibilities for budgets.
6 The long-term plan, just as the budget, must be based on a detailed set of assumptions dealing with market size and market share, product range and selling prices, location of manufacture and manufacturing methods, sources of supplies and services, material prices, labour costs, etc., and organisational changes.

With regard to schedules of the long-term plan, it must always be borne in mind that the plan is an extension of the budget and every attempt should be made to keep the schedules in the same form as the budget schedules.

PART TWO

Marketing Management

Chapter 6

Techniques of Industrial Market Research

E P Danger, Managing Director, Technical Market Research Limited

---

Market reserarch is the *systematic* collection of facts, figures and information about markets with a definite objective in view. Its purpose is to collect and interpret data which can then be used to plan production and promote sales to the best advantage. The need for market research arises because every management decision should be based on the best available information, and not on guesswork or hunch. It is a tool of management and not a substitute for management. It provides the basis on which decisions are made and not the decisions themselves. It is a vital part of long-range planning, but it is equally important in the short term.

Market research is of interest to virtually every company in the engineering industry, whether it is making machines or components, assembling, fabricating, casting or machining, and whether it is building standard products or making them to order. The engineering industry needs market research just as much as any other industry. In fact, it probably needs it more than most because, although it has long been production orientated, it has now been forced into a position, by technological developments and changes in users' needs, where marketing and selling are much more vital than they were in the past.

Changes in the engineering industry are illustrated in Figures 6:1 and 6:2. The first demonstrates deliveries of two typical types of machine tools over an eight year period. It will be noted how demand has fluctuated and, in one case, declined overall.

Figure 6:2 illustrates a more sophisticated problem. Although the output of numerically-controlled machine tools has practically doubled over the period, the value has increased almost fourfold, indicating the increasing sophistication of these tools. Examination of the export figures, on the other hand, shows that deliveries to the home market have been practically static over the whole period (although, of course, the value has increased). This would seem to suggest the need for a much greater sales effort despite the fact that the sales graph based on value would show a strong upward curve.

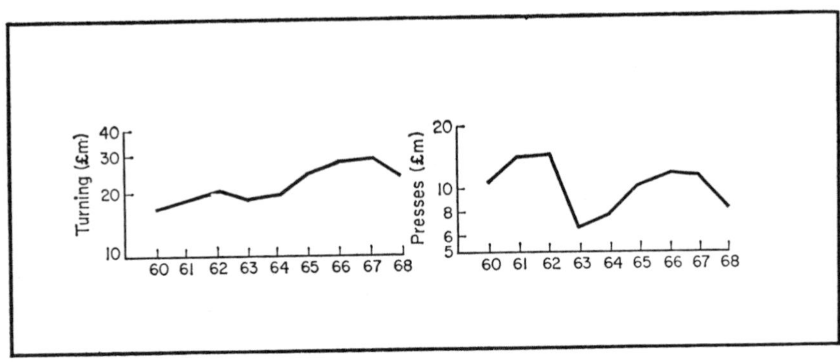

FIGURE 6:1 HOME DELIVERIES OF UK MACHINES TOOLS

Illustrates the fluctuating demand for typical machine tools (Reproduced with permission of the Controller of Her Majesty's Stationery Office)

Almost every company uses market research in a more or less rudimentary way, although it may not be called market research. For example, if the managing director visits customers, that is market research; if the export manager studies overseas conditions, that is

Year	Number	Total £ thousands	Number	Export £ thousands
1966	323	4 161	-	904
1967	458	7 503	-	2 534
1968	558	11 875	109	2 547
1969	543	14 627	189	6 141
1970	600	15 739	241	6 603

FIGURE 6:2 DELIVERIES OF NUMERICALLY-CONTROLLED METALWORKING MACHINE TOOLS

Indicates a static home demand in spite of increased sales value (Reproduced with permission of the Controller of Her Majesty's Stationery Office)

market research; if the sales manager analyses representatives' reports, that is market research. However, information so obtained is seldom coordinated and even less likely to be systematic. Market research needs an objective. In the engineering industry fixing the objective may be even more important than carrying out the research itself and certainly requires a discussion of marketing principles.

Marketing for the engineering industry

There are many definitions of marketing but the simplest is probably 'making a profit from the sale of goods' and this involves production, selling and distribution. Marketing is not just another word for selling but involves consideration of all aspects of a business. Modern marketing principles can be applied to the engineering industry with particular advantage because, in the past, engineering products have usually been sold by waiting for the customer to come and buy them.

This system works very well until there is a recession, with consequent price cutting, or until the changing nature of a user industry puts most of the customers out of business or changes the nature of their demand. Finding new customers for a production-orientated business is no easy task, particularly when there is a great deal of surplus capacity available.

Adopting the marketing approach may require quite a radical change in the thinking of the production-orientated company and in the company's attitude to the market-place. What it really means is finding out what the customer wants, producing what he wants, and then going out and selling it to him. In other words, transferring the initiative from the customer to the manufacturer.

However, it also means that if adequate profits are to be made production must be geared to the requirements of the customer so that he gets what he wants, when he wants it, and at a price that he is willing to pay or which it is economical for him to pay.

Acceptance of the marketing concept means that market research must be used to analyse the nature of the demand and how that demand can be met profitably. A manufacturer might find that he would do best to concentrate on a specific part of the market – which he is well equipped to handle – and to forget about trying to meet every demand made on him. On the other hand, a manufacturer might do better to drop his existing production and get into something entirely new. Yet again, methods of selling or distribution may require radical alteration or should be given a new look.

A metal fabricator, for example, with special skills in the manipulation of stainless steel tubes, who studies his market, could reach the conclusion that he would be well advised to go out and sell the *uses* of stainless steel tubes rather than just look for customers who want tubes. The study could show that a greater degree of specialisation was advantageous or that concentration on a range of standard sizes and shapes would cheapen production and improve profitability. The manufacturer might even discover that his particular skills were in a declining market and that he ought to be looking at something else.

Sound marketing practice requires that a manufacturer should be aware of the changing nature of the market so that new ideas, new methods, and new products are adopted as the need for them arises. Many engineering companies have seen their markets disappear almost overnight because of declining customer industries or because of new techniques. The replacement of metal by plastics is a case in point. Figure 6:3 illustrates this point very graphically.

The reaction to a threat of this kind may be to consider joining the

	1966	1968	1969	1970	1971
Wood	249 (39.8%)	200 (28.0%)	175 (25.9%)	99 (13.6%)	68 (8.8%)
Metal	33 (5.3%)	13 (1.8%)	21 (3.1%)	8 (1.1%)	1 (0.1%)
Glass-fibre	293 (46.8%)	430 (60.1%)	404 (59.6%)	515 (70.8%)	607 (78.3%)
Inflatable and others	51 (8.1%)	72 (10.1%)	77 (11.4%)	106 (14.5%)	99 (12.8%)
Total number of boats	626	715	677	728	775

FIGURE 6:3 CONSTRUCTION MATERIALS OF BOATS EXHIBITED AT THE INTERNATIONAL BOAT SHOW

These statistics show how the use of metal and wood has been replaced by plastics in a typical sector of industry (With acknowledgments to the *Daily Express*)

opposition. At one time many die casters feared the loss of their market to plastics and promptly became plastics fabricators themselves. This is realistic but it requires market research to provide information on which a decision can be based.

Any marketing decision needs market research to put the market into focus, to enable developments to be foreseen and to outline the action that ought to be taken. The principal marketing problems and the questions that might be asked and to which market research can provide an answer are discussed below.

The basic marketing problem

The question that every engineering company should ask itself is: 'Are we in the right business?' and, if the answer is negative: 'What business should we be in?' Many managements would throw up their hands in horror at the very idea that anyone should suggest that they were in the wrong business but the idea is not so crazy as it sounds.

For example, a company making steam locomotives is obviously in the wrong business. The market has virtually disappeared and if the company has not already moved into something else it will soon be out of business. In fact, this happened a few years ago to a number of once prosperous locomotive builders. They failed to see the writing on the wall and very quickly went to the wall. Figures extracted from the 1963 Census of Production and shown in Figure 6:4 tell the story, while Figure 6:5 underlines the decline of an industry even more dramatically.

This is an extreme example but there are many other sectors of the engineering industry which are doing quite well at the present time but whose future is very uncertain. They are serving declining industries and sooner or later their markets will disappear or decline to a point where there is insufficient profit. There may even be a surplus of capacity which will sooner or later be impossible to fill. There was a large and prosperous sector of the engineering industry based on the production of coal gas, but the gas industry has changed out of all recognition in the last few years and those companies which were not

	1958	1963
MANUFACTURED IN RAILWAY WORKSHOPS (Number)		
Steam	61	nil
IC (including electric, etc., transmissions)	294	123
PRIVATE MANUFACTURERS		
Steam	44	nil
IC (including electric, etc., transmissions)	304	348

FIGURE 6:4 MANUFACTURE OF LOCOMOTIVES

These figures provide a dramatic illustration of the decline in steam locomotives (Reproduced with permission of the Controller of Her Majesty's Stationery Office)

	Total	Steam	Diesel	Electric
1959	16 342	14 457	1 800	85
1960	15 961	13 276	2 550	135
1961	15 028	11 691	3 179	158
1962	12 628	8 767	3 683	178
1963	11 304	7 050	4 060	194
1964	9 633	4 973	4 462	198
1965	8 075	2 987	4 811	277
1966	6 991	1 689	4 962	340
1967	5 445	362	4 742	341
1968	4 658	3	4 326	329
1969	4 511	-	4 183	328

FIGURE 6:5 BRITISH RAIL STOCK OF LOCOMOTIVES

An even more dramatic demonstration of the decline of the steam locomotive industry (Reproduced with permission of the Controller of Her Majesty's Stationery Office)

far sighted enough to diversify in time are now out of business, or nearly so.

To answer the basic questions posed above requires market research, but it is seldom possible to provide a definitive answer in terms of figures. What is usually required in a case of this kind is a broad view of the market and its future. In some cases it is very obvious from a projection of official, or semi-official, statistics that a market is a declining one, but in other cases it may only be possible to make an assessment based on the opinions of knowledgeable persons and on an assessment of technological trends.

A company may find that its present technology has a reasonable life-span but it might also be in a situation where replacement of plant at high cost will be required in the near future. The decision then has to be made whether the market will last sufficiently long to secure an adequate return on the capital sunk in new plant. A decision of this kind requires a very detailed analysis of market prospects and development trends. It should take into account such factors as the probable trend of raw material prices and the prospects of markets increasing to such an extent as to take care of rising costs.

If a company is making a standard product, or a range of standard products (as distinct from, say, fabricating to order), it needs to watch the market trends of these products very carefully. Every product has a life-cycle, which may be short or long depending on circumstances. It may be difficult to measure this life-cycle in advance except by comparison with similar circumstances. However, a slow-down in sales growth is a danger signal and a decline in sales an even more marked one. A slow-down in sales growth may indicate that the sales effort needs attention, but it may also be a sign that the product has reached the peak of its life-cycle and will eventually decline and require replacement. Many companies tend to hang on to declining products too long and it will very often be found that such products are not even making a profit.

Long before the latter stage is reached market research should have been used to measure the future market for a suspect product, and if the market research proves that the market is a declining one, then action is necessary. The market share held by the company requires special attention in a case of this kind: a company may actually be achieving a larger share of a declining market becuse its competitors are withdrawing. A smaller share of the market may indicate, on the other hand, that the sales effort needs attention.

A typical product life-cycle is illustrated in Figure 6:6. The point where the sales curve of the old product begins to flatten out is the point where a new product is desirable but it should be introduced even earlier if the profit margins of the existing product begin to fall, despite increasing sales.

There is a strong case for examining the market for every product periodically to check that the overall market is growing and that the company is achieving its fair share. If market research is used wisely, every company will recognise the situation where it must seek new markets or new products in order to maintain profits.

New products

Market research plays a vital part in the whole question of new products and new markets. Apart from helping to decide whether a new product or a new market is required, it can help to decide what

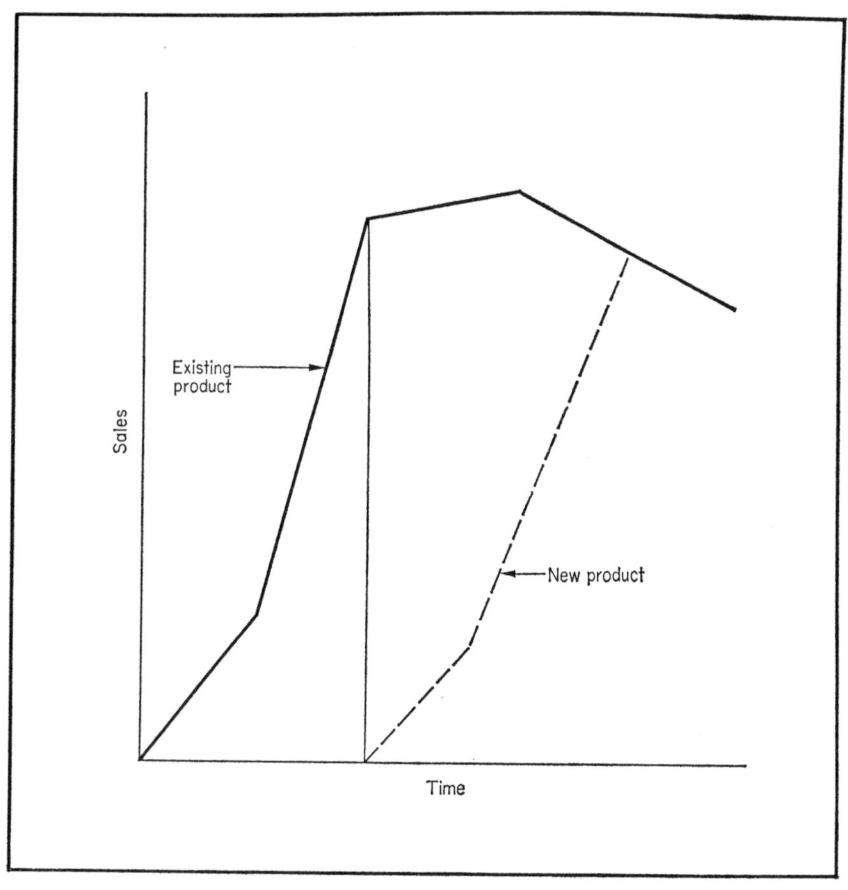

FIGURE 6:6 PRODUCT LIFE-CYCLE

A new product should be introduced at, or before, the point where existing product sales growth begins to flatten out

the new product should be and, most important of all, whether the new product has a viable market.

New products arise in a variety of ways. In some cases a company goes out and looks for them, in some cases they come to light almost by accident, and in other cases they are the result of planned research and development. The latter is a particularly fruitful area for market research. Scientists, technicians, and even management tend to be wildly over-optimistic about their brain-children and there are many companies which have spent vast sums on developing new products which eventually prove to have no market, or at least an unprofitable market.

A company which has a positive research and development programme ought to use market research at all stages in the following way:

1 To make a preliminary assessment of an idea.
2 To make a more detailed study before large sums are spent on research.
3 To make a definitive market study before a new product is developed or goes into production.

In this way, much wasted expenditure can be avoided. Even if the product is a good one, market research will often be able to suggest design changes or modifications which will make the final result more saleable.

Using market research to find new products is practicable but tends to be a rather long and expensive process which may not always show results commensurate with the money expended, unless the area of search can be kept within narrow limits. The main value of market research in the new product-finding process is checking the feasibility of ideas before the process of development gets too far and before the product goes into production.

If the preliminary process of assessment shows that a new product has promise, then a thorough market survey will help to paint the marketing picture, to suggest the most suitable distribution methods, to pinpoint the customers, and to outline the selling methods that should be employed.

There are two important points that should always be remembered in connection with new products in the engineering industry. The first is that the customer for an engineering product is a specialised one and has to be found: it is not a matter of just the ordinary man in the street as with a consumer product; furthermore, the customer may have methods of purchase which are peculiar to a trade or industry, or even specifically to the product. The second important point is that because an engineering company has been successfully selling one product, it does not necessarily mean that it will be able to sell another product; a new product may involve quite a different market and may require quite different selling techniques or a sales force with different characteristics.

Hence, the importance of market research. The aim of the survey should be to find out who the customers are, how they can best be approached, and what characteristics are necessary to meet their needs.

Improving sales

Market research is not always concerned with solving the basic marketing problem or assessing the potential market for new products. Its purpose may be to analyse existing markets and to provide information which will help to increase sales. It will provide the sales manager with a blueprint for more satisfactory selling. This assumes, of course, that the engineering company is satisfied that it is in the right market and that it has the right product mix.

Market research is not, of course, a sales promotion medium, nor is it a short-cut to increased sales, but it can provide positive assistance by, for example, finding new customers and new outlets, calculating the size of the market so that realistic sales targets can be fixed, ascertaining users' needs so that product characteristics meet these needs, discovering the purchasing influence so that promotion may be aimed to the best advantage, assessing the strength of competition so that this can be countered, and outlining better distribution and promotion methods.

The aim of market research may, of course, be to provide the data on which a completely new marketing or selling plan can be based.

Apart from the positive aspects of market research in relation to increasing sales, it may also be very valuable as a means of discovering, or eliminating, those negative factors which may cause static, or even declining, sales. These may include, for example: unsatisfactory distribution or servicing, a poor company image, declining market shares, failure to meet market needs, inadequate promotional material, out of date design, non-competitive prices, increasing or unexpected competition, and competition from new materials or new products.

No company is likely to admit to all, or perhaps any, of these failings but anyone with experience of market research in the engineering industry will know that they are very common faults, and many companies will not be aware of these faults until they take active steps to find out whether they have them. Any management which is worried because sales are not buoyant would do well to check these negative factors and then seek the positive assistance that market research can provide towards increasing sales.

Pricing policy is outside the scope of this chapter but it is worth remembering that market research can be used to find out what competition is doing, and that it may also be used to assess the possible effect of a price increase on sales or to judge the effect of charging higher prices for small orders, to give only two practical examples.

One fault, which is very common in the engineering industry, is inadequate literature, particularly leaflets and brochures which do not describe a product to the best advantage or which omit important information that the buyer needs to know. Comparison with competitive literature or discussion with purchasers will often be very helpful in bringing these faults to light, and this is a market research function.

Improving profits

Increased sales do not necessarily mean increased profits and, if maximum profits are to be achieved, there must be a close coordination between production and sales. In the simplest terms, there is no point in producing goods for which there is no sale, or in increasing production if the increased output cannot find a market. There must be a positive attempt to provide what the customer wants and there must be careful planning ahead so that production and sales keep closely in step.

The dynamics of user industries

One of the most important factors in planning this correlation between production and sales is adequate data about the future technical progress of customer industries; this is particularly so where the main market is one specific industry. The health of that industry, and its future needs, must be watched very closely indeed.

For example, suppliers to the motor industry are particularly sensitive to the economic health of that industry and failure to read the signs correctly, or to read them in time, can lead to trouble. If the motor industry declines, then the engineering industry supplying it also declines and profits begin to tumble. It is very desirable to know about possible trouble well in advance so that action can be initiated to find new customers, or even new products, so that production can be maintained at a profitable level.

Figure 6:7 illustrates the ups and downs of the motor industry over a twenty-year period. Although the broad trend of production has been upwards, there have been substantial falls in production at intervals which, in some cases, have had catastrophic effects on suppliers to the motor industry.

Developments in user industries

Developments in user industries have a significant place in marketing plans and their importance will be appreciated if it is remembered that one of the basic principles of marketing is to provide what the customer wants. If a company is producing a particular type of machine, or piece of equipment, and selling it to certain specialised customers who are themselves in course of change, the company may very well find that its market has declined quite suddenly if it does not see the signs in time. Sudden cutbacks in production will play havoc with profitability.

Unless the situation is examined periodically, or kept under constant review, trouble may arise quite suddenly. If sales are static it may be because the company is taking an increasing share of a declining market, and if the situation has not been appreciated and foreseen a sudden drop in sales will occur at some point, possibly too late to take avoiding action.

Production

Information about user industries and their probable needs is very useful in forecasting the growth of the market and thus ensuring that

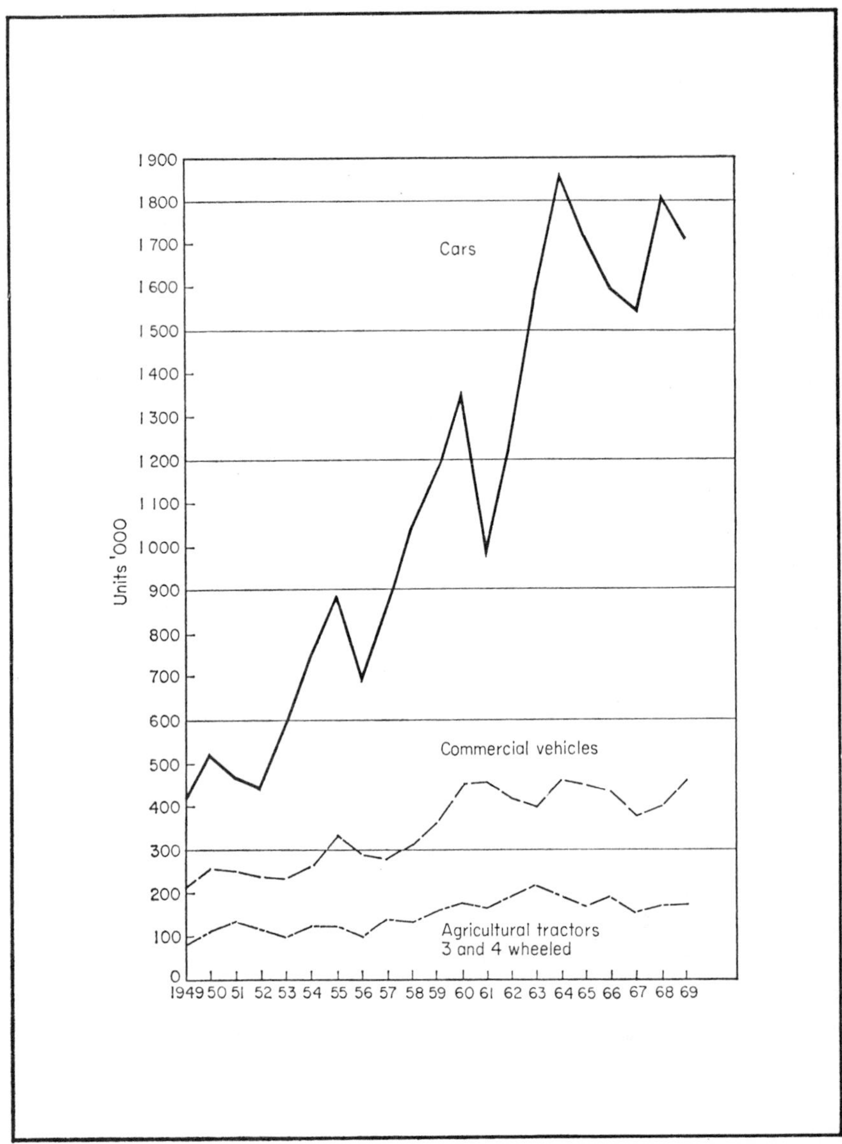

FIGURE 6:7 UK PRODUCTION OF CARS, COMMERCIAL VEHICLES AND AGRICULTURAL TRACTORS

The ups and downs of the motor industry (Reproduced with permission of the Society of Motor Manufacturers and Traders)

production keeps pace with demand in the most profitable way. The assessment of probable demand from customers is not easy and it may be particularly difficult to find a suitable base from which a curve of growth can be projected. It may also be necessary to take into account underlying economic conditions, developments in world trade, the course of raw material prices, and many other factors.

Some general problems

Whether the purpose of market research is to assess the market for new products, to help to increase sales, or to help to improve profitability, there are certain questions of a general nature which will form part of almost every market survey, and particularly so in the engineering industry. These are questions which every management ought to ask itself when considering its marketing policy or position.

The reputation of the company

The reputation of a manufacturer often begins to decline because of a failure to appreciate the changing needs of customers, or because of a failure to keep pace with developments in design, or because its distribution and servicing are not good enough for modern conditions. An engineering company often acquires an old-fashioned image when it has been making a good product for years in a sellers' market. When this latter turns into a buyers' market, or perhaps declines because of changing market needs, the company may well be in difficulties if it does not update its image.

The reputation of a company may suffer because of faults in organisation, failure to make new contacts, or lack of a coherent policy. All these things are very difficult to appraise without a systematic and unbiased look at the situation and market research can be used for this purpose. Even if enquiries prove that there is nothing wrong with the company's reputation, it is useful to know that it is operating on the right lines.

Competition

Information about competition, and what it is doing, is vital to every engineering company if it is to maintain a profitable place in the market. Competition does not only mean knowing the prices charged by other firms which are making exactly the same product; it also means knowing about other products or other materials which may be acquiring part of the market. For example, the extent to which plastics mouldings are taking the place of die castings. Discovering the position with regard to competition is one of the most important functions of market research.

The size of the market

Market size and market shares are an important target for the sales effort and a declining share of an increasing market, or even a static share of an increasing market, is a sure sign of trouble. A declining market is a signal for diversification or new products.

Calculating the size of a market may be a difficult and expensive task and the cost is not always justified. It may be sufficient to discover whether the market is expanding and whether the company's share is expanding with it, and this can usually be effected at reasonable cost. If the company's share of the market is not expanding, it is very important to discover why. The situation may call for an increased sales effort or there may be some other deep-seated reasons which need identifying and correcting.

Users' needs

One of the criticisms frequently levelled against the engineering industry is that it does not pay sufficient attention to users' needs or to the changing needs of the market-place. It is almost always useful to find out whether users are satisfied with what they are getting or whether a specific piece of equipment continues to meet the job characteristics for which it was designed. Technical changes in a process, for example, may call for new machines or methods, and failure to appreciate and meet these changes will eventually affect sales. Market research may be used to make a critical appreciation of users' needs, to obtain their views and to study their requirements.

Trends and developments

The engineer often has difficulty in keeping track of technical developments in his particular field and the effect of these developments on the design of machines and market needs generally. This is particularly the case in the smaller engineering company, where management is fully occupied with day-to-day production problems. Failure to watch what other manufacturers are doing, failure to find out what customers will require next year and the year after, and failure to foresee the effect of new developments in materials and new techniques in manufacture will eventually have a depressing effect on sales.

Market research includes the systematic study of developments, an assessment of the effect of these developments on markets, the review of the progress of other manufacturers, and a means of taking a broad look at markets. It can also include an appreciation of technical advances.

The essentials of industrial market research

As its name implies, industrial market research is concerned with markets of a technical nature and should be distinguished from the better known consumer market research which is concerned with the attitudes of the man, or woman, in the street.

The principal function of market research is to provide answers to those questions which management asks itself, or should ask itself, when seeking to solve marketing problems; the formulation of the appropriate questions requires special consideration in the context of the engineering industry. For example, the prospects for continuing good business often depend on a correct assessment of the future needs of users of a machine and this may, in turn, depend on an assessment of the design of machines. In fact, machine design may be a more important factor in sales than good advertising. Market research, in this case, will be used to find out what the customer needs in terms of design.

This underlines the main difference between industrial market research and consumer market research. The latter is primarily a statistical exercise, while the former seldom is because it is usually concerned with technical questions which have to be answered at a technical level by people who can provide the information required. This normally involves careful selection of the most appropriate sources of information, rather than selection of a statistically accurate sample.

Industrial market research does not necessarily involve contact with sources outside the company. A great deal of very useful data can be obtained by a company from its own resources, such as salesmen's reports, sales statistics, analysis of orders, and similar company records. This valuable source of information is frequently wasted or forgotten. However, at some stage a company will require additional information from users, competitors, customers, experts of various kinds, and others. To seek and collate all this data a company may have its own market research department or it may use outside consultants. Many companies use both and, although there are often arguments about the comparative merits of the in-company researcher and the outside consultant, these arguments are really a waste of time. There is room for both and the decision whether to use one or the other is usually an economic one, but it may be dictated by other circumstances.

Market research is a subject which tends to become surrounded by a mass of semi-scientific jargon which often blinds both the researcher and the company commissioning the research. Basically it is commonsense, plus hard work, plus experience. The latter is particularly important if market research is to be of value to the engineering industry because of the need to seek data at a technical level. The investigator should not only have knowledge of the engineering industry itself, but should also have some knowledge of customer industries because otherwise he may fail to appreciate the viewpoint of the user. Experience in 'digging out' information is also an essential attribute and the value of the result depends very largely on the right combination of technical knowledge and interviewing skill.

Industrial market research is not only a question of facts, important though these are. It is also a question of opinions. The opinions of users, competitors, customers and others is particularly important in, for example, assessing future trends. No one can say with certainty what is going to happen in a year's time, much less in five years' time, but informed opinion about the prospects is the next best thing provided that it *is* informed and that sufficient opinions are taken to ensure a balanced viewpoint.

How industrial market research works

As already stated, industrial market research is the systematic collection of facts, figures, information and opinions about markets of a technical and industrial nature, with a definite objective in view. It follows that the first step in any market survey is to decide the objective – in other words, to pinpoint the problem.

This is by no means so easy as it sounds and is often the most difficult part of the whole operation. It requires that a logical process of thought be applied to the situation which is analysed and translated into a series of questions. The information required to answer these questions is what market research is all about. The experienced professional market researcher faced with a request from management for specific information frequently finds that the real problems are quite different and require quite different information to solve them satisfactorily. Some of the common problems that need to be solved have already been outlined in previous paragraphs.

Once the objective has been fixed and it is known what information is required, the next step is to plan how to obtain that information – the sources of information to be consulted, the extent of the enquiries necessary, whether the information can be obtained from published material or whether extensive field work is required, (if the latter, who is to be approached, and how), and other factors of a similar nature. It is impossible to lay down hard and fast rules about this because much will depend on the speed with which the information is required, whether an exhaustive study or just a preliminary look is necessary, and, above all, the budget available. Planning a survey is mostly common-sense but experience is valuable because it enables mistakes and unnecessary work to be avoided.

Obtaining the information involves two basic processes, desk research and field work, the latter including the use of postal questionnaires. Desk research, as its name implies, is the process of obtaining information by studying published material, statistics, case histories, the trade and technical press. It may also involve study of the material in a company's own files, consulting specialised libraries and generally reading up background material.

Desk research is an essential part of every survey because, at the very least, it helps to 'set the scene' for later stages and, in simplest terms, provides the list of sources of information to be approached. At best it may provide all the information necessary. The diligent and persistent researcher can find a great deal of very useful data by careful reading, by studying government and other statistics, and by scanning the trade and technical press. Here again, the main requirement is common-sense and hard work, but the experienced researcher has the advantage of knowing where to look and what to discard.

Field work provides the mass of information. It involves contact with users, customers, distributors, factors, research associations, consultants, trade bodies and others, according to circumstances. The method of approach may be by means of personal interview, telephone interview, or postal questionnaire, and the choice of method depends very largely on what is required and how extensive the enquiry needs to be. If opinions are required on technical subjects, personal interviews are almost essential. Interviews may be either unstructured or structured. In the former case the investigator 'digs' for information and it follows that the investigator must not only be very experienced but must also have a wide knowledge of the subject under investigation. The structured interview makes use of a questionnaire and can be carried out by a less experienced investigator.

Where wide coverage is necessary, postal questionnaires provide the only economical means of reaching a large enough sample, but in recent years postal questionnaires have been used so widely that there is tending to be some resistance to them, with response rates falling and the quality of replies being less satisfactory.

Many volumes have been written about questionnaire design and about the theory of sample size and selection, but a discussion of these theories is beyond the scope of this chapter. It will suffice to say that questionnaires should be kept as short as possible, as simple as possible, and should be as easy as possible for the respondent to fill in and return. The total number of sources of information that can be approached in any given case is described as the universe and the sample is the proportion of the universe selected for an approach. The sample is frequently fixed on a statistical basis (for example, five per cent of the total universe), but in many cases it must be selective. For example, where an industry is dominated by two or three large firms it is most desirable that one or more of these should be included in the sample, instead of the sample being selected on a strictly random basis.

A study of competition, its methods, products, prices and policies is an essential part of most market surveys but may present difficulties for the company researcher. Engineering companies are often very unwilling to give information to their competitors but there is a growing tendency to exchange information on a much freer basis than was once the case.

The engineering industry is fortunate because some very valuable tables have been produced by the Mechanical Engineering National Economic Development Committee. These tables are entitled *Company Financial Results 1965/66 – 1969/70* and they provide comparative figures on some 350 companies which are a most useful guide to the relative profitability and progress of the companies concerned. The tables are available from the National Economic Development Office.

Finally, the information obtained must be collected together, analysed and interpreted. Conclusions must be drawn and recommendations made. The whole must be presented to management in a form which is easy to assimilate and which will show clearly what has been achieved. There are some differences of opinion about the way in which the result of a market survey should be presented to management but, broadly speaking, the report should include a summary of the information obtained, the sources from whence it was obtained, and the weight to be attached to these sources. The method used in making calculations (for example, of market size) and in reaching conclusions should be clearly stated with fact differentiated from opinion. Most market surveys will include recommendations for future action based on the conclusions reached, but the market researcher must always be very careful that both conclusions and recommendations are based on the information obtained and not on his own personal opinion or on guesses. Any doubts should be clearly stated.

Compilation of a good report does, of course, require a great deal of experience and skill and is best left to the experienced researcher.

Chapter 7

Market Economics and Pricing

Leon Simons, Management Consultant

The purpose of marketing or, indeed, any organisational function is to help best achieve the organisational objective. Consequently, different objectives require different marketing strategies. In this chapter the objective of the chief executive shall be assumed to be the maximisation of trading profit on total investment. *Trading profit* is the profit after deducting bank interest, but before deducting long-term loan interest, taxation and dividends: this is because bank interest is within the control of the chief executive, but these other charges are not. *Total investment* is the capital made available by the board of directors to the chief executive and includes ordinary shareholders' funds (ordinary share capital and reserves), preference capital and loan capital.

The objective of the marketing manager, assuming that the production function is within the direct authority of the chief executive and not of the marketing manager, could, appropriately, be the achievement of an agreed sales budget at least cost within limits set by the chief executive.

The budget must be set by the chief executive and not the marketing manager because it is determined not only by what can be sold, but also by what can be designed, developed and produced. It is a commitment which involves the whole company and not merely the marketing department.

Given a certain production capacity, the optimum product mix must be that at which profit is maximised. One of the key factors in determining the optimum product mix is the price-volume relationship.

Standard and non-standard products

The distinctions between standard and non-standard products are important when discussing the price-volume relationship, but they also have considerable relevance to pricing strategy generally. A standard product can be defined as one which is made to the specification of the producer, and a non-standard product as one which is specified by the customer.

Because standard products are specified by the producer, he determines the products to be included in his range, and very often, although not always, they are made speculatively before orders are received and the product range, irrespective of how big it is, is finite. Non-standard products, on the other hand, are specified by the purchaser and every day, enquiries can be received for items which have never been made before even although they fall into product categories which are within the production capacity of the producer.

Since the size of the range is finite, standard products can be priced in advance by means of a price list and discount structure, and this makes the problem of delegation very simple. The brand or product manager who has authority to set prices for his products can authorise the price list and discount structure for use in the knowledge that the net prices quoted by his subordinates for specific products to specific customers would be exactly the same as he would have quoted had he done the job himself. Moreover, an extremely large business can be conducted with a relatively small number of pricing decisions.

With non-standard products the problem is a much more difficult one. Since unique enquiries are coming in all the time, they cannot be priced in advance, but must be priced on an ad hoc basis. This could necessitate five or ten prices being set for every order received by the company if that is the ratio of enquiries to orders. Thus, the number of pricing decisions to be made in a company with only a few hundred transactions per year could easily run into thousands and, therefore, be outside the ability of whoever should be controlling the pricing policy to do so personally. Accordingly, the pricing of non-standard products has to be delegated and a price list cannot be used as the means of so doing.

For the delegation to take place adequately, an objective set of instructions must be given from manager to subordinate to enable the subordinate to arrive at exactly the same price for an enquiry as the manager would have reached himself. This may be called the criterion of delegated pricing and is referred to later in the chapter.

Price-quality and price-volume relationships

The purchaser of the standard product does not specify it, and although the specification or ingredients may be published by the producer, such information will normally be insufficient to permit the purchaser to obtain a comprehensive idea of the quality of the product such as he would tend to have if he specified it himself. That being so, price is often used as an indicator of quality and people will reject an article as being too cheap (and therefore nasty) just as they will reject it as being too dear. In these circumstances, a producer can underprice as well as overprice himself out of a market.

The buyer of non-standard products, on the other hand, usually has sufficient information or knowledge of the product he is buying to be able to consider the quality more or less objectively without using price as an indicator. He is therefore likely to choose among a number of offers of similar quality on the basis of the lowest price. To the extent that this is true – and it is not 100 per cent true – there is a price-volume relationship. From the producer's point of view, the lower his price level the more he sells; the higher, the less he sells.

Market price

One's ability to sell at a given price depends largely on the prices charged by one's competitors for what appears to be a similar product.

Moreover, all the makers of a given product can collectively price themselves out of their market if their customers can buy substitute products at a sufficiently lower cost to compensate for any loss of value suffered in the substitution.

The sensitivity of the price-volume relationship is quite different as between one product and another depending on competition and substitution possibilities, but is always present to some extent except in the case of a pure monopoly in a necessary product or commodity and this exception is very rare.

One way of differentiating price from those of one's competitors is by differentiating the product. This is the purpose of much brand advertising. The scope for this activity is much greater with standard products, because the buyer must usually assess quality subjectively, than with non-standards where objective knowledge of the product specification makes differentiation extremely difficult.

However, there is no one market price; there is a range of prices at which a product can be sold and, if it is non-standard where there is a price-volume relationship, the lower the price (down to a limit) the better the chance of selling and the higher the price (up to a limit) the smaller the chance. Alternatively, the lower the price level over a period the more will be sold, and vice versa. The lower limit is a price below which the most efficient producer refuses to sell, and the upper limit is a price above which the least discriminating buyer refuses to buy.

The price level should be set so that the revenue generated combines with the expense incurred to maximise profit. Given a good knowledge of the market and one's costs this level can be found by trial and error in a single-product organisation. Where a number of products can be manufactured with the same capacity, the optimum product mix can be obtained with the help of a computer.

The consequence of too high prices is the receipt of less than the desired amount of work, and conversely, too much work follows from too low pricing. When a producer talks of the market price, there is an implied desired volume of sales, since the price level necessary to attract two per cent of an available market is doubtless quite different from the level required to bring twenty per cent.

Prices charged for a company's production must therefore be orientated towards the market level, since any other level will be non-optimal.

The two criteria which must be met by any pricing system have now been established. First, the pricing work must be capable of being delegated. Second, prices must be orientated towards the market.

Conventional pricing

More has been written about the pricing of standard products than about that of non-standards, which is generally thought to be the more difficult problem. Consequently, the remainder of this chapter will concentrate on the latter.

Cost-plus pricing is by far and away the commonest method of pricing non-standards in this and in most other capitalist countries. This is done by working out the cost of the product or job or batch and adding on a percentage for profit to give the quoted price. There are two basic ways of calculating cost: one is the full or absorption cost, and the other is the marginal cost. The former is overwhelmingly the more commonly used.

A simple explanation of the basic difference between the two is that the marginal cost is the direct cost, consisting of direct material, direct labour and direct expenses and ignoring all indirect costs or overheads, while the full cost is the direct cost plus a proportion of overhead:

  Direct material
+ Direct labour
+ Direct expenses
____
  Direct cost = Marginal cost
+ Proportion of overhead = Full cost

The logic behind the use of marginal cost as a basis for price setting is that if a price is achieved in excess of marginal cost, that excess represents a contribution to overhead and profit and the seller is better off by that contribution than if he had not sold at all.

The exponents of full costing as a basis for price setting argue that if the volume of sales on which the allocation of overhead was based is achieved, and if selling prices are obtained in excess of the full cost, then, since all the direct and indirect expenses are absorbed, the seller must make a profit.

Before overheads are allocated to products or jobs, a forecast of sales must be made to estimate the number of units of production which will be available to absorb the overheads. Clearly, the overhead allocated to each unit will be different if one million products are expected to be sold than if the estimate were two million, since the overheads would not vary proportionally if they varied at all.

Overheads are usually allocated first of all to areas of production or cost centres and thence to the products passing through these cost centres. The basis of allocation to cost centres is arbitrary and may be expected turnover, floor space, direct labour, machine-hour capacity, etc.; the choice of any one basis could give a vastly different spread of overheads between cost centres than the choice of another, although apparently equally justifiable.

The allocation of a cost centre's expenses to the jobs passing through it is normally made on the basis of estimated production time, which may or may not turn out to be accurate. A further consequence is that the processes in which the producer is more efficient will tend to have lower costs than those in which he is less efficient: this, in turn, is likely to affect selling prices, despite the fact that the value to the customer will either not differ or may even tend to be greater in the case of the more efficiently made products.

Furthermore, when the factory is busy, there will be more throughput over which to spread the overheads and unit costs will therefore be lower, which is just the time when prices will tend to be higher. Conversely, when there is a slump in trade and work is scarce, unit costs will be higher, as the work available to absorb the overheads shrinks. Any attempt to reflect these increased costs in higher selling prices is likely to exacerbate the problem by making work scarcer still and thus creating a vicious circle.

The foregoing argument shows that there is no relationship between unit cost and the selling prices obtainable in the market. Also, it shows that in the case of full costing the arbitrary allocation of overheads means that the resulting unit costs are not factual.

Let it not be thought, however, that the direct or marginal cost is factual, just because it does not involve the allocation of overheads. Direct material cost is dependent upon the costing method used, for example, first in first out (FIFO), last in first out (LIFO), average cost, etc. If four identical items in store were bought at different times for £10, £11, £11.60 and £13 respectively, the FIFO cost is £10, the LIFO cost is £13 and the average cost is £11.40. The replacement cost, or next in first out, could give yet another answer.

What is called direct labour is seldom direct at all. Today, there are very few examples of direct labour, where wages are paid for a job, which would not be paid if the job were not done. These examples are piece-rates, overtime payments in most cases, and construction site casual labour which is hired for a contract and dismissed on its completion. Apart from these and perhaps a few more cases, wages are paid for attendance on a time basis at the place of work irrespective of how much work is actually done. Production of another few units more or less does not change the amount of wages paid, and consequently the labour cost for these units is nil. The labour is, in fact, indirect and is an overhead. With the trend away from piece-rate payment systems accelerating, and the growing inability or unwillingness of firms to dismiss men because of temporary shortage of work, evidence of true direct labour is becoming more exceptional as time goes on. While the majority of people welcome this tendency, few recognise it inasmuch as they continue to use this archaic distinction between direct and indirect labour.

To summarise this part of the discussion: both full and marginal costing are arbitrary methods of calculating so-called costs which would vary with changes in any one of a large number of implicit assumptions; moreover any selling price based on either method of costing cannot at the same time be based on the price levels ruling in the market in which the goods are sold. Costing is an internal activity which is of no interest to the customer, who is concerned with the value he thinks he gets for the price he has to pay. The confusion is essentially that between input and output. Costing is an attempt to measure input whilst pricing is an attempt to value output.

Common-sense

The reader is invited to ask himself how he has priced any article or service which he, as an individual, has sold. Has he started with the cost to himself and added a percentage for profit, or has he attempted to ascertain what prices similar goods or services were fetching on the market and pitching his own price accordingly? Surely the answer is the same whether he is selling a house, a car, a piece of furniture, a block of shares or anything else – what he thinks the market will bear.

He knows the cost to be quite irrelevant, whether he bought or made the item last week or last year. Just because he bought cheaply, he does not need to sell cheaply, and if he bought dearly he made a mistake which trying to sell dearly will merely compound. Why does this obvious common-sense desert him when he enters the business environment? Is it because it is the company's money instead of his own, or is it great humility that prevents him from believing that so many people have been wrong for so long?

Selling at a loss

Many would agree that pricing against competition rather than on the basis of one's costs sounds fine, but would be inhibited from doing so by the risk of selling 'at a loss'. This fear, however, can easily be unfounded. If full costing is used, one knows that the 'full cost' is not factual. Since one does not know what the cost of a product is, then clearly one does not know if it is selling at a profit or a loss. Yet one cannot continuously lower prices with impunity; there comes a point where selling below a certain price will lose money, and the more that is sold the more money will be lost. Note that this is quite different from selling below full cost where increased volume, by absorbing more overhead, could result in profit.

The real cost of a job or product has to be established and it consists of those costs which are incurred as a result of the decision to make the job or product and which would not be incurred otherwise. This is the true marginal or incremental cost. It consists of the replacement cost of the material (assuming that the material could be used for another job now or in the future), the cost of any labour which would not have arisen if the job in question had not been done, and any other extra costs such as power, packing and delivering. Most other costs such as rates, insurance, etc., are not costs resulting from a decision to make a particular job; they would be precisely the same if the job were or were not made and are costs of a totally different decision, namely the decision to remain in business.

It is essential to analyse costs in relation to the decisions which incurred them, because only in that way can they be properly controlled.

Also, the danger of turning away business would be obviated for the reason that the obtainable price was less than full cost, where that business would make a valuable contribution to overheads and profit.

In retail selling, the term 'loss leader' is commonly used. A supermarket sells sugar below its invoiced cost so that customers are attracted into the store and thus spend money on other 'profitable' goods which they would not otherwise have bought. As a result of selling the sugar at this price, the supermarket makes a bigger profit, so it can hardly be said to be selling at a loss. The fallacy is that the supermarket is not in business merely to sell sugar, and it is idle to separate out the profitability or otherwise of its various items as if they have nothing to do with each other. The same holds true in many other businesses.

It is not being suggested that prices should be set on the basis of incremental or any other cost. It has been clearly stated that prices depend on market forces and have no relationship with cost. Incremental cost should be used as a cut-off point, so that business will be rejected if the market price falls below it.

Two quite separate decisions have been discussed: first, arriving at the market price, which has nothing whatever to do with one's costs, and second, deciding whether to accept or reject the business at the market price; for the latter decision, one should refer to the incremental cost. Traditional cost-plus pricing confuses these two decisions.

Finding the market price

The problem of finding the market price of a non-standard product, the replica of which the seller has never made before, is dealt with, conventionally, in two steps. First, to arrive at the cost of the product or job, and second, to base the price on the cost by the addition of a percentage for profit. Thus:

Product→Cost→Price

The first of these steps has already been proved false, since any number of different costs can be obtained for the same product depending on how they are calculated.

The second step, from cost to price, is no more soundly based than the first. Price is not a function of cost and there is ample evidence to support this. Company chairmen are constantly complaining of their margins being squeezed, meaning that their prices and costs are moving at different rates from each other, if not in different directions altogether. How many firms would go bankrupt if prices moved in line with costs? Certainly, the theory that prices are based on costs is very attractive, and would be very convenient if it were true, but it just does not begin to stand up to the test of reality. Therefore, the product→cost→price process relies on two false premises.

A price has to be derived from a product. Since the price the customer is prepared to pay for one product as opposed to another is determined by the difference he perceives between them, the seller should therefore look at the products through the customer's eyes, as it were, and analyse their characteristics or properties to establish how the customer sets differential values. Thus, the seller will learn to evaluate the product properties himself, and when he receives a specification from a customer he can apply the results of his analysis to it, and so build up prices for different products which appear quite consistent to the customer. This technique can be studied in detail elsewhere[1] but the principles will now be explained briefly.

Product analysis

A product category should be selected, consisting of a range of similar products differing from each other, say, dimensionally: for example, aluminium gravity die castings made to customers' specifications.

A number of samples, perhaps twenty to thirty, should be selected from quotations given to customers and accepted by them in the recent past. The company's salesmen should be asked to identify the variable properties of the product which are parameters of price. This can be done by getting reasons why one sample should fetch a higher price than another, for example, this one is heavier, but that one is bigger dimensionally (less compact) and more complicated but is made from a less expensive alloy, and so on.

When it is felt that all the parameters of price have been identified, units of measurement will have to be selected for each of them so that they can be quantified. Thus, the weight can be measured in pounds (or ounces or grammes), the dimensions of size, length, breadth and height, in inches or centimetres; and complexity perhaps by the number of blocks and independently operated cores in the die. The materials in the alloy are valued at market price on the date of the quotation, not at what the company happened to pay for the materials, which is irrelevant both to the customer and to the company.

The next step is to arrange on a sheet of paper all the samples in ascending order of price with all the quantities of the significant properties tabulated as shown in Figure 7:1.

Sample number	Price (pence)	Material value (pence)	Weight (pounds)	Size of box (cubic inches)	Number of blocks	Number of cores
1	19	5	0.5	5	2	-
2	19.5	2.5	0.3	4	2	1
.	.	.	.	.	.	.
.	.	.	.	.		.
20	96	10	1.4	17	2	2
.	.	.	.	.		.
25	120	20	2.5	24	2	1

FIGURE 7:1 EXAMPLE OF A TABLE RANKING SAMPLE PRODUCT QUOTATIONS

This gives the form of a large simultaneous equation with five variables, which can be solved visually by trial and error or with the aid of a computer. An exact solution will not be found and the line of best fit should be sought. The result would be a formula like this:

$$[(7 \times Weight)+(0.25 \times Box\ size)]\,[No.\ of\ blocks+2\ No.\ of\ cores] +4+Material\ value$$

The constant of 4 in the formula is an existence value which is relatively more important in the smaller items in the range than in the larger.

When this formula is applied to the data in the table, the following results are obtained (the data for sample numbers 3–19 and 21–24 will all have been worked out but are not shown so as to avoid confusing the reader with a mass of figures):

Sample No.

1 $[(7\times 0.5)+(0.25\times 5)]\ [2]+4+5=18.5$

2 $[(7\times 0.3)+(0.25\times 4)]\ [2+2]+4+2.5=18.9$

. . . .

. . . .

20 $[(7\times 1.4)+(0.25\times 17)]\ [2+4]+4+10=98.3$

. . . .

25 $[(7\times 2.5)+(0.25\times 24)]\ [2+2]+4+20=118.0$

The results are close enough for practical purposes to the prices obtained and, assuming that the other samples fitted also, the formula would be used for pricing new enquiries in the same product category. If an inquiry were received for a casting of 0.7 lb weight, 8 cu ins, 3 blocks and material value of 6, the price would be:

$$[(7\times 0.7)+(0.25\times 8)]\ [3]+4+6=30.7$$

A further factor would be used to attract good-sized order quantities and discourage relatively unattractive ones. Otherwise, if competitors quoted quantity-related prices, one would find oneself attracting short-run jobs and overpricing long ones. It is possible, however, that in some cases such as a small jobbing shop, this kind of work-mix would be desirable.

A market factor would take into account different price levels which obtain in various countries, industries, regions, etc. The basic formula excluding the quantity and market factors would give internally consistent prices and this relationship would remain in a given market after the application of the market factor.

Control

There are various other features of the system which provide control mechanisms but which are outside the scope of this chapter.

Summary

Two criteria for any pricing system have already been established: that the pricing decision must be capable of delegation, and that the prices arrived at are geared to the market levels. The system which has been described meets both.

If the formula is applied to a set of data by two clerks, quite independently, they would reach identical results which their manager would also have obtained had he done the job personally. The subjective judgment of the subordinates is completely removed. This is impossible to achieve with any cost-based pricing technique.

The formula prices are derived from actual selling prices and are not related to the company's costs, which clearly do not influence the price which the customer is prepared to pay.

To avoid work being taken on which would detract from the company's profit, the incremental cost will be calculated in a percentage of cases and compared with the formula price.

Finally, there are a number of administrative benefits of pricing in this way. The clerical staff required is considerably less than for conventional methods and the time taken to work out prices is a matter of minutes so that quotations can be given to customers without delay.

References

1 See, for example, *Product Analysis Pricing* by Brown and Jaques, Heinemann Educational Books, 1964.

Chapter 8

Selling Industrial Products

D W Newill, Director, GFM-Chemie Institut and Inplan Limited

Selling to industry covers a wide spectrum of business activity but certain vitally important principles are common in all sectors. Effective selling requires planning, training, experience, organisation and a systematic approach, all of which must be completely orientated towards the customer's needs. It is basically concerned with people and communications, but at the same time it can only succeed if governed by the profit motive.

No mention is made in this chapter of export selling, although the principles outlined can be applied with suitable modification in any industrial market.

Establishing a sales policy and budget

The sales policy is defined as the objectives for the selling function which define the scope and practice of future sales operations. In establishing a sales policy the sales manager operates within certain boundaries. Firstly, company policy; secondly, marketing policy, and thirdly, market or customer factors.

Company policy and marketing policy are closely related and cover matters such as diversification targets and product obsolescence, long-term marketing strategy and short-term tactical policy. For example, potential acquisitions, reciprocity in trading or future rationalisation plans for associated or subsidiary companies are integrated into the company policy. The sales policy must be made to harmonise with corporate and marketing plans.

It is common practice to prepare an annual corporate plan during late summer or early autumn. From this plan and the market forecasts for the following year, guidelines are set for sales management by the company. Within the guidelines, sales managers prepare their draft sales plan and define sales policy for the following year. Company and marketing management then ensure adequate harmonisation between the draft sales policy as stated and the overall company position.

Sales management has two main sources of information in preparing its forward sales policy: field salesmen and sales intelligence or sales department on one side and marketing research and market intelligence on the other side. Information from its own sales force and department provides substantial detail but can be over-subjective. It can, however, be evaluated against the more objective and quantified information obtained from marketing research and marketing intelligence departments.

Armed with sales forecasts, pricing information and general market statistics, the sales manager devises a tactical plan for the following year which covers in detail objectives for the department and sales forces. Examples of objectives include obtaining business from competition at a specific company; an increase in sales in a defined territory or market; the introduction of a new product for long-term evaluation, and the transforming of erratic orders into regular delivery contracts.

The key points in establishing a sales policy are that it must harmonise with corporate and marketing policy and that it must have sufficient flexibility to be amended during periodic reviews. The sales policy also defines the methods by which the objectives will be met and is the basic working document for the regional and field sales managers. Either within the sales policy or in more detailed documents derived from it, all personal sales targets are defined. Each individual industrial salesman has his clearly defined targets and objectives which he has helped management to prepare. The sales policy is converted on the basis of sales, price and competitive forecasts to a detailed statistical breakdown of individual sales targets. Having defined sales policy, the sales manager's next task is to prepare the sales budget.

Sales budget

The sales budget is a detailed breakdown of forward sales estimates and the selling costs and expenses which will be met in reaching the sales targets defined in the sales policy.

Definitions of sales costs and expenses may depend on the division of responsibilities with marketing management but usually cover the full range of fixed and variable expenses. Fixed expenses include items such as components of salaries, depot and office costs or charges, and transport depreciation. Examples of variable expenses are sales commissions and bonuses, publicity, packaging and transportation.

It is usual for a full breakdown of departmental costs to be provided on a monthly basis. With this information and with the forward sales forecasts, sales management is able to allocate expenses and charges to each operation under its control. Subsidiary budgets for sales regions and sales areas, or to autonomous sales units, are provided so that area sales managers are able to exert regular budgetary control.

The development of adequate and meaningful commission schemes and the sensible control of external expenses is completely dependent on detailed budgeting. Sales management is also able to direct sales effort into exactly the right areas at the right time when unforeseen external factors affect the sales plan. For example, highly profitable, large-volume business can be lost or superior competitive products can be introduced to the market, and the correct action could be to drastically reduce selling effort in that sector or market. Good industrial and technical salesmen cannot be hired and fired so that rapid redeployment of resources is essential. Regional and market based budgetary control enables sales management, in this situation, to minimise reduction in profit and to revise the sales policy.

Revision

A sales policy and budget which is approved in the early autumn may require some revision at the end of the year before becoming operative. However, after the start of the operating year it is unwise to revise too frequently. Modifications on the basis of the first quarter's results can be valuable and a suitable time for the second revision is after seven to eight month's trading. This later information is also needed for completing the planning of the following year's policy and budget, and also provides management with quite accurate forecasts of the end-year position.

Prices

Essential information in compiling the sales budget and in sales forecasting are the individual salesmen's price forecasts. Although pricing policies can be defined from company management and marketing management, there are necessary degrees of freedom for sales managers, area managers and individual salesmen. Any tendency on the part of the sales force to reduce selling prices excessively in order to increase turnover can be identified through sales budgets. This will reduce the heavy decline in profitability caused by even moderate price reductions.

Conclusion

The two basic supports for sales management can be summarised as:
The sales policy, which defines objectives, the scale and practice of future operations and the forward sales targets and plan.
The sales budget, which converts sales policy and targets into a detailed financial breakdown of sales income and costs, and which is a control document and essential tool for sales management.

Selling outlets

The basic characteristics of industrial selling are the differing complexities of market structures and product types, coupled with the wide range of types and levels of purchasing decision. Selling to *industry* is thus a basically different process from selling to the mass consumption and general consumer markets; although in certain areas, such as small industrial companies and distributors, there are similarities between consumer and industrial selling, and for the vast majority of industrial sales operations the differences are far greater than the similarities. The factors which govern the exact type of industrial selling outlet are derived from two basic determinants:

1 The structure of the market
2 The characteristics of the produt

Market structure

The two extremes of market structure as defined by the market's 'external shape' are the convergent market and the divergent market. The former, also known as the narrow, singular or vertical market, is one which covers a very few, and possibly only one, industrial application. The latter, also known as the wide, plural or horizontal market, is one which covers a large number of companies or several industrial applications. As the 'external shape' of the market tends from the convergent towards the divergent, so the techniques and problems of selling tend towards those of consumer market selling.

In addition to their 'external shape', industrial markets may be classified according to their 'internal structure' or composition. The two extremes in this instance are the amorphous and the isomorphous markets. The former is homogeneous or shapeless in the sense that clearly defined market segments or components do not exist or cannot be identified. The latter has a clearly defined structure, can be heterogeneous, and is composed of components or market segments.

Product characteristics

The two main groups of industrial products are the *establishment group* and the *production group*. The former group covers products which are purchased by an industrial company in order to maintain its operating capability and which do not form a part of the products manufactured by the company; three sub-groups are *capital equipment, minor and accessory equipment,* and *maintenance and operating goods*. The *production group* covers products which form a physical part of the end product of the company; three sub-groups are *raw materials, processed materials* and *components* and *prefabricated goods*.

Sales planning

An important task for the industrial sales manager, when planning entry to a new market or the launching of a new product, is to analyse the market and product characteristics in relation to the markets in which his sales force is currently operating and in relation to the existing product range. Such an analysis will help to identify fundamental differences in the new sales outlets which can affect the type of salesman to be used, the market shares which can be obtained, the costs of selling, publicity and advertising and the structure and management of the sales department. A major problem is, frequently, whether or not to recruit new industrial salesmen into the existing sales force or to create a separate selling operation. The analysis of sales outlets according to their properties, which are determined by the interaction of product characteristics with market structures, can help to provide an answer to such problems. Figure 8:1 illustrates the forces which determine selling techniques.

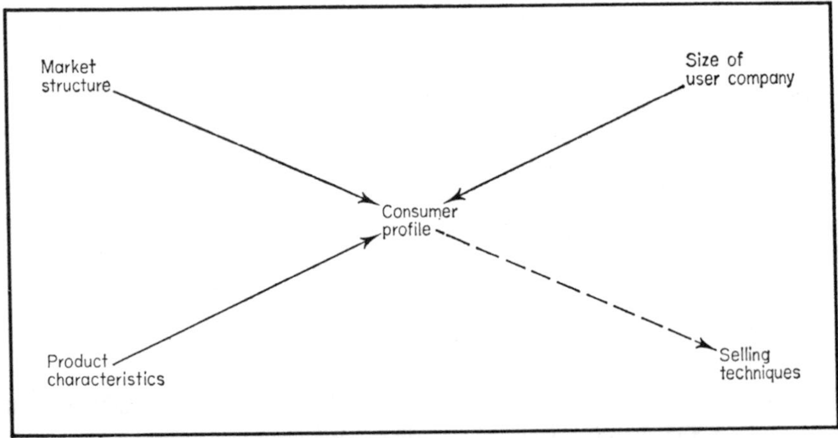

FIGURE 8:1 CONTROLS FOR SELLING TECHNIQUES

Illustration of the interaction between the various forces that determine appropriate selling techniques

Purchasing influences

The number of purchasing influences met by the salesman ranges from one or two in small companies to eight or more in the larger establishments. There is generally some correlation between the average number of executives influencing purchasing decisions and the total purchases of their company. It should be noted that not all purchasing influences are generally concerned with decisions on a given product, although they may be for the larger contracts or, in total, for a product range.

It is also well known that on average over fifty per cent of industrial purchases are made by under five per cent of the establishments and that over eighty per cent are made by about twenty per cent of establishments. A very large proportion of industrial sales effort must therefore be directed towards the market sector comprising the ten to twenty per cent of the largest companies, which are those which also contain the highest number of purchasing influences and, also, the most professional purchasing management.

For the salesman entering a new market there is the inevitable problem of lack of knowledge of product applications and technology and a lack of previous selling records. Information from marketing research and company intelligence is a good starting point but from there it is only the very experienced industrial salesman who will quickly identify the right people to see in the largest companies.

Identification of outlets

For a company already established in a market this presents few problems for the main potential customers. When it is desired to expand into the areas of smaller potential, sales intelligence becomes a more difficult task and the salesman will need the support of planned advertising and direct mailing. In addition, an active sales intelligence operation within the sales department can provide invaluable guidance to the sales force. A combination of experienced industrial salesmen with a well organised sales intelligence function, backed by adequate promotional support, will solve most of the problems to be met in entering new markets and identifying sales outlets.

Publicity and advertising

The main objective of industrial publicity and advertising is to sell the company's products and services through the provision of information. It is generally a tactical and selling tool rather than a strategic tool and has to be very closely geared to sales operations. A research project carried out by the Industrial Marketing Council[1] on the allocation of industrial publicity budgets provides some interesting figures on the average expenditure by industrial companies in Great Britain.

ADVERTISING PERCENTAGE OF PUBLICITY BUDGET	
Techno-commercial and trade journals	34
Direct mail	7
National and regional press	5
LITERATURE	
Sales and technical sales literature, catalogues and films	24
EXHIBITIONS	
Trade and technical exhibitions, demonstrations and symposia	19
PR	
Public relations allocated to selling, trade and technical press relations	11

The research indicated that approximately twenty-five per cent of expenditure on literature could be allocated to direct mail and to exhibition in roughly equal proportions. This would give comparative percentage of publicity budget expenditure figures of:

Advertising	49 per cent
Exhibitions	22 per cent
Literature	18 per cent
PR	11 per cent

Primary requirements in establishing an industrial publicity budget are the measurement of past results, the definition of forward publicity objectives and the integration of the publicity plan within the sales policy. The most widely used method of determining the publicity budget is to measure publicity cost for the previous operating year against sales results by sectors or market segments and then to apply these ratios to the forward sales targets. Additional expenditure may be allocated to areas of increased profitability or for the development of new products and markets. In addition reductions may be essential where sales effort is being directed away from market sectors, or where product applications are declining. The percentage of net sales income allocated to publicity budgets is almost always below five per cent of turnover and most usually in the area of two per cent for companies supplying industrial markets.

It should be noted that expenditure cannot necessarily be moved from one form of publicity to another. For instance, direct mail and technical press advertising programmes are closely related and the value of each method is not always in proportion to the respective costs. Above a defined level of advertising or direct mailing any increases could produce only marginal improvements in results. For this, and other reasons, it is important to be able to measure the effectiveness of each publicity campaign and to have adequate data on media effectiveness. Inquiries received as a result of publicity should be recorded, although it is the actual conversion of inquiries to orders which is really significant.

Advertising

The different purchasing influences can generally be classified into two areas:

1 Production, laboratory and design
2 Purchasing

Techno-commercial and trade press advertising is usually highly effective with the former category but can often be reinforced with advantage for the purchasing area by direct mailing of information sheets, pricing details and catalogues. Direct mail can also be very effective in convergent markets where a high proportion of purchasing influences can be personally identified. Direct mail is very effective when harmonised with press advertising and for presenting a specific offer with clearly identifiable benefits. One or two follow-up mailing shots are frequently worthwhile.

From the previously mentioned research it was found that fifty-three per cent of direct mail shots brought in a two to three per cent return and that ten per cent brought in a return of fourteen per cent or more. Direct mail must use very carefully maintained and, preferably, personalised lists, which can be used selectively. Salesmen should be encouraged to send in amendments and coded additions so that the lists can be used not only to supplement press advertising, but also for invitations to exhibitions, to aid selling campaigns and to reinforce public relations.

Press advertising is expensive and media selection must be based on a careful assessment of the quality of the journal and also on readership research. A check-list at the end of this chapter can be used as a first step in evaluation. Prestige advertising by the company in the national press can give a valuable boost to product advertising. Techno-commercial press advertising and direct mailing should take full advantage of the benefits of such national press advertising.

Literature

Sales literature is frequently produced badly in conflicting sizes and format and fails in its purpose by attempting to present too much, or too little, information. As with advertising, it is necessary to define clearly the objectives of literature, information sheets, price lists and catalogues, and to aim for some degree of standardisation, continuity and quality in style. Films can be used to supplement literature and can be an invaluable aid in introducing new product applications at exhibitions or symposia organised for customers.

Exhibitions

Exhibitions are a means of presenting the company product to a wide range of potential customers and also to have adequate technical and technical sales staff in attendance. The cost is, however, often underestimated in terms of preparation time and staff. Most other promotional or selling activities can be postponed if, for instance, there is some unforseen delay in new product availability. Exhibitions, on the other hand, present a series of firm deadlines and therefore require most detailed and careful planning, coupled with accurate cost estimating. Demonstrations or symposia can be a valuable method of promotion and can be held with advantage during exhibitions. Company personnel used for lecturing should be chosen with care since poor presentation, combined with the numerous difficulties met in organising symposia, can do far more harm than good. A trial run for company staff, attended by local and well-established customers, is some safeguard.

Press relations

There is no substitute for close personal relationships with editorial staff from the techno-commercial press. General press visits should be limited to occasions when the attendance of press representatives is really valuable to all concerned. A major innovation or new product range can be a good reason, whereas minor additions to the factory or laboratories are too often used as an excuse to obtain publicity. Personal visits from a selected journal when editors have the opportunity to tour the factory, to meet production, technical and sales executives and to hold detailed discussions, are most useful and generally well received.

Salesmen should be continually encouraged to submit items for press releases and the effect or the inquiries received should be noted and reported back. Too often PR is regarded as a nuisance and just a means of announcing items of high sales value, by the sales force. Press mentions should be carefully recorded and a measure of their value calculated and correlated with PR costs and inquiries received.

Agencies

Most companies use advertising agencies, the majority of which receive service fees in addition to their commission on advertisements. Advertising and PR agencies can be chosen incorrectly, can be misused and can be expensive. Initially, the greatest care must be taken in selection of an agency and both client lists and examples of creative work should be examined. Certain of the agency's existing clients should be interviewed in addition to companies which are past clients. After selection very close liaison has to be maintained and the agency staff encouraged to identify closely with the company. Media research can be conducted by the company market research department in co-operation with the agency.

Organising and managing the technical sales force

An industrial sales force can be organised in one of two ways: by specialisation or by geographical area. Organisation by specialisation means that salesmen operate within a defined area of product application or by specialised industrial sectors. It has the advantages of giving salesmen greater product knowledge and experience of specific industries, together with better technical and product intelligence. However, it has the disadvantage of reducing call rates and the tendency to have two or more salesmen calling on the same customer. Organisation by geographical area gives salesmen better local knowledge or commercial intelligence and improved customer contacts and relations. There is, on the other hand, the disadvantage of reduced technical and product knowledge. For industrial or technical selling the specialist organisation is generally to be preferred and, with increasing sales volume, can allow some degree of regional breakdown.

For the industrial sales manager organisation of the sales forces is only one of many problems. He has fundamentally two jobs. One is to be a manager and the other to be a salesman. The greatest difficulty is to prevent his selling activities from completely swamping the managerial work.

Recruitment of salesmen

The three requirements for the industrial salesman are:

1 Sales ability, including empathy and ego-drive
2 Product knowledge
3 Market knowledge

It is often overlooked that industrial selling is an activity in which the salesman can be forgotten and can become isolated from his company. The characteristic of ego-drive is therefore essential for the salesman to be fully effective during the inevitable periods of absence from the sales office. Empathy has to be developed to enable the salesman to adapt himself and to sell at all levels from the shop floor to the chief executive, or from purchasing officers to technologists and scientists. Apart from personal qualities, technical knowledge or the ability to acquire an understanding of products and product applications is most important. The general industrial salesman may still require services from a technical sales or sales service department, but he has to be able to deal with a high proportion of problems on his own initiative.

In recruitment the sales manager should also consider both the age and the experience of existing salesmen. If a new sales force is created with all salesmen in the twenty to thirty years age group, there will be invitable problems in ten to fifteen years' time. Variable ambition and managerial potential levels are also important in a well-balanced sales force. At the present time it would be advisable to attempt to build up a good range of European languages.

Training

Sales training falls into two main groups:

1 Initial, consisting of training in the sales office, the product and selling.
2 Continuous, consisting of training in the product and selling.

An initial spell in the sales office coupled with product training is generally of great value. The prospective salesman understands problems to be met in the field, handles inquiries and complaints, overcomes delays in production and becomes generally familiar with the company of which he will be a representative. For many customers he will be the only representative or executive they meet from the company. A well-planned pool of young executives in the sales department helps to overcome many of the difficulties created by resignations or unforseen expansion.

Training in industrial salesmanship is also of the greatest importance and for most sales forces, which are too small to have their own training officer, an outside company should be used. It is very unlikely indeed that effective sales training can be carried out within the company but the outside trainers must be specialist in industrial selling and should be selected with great care. They can initially train staff in the sales department before being moved into the field sales force. Secondly, they can give continuous training at sales meetings or in the field and, thirdly, give refresher courses every two to four years.

Product and product application training is almost always an internal responsibility. New products are inevitably introduced to salesmen but the minor changes which creep into existing products can be overlooked. Product training given to new salesman can therefore also be used for members of the established sales force.

Remuneration

Commission related to profitability is an obvious incentive and is preferable to a simple relationship to turnover, which can result in price cutting and obtaining basically unprofitable business. Suitable ratios of salary to commission cannot be defined easily but the danger of too high a proportion of total income consisting of commission is that salesmen can be unwilling to work on long-term projects and can be upset by failures to deliver or to accept orders. Flexibility of operation of the sales force is also inhibited where commission is too high. Other incentives, such as free holidays for top salesmen, are valuable but, as for all such rewards, must be recognised as fair by the sales force.

Meetings

Sales conferences and regular meetings can easily suffer from attempts to say too much. If there is too big an agenda it is better to take an extra day, since these meetings are of vital importance to field salesmen. They should never become complaint sessions and can be usefully divided into two parts: the first part can cover new products and highlights from operating results or new policies, whilst the second part can be used for training sessions in salesmanship.

Management

Sales managers should ensure that their salesmen and assistant or field sales managers are of a high enough calibre to handle virtually all direct selling. If this is not the case the sales manager becomes merely a senior salesman and ceases to *manage*, with disastrous results for the sales force. Nevertheless, he must be able to sell and to lead the salesmen into major potentials. The sales manager must make spot checks on the sales force and depots to see that the highest standards are maintained and that customer records are adequate and up to date. Checks should also be made to ensure that salesmen are planning both their call programs and the objectives of each sales call.

In giving basic motivation to the sales force the sales manager must encourage a positive enjoyment of selling, recognise results and encourage team spirit, initiative and decision-taking. As a result of the practical problems of working with, say, five to twenty-five salesmen over the entire country, sales managers' contacts can too easily become half-yearly or annual and, as sales forces grow beyond a critical size, field sales managers are absolutely necessary to maintain adequate management.

Sales office

The sales office must identify very closely with field salesmen and feel part of the same team. Reports must be handled efficiently and good communications maintained with salesmen. An intelligence feedback to the sales force is vital and help should be obtained from the market research department. Management also requires a constant analysis of, for example, calls graded by potential, orders per call ratios, call effectiveness assessments, expense and mileage analyses, etc. A salesman who is dispirited or loosing interest can be identified very easily by good analysis and the problems corrected by training or improved communication before it becomes too late. Technical service will be closely linked with the sales office and is a sales function, it must be used very selectively and be directed towards the sectors of greatest profitability. The sales office is, therefore, both an administrative tool and control centre for sales management and also the focal point of sales communications.

Screening customer inquiries

Inquiries are received by the sales department through three channels:

1 The salesman
2 By letter
3 By telephone

In each instance two vitally important conditions must be met: speed of reaction and systematic handling.

Salesman's inquiries

Several stages and components of the screening process can be eliminated by the efficient and trained salesman. He should have an assessment of the sales potential of the inquiry for both the short and long term, and an indication of the competition. He should, in addition, have a clear idea of the customer's problem or reason for raising the inquiry, the urgency and the general market possibilities for wider sales where new product development is involved.

Information provided by the salesman must be checked by the sales office and a series of actions initiated. Further information may be required from field salesmen, sales and market intelligence records may be examined, and the technical feasibility for new products assessed.

Telephone inquiries

The main problem for the sales office staff is to obtain information that is as good as, or better, than that obtained through a salesman's inquiry. Staff who handle telephone inquiries must therefore be experienced inside salesmen well trained in telephone interview techniques. In general a brief report should be issued to initiate action, with a copy to the appropriate salesman indicating what action should be taken by him and asking also for any relevant comments.

Postal inquiries

Postal inquiries range from a simple letter requesting information sheets and prices or a sample, to an invitation to tender for a major contract. Most postal inquiries, however, provide only very limited information. Parallel action to be taken is to notify the salesman or area manager and to check departmental records. An immediate telephone discussion with the originator of the inquiry can frequently save time and improve the efficiency of action taken.

Checking inquiries

Once the sales inquiry has been received and the available information studied, a series of actions can be taken as outlined in the sales inquiry check-list at the end of this chapter. The overriding consideration must be to obtain profitable business and the early classification of an inquiry by probable order potential and priority is thus vital. A number of key points have to be watched. For example, a low priority assessment for an inquiry which could be from a company with a high potential for other products than that in the inquiry, could lose an opportunity for entry by the salesman. Another example of a danger to be met in giving priority assessments to inquiries is that over a time-scale of several months a number of similar inquiries could be turned down, which, if combined, could result in positive or high priority action being taken.

The possibility of developing business through reciprocal trading should also be examined and can be particularly relevant where an inquiry is difficult to handle. The sales office should take care that too many inquiries are not simply passed to the salesman as the easiest course of action. However, inquiries can be a forewarning of new applications or processes and new markets to be developed. The salesman can also help to avoid too low a priority being given to an inquiry or too low a price being quoted where savings in the customer's production costs through using the product would be substantial. These examples of problems which can be met illustrate the great need for careful screening by experienced sales staff.

Recording

Once the screening process has fulfilled the two requirements of speedy reaction and systematic handling, the remaining, and no less important, action is to classify for future reference and any follow-up action. In this way sales intelligence records are built up.

It is important for the sales office and for sales management to be able to identify the reasons why certain sales inquiries do not result in profitable business and to be able to ensure that salesmen and distributors have been taking effective action. The information is also relevant to publicity budgeting when the reasons why inquiries are put to the company are analysed.

Preparation of proposals and quotations

Sales proposals and quotations range from the simple information sheet and standard price list to a detailed document stating the product specification, guarantees, price levels, conditions of sale and delivery. Certain common factors exist, although their relative importance may vary considerably. In many cases the appropriate selling price is defined by the known competitive price and the current pricing policy of the company. In other cases, prices given in tenders can vary by a very considerable degree. In this instance sales management's greatest problem is to derive an accurate measure of the competitive prices offered. Market and sales intelligence records can provide considerable background data on which logical assumptions can be made. The internal costs and marketing policies of competitors must be known and very detailed effort expended in deriving accurate estimates of their quotations, and in deciding whether or not a comparable price should be offered. Where the various prices have to be measured against differing product performance characteristics, the task of sales management become extremely difficult. However, in many cases the price to be quoted is not the dominant factor.

Tactics

Where regular sales may result from acceptance of a quotation, the product life-cycle has to be considered as has the effect on existing sales costs and profitability of the introduction of an increased volume of orders. Planned obsolescence of existing products may require amendment, or diversification plans may be accelerated or retarded as a result of the acceptance of a proposal for a regular sales contract. Marginal costing may be used as a tactical measure to reduce the effectiveness of certain competitors or to gain entry to a major company with potential sales opportunities for other products.

Customer confidence may be increased by inserting product guarantees into the proposal, even if not entirely necessary or even though service or product replacement would take place anyway as a matter of policy. It is most important to assess the professional purchasing capability of the potential customer and to assist the customer's value analysis where the product can have advantages over competitive products in respect of the user's production costs.

Substantial price disadvantages can be overcome in this way.

Sales visits are generally desirable before a proposal and quotations are completed in order that the proposal, which is a basic selling document, is directed in the most effective manner towards decision-taking executives. Lengthy or detailed proposals should be prepared in a format which is easy to read and which, in appearance and quality, harmonises with the product it is designed to sell.

Useful check-lists

Technical journal selection[2]

1 Which journals cover the defined market and product area?
2 How specialist are the editorial staff?
3 What news items are included?
4 How is the editorial space divided?:
 (*a*) Staff articles
 (*b*) Industry contributions
 (*c*) Reprints
 (*d*) Company press releases and syndicated material
5 How is the advertising divided?:
 (*a*) Competitors
 (*b*) Repeat or regular advertising
6 What is the trend over the past three years (by the above classifications) in editorial space and advertising?
7 How do the trends compare with other journals?
8 Readership:
 (*a*) What readership breakdown is published?
 (*b*) Do customers and potential customers read the journal?
 (*c*) What are the results of readership research?
 (*d*) How do readership sectors rate the value of editorial content?
9 What inquiries have been received as a result of previous advertising in the journal in the past three years?
 (*a*) By the company?
 (*b*) By competitors?
 (*c*) What business is received from inquiries?
10 What are the comparative advertising costs when related to available information on readership and inquiries ?

Proposals and quotations[2]

1 Sales budget:
- (*a*) Costs: selling, service, distribution, effect of acceptance
- (*b*) Terms of payment
- (*c*) Distributor discounts
- (*d*) Product life-cycles and profitability

2 Competitors:
- (*a*) Prices and estimated costs
- (*b*) Effect of differing quotations
- (*c*) Product availability

3 Intelligence:
- (*a*) Competitors actually quoting
- (*b*) Competitors' prices and product specifications

4 Distribution:
- (*a*) Distributor policy
- (*b*) Importance of delivery schedules
- (*c*) Effect on forecast deliveries

5 Servicing:
- (*a*) At installation/introduction
- (*b*) Regular and standard
- (*c*) Maintenance or irregular

6 Technical:
- (*a*) Specification standards
- (*b*) Need to demonstrate or sample

7 Pricing:
- (*a*) Effect on budget and general costs
- (*b*) Marginal costing
- (*c*) Price variations and order size
- (*d*) Value of product benefits (value analysis)

8 Legal:
- (*a*) Guarantees
- (*b*) Non-delivery penalties
- (*c*) Conditions: availability, price fluctuations
- (*d*) Duration of contract

9 Future:
- (*a*) Life-cycle of product
- (*b*) Follow-up tactics
- (*c*) Price trends

(*d*) Technological trends
(*e*) Demand trends

10 Selling:
(*a*) Customer purchasing ability/experience
(*b*) Purchasing influence identification

Sales inquiries[2]

1 Potential value:
(*a*) Short term
(*b*) Long term
(*c*) Likely frequency

2 Competition:
(*a*) Existing
(*b*) Potential

3 Pricing:
(*a*) Acceptable price
(*b*) Quotation levels for quantities
(*c*) Sales, service and distribution costs

4 Policy:
(*a*) Reciprocal trading
(*b*) Customer associated/subsidiary companies
(*c*) Distributors

5 Specifications:
(*a*) Competitors
(*b*) Technical opinion

6 Communication:
(*a*) Salesman
(*b*) Area manager
(*c*) Distributor

7 Distribution:
(*a*) Physical distribution problems
(*b*) Distributor availability
(*c*) Stocks held
(*d*) Effect on production schedule
(*e*) Changes in packaging

8 Diversification:
(*a*) New markets or applications involved
(*b*) Similar recent applications noted

(*c*) Product modifications or diversification involved

9 Action:

(*a*) Degree of urgency

(*b*) Executive level involved

(*c*) Sales literature, quotations and price lists

10 Records:

(*a*) Reasons for inquiry

(*b*) File referencing

(*c*) Follow-up action

References

1 *Industrial Publicity Survey*, 1971.

2 See the *Industrial Sales Manual of the European College of Marketing and Marketing Research*.

Chapter 9

Sales Engineering

John Fenton, Director-General, The Institution of Sales Engineers

---

Selling industrial products and sales engineering are very closely intertwined. Much of what has already been discussed in the previous chapter applies equally to sales engineering. Sales engineering can be defined as the selling of a technical product, process or service, where the engineering ability of the salesman and his company is needed to secure an order.

Sometimes a large degree of special design work is involved. Even with some standard ranges of products, the engineering element can be paramount. For example, selling which involves sales engineering includes the following:

1 Machine tools, where production times, tool life, labour involvement, output, running costs, etc., have to be considered.
2 Process pipework and plant, for chemical applications, where each project is specially designed.
3 Process control, to 2 above, similar but involving circuitry and electronics.
4 Hydraulics and pneumatics, for control, automatic operation and many other applications, all involving special circuitry and design.

5 Pumps and valves, where consideration has to be given to corrosive elements, flows, etc.
6 Computers, involving the whole systems analysis process before the right computer and software can be specified.
7 Mechanical handling equipment, (like fork-lift trucks and conveyor systems) where critical path analysis, flow diagrams and work study play an important part.
8 Effluent treatment plant, where the plant has to suit the various kinds of effluent which need treating.
9 Inspection equipment, from simple gauges to radio active isotopes, needs a highly-skilled sales engineer (and there is a built-in objection to buying inspection equipment, for it only results in scrap).
10 Structural steelwork, no building is the same; stresses, subsidence, foundations, load-carrying structures, all have to be considered.

There are many more examples – scientific instruments, electrical gear, electronics, communications equipment, marine equipment, aerospace and nuclear equipment, special-purposes vehicles (like tankers and tippers), refractories, packaging, textile machinery – the list is endless. In fact, there are very few technical products sold to industry which do not require a fair degree of engineering know-how on the part of the salesman.

Probably vending machines and certain types of office equipment would fall into the non-sales engineering category, as might nuts and bolts, some oils and greases, steel stockholding, abrasives, timbers, paper and print. But this is not always so – fasteners are quite complicated· today, with plastics and other materials. The degree of engineering expertise is often considerable.

To sell the wrong lubricating oil for use on a surface grinder could result in a very low grade finish. To supply a tool steel which has to be made into a power-press tool could involve the salesman in highly technical discussions on hardening and tempering, ease of machining, and so on.

Even electronic components sold by the million – like resistors, capacitors, transistors and integrated circuits – can involve the salesman in discussions far above the head of even the most ardent radio ham.

This chapter takes just one company as an example – a company manufacturing and selling a range of machine tools. The principles discussed in the previous chapter will be used in the example, so that every engineer reading this Handbook can see just what is required to ensure that the company is marketing orientated (the customer comes first), and can sell effectively.

The company is question has been established for eighty years. It has a range of products which have been developed over the years and which hold their own in a market that contains six other companies selling similar products in competition.

The company is looking for expansion at the rate of a steady ten per cent each year. The market has been assessed as being stable enough to support this expansion. In addition, the company has production capacity which could be used to manufacture new products if a demand should arise.

The company's sales force comprises ten sales engineers, each having a territory, so that together they cover the whole United Kingdom. There is also a sales office with three estimating engineers supported by a drawing office which handles any necessary design work.

An export sales manager handles all overseas business through a number of agents, resident in the countries where the company operates.

The company just described will serve as a typical example, since it can be taken as fitting the specification of, probably, twenty-five per cent of the British engineering industry. The role of the sales engineers in this company will be considered together with that of the general sales manager. His job is, initially, to ensure that the company's sales effort is as effective as it can be.

The sales engineer as a person

The general sales manager (GSM) needs to take a long look at the ten people he is responsible for in his sales force. Are they capable of sustained effort? Do they need pushing every other week to keep them at it? Can they work without supervision?

The GSM has to understand each of his men; he has to know their likes and dislikes, hobby-horses, strong points, weak points, desires and ambitions. All this is necessary before the GSM will be able to motivate each man effectively to attain whatever goals the company has set.

Sales engineers are complex people, even by definition. They are engineers on one hand, and salesmen on the other. These two beliefs are poles apart in their attitudes and emotions, which is why the job is so difficult to do properly. The background needed by a good sales engineer is set out below.

Engineering ability

He has to be fully conversant with the products he sells, their applications, his competition and its applications (and how this compares with his own), and his customers' business and markets.

To cope with this veritable mountain of technical and commercial knowledge, the sales engineer needs a background in engineering. Otherwise he will be a brilliant man indeed if he can grasp half the technical data involved and appreciate technical problems and their solutions.

Salesmanship

Contrary to popular belief, salesmen are not born, they are made; like every good recipe, if the ingredients are available, it is only up to the chef and the temperature of the oven.

To be a good salesman, a man needs to have certain attitudes of mind and body. The most important of these are as follows:

1 Acceptability to people of all levels.
2 Good health: selling is real hard work.
3 Fluency of communication, both spoken and written.
4 Resilience: the ability to get up and back in fighting.
5 A positive temperament: the ability to make things happen.
6 Sincerity, honesty, integrity and loyalty.
7 Enthusiasm: it spreads quickly.
8 Empathy: the ability to understand why a person holds a particular opinion, without necessarily agreeing with it.

Given most of these qualities in his sales engineer, the GSM can mould them together into a coherent, dynamic whole – and add one final factor as a result of his own leadership. This final factor for the sales engineer is a firm belief in the value and importance of the job he is doing.

Training

Before any sales engineer can actively go out to sell, he has to be thoroughly trained in product applications and company policies and systems. No period in a sales office can fulfil all this unless the period is two years or more.

The GSM will quickly establish the level of competence his sales force shows. If product knowledge, competition knowledge and customer knowledge is lacking, he should quickly organise training to bring this knowledge up to the required level. This training can be handled by members of the company, providing they are competent to present the material in such a way that the sales engineers can comfortably absorb it. Nothing is worse than to see the chief designer waffling on about his pride and joy in a way which bores his listeners to tears; and, what is more important, nothing is achieved either.

Salesmanship training, however, should not be handled by the GSM or any other member of the company unless he has first-hand experience of the techniques involved. This specialised training should be left to the experts, provided they really are experts. If the expertise cannot be found within the company, it may be necessary to use consultants, or approach an advisory organisation. Among these is the Institution of Sales Engineers.

Quite a number of companies believe in putting a new sales engineer out on a territory for six months and *then* giving him some salesmanship training. Most emphatically this is one of the most ludicrous practices ever dreamed up. One need only consider how much damage a man can do, even in one month, if he does not know what he is doing – or why. And it is the company's customers who are being damaged.

Commitment to his responsibilities

The first tasks the GSM has to tackle after he has assessed his man, are the questions of motivation and incentive. How does he make as sure as he can that each and every one of his sales engineers works as hard as he does himself towards achieving the company targets?

Commission schemes, bonuses, holiday prizes and all monetary incentives might help – but most companies ignore one of the finest incentives of all – and one which costs nothing. It is tied up with the sales engineer's belief in the value and importance of the job he is doing.

The sales engineer needs to feel important. He needs encouragement and praise. Sometimes he needs guidance. But above all he needs to be told just where the company is trying to go and what part he must play in getting it there.

This is not achieved simply by being given a quota and being told to get on and make it by the end of the year. It means being involved in the setting of the company target in the first place – being consulted for an accurate assessment of what he feels his territory will produce next year; and it means being part of the numerous meetings and discussions with production, finance, purchasing and market research, where the targets are hashed out in detail, knowing, when the board of directors finally agree the company target, exactly how and why it was fixed where it is fixed; it means knowing, by virtue of his involvement, just how critical it is to his company that the target should be met.

This is total commitment by a man to the objectives of his company. This is what the GSM must strive to achieve. If he succeeds, his sales force will be better motivated than any financial incentive could inspire.

There are a number of methods which the GSM can use to make his sales engineers conscious of their responsibilities: the sales staff should be aware of the following facts:

1 The company employs 1,000 people in total. With a sales force of ten – the only people in direct contact with the customers – this means that the livelihood of 100 workers and their families rests on each sales engineer's shoulders.
2 Each sales engineer is, in effect, an emissary. He *is* the company in the eyes of the customer, for he is the only piece of the company which the customer sees. What he does and says, the company is doing and saying. He therefore has the company image to project.
3 Illustrate to the sales force what would happen to the company's financial position if they failed to make target.

These facts can then be coupled with an example of the company's profit-making situation; for example:

Company target sales	£2,000,000
Cost of manufacture	£1,000,000
	£1,000,000
Administrative overheads	£500,000
	£500,000
Marketing overheads	£300,000
Gross margin	£200,000

This example shows, basically, the profit which the company expects to make if it sells the £2 million of machine-tools it forecast. It can be re-costed on the assumption that the sales force only makes ninety per cent of the target – a ten per cent shortfall – not uncommon, and often not giving rise to concern. One could also assume that three-quarters of the year have passed before management realise the target is not going to be met, so that all raw materials have been purchased and most of the production started or finished for the whole £2 million machines. It is not sound to lay off any labour because, if sales increase in the future, this labour would not be retrievable. Likewise, administration and marketing overheads cannot be reduced without endangering future sales. In fact, at such a time as this, marketing should increase its advertising and promotion expenditure to provide for next year. Thus, the example will be as follows:

Actual sales made (90 per cent)	£1,800,000
Cost of manufacture (committed)	£1,000,000
	£800,000
Administrative overheads	£500,000
	£300,000
Marketing overheads	£300,000
Gross margin	ZERO

Thus, any additional expenditure on advertising would put the company into the red.

Similar examples can be illustrated by the GSM to show the effects of erratic order intake on the company's cash flow, and the effects on profits of the sales force selling more or less of some particular products than the company budgeted to manufacture.

If any financial incentive scheme is introduced, it should be based on profit and not turnover. A profit-conscious sales force will be worth its weight in gold.

Planning sales engineering activities

One of the oldest rules in selling is: 'Plan your work and work your plan'. It is a first-class rule, yet many sales engineers do not adhere to it for long, even if they get as far as deciding on a workable plan in the first place.

Obviously, any plan will not work all the time. There will always be emergency calls, special meetings at short notice and illness to get in the way. But, if a plan works eighty per cent of the time, it should not be thrown away because of the twenty per cent of problems that come up. All an eighty per cent workable plan means is that it takes maybe fourteen months to complete rather than the calculated twelve months; that is far better than having no plan at all. Next year, lessons learned can result in a more accurate plan.

The odd case that is different should never be treated as the rule or the norm. If it is treated as the norm, *all* the statistics will be false. Exceptions should be treated as exceptions.

Planning individual targets

At the beginning of each period of operation, the GSM must make sure each of his sales engineers knows what his target is, and what he needs to do to achieve the target. The latter means he must calculate:

1 How many existing customers he has who will buy again, and how much they will buy.
2 How many calls he can make in the period.
3 How many 'prospects' he must generate to provide the element of new business he requires for his target achievement.

The GSM has past records to call upon when working out what his sales force has to do. These records should tell him how he should divide the targets for each sales engineer in terms of business from existing customers (repeat business) and business from new customers.

In the case of machine tools, this division may be twenty per cent from repeat business and eighty per cent from new customers; it would depend on the product to a great extent. In engineering consumables, the figures might be reversed, that is, eighty per cent from repeat business and twenty per cent from new customers. A lot also depends upon the competition and the rate of expansion planned for the company.

It is assumed that the GSM has divided his target to provide for forty per cent of business from existing customers, and sixty per cent from new customers.

Again, from past records, the GSM can establish the average number of calls his sales engineers make in a day. For machine tools this might be four. However, six or eight calls a day are not uncommon. There are on average twenty working days in each month. So each sales engineer can make on average $4 \times 20 = 80$ calls per month. This is an indisputable fact on which the plan has to be based. The GSM can work at increasing the number of calls his sales engineers make per day, but this comes later.

Existing customers

Priority has to be given to servicing the existing customers, or the competition will steal some of them. Allowing for a certain amount of repeat business coming in semi-automatically – at least with the sales engineer only having to carry out half his usual operations to secure the order – the GSM can probably only afford to allocate twenty-five per cent of the available selling time to the servicing of existing customers. That is twenty calls per month.

Each existing customer needs to be classified in terms of the amount of business he will generate during the planned period and beyond. Customers unlikely to buy again should not be included but should be telephoned once or twice a year so that some contact is maintained. This classification of existing customers can probably be divided into good, medium and small potential business. Thus, the number of customers in each division can be listed.

The next operation is to estimate the frequency at which the sales engineer should call on each division. A call once each month may be necessary for a good division customer; once every three months may be sufficient for a medium division customer. With the number of customers listed and the call frequency determined, a table can be constructed which will show how many calls per month will be necessary to service these existing customers. An example is shown in Figure 9:1.

Division	Number of customers	Call frequency	Calls per month
Good	10	1 month	10
Medium	18	3 months	6
Small	24	6 months	4
	52		20

FIGURE 9:1 TABLE DETERMINING FREQUENCY OF SALES CALLS

This particular table worked first time. However, it is not always this easy. It may be that on the first attempt the GSM or the sales engineer has 100 customers listed; he may feel that he should call on the medium division once every two months and the small division once every three months. The resultant calls per month allocated would be around sixty. Thus, the plan would not work in practice. Then a really critical look at both the customer potential and the call frequency has to be made – and the figures changed until the final plan is workable.

New business

This takes care of the existing customers and leaves sixty calls per month available for new business. But first holidays, exhibitions, meetings and illness have to be allowed for. In a normal year two months can be taken out for these. That means 160 calls per year, or spread evenly over the year, thirteen calls per month. Thus, the true allocation for new business is:

$$60-13=47 \text{ calls per month or } 564 \text{ calls per year.}$$

The GSM is faced with generating sixty per cent of the total target business from new accounts. He breaks this down for each sales engineer, as he did for the existing customer calculations. However, attaining a new business target is far less certain than is the case with existing business. Whether it is attained or not depends largely upon the personal performance of each sales engineer, and it is upon this factor that the GSM has to concentrate.

In this example the actual target for each sales engineer in terms of turnover is probably around £200,000. So the turnover each man needs from new business is £120,000.

From past records, the GSM can establish a figure for *average order value*. Using this figure (assumed to be £5,000) he can calculate the number of actual orders his sales engineer needs to secure to make his target, that is:

$$\frac{120{,}000}{5{,}000}=24 \text{ orders}$$

It is worth noting that with engineering consumables, once an initial order has been secured, there is repeat business. Therefore, in calculating average order value, the value of business from a new account in the first year should be used.

Having established the number of orders needed, the GSM has to measure the performance of each man. He does this by recording the types of calls his sales engineers make on 'prospects'. The section in this chapter devoted to records shows the easiest way for the GSM to get this information. He records the number of calls his sales engineer makes before he gets a written proposal submitted (always, of course, having made sure the proposal was not just requested by the prospect as an easy way of getting rid of the sales engineer). He also records the number of proposals which are submitted and compares this with the number of orders received from the proposals.

These figures, within a period of six months, give the GSM an accurate picture of the effectiveness of his sales engineers on an individual basis. With the figures he can not only calculate whether the target will be achieved, but also what he has to do to improve his sales engineers' performance.

Let us suppose the GSM records these figures for one of his sales engineers and they show, firstly, that for every ten initial calls he makes on prospects he generates one proposal; secondly, for every five proposals submitted, the sales engineer secures one order. From this, the GSM can calculate how many initial calls this sales engineer needs to make to achieve his target of twenty-four orders, that is:

$$10 \times 5 \times 24 = 1{,}200 \text{ calls}$$

As the sales engineer has only 564 calls that he can use for this part of his job it is a foregone conclusion that he will *not* achieve his target. Having ascertained this, the GSM sets about improving the sales engineer's performance so that he *will* achieve the target.

Together with the sales engineer, the GSM looks closely at the sort of prospects the man is calling on. Are they really people who would buy the company's products? Are they in the right sector of the market? Do they need the particular benefits the products can offer, or will they find more benefits in the competition? Is the sales engineer doing sufficient research on each prospect before he starts selling? Is he seeing the right people or *all* the people who will influence the decision to buy or not? Is the sales engineer's method of presentation good enough? Does he use visual aids? Does he ask the right sort of questions? Does he talk about the *benefits* of his product, or waffle on about the technical specification? Does he determine an objective with the prospect as early in the sale as he can? Does he then make sure he gets to that objective? (For example, 'If I can show you that this new machine will increase your production of widgets by ten per cent, will you seriously consider buying it?')

The GSM may have to train his sales engineers in developing opening presentations to the point where objectives are agreed. For example:

> 'One of the headaches in drilling and tapping is tool breakage – I'm sure you'll agree with that, Mr Jones. When a drill or a tap breaks it's usually in the hole. Not only does the tool have to be

replaced, the component usually has to be scrapped. That's not so bad when the component is small, but if it is a larger, more elaborate job you might have to try to reclaim the component, and that costs time and money.

Where do you find tool breakages hurt you most, Mr Jones?

What have you done to improve things? Did it work?

What sort of tool holders do you use?

Have you even tried floating holders, like those used on our Mk. 47B multi-purpose drilling machine?

We had a similar problem at Snooks Engineering, over at Leamington. They changed to our Mk 47B and found it reduced their tool breakage and down-time by 200 per cent. If we could show these sort of savings for your production, Mr Jones, would you be interested in having the Mk 47B?

Can I have a look at your production line, to see exactly what you've got? In about half-an-hour we should be able to establish roughly whether we can help and to what extent.

Can you spare half-an-hour?'

Finally – when a proposal has been submitted – does the sales engineer really try to get final commitment and *ask* for the order?

The GSM is aiming for an improvement in performance so that for every five initial calls made one serious proposal is submitted, and for every four proposals submitted an order is secured. If this happens, the initial calls required to make those twenty-four orders will reduce to:

$$5 \times 4 \times 24 = 480$$

Now the sales engineer has eighty-four calls per year spare which he can use to follow up and improve his sales figures even further.

The individual territory

Having completed the necessary calculations, the GSM can devote some time to making sure his sales engineers cover their territories efficiently. This has a two-fold benefit. It enables the sales engineers to make more calls and also contributes towards reducing expenses – mainly petrol costs. One basic rule exists about territories: the sales engineer does not necessarily have to cover *all of it*. One prospect of a certain size and potential is just as good as another; it is, therefore, best to leave the far-distant prospects alone until all the nearer ones have been dealt with.

The GSM should provide each of his sales engineers with a large-scale map of his territory, mounted on pin-board and with the boundary clearly marked. Main roads are very often used as boundaries for territories. They can be much more effective at times as *spines* with open moorland as boundaries. The GSM should also provide a supply of coloured pins – one colour for each category of customer or prospect. The sales engineer then has one month in which to use his map and pins to work out his plan for covering the territory, based on the calculations already described. At the end of the month, the GSM has a meeting with the sales engineer and together they develop and finalise the plan.

The final phase of instilling into the sales engineers their responsibilities for organising their work is to show them the film *Get Organised* which is available from the Rank Film Library, London.

Reports and customer records

Every company needs to keep the most comprehensive records possible of its customers, their business, buying record, developments, etc. This is the company's very life-blood, yet so often everything is left in the hands of the sales engineer himself, and when he leaves, the records and the life-blood leave with him. The GSM, therefore, has to devise and implement a system of customer records and reporting so that both the company and the sales engineer can operate in the long term in the most efficient way possible. This system should also provide the measurement figures which the GSM needs in order to assess the personal performance of his individual sales engineers.

A good reporting system is one where the amount of writing necessary is kept to the absolute minimum. A sales engineer is employed primarily to sell, not to write reports. However, in sales engineering the accuracy of a report can mean the difference between an order and a rejection. So time spent in perfecting the system is time well spent. Many companies develop their own systems. Many others use one of the standard systems available. This section illustrates one of the standard systems, produced by Sales Control and

 CP A4

CALL PLAN FOR WEEK COMMENCING SALESMAN

	TIME	APPT OR COLD	COMPANY	CONTACT	AIM OF CALL
MONDAY					
TUESDAY					
WEDNESDAY					
THURSDAY					
FRIDAY					

ADVANCE APPOINTMENTS	DATE	TIME	COMPANY	CONTACT	AIM OF CALL

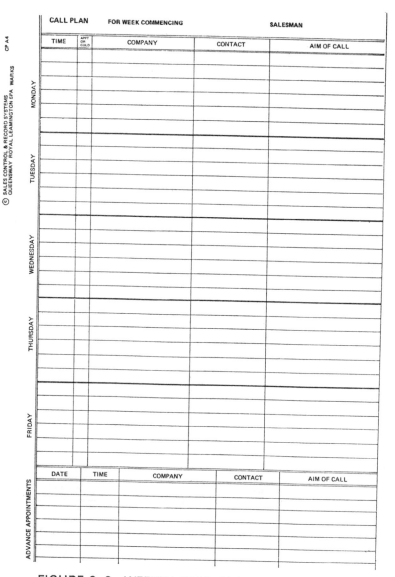

FIGURE 9:2 WEEKLY CALL PLAN—SCRS SYSTEM

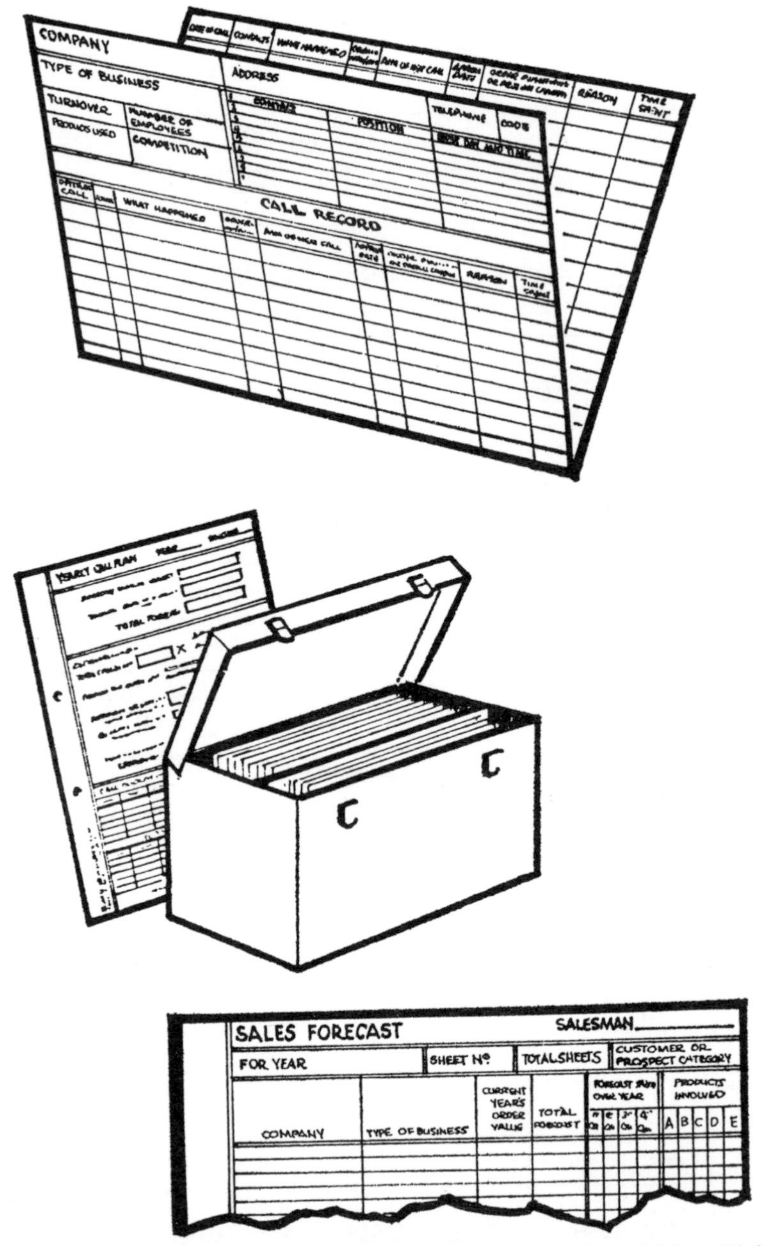

FIGURE 9:3 CUSTOMER RECORD FILE, YEARLY CALL PLAN, SALESMAN'S WEEKLY WORK CASE AND SALES FORECASTING SHEET

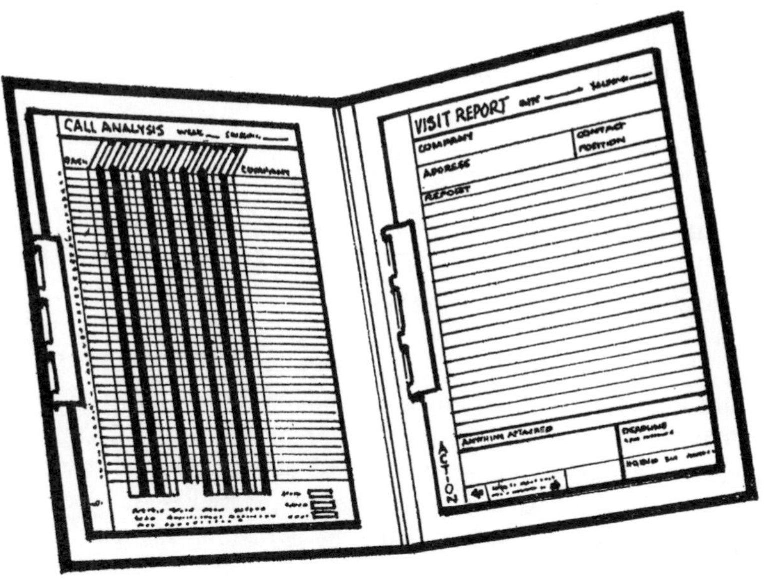

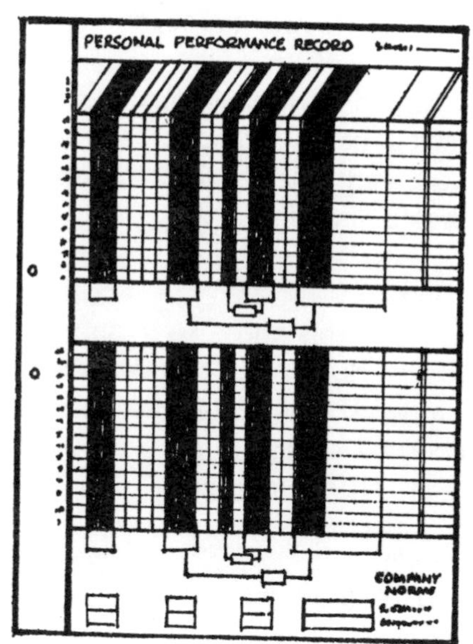

FIGURE 9:4 WEEKLY CALL ANALYSIS, VISIT REPORT AND PERSONAL PERFORMANCE RECORD—SCRS SYSTEM

Record Systems – a division of the Institution of Sales Engineers. The system can be adapted to meet any specific requirements and has been designed for engineering and industrial selling.

Call plan

First, the system should contain a form on which the sales engineer lists his calls for the week. This should be with the GSM by the Wednesday of the previous week.

On this form, for each day of the week, is entered the scheduled time of the call, whether it is by appointment or 'cold' (the GSM should insist on his sales engineers making at least two of their calls per day by appointment, more if possible), the name of the person to be seen, the customer and the aim of the call. The date of the last call made on the customer is also helpful; it makes the sales engineer look up his own record card while he is making his plan. This form is illustrated on Figure 9:2.

Customer record file

The sales engineer has a record file for each customer, which holds information on the customer's name, address, telephone number, trade, products used, contacts, and a list of the calls made and their results. This form is illustrated on Figure 9:3. Once a year, the sales engineer's record files can be used in preparing an accurate forecast of sales from his territory for the year ahead. The SCRS system provides special forms for this and also a simple method by which the sales engineer can work out his overall call plan for the year. A case for holding a week's work of customer record files and the sales engineer's reporting system is provided as part of the SCRS package. These items are shown in Figure 9:3.

Week call analysis

Every call which the sales engineer makes is entered on a weekly call analysis form – illustrated in Figure 9:4. Apart from the name of the company called upon, all entries are either ticks or numbers.

The information enables the GSM to measure personal performance

The totals at the bottom of the weekly analysis forms enable the GSM to summarise various facets of the operation, that is, appointments, cold calls, abortive calls, action obtained, products discussed, etc. These are totalled quarterly, and company norms established. A special personal performance record card is provided for this.

Visit report

If any action is required by the sales engineer from his company, a special visit report form is used. This can have three copies, one of which is returned to the sales engineer when action has been taken. This enables the sales engineer to progress his work and remind his company about any action requests still outstanding. An visit report form is shown in Figure 9 : 4.

Check-lists are very useful when a sales engineer is conducting a survey prior to putting forward a proposal. They enable him to carry out the survey in the shortest possible time and prevent him forgetting to get some vital piece of information, without which the proposal loses impact. Check-lists can be attached to action request forms for this purpose.

Every engineering company encourages its sales engineers to sell standard equipment, or equipment which the company has at least designed and built before. However, there are obviously situations, and they occur quite regularly, when a customer needs something special, which means the involvement of the drawing office and estimating staff before any proposal can be submitted. The action request from the sales engineer therefore has to contain sufficient information to enable the drawing office and estimating staff to carry out their functions as swiftly and as economically as possible. The check-list obviously helps in the compiling of this information, but in involved technical situations, the sales engineer himself will have to discuss requirements in detail with the designers.

The GSM, however, has a different criterion to deal with. He has to decide for each request for a 'special' proposal, whether it will be worth carrying out the necessary work to get as far as the submitting of a full proposal. In some highly technical capital equipment sales,

PROSPECT LIST MONTH________ SALESMAN________

COMPANY	ADDRESS	MAIN CONTACT	BEST LINE OF ATTACK AND REASON	FILE START

FIGURE 9:5 MONTHLY PROSPECT LIST—SCRS SYSTEM

the design and estimating work alone could cost the company £1,000 or so. The time devoted to the particular job could also be spread over six months or more and amount to over 100 hours of the sales engineer's time and the back-up staff's time. This time can probably be costed at an overall £6 per hour.

The GSM, therefore, should be looking critically at his sales engineers' reports and action requests to find sufficient information in them to enable him to make a decision on whether to allow the proposal to be made, or to withdraw from the fight. Of course, the GSM cannot be absolutely right all the time, but he can do his best to make sure that his sales engineer has established the objectives already outlined. For example: Does he determine an objective with the prospect as early in the sale as he can? Does he then make sure he gets to that objective? ('If I can show you that this new machine will increase your production of widgets by ten per cent, will you seriously consider buying it?') Does he ask the right sort of questions? The check list can help here: Has the prospect actually confirmed to the sales engineer that he is satisfied with what has been discussed so far and seriously wants a written proposal? Why does the prospect want a proposal? Who has to make the final decision? How many copies of the proposal will be required? When is the equipment required – and why? Is the expenditure already budgeted by the prospect company? If not, is the money available? If not, will the prospect consider extended credit purchases or leasing? If not, why are you bothering?

If the sales engineer has clarified the above points satisfactorily, the GSM has sufficient information to decide to go ahead. If the sales engineer has *not* obtained all the data, the GSM must get him to verify anything in doubt; if he is still in doubt afterwards, he should send the sales engineer back to the prospect to find out. After the first half-dozen experiences like this, the sales engineer will be doing a proper job at the beginning. Sales engineers should always be encouraged to find out what they are up against. Who else is interested in supplying this equipment? What have they done so far? What are they going to do? He should even go as far as asking how much the job will stand. No one can sell unless they know what they have to sell against; it may be that there is prejudice against the technique or process involved: if so, the prejudice has to be overcome before money is spent; it may be a trade union objection which will prevent a prospect from placing an order; or perhaps the prospect simply considers that there is a more effective way of spending the available money and this has nothing to do with engineering.

All these factors need to be established by the sales engineer before action is taken, quite apart from dealing with the normal problem-solving questions which have to be asked.

Sometimes, of course, it is impossible to secure all the desired information. The situation may be wreathed in politics, be delicate or precarious; then it is up to the GSM to form a conclusion based on instinct and past experience. If in doubt, perhaps the proposal should be submitted; or perhaps a simple outline proposal will suffice to carry the sales engineer through until a more tangible commitment has been obtained from the customer.

Prospecting for new business

The GSM has to make sure that his sales engineers are finding sufficient new prospects to ensure the eventual generation of the required amount of new business. Both the GSM and the sales engineers will know how many new prospects they need from their calculations made for the yearly call plan. The SCRS system provides a prospecting section with which the GSM can control and measure this part of the sales operation – illustrated in Figure 9 : 5.

If a man leaves

The whole of this reporting and record system is supplied to the sales engineer by his company. Therefore the company can and should demand every piece of it back if a sales engineer decides to leave. This should be written into his contract of employment. The man who replaces the departing sales engineer then has a complete record of his new territory with which to start.

Inquiries from advertising

Most engineering companies advertise in order to generate inquiries. The advertisements either have a coupon which the reader fills in and sends off, or a line which says simply: 'send for full details'.

Direct mail shots are designed similarly to generate inquiries.

In machine tools certainly, and in most other areas of engineering, the sales engineer will need to follow up each inquiry before an order is secured. Yet what happens in most companies? The most junior girl in the sales office has the job of dealing with the coupons and inquiries. She types a simple letter to the inquirer:

Dear Sir,

Thank you for inquiring about our multi-purpose rotary drilling machine, as advertised in the *Machinery Gazette*.

I enclose literature on this machine and our other products.

If you require any further information our representative will be happy to call on you.

Yours faithfully,
etc.

Apart from dispensing several times as much literature as is necessary, this operation has one major disadvantage. It reduces the sales engineer's opportunity to talk to the inquirer by thirty per cent and so prevents the company from finding out *why* the inquiry was made. The GSM must find the junior girl something more meaningful to do. Then he can make sure the sales engineers receive the inquiries as quickly as is possible. He also provides all the sales engineers with quantities of literature, large envelopes, visiting cards and a stapler. Then he tells the sales engineers what to do, and makes sure they do it. They telephone each inquirer, saying: 'Thank you for sending in our coupon from the advertisement in *Machinery Gazette*. I've got an awful lot of information I want to send you, but just to make sure I send you what you want – what made you inquire?'

Depending upon the answer he gets, the sales engineer will either make an appointment and see the inquirer, or send him literature through the post, in a hand written envelope, with his card stapled to every brochure: 'Would you mind if I put all this in the post to-night in a handwritten envelope? I want to get the literature to you as quickly as possible and a letter will take a couple of days.' This results in the maximum information being supplied, the maximum number of appointments being made, the minimum amount of literature being used, and the minimum costs arising.

Quotations and proposals

The written, formal proposal from the company to a prospective customer can be quite complex if the product is capital equipment, especially production equipment. A whole book could be written about quotations and proposals. Only the basic concepts and the problems which the sales engineer faces are investigated here.

A typical engineering quotation, which the sales engineer is expected to use to help him secure the order, is shown in Figure 9:6 below:

Dear Sirs,

We beg to thank you for your esteemed inquiry and have pleasure in quoting as follows:

Subject to the terms and conditions stated on the back of this form:

One Model 47B multi-purpose drilling machine.
3 phase 5 hp motor. 6 speed gear box.
No 3 Morse taper spindle. Throat 20 inches.
Depth of drilling adjustable from 2 inches to 16 inches.
Weight 8 cwts. Height overall 6 feet 3 inches.

Price £740 Ex works

Delivery 10/14 weeks. Terms of payment net 30 days.

We trust that the above quotation will prove to be satisfactory and we look forward to the receipt of your esteemed order in due course, when it will receive our most careful attention.

Yours faithfully,

Per Pro ________________

____

E & O E

FIGURE 9:6 EXAMPLE OF A TYPICAL QUOTATION AND PROPOSAL
This example of a typically bad proposal should be compared with the proposal in Figure 9:7

This type of document is primarily a legal document. As such, it has to safeguard the supply company against any chicanery which its customers might throw its way.

However, this legal document in most cases has to serve as the only written evidence of what the sales engineer has spent six months telling a prospective customer. As such, it does a very poor job indeed. Capital equipment, especially, has to obtain the sanction of a board of directors before an order can be placed.

Any board of directors – in fact, any customer at any level – is primarily interested in only one thing: what is in it for him?

The legal quotation document does not even start to show a customer this; in fact it contains every single reason why he should *not* buy the product.

The proposal format

So the GSM quickly removes the Victorian style prose and the deterrents and sets about producing written proposals which his sales engineers can use to SELL with.

The quotation used in Figure 9:6 can be taken as an example and re-written as a selling proposal. This is shown in Figure 9:7.

This format is necessarily longer than the simple quotation, but its effectiveness in securing orders against competition more than makes up for the time taken to prepare it.

The format has four main sections:

1 Objectives
2 Recommendations
3 Price and financial breakdown (or justification)
4 Service

One company selling capital equipment in Britain and using this proposal format is achieving a conversion of one order for ever two proposals submitted. Perhaps this is the proof of the pudding.

Dear Mr Smith,

Our sales engineer, Mr R.B. Jones, has asked me to write to you with details of our multi-purpose drilling machines.

As I understand it, you are looking for a machine which will:

1 Replace an existing drilling machine which no longer provides the accuracy you require.
2 Provide you with plant able to drill any of the components which you have to handle through your production.
3 Enable this to be done with the very minimum of setting and down-time.

I have discussed these requirements in details with Mr Jones and we recommend our Model 47B multi-purpose drilling machine. This will fit the space your existing machine occupies and provide an accuracy of ± 0.0002 inches in each of its three axes.

The machine has a throat-depth suitable to take your largest component comfortably, and its quick traverse and vertical adjustment, coupled with our new system of hydraulically-clamped jigs, enable the setter to change jigs and tools in a matter of minutes.

The installation of the Model 47B will be carried out by our personnel, who will also commission the machine and instruct your setters in the tooling and jigging procedure. Installation can be completed in one day and this can be a Saturday if you prefer.

Price and financial breakdown

The price of the Model 47B is £740 ex works. Delivery, installation and commissioning would be £60, making a total price of £800.

I understand that you depreciate your plant over ten years. We are confident that the Model 47B will retain its accuracy over this period, assuming normal usage.

Together with Mr Jones, I have estimated the savings the new machine would give you in setting and down-time, comparing it with your existing plant. You change jigs on the machine on average ten times each week; each change takes one hour, the loss of production during this hour is about 40 components.

The new machine, with its hydraulic clamping, will enable you to change jigs in 15 minutes. This gives you a saving in setters time of 7½ hours per week and an increase in machined components of 300 per week. Basing the setters time at £2 per hour, this represents a saving of £15 per week, or £750 per year. Over the life of the machine, this saving would be upwards of £7 500, plus the gain in machined components, which we are unable to calculate in financial terms.

After-sales service

As Mr Jones has told you we have a reputation for reliability. With any production equipment this is essential. Our service engineers are supplied with radio-telephones so that they can reach you as quickly as possible if an accident occurs – for example, a forklift truck might damage the motor control gear.

We have installed similar drilling machines at Snooks Engineering Limited, Warwick; Bloggs Pumps Limited, Solihull and Coote and Sons Limited, Birmingham. I know these companies would not mind you asking them what they think of our machines.

I enclose with this proposal our official quotation and a technical leaflet which gives the full specification of the Model 47B.

I hope you decide to install the machine. I know it will give you many years of excellent and trouble-free service.

Yours sincerely,

J.E. Fenton
Commercial Manager

FIGURE 9:7 THE SELLING PROPOSAL

Processing the order

Normally, any order received for goods like machine tools will be an order which refers to a drawing number and proposal supplied by the GSM's company.

If the order is for a standard product, the procedure is simple. However, care must be taken by the sales engineer to ensure that the customer knows exactly what he is going to buy. All extras, attachments, special adaptations, even special paint finishes, must be clearly outlined on the technical specification that accompanies the proposal.

If a customer requires an amendment of any kind to the proposed goods an amended proposal is submitted before, or even after the official order is received. This ties up the special requirements and confirms the price for these and, at the same time, provides the necessary paperwork so that accurate instructions can be passed to the works by the sales department for the manufacture of the goods. It should be a gospel rule that whenever an order is received which differs from the last proposal submitted, a new proposal should be prepared and the price, if different to that shown on the order, should be verified with the customer. This is the only way to make sure the goods actually manufactured are dove-tailed exactly to the customer's final requirements.

There are times when a customer alters a specification when manufacture of the goods is part-completed. Then the sales engineer has a liaison job to do between the customer and his own works. But again, all alterations need to be tied up with the necessary paperwork. Again, price and profit margins can be affected. Written confirmation of alterations after order should be obtained from the customer.

The GSM should work to a hard and fast rule: Works departments do not accept instructions from sales engineers unless passed by the sales office and covered by the necessary amendments to the works order.

After-sales service

The GSM in the example has already committed himself and his company to having a really efficient after-sales service organisation – in the selling proposal. But where production equipment is concerned, a machine forms only a small part of a whole production line and failure of that machine can mean the failure or hold-up of the whole line. In some cases this hold-up can be very expensive indeed for the customer. One transfer unit for machining rear-axle housings costs its owners £20 per minute if it breaks down.

The spares and service organisation has to be in existence *before* a product is launched or, at least, by the time it is launched. The service engineers themselves have to be trained in customer relations and salesmanship. They probably represent the core of the GSM's development program for his future sales engineers. They need control systems, record systems and feedback-generating capabilities, just the same as the sales engineers.

Sales engineering has not been covered in depth in this chapter. Neither has every single factor been mentioned. The writer has tried to show the reader what he needs to look for and to do when he becomes general sales manager. Sales engineers reading this will quickly see that most of what the GSM is going to do they will be able to do for themselves. And they should. It is the quickest way to the GSM's job itself.

Further Reading

1 *Effective Salesmanship for Sales Engineers*, J B Windsor, Institution of Sales Engineers, 1969 and 1971.
2 *Managing a Sales Force,* M T Wilson, Gower Press, 1971.

PART THREE

Administration

Chapter 10

Company Law and Patents

F W Rose, Principal Lecturer in Law, City of Birmingham Polytechnic

---

It is not always appreciated that a company registered under the Companies Acts 1948 and 1967 has a legal existence and personality quite separate and distinct from that of persons holding shares in the company. Many legal formalities must be complied with before such a company comes into existence. When formed the company has rights and liabilities in law which depend upon a careful analysis of the relevant statutory rules.

It may be necessary when an individual makes an agreement with a company to determine its precise power to contract, its financial position and future prospects. If the company is experiencing difficulties in trading profitably, the rights of the shareholders to control the company may be of vital importance.

This chapter attempts to explain some of the more important legal provisions in straightforward, non-technical language that may be understood by the non-lawyer.

Legal status of a public limited company

The relevant statutory rules governing the legal status of a public limited company are contained in the Companies Acts 1948 and 1967. In law a company has an existence separate and distinct from that of the individual members who hold shares in the company. The company:

1 Can own property and members have no rights in that property, their interest is in the shares they hold.
2 Can make contracts with other individuals, companies or members.
3 Will continue to exist irrespective of the death of an individual member, whose shareholding is then taken over by the person who succeeds to his property.
4 Must act through the medium of human agents who will control its affairs, such as directors.

Formation of a public limited company

Reasons for forming a public limited company

A private company is often formed to carry on a family business. Frequently there are only a handful of shareholders, usually members of the same family. A private company may trade successfully for several years, but further expansion will require additional capital which cannot be supplied by existing shareholders. A public company may be formed to take over and carry on the business; members of the private company will exchange their shares for shares in the new public company. The additional capital for such items as land, new buildings and machinery will be provided by issuing shares which the general public may purchase if they wish.

Registration

The company must be registered. This is effected by filing the following documents with the Registrar of Companies:

1 The memorandum of association
2 The articles of association
3 A statement of nominal capital
4 A list of persons consenting to be directors

These formalities are usually dealt with by a solicitor, accountant or a company formation firm specialising in this type of work.

The memorandum of association

This is the charter of the company embodying its constitution and powers. It must state:

1 The name of the company, with 'limited' as the last word
2 The location of the registered office of the company
3 The objects to be carried out by the company
4 A declaration that the liability of members is limited
5 The share capital and its division into shares

The objects clause. This clause states the company's main business objective. It is followed by a large number of ancilliary clauses giving the company power to effect other objects incidental to the main purpose. Examples would include power to buy land, borrow money, and purchase shares in other companies. In practice, the objects clause will be widely drawn to include almost every conceivable business objective, coupled with a declaration that they should be construed as main objectives and not subsidiary powers.

The original purpose of the object's clause was to delimit the company's powers so that capital subscribed by investors could be used only for the company's main and, presumably commercially sound, objective, not in some other subsidiary and risky enterprise in which the investor would not have chosen to place his capital.

The concept of limited liability. An investor who purchases shares must pay to the company the purchase price agreed upon. Usually shares must be fully paid for at the time when they are allotted to a shareholder by the company. If they are only partly paid for, then the shareholder is contingently liable to pay the sum still outstanding, even though the company is in liquidation. Once the shares have been fully paid for, the shareholder's liability is complete. He cannot be required to make further contributions, even if the company fails and is unable to settle debts owed to creditors who have supplied goods and services to the company.

Limited liability is one of the most important attractions of shareholding in a public company. After fully paying for his shares the investor has fixed the amount of money that he is prepared to place at risk. However disastrous the company's financial collapse, he cannot be called upon to pay more.

Articles of association

These govern the internal management of the company, regulating the rights of the members among themselves in such matters as:

1 Appointment and power of directors
2 Issue, transfer and forfeiture of shares
3 Rules regulating meetings of the company
4 Payment of dividends
5 Preparation of accounts and auditing
6 Alterations to the capital structure of the company
7 Rights of different classes of shareholders

It is usual for a company to register its own special set of articles which make specific provisions on matters of internal management, particularly suited to the needs of that individual business.

The prospectus

The usual object of forming a public company is to raise money from the investing public to finance the company's policies of expansion. When the formalities of registration are complete the company will issue a prospectus which sets out:

1 The objects it will pursue.
2 Reports by experts on property owned, its financial position and trading prospects for the future.
3 The names of directors; if the board of directors includes well-known experts it may be an inducement to buy the shares.
4 The details of the company's capital structure.

These details will enable the investor to determine whether he wishes to purchase shares.

A trading certificate will be issued and the company may commence business after a director has filed a statutory declaration with the

Registrar, stating that shares have been sold to an amount not less than the minimum subscription. This is the amount of money which the company must receive in cash in return for allotting shares to in-estors who have offered to purchase them. It is the sum needed:

To finance the purchase of property to be acquired or repay money borrowed for this purpose.

To provide the working capital necessary to give the company a reasonable chance of commercial success, so that it does not fail by being under-capitalised with consequent loss of any money subscribed.

Capital and shares

'he authorised (or nominal) capital is the amount of money that the ompany is authorised by the memorandum of association to raise rom the public, for example, £500,000. In practice the company may ot require this amount immediately, but it can issue shares up to ie limit specified at any time when it wishes to do so.

The issued capital is that part of the nominal capital which has een actually issued to the public for cash or other considerations, ich as land or buildings, in return for an allotment of shares, for xample, an issued capital of £250,000 out of the nominal capital of 500,000. If a subscriber is required to pay only half the amount due n his share allotment, then the capital actually received by the com-any, that is the paid up capital, will be only £125,000 in the above xample. The amount not yet paid up on the shares issued is referred as uncalled capital and it may be declared by the company to be capable of being required from a shareholder except in a winding p of its affairs.

Membership

shareholder is a member of the company entitled to the following ghts:

To attend meetings and vote on issues affecting company policy, including the appointment and removal of directors. He may requisition a meeting if he wishes to discuss any matter of concern.

2 To receive an annual report and accounts giving details of th company's affairs.
3 To share in the profits made in the form of a dividend declare by the directors.
4 To share in the assets of the company if its affairs are wound up provided any property remains when the rights of other creditor with prior claims have been met.
5 To transfer his shares when he wishes by selling or giving them t another person.
6 To present a petition to wind up the company or ask for an orde controlling its affairs.

Different classes of shares

A company usually issues different classes of shares, each having it attractions for the investor.

Preference shareholders are entitled to the following payments i priority to ordinary shareholders:

1 A yearly dividend out of profits, at a fixed though moderat percentage of the capital invested, for example, seven per cen Unless the articles of association state otherwise, arrears c dividend not paid in a previous year when there were no profi are carried forward and must be paid in future years whe sufficient profits are available.
2 Repayments of the capital contributed to the company when is wound up if, as is usual, the articles so provide.

Ordinary shareholders are entitled to:

1 The remainder of profits available for distribution, which wi secure a high rate of dividend if the company is successful. How ever, if a loss results in any trading year the dividend may not b paid at all.
2 Return of capital contributed to the company when it is wour up, if sufficient assets remain to satisfy these claims.

The market value of shares will rise if the company trades succes fully and the ordinary shareholder, in particular, may make a capital profit on selling his shares.

Ordinary shareholders bear the risk of substantial loss if the company fails; consequently, they have a right to vote at meetings and control the company's affairs to the exclusion of preference shareholders who are usually entitled to vote only if :

1 Their dividend is six months in arrear.
2 Their rights as a class are affected by some issue under discussion at the meeting.

Debentures

A company needing finance for a programme of expansion may be reluctant to raise the additional capital required by issuing more shares, for two reasons: first, the money will only be required for a short period of time until the new equipment purchased begins to earn profits, then those profits may be used to refund the capital borrowed and the company may not wish to raise capital on a permanent basis on which a regular dividend must be paid; and second, once shares have been issued a company cannot buy them back when it has sufficient cash available, with the exception of redeemable preference shares which may be issued for the same reason as debentures.

The company borrows money from the lender and in return issues debenture, redeemable at a fixed or determinable time or at the company's option. The debenture holder is entitled to:

A fixed rate of interest which must be paid even if it is paid out of capital, not profits.
Repayment of the principal sum when due.
A charge on the company's property. This means that if the compay fails to repay the loan and interest when due, the debenture holders may satisfy their claims by disposing of the company's assets. These claims have priority over, and must be satisfied before, claims by all types of shareholders.

Acquisition and transfer of shares

When shares are first issued by a company an investor may make an offer to purchase then by submitting an application form. Allotment of shares by the company creates a binding contract with the investor Shares may be issued at a premium; for example, 50p may have to be paid for a share with a nominal or face value of only 25p. This means that existing shares already issued have a market value of 50p, thus the real worth of a share is determined by reference to the marke value, not the face or par value.

A share certificate will be issued by the company stating the name of the shareholder and the extent of his shareholding. The register of members, kept by the company, will record the shareholder's name and address and the number of shares held.

The shares of public companies are quoted on the Stock Exchange and the shareholder can determine the present value of his shares by referring to the Stock Exchange list which is published in leading newspapers. One of the main advantages of shareholding is the ability to sell quickly and realise the value of the shares.

Sale or purchase of shares is frequently effected through a stock broker. The present shareholder executes a form authorising the transfer and hands it to the purchaser together with the shar certificate. It must be stamped by the Inland Revenue and the dut paid depends upon the amount of money being paid by the purchaser The transfer form and the share certificate are forwarded to the company, so that it can enter the new shareholder's name on the register in place of the seller's name. A new share certificate will be issued bearing the new owner's name.

Directors

Every public company must have at least two directors and a secre tary. A proportion of the directors, usually about one third, retire a each annual general meeting, and the members may re-elect them o appoint others in their place. A director may be removed by a ordinary resolution passed by members, but the director may mak representations on the issue showing why he should not be removed

The directors must manage the company's affairs by taking d

cisions at board meetings, otherwise they may be personally liable for their actions. To prevent a conflict of interest and duty a director must not benefit from any contract made by the company, unless he discloses his interest to the board, and does not vote on the matter.

A director will be required to hold a certain number of shares in the company which are called his qualification shares, otherwise he must vacate his office. This gives him a personal interest in furthering the fortunes of the company to the best of his ability.

The articles may provide for the payment of a fixed fee to a director, but his remuneration is often stated in a service contract which he makes with the company. His remuneration must be disclosed in the annual accounts. A director is not entitled to compensation for loss of office or on retirement, unless approved by the shareholders.

The powers of the company, as determined by the memorandum and articles, are usually delegated to the directors insofar as they are not exercised by the company in general meeting. Members in general meeting cannot interfere with the manner in which the directors exercise their powers, unless they alter the articles accordingly. The directors should communicate their policy to the shareholders from time to time. If directors exceed their powers the members may ratify their actions, provided the act is within the powers of the company.

Publicity concerning directors

The company must make available the following information about a director:

1 A register of directors and secretaries must be kept at the registered office and open for public inspection, specifying a director's name, address, nationality, business occupation and other directorships held, except directorships in wholly-owned subsidiaries.
2 A register of directors' interests in the company's shares and debentures must be kept at the registered office or place where the register of members is kept. It must be open for public inspection.
3 Details of a director's service contract must be kept at the registered office, or place where the register of members is kept or

at the company's principal place of business. It must be open for inspection by members.
4 The names of directors must appear on business letters, trade catalogues, circulars and show cards.

Legal liability of directors

Directors are criminally liable and subject to payment of a penalty if they fail to effect their duties as specified in the Companies Act 1948, such as:

1 Keeping a register of members, a register of directors and secretaries and a register of mortgages and charges on the company's property.
2 Keeping proper accounts and ensuring preparation of annual accounts and a directors' report.
3 Making an annual return to the registrar giving the address of the registered office, particulars of directors and secretaries, indebtedness on registered charges, details of share capital, a list of members, copies of the last balance sheet and the profit and loss account.
4 Forwarding to the registrar copies of special and extraordinary resolutions.
5 Calling an annual general meeting each year.
6 Making a return to the registrar of allotment of shares within one month of the allotment.

Directors are civilly liable to pay damages to the company or a third party if:

1 They commit an act that is beyond the powers of the company, as by paying dividends out of capital instead of profits.
2 They act negligently, by failing to exercise that degree of care that is to be expected from a prudent person when conducting the affairs of a company. If, for example, they leave the company's money in the hands of a stockbroker for an unreasonable length of time without checking to determine whether it has been properly invested as required.
3 They act dishonestly, in breach of their duty as trustees for the

company, where for example, they make a call on shareholders by requesting payment of sums still outstanding on shares, but exempting their own shares from this requirement.

Meetings

The company is obliged to hold various types of meetings from time to time to transact business.

A public company must hold a statutory meeting between one month and three months from the date of entitlement to commence business. Fourteen days' notice of the meeting must be given. This gives members a chance to meet the directors and discuss matters arising from the company's formation.

An annual general meeting must be held every year to deal with:

1 Declaration of dividends.
2 Consideration of the accounts and balance sheet and the report of directors and auditors.
3 Appointment of directors.
4 Appointment and fixing of the remuneration of auditors.

Members must be given twenty-one days' notice of the meeting.

An extraordinary general meeting may be called by directors if important business needs to be transacted which cannot await the next annual general meeting. Holders of one tenth of the paid up share capital with voting rights may requisition such a meeting, even against the directors' wishes. Members must be given fourteen days' notice of the meeting.

The rights of various classes of shareholders cannot be varied unless they consent at a meeting of that class, for example, where it is proposed that, in future, preference shareholders' dividends are to be non-cumulative instead of cumulative.

Dividends

Dividends are trading profits divided among members in proportion to the number of shares held. Dividends must not be paid out of capital. A loss of circulating capital must be made good before a dividend is declared. Circulating capital, such as a company's stock in trade, is property purchased or produced with the intention of selling it at a profit. A loss of fixed capital does not have to be provided for before profits can be used to pay dividends. Fixed capital is property acquired for retention and used so that a profit can be made, for example, plant and machinery used to produce goods that are then sold at a profit. Sums may be set aside from profit to allow for depreciation to fixed assets of this type.

The dividend is declared as a percentage of the share's nominal value, for example a thirty per cent dividend for each 50p share held. The market value of the shares will be probably higher than the par value, say £1.50, consequently the real return on capital for a recent purchaser will be a more modest ten per cent. A preference shareholder's dividend is usually at a fixed percentage, but ordinary shareholders will receive a dividend varying annually as the level of profits changes.

The directors are responsible for fixing the rate of dividend, with the sanction of the general meeting. Shareholders cannot demand a dividend if the directors refuse to declare one, even though the annual profits seem to warrant some payment. Profits do not have to be distributed as dividends, as the directors may think it wiser to use them to offset past losses, or to transfer them to reserve to meet future liabilities. Once a dividend has been declared, however, a shareholder may sue to recover the sum he is entitled to receive if payment is not made.

An increase in the value of the company's assets may be used to pay a dividend, unless the articles provide otherwise, for example where a supposedly bad debt of a substantial amount is unexpectedly paid off. The whole pattern of the accounts for the year must be examined, however, and if other assets have depreciated in value a dividend may not be justified out of the appreciation of one capital asset alone.

Patents

A patent is a grant by the Crown to an inventor giving him the sole right to utilise his invention for a specified period.

Procedure for the grant of a patent

An application on the prescribed form for Letters Patent, must be forwarded to the Comptroller General of Patents at the Patent Office by:

1 The true and first inventor, or,
2 The person to whom the invention has been assigned, together with the name of the inventor and his consent to the application.

A complete specification of the invention must be submitted to an examiner. If it is possible to submit a provisional specification only, then a complete specification must be filed within twelve months of making the application, otherwise it is abandoned.

Priority of a claim dates from the time of making the first application. The claim then takes precedence over any later application for a patent in respect of the same invention.

International convention for the protection of industrial property

This convention is adhered to by all important industrial countries throughout the world. If a patent application is filed in one convention country and an application for the same invention is filed in other convention countries within a period of twelve months, then these other applications have the same priority date as the original application. An applicant in the United Kingdom should file all foreign applications within twelve months of filing the complete specification in the United Kingdom.

Reasons for refusing a patent grant

The grant of a patent may be refused even though it has not been opposed if the comptroller learns that the invention has been published already or the invention is important in relation to defence; in the latter case the application will be held up until consent is given by the government department currently handling defence matters.

Opposition to a grant

If the examiner of the patent reports favourably, the specification will be advertised. It may be inspected and opposed by anyone on the following grounds:

1 That the applicant obtained the invention from the complainant.
2 That the invention had been claimed in a prior complete specification during the last fifty years.
3 That the invention has been claimed already in a complete specification which, although not published at the priority date of the applicant's claim, had been deposited pursuant to an application for a patent which has an earlier priority date.
4 That the invention has been openly used in the United Kingdom before the date of the present application.
5 That the invention is obvious and uninventive.
6 That the subject matter of the claim is not an invention within the meaning of the Patents Act 1949; for example, the subject matter must be a process or article resulting from Man's creation, it cannot be a mere idea; the claim must have some utility or advantage, however slight, such as producing a new and useful device or producing an old device in some new and improved form.
7 That the complete specification is insufficient.
8 That, in the case of a convention application, the application was not made within twelve months from the date of filing the first application in the convention country.

Revocation of a patent

Application may be made to the comptroller within twelve months of granting a patent, by any person who was entitled to oppose it on one of the grounds specified. The comptroller may revoke the patent if he could have refused to grant it in the first place, had he been aware of the present reasons for opposition. There may be an appeal from his decision to the Court.

A patent may be revoked on petition to the Court for one of the following reasons:

1 That the patent was obtained by a person disentitled to it because of a false suggestion or representation.
2 That the pátent contravenes the rights of the applicant who is the true inventor.
3 That the invention is not useful, or novel, or its intended use is contrary to the law.
4 That the complete specification either describes the invention insufficiently or does not state the best method of which the applicant is aware of performing it.
5 That the patentee has not allowed the invention to be used by the Crown upon reasonable terms, as requested.

Grant of a patent

The comptroller will grant a patent to the applicant if:

1 The examiner reports favourably after examining the complete specification, and
2 There is no opposition to the grant, or, alternatively, any opposition fails.

The patent dates from the time when the complete specification was filed, but proceedings cannot be taken in respect of any infringements of the patentee's rights which occured before that date.

Any government department may use any invention for any purpose if this is necessary for the efficient prosecution of any war or maintaining supplies and services essential to the life of the community.

Rights of the patentee

A patentee is the person to whom a patent is granted. The patentee is entitled to the following rights:

1 The sole rights and profits resulting from his invention while the patent lasts, that is, sixteen years. This period may be extended by a further five years, or ten years in exceptional cases.
2 To claim damages for infringement of his rights, or alternatively an account of any profits made because of the infringement,

except in cases where the infringement was innocent.

3 To request the granting of a court order (injunction) to prevent continued violation of the patent rights.
4 To grant a licence to other persons to exploit the invention.
5 To transfer his rights absolutely to another person.
6 To transfer his rights conditionally by imposing restrictions as to the time during which and the area over which the patent may be exploited.
7 To secure a 'patent of addition' to the original patent, to cover any changes to the original invention. This will last for the same period as the original patent.

Compulsory licences

After three years from the granting of a patent, application may be made to the comptroller for a compulsory licence by a person interested in the patent. It may be alleged that the monopoly rights granted by the patent are being abused for one of the following reasons:

1 The invention is not being commercially exploited or worked to its fullest extent in the United Kingdom.
2 The demand for the patented article in the United Kingdom is not being met to an adequate extent or on reasonable terms.
3 The industrial output and development in the United Kingdom is being hindered by the patentee's refusal to allow others to exploit the invention by granting a licence or only upon unreasonable terms.

The comptroller may order the grant of a licence on such terms as he thinks fit, subject to an appeal to the Court.

An employer's right to his employee's invention

The employer will be the first and trustee inventor, where the employee makes the invention as a result of guided research under the employer's instruction. Though the employee be the true and first inventor, he cannot claim the benefit of any patent where:

1 He agrees in his contract of employment to assign to the employer inventions made during the period of his employment.
2 In the absence of an express agreement it would be a breach of good faith for the employee to so act, as where making inventions is his job or a by-product of his work or the invention results from the provision by the employer of all necessary facilities.

An invention patented in the joint names of employer and employee belongs to the employer, since the employee holds his interest in the invention for the employer's benefit, unless there is an express agreement contradicting this implied assumption.

Chapter 11

Contracts between Companies

F W Rose, Principal Lecturer in Law, City of Birmingham Polytechnic

---

There are several essential elements that must be present before an agreement becomes a contract binding in law. Although the examples given concentrate on the sale of goods, the legal requirements are the same for all types of contract, whether the subject matter is a contract for the sale of goods or supply of a service by one company to another, or by a company to a private individual (or vice versa), or a contract of employment between employer and employee.

Offer and acceptance

An offer is a definite indication by one party, that he is willing to contract with another party on specified terms. A binding legal contract will come into existence if the terms are accepted without qualification and this fact is brought to the attention of the party making the offer. The conclusion of a contract is often preceded by lengthy discussions between the parties, but from these negotiations it must be possible to extract a firm offer followed by a firm acceptance

Company B may ask further questions to induce better terms from Company A, but without intending to reject the original offer which will be accepted without qualification if better terms cannot be secured, for example, whether a total purchase price of £2,000 can be paid in instalments.

Any variation between the terms of the offer and the acceptance prevents the formation of a contract. For example, if Company A offers to sell Company B 100 office desks at £20 each, the offer is not accepted if Company B agrees to buy at £18 each. Company B has rejected the original offer and made a counter-offer which is capable of acceptance by Company A. If Company A rejects the counter offer, Company B cannot accept the original offer, unless Company A agrees. By this time Company A may have sold the goods to Company C. Company B cannot sue Company A for 2,000 damages for breach of contract if desks of the same type have to be purchased elsewhere for £22 each.

Keeping the offer open for a stipulated time

If a company offers to sell goods on stated terms, the company to whom the offer is made may be allowed a period of time to reach its decision. If an acceptance is communicated before the time allowed has elapsed, then a binding contract comes into existence. Although the company making the offer may feel morally bound to allow the company to whom the offer is made the stipulated period of time for reflection, the offer may be revoked at any time before notification of acceptance, even if the stipulated period for consideration has not ended. This right may be exercised where changed circumstances render conclusion of the contract undesirable, for example, where the market price of the goods has risen.

To safeguard its position the company to whom the offer is made may take an 'option' on the goods. This is a separate, binding contract whereby a period of time is given to reach a final decision on purchase. If during the period of the option the offer is revoked, the company making the offer commits a breach of contract for which damages are recoverable. Since the option itself is a contract, it must satisfy all the essential requirements of a contract. This usually means that the company making the offer must be paid for granting the option.

Lapse and revocation of an offer

An offer lapses if it is not accepted within the stipulated time. Where a given period of time for acceptance is not prescribed in the offer, there must be acceptance within the time that is 'reasonable' in the circumstances of the case.

An offer may be revoked any time before acceptance, but revocation is effective only when actually communicated to the party to whom the offer was made. It is important to choose a reliable means of communication, so that the company to whom the offer is made cannot claim that it has not heard of the revocation. If the post is used, a revocation is effective only when it is actually received. If the communication is lost in the post the revocation is ineffective. Notification of the revocation may be made through some reliable source, such as the company's sales manager.

Need for a special method of acceptance

The company making the offer may request an acceptance in a particular form, such as telephone or telegram, a likely possibility where a speedy answer is required. Acceptance by another method, for instance a letter, would then be invalid. If the method of acceptance were quicker than the one prescribed by the offeror, such as a telegram instead of a letter, this would probably be a valid acceptance.

Where a speedy reply is not required, but a particular method of acceptance is stipulated, use of the alternative method will not invalidate the acceptance if the circumstances suggest that there was a choice. For example, pending execution of a standard written agreement containing the contractual terms, an informal letter of acceptance may suffice, especially if the party making the offer expressly or by conduct waives the condition as to the special mode of acceptance.

Postal acceptance of an offer

A postal acceptance is permissible whenever the parties can be taken to have contemplated this possibility, for example, if the offer itself was made by post or where a few days have been allowed for consideration of the offer. The acceptance is complete as soon as the letter of acceptance is posted, and a legally binding contract exists even if the letter is lost in the post and is never received by the company making the offer. Before selling the goods to another buyer, the seller should, in the absence of any communication from the first intended buyer, determine whether he intends to accept the offer, for if the letter has been lost in the post the seller may finish up with two binding agreements in respect of the same goods.

Tenders

A company may invite a tender from businessmen for the supply of specified goods or services. Every tender submitted is an offer and the company can accept any tender to bring a binding contract into existence.

Where tenders are invited for the supply of goods or services as and when demanded, the company submitting the successful tender is making a standing offer. There is a separate acceptance by the company requiring the goods or services each time an order is placed with the party who has submitted the tender. A fresh contract is made each time an order is placed.

Where this type of agreement includes an estimate of the quantity required, there is no obligation to order goods of any particular quantity or indeed any goods at all. On the other hand, if the buyer undertakes to purchase all his requirements in relation to specified goods from the person whose tender is accepted, there is a breach of contract if the goods are bought elsewhere.

The standing offer may be revoked at any time by the party making it, except in relation to any goods or services that have been ordered. To prevent this happening there is usually a binding undertaking between the parties to keep the standing offer open for a stipulated period. This usually means that a sum of money must be paid to the party making the standing offer.

Consideration

The majority of contracts made are simple contracts and the presence of valuable consideration is essential to their validity. This means that each party to the contract must confer a benefit on the other party in return for the benefit received. If Company A sells goods to

Company B for £1,000, Company A loses the goods but receives the purchase price of £1,000. Company B has to pay the £1,000 but receives the benefit of the goods in return.

Consideration is a more complex doctrine than this simple illustration may suggest. It can take the form of an exchange of promises, with Company A promising to sell and deliver goods by 1 January and Company B agreeing to accept and pay £1,000 for them. If Company A refuses to deliver the goods on 1 January, then Company B may sue for breach of contract or, alternatively, if Company B refuses to accept delivery, Company A may sue for breach of contract.

Consideration must be valuable. It must have an economic character and be worth something. The Court will not determine how much the goods sold are worth and then determine whether the price paid is adequate. It is for businessmen, not courts, to make commercially sound agreements. No attempt is made to balance the respective promises or acts of the parties to determine whether the bargain is fair, provided each party has received some benefit.

Form of a contract

In most cases a contract does not have to be concluded in writing, but writing is useful since the precise terms agreed upon are then easily ascertainable. The following contracts must be in a written form however:

1 Bills of exchange, promissory notes and cheques
2 Contracts of marine insurance
3 Hire-purchase contracts
4 Contracts for the transfer of shares in a public company

Although writing is not essential at the time when the contract is made, there are two cases where writing is needed for purposes of evidence, these are:

1 Contracts of guarantee whereby A promises B that he will settle C's debts to B if C cannot meet his own commitments.
2 Contracts to sell or lease land.

If the writing does not exist the contract cannot be enforced in a court of law. The written document may be quite informal: a letter will suffice, provided it includes:

1 The names of the parties, or a sufficient description of them.
2 A description of the subject matter.
3 All material terms.
4 Consideration, except in a contract of guarantee.
5 The signature of the person being sued or his agent.

A few contracts must be embodied in a deed, that is a written agreement, that is signed by the parties, sealed and delivered. Such contracts are:

1 A conveyance of land or interest in land, including a lease for a term exceeding three years.
2 Gifts; a promise to give embodied in a deed is binding and enforceable, although consideration is not provided in return by the recipient.

Intention to create legal relations

If an agreement is supported by consideration it is assumed that the parties intended it to be legally enforceable one against the other, especially if it relates to a commercial matter. The parties are free, however, to state expressly that their agreement is not intended to be legally binding. Then it is an obligation binding in honour only and not subject to the jurisdiction of the courts. For example, collective agreements between unions and management may fall into this category if there is an express declaration to that effect.

Capacity to make a contract

A company does not have contractual power to negotiate an agreement which falls outside the scope of its objects clause. Any such agreement is void and ineffective, and beyond the powers of the company (*ultra vires*), even though the other contracting party was unaware of this fact. The memorandum and articles of a company, which are documents setting out its powers, may be inspected by anyone at the Companies Registry before an agreement is concluded. In law, a contracting party is deemed to know the contents of these documents and be aware of the precise extent of the company's contractual powers.

An *ultra vires* contract is enforceable against a company if the subject matter is fairly incidental to its main objects, though not specifically authorised by the memorandum. For example, a trading company may lease premises for the purposes of carrying out its business.

A contract with a company may appear to be valid and enforceable on the face of it, and an inspection of the memorandum would not have suggested otherwise. In such cases the other contracting party may enforce it against the company, even if it is *ultra vires*. For example, a supplier of fuel may recover its cost from the company, even though it has been purchased by the company for an *ultra vires* purpose, if the supplier can show that the fuel is also needed for carrying out objects duly authorised by the memorandum.

A company is a non human entity and its affairs are conducted through the medium of agents, such as directors. A director may exceed his authority when negotiating a contract, although the company itself may have power to conclude that type of agreement. The contract is enforceable against the company if the director's actions are ratified by shareholders, or, an inspection of the memorandum and articles would not have suggested that the director was acting outside the scope of his powers; his restricted authority to contract may be a matter of internal company management of which the other contracting party is unaware.

Mistakes in the contract

A contract may have been concluded under a misapprehension as to a material fact. Where both parties mistakenly believe the subject matter of the contract to be in existence when this is not so, then the contract is void, for example, where the goods have been destroyed by fire, the buyer is not obliged to pay for the goods.

A mistake by both parties concerning the quality of the subject matter does not avoid the contract, where they have agreed on the same terms on the same subject matter, if for example, A and B mistakenly believe that land about to be sold has valuable mineral deposits. The buyer cannot claim his money back and return the land. In this situation the court may be willing on occasions to set the contract aside, thus relieving the party who suffers most because of the mistake. This would only apply on terms which are fair as between both parties, for example, allowing the seller to claim any expenses incurred.

A binding contract does not exist if the parties have negotiated completely at cross-purposes and made a mistake as to the identity of the subject matter. For example, one party intends to sell a cargo leaving New York in March on board a ship named 'Eastern Star', while the buyer intends to purchase the cargo on board a similarly named vessel leaving New York in January. The ambiguity of the circumstances make it impossible for the court to determine with reasonable certainty which cargo is the subject matter of the contract. Conversely, an enforceable contract will exist on the terms as understood by one of the parties, if the mistake is basically the fault of one party only. For example, if a purchaser buys land mistakenly believing that it is more extensive in area than the plot being sold, he cannot avoid the contract simply because he failed to check the specifications of the sale which were readily available to him.

A contract is void if one party is mistaken as to a fundamental fact concerning the subject matter and the other party knows of the mistake and takes advantage of it. If Company A offers to sell goods to Company B for £1,250 when Company B's previous offer to buy at £2,000 had already been refused, it is obvious that Company A really intended the price to be £2,250. Company B cannot accept the offer of £1,250 and enforce the agreement against Company A. On the other hand, if one party's mistake is not appreciated by the other party who accepts in ignorance of that mistake, then a binding contract exists. If Company A offers to sell goods at £350 when, because of an arithmetical error, £400 was intended, an acceptance of the offer by Company B is binding, provided the circumstances do not suggest that an obvious mistake has been made in the price charged.

Mistaken signature

A party may be induced to sign a written document embodying an agreement which is fundamentally different in nature from the obligation he intended to assume and the party inducing him to sign may be aware of the mistake. The mistaken party can escape liability in pursuance of the agreement only in the most exceptional cases, such as blindness or illiteracy. Company representatives signing contractual documents should carefully scrutinise the contents of the agreement and ensure that the agreement being signed is the agreement that they intend to sign and that all the individual terms are acceptable and have not been altered contrary to any verbal understanding that preceded the execution of a formal written document.

Misrepresentation

A company may be induced to contract because of misrepresentation by the other party. A misrepresentation is defined as a false statement of a fact that is material to the agreement, made by one party to the other during negotiations leading to the agreement, which was intended to operate and did operate as an inducement to enter the contract.

A false representation may be either fraudulent or innocent and it renders the contract voidable. The party misled may have the contract set aside if desired.

A false representation is fraudulent if it is made with knowledge of the falsity, or without belief in its truth, or recklessly not caring whether it is true or false. Honest belief in the truth of a statement negatives deceit, even though the representation is stupid, careless or negligent. A belief is not honest, however, if the representor deliberately shuts his eyes to the true facts or purposely abstains from investigating them. The aggrieved party may either avoid the contract with or without suing for damages for deceit, or affirm the contract and also seek damages.

A false representation is innocent if the representor believes his assertion to be true and does not intend to deceive the party misled. The main remedy is to avoid the contract, but damages may be claimed also.

A contract cannot be avoided (rescinded) where the aggrieved party elects to waive his rights by affirming the contract, for example, if he takes benefits provided by the contract with full knowledge of the misrepresentation, whether innocent or fraudulent, as by using goods purchased.

A contract induced by fraudulent misrepresentation must be avoided within six years of either discovery of the fraud, or the time when it could have been discovered by using reasonable diligence. There are no precise time limits during which a contract induced by innocent misrepresentation must be avoided, but a period of delay less than six years may be too long. For example, a delay of two weeks may be too long where a shareholder has been induced to purchase shares on the faith of a false statement issued by the company in the prospectus.

If the parties cannot be restored to their original positions by taking back the purchase price and goods respectively, then the contract cannot be rescinded. A buyer may have radically altered the property he purchased before discovering the misrepresentation or electing to rescind the contract; for example, there may have been substantial extractions from a mine that has been purchased. Damages may be recovered, however, to compensate the party misled where the property is now worth much less than he anticipated because of the misrepresentation.

It is too late to rescind where property sold has already been sold again to a third party who now has rights to the property in question.

Damages for breach of contract

If one party has broken the terms of a valid contract, the innocent party is entitled to recover damages for any loss suffered. He must be restored to the position he would have been in if the particular damage suffered had not occurred, insofar as money can be sufficient compensation.

Recovery may be confined to those losses that arise naturally in the usual course of events from the breach, and are thus assumed to be within the contemplation of the defaulting party. In a contract for the sale of goods, where there is a market for the goods, the measure of damages recoverable by the buyer is the difference between the contract price and the market price of goods at the time when the seller ought to have delivered them. The buyer can purchase goods similar to the contract goods in the market. On the other hand, if the buyer has refused to accept delivery, the seller recovers the sum by which the market price falls short of the contract price at the time when the goods ought to have been accepted. The seller can dispose of the contract goods in the market.

If there is no available market but the buyer has agreed to resell the goods, the resale price may be taken as representing their value. The buyer's damages will be the difference between the sale and resale prices, though the seller is unaware of the sub-sale. A loss of profit is recoverable for breach of a trading contract made between experienced parties if they can be taken to understand the ordinary practices and exigencies of one another's business.

If the seller is a dealer selling goods at a standard market price, this will be the same as the contract price, for example, the contract price and the market price of machinery may be £5,000. For refusal to accept delivery the seller may recover from the buyer the profit that he would have made if the sale had been completed. Even if the item is readily sold to a new buyer, the seller has made the profit on one sale only instead of upon two sales in cases where he has plenty of stock for disposal. Conversely, if a particular item can be sold as quickly as it comes into the seller's stock, the buyer's default is a matter of indifference to the seller. In such cases only nominal damages are recoverable; for example, where a certain type of machinery is in short supply because of strikes.

Owing to special circumstances known at the time of contracting to the party ultimately committing a breach, a loss may be suffered outside the usual course of events. The defaulting party must pay damages in respect of the exceptional loss. For example, a vendor of land may know that the purchaser intends to develop the property and make a large profit. If the seller refuses to complete the sale he is accountable for this loss of profit.

The amount of damages awarded may be reduced to reflect a claimant's liability to reduce the losses suffered, if this is possible, as by selling or buying goods elsewhere.

Distinction between liquidated and unliquidated damages

Damages are unliquidated where one party to a contract sues the other to recover whatever sum the court holds to be the proper measure of damages, in the circumstances. A contract may provide that, in the event of a breach, the innocent party may recover from the defaulting party a sum stated in the contract itself: this sum is called liquidated damages. This type of arrangement has the advantage of saving the time, trouble and expense of litigation should a breach of contract occur. Only the agreed sum is recoverable, even if the actual loss suffered greatly exceeds the sum fixed by the contract. If damages are to be assessed by the contract itself, it is essential to estimate with precision the monetary effect of any possible breach.

Distinction between liquidated damages and a penalty

A sum agreed as payable in the event of a breach of the contract may be liquidated damages or a penalty. The distinction is of vital importance. If the sum is liquidated damages it can be recovered from the party in default. It is regarded as a genuine pre-estimate of the damage suffered by the innocent party.

If the sum fixed by the contract is deemed to be a penalty, then essentially it is a threat held against the party likely to violate the contractual obligations. The intention of a penalty is to attempt to compel performance of the contract by severely punishing the party who refuses to implement it. The defaulting party is made liable to pay an extravagant sum, exceeding the greatest loss that could possibly result from the breach. A penalty is irrecoverable and the injured party is limited to recovering the actual loss he has suffered. If a company wishes to guard against breach of contract, a penalty clause is not the method to use.

An example will illustrate the practical operation of these rules. Company A may agree to install machinery on the premises of Company B. A term of the contract may provide that if the work is not completed by 1 January, then for every extra working day taken to complete the installation Company A must pay Company B £100. If a delay of twenty working days results in lost production and lost profits of £2,000, this sum is recoverable from Company A as liquidated damages if the sum is a genuine pre-estimate of the loss likely to be incurred. In the same circumstances, if the actual loss is £3,000, only £2,000 is recoverable. Here Company B is confined in its claim to the genuine, though incorrect, pre-estimate of the likely loss.

On the other hand, if Company B's maximum loss of profit for one day's lost production could not possibly exceed £20, the clause in the contract stipulating that £100 will be recoverable is a penalty. The court will disregard the clause and only the actual loss suffered will be recovered by Company B.

Specific performance

Damages may be an inadequate remedy and the Court may order the defaulting party to perform specifically the obligation undertaken in the contract. This is a discretionary remedy usually given for breach of a contract to sell or lease land, or sell chattels with unique qualities. In these cases it may be difficult for the disappointed purchaser to acquire similar property elsewhere.

Chapter 12

Organisation and Methods

H W Mount, Management Consultant

Since the end of World War II, and particularly during the past decade, a transformation has taken place in the office function.

In the first place there has been a marked change in the status of white collar workers compared with other sections of the working population. The pay and social differentials which they previously enjoyed have been steadily eroded, so that entry into office employment no longer has the attraction that it once possessed. As a consequence there has been a general lowering of relative calibre among recruits to office jobs. This has been coupled with the growth in the proportion of women employed in offices which, in turn, has given rise to very much higher rates of staff turnover.

Coinciding with the changes mentioned in the preceding paragraph, there has been what is often called the information explosion. Governments and other public authorities make increasing demands on industry and commerce for statistical and other information; the growth in size, scope and complexity of modern enterprises requires an ever-increasing volume of information for planning and controlling the various activities, while the requirements of new technology and management services frequently result in a need for additional information of a specialist type.

The advent of the so-called affluent society has had its own impact on the information processing scene – larger volumes of sales transactions, the creation of records for hire-purchase, credit trading and so on. Although the computer has alleviated the clerical and administrative burden stemming from these developments, the application of electronic data processing methods has itself created the need for new thinking in dealing with the organisational and associated problems which are involved.

A further, and most significant, development has been the growing influence of trade union representation among office workers. This trend was clearly discernible before the passing of the Industrial Relations Act 1971, but the advent of that legislation has given an added impetus to the formal organisation of administrative and clerical employees throughout industry and commerce.

The influences described in the foregoing paragraphs have resulted in a steeply rising incidence of administrative and clerical costs, coupled with the emergence of a host of new problems relating to the maintenance of an effective office function. Office management has, as a consequence, assumed an increasingly important role throughout industry, commerce and the public sector. More and more professionalism is entering into this role and considerable advances have been made in the management techniques that are available. The more important of these are described in this chapter. The reader is referred to Chapter 13 also, since layout and office planning are important elements in office management.

Contribution of organisation and methods studies

Organisation and methods (O and M) is the term used to describe the study of administrative and clerical work with the object of improving its effectiveness. As the term implies, it comprises the following two main fields of enquiry:

Organisation – covering the deployment and grouping of facilities in order to secure a stated objective. In its wide sense this would embrace personnel, materials, equipment and premises. In O and M work the emphasis is upon the organisation structure, dealing with lines of authority and communication between departments, sections and individuals.

Methods – which is concerned with *how* a stated objective is to be achieved. Included here are questions of procedures, documentation, the use of equipment, etc.

Establishing objectives

The basic aims of the office function within an organisation may be stated as:

1 The recording of essential facts and figures and their production as required.
2 The production of information for management purposes.
3 The provision of an effective administrative and clerical service to all parts of the undertaking.

Where the operations involve contact with members of the public or outside organisations the office has a further vital role in maintaining good external relations.

The prime purpose of O and M is to increase the contribution of the office function to the achievement of the organisation's objectives. Before applying O and M techniques it is, therefore, important to have an appreciation of the true role and aims of the enterprise, combined with a clear understanding of the objectives and functions of its constituent parts and how these contribute to the attainment of the overall aims. It should further be established whether any changes are likely to occur in the short term and, if so, the probable direction and extent of these.

The approach to organisation and methods studies

The crucial factors on which the success of O and M depends are, first, the support of top management and, secondly, the co-operation of all those who are involved in any way in the studies or subsequent introduction of agreed changes in organisation, procedures or methods. The achievement of the necessary support and co-operation requires:

1 Clear agreement on the part of management concerning the objectives of the O and M studies.
2 An understanding of these objectives among all the people in-

volved, coupled with an appreciation of the procedures and techniques used to attain them.
3 Close and continuing attention to the human relations aspect of the work.

O and M cannot be employed effectively in isolation within an organisation. It must be closely linked with other management techniques or developments which affect the administrative or information processing arrangements. Where computers are involved the need to associate O and M with feasibility studies and systems analysis work is evident. Similarly, the introduction of new techniques or operational changes in the fields of marketing, production, personnel, finance and accounting have an impact on the office function which demands that attention be given to the associated questions of organisation, procedures and methods.

Conduct of organisation and methods work

Organisation and methods assignments normally comprise the following three phases:

1 Preliminary survey
2 Investigation and analysis, leading to the preparation of proposals
3 Implementation of agreed proposals

Preliminary survey

The main purposes of the preliminary survey are to gain an appreciation of the overall operations in the relevant departments or sections of the business and to identify those areas having the greatest potential for the application of detailed study and analysis. The survey will encompass the facets set out below.

The organisation structure will be surveyed and where it is portrayed by an existing organisation chart, checks should be made to ascertain that it is up to date and factual in its presentation of lines of authority and communication between departments, sections and individuals. Where a chart does not exist it will be necessary to prepare one in sufficient detail to obtain a clear understanding of the organisation structure, together with the functions and responsibilities of the executives and staff groupings shown thereon.

The more important documents used in the departments or sections under review will be assembled and examined to determine their purpose, content, origin and distribution.

The flow of information and documents, with notes of the principal activities undertaken by the various groups or individuals concerned in the processing of the work, will be surveyed. The preparation of simple flow charts will facilitate an understanding of the overall picture in this connection (see, for example, Figure 12:1). Details will be assembled relating to staff numbers and costs, broken down into categories within departments, sections or other groupings and distinguishing between male and female employees. Information should be obtained concerning staff turnover rates, overtime hours and costs and the extent to which temporary staff have been employed, with the costs of such staff.

Next, the survey will examine the average volumes of transactions or other appropriate indices of work-loads, noting seasonal peaks and the factors which influence fluctuations in volume.

In addition to the foregoing items of specific information, notes should be made during the survey of apparent defects in organisation, procedures or methods. The more important of these are: illogical grouping of staff, incorrect allocation, or overlapping, of their responsibilities or duties, inequitable treatment of staff as between sections; failure to delegate on the part of managerial and supervisory personnel, lack of balance in the work-load as between departments, sections or individuals; lack of opportunity for staff to identify their jobs with the aims and practical operations of the enterprise; inadequate communications; existence of work backlogs and failure to maintain required time-scales in the preparation or distribution of information; the incidence of errors and the causes; an apparent over-elaboration of system as evidenced by the number of forms, records or reports, or by the channels through which information is passed; poor or inadequate equipment, poor or inadequate working conditions.

Selecting a starting point for detailed investigations

One of the main objects of carrying out a preliminary survey is to

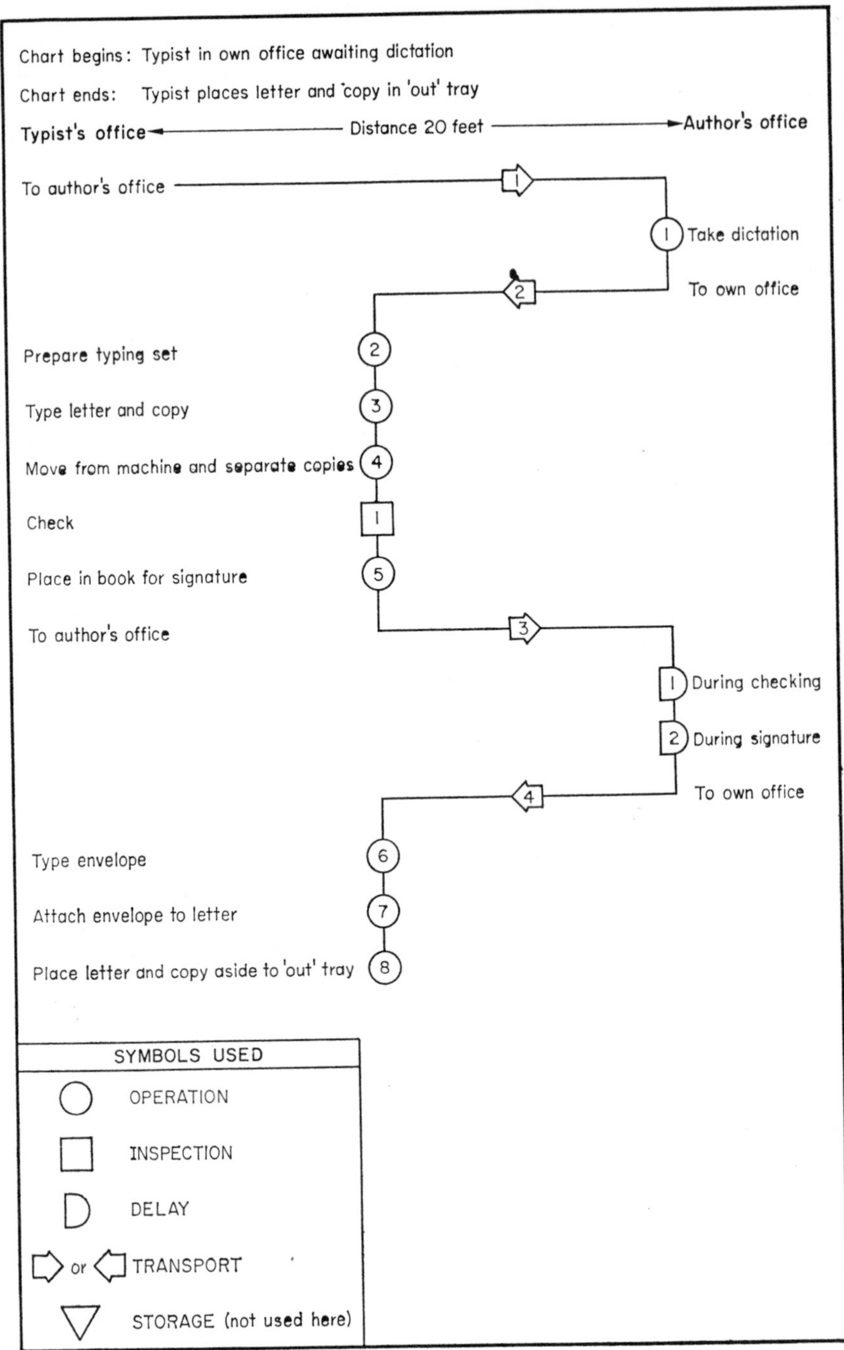

FIGURE 12:1 FLOW DIAGRAM

A simple example of a flow diagram—writing a letter using a shorthand typist (Reproduced with permission of the British Institute of Management) The symbols are the standard symbols laid down by ASME (American Society of Mechanical Engineers) in 1947 and in common use since

identify those activities or areas of work which would yield the greatest benefits from detailed study and analysis. The time-scale is important in this context. Where O and M is being introduced for the first time, it is desirable to select a fairly straightforward procedure which is capable of investigation in a reasonably short space of time and where improvements or economies can be easily and quickly demonstrated. Further assignments will be viewed very much in the light of earlier results and the selection of the first project is, therefore, of particular significance.

Subject to the consideration mentioned in the preceding paragraph, where there is a head office and a branch or district organisation, it can be psychologically beneficial to choose a headquarters project as the first assignment. It is desirable initially to avoid contentious matters which may be the subject of dispute between departmental executives, although there will be occasions when the existence of such a dispute is itself the reason for carrying out detailed investigations. Similarly, it is desirable, at the outset, to avoid the investigation of procedures which have only recently been introduced under the sponsorship of a departmental executive.

Investigation and analysis

The success of O and M work depends a great deal upon pre-planning and the adoption of a systematic means of data-collection, analysis and the development of proposals. Arrangements should incorporate, and link, the various areas of study. In the majority of cases it will be found that seven fields of enquiry are involved:

1 Personnel.
2 Procedures, including work-flow, the method of performing individual operations and the provision of controls.
3 Forms, records, reports and other documentation.
4 Filing methods and other arrangements for the retention of information.
5 Office layout.
6 Equipment.
7 Communications.

The achievement of a stated result from the procedure or operation under investigation should be kept firmly in mind throughout the investigation, analysis and the formulation of proposals. It should be carried out in the shortest possible time, with the least amount of effort and at the lowest overall cost.

The means by which office work may be rendered more effective can be indicated quite simply by the four key-words:

1 Eliminate
2 Combine
3 Simplify
4 Improve

In his analysis of existing procedures, methods and documentation, the investigator should test every aspect of the work by reference to the contribution which it makes to the attainment of the stated objective. Using this test in conjunction with a detailed analysis of staff duties, documentation, procedures and methods will reveal unnecessary operations, paperwork or movement. Examples of the items that can frequently be eliminated as a result of such inquiries are: returns or reports of no value or whose value is, at least, doubtful; copies of documents which are not used by the recipients in the performance of the functions for which they are responsible; unnecessary records; and unnecessary movement of paperwork.

In addition to the opportunities for eliminating unnecessary work or documentation, the analysis will reveal possibilities of combining forms, records or reports to avoid duplication. Duplicated information is a common cause of waste in many offices, particularly in larger undertakings where there may be a tendency for different departments to build up their own sources of reference independently of the requirements of other parts of the organisation. In such circumstances it is often possible to combine similar records in a location suitable to the prime user, at the same time providing an adequate service for the supply of essential information to other departments or sections.

Where it is not feasible either to eliminate or to combine procedures or the associated documentation, there should be a critical examination aimed at simplifying or improving them. Aspects requiring attention under this heading will be revealed by the existence of complicated or cumbersome systems or methods of handling the work, together with unsuitable forms, records or reports. The rectification of such weaknesses may involve detailed method study and will, almost inevitably, call for the re-design of documentation. Close attention must be given to the flow of work and to the conditions at the various work stations. The studies should include a careful analysis and review of all equipment in use, combined with a detailed assessment of the advantages that could accrue from the introduction of more advanced or improved equipment.

The formulation of proposals

It will be recalled that the first essential in starting an O and M investigation is the determination of the basic objectives of the departments or sections with which the inquiries are concerned. It was also emphasised that all administrative or clerical work should be examined in the light of its contribution or otherwise to the attainment of stated objectives. This fundamental test should be applied throughout the review of present practice.

The detailed studies should have established the following information:

1 What is being done
2 Who is doing it
3 Where it is being done
4 When it is being done
5 How it is being done

The critical review leading to the formulation of proposals for improved working involves the application of the question 'Why?' to each significant fact arising from the investigations. Ideas concerning possible improvements will, in practice, emerge during the investigatory stages and these should be tested against the detailed information assembled in the course of the inquiries.

Implementation

Organisation and methods studies can be justified only if they result in worthwhile economies and an increase in the effectiveness of administrative and clerical work. O and M work will be judged by the results achieved and this implies that proposals must be implemented with thoroughness and at a reasonable speed.

Nowhere is the need for co-operation at all levels of management and staff more in evidence than in the introduction of revisions in organisation, procedures or methods. The acceptance of change depends essentially upon the existence of good human relations, coupled with an understanding of the need for the new arrangements. This is best achieved by personal contact. It is, therefore, good practice to hold meetings of the managers, supervisors and other staff involved so that the scheme may be fully explained and discussed prior to its introduction.

A list of requirements should be drawn up covering the various aspects that require attention before the scheme is finally installed. This would normally include:

1 The extent to which other departments are concerned and the action required of them.
2 The provision of suitable office accommodation (if necessary) to operate the new procedures or methods.
3 The supply of the necessary equipment.
4 Staffing requirements and the extent to which re-deployment and/or staff training will be necessary.
5 Where customers, suppliers or other outside bodies are concerned, the manner in which they should be approached.

For one reason or another it may not be considered desirable to introduce the entire scheme at the outset. In this event consideration could be given to the introduction of the new arrangements in one of the following ways:

1 A pilot scheme, where the proposals may be applied to a selected part of the organisation.
2 A proving run, where the new arrangements may be operated alongside the old.
3 A change-over by stages, where certain aspects of the work may be dealt with in advance of others.

The selection of the most suitable means of implementation will depend upon the nature of the operations and the surrounding circumstances. Thus, where mechanised methods are being introduced in place of a manual system, there can be considerable advantage in arranging a proving run of sufficient duration to ensure that the operators, machines, service sections, etc., are functioning satisfactorily before relinquishing the existing procedures and controls.

Use of clerical work measurement

One of the most difficult areas in O and M work has been the factual evaluation of results and, in particular, the setting of appropriate staffing levels to handle prescribed volumes of work.

Considerable advances have been made in recent years in the techniques available for the measurement and evaluation of office work. Selection of the most appropriate technique will depend primarily upon the purposes for which the measurement is required and its application will normally follow an analysis of the work as described in the section dealing with O and M studies. The measurement techniques most commonly used in clerical work are outlined below.

Self-recording

This entails the preparation of reports by individuals of the amount of time spent on each activity or duty during the working day, with a note of their output. It is useful in providing a broad estimate of the time taken per unit of output in each activity and in building up a general picture of the work-load. It is less accurate than other methods and relies upon people to report accurately. Moreover, the work values are reported times, as distinct from the times that should be allowed for the performance of the duties.

Estimating

This is a means of assessing the time required to carry out work, based on a knowledge and experience of similar work. It is, therefore, dependent on judgment as distinct from measurement and is liable to error. It is, however, useful as a rough check on work-load and may be sufficiently accurate for minor items of work.

Batch control

Work is issued in batches of known size and a record is made of the time taken to complete each batch. It is particularly valuable from the standpoint of supervisory control and as an aid in attaining an effective flow of work. The work values derived from batch control are, of course, based on actual times taken, as distinct from times that should be allowed. On the other hand, the system enables a direct comparison to be made of the performances of individual members of staff.

Activity sampling

This is a technique in which large numbers of instantaneous observations of a group of staff, processes or machines are made over a period of time. Each observation records what is happening at that moment, and the percentage of observations recorded for a particular activity or delay is a measure of the proportion of time during which the activity or delay occurs.

The purpose of activity sampling is to establish for a group of people or machines how much time is spent on different activities. The use of a rating factor or performance assessment in conjunction with activity sampling enables the work content to be determined in addition to the allocation of time.

The technique is not suitable for infrequently occurring activities. Accuracy of the results is affected by the number of observations, but the confidence limits can be defined statistically. It has the advantage of enabling several people to be included in a single study and it is generally accepted by the staff. It is a method of obtaining information which, otherwise, could only be secured at a disproportionate cost.

Group timing technique

This is a form of activity sampling in which observations are made on a group of staff at short and regular intervals, with their output being recorded. The time spent on each activity is found by multiplying the number of observations of that activity by the sampling interval. The observer is present during the whole of the study and the results are more detailed than those obtained from random sampling, where the application of performance rating can be more difficult.

Time study

A watch or similar device is used to record the time taken to complete each element involved in performing an operation or processing a piece of work. By applying performance rating factors, standard time-values can be derived for the various tasks.

The timing may be carried out by stop-watch, wrist-watch or wall clock, while in some instances, tape-recorders or cine cameras are used to obtain the required information. The choice of method will depend partly upon the degree of accuracy required, partly upon convenience and partly upon staff reaction. In general, office staff react adversely to direct time study and it is, therefore, not widely used for clerical work except, possibly, in those areas where the work is highly mechanised.

Production study

This is a general study of the work performed by an individual over a period of time (usually a full day), performance ratings and output being recorded at prescribed intervals. In this way it can be verified that all the work of the individual is covered by time standards, with an overall check on the accuracy of such standards.

The technique involves the maintenance of an accurate record of work completed, together with a note of non-working periods and the reasons for these.

Predetermined standards

As its name implies, this technique involves the application of known work values to prescribed component parts of a job. Once the elements, or sequences of elements, in a task have been identified, the appropriate time-values can be read off from tables. The standards used are frequently based on the methods-time measurement (MTM) system, which has a wide application over an extensive range of activities. An important feature of the technique is that it establishes the times that clerical operations should take and thus enables standards to be set based on known levels of performance. A further advantage is provided by the ability to measure in advance the work content of new or changed procedures or methods. The system involves a detailed analysis of the work which, in turn, directs attention to the opportunities for simplifying or improving existing practices. It permits the establishment of a continuing control over clerical activities so that staff levels and costs may be directly related to fluctuations in work-load.

MTM data system

This is the most recent development in clerical work measurement. The system is based on a combination of statistical techniques and the MTM principles mentioned above. Its purpose is to provide an economical method of measuring, within defined limits of accuracy, both repetitive clerical tasks and those which may be subject to random variations in work content and frequency of occurrence.

The system possesses the following advantages:

1 Low cost of application
2 Known reliability and accuracy
3 Consistency between analysts
4 Consistency between areas of application
5 Compatibility with other MTM/MTM-2 derived standards
6 Maximum transferability of data blocks between work areas
7 Low cost of transfer and validation
8 Provision of comprehensive control standards
9 Highly descriptive of work methods used

Multiple regression analysis (MRA)

This is the means of determining the units of work to be produced from variable inputs and/or outputs to the system. Its purpose is to establish the allowed time for each day's work, where a clerk or a group of clerks are engaged on a variety of independent jobs, but where the work done can be expressed in terms of a few easily-recorded activities. The method involves the writing of a series of simultaneous equations (one for each day of the period of assessment) linking the units of work produced with that day's quantities of the various inputs and/or outputs. The calculations are frequently processed by a computer, for which programs are readily available.

Document control

The proliferation of forms, records and reports is a common cause of inflated overhead costs in offices. There are few organisations where a sytematic review of documentation, combined with suitable controls, would not pay handsome dividends.

The subject is logically within the orbit of organisation and methods studies, which have been discussed earlier in this chapter and, where an O and M function exists, forms control should be one of its specific responsibilities. Even where O and M, as such, is not an on-going activity within the organisation, it is most desirable that a suitable person be nominated to exercise the necessary coordination and control in this important area. It is, however, essential that this work should be undertaken in close collaboration with the users of the various documents.

In designing and maintaining a system of document control, careful attention should be given to forms, records or reports which are produced internally within departments or sections. One effect of the widespread use of cheap and simple copying and duplicating equipment has been an upsurge in the production of such documents to meet what is considered to be an immediate local requirement. Once established, the paper-work is perpetuated without reference to the contribution which it may, or may not, be making to the operational requirements of the undertaking.

Where computers are involved there exist opportunities for the production of vast quantities of hard-copy output which, if not strictly controlled, could defeat the purpose for which it has been designed. Examples are not difficult to find where the sheer volume of output information is beyond the capacity of the recipients to digest it, let alone take intelligent decisions upon it.

The tests which must be applied to office documents of all descriptions are basically similar to those which have already been mentioned in relation to O and M studies:

1 What is the precise purpose of the information contained in the document?
2 How does this information contribute to the effective performance of the functions and responsibilities of the recipients?
3 What would be the effect if the information were not, in fact, available?
4 Is the information produced in the most economic or effective manner?
5 Is it presented in a manner best suited to the needs of the users?
6 What is the estimated period of time during which the information should remain available? What arrangements should be made for its storage and retrieval during this period?

The two key-words in any review of documentation are *information* and *action*. There are many situations where there is a preponderance of information with insufficient action, and others where action is taken on inadequate or defective information. Both are equally undesirable. The objective should be to strike the most effective balance in the light of prevailing circumstances, always bearing in mind that cost is usually a steeply rising factor in the development of any information system.

A simple, practical first step in a paper work review is to assemble examples of all forms, records and reports in use within the organisation, department or section which is the subject of inquiry. If the sample documents are collected in triplicate this will enable them to be classified and filed:

1 In series by alphabetical or numerical reference, thus constituting a master index.
2 By department or section.
3 By topic or subject matter.

Care should be taken to include all documents in use, whether they are official company forms or internally-produced items designed and used by individuals for their personal requirements – the latter type frequently out-number the former and they may, in fact, play a more important role in the processing of the work.

A further matter to which attention should be directed is the production of copies of memoranda, letters or other similar documents and their distribution among the various departments, sections or individuals.

The following details should be obtained concerning each sample document:

1 Title and reference number (if any).
2 Size and colour.
3 The number of sheets in the set.
4 The approximate annual usage.
5 The originator.
6 Method of preparation.
7 Distribution.
8 The purpose of the document.
9 A summary of the procedure in which the document is used.
10 Notes of any special requirements concerning the preparation or use of the document; for example, different design characteristics would be involved where forms were to be originated by members of the public or by non-clerical personnel, as distinct from skilled clerical staff.

The objectives of the overall review are to: eliminate any unnecessary documentation and combine two or more documents into one whenever practicable; simplify or improve existing documents following a justification of their continuing use; prepare new or substitute documents where the review has shown this to be necessary.

The opportunity of reviewing the methods of distribution, filing or storage should be taken. Bearing in mind that the study is essentially concerned with information and that paper is merely a vehicle, consideration should be given to the possibility of employing some entirely different medium; for example, telex, telephone or microfilm.

As has been stated, the review of existing documentation constitutes a first step in the introduction of a paperwork control system. To secure lasting benefits it will be necessary to carry out periodical reappraisals and to establish a discipline whereby any new or revised forms, records or routine reports are cleared through the section or individual nominated for this responsibility. The exercise of this function calls for a sound knowledge of form design, together with a detailed understanding of the requirements of the users of the documents. This should be combined with an appreciation of office machinery or equipment characteristics where these facilities are used in the processing of the material.

The exercise of the control function is aided considerably by the introduction and maintenance of a uniform classification and coding system for the forms and other documents used throughout the organisation. There are also substantial advantages to be secured by standardising as far as possible on paper-sizes, type styles and quality. Attention to these details can result in significant savings in filing space and equipment. Print costs and paper purchasing cost will be reduced through the opportunities for bulk buying.

An effective document control procedure should incorporate arrangements for the systematic disposal of unwanted papers. This entails the agreement of maximum retention periods for the various documents, including correspondence items. The general tendency in offices is to keep far too many out-of-date records, reports, copy letters and similar items. The cluttering up of files and storage areas with such unnecessary material, besides hindering the conduct of the day-to-day business, can be extremely costly where office space is at a premium. Where it is essential to retain papers for extended periods, consideration should be given to their transfer to cheaper storage areas or to the use of microfilmed records.

In the same way that an appraisal of existing documentation can produce substantial savings and other benefits, so can an overall review of files and records result in worthwhile economies and lead to more effective working. Such a review should be undertaken in the light of the retention periods already mentioned. Once agreed, these periods should be strictly adhered to. If a simple coding system is used to indicate the appropriate retention periods *before* the documents are placed on file, the persons responsible for file maintenance are able to operate a continuous programme whereby the records are either transferred to less active sections or finally destroyed, as necessary.

Selection of office equipment

It would be difficult to overestimate the contribution which the office equipment industry has made to the effective conduct of business during recent years. The advent of the computer has revolutionised the whole field of data processing and information handling, while in practically every other area of administrative and office work, machinery and equipment of various types have transformed old practices and procedures.

Although the introduction of appropriate equipment can produce substantial economies and other benefits, mistakes in selection or application can be costly – not only in monetary terms, but also in the general disruption of the day-to-day work. The latter result can frequently give rise to a deterioration of relationships with customers or outside bodies.

A decision to introduce new or improved equipment will, in general, be justified if certain criteria are met. First, if there is a net reduction in operating cost, while maintaining the required level of effectiveness; since staff costs are the main ingredient of office expense, this implies that the existing work-load will be handled by a reduced number of people or that additional output will be achieved without a proportionate increase in the number of employees. Second, if the equipment will permit the production of essential information which cannot be obtained within the required time-scale without its use.

In addition to these fundamental criteria, consideration should be given to possible supporting advantages; for example, the removal of the drudgery from routine manual tasks or improvement in the quality of work and the avoidance of detailed internal checking.

Care should be taken to avoid the mere substitution of mechanical for manual methods, without positive and defined attendant advantages. Where the equipment is to be used at a particular stage in the processing of information it should be viewed in the context of the overall system which, in turn, should, preferably, have been the subject of detailed O and M studies. The important principle here is to ensure that the equipment serves the system, rather than to try to build the system round the equipment.

The starting point in the selection of specific items of equipment must be a clear understanding of what is required by way of end-product. It is only after agreement has been reached on this requirement that attention can be given to the detailed characteristics of individual products. These will include:

1 Complexity and the degree of operator training that will be required.
2 Flexibility in operation; for example, the ability to handle a number of routines.
3 The availability of installation, servicing and maintenance facilities.
4 The estimated life of the equipment.
5 Cost, including installation expense, annual charges, staff costs, replacement costs, etc.
6 Delivery periods.
7 Peripheral or ancillary requirements, for example, special supplies, materials or stationery.
8 General support services, such as the availability of substitute equipment in the event of breakdown or the possibility of using bureaux or sub-contract facilities.

In addition, regard should be had to users' reports on similar equipment. The opportunity should be taken, wherever possible, of visiting installations engaged on routines which are comparable with those contemplated.

The ever-widening range and technical complexity of office machinery and other equipment has created the need for specialists in the different fields of application. The work of the specialists depends in large measure upon the understanding and support of senior management for its success. It should, therefore, be part of the role of office management to be aware of the facilities that are available and to keep abreast of new developments in this, and related, fields.

Further reading

Office Organisation and Method by G J Mills and O W Standingford, Pitman, 1968.

Office Administration Handbook edited by J C Aspley, The Dartnell Corporation, 1967.

Productivity Improvements in the Office by J E Bayhylle, Kogan Page, 1969.

The Disposal and Retention of Documents, The Institute of Chartered Secretaries and Administrators, 1970.

Procedure and Process Charts by L G S Mason, The Institute of Administrative Management, 1972.

The Measurement and Control of Office Costs by S A Birn, *et al* McGraw-Hill, 1961.

Work Measurement in the Office by E V Grillo and C J Berg, McGraw-Hill, 1959.

Chapter 13

Planning Office Space

P Lebus, Managing Director, C E Planning Limited

The planning and layout of office accommodation are becoming matters of increasing management concern. The introduction of the Offices, Shops and Railway Premises Act in 1963 encouraged the examination of the working environment in a more critical light, and it was seen that many offices fell short of the standards that were desirable for efficiency and staff welfare. As fast as offices were planned, the organisation or equipment changed and the layout became invalid.

Recent developments in office space planning have therefore led to new types of layout based on more analytical methods. By this means management is ensuring that office accommodation is no longer a hazard over which there is little or no control, but that it makes a positive contribution to company efficiency and good staff relations.

The planning of layouts involves the consideration of many factors and the application of a number of techniques in a logical manner. For clarity, the process can be thought of as four interlocking phases:

1 Information
2 Analysis
3 Solution
4 Implementation

Information

The collection of primary information is fundamental and is the essential first step in all planning. The facts must be established and weighed against each other to ensure the right priorities and to create the basis for all that follows. The success of the project will depend on being aware of individual needs and balancing these with corporate objectives.

The most comprehensive method of obtaining this information is by the use of staff questionnaires together with a number of interviews. It is most important at this stage to obtain an unbiased picture of the type of work that is undertaken by each individual. Questions should be phrased to establish that an individual is not only an engineer, or an accountant, or a typist, but that a significant portion of his time is spent reading or writing or on a drawing board or at meetings and so on. The number of visitors that can be expected and their frequency of arrival is important, as well as the degree of confidentiality of the work that is being performed. The need for freedom from distraction and communication with others should be determined, and the need for furniture, storage and equipment should be calculated.

A question asking how many filing units are needed usually receives an answer which is significantly too high. A more realistic estimate can be obtained by assessing the quantity and type of information that must be stored, together with the necessary retrieval times.

In addition to individual needs, staff numbers today and for at least two years into the future must be established. Likely changes in company organisation, office systems and equipment should be forecast. Even the type of people to be accommodated must be known, as their age group, sex, background, and status will have an influence on the type of layout that is desirable and that will be acceptable.

The pattern of communications within the organisation should be established. This is a function of the paper flow, the use of telephones and the amount of personal contact. Each organisation will need to weigh these factors to reflect their particular methods of working. For example, the production control department might rate paper flow and telephone contact very highly, whereas a design team might need personal contact with frequent discussions or longer meetings. It must be remembered that the existing location of departments, and the layout and design of the building, will have a considerable influence on the existing ratio of telephone and personal contacts. It is common to find that some personal communication links have grown up for no other reason than that the people are housed in adjacent areas, and conversely that departments which should be working closely together have a weak link as the result of being placed on different floors or in different buildings. These links should be adjusted accordingly.

Every organisation is constantly changing, and therefore the information that is gathered must be regularly checked to ensure that the final layout is up-to-date.

Analysis

The purpose of this stage is to establish space standards and relationship patterns, and to assess different types of layouts.

Space standards

Space standards should be based on an analysis of functional requirements. These can be summarised as:

1 Work content
2 Furniture and equipment
3 Storage
4 Need for privacy
5 Type of layout
6 Number of visitors or meetings
7 Access

Each of these factors affects the need for space, although some overlap in their influence.

The characteristics of a building, such as the size and shape of office areas and the acoustic properties of the rooms, can have a major influence on the space that must be allocated to an individual. For instance, a building which is 42ft deep with a 6ft central corridor and has a window module of 5ft, would dictate that the minimum size for a private office is 18ft by 10ft, namely, 180 sq ft (or 210 sq ft including corridor space). This is likely to be considerably in excess of the theoretical space standards needed by most staff. In addition, when open layouts are used and some privacy is required, the acoustics of the room will determine the minimum distances between individuals.

Relationship patterns

The relationship pattern within the company can be established by the sequence of steps illustrated in Figure 13:1. A survey is carried out to determine the existing pattern of telephone calls, paper flow and visits. This can be done by individual record, sampling, estimate or observation. The results should be summarised into a matrix which will show the comparative figures. Any major bias resulting from the present location of departments or individuals should be established by interview, and the results weighted to reflect this. Further adjustments can be made in order to further company policy. By this means communication links can be either encouraged or discouraged.

This modified matrix should be used to create a relationship diagram (Figure 13:2), which can be used as a basis for locating activities. The thicker lines denote the stronger relationship links and therefore should be kept as short as possible. In due course, when space requirements have been finalised and the shape and size of the accommodation is known, the relationship diagram is used to create a block diagram allocating space to each department (see Figure 13:1).

Layout types

One of the commonest errors in office planning is to decide which type of layout will be used without reference to the specific needs of each function. It is now usual to find companies that have taken an arbitrary decision to introduce landscaped layouts into their offices regardless of whether it is appropriate for either the organisation or the building.

There are at least six types of layout now in common use and each has a number of advantages and disadvantages. It is only by considering each on its merits that a realistic decision can be taken to answer the needs of the company.

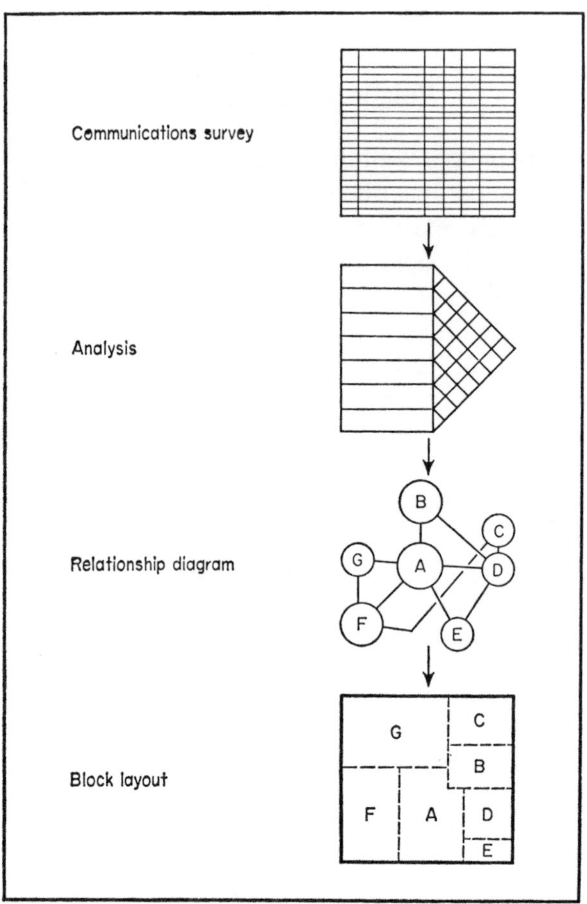

FIGURE 13:1 CREATION OF A BLOCK LAYOUT

This shows the four steps in the analysis of communications which are used to determine the relationship pattern within an organisation and the optimum layout of departments or functions

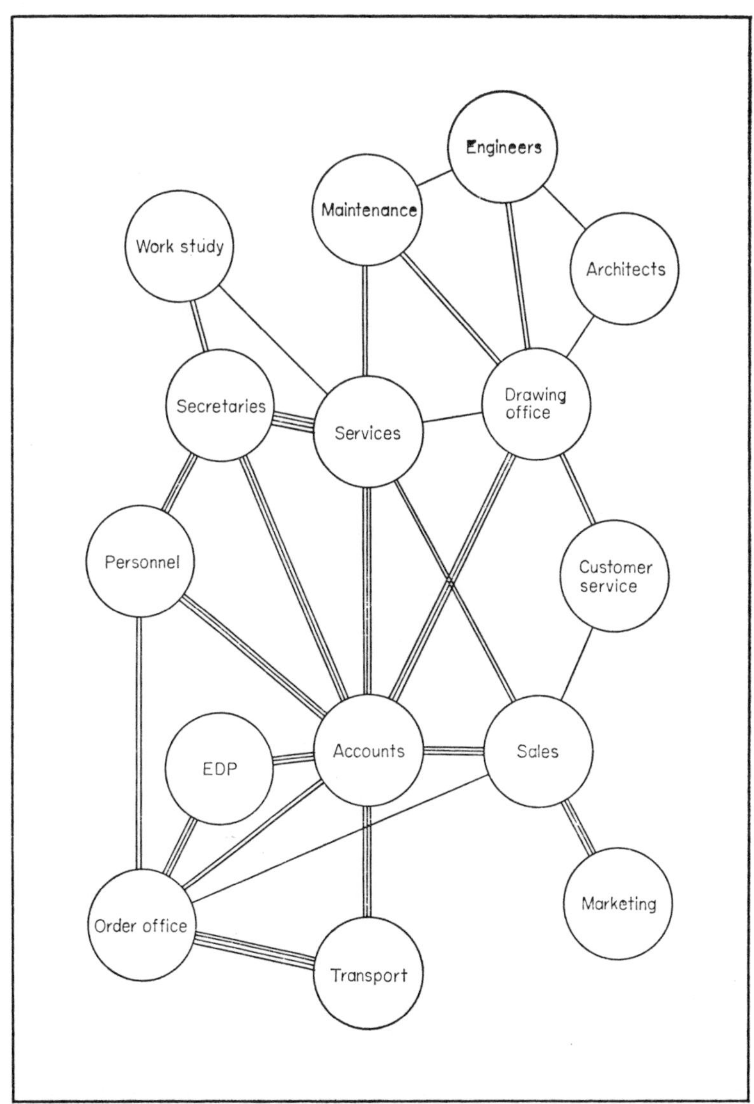

FIGURE 13:2 RELATIONSHIP DIAGRAM

This shows the volume of communications between departments. This can reflect the present situation or be used to show future intentions

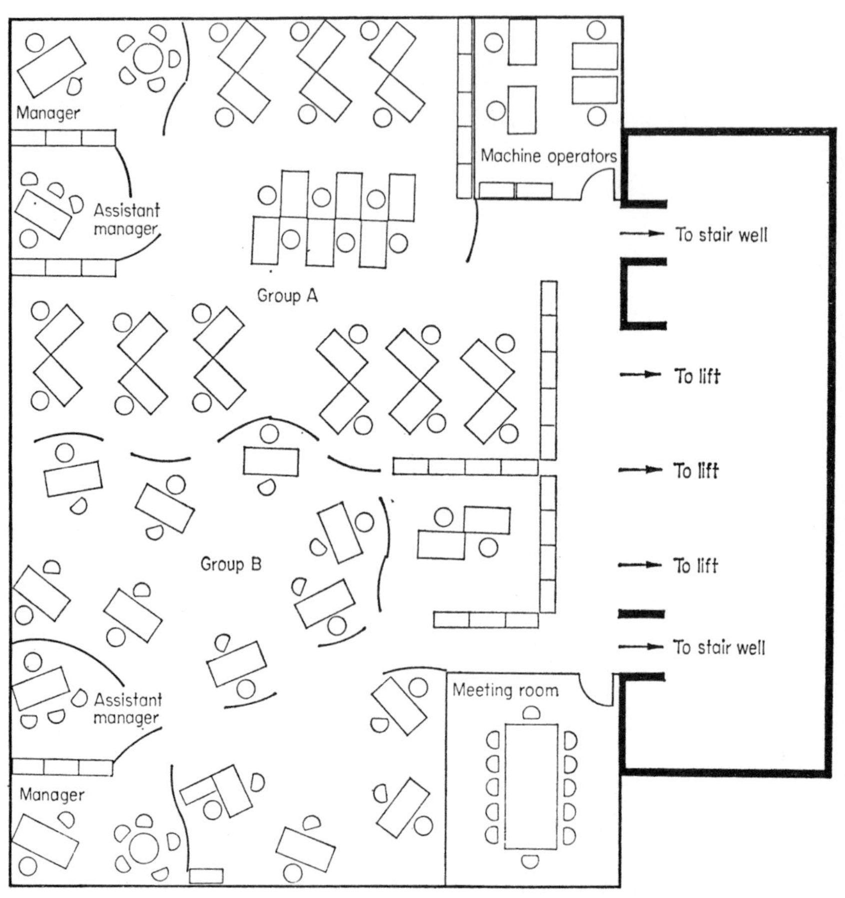

FIGURE 13:3 TYPICAL OPEN-SPACE OR LANDSCAPED OFFICE

This illustrates the informal layout, and the use of screens and planters to define groups and individuals

Open Space. A layout which is currently in fashion is the open space or landscaped office. This type of layout planning involves a fairly large number of people in one room. No fixed partitions are used and individuals are grouped in sections and departments. Figure 13:3 shows the informal distribution of furniture and equipment that is used. Privacy and freedom from undue distraction is achieved with shoulder high free-standing screens and boxes of indoor plants. A very high degree of flexibility is possible and reorganisation can be reflected by the simple movement of a few pieces of furniture. Communications are good and there are no barriers to inhibit conversation or discourage meetings.

Care must be taken to avoid the problem of over communication. Individuals may find themselves brought into conversations or involved in problems which are outside their normal work. For instance, an electrical engineer may usefully join in discussions with a civil engineer on the design of a common project. However, he will not want to be disturbed by a discussion between two civil engineers on the use of light-weight concrete. It is problems such as these that the detailed layout must be designed to avoid.

Acoustics play a very large part in the success of this type of layout. Noise levels must be such as to provide adequate masking without creating undesirable distraction. This will be promoted by using a large room which is as deep as possible and can accommodate at least fifty people. Nevertheless, it should be mentioned that several successful open space offices have been created for as few as thirty people. The critical number of people will, of course, be affected by the acoustic properties of the room, the intensity of noise production and the need for freedom from distraction by the staff. The achievement of the correct acoustic environment can be aided by the use of artificial noise sources.

Open plan. The layout which the landscaped office was designed to replace, is the open plan office. This is still in wide use for drawing offices and large scale routine paper handling departments. Figure 13:4 illustrates the straight line layout that is used. There are no fixed partitions and little, if any, screening. Space utilisation is high and the flow of paper can be good; however, it is virtually impossible to achieve any degree of privacy, and distraction can be bad. Management is usually accommodated in separate offices so that it can work efficiently. The use of this layout in drawing offices avoids some of

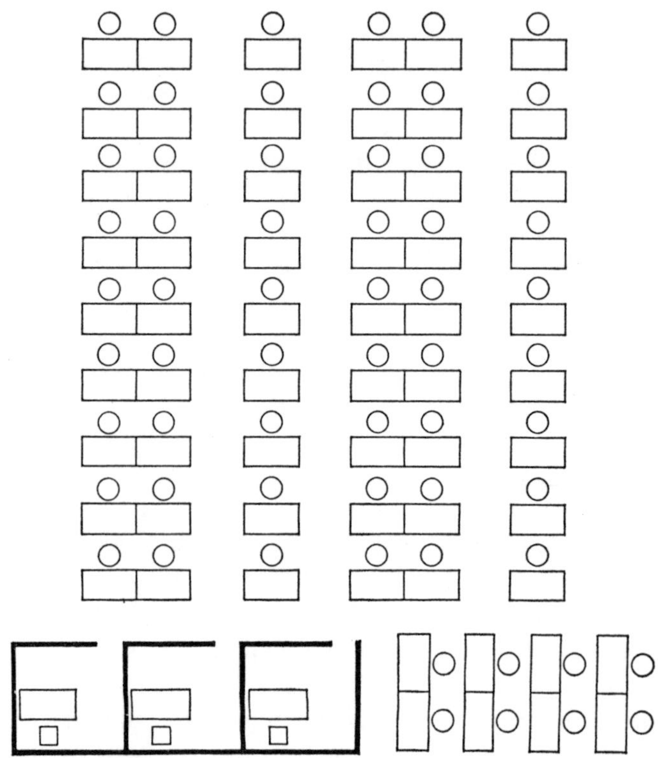

FIGURE 13:4 OPEN-PLAN OFFICE

This illustrates the rigid layout normally used, and shows the high level of distraction to be expected. Space utilisation is good

these disadvantages. The bulky furniture breaks up the sound pattern and the drawing boards afford some reduction in visual distraction.

Cellular. Cellular offices, when used by individuals, achieve a high degree of privacy and freedom from distraction. Communications are not good and relationships tend to become more formalised. Flexibility of use is low, and any change of office size may require a large number of partition moves. Space utilisation is usually poor when the building module dictates large offices. Spare space is often wasted when it becomes available in the wrong part of the floor.

The cellular office which is shared by several people has the worst of all worlds. It has the disadvantages of inflexibility, poor space utilisation and bad communications, and at the same time, because of its small size, gives the highest levels of distraction and lack of privacy. However, the design of the building or the special requirements of the company may dictate its use.

Half-height partitions. The layout using half-height partitions is still in common use. Fixed partitions from four to six feet high are installed, creating small office areas for groups or individuals. This gives some privacy and meets the regulations for day lighting and ventilation for internal offices. However, space utilisation and flexibility are lower than with either the landscaped or open plan layout.

Carrel. A new type of layout which is being promoted by many furniture suppliers is the carrel. This consists of a number of individual work stations. The furniture is designed to provide an integrated system of work top, storage and screening. The furniture can surround the worker on two or three sides, or even on all four sides with a small entrance gap. This provides more flexibility than the cellular layout, and more privacy than the open plan. However, communications are poor and so this is most appropriate for the individual research type of operation.

A means of determining the most appropriate layout is illustrated in Figure 13:5. Each type of layout is listed and factors are graded according to their influence. This provides an absolute rating which is a function of the type of layout and makes no reference to the organisation or company that is being considered.

A weighting column can be included in the table so that the requirements of the organisation are taken into account. For instance, an engineering design office might well put a high rating on communications and flexibility and a relatively low rating on privacy. On

	Open Space	Open Plan	Cellular		Half-height partition	Carrel
			Individual	Shared		
Privacy	xx		xxx	x	x	xx
Freedom from distraction	xx	x	xxx		x	xx
Communication	xxx	xxx		x	xx	x
Flexibility	xxx	xx			x	x
Supervision	xx	xxx		x	x	
Work flow	xxx	xxx		x	x	
Space utilisation	xxx	xxx		x	x	xx

FIGURE 13:5 CHARACTERISTICS OF LAYOUTS

This table illustrates the relative merits of six types of layout. The greater the number of xs, the better is the result

the other hand a solicitor's office would put a very high rating on privacy while having little need for flexibility. Each department within the company may have a different set of weighting factors which should be used to produce a weighted total for each layout. This should indicate the most appropriate layout for each function. It must be remembered that, in common with every semi-automatic procedure, the answers will be only as good as the information or judgment that is fed in.

Solution

Decisions concerning space requirements, relationship patterns, types of layout and block layouts follow from the recommendations during the analysis phase. The block diagram should be split on to individual floors and modified to ensure that it fits within the shell of the building. This is followed by the creation of the detailed layout, which is the most crucial part of the whole process. At this time the immediate working environment of each individual in the organisation is decided. The result will have a major influence on his ability and inclination to be efficient. If the working conditions are not right he will work more slowly or make more mistakes.

In an open space office, the layout for each person will have an influence on all those others whose areas adjoin his. Requirements for privacy or freedom from distraction must be recalled and each piece of furniture or screening positioned to ensure that this is achieved.

It is most important to visualise the plan in three dimensions. The height of screens and storage units can be very misleading when viewed on a normal two dimensional plan. It is common to provide totally inadequate privacy for this reason. The temptation to make pretty patterns or to create change for change's sake should be resisted. No one within the office will ever see it from the same bird's eye view as is shown on the plan.

Groups must be identified so that each person feels part of the team, but at the same time is given a feeling of individual treatment. Furniture should be used to encourage staff to walk along the access ways and to prevent them walking through departments, which can be most distracting and annoying.

In an engineers' office, the storage and retrieval of information is of paramount importance. In many cases the volume of drawings and reference material dictates some form of centralised filing. When considering this, the tail must not be allowed to wag the dog – the filing system must not impair operational efficiency. All too often reference books are not used because it is too much effort to get them and then return them. The layout must therefore be planned to encourage the use of information through the correct location and type of storage facilities.

The provision of services such as telephone and power can control the layout of staff. Considerable flexibility can be achieved when a floor grid of service points is provided at approximately five feet centres. This allows alterations to be made to the layout with the minimum disturbance. The lack of such a grid will determine the position of each person requiring a service outlet, if trailing wires are to be avoided.

Figure 13:6 shows a typical landscaped layout with departments and access ways clearly defined. Some members of senior management

FIGURE 13: 6 LANDSCAPED LAYOUT

This illustrates the different treatment for each grade of staff or function

have private offices. It can be seen that the other managers are given different treatment from junior clerical staff, and that assistant managers have a compromise layout which provides them with some privacy without wasting space.

Implementation

The physical laying out of an office should be supervised by the person who created the plans. He will be aware of all the objectives and can ensure that they are achieved on the ground. The three dimensional sight angles can be seen and any modifications that are necessary should be made. It is common for a change of alignment of only ten degrees or two to three inches to cause the difference between considerable distraction and peace.

Each chair should be sat in and final adjustments made to ensure that furniture and equipment are in position for efficient use, that all work surfaces can be utilised and that access ways are clearly marked.

On the day of occupation a number of further modifications may be necessary to bring the layout into line with those factors which a few occupants will have forgotten. These are the only alterations that should be made initially, as it may be some weeks before the occupants are thoroughly settled into the new layout.

It must be remembered that this layout is appropriate for this particular organisation at this particular point in time. However, as all organisations are constantly changing in size, organisation, methods and equipment, the layout should be used to reflect these changes and not allowed to develop into a strait-jacket which will become increasingly constricting with time.

Government legislation

Since August 1964, it has been necessary to consider the Offices, Shops and Railway Premises Act when planning office accommodation. A number of minimum standards are defined which must be met by all office premises. Major alterations to the building or a layout should be notified to the local authority in order to obtain the appropriate permission.

There are a number of provisions, in the original act and in a number of subsequent orders and regulations, which are encountered on a frequent basis during office space planning.

Temperature control

A temperature of at least sixteen degrees centigrade must be attained within one hour in any room in which people work for more than short periods. A thermometer must be prominently displayed on each floor of the office building. (It should be noted that this temperature is four to five degrees centigrade below that normally considered appropriate for office work.)

Ventilation

Adequate supplies of either fresh or artifically purified air must be provided in every room where staff are working.

Lighting

Good lighting must be provided, using either natural or artificial means. The Minister may prescribe a standard of lighting which would become obligatory. (In the meantime, companies are encouraged to use the Illuminating Engineering Society's code as a minimum; however, there is no statutory obligation to do so.)

Noise

The Minister can make regulations to control noise or vibrations; however, no such regulations have yet been introduced.

Space and overcrowding

Overcrowding, such as to endanger the health of workers, must be avoided. Both the number of people and the quantity of furniture will be taken into açcount in any decision on overcrowding. When the ceiling height is 10ft or above, each person habitually employed at a time in such a room must have a minimum of 40 sq ft. When the ceiling height is below 10ft, a minimum of 400 cubic feet must be provided for each person. Both of these standards relate to the average for people employed within a single room. This section is administered by the Public Health Inspectorate.

Cleanliness

Normal cleanliness should be maintained, and floors and steps should be cleaned at least once a week.

Sanitation and washing facilities

The following schedules should be observed. The facilities must be kept clean and properly maintained, lighted and ventilated. When a number of firms share conveniences, all workers should be added together when making these calculations.

Schedule 1: Scale of sanitary accommodation to be provided separately for persons of each sex. This scale is to be used for females. It is also to be used for males when the urinal accommodation does not meet the requirements of Schedule 2.

Number of persons of each sex regularly employed to work in the premises at any one time	Number of water closets
1 – 15	1
16 – 30	2
31 – 50	3
51 – 75	4
76 – 100	5
Exceeding 100	5, plus 1 for every 25 persons (or fraction thereof) in excess of 100

Schedule 2: Scale of sanitary accommodation to be provided for males where urinals are installed.

Number of male persons regularly employed to work in the premises at any one time	Number of water closets	Units of urinal accommodation
1 – 15	1	–
16 – 20	1	1
21 – 30	2	1
31 – 45	2	2
46 – 60	3	2
61 – 75	3	3
76 – 90	4	3
91 – 100	4	4
Exceeding 100	4	4
	with the addition of one sanitary convenience for every 25 persons (or fraction thereof) in excess of 100. A sanitary convenience is either a water closet or urinal; however, of the additional number not less than three-quarters shall be water closets.	

Schedule 3: Scale of washing facilities to be provided.

Number of persons regularly employed to work in the premises at any one time (or, where separate accommodation for the sexes is required to be provided, number of such persons of each sex)	Number of wash-basins
1 – 15	1
16 – 30	2
31 – 50	3
51 – 75	4
76 – 100	5
Exceeding 100	5, plus 1 for every 25 persons (or fraction thereof) in excess of 100

Drinking water

A supply of wholesome drinking water must be provided, although this does not need to be a piped supply.

Facilities for storing and drying clothing

These must be provided in every building.

Safety

This section covers the prevention of accidents due to bad maintenance and untidiness, as well as the use of all types of machinery. Seven sections in the Act deal with this:

1 Section 16: Security of floors, passages and stairs
2 Section 17: Safeguarding machinery
3 Section 18: Young persons
4 Section 19: Beginners
5 Section 20: Safety regulations

6 Section 22: The powers of the courts
7 Section 23: Heavy work

First-aid

This section covers the entire field of first-aid and lays down certain basic principles. A readily accessible first-aid box or cupboard must be provided for every premises. There must be an additional box for every 150 persons or fraction thereof in addition to the first 150 actually at work on the premises. Where more than 150 people work at any one time, the person in charge of the first-aid box should be qualified in first-aid and available during working hours. This section goes on to specify the contents of the first-aid box or cupboard depending on the number of workers. The Offices, Shops and Railway Premises First Aid Order 1964, should be used when establishing requirements.

Fire

Adequate means of escape, fire alarms and fire fighting equipment must be provided. A fire certificate is necessary if more than twenty people are employed or more than ten people work above ground level. The certificates are provided after inspection by the local fire authority. A useful guide to the requirements in this section is provided by *Means of Escape in Case of Fire in Offices, Shops and Railway Premises* (New Series No. 40, HMSO).

The regulations are applicable to offices throughout the United Kingdom but excluding Northern Ireland. In addition to this there are a number of local authority regulations and by-laws which should be observed. If there is a doubt as to the acceptability of any office alterations, it is advisable to check them with the local authority.

Chapter 14

Data Processing Applications

D A Barrett, Manager, Systems Development, K and H Business Consultants Limited

---

This chapter deals with the use of computers in management. The type of computer most significant in this area is the 'stored-program digital computer'; all subsequent references to computers should be taken as relating to this specific type of machine.

What is a computer?

It is a useful analogy to compare a computer with a clerk; to compare the functions of a clerk and his equipment with the various pieces of hardware which can be attached to a computer. This analogy is illustrated in Figure 14:1. The clerk sitting at his desk has what may be described as a logical unit situated between the ears; he has a scratch-pad for calculations to one side of his desk and a book of procedures that define the actions he should take under a variety of circumstances on the other side.

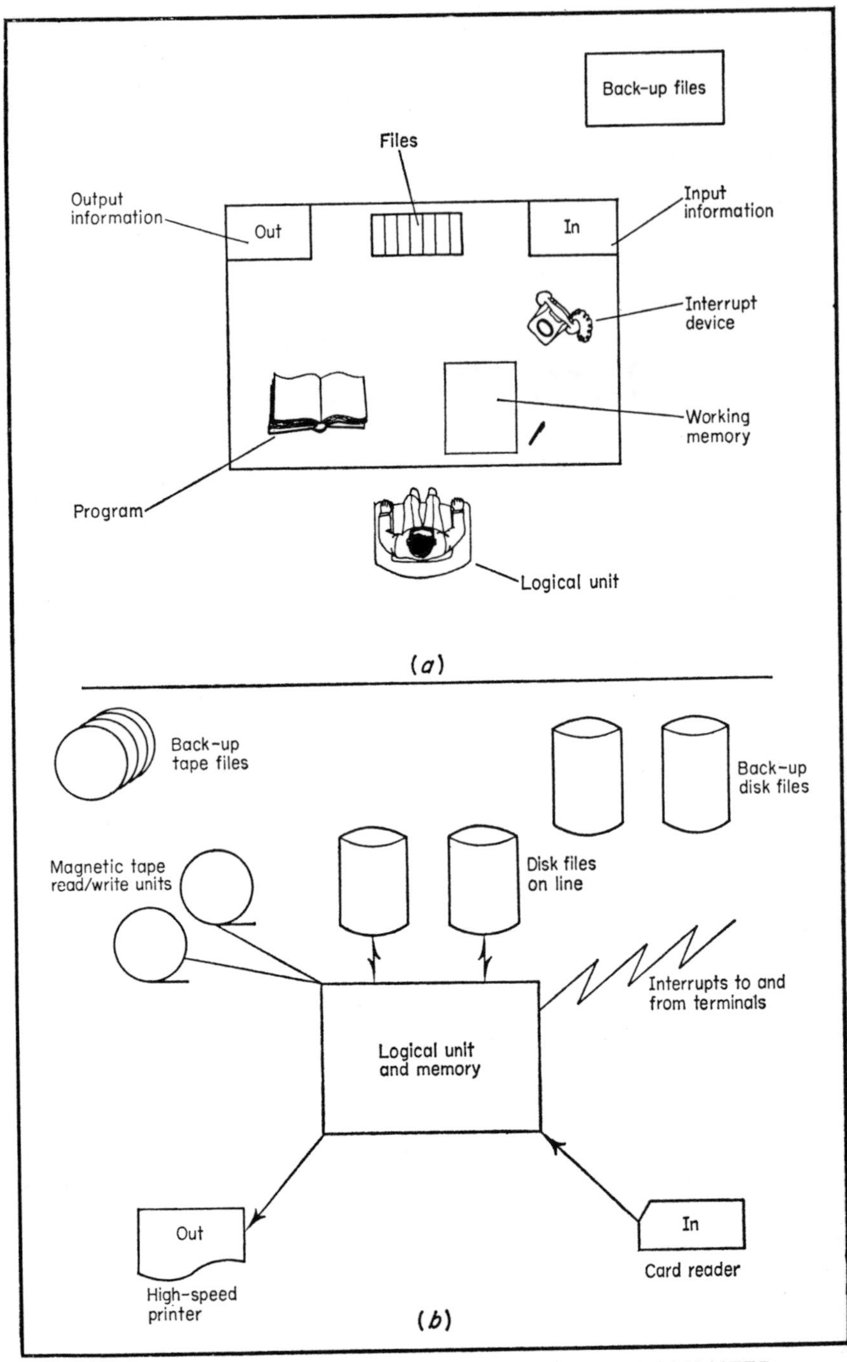

FIGURE 14:1 BASIC ARRANGEMENT OF A COMPUTER

At (a) the principal functions of a clerk are illustrated, and their counterparts in the computer can be compared by reference to (b)

The central memory of a computer carries out the functions of both the scratch-pad and the book of procedures. Any part of this 'memory' may be used to contain instructions (procedures) or to hold the result of intermediate calculations. The logical unit will follow these procedures and use the scratch-pad with considerably more speed and fidelity than the clerk. However, it has a very literal mind, and will follow both correct and obviously incorrect instructions with equal enthusiasm. This can be thought of as a perpetual work-to-rule situation. Furthermore, it is capable of understanding only a limited range of instructions; one of the more interesting tasks in computer work is that of the systems analyst and the programmer, who have to analyse the procedures to be carried out, and break them down into combinations of these simple elementary instructions.

The computer 'learns' the set of procedures very rapidly, although it can be a complex, time-consuming operation to set them up. It will generally be used for only one task, or at most a small number of tasks, at any one time, and can be converted from one task to another simply by switching the instruction book. In contrast, the first eighteen or so years of the clerk's existence is spent in setting up one large comprehensive multi-purpose program which is permanently resident in the memory. For this, and perhaps other, reasons the clerk is generally more prone to error within the limited area defined by a simple task.

To carry the analogy further, the clerk may well have an in-tray and an out-tray to either side of his desk, containing items to be processed, and the results of such processing, respectively. This corresponds to the input and output devices of the computer. Generally, the in-tray will be represented by a machine for reading punched cards or punched paper tape. The out-tray will correspond to a high-speed printer capable of producing a greater quantity of information per minute than a large number of clerks. (The relative *quality* of such information may be more difficult to vouch for.)

There may also be a number of ledgers and files on the clerk's desk, and a larger number on shelves and in cabinets in his office. These correspond quite closely to removable disk-packs attached to the computer. There will be a limited number of disk-drives, each capable of holding, reading from, and writing on a disk-pack, attached to the computer. The packs currently held by these drives, each capable of containing as much information as a small ledger, will be equivalent to the books actually on the desk. Other packs stored ready for use are equivalent to books or ledgers available within the office.

A computer may also have magnetic tape-drives attached to it for similar information storage purposes. These have a disadvantage against disk-units or books in that it is not possible to look up a single item of information in the middle of the file without reading through all the preceding information. This is a disadvantage comparable to the difference between a record-player and a tape-recorder, whereby one can play a single track in the middle of a record quite easily, but a tape-recorder has to be wound on to the section one desires to hear. However, when it is necessary to look at every individual item in a file, magnetic tapes and tape-drives are cheaper than disk-packs and disk-drives.

Lastly, the clerk may have a telephone on his desk, by which he may be (and often is) interrupted from his current task in order to perform some unrelated function. This also has an equivalent in the 'terminal' or other inquiry device which can be attached to a computer in order to allow interruptions of its current task in order to carry out operations of immediate interest or urgency.

It must be remembered that the above is only an analogy, though quite an illuminating one, which serves to introduce many important aspects of the computer and to explain some of the technical terms of the field. In principle the computer can carry out extremely large volumes of calculation, or process very large quantities of information at great speed. It is relatively inflexible, and is usually more suited to well-defined operations of limited scope. It is not often good at dealing with the unexpected. It is also an expensive piece of equipment.

When comparing the relative cost and performance of computers and manual methods in different situations it should be borne in mind that the human being is currently the only general purpose computer which can be mass-produced with pleasure by unskilled labour.

Computers in management

Most engineers will be familiar with the computer as an engine for performing large quantities of arithmetic at high speed. However, there is another aspect of computer work which becomes more significant in the management environment. This can be expressed as a switch of emphasis from the arithmetic to the logical capabilities of the machine. In most management applications, the computer is used as an information processing device which can collect, organise, summarise and distribute information.

The simplest management applications can be described as the collection, organisation and distribution of information. An example is a standard invoicing procedure, in which items to be billed are collected, organised by customer, associated with a name/address list, and distributed to the clients of a company. A summarisation function may also apply, whereby the total debt of each customer is summarised and retained for later comparison with payments, production of monthly statements, and so on. A logical selection function might also be invoked, using the criteria of size of outstanding debt, time elapsed without payment, and other similar factors. Such selected information could then be distributed to the appropriate customer and/or to the company's accounts department.

Data capture

The weakest point of systems of this type is the first stage, the collection of information. Large quantities of data must be presented to the computer in machine-readable form. Traditionally this involves punching coded cards or paper tape from documents, an operation similar to typing, with the corresponding possibility of human error in the reading and interpretation of the documents. Plain finger trouble can often be eliminated by the use of proper verification procedures. These procedures involve the repetition of the typing operation using a machine which compares the second keying operation with the contents of the cards or paper tape and signals any discrepancy. This verification doubles the time and cost of the preparation of input data, but it is unwise to omit it.

Since the collection of data is so error-prone and costly, two general approaches have been taken to improve the situation. The first approach has been to develop new methods of collecting information. A notable example is the development of optical character reading equipment, which enables the computer to read directly from typewritten or carefully hand-written documents. Such equipment works with remarkable reliability, but is still rather costly and limited in its applications.

Television screens with typewriter keyboards which are wired directly into a computer can also provide some improvement in the data collection process. Because of the direct input to a computer, the information provided can be scanned immediately, and any obvious errors or anomalies can be displayed on the screen for correction. These remote television screens (often known as cathode ray terminals or CRTs for short) can also enable the originator of the information to submit it directly to the computer, so that the input of a particular piece of information becomes the complete responsibility of one individual.

Other input devices attempt to collect data as a spin-off from some process which has to take place for other reasons; for example, devices for reading cash-register paper rolls, or recording devices from time clocks, badge readers, and the like.

The second main approach is to ensure that once a piece of information has been given to the computer, full use is made of it, and that it is available to all users of the machine. In many cases, redundant information is collected by computer systems used by different departments of the same company, because the data is required in a slightly different form or through simple lack of co-ordination. The ultimate development of this line of thinking is enshrined in the concept of a 'data base' to be used by a 'total information system'. These currently popular phrases imply that information which has been collected should be amalgamated into a central information storage facility containing data cross-referenced under the major headings and categories used by the company, and available for access from any computer-based system within the organisation. The concept is logical in principle, but difficult to achieve in practice, particularly at a reasonable cost.

On-line systems

The television screen terminal on the desk of the managing director has been a dream of both computer technicians and managers for some time. In principle, current information about any aspect of a company's operations could be provided at the touch of a key through such a device, although there is some question whether *current* information is exactly what the chief executive needs. Present equipment is certainly able to produce such a service. The difficulty lies in the organisation of information systems to support the operation; the problem is in the 'software' rather than the 'hardware' capabilities.

It has been true for some time that computer manufacturers have been producing equipment far in advance of the abilities of systems designers to make full use of it. The relevant hardware factors in this case are 'multi-processors' and 'random access devices'.

Multi-processing implies that a computer has the capability of being interrupted from a routine task in order to process an inquiry. Random access devices are storage devices, such as disk-packs or drums, which allow the access of a piece of information in the middle of a file without having to search through all the preceding information on the file.

Given these possibilities, quite large numbers of remote terminals can be attached to a computer, making information potentially available at many points in the company. The cathode ray terminal is a particularly good device for this purpose, as it enables both the entry and the extraction of data, and allows the access of only one page of information at a time, thus discouraging the production of vast quantities of paper and encouraging the use of the computer to select and summarise information before providing it to the user.

The logical procedures behind these uses of a computer are complex and difficult; particularly so because the methods by which people may enter or extract data must be designed to be fool-proof and easy to use. Large numbers of people with little knowledge of computers must be capable of using these procedures after the minimum of training.

Applications

A large percentage of commercial applications of computers consists of the mechanisation of clearly defined manual procedures. These were generally to be found in the payroll and accounts departments; and provided easy areas of conversion that produced clearly defined benefits. These obvious areas of application have become well known and defined, and attention is now being turned to applications which impinge directly on the operations of a company, rather than on the overhead and administration procedures.

These newer applications tend to be more difficult and expensive to set up, and there is always doubt whether they will be usable in practice; or, however effective they may be, whether they will be used by the people they were designed to help. There may be three technical functions contributing to the design of such a system.

Firstly, the potential user of the system, who will often not be aware of the range of possibilities offered to him by the computer department, will define the main requirements.

Secondly, there may be an operations research department, whose advice and theoretical knowledge should be invaluable in the development of a complex system. They may not be aware of the areas of greatest potential saving within the company, and may be tempted to concentrate on those areas where the problems are immediately suitable to operational research techniques or where the user response is particularly enthusiastic.

The third contributor will be the computer department, which may not be fully conversant with either the user's problems or the theoretical techniques which may be applied to them.

There is an obvious necessity for some co-ordinating force which will identify the areas in which the use of computers will provide the greatest return, and which will direct the energies of the appropriate user and technical departments to these areas, and ensure that as much communication and co-operation as possible occurs between them.

The majority of computer applications are quite simple in principle. They can be divided into three very broad categories for convenience. These are:

1 Commercial applications, characterised by large amounts of data and relatively simple calculations.
2 Engineering and scientific calculations, characterised by carrying out large amounts of calculation on limited amounts of data.
3 Sophisticated applications, which may imply complex logical procedures, direct response from computer to user in a practical situation, direct reading and control of instruments by the computer, and the like.

Commercial applications

There are many 'bread and butter' applications in this area, which may include payroll, invoicing, cost accounting, sales analysis, stock recording, man-hours recording, order processing and market research.

Engineering calculations

These are extremely varied, and cover a wide range of problems. Usually the vast majority cover the use of a computer as the extension of a calculating machine. Some of these applications can become extremely complicated, as in the case of structural analysis, automatic design programs and the like. Engineers will already be familiar with a variety of these applications.

It is now becoming reasonably economical to produce the results of many engineering calculations in the form of graphs or drawings directly from the computer. The equipment used for this purpose, 'digital graph plotters', is becoming more efficient and less expensive. Furthermore, when a digital computer is asked to control a plotter, and so produce graphic output, it is necessary to specify every tiny movement of the pen which carries out the actual drawing. Plotter manufacturers are now providing excellent pre-written routines, which makes this operation relatively simple to set up. Obviously, this kind of output can have great advantages in time-saving and in accuracy when detailed drawings are required from the results of a computer calculation.

Sophisticated applications

Operational research can be described, with some justice, as a series of techniques in search of a problem. The theoretical techniques of operational research can provide excellent solutions to a range of clearly defined problems. If the practical situation falls completely within the terms of reference of one of these techniques, then it can be relied upon to produce usable results. However, it is often the case that available methods will solve a limited part of a practical situation, or will handle a large percentage of cases, leaving exceptional conditions to be resolved by human intervention. Under these circumstances, any solution will necessarily be partial. The difficulty lies in the transmission of the partial solution and its implications to the user, who will probably be using a very different set of rules and approaches to solve the same problem.

It is difficult to give a fully acceptable definition of the term 'operational research'. In essence, it is the application of mathematical principles to practical problems of decision-making. However, the term has come to be more widely used to cover a variety of advanced methods of calculation. Some of the techniques worth mentioning under the heading of sophisticated applications, either because they use complex mathematical procedures, or involve technical complications such as real-time response on the part of the computer, are:

Linear programming. This is a method of balancing a situation which depends on a number of different factors defined by linear equations (hence 'linear' programming), so as to deduce the most profitable or least costly strategy. Typical applications are the control of petroleum distillation, feed mix for livestock, least-cost methods of redistributing rolling-stock or lorries, and so on.

Traffic flow analysis. This is partly a statistical exercise, in the interpretation of road traffic surveys, and partly a computation or simulation exercise to deduce the implications of, say, proposed new roads, traffic lights, roundabouts, etc.

Route scheduling. This is the technique used to detect minimum cost routes for the distribution of goods from a warehouse to several outlets using a limited lorry fleet, or the setting up of bus timetables, and so on.

Inventory control. This is the automatic re-ordering of goods in a warehouse, factory or store based on statistical analysis of the sales pattern of each item, with the objective of minimising the amount of money tied up in inventory and minimising the inconvenience due to stock-outs.

Simulation techniques. These involve the construction of a mathematical model to represent the operation of some real process, and the exploration of different policies and their effect on the model to deduce what might happen in practice, without actually going to the expense or risk of trial and error in the real environment.

Seat reservation systems. These may be used for airlines, for example.

Process control, where the computer is directly altering control valves, and so on, as in oil refineries, steel works and the like.

Critical path analysis.

Management involvement

In computer applications, there are a number of trade-off situations which are properly the province of management decision, but which are often left to pass by default or left to the judgment of computer personnel. For example, there is a balance between the cost of setting up (programming) a computer application, and its eventual running cost. The major choice in this case is that of which computer language to use. There are a number of programming languages available for any given machine, which are more or less difficult to use. If one of the more difficult languages is chosen, it will, of course, take more time, and will cost more, for the computer department to set up the application; but the eventual usage of computer time when the system is in operation (the running cost) will be less. Conversely, the use of one of the easier languages will reduce the set-up cost and increase the running cost, both by causing slower execution of the job and by using a larger fraction of the computer's memory. (This last is significant in the case of large computers capable of carrying out many simultaneous tasks, providing that enough memory is available.)

Other trade-off situations occur between the speed of execution of a job and the amount of computer memory used, the simplicity of design of the system and its efficiency, and so on. In many cases these considerations are ignored in the interests of standardisation (say, on the use of one particular computer language for all applications), or through total priority being given to getting an application operational in the minimum time. Often the decision is taken which will minimise the effort of the computer department, which sometimes over-values the time of computer personnel relative to the cost of, say, computer time. There is always a temptation to measure the performance of the computer department in terms of the number of tasks made operational, rather than from the quality of the result, which is notoriously difficult to evaluate.

The management of computers

In contrast to the management problems in which the computer may be of use, one must consider the problems of management which the computer itself creates. How should the computing facilities of a company be organised, managed, costed; what are the advantages and relative costs of the alternative approaches?

The current computerised operations of a company will need a certain power of computing equipment, and will justify a certain expenditure in terms of machinery and personnel. Planned future operations will have similar figures associated with them. One must decide what can be done with advantage by a computer; how much it will cost to develop; how much it will cost to operate; what are the relative advantages over manual methods. These questions are often difficult to answer with any certainty, even for specialists in the field. Costs are frequently under-estimated. Savings are often badly estimated, particularly when they refer to economies due to staff reduction, which have been known not to materialise.

When considering a new application of computers, an organisation has two main problems. First, it may need to expand existing computer facilities. This may be done by obtaining additional equipment, by obtaining a terminal to a large machine, or by the use of outside service bureaux. Second, it may carry out the development of the new system by current personnel, by the use of programming consultants, or by the use of service bureaux.

In the case of a company with little or no previous experience of computer operations, it is often wise to implement the first few applications at an outside service bureau. This technique will allow the accumulation of experience of computers by personnel at all levels of the company without incurring the large capital cost of setting up an in-house operation. The costs will be known in advance, from the estimate received from the bureau, and it will be possible to measure the costs and advantages with reasonable accuracy when the job is running.

There are, of course, corresponding disadvantages. One would expect the cost of a bureau operation to be greater than the cost of one's own operation (assuming it to be reasonably efficient) because of the elimination of the profit factor. Also, the eventual transfer of the operation to in-house computing may be difficult because a different type of computer may be involved, or because different programming languages or techniques have been adopted. Further, the technical understanding of the system will be outside the company itself, which may make it difficult to alter and maintain the system once it has been transferred.

A similar approach with perhaps fewer disadvantages is to set up a small programming team within the organisation, which may become the nucleus of an eventual data processing department. The three or four people involved will be assigned the task of producing the first few systems, and will buy raw machine-time from a convenient bureau or bureaux. This will ensure that the relevant expertise is more likely to remain within the company, and that the only major cost will be that of the machine-time itself. This programming team can then be expanded step by step as further applications are set in motion; and the decision to buy one's own machine can be taken as soon as regular expenditure on bureau machine-time becomes a significant proportion of the cost of buying a suitable machine.

The advantages of an in-house machine will be a (presumably) lower unit cost of machine-time, the possibility of setting one's own priorities for machine usage (and hence faster turn-round of critical work) and the ability to attach special equipment to the machine, which may not have been available at the bureau.

An increasingly popular alternative to buying one's own machine is to buy a terminal to a large bureau's machine. This allows access to a large, fast computer at relatively low cost through local facilities. Current developments in data transmission make this a viable proposition, especially if some of the applications require or can use to advantage the large computer memory thus made available.

A large organisation may have an equivalent choice to make. It is possible to set up a large central computer, with terminals at each of the main locations, with a centralised computer department, or to have a number of smaller machines local to the individual operations; or, of course, one could use a combination of the two. The advantages of centralised operation, in terms of cost and central control must be balanced against the communication problems between remote users and the central department.

It is usually difficult for the user to communicate his requirements to the computer staff, and for computer staff lacking particular expertise in that area to understand fully such requirements, and to communicate back the possibilities and limitations inherent in the use of a computer for the application in question. The remoteness of a central department will not improve this situation. Even the avoidance of duplication of development effort implied by a central operation may be a mixed blessing. If several individual teams are working on the same problem in different locations, there is a chance that one of these teams will come up with a good solution, and proper liaison would ensure that this solution is adopted throughout the organisation.

Costing computer-time

There are two main financial approaches to the spreading of computer costs. One is to consider the computer department as an overhead, to be apportioned between functional departments, and the other is to charge an appropriate rate to each user for each job. The first approach has the advantage of simplicity. Internal charges for computer work will always balance exactly with costs. No effort will be wasted in internal accounting of the cost of each job between departments. Department managers will be less reluctant to use the available facilities, since they are paying for the computer anyway, and there will be no extra cost on their budget. The disadvantages are that little thought will be given to whether an application is suitable or economic, and there will be no incentive to keep the use of the computer efficient. Although it is an attractive concept to consider computing power available like tap-water, such an approach will encourage inefficiency and disproportionate expenditure on computing equipment.

Computers come in a wide range of sizes, speeds and prices. In general, a more expensive machine will be able to carry out a given job more quickly than a cheaper machine. This must be subject to the restriction that some kinds of calculation will be very cramped and difficult to carry out on the smaller equipment. On the other hand, a large machine may outrun its own input and output speeds, because it is capable of performing all the necessary calculations much faster than the time needed to read in the data or to print out the results. Thus, in a broad sense, the smaller machines are less suitable for scientific and engineering applications whilst the larger machines are probably less suitable for commercial use.

The cost of computer-time can vary between £10 and £1,000 per hour. In individual cases it is the cost performance obtainable for the particular range of jobs that becomes important. In other words, it is necessary to assess the amount of work performed for every pound spent. Some computer companies and bureaux are willing to provide free 'benchmark' tests that enable potential users or purchasers to make cost comparisons between different types of equipment or computer services.

The implementation of systems

Consider the various stages through which a computer application is implemented. The first stage is a definition of objectives by the ultimate user of the system. These objectives will be transmitted to a computer specialist who may or may not comprehend them. He will estimate the cost and difficulty of each major objective, and may suggest limitation of the objectives to those most adaptable to machine operation, and may also suggest expansions which can easily be achieved from the information storage implied by the initial set. He will then agree a general solution with the user, who may or may not understand the implications of this solution.

The specialist will explain his system to a technician or 'programmer', who may or may not understand the system. The programmer will then set up a series of instructions for the computer (which can be loosely thought of as explaining the system to the computer) to enable it to carry out the required processes. These instructions may or may not be accurate, and probably will not allow for a large variety of practical situations which were not envisaged at any of the stages set out above.

The system will be tested on sample information until many of the misunderstandings and omissions involved in the stages of communication have been rectified. The system can then be used in practice, and exceptional conditions which have not been allowed for will occur from time to time, and the system must be modified or expanded to cater for them. Finally the user (who may or may not wish to recognise his offspring), will decide whether the system meets his requirements and whether the associated running costs are acceptable, or whether the system should be abandoned altogether.

The time-scale of these processes may be anything from a few weeks to a few years, depending on the difficulty of the system, the skill of the personnel, and the extent of data-collection and organisational procedures associated with the system.

At the first stage, it may be that the computer specialist will recognise that the user's problem has been solved in a general way by a pre-written program package supplied by the computer manufacturer or by a software organisation. In this case, he will attempt to discover whether the user's requirements can be forced to fit within the limitations of the pre-written programs, and whether it is better to work within these limitations and buy the package, which will presumably be less costly than the development of a new system. He will also be interested in the operating cost and reliability of the package, and in maintenance conditions in case errors are discovered in it. He will also have to bear in mind the fact that the package will be difficult to modify in case the user's requirements change or expand. One advantage of a package program is that it will be available immediately, and experiments can be made with it to determine whether, in fact, it fits the problem closely enough to be practical.

Another alternative may be to have the system developed by a programming bureau, particularly if there is one which specialises in the application in question. This may have the disadvantage of lack of continuity and a high cost of subsequent modification of the system, although the same problem may occur in the company's own computer department if there is a high turnover of personnel.

The theoretical answer to these problems of continuity of knowledge of a system is good documentation of the techniques and methods used within the computer system. However, an adequate standard of such documentation is difficult to maintain, particularly in complex systems, and it is also costly.

Budgeting and control

Typically, the cost of a company's computer operation will be divided into three approximately equal sections. These comprise:

1 The cost of the hardware, that is, the computer itself and associated input and output devices.
2 The cost of the operational staff, data preparation, space taken up by the department, and other operating expenses, such as punched cards, paper, etc.
3 The cost of systems and programming.

This last item will itself be divided into two approximately equal sections; the cost of maintenance, keeping current applications running smoothly, making minor improvements and adjustments to adapt to changing external factors, such as tax rates, and other maintenance functions, and on the other hand the cost of developing new applications. This limited development budget applies to an area which can have the most significant effects on the whole organisation, and must therefore be used as wisely as possible.

The manager responsible for the computer effort of the company must therefore keep in mind the following questions: which areas of the operation of the company could provide the largest pay-off from computerisation; how much will the development of the relevant systems absorb of the development budget, and for how long; can the operations research function devise adequate techniques for the problem; will the appropriate user department or departments take advantage of the facilities once they have been provided; is the computer department capable of developing the application, and if so, is it capable of running it when it is developed?

The results of such an analysis may cause the manager to choose alternative applications, or to change some of the parameters mentioned above, possibly by starting a comprehensive education program in departments of high potential in order to familiarise them with computer concepts and make them more likely to accept an automated system. If such decisions are allowed to go by default, or are delegated to personnel with an insufficiently broad view of the total operations and potential benefits of the company, optimum results are unlikely to be achieved.

PART FOUR

Personnel, Human Relations and Training

Chapter 15

Manpower Planning

E S M Chadwick, Director, Technical and Management Consultants Limited

---

The need for companies to take a searching look at their future manpower requirements has become more and more evident, and manpower planning is more important for management than it has ever been. There are three main arguments in favour of manpower planning at the level of the firm. Firstly, there is considerable evidence to indicate that for some time to come there will be a shortage of quality manpower, particularly technological and scientific manpower, the demand for which is steadily increasing. Secondly, changes in manpower requirements in skill terms are likely to be much more rapid in the future than they have been in the past. No longer is a man able to learn a skill in his youth which will carry him through the whole of his working life; it is probable that the young, and the not so young man will have to change his skill once, or even twice, in the course of his working life. Thirdly, the ever-increasing costs of manpower. Demands for higher standards of living and increased leisure are tending to push these up at an even faster rate.

Assuming that the *average* stay in a company of a newly recruited graduate engineer is twelve years, and that such a recruit makes normal, but not exceptional, advancement; then the cost in salary alone over the twelve-year period is likely to be (on current values) of the order of £30,000. If, however, one adds on the other costs of staff-pensions, National Insurance payments, various fringe benefits, accommodation and office services, etc., then the total cost is of the order of £50,000.

No one contemplating the purchase of a piece of plant or equipment, with a similar life-span, costing that amount would do so without the most careful study of its suitability for the purpose for which it was intended, its capacity, the means by which that capacity could be utilised to the full, its place in the scheme of production, and the expected return on the investment. Few companies apply the same level of criteria or consideration to manpower. The reason for this difference in approach lies in the traditional attitude to manpower as a cost rather than as an investment. Yet while machinery depreciates and eventually becomes obsolete, properly developed manpower can continue to grow in usefulness and capacity.

The view that there is likely to be a shortage of quality staff over the longer term, or that one presently exists, is not universally shared. Some take the view that there is considerable under-use of talents and abilities, and that there is a large, as yet untapped, potential for the exercise of higher skills if only adequate training and education can be made available. This, in itself, is a very large subject. The objective of manpower planning is, and must be, to improve manpower utilisation and to ensure that there is available manpower of the right number and the right quality to meet the present and future needs of the organisation. It must, therefore, produce, *inter alia*, a realistic recruitment policy and plan and must be very much concerned with costs and productivity.

Role and content of manpower planning

Manpower planning has to reconcile two apparently different sets of views: those concerned with the accepted managerial yardsticks of costs, trends, projections, and so on, and those involved in the more traditional staff management approach of 'concern for individuals'. There are people, particularly in the older age groups who have long been concerned with personnel management, who see planning as a de-humanising process. In fact, the contrary is the case. These two viewpoints are not in opposition but complement each other. The really skilful manager is the man who is equipped to consider the immediate implication of an individual case in a long-term company and national context. Decisions and advice given after consideration of both short- and long-term factors is likely to be of more value both to the individual involved and to the management.

Manpower planning, in its broadest sense, covers all those activities traditionally associated with the management of personnel – records, recruitment, selection, training and development, appraisal, career planning, management succession, and so on. But it is important, both for analytical purposes and ultimately for executive purposes, to disentangle these activities and to think of them as a number of sequential phases. It has been found convenient to think of three main phases. These are illustrated in Figure 15:1. They are:

Phase 1: The development of manpower objectives. This is concerned with the development of forecasts of the manpower necessary to fulfil the company's *corporate* objectives; with looking at the totality of situations rather than at individuals. In this phase, analysis, forecasting and the setting of targets is carried out in terms of total numbers, skill groups, organisational groups, total costs, etc. It is concerned with detailed analysis in order to identify and foresee problem areas, to assess future demands and to establish how those demands may be met. It is directed towards the development of manpower *strategy* as an integral part of company strategy.

Phase 2: The management of manpower. In this phase, the question is one of managing manpower resources to meet objectives and the development, in more specific and individual terms, of recruitment plans, training and development plans, succession plans, appraisal systems, etc.

Phase 3: Control and evaluation. This concerns the continual evaluation and amendment of plans in the light of achievement and changing circumstances. Planning starts from a given factual position and tries to look ahead through a range of possibilities. Evaluation in this context means thoroughly checking forecasts and forecasting methods against what eventually happens, and making such revisions as may prove necessary. Any planning activity must have a system for this regular checking built into it. In other words, planning must be a continuing process.

The components of the second phase are fairly familiar in industry

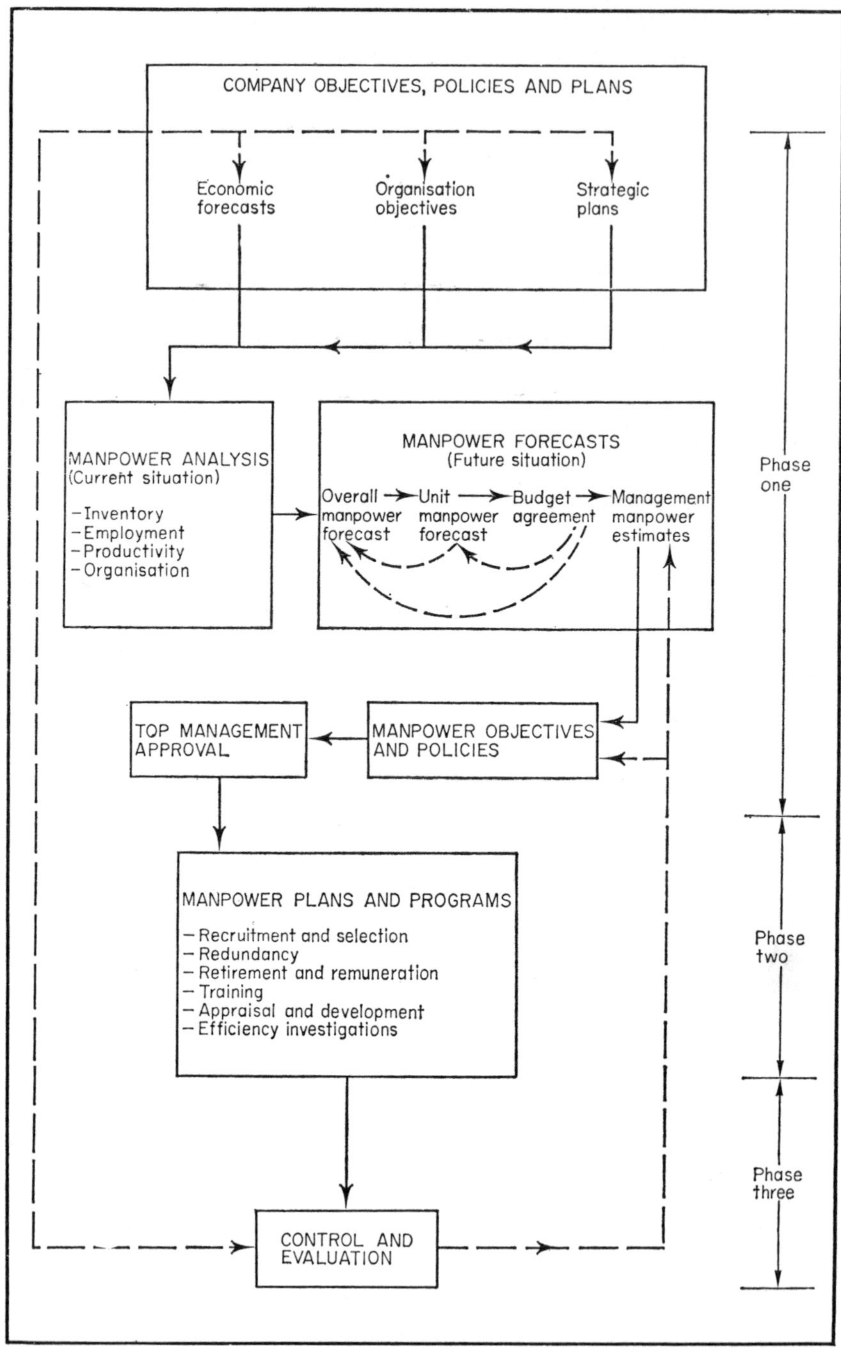

FIGURE 15:1 A PROCEDURE FOR MANPOWER PLANNING

Here, the three phases of manpower planning are shown in their logical sequence, together with the information feed-back loop which must result from the final phase of control and evaluation

and are often taken to be synonymous with manpower planning. They are a part, but not the whole. Phase 1, on the other hand, while obviously supplying the general context in which phase 2 must operate, is much less familiar and it is in this area that recent developments in thinking on manpower planning have occurred.

It is the ultimate aim of any complete system of manpower planning that all three phases should be fully integrated (see Figure 15:1). It is equally clear that manpower planning must be fully integrated with the company plan. Indeed, without a company plan, there can be no realistic manpower planning.

This chapter deals primarily with phase 1. Various aspects of phase 2 are dealt with in other chapters. It is essential that this first phase of manpower planning is well understood if the vital second phase is not to take on an atmosphere of uncertainty and become an operation entirely concerned with short-term tactics, without any particular strategy in mind. The equally vital, and again less familiar, third phase will also be discussed here.

Time-scale

How far ahead should one attempt to plan? Obviously, as one looks forward in time, forecasts become increasingly tentative. As a generalisation, one can say that the plan period should be that which, having regard to the particular circumstances of the time and the activity, will give the lead-time necessary to deal with most manpower situations. If, for example, the time between the decision to re-equip and the installation and operation of the new equipment is, say, two years, then one must look ahead at least that time to assess the manpower implications in terms of numbers and skills. If there is significant recruitment through apprenticeships whereby productive work is five years removed from recruitment, then for that category of employee one should look five years ahead. On the other hand, occasional operating or organisational situations can render some aspects of the future so unpredictable that, for the time being, planning in any detail has to be very short-term but even with such situations, the need for the development of a broad strategy remains.

It is also true that for some activities and for some individual career developments plans, five years can be a comparatively short period. Consequently, in some individual cases, a five-year planning period, although only possible to cover part of the plan concerning an individual, is a *practical* period for looking ahead in terms of the actual action contributing to the long-term aim.

Limitations of manpower planning

It is important to bear in mind what can reasonably be expected of planning. The aim is the reduction of uncertainty, but the possibility of doing this varies inversely with time. It must be appreciated that the forecasts covering the later years of the planning period are increasingly tentative. If may be more appropriate to think of the five-year period as comprising a two-year plan (a plan implying action), followed by a three-year forecast (indicating the broad path to be followed).

Manpower does not lend itself to precise measurement and docketing; it oftens behaves in a quite unpredictable way. The trading and technical situation is also fluid and targets and plans have often to be radically adjusted at short notice. Consequently, the manpower planning activity shares, in a particularly acute way, the essential characteristic of all planning in an uncertain world – it is a never-ending adjustment of expectations and aims to meet changing goals within a very uncertain environment. Its language and results will, of necessity, be probablistic in nature and will *not* be inflexible commitments to some postulated single course of events.

Above all, it is not a new and revolutionary approach to problems that have only recently been identified; much of it has long been common practice in many companies. What manpower planning, as here described, sets out to do is to bring these practices together into a systematic approach that directs attention to the future and to identification of potential but avoidable manpower problems.

This chapter sets out to describe a number of possible analytical approaches which have been found to be useful. But there is no single universally applicable *system* of manpower planning, though the concepts have been found to have general applicability. It is for each company to consider the various methods which seem appropriate to its own situation. The check-list given in Figure 15:2 may be helpful in identifying particular needs.

	Room for improvement	Adequate	Good — no weaknesses
1 Top management and organisational support for manpower plans and programs			
2 An adequate information system on manpower			
3 Anticipation of future manpower requirements			
4 Integration of manpower programs with overall company objectives			
5 Anticipation of organisational changes and preparing for their manpower implications			
6 Recruitment of necessary number of well-qualified staff at each level			
7 Effective placement of newly-engaged graduate/professional staff to make them productive			
8 Filling key middle and top management posts with well-qualified staff			
9 Management of age structure to minimise wastage problems and avoid promotion blockages			
10 Reducing wastage at all levels			
11 Providing significant jobs for managers throughout their career			

FIGURE 15:2 MANPOWER PLANNING CHECK-LIST

The purpose of this check-list is to evaluate the effectiveness of manpower planning in a company. It does not claim to cover every point of manpower management, but is a starting point for the development of an evaluation system related to the needs of a particular company. The aim is to help identify those areas where manpower management is underdeveloped and where further planning and development are needed

12 Evaluating the current performance of all staff			
13 Evaluating the potential of all staff for promotion and of managers for higher responsibilities			
14 Providing sound promotion and career opportunities for all staff with potential			
15 Motivating managers to develop their subordinates			
16 Development of managers for higher-level responsibilities			
17 Keeping the remuneration system up-to-date and effective as a motivator			
18 Investigation into the causes and solutions of serious manpower problems			
19 Measuring productivity improvements			
20 Maintenance of a system that enables the cost of manpower and its contribution to the company effort to be evaluated			
21 Maintenance of a comprehensive and systematic program of training to enable staff to adapt to new procedures and techniques and to equip them for higher responsibilities			
22 Maintenance of a sound and flexible organisation structure			
23 Integration of the manpower management program			

FIGURE 15:2 MANPOWER PLANNING CHECK-LIST continued

Analysis and forecasting

It is axiomatic that no forecast is any better than the data upon which it is based and the judgment of the forecaster. It follows that the first essential of any planning and forecasting is data and analysis of the data in order to reveal trends, changes that have taken place in company activities and objectives and their influence upon manpower requirements. Only then can one consider future changes in company objectives and their manpower implications.

Manpower data traditionally tends to be organised with the primary aim of supplying information on individuals. For planning purposes it is vital that such information should be organised in a manner which permits information to be easily available on groups, and in such a way that it can be sorted and arranged to illustrate not only the present position in any group or combination of groups, but also the changes that have taken place over time and to measure the trends that have become apparent. Various systems are available for this purpose from simple needle-sorting punch card systems up to computers. The decision as to which to use will depend on cost, facilities already available, the size of company, and so on.

The present position and the analysis of trends

In manpower planning there are three basic elements to be considered: the present stock of manpower; wastage; and future requirements for manpower. By a proper analysis of present manpower and wastage rates, for example, conclusions can be reached as to how much of the labour force will still be there in five or ten years' time. Figure 15:3 shows such an analysis and projection by age groups. Analysis should also be done by category, department, sex, etc.

The starting point of any plan (and any control system) must be a careful analysis of the position as it exists at the beginning of the planning period. Information will be needed in a series of permutations according to the needs of the company. The following are the basic 'building blocks' that will probably be needed in most circumstances:

1 Present total manpower.
2 Manpower resources by appropriate planning groups, for

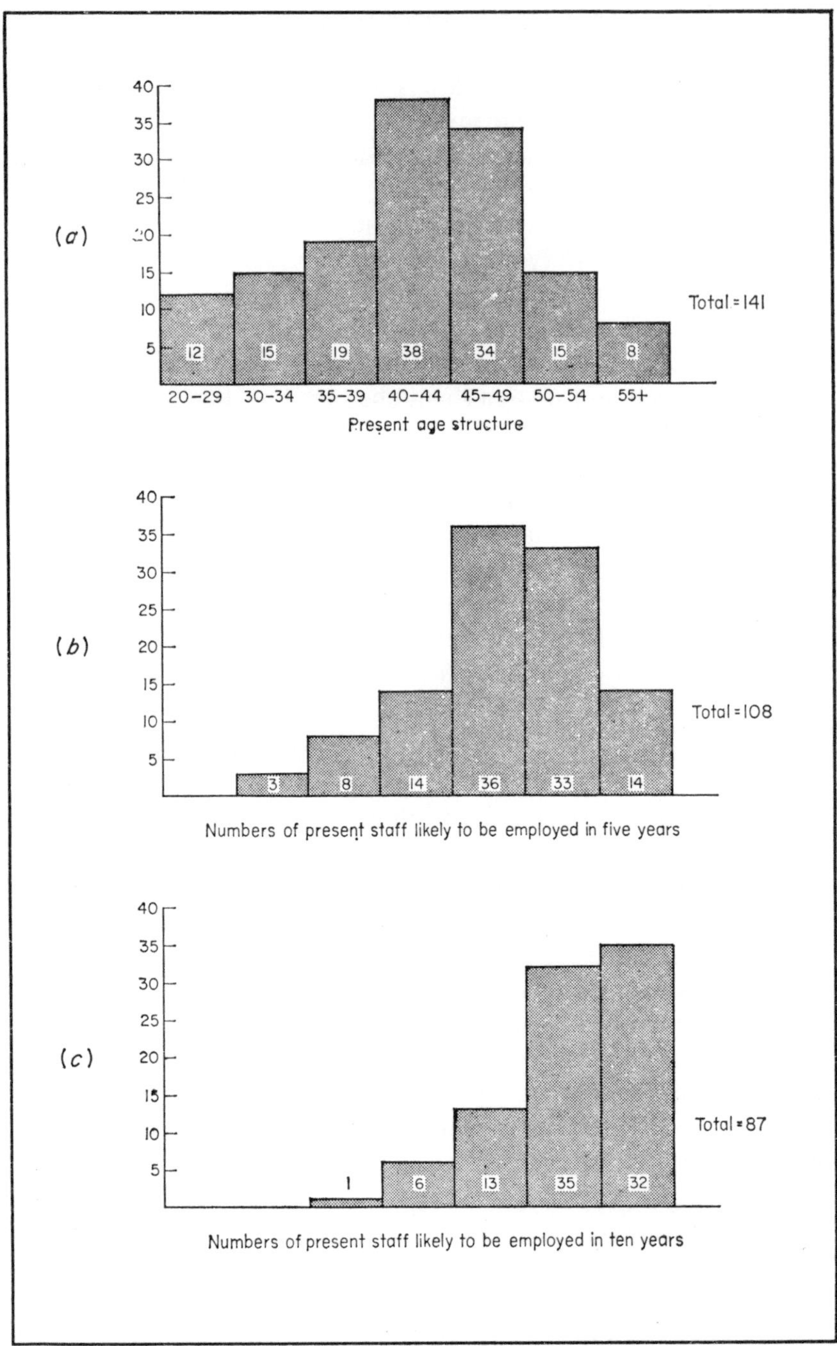

FIGURE 15:3 AGE ANALYSIS

The present age structure of a category of staff and projections showing the numbers retained and their age groupings in five and ten years' time

example, sex, grade, function/department, profession/skill, qualification, age group, and length of service.

3 Total manpower costs.
4 Total costs by appropriate component elements, for example, salaries, wages, pension contributions, welfare, canteen, etc.
5 Costs by functions/departments.
6 Costs indices and ratios (see control and evaluation below).
7 Total numbers related to sales, production, or such other criteria as may be appropriate, in physical and financial terms.
8 Attrition and retention rates by appropriate groups, that is, overall, by function/department, profession, sex, age group, etc.
9 Recruitment patterns by age, education, etc., for each function/department.
10 Resources of promotable staff.

The pampower pattern revealed by this analysis will be operating in a specific context and the manpower plan will have to keep this context in mind. Obviously a large number of subtle pressures will be at work and these pressures will vary from company to company. Many of them will not normally be of immediate day-to-day concern to management but they underline how important it is to keep informed. Among the questions to be borne in mind will be: the general position of the company in relation to national policies, both economic and social; the company's market share in relation to other companies; the position of the labour market for the various categories employed.

Forecasting future manpower requirements

Future manpower requirements are self-evidently governed by the company's corporate plan and they can only be considered in that context. Indeed, without a corporate plan there can be no realistic manpower plan. It follows that no forecast for the forward demand of manpower can be more precise than the formulation of the company's overall objectives. Clearly, it is also important that a company's objectives should be so stated as to be interpretable in terms of manpower involvement. The factors affecting manpower demand fall into two main groups: trading and production patterns, and

Estimates of staff numbers 1971-76

Functional sector ....

Department ....

			Increases and decreases in requirements and year end balances				
Categories of staff	Actual number at time of estimate	Expected number at year end 1970	Estimated		Forecast		
			1971	1972	1973	1974	1975
			– + =	– + =	– + =	– + =	– + =
Totals							

Brief statement of reasons for increases and/or decreases:

Signed __________________
Departmental Manager Date __________

Signed __________________ Date __________
General Manager

FIGURE 15:4 MANPOWER FORECAST SHEET

A method of collecting information on anticipated manpower changes

	Manpower age brackets								
	20-24	25-29	30-34	35-39	40-44	45-49	50-54	55-59	TOTAL
A Present strength	12	31	28	55	33	29	19	23	230
B Anticipated intake for 5 years	21	30	9						60
C Average retention rate (percentage)	92	94	95.5	97.5	99	99	97.5	87.5	-
D Anticipated retention of present employees after 5 years	8	23	23	50	31	27	14	-	176
	↘	↘	↘	↘	↘	↘	↘		
E Corrected age brackets for retained employees	0	8	23	23	50	31	27	14	176
F Anticipated retention of intake after 5 years	11	24	16	3					54
G Forecast strength in 5 years	11	32	39	26	50	31	27	14	230
H Net change after 5 years	-1	+1	+11	-29	+17	+2	+8	-9	0

FIGURE 15:5 DERIVATION OF THE QUANTITATIVE FIVE-YEAR FORECAST FOR A FUNCTION

This forecast is on the basis of nil expansion and present recruitment and wastage patterns

technological change. Some indication of the extent to which volume and patterns of trade, and technological change affect manpower will have been gathered from the analyses which have been described in previous paragraphs.

The method of calculating actual manpower needs against stated work targets, as indicated from the corporate plan, will depend on the type of manpower in question. On the shop floor it may be a matter of simple output volume to manpower relationships, with due allowances for technological developments. At the higher levels, ratios of manpower to volume of work are less likely to be valid, and it then becomes necessary to define the form of future management roles.

A means by which this sort of information can be gathered is given in Figure 15:4. It is emphasised than any changes from the present position have to be substantiated.

Information, estimates and forecasts so gathered need to be carefully analysed and evaluated in a variety of ways. An example of one such analysis and a method of its presentation is given in Figure 15:5. This shows the present strength by age groups, the retention rate over the next five years, anticipated recruitment and the forecast strength by the age groupings then applicable. For the purpose of this example, it has been assumed that there will be no expansion (or contraction) of numbers and that present recruitment and wastage patterns will continue. Should any of these three factors change, or be changed, only the arithmetic would need amendment, the principle remains.

It is not enough, however, just to build up manpower requirements in this way and to accept the present position as satisfactory. Indeed, the very act of collecting and analysing information in the way that has been described tends to raise questions. Does one really need so many laboratory technicians, or engineers, or chemists? Could one do as well with fewer highly-qualified staff and more support staff? Such questions may well make the planner go back and look again at some of the estimates for parts of the organisation and review them in the light of what has been found.

Nor should one merely equate supply and demand. To do so will only perpetuate the misuse or under-use of manpower, where it exists. It is, therefore, essential that the manpower planning activity goes hand-in-hand with productivity studies and other studies of manpower utilisation. One needs also to give particular consideration to the composition of the overall manpower profile, the proportions of

Grade group	Existing jobs at year-end 1971	Vacancies arising due to					Possibilities to fill vacancies			Surplus of promotable staff
		Retirement	Promotion	Wastage	New jobs by year-end 1973	Total	Promotion	Recruitment	Total	
Male										
A										
B										
C										
D										
Total										
Female										
C										
D										
Total										

FIGURE 15:6 RECRUITMENT TARGETS 1972, 1973

Analysis of recruitment needs by grade level. Numbers and definitions of levels would depend on particular company organisation. A form of staff appraisal, such as forms part of phase 2 of manpower planning would be essential to arrive at a realistic assessment of promotable staff various levels of skills in each of the main employment categories.

Out of these studies, and analyses, one is able to build up realistic recruitment targets (Figure 15:6). This shows the expected vacancies arising over the next two years by grade level from retirement, wastage and additional jobs, and how it is expected they can be filled, that is by promotion or recruitment. In the case of recruitment, a further analysis by age group, as shown in Figure 15:5, is necessary.

What has been said up to now has been concerned with the medium-term demand for manpower. The longer-term picture must also be kept in mind, even though this may have no immediate influence. The factors here include the local and national environment, the size and shape of the firm in fifteen to twenty years time, its share of the market, what the market will be, demographic projections and the rate of technological change.

Equally, one must look at the supply position. It is no good setting requirements that cannot be met. A study of the availability of the different types of manpower will be needed. The ability of the industry and the firm itself to attract recruits must also be considered. This is true of both the short and longer term.

The question of supply is not nearly so difficult as it might at first seem. All the manpower that can enter into planning studies over the time-scale is already in existence; it is simply a matter of finding out where it is and what will be done with it in terms of education. The

Year	Total UK working population (000s)	Year	Total UK working population (000s)
1967	26 196	1973	26 168
1968	26 204	1974	25 979
1969	26 206	1975	26 049
1970	26 196	1976	26 144
1971	26 203	1977	26 284
1972	26 201	1978	27 023

FIGURE 15:7 FORWARD PROJECTIONS OF THE WORKING POPULATION OF THE UK, 1967–1981

These forecasts were prepared by the Department of Employment and Productivity

numbers and subjects of study in the top classes of education are known and since, of all things, the education system is slowest to change, reasonable forecasts can be made. Obviously, the size of the total working population has some bearing on this (Figure 15:7).

It will be seen in Figure 15:7 that, up to 1974 when there is a marked fall due to the raising of the school leaving age, the numbers are very consistent. The present level is not expected to be regained thereafter until 1977. From this, it is apparent that, in a period which will see great emphasis on increasing output to restore the country's economic fortunes, manpower is going to be extremely limited.

But as important, if not more important than the mere numbers, is the matter of quality and the ability of the educational system, and industrial training in its many forms, to provide the skills which will be required as a result of changing technology. The problem of manpower obsolescence at all levels is real and urgent. A high proportion, it may be as much as fifty per cent, of a company's present manpower may still be in its employment fifteen years from now (see Figure 15:3). Will they have the knowledge and skills which will then be required of them? Manpower planning has thrown up the need for some form of occupational/skill classification which can be used to indicate the changing pattern of skill requirements and the changing manpower profile.

Projections

What has been discussed up to this point is the assessment of manpower needs to meet task objectives, the supply of manpower and environmental influences and constraints. Another aspect of manpower planning is the use of mathematically based prediction techniques to detect trends, to assist in policy decisions to indicate the futurity in present courses of action, to assess the probable future consequences of alternative possibilities. They have been found to be particularly useful in examining wastage – a whole subject in its own right – and the development of balanced recruitment policies directed towards a stable age structure.

These projections are not an alternative to managerial manpower forecasting such as has been discussed but are supplementary to it. They are generally only applicable in larger companies but the approach, if not the mathematics, can be used universally.

For the purposes of projections, the basic need is for a bank of historical data over a minimum of five years. From such a store of information, it is possible to extract such essential factors as turnover rates in whatever category is required, related to age and/or length of service, movements within or between categories, the probability of promotion between grades as related to age, length of service, and qualifications. By this means one is able to gain insights into, and an understanding of, situations and the relationships which brought them about; to isolate problem areas, present or future, and the action needed for their solution. By establishing this picture of how the system has worked, it also becomes possible to consider projections of the future to assist in policy decisions by indicating the probable future consequences in alternative courses of action. There is, of course, no method of establishing a staff position which, in five years time, will *inevitably* be achieved; decisions can, however, be made which will, in all probability, approximate to that position. The aim is to examine a variety of trends and see whether the projected position achieved by these trends is satisfactory or not. The *executive decision* lies in deciding what position is desirable, what trend produces this position, and what action, if any, is necessary in order to produce that trend.

This method of approach, which is the one that appears most to engender distrust or, perhaps, fear of manpower planning as it has developed, has the object of attempting to see a problem as it really is, not what people think it is. In order to take a decision, one must have solved a problem, and to do that one must see the problem as it really is.

It is a matter of making logical deductions in relation to a situation in which some, at least, of the elements have been measured. Logical analysis of this type of situation cannot be taken very far before running into mathematics. The choice is therefore either to go into the mathematics or to stop the logic short at that point. Everything depends on how much analysis is needed to solve the problem. If logic stops short, the chances are that the problem has not been solved and the decision is, therefore, likely to be wrong, and the consequences that flow from it are not those that were being aimed at.

The choice is not between something simple and good and something difficult and not to be trusted, but between something which gives the right (or best available) answer and something based on intuition and guesswork, the consequences of which cannot be foreseen.

Control and evaluation

Two broad and complementary approaches to the control and evaluation of the manpower plan are necessary, one in terms of numerical trends and the other in terms of costs and costs criteria.

Assuming that the planning period is five years, then the plan prepared in 1971 would go through to the end of 1976. In the autumn of 1972, the plan should have been reviewed and up-dated where necessary and extended to include 1977. The first step is, as has been stated, the review and up-dating of the corporate plan. This normally takes the form of a package of expectations and objectives, all of which are considered mutually consistent and feasible. The strategy for achieving these objectives determines the form of organisation to be used and the amount and form of resources required, including manpower.

In this review, management will want to question the degree to which the various specific goals of the manpower plan were achieved. This can be shown by the use of a number of numerical controls and gauges, such as changes in numbers by total/department/function, changes in wastage (turnover) rates and the reasons for wastage, changing age structures and their implications, all related to the original targets set.

Another approach which has been found useful in giving a comparative picture of the contribution being made by personnel to the operation of the company is the development of cost ratios.

The concept of productivity is very complex in practice and raises considerable theoretical questions of definition and data. Nevertheless, a number of simple indices can be used to illustrate the changing contribution and costs of manpower. It should be emphasised, however, that these give no more than a 'broad-brush' view and should be treated with caution, particularly in making any sort of comparison between one function and another and, more particularly, between different companies. Reliance on a single index could itself be misleading but, taken together, they can give an indication of trends and the movement of manpower costs related to company activities as a whole (Figure 15:8).

Year	Present	1972	1973	1974	1975	1975
Sales index-units	100					
Production index	100					
Sales proceeds index	100					
Manpower costs index	100					
Staff costs per sales or prod-units	100					
Total staff costs / Total operation cost	100					

FIGURE 15:8 INDEX APPROACH FOR ASSESSING TRENDS IN CONTRIBUTION MADE BY MANPOWER

Indices which, together, may be used to give a view of trends and the changing contribution and costs of manpower

Conclusion

The need to plan manpower as one does other resources has only recently been recognised, yet it is true to say that the prosperity and growth of any company rests, in the end, on the quality of its manpower and the extent to which their talents and abilities are utilised to the full.

Manpower planning is concerned with safeguarding the future, with preventing the loss of opportunities through lack of appropriate human abilities and the wastefulness of 'over-braining' the organisation. It emphasises the need for rationalisation in keeping with modern needs and technological capabilities and the development of organisation structures to match.

It is not some separate, rather esoteric, activity carried on by a few people in back rooms in large companies. It is, or should be, part of the normal conduct of business which can, and has been, successfully and advantageously practised in a wide range of companies in size, background and activity.

At the beginning it can appear to be a large and somewhat daunting task; it certainly needs perseverance and determination to achieve results. It is something which is best learned by doing. It is better to start simply, linking planning with an existing system, such as annual budgeting, and building from there.

Further reading

1 E S M Chadwick, Integrating Enterprise Manpower Planning with External Manpower Planning and Programmes, O E C D 1970.
2 E S M Chadwick and R H E Duffett, Model Building in Manpower Planning and Staff Management, in *Mathematical Model Building in Economics and Industry*, Charles Griffin and Co Ltd, 1970.
3 E S M Chadwick, E K Ferguson and R H E Duffett, A Guide to Manpower Planning, a British Petroleum Company private publication, 1969.
4 John R Hinricks, High Talent Personnel – Managing a Critical Resource, American Management Association, 1966.
5 A Young and G Almond, Predicting Distributions of Staff, *Computer Journal* 3, 246–250.

Chapter 16

Recruitment and Selection

F A Sneath, Lecturer, Department of Occupational Psychology, Birkbeck College, University of London

---

Manpower is often a firm's most important asset, and it is becoming increasingly costly. Firms need to pay attention to the quality of new staff recruited, and of supervisors and managers selected from existing staff. Recruitment and selection aim to obtain the right man for a particular job, at a reasonable cost. The cost will vary with the importance of the job. To engage a stores labourer who turns out to be clumsy in handling goods may be an embarrassment. To promote the wrong man as sales director may be a disaster.

Selection is concerned both with finding a man who can do a particular job satisfactorily, and with his satisfaction – his willingness to do the job to the standard required. In a broader sense, it is concerned with what the man can contribute to the firm's efficiency, and how the firm can help him to develop as a person in a worthwhile job.

Main steps

The manager concerned must first establish that the firm needs, and can afford, to fill the vacancy or create a new post. The firm must then describe the job and the person needed to do it, contact sufficient candidates, and assess their ability and their willingness to do the job. For the best results, a systematic procedure, as set out below, is recommended. Some of the steps may be omitted or modified.

Step 1: Indentifying the job requirements
1 Consider the job in its context
2 Prepare or revise the job specification
Step 2: Reaching candidates
1 Draft an advertisement or notification about the vacancy
2 Contact applicants through employment agencies or direct
3 Provide applicants with details about the job and the firm, and with application forms
Step 3: Assessing candidates
1 Prepare a short-list of candidates and explore their backgrounds
2 Apply assessment devices of known usefulness
3 Interview the short-listed candidates
4 Reach a decision and notify the candidates and others concerned
Step 4: Installing the new entrant
1 Arrange for a medical examination
2 Provide suitable induction training
Step 5: Follow-up
Keep records of the selection, training and progress of entrants.

Usually the personnel department, co-operating with the department concerned, will be responsible for most steps except the final decision. In small firms the line manager may find himself responsible for many of them. How far these steps are carried out, and in what order, depends on such points as these:

1 What is the type of job? production, marketing, office services?
2 What is the level of job? unskilled, semi-skilled, technical, clerical, professional?
3 Do several vacancies exist for the same type of job? Are related jobs to be filled from the same group of applicants?
4 Will formal training be given (for example, apprenticeships), or will training be on the job? What degree of experience is needed?
5 Are candidates to be chosen with a view to later promotion?

The cost of the steps must be considered. They include advertising, and paying candidates' fares and expenses, but also the cost of using outside agencies, and of staff time and energy. Grouping similar jobs together for recruitment allows the most effective and economical allocation of suitable candidates to the jobs available. Clerical staff may be recruited centrally for all departments, for example. Again, some firms give all their engineering apprentices a common first-year course, and their final placement depends on their performance in various departments, and their interests.

Identifying job requirements through job analysis

Job analysis is central to successful selection, as it may be to other management functions described in this book – effective training, fair payment systems, or organisation and methods. Job analysis needs close co-operation between the personnel department and the line managers concerned. The methods used may include doing or observing the job, and discussing it with workers and supervisors. Job analysis should establish those characteristics which separate successful from less successful workers. It is often easier to identify reasons for failure than reasons for success. Job analysis should therefore focus on common reasons for unsatisfactory performance by workers in their training or on the job. Certain tasks or parts of the job may be frequent stumbling blocks, which many workers find difficult or take a long time to master. Similarly, certain physical or social conditions of work may cause discontent, such as excessive noise, dirt, danger, close supervision or isolation. If such conditions cannot easily be remedied, there is little point in recruiting staff who will not tolerate them for long.

Job analysis results in a job description, which should be in specific terms, and pay attention to common difficulties and distastes met by workers on the job. Most firms hope to recruit hard-working, loyal and responsible staff; but the job description has to answer the question 'responsible for what?' Routine duties and responsibilities need to be distinguished from occasional or emergency ones.

The seven point plan

To the job description will be added the personal requirements of the job, as far as they are known or can be inferred. These requirements should be listed in a systematic way. One such system, widely used in selection and allocation, is the Seven Point Plan devised by Professor Alec Rodger of Birkbeck College[1]. This covers:

1 Physical requirements of the job, for example, robustness, normal vision or hearing; freedom from particular complaints; agreeableness of appearance, bearing and speech.
2 Educational and occupational attainments normally needed for entry, and for advancement.
3 Range of intelligence needed for the job, often expressed broadly in terms of general level of education.
4 Specialised aptitudes which may be useful, such as manual dexterity, mechanical aptitude, facility with words or figures.
5 Job or leisure interests which may be an advantage; for example, interest in reading or studying, practical things, outdoor activities, dealing with or helping other people, or artistic activities.
6 Qualities of disposition which are desirable, such as acceptability to others, leadership, dependability, self-reliance.
7 Any special circumstances of the job, such as mobility.

It is important to distinguish requirements which are *essential* to do the job properly or cope with the training needed from qualities which are merely *desirable*. To set standards of physical fitness or education too high is to rule out applicants who may be well qualified otherwise.

Job requirements may vary, and should be kept under constant review. When local labour is in short supply, the firm may have to lower its standards, rather than raise its pay rates or advertise more widely. The demands of a changing technology, the introduction of a new process, or newly created channels of promotion, may each alter the job requirements.

The final working document of the selector is the *job specification*. This includes the job description, the job requirements, and the benefits and rewards of the job – not only rates of pay, but such things as fringe benefits and promotion prospects. There is also the 'context' of the job, how it fits in with other jobs, how far sideways transfer is possible, and so on.

Occasionally a firm job specification cannot be drawn up. The job may be new. At senior levels, the way the job develops may depend on the man finally chosen to take it. For example, the head of production may need freedom to develop and organise his department. Even then, the selector should try to forecast the type of person required, or draw up alternative specifications which are equally acceptable.

Reaching candidates

The vacancy needs to be made known to possible applicants. A source of applicants may already exist, amongst former workers who might return, or candidates for previous vacancies. People may have inquired about jobs on the off-chance, especially if they have friends or relatives working in the firm. For supervisory jobs, the firm may wish to promote internally, rather than advertise outside.

Lower levels of jobs may be filled by local advertising. For skilled or highly-qualified staff, regional or national advertising may be needed. In drafting the advertisement, the aim is to attract enough applicants to allow the firm some freedom of choice, but not too many. Attractive features of the job will be mentioned, but lavish promises of high earnings or rapid promotion are unwise. Indeed, essential requirements which might deter some applicants (such as occasional week-end work) may need mentioning.

Sometimes firms need to use box numbers for particular vacancies. This is cheaper than display advertising, and may be adequate for lowly skilled jobs. For other jobs a firm may not want to publicise its vacancies or pay scales. But generally the firm's reputation will be enhanced by appropriate and well-designed advertising.

Employment agencies

Employment agencies can be a useful source of applicants. The public agencies are those of the Department of Employment and the Youth Employment Service. The Department of Employment can supply adult candidates for all levels of job. Up to the skilled level these will usually be unemployed people seeking work. Through the Professional and Executive Register, the Department covers higher staff levels, including those who are unemployed and those who may be thinking about changing their jobs. A special section deals with the rehabilitation, training and employment of the disabled. The Youth Employment Service advises and places young school leavers and those at work under the age of eighteen. It can be particularly useful in recruiting for craft apprenticeships.

Private employment agencies are widely used for female clerical staff (both permanent and temporary). Some may specialise in other groups, such as accounting, sales and computer staff.

For jobs requiring professionally qualified young men and women or graduates, firms may contact colleges of technology, polytechnics and university appointments boards. There are placement services for some special groups, such as ex-servicemen, ex-prisoners and others. Some trade unions keep registers of members seeking work.

When the firm has contacted a sufficient number of applicants, it can send out application forms and details about the job. The application form should be clear and easy to fill in. It should cover personal particulars, education and job record, and other points if they can be conveniently included and are relevant to success in the job or the firm. The design of the form may vary with the type or level of job, but in any case it should give enough space for selectors to make notes about the candidates.

The letter giving details of the job will be based on the job specification. As in the advertisement, unattractive but essential features of the job need not be omitted, since they will discourage casual applicants from going further.

Assessing candidates

Completed application forms, when they are received, can be sorted into three groups. Outsiders, who are well below the minimum requirements or otherwise quite unsuitable, should be informed of their rejection immediately. Likely candidates who seem well up to standard can be invited to interview. In between is the third group, consisting of those who do not quite meet the specified requirements but may have other advantages (such as wider experience than would be expected). Whether the short-list to be drawn up includes the borderline candidates as well as the best group depends on the numbers coming forward. For a single post, not more than half-a-dozen candidates would usually be seen. For several vacancies, the short-list is usually up to three or four times as long as the number of vacancies, except in times of extreme shortage of labour.

Selectors should guard against reading too much into the application forms. Some candidates may be too well qualified for the job, and may not stay long in it. Others may be able to produce impressive paper qualifications and experience which are exaggerated. At this stage, therefore, the firm can explore the background of the short-listed candidates, by taking up references from schools, colleges or employers. Many applicants, however, will not wish their present employers to be approached unless they are to be offered a post.

When inviting references from schools or employers, the firm should preferably ask them to cover specific points. For important jobs, a summary of the job description may be enclosed. Confidential information may be obtained or amplified by telephone. The value of a reference depends on how well the referee has known the candidate, and whether he is willing, and able, to report frankly on his behaviour and attitudes. Selectors can seldom check on these conditions unless they already know and trust the referee. The 'open reference' produced by many candidates and addressed 'to whom it may concern' usually consists of vague or useless generalities.

Assessment methods

Apart from the interview (considered below), assessment methods include selection tests, questionnaires about interests or qualities of disposition, and group exercises. A selection test is a standard task or set of problems, given in the same way to all candidates, and marked under an objective scheme. Such tests may be paper-and-pencil tests of intelligence, or of attainment and knowledge. Others may be practical, like tests of dexterity, or 'job samples' like tests of typing speed and accuracy.

Tests can play a useful but limited part in selection and allocation schemes, if they can be shown to be relevant to important job requirements, or to predict later success or progress on the job. There is very little evidence for the value of so-called 'personality inventories' in most selection situations. However, group discussions or similar exercises with groups of candidates can sometimes give useful clues about individual members to experienced observers.

Using tests presents many difficulties. Staff need training and supervision to administer the tests, so that every candidate has a fair chance to work at his best. Interpreting the test results needs care, especially if the candidates come from widely differing educational and social backgrounds. Many tests are only supplied when they are to be used by psychologists or under their direct supervision. Any firm wishing to introduce tests should get in touch with experts in this field – reputable occupational psychologists[2] or a leading test agency[3].

The interview

The interview is by far the most common method of assessment. It is flexible, relatively cheap, and acceptable to candidates and to management. But interviewers who are inexperienced or careless can often reach wrong decisions about candidates. To be effective, the interview needs care and preparation. Selection interviews may be an important part of a line manager's job, if only occasionally.

The purposes of the selection interview are:

1 To check and amplify the available information about the candidate.
2 To assess how far his capacities and previous experience meet the present and future requirements of the job and the firm.
3 To get some idea of his social skills and motivation, and how well he will fit in with his future colleagues.
4 To inform him about the firm, the job, and future developments.
5 To develop and maintain good relations between the firm and the candidate.

In addition, if the candidate is promising and may receive offers from other employers, the interview may be used to 'sell' the job to the candidate.

To carry out these aims effectively and fairly with all candidates, the interviewer needs a clear idea of what he wants to find out, and of how his interview fits in with other parts of the selection procedure.

The interviewer should study all the available information about the candidates, in conjunction with the job specification. He can then decide what he needs to explore, and note any unexplained gaps or inconsistencies for tactful probing. He should prepare himself to answer questions which candidates may ask about the job or the firm.

Interviews should be planned ahead so that candidates are given ample notice. The length of each interview will vary according to the level of job. It is difficult to achieve much in less than twenty minutes, and for important appointments an hour or more may be needed. Timetabling the interviews should allow for writing up notes (and discussions with colleagues if necessary) at the end of each interview. Suitable arrangements should be made for the reception of candidates. The interviews themselves should preferably be uninterrupted and in a comfortable setting.

The interviewer can usefully start by introducing himself and his position or function. Some candidates may not know what to expect, and the interviewer can outline what he hopes to cover. From the start his manner should be friendly and business-like, and he should show an interest in what the candidate has to say. He should encourage the candidate to talk about his strengths; but he should not be afraid to explore any less good points in a tactful way. In doing so, he is comparing the candidate both with the job specification and with the other candidates, so that they can all be rated for suitability or arranged in order of merit.

The interviewer should keep to some system, such as the Seven Point Plan referred to earlier. He need not ask all the candidates the same questions, but should aim to deal with the important topics in a methodical and comprehensive way.

The early stages of the interview often cover the candidate's job record, and particularly his most recent job. The interviewer needs to discover the actual responsibilities of the candidate's most recent (or present) job and how well he has coped with them. Relevant experience and past performance are likely to be good guides to future behaviour in the job. These will not be available for young people starting work for the first time; and for them their schooling and any part-time or holiday jobs should be explored. The interviewer will need to cover the training and qualifications of candidates at the skilled or professional level.

Early family history may sometimes be relevant. For example, a man who had to leave school early and gained qualifications by part-time study may have shown unusual determination. Present family background may be touched on, if it is essential to the job (which might call for shift-work or much travelling); but personal matters should not be probed too far. However, the candidate's plans for the future and his reasons for applying for the job are relevant questions. It is worth asking him what he hopes to get out of the job, and to contribute to the job and the firm.

The interviewer can also tell the candidate about job prospects and the people with whom he would be expected to work. He can be shown how the job fits into the department and the firm. Any questions about training facilities, or prospects of promotion or transfer, should be dealt with frankly, since at this stage the firm is also being assessed by the candidate, as well as the other way round.

Towards the end of the interview, the interviewer can sum up briefly, and invite the candidate to raise any final questions or clear up doubts. Often the interviewer will not be in a position to tell the candidate whether he has been successful; but at any rate he should say what the next step will be.

In all but the shortest interviews, the interviewer will need to take notes of the main points discussed, without holding up the interview. Brief notes can be made on the application form or on an interview record form with appropriate headings, to be written up afterwards.

Board interviews or interviewing panels are sometimes used for selection or promotion at more senior levels. This may be for administrative reasons rather than for efficient selection as such, so that the interests of several departments are represented. For the most senior appointments, the full board of directors may wish to see the short-listed candidates, since the board is responsible for the efficiency of the firm. Here the personnel department and the manager most closely concerned with the job may have done much of the work beforehand following detailed interviews, and may have drawn up an order of preference.

If the panel is to do more than approve previous suggestions, it will function best if it contains not more than three or four people. Each member needs to brief himself about the job specification and the candidates. Members need also to agree their selection standards, and to divide up the areas to be discussed with candidates according to their own backgrounds and functions.

Common weaknesses of untrained interviewers (whether working individually or on a panel) include the following:

1 Lack of preparation or system.
2 Talking too much or off the point.
3 Not listening to what the candidate is saying.
4 Jumping to unjustified conclusions.
5 Asking 'leading questions' which strongly suggests the answer expected (for example, 'I suppose you got on really well with your boss, did you?').
6 Asking 'closed questions' which can be answered 'yes' or 'no'.

The interviewer should distrust his 'intuitions' until he has collected evidence to back them up. He may favour – or dislike – people with red hair or a Scottish accent. A candidate may remind him of someone who had previously done very well or particularly badly in the firm. He should be aware of such possible biases. There are several books available which will help the inexperienced interviewer to improve his performance[4].

The final stages

The final decision about candidates will be made either by the line manager concerned, or in discussion with the personnel department. The successful candidate should be notified as soon as possible. Any strong runners-up may not be contacted till later, since the man selected may decline the offer. Some candidates may be given conditional offers, subject to passing an examination or completing a course. The unsuccessful candidates will be sent a courteous letter of rejection

Firms' pension schemes usually require a medical examination for the successful candidate. If physical health or freedom from certain defects is important in a particular job, a medical examination will be arranged for all short-listed candidates.

Selection does not end with recruitment. Selectors should keep in touch with the arrangements for induction and training, which may need adapting for the successful candidate. Still more important, they should follow up the progress of the candidate in the job, so that they can check their own effectiveness and keep their procedures up-to-date.

The use of consultants

A wide service is offered by selection and recruitment consultants. They may offer the following services:

1 Producing and checking job specifications
2 Drafting and placing advertisements
3 Appraising the replies and advising on a short-list
4 Applying selection tests and carrying out preliminary interviews

Some consultants also maintain a register of well-qualified candidates, and may be prepared to seek out men with specialist experience who could be persuaded to apply. They may also offer other management services.

There are several advantages in using consultants. They have resources and expertise not often available in small firms. They can preserve confidentiality both for the firm and the candidates. Well-qualified outsiders are able to compete on equal terms with staff inside the firm. It is often helpful for a knowledgeable person from outside to check the job specification for new or senior posts, or to assess candidates with unusual technical qualifications. Consultants can save time and effort. They cope promptly and smoothly with administrative problems concerned with inquiries and short-lists.

The firm, however, must allow the consultants some freedom to explore widely around the job itself, to study other people who would be working with the new man, and to understand the atmosphere of the department and the firm. Some firms will want the type of man who will fit in comfortably with their traditions and their outlook. Other firms may employ consultants to bring in 'fresh blood', and to challenge accepted practices and ideas.

The smaller firm may sometimes wish for advice on recruitment and selection generally, rather than on filling a particular post. The British Institute of Management, the Institute of Personnel Management, and the Industrial Society can provide details of training courses and selection methods. Departments of management and business studies in polytechnics and colleges of technology have staff available to give advice. There are also the advisory services of the Department of Employment and the Industrial Training Boards. Finally, a comprehensive and up-to-date survey of recruitment principles and practices is contained in the *Recruitment Handbook* edited by Bernard Ungerson (1970), and published by the Gower Press.

References

1 *The Seven Point Plan* by A Rodger, National Institute of Industrial Psychology, 1970.
2 The British Psychological Society, 18–19 Albemarle Street, London W1X 4DN, can put inquirers in touch with suitable advisers.
3 The National Institute of Industrial Psychology, 14 Welbeck Street, London W1M 8DR and the National Foundation for Educational Research, The Mere, Upton Park, Slough, Bucks., are two examples.
4 For example: *The Skills of Interviewing* by E Sidney and M Brown, Tavistock Publications, 1961; and *Assessment through Interviewing* by G Shouksmith, Pergamon Press, 1968.

Chapter 17

Payment Structures and Incentives

G L Buckingham, General Manager, Personnel, Gallaher Limited; Director, North, Paul and Associates Limited

---

Although many systematic examinations of people's motives for working have revealed that pay is not the primary motivating factor for many of them, it is both the source and the symbol of much of the conflict in our industrial society. The profit motive does not only apply to the business; it is considered to be the reason why men and women work in our increasingly materialistic society.

Whatever its motivating effect, the employee's wage or salary is his livelihood, his means of maintaining and, wherever possible, of improving his standard of living. In addition, pay is an important symbol: a tangible expression by the employer of an employee's worth and a mathematical expression of the individual's value in society. As such, pay has important status connotations which is one of the reasons why differentials are so important to employees and are so often a source of conflict and dispute.

On the other hand, the wage and salary bill is a cost to the employer and, in all but the most capital intensive industries, a very substantial cost. The employer seeks to contain and, if possible, to reduce this cost. This is at variance with the employee's basic desire for more money to improve his standard of living and/or to combat inflation. Thus pay becomes a primary source of industrial conflict. It is the principal battleground over which the trade unions and employers fight. As a result, many managers and engineers are increasingly involved in the wide variety of disputes and negotiations over pay which take place in modern industry.

Principles of payment

It is important, therefore, to establish certain principles of payment on the basis of which pay relationships and systems can be established and problems resolved. As a starting point it is helpful to consider such principles in terms of expectations. There are, on the one hand, the employee's expectations for a rising standard of living and earnings consistent with his market value, allied to internal criteria relating to differentials within the organisation. These the employee expects to be reasonably consistent with the contribution he makes and the skills and effort that he applies. The company, on the other hand, expects to be able to recruit and retain the calibre of employee required to carry out its operations and to obtain high standards of performance, flexible working arrangements and so on.

Some of these expectations conflict but some do not. Common to both, for example, is the expectation that the payment system should reflect the importance of the jobs within the organisation. This means that the basis of any payment system in an organisation should be an agreed set of differentials between common groups of jobs at various levels and in common functions within the organisation.

Importance of differentials

It has been said that almost all payment problems in industry are basically problems of differentials. If this is an over-statement, there is no doubt that such problems are a major cause of pressures upon wage and salary structures and of disputes between employees and management.

However, many of these problems need never occur. There is now a substantial body of evidence supported by a large number of practical applications which shows that 'there exist shared social norms of what constitutes a fair or equitable payment for any given level of work, these norms being intuitively known by each individual'.[1] This evidence that we share with other people's consistent views about the relative level of pay which is fair for any job, is of fundamental importance. It should be used to establish the basis of any wage and salary structure.

Pay and performance

One of the most controversial aspects of any payment question is the relationship of payment level to performance. Arguments about the value and importance of incentive systems have been raging for many years and will doubtless continue for many more. On the one hand, a strong body of opinion views financial incentives as the principal means of obtaining satisfactory performance standards from employees. Piecework and payment by results systems are an integral part of many wage payment systems, notably in the engineering, textile and clothing industries. In a detailed analysis of payment by results systems, the now defunct National Board for Prices and Incomes reported that: 'We are on the whole satisfied that conventional payment by results systems can be a useful tool for raising effort in situations of low performance'.[2]

However, there are many critics of the use of financial incentives in wage and salary systems. The criticisms are particularly directed at piecework and badly-designed incentive schemes. Dr W E J McCarthy for example, wrote a few years ago in his article entitled 'The Piecework Jungle' which appeared in *New Society*, 'Piecework is about money. The worker gets paid by what he produces. The trouble with this is that in the long run it leads to a loss of management control. If management wants to move the worker about, the worker resists because it may lead to a loss of money. If management wants to change the system of work arrangements, the worker again would resist because it may lead to loss of money. If management tries to introduce quality control, the worker is bound to resist because this will probably lead to a loss of money; so in all these ways it leads to resistance on the part of the workers to changes introduced by management'. To this catalogue of problems, which applies to a variety of loosely designed incentive arrangements, one may add that such systems can provide countless opportunities for employees and their shop stewards to exert heavy negotiating pressures on management.

Faced with conflicting evidence of the pros and cons of incentives, one may be helped by studying further evidence produced and analysed by Dr Elliot Jacques. He has identified a prime relationship between the level of work done, the level of pay for that work and the capacity or ability of the individual. When these three elements are in balance then, Dr Jacques claims, the individual is satisfied both financially and in non-financial terms as well. Jacques points out that the individual's capacity increases in his working situation over a period of time and notes that, while many salary structures provide pay increases over the years so as to maintain some sort of balance between pay and capacity, many wage systems do not. For example, a tradesman completes his apprenticeship at twenty years of age and is therefore regarded by his union and paid by management on the basis that he is able to perform a range of work similar in scope and technical complexity to that undertaken by a craftsman of twenty years experience. The older and more experienced man rarely has his capacity recognised in payment terms.

These problems encountered with financial incentives arise in most cases from bad design of the payment system or incorrect application and insufficient control. These problems can be overcome; a sound set of principles on which a company can base its policies on incentives and the relationship of pay and performance in both wages and salary systems may be summarised as follows: in an economic environment there should be some financial reward related to achievement and the capacity of the employee; financial incentives have an important, but in many cases not over-riding, contribution to make within the total motivational pattern. The less interesting and satisfying the job and the more the job holder is circumscribed, the greater the need for financial recognition of achievement and some degree of individual control over pay.

Thus, there is now a sufficient body of knowledge on which to base soundly designed wage and salary structures and payment systems and sufficient experience and understanding to ensure that such systems are properly applied and maintained.

Design of the payment system

There are two distinct factors in the design of a wage or a salary structure. Firstly, the structure must be founded on the relationship of jobs to each other so that acceptable differentials can be established. Secondly, the system of payment must be considered and decisions taken on the application of financial incentives or the basis of, and criteria for, pay progression. These two factors are considered separately in the subsequent sections.

Job evaluation as the basis for payment structures

The foundation of a properly designed wage or salary structure is the grouping or grading of jobs into qualitatively similar categories. The aim must be to establish acceptable pay relationships between different levels of job within the same job population; for example, all manual jobs in a factory or all clerical jobs in a group of offices. To meet this need many companies are introducing graded payment structures which group together all jobs of similar worth or responsibility.

This process of grading the jobs is the foundation of a properly designed payment structure. It is achieved by one of a variety of job evaluation techniques. (For a description of the various types of job evaluation system see *Job Evaluation Report No. 83* of the National Board for Prices and Incomes, September 1968.) While no one method has become universal, the most common is that based upon an appropriate factor plan. Under this method a number of points are given to a range of factors selected to cover the most important aspects of the job population which is being evaluated. The factors vary according to the jobs being evaluated. Management jobs may be assessed against such factors as 'supervisory responsibility', 'technical complexity' and 'level of decisions'. For jobs in a factory, factors such as 'skill requirements', 'responsibility for materials and/or equipment' and 'working conditions' are used. As the factors vary, so do the number of points (the weighting) given to each factor. This allocation of points under this factor plan system produces one of the major fallacies about job evaluation, namely, that it is a scientific, or at the very least, an objective technique.

However, as the National Board for Prices and Incomes recognised in its report, acceptability is the key to an effective job evaluation system and it is essentially a subjective matter. As mentioned earlier in this chapter, people have very consistent views about the relative importance of jobs and thus it is possible to obtain a consensus of opinion to ensure acceptable evaluation results.

The latest job evaluation methods are based on this principle of consensus. They also recognise that all a job evaluation system can do is to place the jobs of any given job population into an agreed rank order. It really cannot do more than this. It does not, of itself, establish the grades or groupings of jobs.

Paired comparisons

The new methods of job evaluation which set out to establish an acceptable rank order of jobs vary in detail but have at least two features in common. Firstly, they emphasise participation; judges involved are not only managers but also representatives of the employees to be covered by the payment structure which is being established. Secondly, these systems use a paired comparison method to establish or to assist in producing the rank order.

In the paired comparison method of job ranking a representative sample of jobs is selected from the job population. Every job in the sample is compared with every other job in the sample so that all possible combination of jobs are included. The forms are laid out in the manner shown in Figure 17:1. The total number of such comparisons is large and is calculated by the formula:

$$\frac{N \times (N-1)}{2}$$

where N is the number of jobs in the sample.

An appropriate group of judges is chosen and they study all the jobs carefully, using job descriptions to assist them. The judges then prefer one job of each pair on the basis of the overall worth or importance of the job. In some paired comparison systems the judges further qualify their preference by allocating ten points between each pair, as shown in the example above. Thus, the maintenance fitter is only narrowly preferred to the instrument mechanic, whereas the

Job number	Job title	Score		Job number	Job title
1	Instrument mechanic	4	6	2	Maintenance fitter
2	Maintenance fitter	7	3	3	Capstan setter operator
3	Capstan setter operator	8	2	4	Storeman
	AND SO ON				

FIGURE 17:1 FORM OF JOB SAMPLE RANKING BY PAIRED COMPARISON

job of capstan setter operator has been judged to be considerably more important than that of the storeman.

Each judge assesses a proportion of the total number of comparisons and the judges' scores are then totalled by a computer program which produces the overall rank order of jobs and the degree of agreement between judges. Perfect agreement would be 100 per cent and this system almost invariably produces above 85 per cent agreement and frequently above 90 per cent agreement.

The rank order is considered by the panel of judges, and individual judges' decisions which do not agree with the rank order are discussed and a final rank order of jobs agreed.

Thus, by this method, a rank order of bench-mark jobs is quickly achieved on a basis which ensures the acceptability of the result.

Establishing a graded structure

No system of job evaluation will, in itself, determine the grade structure of a given job population. The type of structure will be determined by the interaction of a number of factors.

1 Qualitative differences in groups of jobs in the population, for example, putting skilled and semi-skilled jobs in the same grade is likely to be unacceptable.

2 The type of technology; for example, a narrow range of semi-skilled assembly work will demand relatively few grades, but a wider range from simple process control to sophisticated fitting and testing will need a larger number of grades.
3 The type of career progression required, by means of which promotion through the grades is provided.
4 The existing pattern of differentials and payment levels. This is a most significant factor and requires close and thorough analysis.
5 The more grades that are established, the greater the likelihood of boundary disputes about grading and the easier it is for employees to apply pressure for re-grading.
6 In manual worker categories, the fewer the grades (within reason), the fewer the barriers to labour flexibility and mobility.

The above factors should be considered in consultation with the trade unions wherever negotiating rights exist. Decisions on the number of grades should be provisional until their cost implications have been examined in detail. This is covered more fully in the last section of this chapter.

Once definitive grade proposals have been established and agreed, then the remaining jobs in the job population must be allocated to the grade structure, by careful comparison with the bench-mark jobs. If a number of problems remain, a further ranking exercise can be undertaken to resolve the grading of jobs where uncertainty exists. This can be done by taking such jobs, together with a sample of bench-mark jobs, and carrying out a final paired comparison exercise. Once all jobs have been graded a complete wage or salary analysis should be undertaken to identify the implications for all employees affected.

Equal pay

Industry is now confronted with the need to implement the Equal Pay Act. The aim of the Act is to eliminate discrimination between men and women in respect of pay and other terms and conditions of employment. It requires that after 1975 no collective agreement should differentiate between men and women over basic rates of pay and terms and conditions of employment. This will affect many companies' wage and salary structures, since adjustments to the basic female rates of pay will fundamentally change existing differentials.

But the Act goes further than this. It establishes the legal right of the woman to equal treatment, when she is employed on work of the same or broadly similar nature to that of men or on a job which, though different from those done by men, has been given an equal value under a job evaluation scheme.

Such job evaluation schemes must not, themselves, discriminate against women employees by reason of the factors used or points awarded. Thus, where job evaluation schemes exist which cover male and female employees, they should be carefully reviewed to examine the effect on pay relationships that the Equal Pay Act will have.

In many cases it may be necessary to consider re-evaluation to ensure that correct relationships for men and women are established. Where this needs to be done, a quick and acceptable method of re-evaluation is that described in the preceding sections of this chapter.

The Equal Pay Act, therefore, will have a strong impact on many companies' wage and salary structures. Companies which employ large numbers of women will find that the potential costs are high and that careful planning of their equal pay programme is a matter of high priority.

Relating wages and performance

The relationship of pay to performance varies in its application to wage and salary systems. It is appropriate to consider them separately.

Incentives and wage systems

Carefully designed incentive schemes provide a stimulus to employees to achieve high performance in their jobs. It is essential, however, to ensure that incentive arrangements are consistent with the requirements of the jobs and do not encourage the misuse of time, resources and materials.

The type of incentive scheme is closely affected by the type of measured standard available for the work concerned. Incentive schemes are commonly based on the following, as appropriate:

1 Output, in unit time
2 Quality, measured by percentage of rejects
3 Yield of a process or from a given material
4 Utilisation of machines, equipment or process
5 Cost of manhours related to performance

Depending on the job, the measure of performance and the type of such standard, incentive schemes may be tightly linked to short-term achievement (for example, mass and large batch production), more loosely linked to longer-term achievement (for example, maintenance, toolroom, small batch work), or linked to relative improvements rather than precisely measured standards, for example, inspection, stores, transport work. (The last is also suitable for yield indices.)

To summarise, therefore, the answers to the following questions will clarify the types of incentive scheme appropriate to a particular activity: what is the main purpose of the activity in terms of the unit objectives: is it machine or plant utilisation, material yield, adherence to production or dispatch schedules, quality? What influences can the job holders exert on the operation and how is this affected? What variability can they introduce into the operation and what degree of control have they? What is the relationship between this operation and other parts of the process or activity?

Types of Incentive Scheme

There are many types of incentive scheme for manual workers. The most widespread type is that which relates pay to the performance of either individuals or small groups of workers and which measures performance in units of time on the basis of the work-content in the job.

The share of the savings in hours worked which the employee receives determines the 'bonus curve', that is, the relationship between pay and employee performance. There are a great many variations in the design of 'bonus curves' but most fall into the following broad categories:

Directly proportional or constant cost. This is so called because changes in earnings are directly proportional to changes in output, and the labour cost per unit of output is constant above an established minimum payment level (the basic rate). Thus, no labour cost savings accrue to the company from increased output, but it benefits from the improvement in over-recovery of overheads, improved plant utilisation, etc. Virtually all the work done needs to be measured with precision, and elaborate arrangements are usually required to deal with unmeasured work, method or design changes, time lost by operators and payments for indirect workers. This type of scheme usually provides for a basic rate for all output or performance below a level of seventy-five performance on the British Standard scale, and a set amount per standard minute of output for all output above the seventy-five performance level, this amount being determined by the cost of a standard minute at the 75 British Standard level. Directly proportional schemes may be modified to incorporate quality, material economy or other appropriate factors.

'Geared' variants of directly proportional schemes. These provide reducing labour costs as output rises. This is achieved, for example, by paying the same bonus amount at standard performance as a directly proportional scheme, but starting from a lower performance level. Under such a scheme, known as the '50 plus a half', bonus is paid from a fifty British Standard performance level, but at half the rate per standard minute.

Amount of payment

Earnings levels at standard performance (100 British Standards Institution scale) will be determined by a number of factors in the existing situation of which the most important are:

1 Current 40 hour earnings of the employees in each grade
2 The increase in productivity available across the establishment
3 Local market levels of pay

The incentive element of pay should not exceed 25 per cent of total 40 hour earnings at standard performance (100 on the BSI scale). This proportion is suitable for many types of incentive scheme, particularly those based on the measure of work content.

Where schemes based on relative standards, for example improvements in machine utilisation are introduced, the incentive element may be smaller than 25 per cent of total earnings. An amount less than 10 per cent is unlikely to have a positive motivational effect and is recommended as the minimum.

Stability of earnings

A major consideration in the design of an incentive scheme is the degree of earnings stability which the scheme provides. Schemes can be structured, in theory, anywhere between *direct piecework,* when the employee is paid nothing if he fails to produce output, to *measured daywork* whereby the employee is guaranteed a rate of pay, unless the company can demonstrate that any fall in output is specifically the employee's responsibility.

Under direct piecework, the company incurs no labour cost if it fails to provide work and the employee suffers accordingly; under a measured daywork scheme, labour costs escalate if the company is unable to maintain a flow of work to its employees. It follows, therefore, that a company should only introduce a contractually-based scheme of measured daywork when it can be certain of ensuring that the flow of work will be maintained.

Employees, on the other hand, expect a resonable degree of earnings stability. They are adept at manipulating incentive schemes to achieve this end, often by putting pressure on standards or demanding allowances.

It is recommended, therefore, that all incentive schemes should provide for a degree of stabilisation of earnings. This can be achieved in a number of ways, of which the following two are particularly appropriate.

Performance Bands. Bands of performance, for example, 75–80, 81–86, 87–92, 93–98, etc., are established, each of which has a pay increment (related to the basic rate) attached to it. All employees whose performance falls within a particular band, therefore, receive the same bonus increment.

Averaging performance over time. Employees' performance is averaged over a period of time, for example, one week or one month, and bonuses are paid on this average performance. The less precise the standard of measurement, the longer the period over which bonus should be averaged.

One of the real problems of a variable element is its application to situations which cannot be measured. Where direct measurement of work content is inappropriate, statistical techniques and financial ratios are capable of widespread application. Finally, it must be emphasised that incentive arrangements of whatever kind are only part of the total industrial relations system. They are an integral and interacting part of it and must be carefully controlled and monitored.

Relating salaries and performance

Staff salary structures comprise a basic rate element for job worth and, desirably, an element to recognise personal performance and an element to acknowledge age/service.

The most controversial aspect of the design and administration of salary structures is the introduction of a personal performance element. Unless these are carefully controlled they are regarded by employees as being unfair and too subjective, as they leave part of their salary to the whim of the boss.

Nevertheless, it is suggested that it is desirable to provide within a staff salary structure the opportunity to recognise above- and below-average performance in the job. Such recognition is one of the most tangible expressions by a company of its opinion of the employee's performance. Although the final amount in question may be small, it can have a considerable psychological impact.

Devising the system of salary progression

A performance-based progression system should not require a complicated assessment plan. The application of any such system should be kept simple. Accordingly, it is suggested that employees should be classified into one of the following:

1 Outstanding performance in the job
2 Above average performance in the job
3 Satisfactory performance in the job
4 Adequate performance in the job
5 Below average performance in the job

In some cases for junior staff the classification may be more appropriately limited to 2, 3 and 4 above.

Salary progression procedure

The following suggestions set out a relatively simple procedure for determining salary progression:

Variable speed of progression to a grade maximum. This method of operating the progression through each grade of a salary structure is based on establishing a defined year of attainment for the achievement of the grade maximum. For example, assuming a normal rate of progression through a grade over a five-year period, the average employee in the grade will receive annual increments of one fifth of the total grade range for five years as he or she progresses from the grade minimum to grade maximum. Thus:

Total grade range	£500
Normal increment (average classification)	$\frac{500}{5}$=£100 per annum

The system provides for the recognition of above or below average development in the job by permitting variation in the year of attainment of grade maximum. For example, an above-average employee in the grade illustrated above could have his or her year of attainment reduced to four years; thus his or her increment will be:

$$\frac{500}{4}=£124 \text{ per annum}$$

Similarly, an employee classified as 'adequate' would have his or her year of attainment of grade maximum extended by a year, that is:

$$\frac{500}{6}=£83 \text{ (approximately) per annum}$$

It will be noted that in each case the employee receives a definite salary increase each year, thus ensuring recognition for service. It is suggested that any manager should be able to classify the performance of his subordinates into one of these three categories and get the employees concerned to accept such classification. The differences in annual increase are not financially large, but have a strong symbolic impact.

Variable grade maximum. Varying the amount of salary increases by varying the period of progression to the grade maximum provides one method of differentiating between different performance standards. A further means of distinguishing between differing performance standards is to provide differing financial career structures within each grade. This can be done by establishing more than one grade maximum for each grade. For example, five maxima for each grade might be established to provide a performance classification as follows:

1 Outstanding: 10 per cent above grade maximum
2 Above average: 5 per cent above grade maximum
3 Average: grade maximum
4 Adequate: 5 per cent below grade maximum
5 Below average: 10 per cent below grade maximum

Under this system two alternative methods of progression can be used. Firstly, a fixed year of attainment to whichever of the above classifications the employee is allocated by his or her manager, that is, if the standard rate of progression is five years, salary increments for employees will differ according to which of the above maxima he or she is allocated. Secondly, this system can be combined with a system of varying the year of attainment of the grade maxima (as with the variable speed of progression to a grade maximum above). Such a scheme gives greater flexibility in the administration of the salary policy, yet keeps it within defined limits. It ensures that employees whose performance differs do not, after a certain period in a job, reach the same salary level. Although more complex administratively, it is also more flexible than the systems outlined above and may be more appropriate for senior staff.

Implementing a new payment system

Rationalising an unfair or distorted wage or salary situation can prove expensive. It is essential to cost out in detail the effects of introducing a graded structure. This requires a complete earnings analysis covering all employees who are to be paid under the new structure. This analysis is relatively straightforward as far as salaried employees are concerned.

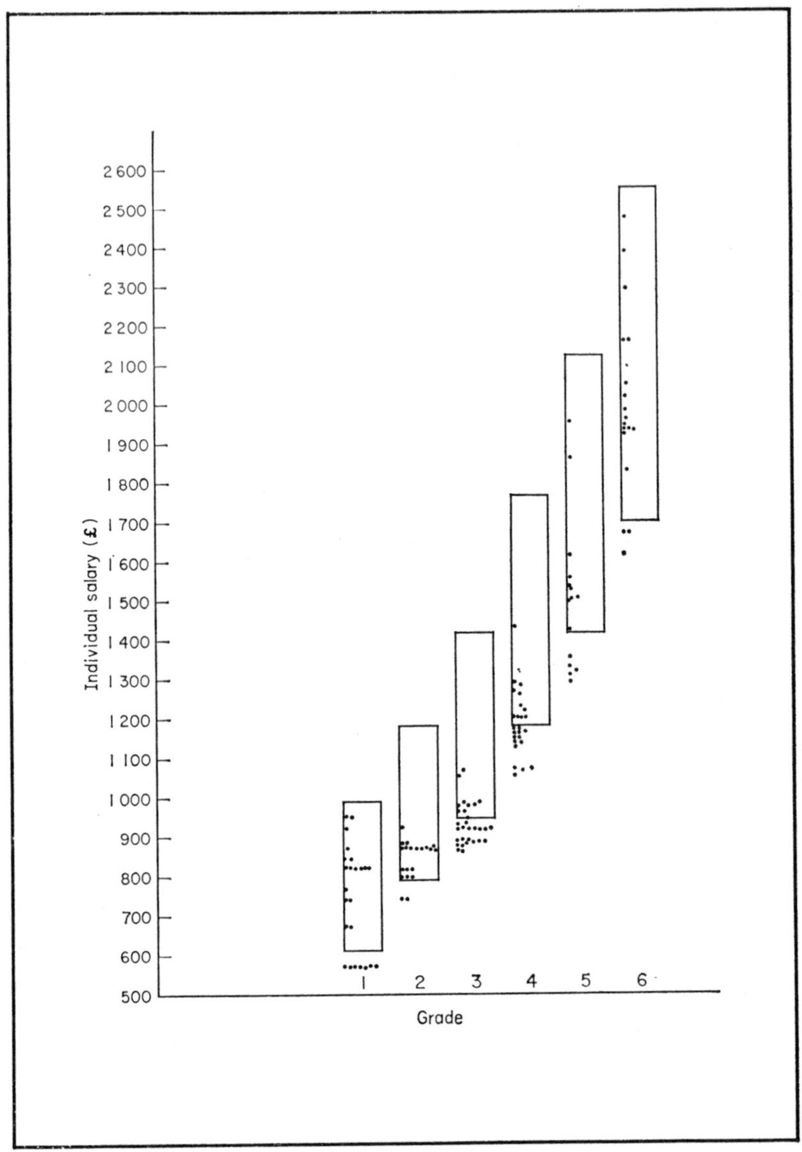

FIGURE 17:2 ANALYSIS OF STAFF SALARIES

Each dot in the graph represents the earnings of an individual member of staff. In this example the dots have been grouped to show the distribution of salaries that would exist if a six-grade salary structure were to be introduced into the company

An example of the earnings distribution of a group of salaried staff is shown in Figure 17:2. The jobs of these staff had been evaluated using the paired comparison system described earlier in this chapter. Certain problems arose among both management and employees on the number of grades into which the jobs were to be grouped. Eventually it was proposed to establish the six grade structure as shown. Each dot is the individual salary of one of the staff concerned and the pairs of horizontal lines show the grade's minimum and maximum salaries proposed. It only remained to establish the policy for progressing employees through the appropriate salary range for a detailed and accurate cost figure to be obtained by comparing each individual's present salary with his or her theoretical entitlement under the new grade and salary progression criteria.

The analysis of hourly-paid employees' earnings is more complex, particularly if they are paid under a payment-by-results scheme. In many cases the make-up of such employees' pay involves such items as the basic rate, over-rates for skill, etc., incentive earnings, special allowances (for example, for tools, working conditions, etc.,) and, overtime and other premiums.

It is essential to establish a uniform basis for comparison in such cases and by far the most useful and informative comparisons are of earnings for the normal working week. While such information is sometimes surprisingly difficult to take out from the company payroll, it permits a meaningful analysis of differentials and pay relationships to be made.

An example of such an analysis is given in Figure 17:3. As with the previous example, a job evaluation exercise had been undertaken and the earnings of the employees affected are shown against a number of proposed grades to which their jobs had been allocated. This form of presentation also permits the performance or incentive element to be shown where an incentive scheme exists, as in this example. The proposed basic or grade pay is shown at the 75 BSI performance level and the incentive earnings for 100 BSI performance are shown for each grade. Clearly, the actual cost of introducing this structure depends on two variables for each employee, namely, his current earnings and his current performance level.

In such a situation it is only possible to obtain an approximate rationalisation cost by making overall estimates of the productivity

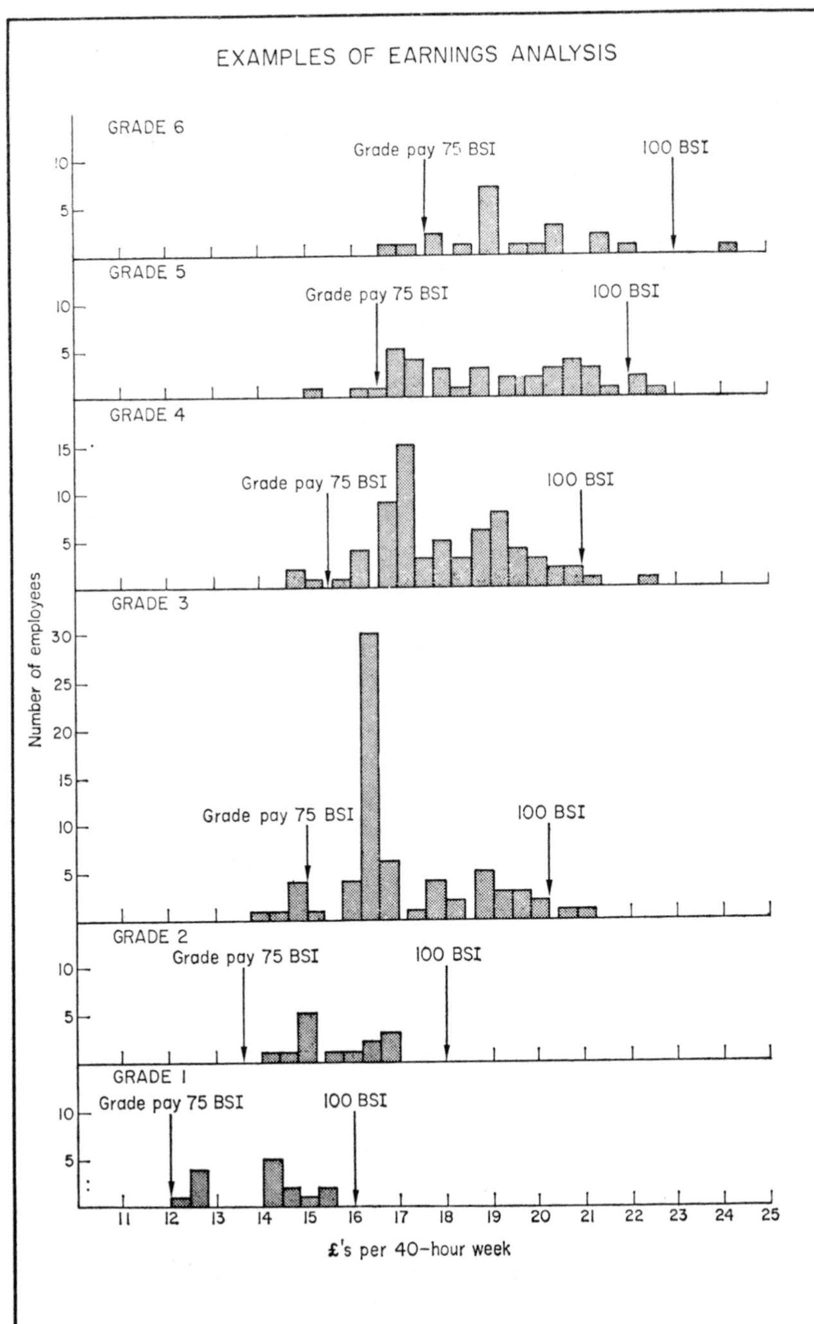

FIGURE 17:3 ANALYSIS OF WAGES

This diagram has a purpose similar to that of Figure 17:2, but is designed to cope with the more complex problem of wage earnings. This form of presentation allows the performance or incentive element of earnings to be shown, where such a scheme exists

potential available, through the use of such techniques as rated activity sampling.

Maintaining the payment structure

Once a rationalised payment structure has been introduced, careful control is required. It is essential to establish the criteria by which new or expanded jobs are placed in the structure if fair differentials are to be maintained. The structure should be integrated into properly defined collective bargaining arrangements where it covers union members with negotiating rights. The Industrial Relations Act requires companies to define bargaining units carefully; it cannot be emphasised too strongly that such bargaining units must be consistent with the wage or salary structures established for groups of employees.

Where pay is a negotiating matter, levels of pay will be reviewed regularly, generally by the unions submitting wage or salary claims. Such negotiations should always attempt to maintain existing differentials and should cover all employees paid under the wage or salary structure. Once small pressure groups are allowed to negotiate separately within a defined pay situation, the system of agreed differentials is quickly upset and the way is then open for continued leapfrogging pressures on management which will have only itself to blame.

If the payment structure covers employees who are not union members, the company is well advised to keep levels of pay under close review, with particular reference to the labour market situation, the cost of living and company prosperity. Regular reviews and adjustments to pay based on these criteria are necessary if the pay situation is to be maintained on an equitable basis.

Finally, it is suggested that consideration be given to a more constructive and dynamic pay review mechanism – a 'share of prosperity element'. This additional tier to the structure provides for the regular review of pay levels by reference to the performance of those covered by the payment structure. It is necessary to establish an index as the basis for such a share of prosperity element and this requires a reasonably consistent ratio between a measure of total activity on the one hand, and a measure of performance on the other. The measure of activity should be as closely related to participants as possible; that of performance as broadly based as possible.

These conditions are often best fulfilled by an index based on the relationship between total wages (or salaries) and added value (that is, the selling price of the product less the cost of raw materials and bought in parts). However other measures can also be used, dependent upon the groups of employees covered. Such an element introduces economic realism into the wage or salary system and acts as a focus for improved performance by all those affected by the index. It can act as a central feature of the company's communication structure, focusing attention on the need for meaningful discussions on productivity improvement.[3]

A company which introduces a share of prosperity element into its payment systems is recognising that pay can be a dynamic in its employee relations situation and not merely a source of continual conflict. While conflict on pay will never disappear, it can be reduced in many British companies and used more constructively than is unfortunately the case today. If this is to be achieved, pay problems must be tackled on the basis of principle and not expediency.

References

1 *Equitable Payment* by Elliott Jacques, Pelican Books, p. 21, para. 5.
2 *Report 65 – Payment by Results Systems,* National Board for Prices and Incomes, 1968, Ch. 10, para. 245.
3 For a more detailed explanation of the 'share prosperity element' see *Productivity Agreements and Wage Systems* by North and Buckingham, Gower Press, 1969.

Chapter 18

Legal Aspects of the Employer/Employee Relationship

F W Rose, Principal Lecturer in Law, City of Birmingham Polytechnic

---

The legal relationship that exists between an employer and his employee gives rise to many complex rights and duties. The full implications of this relationship are not always understood by the parties themselves. Some of the problems associated with employment will be considered in this chapter.

When a person is offered a job he acquires the status of an employee. He is entitled, in appropriate circumstances, to receive his salary, notice of dismissal, a pension or redundancy payment and working conditions as laid down by statute. In recent years Parliament has greatly increased the rights of employees. The employer or his delegate should be aware of the background and general nature of those duties that are owed to an individual employee and the workforce as a whole.

Contracts of employment

To be valid a contract of employment must satisfy all the essential elements of a legally enforceable contract including:

1 Offer and acceptance
2 Valuable consideration
3 Intention to create legal relations
4 Capacity
5 Absence of any vitiating element, such as mistake or misrepresentation

Some of these essential elements have been discussed in Chapter 11, but those elements that are especially important in a contract of employment are discussed here.

Employing persons under the age of 18

A person ceases to be a minor and has full contractual capacity at the first moment of his or her eighteenth birthday. Many contracts concluded by a minor are void. All contracts for his instruction (that is apprenticeship) or employment are enforceable against him, however, provided such contracts are for his benefit. It is essential for a minor to be allowed to earn a livelihood and negotiate a valid and enforceable agreement for this purpose.

The burden of proving that the contract as a whole benefits the minor lies on the party alleging it, usually the employer. As in any other contract, there will be stipulations that benefit the employer and stipulations that benefit the minor. It is not necessary to establish that every single term benefits the minor. The contract should contain only clauses that are usual and customary in the type of employment undertaken.

A contract of employment that is not beneficial to the minor is voidable at his option. This means that the minor can either regard the contract as binding, in which case the employer must observe his part of the bargain, or rescind during minority or within a reasonable time after attaining majority age.

Misrepresentation

A contract of employment is not a contract of utmost good faith (*uberrimae fidei*), consequently there is no obligation on the employee to inform his prospective employer of factors that might result in the employer declining to make any offer of employment. It is the duty of the employer to discover the facts for himself by question and inquiries.

Written details of a contract of employment

Even though a legally binding contract of employment exists, the statutory requirements of the Contracts of Employment Act 1972 must be satisfied.

The employer must, within thirteen weeks after the beginning of an employee's period of employment, supply him with written particulars of his work, unless these are contained in a written contract of which the employee has a copy or reasonable access to a copy. Any change in the terms of service must be communicated within one month of the change. Details must be given of :

1 The name of employer and employee.
2 The date when the employment began.
3 The rate of remuneration and the intervals at which it is paid.
4 Any terms and conditions relating to hours of work, holidays and holiday pay, sickness and sickness pay (if any) and pensions and pension schemes (if any).
5 The length of notice which the employer must give, and which he is entitled to receive, when the contract of employment is terminated.
6 Particulars enabling the employee to calculate his entitlement to holidays, holiday pay and accrued pay when he leaves the employment before arrival of the time for taking a paid holiday.
7 The employee's right to join or refuse to join a trade union.
8 An explanation of the procedure available to an employee with a grievance in relation to his employment, or a reference to a reasonably accessible document explaining the procedure.

An employee who does not receive the required particulars may refer the matter to an industrial tribunal and the employer may be fined up to £20.

Certain employees are not entitled to written particulars under the Act:

1 Civil servants and members of the armed forces.
2 Dock workers, skippers and seamen.
3 Independent contractors.
4 Persons whose hours of employment are less than twenty-one hours a week.
5 Employees engaged on work wholly or mainly outside Great Britain.
6 An employee who is the father, mother, husband, wife, son or daughter of the employer.
7 A partner.

Restricting an employee's spare-time activities

An employer wishing to prevent an employee from engaging in paid spare-time work must insert an express term to this effect in the contract of employment. In the absence of an express term the employee will be restrained in only one instance. He will be in breach of his implied duty of good faith and liable to summary dismissal or restraint by court order (injunction) if he works for his employer's actual or potential rival, or discloses confidential information or techniques made known to him by his employer.

Payment of wages and salaries

The remuneration to be paid by the employer to the employee is usually fixed after negotiations, and stipulated in one of the principal terms of the contract of employment.

If the contract does not fix the wages payable, the employer may be sued for a sum that is deemed to be reasonable, after taking into account the circumstances of the individual case and the negotiations between the parties (a *quantum meruit* claim). For example, a contract of employment, believed to be valid, may turn out to be void if the person who made the appointment acted without authority; then the employee may claim reasonable payment for services provided.

Methods of payment

The Truck Acts requiring payment of workmen in cash, has been modified in its effect by the Payment of Wages Act 1960. Payment of wages by cheque or directly into a bank account assists the increased mechanisation in the wages office of larger companies. It also removes the need to transfer large sums of money from a bank to the employer's place of business with the attendant risk of theft.

An employee's wages may be paid by cheque, money order, postal order or directly into his own personal bank account or an account held jointly with others, provided he has made a written request to this effect and the employer accedes to it. The employer may refuse the employee's request by giving him written notice within fourteen days.

Although the employee may not have consented to payment of wages in a form other than cash, the employer may post the employee's wages to him in the form of a postal order or money order where the employee is working away from the place where wage payments take place, or absent from work because of injury or illness; this is so unless the employee has given written notice to the employer that this method of payment is not acceptable.

The employer or employee may at any time, by written notice, cancel the agreement to make payment by any of the methods under discussion.

At or before the time of payment by one of these methods, the employer must give the employee a statement, in writing, of:

1 The gross amount of wages payable.
2 Each deduction made with details, for example, tax, national insurance and graduated pension payments.
3 The net amount payable.

Equal pay for women

The object of the Equal Pay Act 1970 is to eliminate discrimination on grounds of sex in relation to wages and other conditions of employment. The statute will become effective on 29 December 1975. From that date onwards a term will be implied in every woman's contract of employment that she must be employed on the same conditions and paid the same wages as a man, where she is engaged upon the same or similar work, or work of a different nature which has been rated as equivalent to a man's work, following a job evaluation that has taken account of the effort and skill required.

Equal treatment for men and women is not required where the terms of a woman's employment are more favourable because the employer is observing statutory regulations that protect female employees. For example, the Factories Act 1961 clearly stipulates the permitted hours of employment for women engaged in factories, these hours of work being less demanding that those required from some male employees. Nor is equal treatment required where they receive special treatment in connection with a birth, expected birth, retirement, marriage or death.

If the employer fails to pay women the same wages as men in circumstances where such payment is required, then the matter may be referred for decision to an industrial tribunal within two years. The employer must show that any pay differential between the sexes results from material differences in the work undertaken.

A collective agreement between trade unions and employer fixing different rates of pay for men and women may be amended by the Industrial Court at the request of the Secretary of State for Employment. Any female employee whose salary is fixed in her contract of employment by reference to the terms of that collective agreement is entitled to wages at the new amended rate. Wages regulation orders may also be amended to remove any discrimination in wage rates between men and women.

Fair wage payments in government contracts

A resolution passed by the House of Commons in 1946 states that in all government contracts a fair wage clause should be inserted requiring contractors to:

1 Pay wage rates and observe hours and conditions not less favourable than those commonly accepted in the district. In the absence of a commonly accepted standard, terms equal to those observed by other employers in the industry concerned must be granted.
2 Comply in respect of all employees, not only employees directly engaged on the government contract. Before being placed on the list of firms invited to tender for government contracts, the contractor must show compliance with those terms for the preceding three months.
3 Allow their workers to join a trade union.
4 Display a copy of the resolution in every workplace used by the contractor during the continuance of the employment.
5 Ensure the observance of the resolution by subcontractors employed by them in performance of the government contract.

Any dispute concerning the implementation of the clause must be referred to the Secretary of State for Employment. If it is not settled there may be a reference to the Industrial Arbitration Board for settlement of the issue.

This resolution does not have the force of law. Its main purpose is to ensure that government contractors set a good example to other classes of employers, by paying the generally accepted current wage for the type of work undertaken.

The terms and conditions of the Employment Act 1959

The provisions of *s*8 of this Act as set out below take into account changes made by the Industrial Relations Act 1971. If an employer is not observing the generally accepted terms and conditions of employment in respect of an employee, the issue may be reported by a registered trade union or employers' association to the Secretary of State for Employment. The following conditions must be satisfied: the terms and conditions of the employment in question must have been settled by agreement, with the intention that they are to be generally applied in employment of that type or in a particular district; the agreement must have been concluded by organisations of employers and organisations of workers representing a substantial number of employees in the relevant employment.

If the Secretary of State cannot settle the claim it may be referred to the Industrial Arbitration Board. If the claim is well founded, the Board may make an award requiring the employer concerned to observe the recognised terms and conditions in respect of all employees of the relevant description employed by him. The award becomes effective as an implied term of the employee's contract of employment.

Statutory regulation of wages

Despite the growth in the twentieth century of powerful trade unions with the ability to bargain collectively to secure better wages for their members, there are still sections of employees unprotected by a strong trade union. In these areas of employment legislation is essential to ensure payment of a reasonable wage. About four million workers are now protected in this way.

Wages councils are established by the Secretary of State for Employment on his own initiative or after representations from organisations of workers and employers. They are composed of not more than three independent persons, one of whom acts as chairman, and an equal number of representatives for employers and workers.

A wages council has power to draft a wages regulation proposal for fixing the wages to be paid by employers to all or any of the workers concerned, either generally or for particular work, and the holidays to be allowed.

These proposals must be published and employers and employees affected must be notified, if practicable. The employer must place a copy of the proposals at a place where they may be studied by workers. If desired both employers and workers may make written representations to the wages council concerning the proposals and they may be amended in the light of these suggestions.

The final draft is submitted to the Secretary of State and he may give the wages order immediate statutory force, or resubmit it to the wages council for further consideration. Employers and employees will be informed of the new statutory minimum wage payment for employment covered by the order.

If any employer fails to pay the statutory minimum wage, or to allow the holiday or holiday pay as specified in the order then he may be fined and he can be ordered to pay the difference between the actual pay received by the worker and the statutory minimum due to him.

The Secretary of State may abolish a wages council if it is no longer necessary for maintaining a reasonable standard of remuneration.

Termination of employment

The contract of employment may expressly state that the employment is to continue for a fixed period, or until a specified task has been performed. In these circumstances the contract will be terminated automatically at the end of the period specified, or when the task is completed. Neither party can terminate the agreement by giving notice. It is possible, though unusual, to have a contract of service for life.

A contract of employment does not usually specify the period for which it will last. Often the parties contemplate a continuing relationship until some event occurs which brings the agreement to an end. Examples are dismissal, giving the period of notice specified in the contract, or the employee's death.

Statutory periods of notice

In the absence of an express term in the contract fixing the length of notice, reference may be made to the Contracts of Employment Act 1972. The employer must give the following minimum periods of notice:

1 One week, to an employee employed continuously for thirteen weeks or more, but less than two years.
2 Two weeks to an employee with continuous employment of two years, but less than five years.
3 Four weeks, to an employee with continuous employment of five years, but less than ten years.
4 Six weeks for continuous employment over ten years, but less than fifteen years.
5 Eight weeks for over fifteen years continuous employment.

An employee who has been continuously employed for twenty-six weeks or more must give one week's notice (*s*1(2)).

The contract of employment may, if required, provide for a period of notice that is longer than the period set out in the Act. Where the employer and employee have not expressly agreed upon a period of notice, an employee may claim that the minimum period of notice stipulated by the Act is shorter than that required by custom or the period that is 'reasonable' in the circumstances.

Instant dismissal without notice

An employer may be justified in dismissing an employee without giving him the period of notice required under the contract of employment, or the Contracts of Employment Act 1963. In these cases of instant or summary dismissal the employee cannot sue for wrongful dismissal and he is only entitled to wages earned up until the time of dismissal.

Where an employee is properly dismissed without notice for misconduct, he cannot recover wages for the time during which he worked between the last payment of wages and his subsequent dismissal, unless there is an express term in the contract providing otherwise.

Illness and injury

Where illness causes permanent incapacity, it may frustrate the commercial purpose of the contract and justify summary dismissal, depending upon:

1 The terms of the contract
2 The nature of the work
3 Whether a substitute is required immediately
4 The expected duration of the incapacity
5 The length of service
6 The status of the employee

In these cases an employer can dismiss a sick employee by giving him the requisite notice. This is better than relying on frustration, where the period of notice necessary is relatively short.

The employer cannot claim damages for losses suffered by being deprived of the employee's services, which may be extensive where an employee has highly specialised abilities, for example, a company director.

If the illness or incapacity does not completely prevent the employee from working, the contract of employment is discharged only if the incapacity makes a fundamental difference to the employer by going to the root of the agreement. Many highly paid executives are expected to work for long hours under pressure, and inability to cope completely with the demands of the job, as where ill health necessitates employment for less than a full working week, may justify summary dismissal.

A temporary illness does not usually frustrate the commercial purpose of a contract of employment. In the case of Storey *v* Fulham Steel Works (1907) a works manager had five months absence due to illness, after working two years of his five year contract. The employer was not entitled to regard the contract as discharged.

The contract of service may include an express term covering the right to wages during temporary illness. In the absence of such a term a custom may be applicable. In cases not covered by an express term or custom there is a right to payment during illness.

Disobedience

An employee may be dismissed for refusing to obey the employer's lawful orders, if they are reasonable and not inconsistent with the type of work that the employee is engaged to perform.

To warrant dismissal the employee's disobedience must be wilful, showing a complete disregard of the essential conditions of the contract of service. A single disobedient act suffices if it manifests an intention by the employee to repudiate the whole contract of employment or one of its essential terms, but it need not in itself be of a serious character. In Pepper *v* Webb (1970) a head gardener was justifiably dismissed on the spot after refusing to put new plants in the garden to ensure their survival and addressing his employer in a vulgar and insolent fashion.

Incompetence and negligence

Summary dismissal is justifiable if an employee is unable to carry out the kind of work that he is employed to do. He cannot be dismissed for his inability to do work that he never claimed that he was competent to perform.

An employee may be dismissed instantly if he commits a negligent act or series of negligent acts which are sufficiently serious to strike at the root of the whole contract, where, for example, the manager of a printing press causes serious damage by forgetting to adjust it before use. If the circumstances are not sufficiently serious to warrant dismissal the employer can only claim damages from the employee for any loss he has caused, and terminate the contract by giving the appropriate period of notice.

Dishonesty

It is an implied term in all contracts of employment that an employee will be honest. Even minor dishonesty during working hours will justify summary dismissal. For example, an employee in charge of ready cash must not borrow a sum of money, even though he intends to replace it and does replace it within a few hours, if he knows that the employer would disapprove of such conduct.

Misbehaviour

The degree of misbehaviour required to warrant instant dismissal depends upon the nature of the employment and the duties of the employee. A higher standard may be expected where there is a close personal contact between the employee and his immediate superior. The misconduct must go to the root of the contract and show an unwillingness to observe the conditions of employment.

Misbehaviour on one occasion only, such as loss of temper or use of bad language, does not justify dismissal on the spot. A single act may suffice if it is so exceptional that the employer cannot be expected to continue the relationship. For example, a manager of a life assurance office must not insure a particular risk when he has been expressly instructed not to do so, since the action could result in considerable monetary loss for his employer.

Misbehaviour outside working hours

The employee is free to use his spare time as he pleases, provided that any acts of misconduct do not seriously affect the employee's work during business hours. If his work is detrimentally affected the contract is repudiated. Moral misconduct by the employee in his own time will not justify summary dismissal, unless the employee is engaged in domestic service.

If an employee commits a serious wrong outside working hours, for example, an assault on a fellow employee, such that it is unsafe for the employer to continue the contract of service, then summary dismissal is permissible.

Termination by the employee without notice

The employee also has the right to regard the contract of employment as discharged, leaving him free to terminate his employment without giving the length of notice usually required, in the following circumstances:

1 Where the employer is guilty of misconduct. For example, ill-treating, assaulting staff or making improper advances.
2 Where the employee's life or health are at risk.
3 Where the risks anticipated by the employer and employee are increased as the result of a significant change in circumstances. For example, where the outbreak of war or civil strife in a certain area makes completion of a task by the employee unduly hazardous, where the terms of his contract do not require him to accept such risks.
4 Where the employer wilfully neglects to discharge his duties under the contract. For example, not paying wages at the time when they fall due or not providing safe working conditions.

An employee cannot summarily terminate his contract of employment by paying over a sum equivalent to his wages in lieu of notice.

Damages for wrongful dismissal

An employee wrongfully dismissed may recover damages for the wages he would have earned during the period of notice to which he was entitled. He must seek alternative employment however, and try to reduce his loss. Compensation is not recoverable for abusive dismissal, injured feelings or difficulty in securing another position. If the employee leaves his employment without giving notice, the employer must try to fill the vacancy. The cost of finding a replacement is the reasonably foreseeable loss that the employer may recover as damages. Substantial damages may be claimed where a responsible post is vacated in this way.

A breach of contract may be anticipatory, occurring before the date agreed upon for performance of the contract. The party detrimentally affected can sue for damages immediately. It is unnecessary to wait for the due date of performance.

Compelling an employee to fulfil his contract

A contract of employment is not directly enforceable at the employer's request. The court will not order an employee specifically to perform those tasks that he has contractually bound himself to undertake. It would be impossible for the court to supervise effectively the actions of the employee to ensure that he observed a decree of specific performance. Further, it is undesirable to keep persons tied together in a business relationship when the tie has become odious, thus turning a contract of service into a contract of servitude. The employer is limited to a remedy in damages.

Contracts of employment for a fixed period of time often embody positive promises, such as a promise to carry out various duties stipulated. There may also be negative promises, such as a promise not to work for competitors for the duration of the contract. If the employee refuses to carry out his positive promise, a decree of specific performance will not be granted to make him carry out his work. On the other hand an injunction may be granted to prevent him working for his employer's competitors until the period of the contract expires.

Injunctions are usually issued only against an employee with specialised skills earning a high salary, such as a director, engineer or designer. For example, a company may employ a highly qualified and well established engineer for a fixed period of time, say five years, to assist in a proposed scheme of expansion. He may be contractually bound to give the whole of his time to the company's business and not to work for any other person as an engineer while the contract of employment is in existence. This contract will not be specifically enforced. Further any injunction granted to restrain his breach of contract by preventing him from working for the employer's competitors during the period of the contract of employment, must be limited in its effect to the type of work specified in that contract, namely engineering. The engineer is free to engage in other remunerative activities, although, presumably, less highly paid, during the period of restraint. There is a reluctance to grant an injunction the effect of which is to compel the employee to perform his contract or starve. Since the employee will usually wish to work only in his own specialised field, he will be induced to fulfil the original contract of employment.

If an employee agrees to give the whole of his time to his employer during the term of his employment, a clause that is not unusual in many contracts of employment, this is a purely affirmative contract for personal services. A negative promise will not be implied to prevent the employee from serving another employer in his spare time, provided such work does not compete with that of his employer.

Provision of references

An employer is not under any duty to provide an employee with a reference or testimonial, unless there is a term in the contract to that effect. If a reference is given, however, the employer must not defame the employee. A statement is defamatory if it tends to lower the employee in the estimation of right-thinking members of society. The person making the defamatory statement may be liable for damages in tort, for either slander (in respect of spoken words) or libel (if the defamation is in some permanent form, like writing).

To succeed in any action the employee has the burden of proving that the statement was defamatory and that it referred to him. There must also be publication, that is communication to a party other than the person defamed. No action lies for defamation in an open reference handed to the employee personally, for any subsequent publication must be by the employee himself. In cases of slander there is the additional burden of showing either an imputation of incapacity in relation to the employee's trade, profession or occupation or, alternatively, special loss such as loss of a position that might otherwise have been secured.

Defences

The employer may have one of the following two defences to any action, and if the defence is successful it will negative liability.

Firstly, that the statements made about the employee were substantially true, for no one is entitled to a reputation that is unwarranted. This is a defence of justification.

Secondly, there is the more usual and useful defence of qualified privilege, where for example, an employer provides a reference for the guidance of a potential employer who might offer the employee a situation. Here the statement is made to someone having a justifiable interest in receiving it. An employer will not be in breach of his duty to his employee, if the reference is not entirely true, provided it was not made maliciously. The defence of qualified privilege is lost if the employee establishes malice. He may prove that the employer did not, himself, believe the statement to be true, or that he made a false statement with spite, or that it was published to someone without justifiable interest in receiving it.

If an employer gives a good reference, but later rescinds it, the second communication is also privileged. There is a duty to inform the new employer of a former employee's dishonest acts which are discovered after termination of the employment. Where the employer supplies a reference unrequested, he will have to bring in stronger evidence to show good faith than in cases where a reference is requested.

Liability of a false reference

An employer may be sued for deceit by the person misled if he recommends an employee by making untrue statements fraudulently. A statement is made fraudulently if it is made knowing of the untruth, or without belief in its truth, or recklessly not caring whether it is true or false. The reference must be given with the intention that it should be acted upon and it must have been acted upon by the person suing, usually a potential employer. The misconduct of the employee recommended renders the employer supplying the reference liable, even though he acted without malice or hope of gain. Further, following the House of Lords decision in Hedly Bryne and Company Limited *v* Heller and Partners Limited (1963), liability is established where a reference is merely misleading, if, for example, it contains a careless mis-statement, causing monetary loss to the person relying on the reference. The employer should clearly state, when giving the reference, that he cannot he held responsible for its accuracy, then all responsibility for any careless mis-statements is effectively negatived.

Restraining employees from disclosing trade secrets

It is important to determine the extent to which an employer can restrain his employee, after termination of the contract of employment, from:

1 Entering the service of a competitor
2 Operating a competing business
3 Divulging trade secrets acquired during employment
4 Enticing away customers by use of a list compiled in the course of employment

These interests cannot be protected by the grant of a patent. Protection against these four contingencies should be secured by inserting an express term (or covenant) in the contract of employment. It is inadvisable to draft a restraint clause in very wide terms to protect the employer's proprietary interest against all possible forms of competition from a former employee. By seeking too much protection the employer may lose the right to any protection at all, for an unduly wide covenant is void and unenforceable against the employee who agreed to be bound by it.

Test of reasonableness

The covenant in restraint of trade must be reasonable both from the point of view of the general public, who have an interest in allowing every person to carry on his trade freely, and as between the employer and employee who are the parties to it. Attention is mainly confined to this second aspect of reasonableness. The employer purchases the employee's skills for the duration of the employment only. Thereafter the employee is free to offer his services elsewhere, even if it is to the employer's competitor. Further, an employee in need of work cannot force his own terms on the employer and he may accept a restraint on his future activities after leaving the employment at the employer's insistence.

Trade secrets and trade connections

Any restraint taken to prevent mere competition by the employee after leaving the employer's service is void. A restraint is valid only if it prevents the employee from using trade secrets or trade connections acquired while in his employment in a manner contrary to the employer's best interests.

The employer is entitled to prevent his customers being enticed away by his former employee. To justify any restraint imposed the employer must show that the employee has had close personal and recurring contact with customers. If customers have placed reliance upon the employee's skill and judgment they will probably transfer their custom to him if he establishes his own business or joins the business of a competitor.

The area and duration of the restraint

The employer must prove that the geographical area of the restraint was no wider than necessary to protect his proprietary interest. A world-wide restraint may be reasonable if the employer's business is world-wide, provided the employee's influence also covers such an extensive area. In other cases a restraint covering a five mile radius from the employer's place of business may be too wide if customers are drawn from a smaller area.

The duration of the restraint is also important and its reasonableness is judged by reference to the length of time it will take for the employee's influence, contacts and knowledge of secret processes to become obsolete. In some cases a lifetime restraint may be reasonable if the area over which the restraint is exercised is narrowly circumscribed. The two aspects of the restraint, area and time, must be considered together and their total effect assessed.

Redundancy payments

The object of the Redundancy Payments Act 1965 is to provide monetary compensation to an employee who loses his job. The amount payable is dependent upon the length of service with the employer. The Act recognises that an employee has a proprietary interest in his job. It is is not possible to contract out of the Act. Disputes concerning the right to, and the amount of, a redundancy payment, and an employer's right to claim a rebate from the National Redundancy Fund after he has made a payment to an employee, will be determined by an industrial tribunal.

Meaning of redundancy

If an employee is dismissed wholly or mainly, though not necessarily exclusively, for one of the following reasons, then he is entitled to a redundancy payment:

1 Where the employer either ceases to carry on the business in the particular place where the employee was employed or closes down the business altogether.
2 Where the employer no longer needs the employee's services, although the business has not closed down.

An employee is not entitled to a redundancy payment where he has unreasonably refused either a renewal of his contract on the old terms, without any break in the continuity of employment, or a written offer of suitable alternative employment, sufficiently detailed to enable him to appreciate what is involved and taking effect not later than four weeks from the termination of the existing contract.

The employee is entitled to a redundancy payment after refusing alternative work offered, if he can establish that it was unsuitable and and that his refusal was reasonable considering such matters as his skills, the type of work offered, the nature of the previous work, the wages, travelling problems and family situations, any loss of fringe benefits, health or physical disabilities and lack of permanency in the work offered. The employee's personal preferences are not relevant.

Meaning of dismissal

An employee is dismissed and may claim a redundancy payment if his contract of employment is terminated by the employer, with or without notice. If a dismissed employee claims redundancy pay, the employer must prove that his dismissal was not due to redundancy, but for some other reason, such as misconduct, refusal to obey orders, insubordination or lack of co-operation.

An employee is considered to have been dismissed and may claim a redundancy payment if:

1 A fixed-term contract expires without being renewed, unless in the case of a contract for two years or more the employee waives his rights to a redundancy payment before the contract expires.
2 The business closes down as a result of the employer's death and his contract is terminated, but not where the business is continued and the employee is re-engaged within eight weeks of such death.
3 The employee terminates the contract without notice, where entitled to do so because of the employer's conduct; for example, where the employer is unable to provide remunerative employment for a period of time and there does not seem to be any opportunity of continuing the employment for the normal number of working hours fixed by the contract of employment.

When payment must be made

A claim may be made by an employee who has been continuously employed for two years, but is then dismissed because of redundancy. Any week worked by the employee before he was eighteen years old does not count.

To establish continuous employment where there has been a change in the ownership of a business, an employee must show a transfer from previous to present owner of the entire property and business, with the previous owner terminating employment and the new owner renewing the employee's contract. Consequently if the employee is later dismissed, laid off, or put on short time, employment has been continuous for the purposes of a redundancy claim. (*s*13)

If the new owner offers employment, which is refused, the employee cannot claim any payment if the terms of employment are the same as before and without any break in employment, or the terms differ, but are suitable and made in writing before the change of ownership, provided there is not a break in employment of over four weeks. For *s*13 to be applicable the ownership of a business must be transferred, not merely an asset therein.

Calculating the payment due

The employer is responsible for making the redundancy payment and also supplying a written statement stating the method of calculation.

The period during which the employee has been continuously employed by the employer is determined by reckoning backwards from the date on which notice of dismissal expires or a contract for a fixed term ends. The maximum number of years that can be taken into account is twenty. The years of continuous employment are separated into three categories:

1 Years when the employee was aged forty-one but less than sixty-five (sixty in the case of women) which are then multiplied by one-and-a-half.
2 Years when the employee was twenty-two years old but less than forty-one years old, which are then multiplied by one.
3 Years when the employee was aged twenty-one or less, excepting any period worked before he was eighteen years old, which are then multiplied by a half.

The figures so determined must be added together and multiplied by the employee's 'week's pay' to give the total redundancy payment. In most cases the 'week's pay' is the minimum remuneration to which the employee is entitled in the week immediately preceding the date when his employment terminated, but earnings over £40 in that week are excluded.

Since the maximum number of years is twenty multiplied by one-and-a-half and the maximum for the week's pay is £40, the maximum redundancy payment is £1,200. A payment does not affect entitlement to unemployment benefit, nor is it taxable under Schedule E.

An employee must make his claim within six months of the termination of his employment, unless the issue has been referred to a tribunal for determination.

Employees not entitled to a redundancy payment

The statute does not cover:

1 Persons with a fixed-term contract for two years or more, entered into before 6 December 1965, other than apprentices.
2 Registered dock workers engaged on dock work.
3 Persons employed on a fishing vessel where remuneration is solely from a share of the profits.
4 Crown servants.
5 National Health Service employees.
6 Domestic servants related to their employer.
7 Persons employed outside Great Britain, except those who 'ordinarily' work here.
8 Independent contractors.
9 Employees working less than twenty-one hours per week (on average).
10 An employee who is the employer's spouse.
11 Persons whose notice expires after their sixty-fifth birthday in the case of men, or after their sixtieth birthday in the case of women.

An employee entitled to a pension, gratuity or superannuation allowance payable on leaving his employment is not entitled to a redundancy payment if the sum received equals or exceeds the redundancy claim. Where the pension or other payment is less than the redundancy payment otherwise payable, then the redundancy payment is reduced to take the pension into account.

A redundancy payment is not payable to any employee who receives a similar payment on leaving his employment under an agreement made between an employers' organisation and a trade union. These private arrangements are more suitable where a long continuous period of employment, a necessary pre-requisite to a redundancy payment, may not be possible, as in the building trade.

Chapter 19

The Industrial Relations Act

Darek Celinski, Personnel Manager, Herbert Ingersoll Limited

The Industrial Relations Act 1971 is the first comprehensive body of industrial relations legislation in British history. Relationships between employers and employees in all other advanced industrialised countries have been regulated by law for years. For the first time British employers and employees now find themselves subject to legal obligations similar to those controlling their counterparts in other advanced countries.

The Industrial Relations Act is a long and complicated legal document although its overall aim is simple: to promote good industrial relations. It seeks to achieve its aim by encouraging improvements in the way human relations are conducted in industry and commerce. Its provisions establish an entirely new framework of civil law which imposes new obligations on employers and confers new rights on employees.

Throughout the Act, the accent is on encouragement to resolve industrial problems by voluntary means. Provisions of the Act require the setting up of voluntary systems and clearly-defined procedures for arriving at agreements and settlement of disputes. The aim is to promote such relationships within companies that applications to industrial courts to resolve disputes are made only as the last resort.

Even in these cases, the provisions are framed in such a way as to allow the parties to any proceedings to avail themselves of all opportunities for conciliation.

In the context of the Act, the word 'worker' is used to denote any individual who works or seeks to work under a contract of employment. Thus, the provisions of the Act apply to each and every employee and potential employee in a company: manual, white-collar and managerial. The Act does not apply to the police force or armed services.

The Royal Assent of the Industrial Relations Act in August 1971 marks the end of a long search, by successive governments and over a number of years, for a method of making relations in industry more harmonious. The major landmarks in this search are: the Donovan Report, produced after three years of study and deliberation by a Royal Commission (chaired by Lord Donovan) that was set up in 1964 by the Labour Government; the Conservative document *Fair Deal at Work* which was published in April 1968; the Labour document *In Place of Strife* which was published in January 1969; and finally, the 1971 Act, drafted and guided through Parliament by the Conservative Government. It contains 187 pages of complex legislation. Authoritative interpretation of its provisions can be given only by the industrial courts and tribunals.

The Act introduces major changes in the existing legal framework of industrial relations. It amends the laws relating to employers and workers and to organisations of employers and organisations of workers. It removes proceedings resulting from actions in the course of industrial disputes from the jurisdiction of civil courts to that of the industrial courts and tribunals.

General principles

All provisions of the Act are based on four general principles which are stated as follows:

(a) the principle of collective bargaining freely conducted on behalf of workers and employers and with due regard to the general interests of the community;

(b) the principle of developing and maintaining orderly procedures in industry for the peaceful and expeditious settlement of disputes by negotiation, conciliation or arbitration, with due regard to the general interests of the community;
(c) the principle of free association of workers in independent trade unions, and of employers in employers' associations, so organised as to be representative, responsible and effective bodies for regulating relations between employers and workers; and
(d) the principle of freedom and security for workers, protected by adequate safeguards against unfair industrial practices, whether on the part of employers or others.

Main elements

The general principles of the Act are fulfilled by seven main elements contained in the new legislation. These are listed below and are also shown in Figure 19 : 1 :

1 New system of informal and expert judicial and administrative institutions which, together, are involved in the implementation, administration and enforcement of the provisions of the Act.
2 New system of registration for trade unions and employers' associations which confers on registered organisations certain privileges, concessions and immunities while safeguarding the rights of individuals.
3 New protection for the community in emergency situations. This gives the power of intervention by the Secretary of State for Employment when an industrial action may threaten to cause a serious national emergency.
4 New rights and protection for employees: freedom to belong or not to belong to a trade union; protection against unfair dismissal; more detailed statement of terms and conditions of employment; longer periods of notice of termination of employment; the right to complain to an industrial tribunal; the right to receive information about the affairs of the employers.
5 New concept, both in industrial relations and in the law, of unfair industrial practices. Unfair practices are defined as specific

actions which prevent or deter persons or organisations from exercising their lawful rights or from performing their duties as required by legislation.

6 New methods of settling disputes by establishing bargaining units and improving procedures for the peaceful and expeditious resolving of disputes by negotiation, conciliation or arbitration.

7 Code of Industrial Relations Practice – a handbook which provides guidance on the principal means of raising the standards of conduct in industry. The Secretary of State for Employment, in his foreword to this new document, writes: 'An essential part of the Government's policy for industrial relations is to produce a code of practice, the purpose of which is to set standards and give practical guidance on the conduct of industrial relations and the development of policies to improve human relations in all types of employment'.

The above seven elements provide new foundations for the future development of industrial relations in business organisations. Each element contains numerous provisions of the Act and details are provided in official publications obtainable free from the Department of Employment. This chapter outlines the main features of the seven elements.

Institutions

The tasks of implementation, administration and enforcement of the provisions of the Act are entrusted to institutions specially designed for the purpose. Administrative duties are assigned to the Secretary of State for Employment, the Commission on Industrial Relations (CIR) and the Chief Registrar of Trade Unions and Employers' Associations.

The Commission on Industrial Relations plays a leading role under the Act. It seeks to achieve its results not by enforcement and sanctions but through voluntary acceptance, both by unions and employers, of the impartial and expert advice it offers. It consists of six to fifteen full- or part-time members with special knowledge of industrial relations. The Commission is not a court of law.

The judicial system set up by the Act is two-tier, comprising the National Industrial Relations Court (the Industrial Court) and the

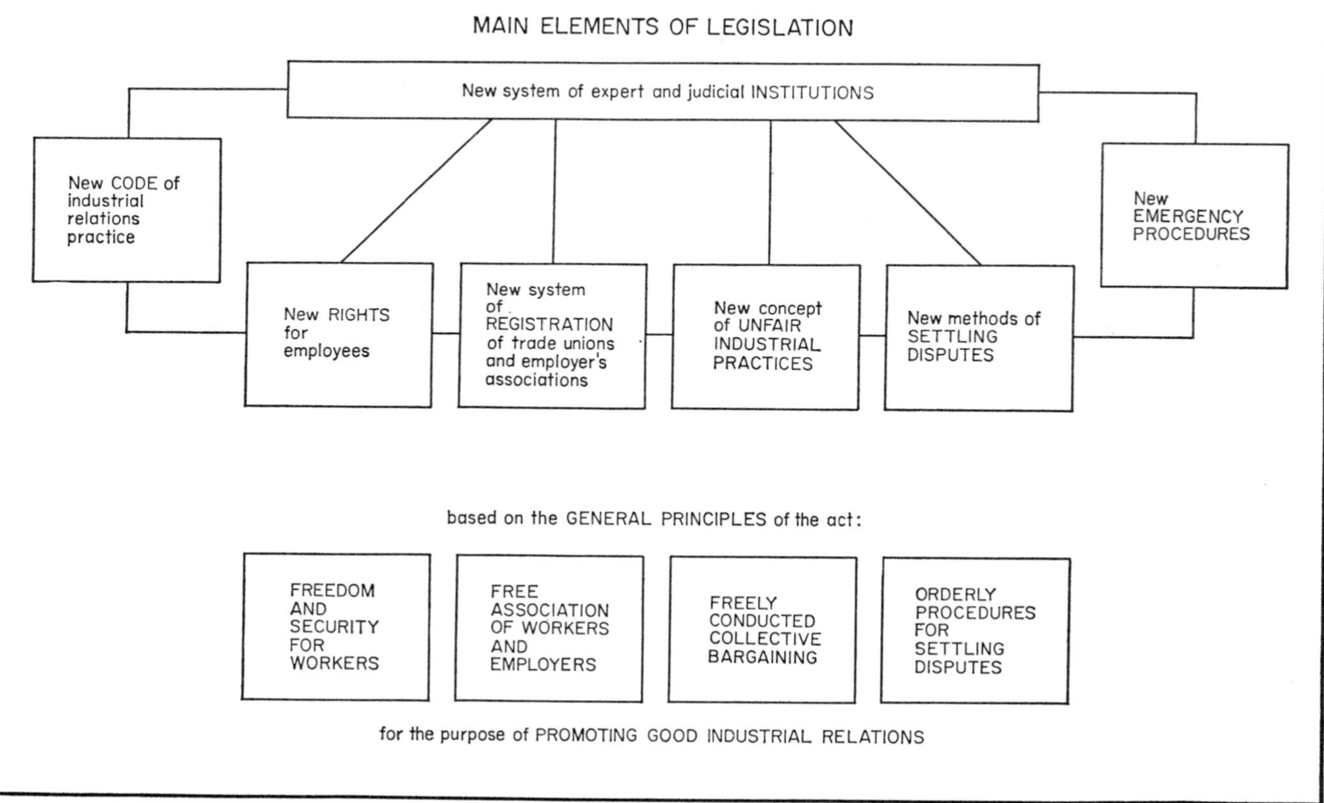

FIGURE 19:1 THE INDUSTRIAL RELATIONS ACT 1971
The general principles and main elements of legislation

industrial tribunals. The National Industrial Relations Court is given the status of a High Court and is quite independent of the Government. Composed of lay members as well as judges, it adjudicates the more important cases arising under the Act. Similarly composed, the industrial tribunals are independent judicial bodies; their jurisdiction also extends to hearing cases under other related legislation – the Redundancy Act, the Industrial Training Act, the Contracts of Employment Act, Redundancy Payments Act, Docks and Harbours Act, Selective Employment Payments Act and Equal Pay Act. The Industrial Arbitration Board comprises independent persons, together with representatives of workers and employers. Its work under the Act relates to terms and conditions of employment.

The Act extends the conciliation service provided by the Department of Employment and Productivity. Additional conciliation officers have been appointed to try to achieve voluntary settlement of industrial relations issues.

Figure 19:2 shows in diagrammatic form the various institutions under the Act and outlines their corresponding functions and judicial responsibilities.

System of registration of trade unions and employers' associations

It is a fundamental feature of the Act that only those organisations which register with the new Registrar of Trade Unions and Employers' Associations can enjoy various privileges, concessions and immunities under the law.

The Act establishes the office of Chief Registrar of Trade Unions and Employers' Associations. It is his duty to ensure that the rules and standards of administration of registered organisations comply with the requirements of the Act. Any organisation of workers and employers which has power to alter its own rules and to control its own property and funds is eligible for registration. There are three registers: Permanent, Provisional and Special.

All organisations which before the passing of the Act were registered under the Trade Unions Act 1871–1964 were transferred automatically to the Provisional Register. This gave them protection from some form of legal action for a limited period while the

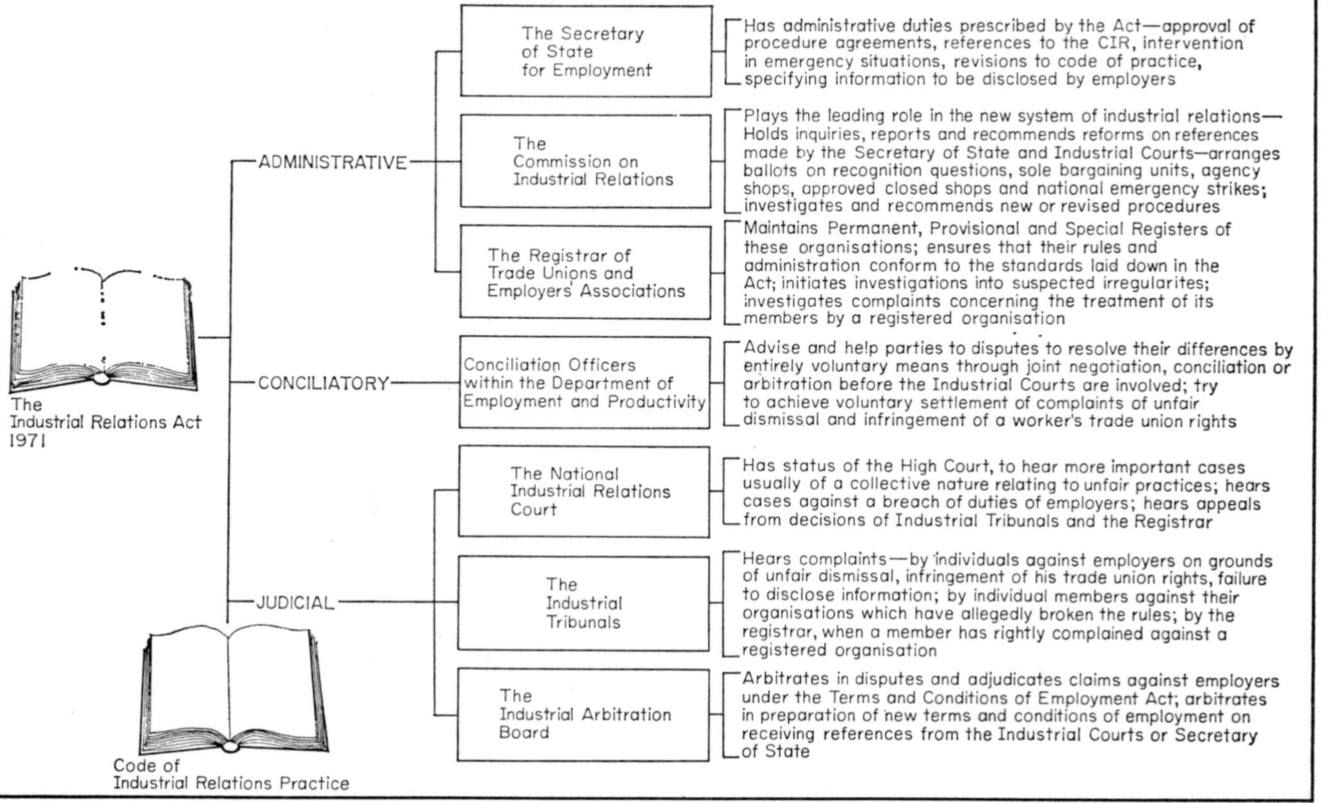

FIGURE 19:2 THE SYSTEM OF EXPERT AND JUDICIAL INSTITUTIONS

The Code of Industrial Relations Practice complements the provisions of the Industrial Relations Act. The main functions and judicial responsibilities of the institutions are shown opposite their titles

Registrar determined their eligibility to be transferred to the Permanent Register.

The Special Register has been set up for certain organisations which are not trade unions nor employers' associations, but are engaged in industrial relations. Professional organisations, chartered bodies and registered companies which meet the conditions laid down in the Act are eligible for registration on the Special Register. This gives the organisations which negotiate on behalf of their members the obligations and benefits of trade union status, but does not prejudice their position as chartered bodies.

The Registrar has power to apply to the Industrial Court for cancellation of the registration of any organisation which has failed to comply with the rules and requirements imposed on it under the Act. He is empowered to initiate investigations into suspected irregularities and complaints concerning the treatment of its members by a registered organisation. The National Industrial Relations Court has the power to hear appeals arising from the decisions of the Registrar. The industrial tribunals adjudicate cases where the Registrar finds that a member has rightly complained against a registered organisation.

The advantages from registration, especially for the trade unions, are considerable. The following immunities, concessions and privileges are provided for the registered trade unions and other organisations while the exact reverse applies if they are unregistered. Registered trade unions:

1 May call members out on strike in breach of their contracts of employment without committing (except in certain circumstances) an unfair industrial practice.
2 May use the procedures laid down in the Act for obtaining recognition rights, that is, an agency shop or an approved closed shop.
3 Have a right to receive information from employers for collective bargaining.
4 Have the protection of limits on the amounts of compensation which the Industrial Court may award against them.
5 Will continue to enjoy tax concessions for their provident funds.
6 Their officials will not be liable to pay awards of compensation if they have acted within their authority.

However, registration does not exempt a trade union from a complaint to the Industrial Court or an industrial tribunal if it has committed an unfair industrial practice. A registered organisation may be removed from the register if it so desires.

Protection for the community in emergency situations

The Act establishes new procedures which are designed to protect the community in situations which threaten the economy or public health and safety. These are termed emergency procedures. They empower the Secretary of State for Employment to intervene in industrial disputes where it appears to him that the effects of any industrial action may cause a serious national emergency.

When the Secretary of State is satisfied that a deferment of industrial action would help to bring about a settlement by negotiation, he may apply to the Industrial Court for a deferment order ('cooling off' period). The Court's order will require those who are organising industrial action to defer or discontinue the action for a period up to a maximum of sixty days. If no settlement is achieved during this period there is nothing then to prevent the industrial action taking place.

Emergency procedures provide for an alternative course of action by the Secretary of State. When he believes that there is some doubt whether the workers concerned support the industrial action or have had an opportunity to express their wishes, he may apply to the Court for an order to conduct a ballot.

Ballots are secret and conducted under the supervision of the Commission on Industrial Relations. The Commission may either invite the registered trade union involved in the dispute to conduct the ballot or conduct it by itself. Those responsible for calling and organising the industrial action must refrain from their actions while the ballot is being conducted. Once the Commission has reported the results of the ballot, even if it shows that a majority is opposed to taking industrial action, those responsible are free to recommence their activities and to organise such action.

Industrial actions are strikes and other concerted courses of conduct which, in furtherance of an industrial dispute, prevent, reduce or interfere with the production of goods or the provision of services.

Rights of employees

The Act introduces new concepts, new safeguards and establishes new rights of employees in relation to both employers and trade unions.

The Act gives every employee the right to belong to a trade union, to participate in its activities and to hold a union office. Equally, every employee has the legal right to choose not to belong to a trade union. These rights are statutory provisions in the employees' standard terms and conditions of employment. An employee who claims that his employer has prevented his joining a union, or penalised him for doing so, is entitled to complain to an industrial tribunal. By the same token, it is an unfair industrial practice by an employer to compel an employee to join a trade union. However, when an employer encourages an employee to join a union, it is not unfair.

The Act recognises a need for special arrangements to be made in some circumstances regarding union membership and introduces agency shop and approved closed shop concepts.

An agency shop can be established by voluntary agreement between an employer and a registered trade union. However, where an employer is unwilling to enter into agreement voluntarily, either he or the registered trade union may apply to the Industrial Court to have the issue decided. The Court will ask the Commission on Industrial Relations to arrange a ballot of the group of employees to whom the agency shop agreement would apply. If a majority of the employees eligible to vote, or two-thirds of those actually voting, favour the introduction of an agency shop, the employer will be under a statutory duty to conclude the agreement. If the required majority is not in favour, the Industrial Court will make an order to bar an agency shop agreement for the next two years.

Where an agency shop agreement is in force, it is a condition of employment for those employees covered by the agreement to belong to the trade union concerned. Thus, the employer may dismiss an employee who refuses or fails to join the union, unless he takes one of two options open to him. One is to pay the basic subscription to the union in lieu of membership dues and the second, in the case of conscientious objection, to an agreed charity.

The Act renders unenforceable all existing closed shop agreements but permits, in exceptional circumstances, an approved post-entry closed shop. Pre-entry closed shop agreements, where workers must be members of a union before they can be engaged, became invalidated by the Act.

To establish an approved post-entry closed shop, the employer and the registered trade union are required to make a joint application to the Industrial Court. The Court will ask the Commission on Industrial Relations to examine the situation and to satisfy itself that there is a real need for the agreement. If the Commission concludes that a post-entry closed shop is justified, it will report its conclusion to the Industrial Court. The next step will be to hold a ballot to determine whether the proposed agreement has the support of the majority of the employees who would be bound by it. Application for a ballot must be supported by no less than one-fifth of those affected.

Where a post-entry closed shop agreement is in force, it is a condition of employment of those employees covered by the agreement to belong to the trade union concerned. Thus, the employer may refuse to engage, or may dismiss or penalise, an employee who refuses to belong to the union unless the employee is a conscientious objector and agrees to pay an appropriate contribution to an agreed charity.

Where a significant proportion of the workers covered by an agency shop or closed shop agreement wish to have it terminated, the Act provides the opportunity for holding a ballot to determine the wishes of the majority. Such a ballot will be held if a request for it is supported in writing by not less than one-fifth of those covered by the agreement and provided that the application is not made within two years of a previous ballot.

One of the new safeguards established by the Act for every employee is his protection against unfair dismissal. An employee who claims that he was unfairly dismissed is entitled to complain to an industrial tribunal. If the tribunal upholds the complaint, it will recommend re-engagement or award compensation up to a limit of 104 weeks' pay or £4,160 whichever is the less.

Any dismissal will be regarded as unfair unless the employer can prove that it was due to the employee's capability, qualifications, conduct or on the grounds of redundancy. 'Capability' is assessed by reference to skill, aptitude, health or other physical or mental qualities. 'Qualifications' means any degree, diploma, or other academic, technical or professional qualifications, relevant to the position which the employee held. Dismissal on grounds of redundancy is fair provided that the employee was not selected because he exercised his statutory right to belong to a trade union or for taking part in its activities.

The Act amends the Contracts of Employment Act. It requires an employer to issue each employee with a written statement of his main terms and conditions of employment which includes the following additional information:

1 Sufficient information about holidays (including public holidays) and holiday pay to enable the employee's entitlement, including any entitlement to accrued holiday pay on the termination of his employment, to be precisely calculated.
2 Information about the employee's rights in relation to trade union membership and activity and, where appropriate, details of how any agency shop agreement or approved closed shop agreement that applies to him affects his rights.
3 Information as to whom the employee should apply if he has a grievance about his employment, how the application should be made, and the procedure for dealing with the matter.

Additions to written statements required by this Act may be treated as though they were changes to particulars in written statements already issued.

Another amendment to the Contracts of Employment Act extends the minimum length of notice for termination of employment for long service employees. The scales, including the new provisions, are now as follows:

1 After thirteen weeks of employment: one week's notice
2 After two years of employment: two weeks' notice
3 After five years of employment: four weeks' notice
4 After ten years of employment: six weeks' notice
5 After fifteen years of employment: eight weeks' notice

The employees, after thirteen weeks of employment, are required to give the company one week's notice, irrespective of the number of years of continuous employment. Staff employees who are on 'one month's notice on either side' are not affected by these minimum scales until ten years of continuous employment have been completed.

The Act places a duty on employers of more than 350 persons, whether employed in the same or different places, to issue to their employees annual written statements relating to their undertakings. The Secretary of State is empowered to make regulations to specify the information which the statements should contain. As a first step management may make available, in the most convenient form, the substance of the information which is supplied to shareholders or published in annual reports. If an employer fails to issue a statement within six months of the end of the financial year to which it relates, any employee concerned may complain to an industrial tribunal.

Concept of unfair industrial practice

This concept is new, both in industrial relations and in law. Unfair practices are defined as specific actions which prevent or deter persons or organisations from performing their duties as required by legislation. Any organisation or individual committing an unfair industrial practice may be complained against in the Industrial Court or before an industrial tribunal.

It is not an unfair practice to strike. The Act prevents any court from making any order either compelling an employee to stay at work against his wishes or requiring him to go on strike against his wishes. Also, peaceful picketing in furtherance of an industrial dispute is not unfair except where this involves the picketing of any individual's home.

The list of unfair industrial practices is in three sections, involving action by an employer or employers' association, a registered or unregistered trade union, and either of the above categories.

Unfair industrial practice by an employer is to:

1 Dismiss an employee unfairly.
2 Infringe an employee's right to join a trade union, take part in its activities and/or hold an office.

3 Infringe an employee's right not to join a trade union.
4 Refuse to employ an individual because of his union membership or non-membership.
5 Fail to negotiate seriously with a trade union where the Industrial Court has made an order that the union is to be the sole bargaining agent for the bargaining unit.
6 Conduct or threaten a lock-out to induce or attempt to induce anyone to refrain from making an application to the Industrial Court about the recognition of a sole bargaining agent or withdrawal of such recognition.

Unfair industrial practice by trade unions (registered, and unregistered) is to:

1 Induce an employer not to perform his duty to enter into an agency shop agreement after a ballot has shown a majority of employees to be in favour of one.
2 Induce an employer to enter into an agency shop agreement after an application has been made for a ballot.
3 Organise or threaten a strike or irregular industrial action short of a strike to induce an employer not to comply with relevant provisions of the Act.

There are many more industrial practices listed which are unfair and may be committed by either side. They generally refer to breaking legally enforceable agreements and acting or threatening to act in contravention of the provisions and procedures laid down in the Act.

Collective bargaining

The provisions of the Act aim to establish within companies a stable and effective bargaining structure as the basis of good industrial relations. Basically, the new methods of settling disputes take the form of establishing bargaining units and improving procedures for handling all industrial relations matters.

A bargaining unit is made up of those employees of an establishment who constitute a common interest group. Common interest means that they perform work of similar nature, are subject to similar terms and conditions of employment and are able to act jointly on matters common to them. When composition of one or more of these units is defined and agreed with the employer, they are able to bargain. Thus, the rights recognised by an employer to negotiate on behalf of all or some of the employees comprised in a bargaining unit are called the bargaining rights. These rights are to negotiate with the employer with a view to conclude or modify one or more collective agreements. Any agreements or arrangements between employers and employees or their representatives, which are in force and relate to matters of procedure or matters of substance, are known as collective agreements.

The procedure agreements regulate all procedural relationships between an employer and his employees. All employees of an employer should be covered by appropriate agreements, which specify:

1 Machinery for consultation for the settlement by negotiation or arbitration of terms and conditions of employment and other questions.
2 Negotiating rights.
3 Facilities for officials of trade unions.
4 Procedures relating to dismissal.
5 Procedures relating to matters of discipline other than dismissal.
6 Procedures relating to grievances of individual employees.

Matters of substance cover such provisions as wages and salaries, overtime rates, bonuses, holiday entitlement, hours of work, shift-working and similar issues.

The Act creates a new presumption in law that written collective agreements are to be regarded as legally binding unless they contain express provision to the contrary. A breach of legally binding agreements is an unfair industrial practice and an injured party may complain to the Industrial Court. This presumption applies to any written settlement governing terms and conditions of employment and industrial relations procedures.

An additional effect of this presumption in law must be the care with which agreements are being drawn up since the passing of the Act. Defective procedures, and disputes over their interpretation, seriously hinder the development and maintenance of good industrial relations. Thus, the precise and unambiguous wording of all collective agreements acquires special importance. Even if it is intended for an agreement not to be binding in law, and an appropriate disclaimer is inserted, the likely tendency is towards greater care and precision in thinking about and making, drafting and keeping agreements.

One of the provisions of the Act concerning the obligations of parties to collective agreements is that they should not only keep the agreements themselves but should do all they reasonably can to ensure that their members and agents act in a way which is consistent with obligations undertaken by the parties themselves.

If full agreement between the parties is not reached, it is now possible for either party to seek an order of the Industrial Court giving the force of a legally binding collective agreement. However, agreements reached voluntarily are always to be preferred.

The formal arrangements for collective bargaining, bargaining units and recognition of their negotiating rights are provided for by the Act. For the first time, the registered trade unions are given a legal right to be recognised by an employer, when their members constitute the prescribed majority within a bargaining unit. Thus, legislation provides for systems of negotiating rights, bargaining agents, sole bargaining agents, joint negotiating panels and joint negotiating panels of trade unions.

A sole bargaining agent in relation to a bargaining unit is a registered organisation of workers which has negotiating rights to the exclusion of all other organisations of workers.

A joint negotiating panel is a body consisting of representatives of two or more organisations of workers which is established for purposes of collective bargaining and is authorised by and on behalf of those organisations to enter into collective agreements on their behalf. A joint negotiating panel of trade unions is a negotiating panel where all the organisations of workers represented on it are trade unions.

Code of Industrial Relations Practice

The Code of Industrial Relations Practice serves a similar purpose in the field of industrial relations to that served by the Highway

Code in the field of regulating traffic on the roads. Naturally, this analogy cannot be taken much further as there are some fundamental differences between the two codes. While the Highway Code deals with very precise situations, the Code of Practice deals with relationships between employers and employees in a wide variety of situations which defy precise description and need to be treated in very general terms.

As with the Highway Code, provisions of the Code of Practice are not legally enforceable, although they are admissible in evidence in industrial courts and tribunals. Thus, compliance or non-compliance with the relevant provisions of the Code will be taken into account for the purpose of determining liability and, where applicable, the awarding of compensation.

There is practically nothing in the code itself which is fundamentally new to industry. Most of its provisions are based on practices well established and proved in companies where good industrial relations already exist. Thus, the practical effect of the Code, when its provisions become fully implemented, will be to extend the standards of the best firms throughout industry.

Experience suggests that good relations between employers and employees in companies do not just happen spontaneously. Where these exist they have invariably been created by deliberate and sustained effort of the management. Such companies, after detailed study of the Code, will no doubt recognise many of their own policies and practices. They may find that there are very few actions needed on their part to comply fully with the provisions of the Code. On the other hand, companies with unsatisfactory relations may find a great deal of work which requires their urgent attention.

The underlying principle of the Code of Practice is an endeavour to re-shape the pattern of industrial relations practices so that the fundamental conditions for good relations between management and employees can be created within a company. The Code gives guidance for creating such conditions. This guidance does not confine itself to the procedural aspects of industrial relations such as collective agreements and negotiating machinery; it is also concerned with human relations and, therefore, with policies and practices which shape attitudes and affect the individual employee in the performance of his job.

The Code of Industrial Relations Practice has thirty-one pages, its provisions are stated in 133 paragraphs grouped under seven headings: Responsibilities, Employment Policies, Communication and Consultation, Collective Bargaining, Employee Representation, Grievance and Disputes Procedures, and Disciplinary Procedures.

The two-page introduction includes a statement of the themes which underlie the Code. These are given as follows:

1 The vital role of collective bargaining carried out in a reasonable and constructive manner between employers and strong representative trade unions.
2 The importance of good human relations between employers and employees in every establishment, based on trust and confidence.

In any undertaking, management needs to use its resources efficiently while employees look for continuity of employment, security of earnings and satisfaction in their work. Both have a common interest in the undertaking's success because without it their aims cannot be achieved. But some conflicts of interest are bound to arise. With good industrial relations they can be resolved in a responsible and constructive way. Good industrial relations are a joint responsibility.

Just as the motorist uses the Highway Code (rather than the Road Traffic Acts) to regulate his day-to-day driving, so company management should look to the Code of Practice to regulate its everyday industrial relations. Managers will, of course, require the full text of the Code when working on the implementation of its provisions. A diagrammatic summary of the Code is given in Figure 19:3.

The Code is so organised that its broad principles are stated in one or more paragraphs immediately following each main heading, subsequent paragraphs under the same heading deal with more detailed requirements. In the summary which follows, the key paragraphs – numbered as in the Code – are given in full, while the ensuing detailed recommendations are very briefly summarised.

Responsibilities

Management

1 The principal aim of management is to conduct the business of the undertaking successfully. Good industrial relations need to be developed within the framework of an efficient organisation and they will in turn help management to achieve this aim.

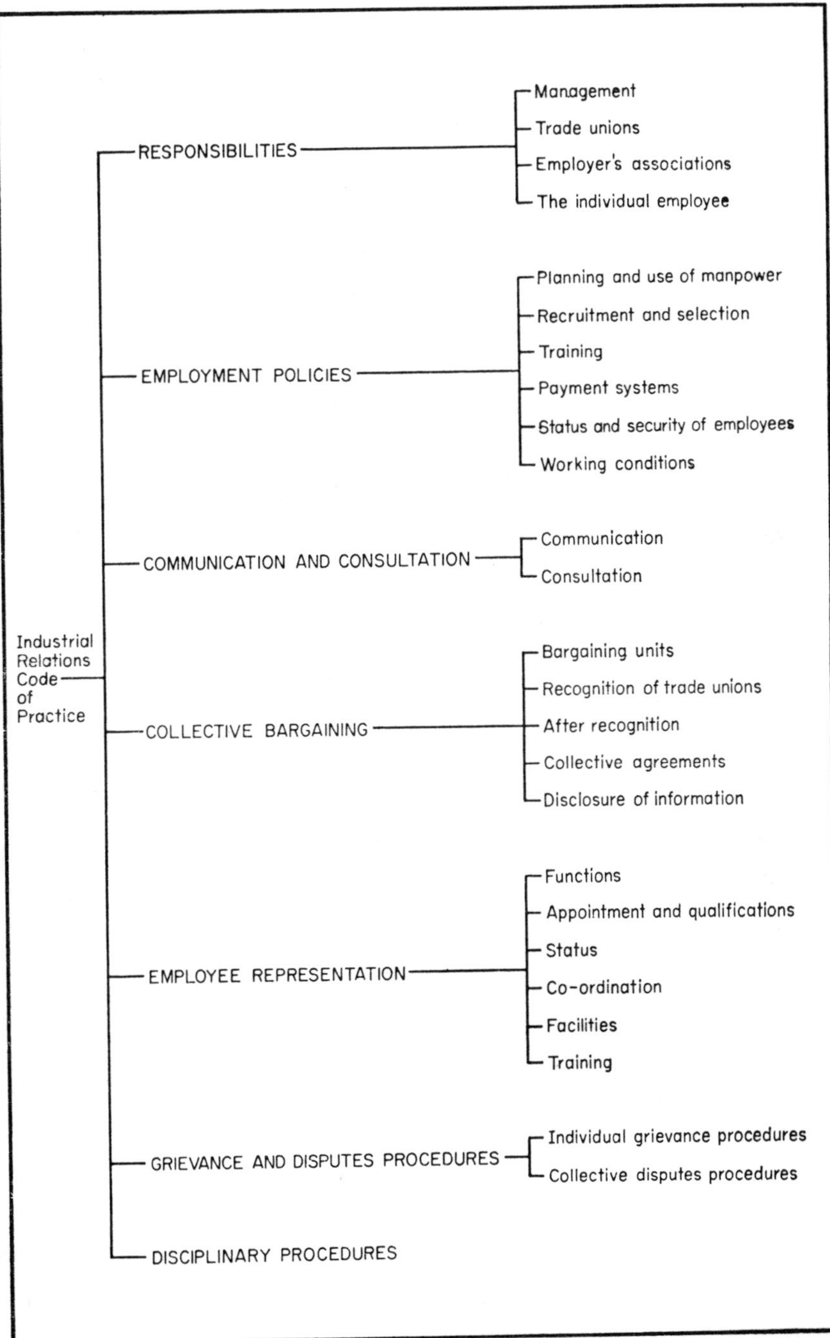

FIGURE 19:3 THE INDUSTRIAL RELATIONS CODE OF PRACTICE

This is a summary of the Code, showing how its contents are organised

2 One of management's major objectives should therefore be to develop effective industrial relations policies which command the confidence of employees. Managers at the highest level should give, and show that they give, just as much attention to industrial relations as to such functions as finance, marketing, production or administration.

3 Good industrial relations are the joint responsibility of management and of employees and trade unions representing them. But the primary responsibility for their promotion rests with management. It should therefore take the initiative in creating and developing them.

The subsequent six paragraphs under this heading detail management responsibilities for effective arrangements for negotiation, consultation, communication, and for settling grievances and disputes. Also, for the organisation of work, for the training of line managers (including supervisors and personnel managers) in industrial relations, for effectiveness of the supervisor (who is in a key position to influence industrial relations), for providing as far as practicable for the employees' job satisfaction.

Trade unions

10 The principal aim of trade unions is to promote their members' interests. They can do this only if the undertakings in which their members are employed prosper. They therefore have an interest in the success of those undertakings and an essential contribution to make to it by co-operating in measures to promote efficiency. They also share with management the responsibility for good industrial relations.

The subsequent four paragraphs under this heading detail trade unions' responsibilities for maintaining jointly with employers' associations and individual managements effective arrangements for negotiation, consultation and communication and for settling grievances and disputes. Also, for ensuring that officials (including shop stewards), look after their members' interests in an efficient and responsible way, for the effectiveness of their organisation and for having the authority and resources needed to carry out their functions.

Employers' associations

15 The principal aim of employers' associations is to promote those interests of their members which can best be served by co-operation at industry or other appropriate levels.

The subsequent two paragraphs under this heading detail the responsibilities of employers' associations for assistance and advice to their members. Also, the need of associations for authority, resources and information to be able to carry out their functions.

The individual employee

18 The individual employee has obligations to his employer, to his trade union if he belongs to one, and to his fellow employees. He shares responsibility for the state of industrial relations in the establishment where he works and his attitudes and conduct can have a decisive influence on them.

There are five more paragraphs under this heading. The first one deals with the legal relationship between employer and employee derived from the contract of employment. Next comes the requirement that each employee should satisfy himself that he understands the terms of his contract and abides by them. Additionally, he should make himself familiar with any procedures for dealing with grievances and make use of them when the need arises. The last three paragraphs refer to professional employees and their special obligations.

Employment policies

24 Clear and comprehensive employment policies are essential to good relations between management and employees. They help management to make the most effective use of its manpower resources and give each employee opportunity to develop his potential.

There are twenty-six further paragraphs under the overall heading of employment policies. The first three are general: management is responsible for initiating these policies, it is unlawful to discriminate on grounds of colour, race or ethnic or national origins in respect of recruitment, conditions of employment, training, promotion and dismissal.

The remaining paragraphs are grouped under six separate subheadings. These deal in detail with the following employment policies each a major subject in its own right):

1 Planning and use of manpower
2 Recruitment and selection

3 Training
4 Payment systems
5 Status and security of employees
6 Working conditions

Communication and consultation

51 Communication and consultation are essential in all establishments. They are necessary to promote operational efficiency and mutual understanding, as well as the individual employee's sense of satisfaction and involvement in his job. Management, employee representatives and trade unions should co-operate in ensuring that effective communication and consultation take place.

There are nineteen further paragraphs under this heading. The first two stress the importance of communication and consultation in times of change. The subsequent paragraphs are grouped under the two sub-headings of communication and consultation.

Communication

54 In its day-to-day conduct of business, management needs both to give information to employees and to receive information from them. Effective arrangements should be made to facilitate this two-way flow.

The subsequent paragraphs under this sub-heading stress the importance of communication by word of mouth and define the information to be provided.

Consultation

65 Consultation means jointly examining and discussing problems of concern to both management and employees. It involves seeking mutually acceptable solutions through a genuine exchange of views and information.

The subsequent paragraphs under this sub-heading emphasise that consultation between management and employees or their representatives about operational and other day-to-day matters is necessary in all establishments, whatever their size. Establishments with more than 250 employees should have systematic arrangements for management and employee representatives to meet regularly.

Collective bargaining

71 Freely conducted collective bargaining is a joint activity which establishes a framework for relations between management and employees. It requires from both sides a reasonable and constructive approach in negotiation, with due regard to the general interests of the community, and a determination to abide by agreements which have been made.

There are twenty-seven further paragraphs under the overall heading of collective bargaining. The first two paragraphs explain that collective bargaining for the same group of employees may be conducted at different levels about different subjects: industry level, group of establishments level or a single establishment level. In such cases, the matters to be bargained about at each level should be defined by agreement.

The remaining paragraphs are grouped under five sub-headings, as follows:

Bargaining Units
74 Collective bargaining in an establishment or undertaking is conducted in relation to defined groups of employees which can appropriately be covered by one negotiating process. In the Industrial Relations Act and in the Code these are called 'bargaining units'.

Other paragraphs under this sub-heading define the composition of bargaining units. They also explain the steps which may be taken when management and unions are unable to reach voluntary agreement for establishing a bargaining unit.

Recognition of trade unions
82 A trade union may claim recognition for negotiating purposes either where management has already agreed bargaining arrangements with other unions or where no arrangements exist.

The subsequent paragraphs under this sub-heading describe the process of recognition and emphasise the need for voluntary settlement of claims for recognition of trade unions.

After recognition
87 Relations between management and trade unions which it recognises for negotiating purposes should be based on agreed pro-

cedures which provide a clear set of rules and a sound basis for resolving conflicts of interest.

The subsequent two paragraphs recommend management to provide reasonable facilities for recognised unions to keep in touch with their members and to encourage personal contact between managers and officials of the union, including shop stewards. Contacts should not be left until trouble arises.

Collective agreements

90 Collective agreements deal with matters of procedure and matters of substance which are of joint concern to management and employees. A single agreement may contain provisions of both kinds or they may be dealt with in separate agreements. In either case, the agreement should be in writing and there should be agreed arrangements for checking that procedural provisions have not become out of date.

The subsequent paragraphs under this sub-heading cover details of collective agreements about procedures: constitution of parties, arrangements, facilities, scope. Substantive collective agreements settle terms and conditions of employment. They cover: wages and salaries, overtime rates, hours of work, holiday entitlement and pay, techniques for determining levels of performance and job grading and similar provisions.

Disclosure of information

96 Collective bargaining can be conducted responsibly only if management and unions have adequate information on the matters being negotiated.

The subsequent paragraphs under this sub-heading recommend to management to meet all reasonable requests from trade unions for information which is relevant to the negotiations in hand. In particular, it should make available the information which is supplied to shareholders or published in annual reports. Management is not obliged to disclose certain kinds of information which would be of advantage to a competitor.

Employee representation at the place of work

99 Employees need representatives to put forward their collective views to management and to safeguard their interests in consultation and negotiation. It is also an advantage for management to deal with representatives who can speak for their fellow employees.

There are a further twenty paragraphs under this heading. The first three describe the responsibilities of employees who are accredited as union representatives and usually given the title of 'shop steward'. The remaining paragraphs are grouped under six sub-headings as follows:

Functions

103 A shop steward's functions at the place of work cover:

i trade union matters such as recruitment, maintaining membership and collecting contributions;

ii industrial relations matters such as handling members' grievances, negotiation and consultation.

All functions of a shop steward in the individual establishment should be clearly defined by agreement between the parties. A shop steward should observe all agreements to which his union is a party and should take all reasonable steps to ensure that those whom he represents also observe them.

Appointment and qualifications

106 Trade unions and management should seek agreement on:

i the number of shop stewards needed in the establishment, including senior stewards and deputies;

ii the work groups for which each steward is responsible.

Both will depend on the size and organisation of the establishment and the number of union members employed. The trade union should decide on any conditions of eligibility. Management should offer the trade union facilities to conduct elections. The trade union should notify management in writing when shop stewards are appointed and when changes are made.

Status

110 Trade unions should:

i give their shop stewards written credentials, setting out their powers and duties within the union, including any authority to call for industrial action;

ii seek agreement with management on the issue of joint written credentials setting out the relevant rights and obligations of the stewards and of management.

All credentials should state the period of office of the shop steward and the work group he represents.

Co-ordination

112 In an establishment where there are a number of shop stewards of one trade union, they should consider electing a senior steward to co-ordinate their activities.

Where there are more than one union, they should seek agreement with management to elect one steward to represent all the members in the establishment and to co-ordinate all union activities.

Facilities

116 The facilities needed by shop stewards will depend on their functions. The nature and extent of these facilities should be agreed between trade unions and management. As a minimum, they should be given:

i time off from the job to the extent reasonably required for their industrial relations functions; permission should be sought from the appropriate manager and should not be unreasonably withheld;

ii maintenance of earnings while carrying out these functions.

The subsequent paragraph recommends that management should also make available other facilities appropriate to the circumstances. These may include: lists of new employees, accommodation for meetings, access to a telephone and provision of notice boards, and the use of office facilities.

Training

118 Trade unions and management should:

i review the type of training most appropriate for the steward's needs and take all reasonable steps to ensure that stewards receive the training they require;

ii seek to agree on the arrangements for leave from the job to attend training courses, including compensation for loss of earnings;

iii accept joint responsibility for training in the use of arrangements for communication and consultation and for handling grievances.

The next paragraph deals with shop stewards' need to be informed by their union about its policies and by their management about its employment policies.

Grievance and disputes procedure

120 All employees have a right to seek redress for grievances relating to their employment. Each employee must be told how he can do so.

There are a further nine paragraphs under this heading. The first three require management to make arrangements and establish procedures for settling individual grievances and collective disputes. These are further expanded under two sub-headings:

Individual grievance procedure

124 The aim of the procedure should be to settle the grievance fairly and as near as possible to the point of origin. It should be simple and rapid in operation.

The next paragraph states that the procedure should be in writing; the grievance should normally be discussed first between the employee and his immediate supervisor; the employee should be accompanied at the next stage of the procedure by his shop steward if he so wishes; there should be a right of appeal.

Collective disputes procedures

126 Disputes are broadly of two kinds:

i disputes of right, which relate to the application or interpretation of existing agreements or contracts of employment;

ii disputes of interest, which relate to claims by employees or proposals by management about terms and conditions of employment.

The subsequent four paragraphs under this sub-heading describe in some detail the form and the stages of the procedure. Reference is made to independent conciliation and arbitration facilities available to help with settling collective disputes.

Disciplinary procedures

130 Management should ensure that fair and effective arrangements exist for dealing with disciplinary matters. These should be agreed with employee representatives or trade unions concerned and should provide for full and speedy consideration by management of all the relevant facts. There should be a formal procedure except in very small establishments where there is close personal contact between the employer and his employees.

The subsequent three paragraphs under this heading are the final ones of the Code. They detail the steps in the procedure which should be in writing and made known to each employee.

It may be appropriate to finish the above summary of the Code of Industrial Relations Practice by quoting from the Introduction to it. Under the heading 'Application and Use' it says:

> The Code applies wherever people are employed. Most of it will apply in most employment situations. But some of the detailed provisions may need to be adapted to suit particular circumstances, especially in small establishments, or particular types of employment. Any adaptations should be consistent with the Code's general intentions.

In many cases, changes will be needed to meet the standards set by the Code. Where they cannot be made at once, those concerned should ensure that there is reasonable and continuing progress towards achieving the Code's standards.

The Code complements the provisions of the Industrial Relations Act. It provides guide-lines for all concerned with the day-to-day problems of industrial relations, as well as for the Commission on Industrial Relations and for Courts of Inquiry and similar bodies.

The Code imposes no legal obligations. Failure to observe it does not by itself render anyone liable to proceedings. But Section 4 of the Industrial Relations Act requires any relevant provisions to be taken into account in proceedings under the Act before the National Industrial Relations Court or an industrial tribunal.

The Code sets standards which reflect existing good industrial relations practice. It is not meant to restrict innovation and experiment or to inhibit improvements on those standards.

Chapter 20

Management by Objectives

Frederick A Rose, Director, Urwick International Limited

The perennial problem confronting most business concerns is that of continuously seeking improvement in overall performance; in today's technologically and commercially complex business environment, this is no easy task. There is no single panacea for improving performance, but there is a vital need for all concerned with the success of a business to take a hard, constructive and self-critical look at the way it gets results and what it should be doing to ensure future success. In so doing the aim should be to sharpen the way it plans, the way it gets things done, the way it controls, the way it organises its resources, the way it solves its problems and the way in which it motivates and develops its people.

Done well, such an appraisal will indicate the need for a style of management which concentrates on the real profit influencing activites of the business and which is based on a continuous, co-ordinated and soundly-motivated effort throughout the organisation to achieve desired results. This is the style of management by objectives (MBO), a system of management which fully integrates planning for the achievement of desired results with the disciplines to put plans into action effectively and ensure the fullest contribution of personnel at all levels to the achievement of those results.

Not everyone will agree with this meaning of MBO. It would be surprising if most engineers were not familar, to some degree, with the term MBO. What is surprising is the number of different interpretations and understandings of what MBO is and how it really works in practice. This array of understanding, or misunderstanding, stems from the different directions the development of MBO has taken since its concepts were first distinguished by Drucker in the early fifties[1]. To some, MBO is concerned only with the broad directional objectives for a business, to others its value is seen in man-to-man target setting, while yet others view it as a strictly behavioural instrument aimed at changing attitudes and behaviour. It is common, for example, to find so-called MBO in the guise of a revamped personnel appraisal system. It is only when these different interpretations are pulled together and refined within an overall framework of sound management practice that the real benefits of MBO as a complete management system can be secured. An authoritative paper by the National Industrial Conference Board in the United States[2] confirms this view.

It is not the purpose of this chapter to embark on a philosophical discourse on the relative merits of the various views of MBO; for this readers should study an excellent paper by Peter Hives[3]. Rather it is concerned with giving the practising engineer an insight into the practical realities of the MBO system. Presentation in this way has its dangers, particularly for the engineer, who, by virtue of his training and experience, is usually highly numerate and quantification orientated. The real danger is that the engineer will be attracted by his affinity with the logic, mechanics and systems of MBO at the risk of ignoring its considerable human aspects. The reader is advised to pay due regard to the comments on these human aspects which are implicit in every stage of the MBO system.

Any definition of MBO is made at the risk of attracting criticism depending on the point of view from which it is approached, but one which has much to commend it, and which is in keeping with the concepts described in this chapter, is attributed to John Humble[4]. He says:

> 'Management by objectives is a dynamic system which seeks to integrate the company's need to clarify and achieve its profit and growth goals with the manager's need to contribute and to develop himself. It is a demanding and rewarding style of managing a business.'

This definition is rich in the spirit of MBO in that it underlines the integration of company and individual needs in seeking to secure desired business results; an integration which cannot be meaningful without active participation of all levels of management on both a team and an individual basis in clarifying what those results should be and in creating the environment in which they can be achieved.

The management by objectives system

When an effective system of MBO is operating in an organisation there is a continuous process of:

1 Keeping under review and revising, where appropriate, the strategies for the business and the plans to put these into effect.
2 Clarification and definition of the objectives of units and functions of the business and the related action-plans concerned with critical result activities.
3 Clarification and definition of the contribution of individual managers to company and unit objectives and gaining their acceptance of, and commitment to, the achievement of agreed results.
4 Creating and maintaining conditions in which it is possible to achieve agreed results, notably, an organisation structure and environment which gives a manager maximum freedom and flexibility to exercise his full capabilities in pursuit of desired results, and control information in a form and at a frequency which enables a manager to exercise effective self-control over progress towards desired results and which forms a common basis in the management hierarchy for assessing achievement.
5 Systematically reviewing progress towards desired results on both a unit and individual basis and using the output of such reviews to plan further action for improvement.
6 Systematically reviewing the quality of managerial resources based on the needs of the company and in terms of each manager's performance on the job. Developing and executing training and development plans to help each manager to overcome his weaknesses, to build on his strengths and to accept a responsibility for self-development.
7 Strengthening a manager's motivation by effective selection, salary and succession planning.

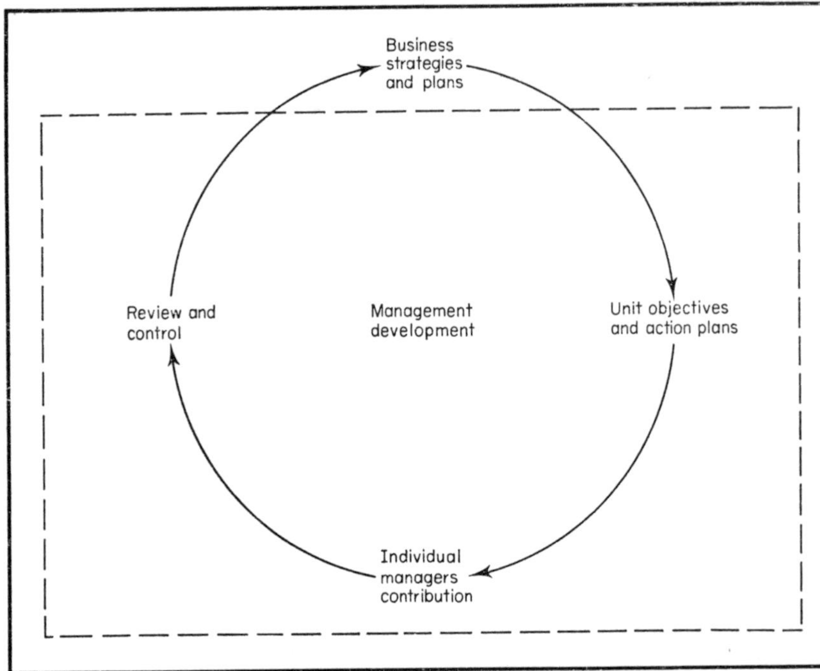

FIGURE 20:1 MANAGEMENT BY OBJECTIVES AS A DYNAMIC SYSTEM

Illustrating the dynamic nature of an MBO system and the inter-dependenc of its elements

The interdependence of these elements of MBO and the dynami nature of the system is illustrated in Figure 20:1.

Business strategies and plans

The overriding objective of any business must be to maximise, in bot the short and long term, the return on the resources which it employs The outstanding entrepreneur, by virtue of experience, flair and in tuition, will sense the action he needs to take to achieve this objective unfortunately entrepreneurs of this calibre are in short suppl Normally this overriding objective can only be satisfied effectivel through the medium of a sound business planning framework.

Business planning of this kind, to be effective must be done in th

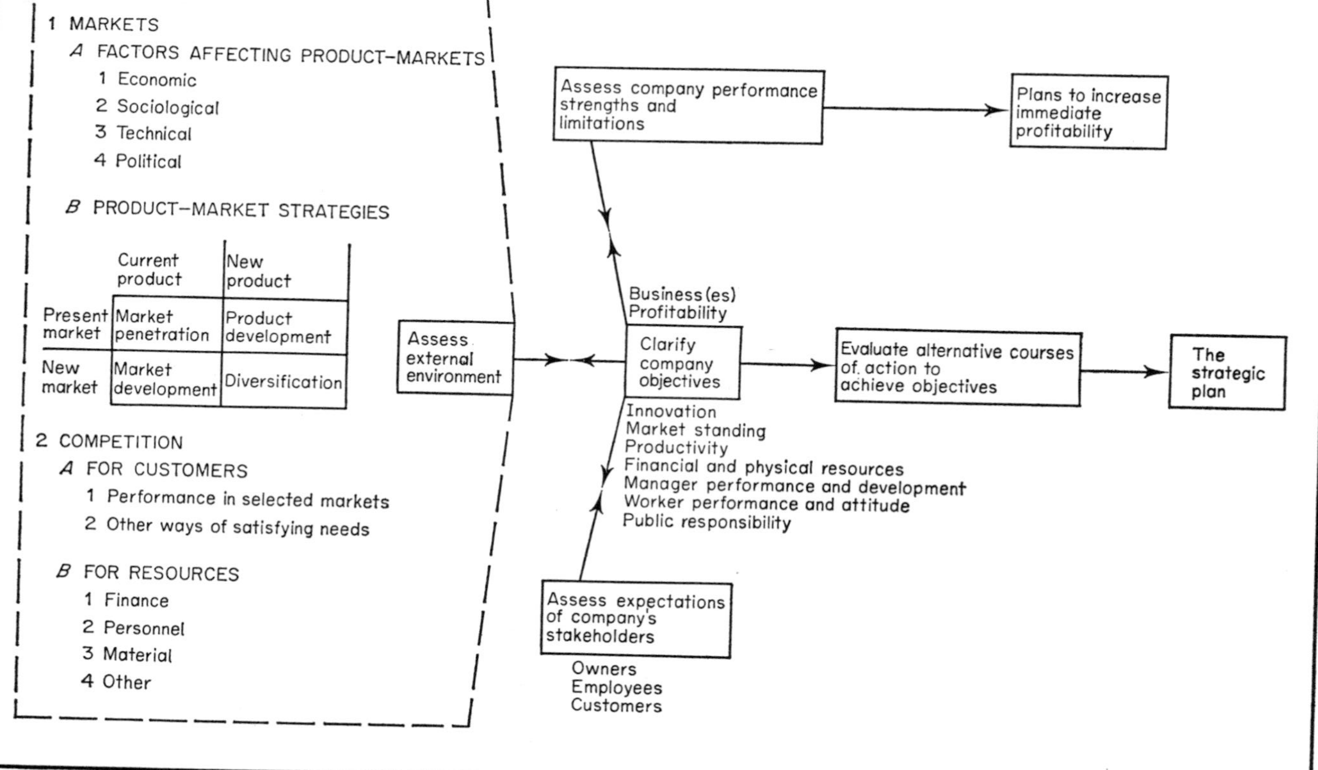

FIGURE 20:2 APPROACH TO DETERMINING BUSINESS STRATEGIES

This illustrates the process of determining business strategies in order to arrive at a strategic plan

context of a critical analysis of the organisation's strengths and weaknesses, of the threats and opportunities arising from the external environment in which it operates and of the expectations of the shareholders, employers, employees and customers. This kind of critical analysis leads to the development of long-term strategies and plans designed to secure the desired future profitability and growth of the business.

Figure 20:2 illustrates the process of determining business strategies culminating in the formulation of a strategic plan. Figure 20:3 shows how a strategic plan is broken down into a typical range of shorter-term tactical plans resulting in the determination of unit and functional objectives on which individual manager contributions will be based. The degree of complexity of this planning process will depend on the nature, size and diversity of the business activity.

This process of analysis, determination of corporate objectives, strategic and tactical plans, is clearly a task for the top management team of a business and would seem to be the logical starting point for ultimately determining the contribution of individual managers. In practice, experience shows that this planning process, if conducted within an 'ivory tower' atmosphere exclusively of the senior executive team, will prove to be a sterile exercise. It will fail because it lacks the penetration in depth within the organisation necessary to unearth the essential data and information which forms the basis for strategic and tactical decision-making; it will almost certainly fail to secure the effective motivation and commitment of individual managers to the achievement of desired results and because it lacks a vehicle for stimulating required action at all levels of the organisation.

The real essence of MBO is in achieving the integration of corporate and individual objectives and in motivating and securing the commitment of individual managers to the achievement of desired results. Experience suggests that in most situations it is only necessar for top management first to set down the basic corporate objective for profitability and growth together with broad policy guidelines an constraints and then to allow the MBO process to develop within th units and functions of the business. In this way: the detailed analysi within the units and functions of the business will provide the dat input to the planning process at corporate level; the whole range c objectives, and plans for achievement, can be gradually developed an integrated throughout the organisation in keeping with the real need

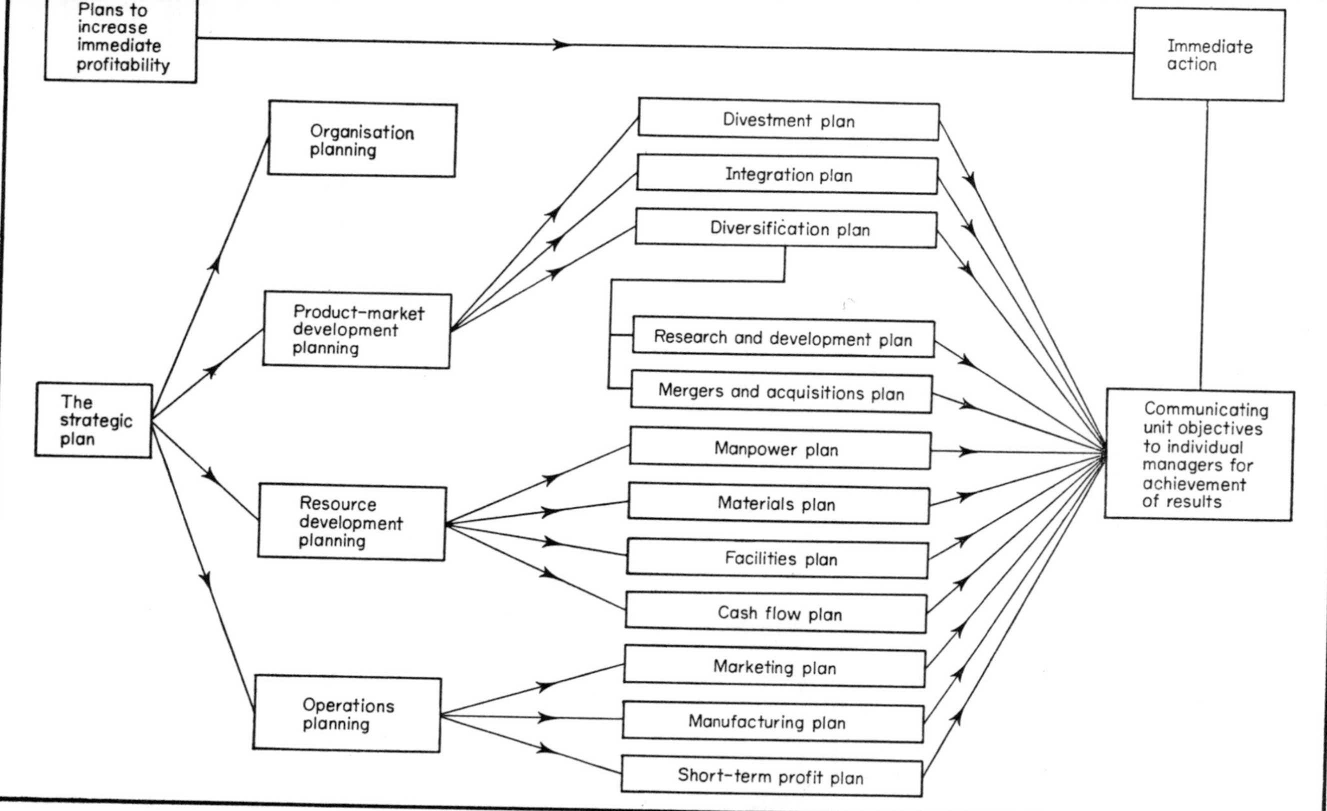

FIGURE 20:3 THE TACTICAL PLANNING STAGE

The overall strategic plan breaks down into shorter-range plans and unit objectives of the business; a vehicle will be created for the effective identification and pursuit of unit and functional objectives and the related contributions of individual managers; participation of managers at all levels in the organisation in the business planning process is secured and their commitment to the achievement of desired results obtained.

The development of objectives and complementary plans for achievement within the constituent units and functions of a business is therefore one of the main keys to the success of MBO. It is upon this aspect that the remainder of this chapter will concentrate; it is represented in Figure 20:1 by the activities within the dotted lines.

Setting unit and functional objectives

The first step in the MBO process at unit and functional level is to determine objectives and this, in turn, requires the management team to proceed through a number of discrete stages of analysis and definition. These are:

1 Define purpose
2 Identify key areas
3 Critical search and analysis
4 Observe policy constraints and guidelines
5 Define objectives

Definition of purpose

In order to be socially acceptable every enterprise must have a reason for existing which is approved by the society in which it operates. This applies not only to the total enterprise but also to its constituent parts, its units and functions. Management should take the view that a unit or function will continue to exist so long as its 'publics' continue to support it, buy its services or gain satisfaction from its activities. 'Publics' in this context may be other units or functions within the same organisation or the external community at large. The aim, therefore, is for the units and functions to define their purpose in terms of the nature of the service, benefits or satisfactions they believe they can and should provide, and the groups of people at whom the service is directed or who they believe can be persuaded to accept the service.

Taking a practical example for the manufacturing unit or production function of an organisation, its purpose could be expressed as: 'To contribute effectively to the planned growth and profitability of the enterprise by maintaining the production resources and producing goods at a cost, quality, quantity and in terms of delivery, needed to satisfy the demands of the market as interpreted by the marketing function'.

Definition of purpose looks deceptively simple but in practice it creates considerable debate among the management team of a unit and between the managers in different units and functions of an organisation. Such debate is beneficial as, often for the first time managers, as a team, are seeking to clarify and gain understanding and acceptance of the mission of the unit. This is an essential prerequisite for the next stage in the process, that of identifying *key areas*.

Identification of key areas

A key area is a grouping of management activities which have a common purpose to produce end results which have an important bearing on the current and/or future success of the enterprise. Identifying key areas is the application of the principle of 'concentration' in management. The aim of the management team, through discussion and analysis, is to agree those activities in which sound performance is vital to success and which, if neglected, could seriously jeopardise the effectiveness of the unit. Typical key areas at company level could be:

1 Profitability
2 Market standing
3 Productivity
4 Financial and physical resources
5 Innovation
6 Manager performance and development
7 Worker performance and attitude
8 Product range and quality

While those typical for a manufacturing unit or production function could be:

1 Material cost control
2 Labour cost control
3 Quality
4 Delivery
5 Utilisation of human resources
6 Utilisation of physical resources
7 Productivity
8 Management development
9 Innovation
10 Industrial relations

There is no such thing as an ideal list of key areas which can be applied universally to suit all situations. The management team must work out key areas to suit the particular circumstances of its own situation. Another way of looking at key areas is that most businesses exercise cost control by identifying *cost centres*; key areas generate management action to improve results by identifying *action centres*. This identification of key areas by the management team is one further stage in clarifying the understanding of managers as to what is important for the success of their unit and gaining their commitment to such improvements in these areas.

Critical search and analysis

The next stage is for the management team to carry out a critical 'search and analysis' process in each of the agreed key areas. The purpose of this search and analysis is to take a deep and critical look at the internal strengths and weaknesses of the organisational unit and to make a searching assessment of its problems and opportunities. The aim is to guide management towards identifying priorities for the maintenance of critical results and for improvement action as a basis for developing meaningful objectives. The search and analysis process in each key area is outlined in Figure 20:4.

The depth and breadth of this analysis is not a task for one man or, indeed, a single level of management. It is usual to establish multi-discipline, multi-level task-forces for the analysis in each key area, the members being selected for their contribution of knowledge, expertise and experience in that area.

The output of this search and analysis provides the foundation for

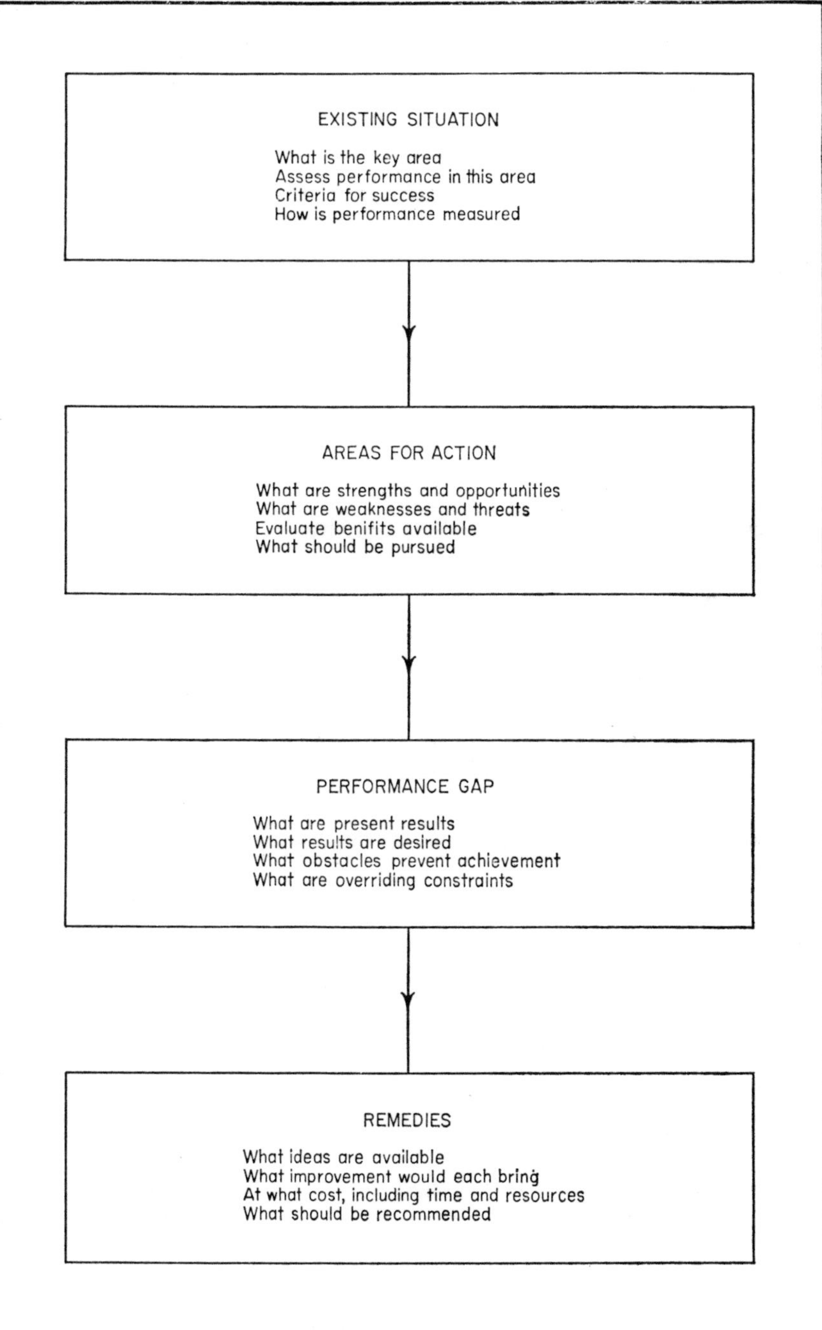

FIGURE 20:4 SEARCH AND ANALYSIS PROCESS

Shows the steps of a search and analysis process within a key area. The outcome of this process provides the foundation for developing purposeful objectives and appropriate plans of action

the development of purposeful objectives and realistic plans for implementing the necessary action. Done well it will produce an imaginative but practical review of all the major opportunities for improvement.

Policy constraints and guidelines

Before moving on to develop specific objectives unit management must recognise that it may not have complete freedom in this connection. Normally, constraints and guidelines are set down by the top management of the organisation of which the unit is a part and the implications of these have to be observed when developing objectives. Characteristically, the constraints and guidelines set down by top management are, firstly, in terms of profitability and growth and, secondly, with respect to a whole collection of issues which have been decided at strategic level. Typically, policy statements could read:

1 'This company will not diversify into any business activity displaying an overall annual growth of less than ten per cent in the past five years.'
2 'Due to the competitive labour market in this area it is the company's policy to train and develop skilled human resources rather than recruit in order to minimise the risks of wage escalation.'
3 'It is the company's policy not to increase the scale of operations in X and Y areas.'

Thus policy guidelines and constraints usually include:

1 Preferred ways of dealing with expected situations
2 Specific limitations within which managers must operate
3 How the company intends to react to assumed situations
4 General guidelines indicating the boundaries of managers' freedom of action
5 The ways and means selected for the achievement of specific objectives

The statements of policy constraints and guidelines may not exist and may have to be requested as they are needed to complete the data and information base from which the unit objectives will be developed.

Setting unit objectives

The foregoing analysis, from determining the purpose through to taking account of policy constraints and guidelines, has created the information base from which objectives can be developed. This is now the decision-making stage; this is what setting objectives is all about, taking decisions in the light of all relevant information.

This is where priorities are determined. Invariably management is presented with more options for improving results than it has resources to tackle them effectively. The difficulty is not so much in setting the objectives but in choosing the right ones in the light of projected benefits and the overall cost of their attainment.

Deciding on the objectives which the unit aims to achieve involves the management team in:

1 Determining priorities from the possibilities available using a sound basis, usually financial, for assessing relative values.
2 Selecting from this ranking order of priorities the areas in which objectives should be set and which represent a challenging but realistic task for management.
3 In each area deciding the extent of the change or improvement to be achieved.
4 Deciding the pace or period of the change or improvement.
5 Forecasting the resources required and deciding how they will be committed.
6 Establishing the viability of the objectives in terms of the means of achieving them and the probability of success.

This process can be complex and the use of a decision-tree similar to that shown in Figure 20:5 will aid the setting of objectives.

All objectives must be stated in purposeful terms and it is useful to bear in mind the following definition of an objective: 'A statement of intent which requires a manager or a number of managers to take coordinated action to maintain, or improve by a specified amount and in a specified time, the level of results being achieved in a given situation.'

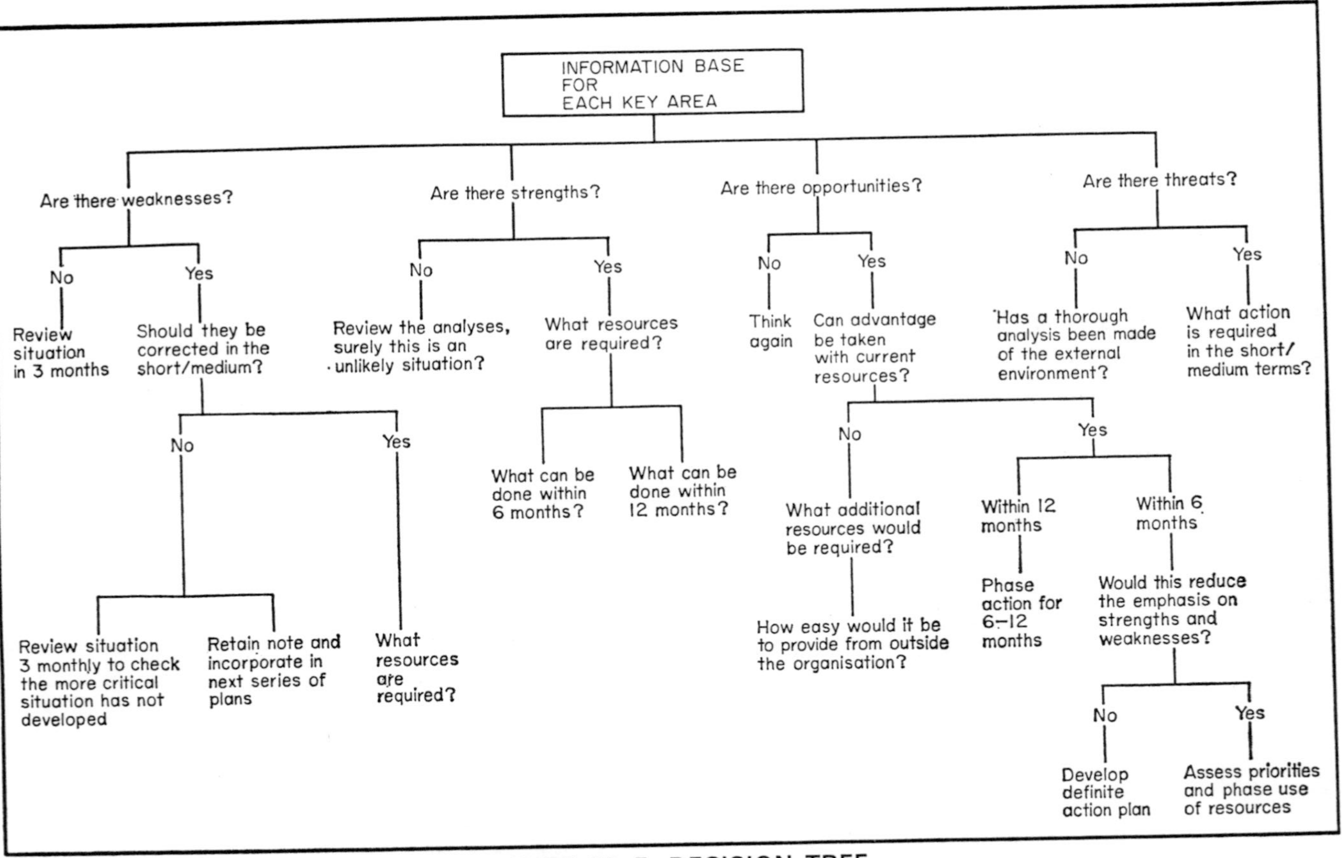

FIGURE 20:5 DECISION TREE

An aid to the setting of objectives

Essentially, sound objectives provide a meaningful guide to action and suggest the type of action required; they should suggest the means of measuring achievement and present a challenging but realistic task for management; they should also recognise all constraints and relate to other objectives within the same organisation. For example: 'To reduce scrap in the turning section from eight per cent to five per cent as measured by weekly batch inspection returns over the next four month period' and: 'To increase numerically-controlled machining centre utilisation from seventy-three per cent to eighty per cent, measured as a percentage of the available machine time by 1 December' are both well-stated objectives.

Engineers are often faced with the need to develop two basic types of objectives, those concerned with the ongoing management process and those concerned with specific projects. The features of on-going objectives are:

1 They relate to factors that usually can be measured over a long period of time.
2 They are likely to demand monitoring techniques that are, or could be, a permanent feature of the management control system.
3 Performance monitoring can be achieved by means of fixed frequency reviews.

The transient or project objectives are best separated from the on-going kind unless the project is very long-term, as difficulties arise in monitoring projects through fixed frequency reviews. Project events are liable to change quickly and to be connected with activities of varying pace and time-span. Once this is recognised objectives can be geared to major project events rather than fixed points in time. The management control process is made more specific to the project.

There is one further cardinal point to be recognised in developing unit or functional objectives: they cannot stand in isolation. Unit objectives must be integrated vertically with overall company objectives and laterally with the objectives of other units and functions within the company. It is unrealistic to expect that what subordinate management units believe can and should be done will coincide exactly with the views of company top management or with the needs arising from the examination of strategic issues. Thus, a series of vertical trade-offs has to be made between the objectives of the company and those of constituent units and functions.

Equally, lateral trade-offs between functions and units within the organisation have to be made in the objective-setting process. For example, in planning to meet corporate objectives a manufacturing unit or production function may develop its own objectives for new production methods requiring capital expenditure, recruitment of labour and/or training of personnel in new skills: this would involve the financial and personnel functions; or it might develop objectives for new wage systems affecting labour costs and the industrial relations policy of the organisation: this would involve the financial, personnel and management services functions; and objectives for product modifications which would involve the product development and marketing functions.

This combination of vertical and lateral trade-offs is essential to arrive at mutually acceptable objectives throughout the organisation and to achieve complete integration of objectives from the top to the bottom of the entire organisation.

Most managers are accustomed to this trade-off practice on an *ad hoc* or crisis basis but experience suggests that too few are experienced in dealing with this aspect on a consistent and planned basis. Exposure to group or team activity to develop interrelated objectives in this way is often new territory for the manager and may require training to acquire the skills necessary to make an effective contribution. Certainly, experience shows that managers in all functions benefit by reaching a better understanding with their counterparts in other functions as to how their various activities interrelate and how their efforts can be integrated to the benefit of the organisation as a whole.

Unit action plans

Merely to have set objectives does not ensure their achievement. Management must think through the action required so that a credible plan exists which guides the team contributing to the action and allows progress to be reviewed regularly.

Although in many cases the objective will have been formed with the approach already apparent, there will be occasions when the first step in action planning will be to select from a number of alternatives the method to be adopted for the achievement of the objective. There may be other occasions when management cannot determine objectives until the consequences of a number of alternative courses of action have been evaluated. In such cases the development of an outline action plan may precede the setting of an objective. Whatever the sequence of events, every objective, once determined, must be supported by a clear plan of action.

The extent to which future action can be planned will vary. In some cases plans can be developed with confidence to cover a complete year or more; in other cases initial action may have to be confined to the short term. Whatever the circumstances, every objective should be supported by an action plan which stipulates the action required, the manager or managers responsible for the action and the target completion date. A typical format for a unit action plan is shown in Figure 20:6. Questions which can be posed to test the effectiveness of an action plan are:

1 Is the problem clearly stated?
2 Is the desired end result clearly stated?
3 Is the action required clearly and simply stated?
4 Where the problem is complex, is step-by-step action detailed?
5 Are priorities defined?
6 Are progress dates realistic?
7 Has action been delegated to specific managers?
8 Do associated managers realise that action is to be taken?
9 Are specialist or support departments included in the resources used?
10 Is the plan realistic in terms of the work-loading of individual managers?

Particular care should be taken to evaluate the work involved in an action plan and to compare it with the capacity of the managers committed to it, otherwise experience shows that achievement of desired results and target dates will be at risk. There is a real danger of under-estimating the work involved or over-estimating the resources available. It is particularly important when committing resources to one objective that account is taken of the resources already committed to other objectives. It is always necessary to balance the unit's resources between the conflicting demands of the unit's objectives.

Action plans developed in this way, stemming as they do from the

ACTION PLAN NUMBER X				
KEY AREA		PERIOD	to	
End result aimed for	Details of action required	Action by	Progress date	Notes

FIGURE 20:6 UNIT ACTION PLAN

This is a typical format for the compilation of unit action plans

unit's objectives, not only identify the unit's management team with the results to which it is committed, but form a sound basis for review and control of progress towards achieving those results.

The process so far, from defining purpose through to developing unit action plans, has been concerned with creating a planning framework for the unit as a basis for management action tied in with the overall company objectives. This part of the process is illustrated in the upper half of Figure 20:7. It has involved the management team of the unit and, in doing so, it has not only created better understanding throughout the organisation as to what is important in terms of results, but has placed a premium on the inter-personal skills of managers. Experience shows that the process of analysis, discussion and decision-making as a team often demands a higher order of inter-personal skills than managers are accustomed to using and, in fact, often more than they possess by virtue of previous experience.

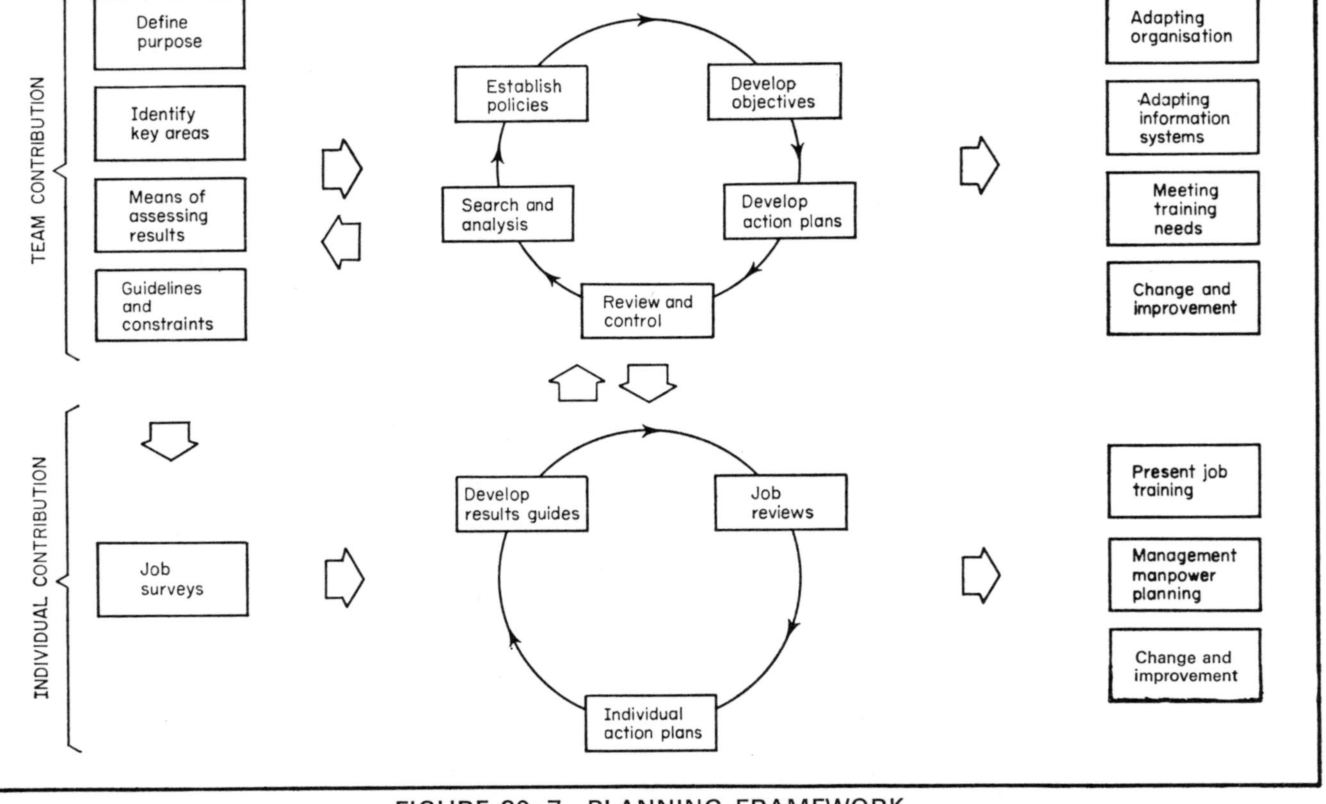

FIGURE 20:7 PLANNING FRAMEWORK

Two processes are shown here. In the upper half of the diagram team contribution leads to a planning framework for management action, linked to overall company objectives. The contributions necessary from individuals are illustrated in the lower half

Such skills have to be acquired and developed and it is in this respect particularly that an outside specialist adviser can make a significant contribution. Preoccupation with the mechanics and systems of the process at the expense of these very real human factors will result in greatly diminished benefits from the MBO process and, at best, will produce only short-term advantages.

The individual manager's contribution

The process so far has been concerned with setting up the planning framework and has created a clear understanding of what is important for the unit to achieve in terms of results. It is now appropriate to examine closely the contribution of individual managers down through the structure and to ensure that what each manager does as an individual is co-ordinated with, and appropriate to, the needs of the unit and, in turn, the company.

The stages involved in this process are:

1 Job analysis
2 Prepare results guides
3 Prepare individual action plans
4 Job and potential reviews

The process is illustrated in the lower half of Figure 20:7.

Job analysis

The key areas of the unit's activities previously determined are now used as a basis for an initial assessment of the contribution of individual managers. The technique used is called *results influence analysis* and its purpose is to build up a matrix of the broad contributions of each manager to each key area. A typical format for this matrix is shown in Figure 20:8. This analysis is carried out by the top management team of the unit and provides the basis for discussion with individual managers about their precise contributions in the next stage, determining the *result guides* for each manager.

Key area \ Manager		Production manager	Personnel officer	Cost accountant
1	Labour cost control	✓		✓
2	Industrial relations	✓	✓	
3	Manager development	✓	✓	✓
4	Plant utilisation	✓		
5	Innovation			

FIGURE 20:8 RESULTS INFLUENCE ANALYSIS

Here is a typical format for a results influence analysis. Its purpose is to build up a matrix of the broad contribution of each manager to each key area

Results guides

Each manager, in consultation with his immediate superior, analyses his job using the results influence analysis as a framework of reference. The purpose of this analysis is to identify the key tasks which form the manager's contribution in each key area. He is concerned not only with stating what these tasks are in a meaningful form but also with agreeing with his superior the standards of performance which indicate when each task is being done well and the information he should use for self-control towards achievement.

A results guide is a list of those tasks a job holder is required to perform which have an important bearing on the attainment of good results in the key areas of his unit, and a check-list of the currently feasible results which an individual has committed himself to attain or maintain in respect of his key tasks.

When initially completed it is also, in effect, a survey of the factors which currently prevent the attainment of better results, and suggestions for alleviating those factors. Figure 20:9 illustrates a typical format for a results guide, while Figure 20:10 gives some practical examples.

Ref.	NAME KEY AREA / KEY TASKS	JOB TITLE PERFORMANCE STANDARDS Description of the important conditions to be achieved and maintained in each KA	DEPARTMENT / DIVISION MEANS OF MEASURING PERFORMANCE
	This column should state the primary sub-division of the outputs of the job – *the key area* (KA) and concise descriptions of the key tasks contributing to each KA Description should be kept down to a minimum consistent with long-term understanding. If a key task runs to ten words or more it probably includes factors that are really standards of performance and should be in the next column. NB. *This should not be a description of how the job is done.*	Against each key task one describes the conditions which will exist or the results which will be achieved when the task is performed to the full satisfaction of one's superior, under the operating conditions that are likely to apply during the next 3, 6, or 12 months. Each standard should be an indicator towards achieving the main purpose of the job. *It is essential to be realistic.* A profile of several parameters may be necessary to give a true picture of the objectives. NB. Standards may be drafted in terms of: – Quantity	What control information is available, or can be made available to enable monitoring of the success of the action in achieving the level of performance indicated in the Performance Standards column. One should think in terms of: – Returns – Inspections and checks – Reports – Meetings – Measurements NB. *It should be kept simple: Is the control worth the expense?*

FIGURE 20:9 TYPICAL RESULTS GUIDE FORMAT

In this typical example of a results guide form, entries have been made to indicate the method of completion

KEY AREAS / KEY TASKS	PERFORMANCE STANDARDS	CONTROL DATA
1 *Resource utilisation* To exercise effective control over utilisation of resources	1 Value of material wastage not more than x% of total costs in any week 2 Labour performance index maintained at not less than y% 3 Average machine utilisation not less than z% in any week	Weekly cost analysis Weekly productivity returns Weekly utilisation analysis
2 *Cost control* To ensure costs are controlled within agreed budgets	All key aspects of budget controlled within x%	Monthly control statements
3 *Customer service* To maintain a satisfactory delivery service to customers compatible with budgeted costs	1 Not less than 94% of orders received to be delivered within 4 weeks 2 Not more than 5% of orders to be delivered within 6 weeks 3 Not more than 1% of orders to be delivered within 10 weeks 4 Value of stocks not to exceed £x and £y on average for the two half-yearly periods	Monthly sales satistics print out (computer program to be modified to give percentage orders delivered within 4, 6 and 10 weeks) Quarterly balance sheet figures reported within 15 days of end of quarter
4 *Industrial relations* To create and maintain a harmonious industrial relations climate	1 Lost time due to disputes does not exceed x% of available man hours 2 Personnel turnover does not exceed y% on an annual basis 3 Changes in work methods accepted by the workforce within 3 weeks of initial talks	Monthly labour utilisation analysis Monthly annual report Project progress reports
5 *Innovation* To maintain and execute a product development program that reflects market needs	1 Product development schedule for the ensuing year agreed with the Managing Director by month 9 2 Sales value of products introduced in current year to be not less than x% of total sales value	Monthly senior executives meeting Monthly sales statistics

FIGURE 20:10 TYPICAL RESULTS GUIDE ENTRIES

Here is an example of a results guide containing sample entries. The extracts shown do not all relate to the same job

Basically a results guide consists of three columns. Column 1 provides for listing those key areas of the unit to which the job makes a significant contribution. Under each key area is listed the actual tasks the job holder performs. Column 2 is read across from each key task and records the agreed currently feasible level of results. Column 3 is read across from column 2 and records the basis to be used for comparing the actual level of performance with the target.

The results guide is much more than a mere reference document. It is something to be *used*. It provides the basis for continual self control of performance by the job holder, and the basis for periodic reviews between the job holder and his superior so that they can jointly assess how the job is going and whether corrective action is needed. It assists identification of where the job holder needs guidance and assistance from his superior and leads to the identification of the training a job holder needs to do his present job better. It also leads to the formulation of specific individual action plans and identifies organisational dilemmas such as, lack of necessary supporting action from service functions, lack of proper feedback of control information and lack of clear-cut policy guidelines.

The dynamic nature of the results guide is important; so too is the participative process between superior and subordinate in its development.

Individual action plans

The process of analysis of key tasks, performance standards and control information involved in the development of the results guides will identify obstacles to the achievement of desired results and opportunities for improved performance. It is important to focus each manager's attention on these problems and opportunities and this is done through the use of individual action plans for each manager.

An individual action plan itemises two or three specific courses of action which the superior and subordinate agree are priorities to be tackled in the short term – typically, three months. Specifically, the action should be related to changing the conditions currently existing in the chosen areas.

For each item included in the action plan, the following should be specified:

1 What the problem or opportunity is, that is, a clear definition of what gives rise to the need for specific action.
2 The end results aimed for in the period covered by the action plan, that is, a description of the conditions that should exist when the action plan is formally reviewed.
3 A breakdown of the action required to achieve the end results. This step, to a large extent, measures the feasibility of the proposed course of action. The breakdown of action not only includes action by the job holder but also enumerates supporting action for which his superior contracts to provide or arrange.

Figure 20:11 illustrates a practical example of an individual action plan. Individual action plans are agreed between superior and subordinate following the development of the results guide and successively following each job review, which, typically, is at a frequency of about three months.

Job and potential reviews

The review process is a key aspect of the MBO system. Essentially it consists of three inter-related parts:

1 The informal review process
2 The formal job review
3 The overall assessment and potential review

The informal review process is, essentially, self-control by the manager as he monitors progress towards agreed results. It requires relevant control information focused on each key area of his activity. The superior, although holding each subordinate accountable for achieving agreed results, needs to monitor progress of the subordinates through a somewhat coarser set of information. However, this overall monitoring by the superior is not intended to result in interference with the subordinate's progress. Where progress is satisfactory the manager should be allowed generally to manage by 'self-control'.

Where progress is unsatisfactory, the superior should provide guidance and coaching to assist the subordinate to get back on target. It is important that the subordinate be encouraged to initiate this type of discussion as a 'learning need', highlighted through his own critical

NAME: J GREEN, TECHNICAL SALES MANAGER: AREA 1		
Key Area Ref.	**Suggestion, that is, made before or during the review meeting**	**Action**
1a	Sales of products G, J, S and V are below our current performance standard because some sub-standard batches have found their way to customers I suggest that to get sales back to 75% of budget we must withdraw all sub-standard stocks and replace them	1 Locate all sub-standard stocks of products G, J, S and V in this area and determine the quantities involved J G 2 Arrange with factory for the necessary replacement stocks, and the treatment of the returns J G 3 Prepare a programme for replacement and arrange with distribution manager for the sub-standard stocks to be withdrawn and replaced JG 4 Decide the approach to be made to all customers including the storing, and the demonstration of samples of new stock J G 5 Brief all salesmen involved J G 6 Monitor achievement of plan J G
	Sales of products E, K, N, R, T and X are unsatisfactory due to shortage of supplies from factory	7 Draw attention of GSM to the shortages and initiate corrective action R B 8 Check whether this area gets its share of these products R B
	Poor sales performance does not come to light until the end of each month. Control information should be more frequent (say, weekly) and available within a day or so of the week ending	9 Negotiate with sales administration manager for weekly information on the sales volume of each product group J G
6a	We are not receiving from the sales force the competitor/market information because we are not clear in our own minds what this information should cover	1 RSM and ASM separately to draft a check-list of information requirements R B and J G 2 Agree check list R B and J G 3 Design and agree procedures and simple forms J G 4 Brief sales force at regular sales meeting J G
	Administrative costs in the regional office are too high. We will investigate both the information needs and the methods for providing the information	1 Identify all the information being provided by the regional office J G 2 Determine information requirements including frequency and accuracy J G 3 Arrange meeting with the 3 ASMs and the administration manager to consider possible improvements to the information

FIGURE 20:11 INDIVIDUAL ACTION PLAN

This is a practical example of an individual action plan. Such plans are agreed between the individual and his superior after development of the results guide analysis of the reasons for current or potential failure to achieve agreed results.

The formal job review meeting held at regular and agreed intervals is, essentially, a dialogue between the job holder and his superior. The purpose of the formal job review is to establish the contribution that each individual job can make to the unit objectives through the

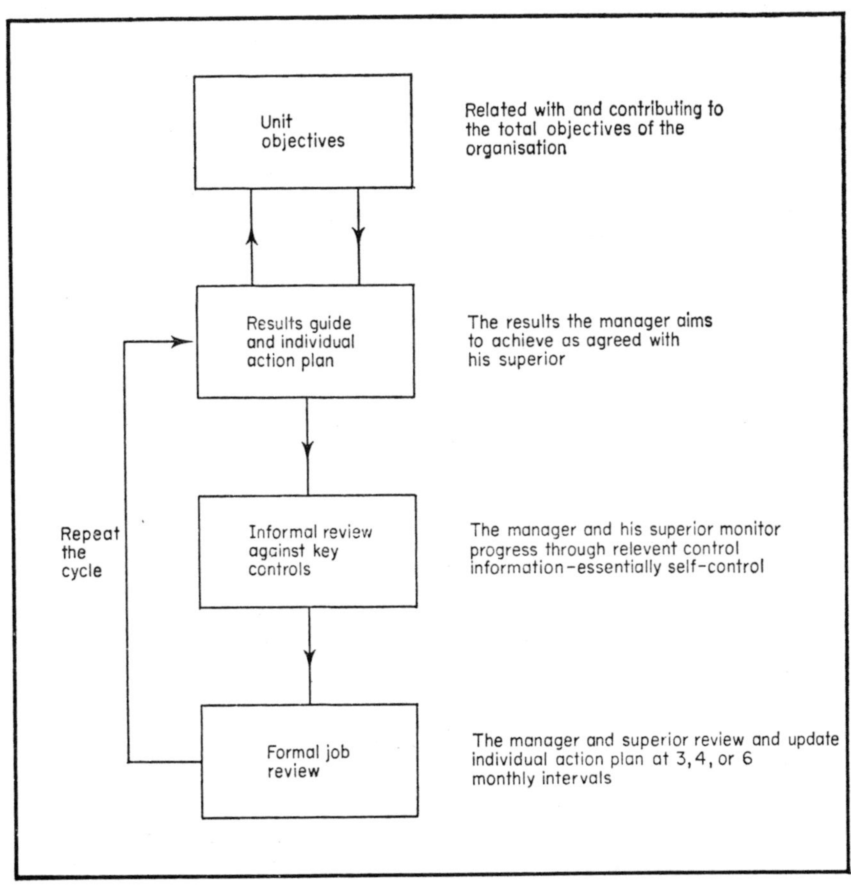

FIGURE 20:12 BASIC REVIEW CYCLE

Job reviews are conducted regularly for managers at each level in the organisation. The frequency will depend on the job level and the calibre of the individual but job reviews serve the same purpose at all levels and all follow the above cycle

activities of the current manager, agree the action that is required to provide each manager with an appropriate working environment, particularly, in respect of organisational arrangements and limits of authority, and to satisfy and/or agree action to satisfy the critical learning needs related to the manager's current job.

The job review serves the same purpose at each level in the organisation, although the frequency between reviews may vary according to the level of the job in the structure and the calibre of the manager. The emphasis of a job review is on what can be done to sustain and improve on current results; it is essentially a job planning, coaching and counselling process. This basic review cycle is illustrated in Figure 20:12.

Experience shows that certain criteria are fundamental to successful reviews. The job holder needs to feel at ease and be encouraged to participate, indeed to take the initiative. There needs to be a constructive structure to the review meeting, and the discussion should be forward-looking rather than an inquest or post mortem on the past; the only reason for considering failure to achieve agreed results should be the insight it gives into the action to be planned to secure improvements. The meeting needs to be seen as an integral part of the normal functioning of line management.

Failure to recognise and satisfy these criteria can result in considerable disillusionment with the MBO concept. The continuous process of informal reviews and formal job reviews demands considerable inter-personal skills and is often an aspect in which most managers require special guidance.

The overall assessment and potential review is carried out, typically, on an annual basis. The review is undertaken by each manager's superior and is concerned with providing a concise statement of:

1 A measure of the total contribution of the job holder to the key objectives of the unit, taking account of quantitative and relevant qualitative criteria.
2 The particular strengths exhibited by the job holder in achieving his agreed individual results during the past year, with particular emphasis on where the job holder has achieved substantially above-standard performance and made positive progress in combating any deteriorating situation, even though the specific objectives may not have been achieved.

3 The weaknesses exhibited by the job holder in non-achievement of agreed results.
4 The job holder's contribution to project or team activity where relevant.
5 The potential that the job holder has for promotion to a job in the same or another function or transfer to another job at the same approximate level as part of his personal development program.
6 The training and personal development requirements of the job holder in terms of his current and future potential jobs which cannot be satisfied through personal counselling and coaching by his superior.

The output of this overall assessment provides the raw material input for the organisation's management development program and management succession planning, as well as providing guidelines for financial reward in the context of the organisation's compensation policy. It would be unrealistic to suggest that compensation is unrelated to overall contribution of the job holder. However, experience shows that compensation reviews should be carried out quite separately from all other reviews in order to avoid pre-occupation with financial rewards when considering the personal development needs of the job holder in the context of achieving improved results in his job.

Management development

An effective management development activity is the cornerstone of successful MBO and in fact is right at the heart of the process. MBO is concerned with securing the desired results of an organisation and these results have to be secured through the activities of people. It is therefore vital to ensure that managers are equipped technically and personally to make an effective contribution. This means that the knowledge, experience, attitude and behaviour of managers must be subject to continuous review and development. Only in this way will the managerial competence and resources match the needs of the organisation while at the same time satisfying the needs of the individual manager to make an effective contribution, to have this recognised, and to develop himself.

Both practical experience and academic research confirm that when people really understand the need for change and improvement and share in securing it in a constructive and understanding climate, they have the capacity to commit themselves. Perhaps the most underutilised resource in any business is the ability people have to improve themselves in a creative and imaginative way, given the climate in which to do so. The conclusion to be drawn from this is that the major impact of management development can be made in the actual job situation; experience supports this view.

Personal counselling and coaching by the manager of his subordinates on the job is therefore the main vehicle for effective management development. The processes of defining objectives, unit action plans, job analysis and definition, individual action plans and job reviews all provide a first-class opportunity for this counselling and coaching. It is the superior who knows, or should know, better than anyone else the strengths and weaknesses of his subordinates; it is the superior who has the opportunity to agree tasks with his subordinates that will help them overcome weaknesses and build on strengths. His responsibility for management development is clear.

Experience indicates that the lack of sound counselling and coaching practices is a major cause of failure of the MBO system. Unfortunately, this is an area of management practice which has been neglected and the potential for failure of the MBO system is therefore very real. Sound counselling and coaching cannot be 'switched on' overnight, it requires a build up of mutual confidence and understanding between superior and subordinates and, often, a change in managerial style and attitude. It is frequently an area in which specialist advice and guidance is needed. Readers are advised to study an excellent short article by Edwin Singer[5] for more information on the subject.

Formal management training has its place in the management development activity but only as a supplement to provide training that cannot be given on the job. It is usually concerned with individual and group training, both in-company and external, designed to equip managers with new knowledge. The process in arriving at formal management training needs is illustrated in Figure 20:13. It will be seen that such training is strictly job related, designed either to secure improved performance in the current job, or to prepare the job holder for a future job.

The full aspects of management development within the context of the MBO system are illustrated in Figure 20:14.

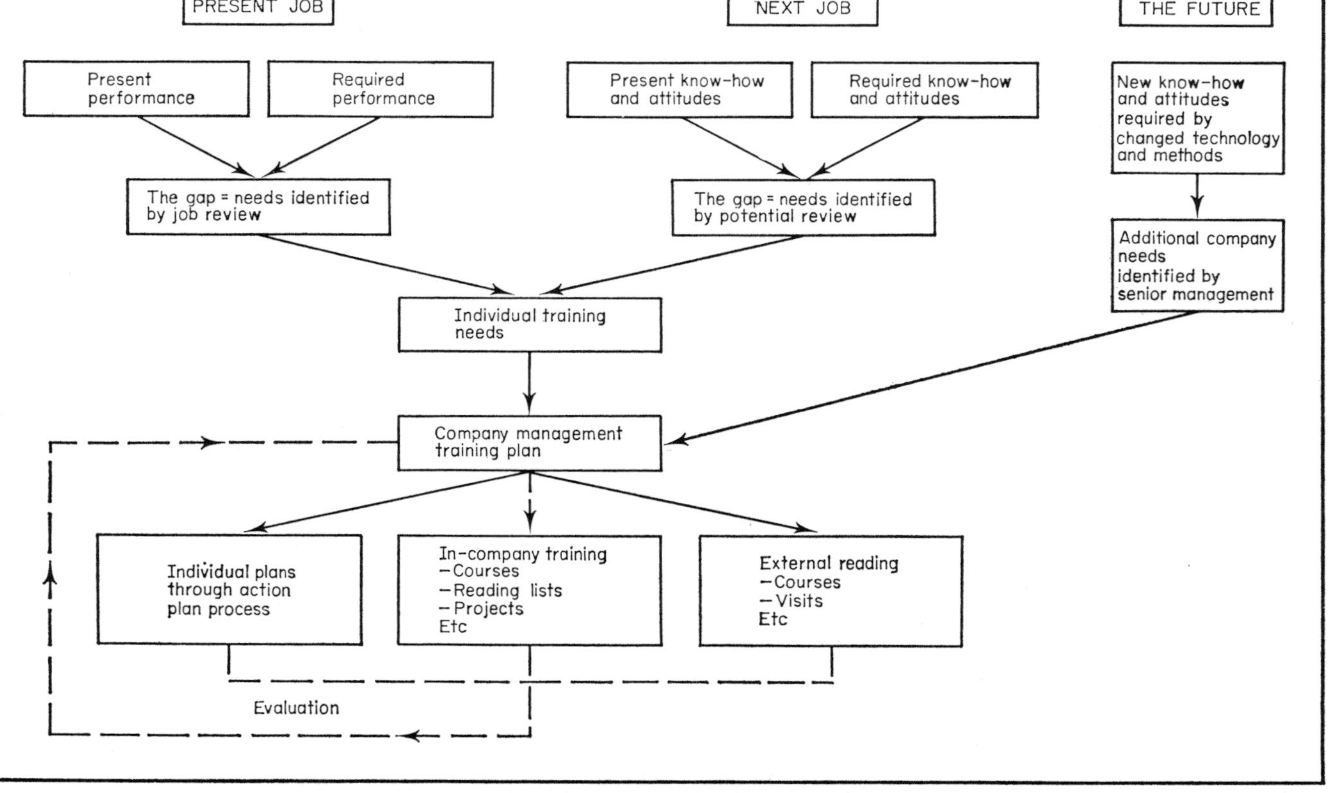

FIGURE 20:13 MANAGEMENT TRAINING PROCESS

Management training is strictly job related. It is designed either to improve current job performance or to prepare the individual for a future job

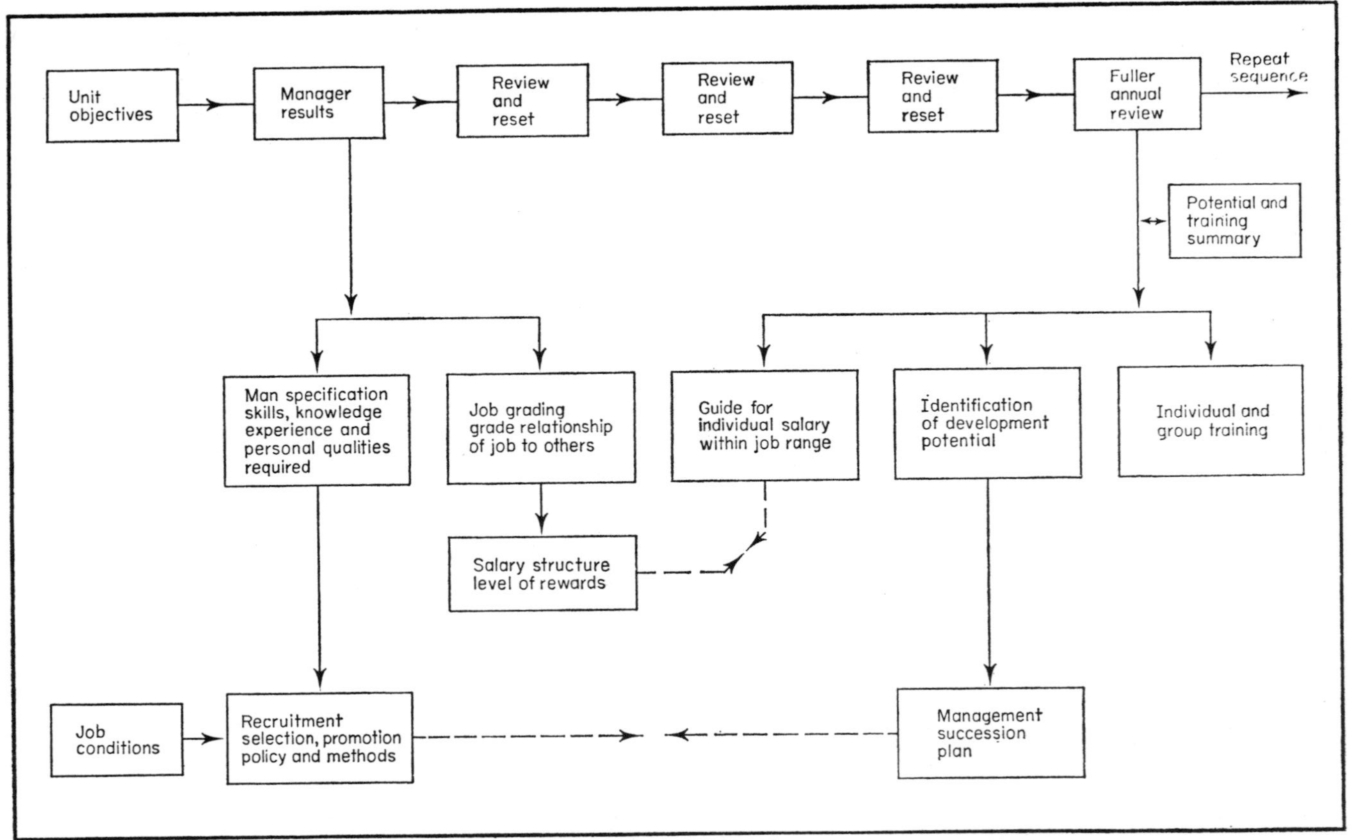

FIGURE 20:14 IMPROVING MANAGEMENT PERFORMANCE

Characteristics of successful MBO

The problems of integrating and consolidating MBO as *the* way of managing and of maintaining its momentum, are often underestimated. MBO is deceptively simple in concept but extremely demanding in implementation; it calls into question long-standing customs, organisational concepts and management practices and these are often deeply entrenched.

Successful MBO demands a high degree of courage, tenacity and patience on the part of top management in particular, and a wide measure of co-operation and understanding at all levels of an organisation to implement the changes which are inevitable to secure improved results. Experience suggests that in the majority of situations, these things do not happen automatically, they have to be worked for.

The success and survival of the MBO system depends so much on how it is introduced and how it is nurtured during the early stages. It is essential that the adoption of MBO is preceded by a perceptive survey of the business to ensure that it is free from overriding constraints in the form of abnormal business pressures and organisational malfunctions. For example, if an attempt is made to use MBO to provoke an unrealistically large leap forward in a managerial backwood, it will probably fail.

Careful and thorough briefing of personnel at all levels must be carried out in order to explain what MBO is, how it will affect the organisation as a whole and the people in it, and to convey the commitment and expectations of top management. The importance of this briefing program cannot be overstressed; it provides the opportunity to establish the resolve of management at all levels that their MBO is going to be a success.

Management at all levels must be sensitive to the need of its subordinates to make an effective contribution at all stages of the MBO process. This sensitivity is perhaps best displayed in a sympathetic and understanding attitude towards the probable lack of inter-personal skills which will be exhibited by subordinates when working in teams and in day-to-day contact with their superiors. The superiors must be alert to their own shortcomings in this respect and be ready to seek expert advice and guidance.

Positive evidence must be provided at an early stage of the introduction, of the benefits being obtained from MBO; this will tend to reinforce the resolve of managers. Experience suggests that the short-term benefits available have little to do with the elegance of the procedures adopted; what is important is the thoroughness of the groundwork done in creating the planning framework and particularly in identifying and provoking priority action for improvement.

Top management must be, and must be seen to be, wholly committed to MBO as the way of managing. This commitment will be tested time and again during the introduction of MBO as it is forced to take decisions which affect the contribution of its subordinates. Apparent disinterest or procrastination at top management level can create serious disillusionment among subordinates and can lead to the whole concept of MBO becoming discredited.

This last point is of crucial importance because perhaps the most important factor in consolidating MBO as a way of managing and maintaining its momentum, is the creation and fostering of the right climate. This requires that top management be deeply involved on a continuous basis in the entire MBO process, infecting the organisation by practical example, with its obvious confidence in, and dependence on, MBO.

MBO would be little more than a logical but somewhat mechanistic process if it was merely a codification of the procedures outline in this chapter. It is to be hoped that it is seen as being much more than this for, to quote John Humble: 'There seems to be an extraordinary human capacity to convert the most exciting, vital and dynamic concepts of management into dreary, mechanistic routines'. Experience shows that many MBO applications have finished up this way through lack of continuous top management involvement – its responsibility for success or failure is clear.

Done well, MBO brings substantial benefits to an organisation. Those most widely and consistently reported are:

1 A structured and logical discipline for identifying and concentrating on those things that are most important for obtaining improved business results.
2 The corporate organisation and individual managers within it improve their planning capabilities leading to the subsequent self-discipline to secure desired results.
3 A marked increase in individual commitment to securing desired business results at all levels of the organisation.

4 The gaining of new perspectives on what the organisation *is* doing and what it *should be* doing to improve results.
5 Balanced attention to a variety of organisation purposes.
6 Greatly improved ability to generate enthusiasm, build morale and establish effective team-work among organisation units in pursuit of improved results.
7 An effective vehicle for significantly improving the performance of personnel at all levels through planned development to meet the current and future needs of the business.
8 A measurable improvement in business results.

Given the dedicated involvement of top management and the creation and maintenance of the right climate in which human effort and talent is motivated to be utilised fully, MBO as described in this chapter can bring these benefits to any organisation.

References

1 *The Practice of Management*, by Peter Drucker, Heinemann, 1955.
2 *Managing by – and with – Objectives*, National Industrial Conference Board, Studies in Personnel Policy No. 212, 1968.
3 'The MBO movement', P Hives, *Management by Objectives* Vol. 1 No. 1 July 1971.
4 *Management by Objectives in Action*, J W Humble, McGraw Hill, 1970.
5 'Overlooking coaching', E Singer, *Personnel Management*, November 1969.

Films

There are six colour films on MBO which, with their guide material, provide a useful basis for further study and discussion of the subject.

MANAGEMENT BY OBJECTIVES – An Introduction to the Subject.

DEFINING THE MANAGER'S JOB.
PERFORMANCE AND POTENTIAL REVIEW.
MANAGEMENT TRAINING.
FOCUS THE FUTURE – A Practical approach to Long Range Planning.
COLT – A CASE HISTORY – MBO in Action in a medium-sized engineering company.

For details:
EMI Special Films Unit, Dean House, Soho Square, London, WIV 5FA.

Chapter 21

Training within Companies

Darek Celinski, Personnel Manager, Herbert-Ingersoll Limited

The overall objective of all training within a company is to produce tangible economic benefits. Such benefits may often be marginal, but they are always cumulative and occasionally dramatic. If training is to bring real benefits to companies, it should cost less to provide than the value which results from it. In effect, training should cost companies nothing. Through striving to meet this requirement, industrial training became job-related and, therefore, the antithesis of education.

It is not easy to distinguish clearly between training and education. Perhaps the most useful distinction is to accept that training aims at the achievement of specific and precise ends while education is an open-ended and continuous process in which there are no clearly definable objectives to be reached.

The essential steps in making any training effective is to identify correctly the learning needs and to use the most economical methods of satisfying them. This makes the services of a trained specialist essential. Although this chapter deals only with training within companies, the importance of relevant external courses should not be forgotten.

The present day effectiveness of training in companies is founded on two parallel developments. Firstly, developments of methods of job analysis; these methods provide a means for identifying the requirements of any job in terms of knowledge, skills and attitudes; in turn, these terms are used to define precisely the objectives of all training to be provided; the same terms are used to find out whether or not training objectives have been achieved in each case. Secondly, developments of new and better training methods; these have made the process of learning by adults in industry far more effective; especially valuable are the participative methods of training.

Learning is a continuous process inseparable from working. However, in all companies situations develop which give rise to special requirements for more intensive learning. In these situations, systematic in-company training has the great virtue of significantly increasing the efficiency of this learning. At the same time, it improves vertical and horizontal interfaces as well as enhancing the effectiveness of procedures and organisation.

Induction training

Everybody on joining a company, whether experienced or inexperienced and regardless of the type and level of the job, needs time for familiarisation with the new environment, the company, the department, and finally, to become fully effective in the job itself.

In the past, this process of familiarisation was by 'exposure' – informal, often casual and sometimes left to pure chance. Experienced colleagues, foremen, section leaders or managers, as appropriate, usually did their best for new starters. Inevitably, and eventually, a new employee became familiar with the new environment and acquired the requisite knowledge. In due course, he or she, settled down and became effective in the new job.

Nowadays, systematic induction training brings to companies distinct benefits. It brings new employees to the required level of effectiveness faster than did the previous informal method. It improves the quality of learning because it is systematic and consistent. It ensures that no aspect of the necessary knowledge is overlooked and adds to the accuracy and reliability of the information provided. The Industrial Relations Code of Practice (paragraph 33) states: 'Management should ensure that the new employees are given . . . induction training.'

Method

The fundamentals of good induction training require that all training is presented by persons who, themselves, have been trained in systematic training techniques; that it follows the plan, prepared in advance as an induction training manual, which contains the relevant instruction schedules; and that the total volume of knowledge which a new employee needs to acquire is presented in units of instruction which are small enough to be mastered properly and efficiently.

There may be a number of ways of satisfying the above requirements; however, one engineering company has organised its induction training as follows:

In order to meet the first requirement, a person in each of the company's departments has been appointed to help with induction training as and when a new employee joins them. The supervisors of manufacturing sections were included automatically. In other departments (for example, finance, production planning, design and engineering offices) senior but non-supervisory staff were asked to volunteer. The training officer's secretary became responsible for induction training of all newly appointed secretarial, short-hand and typing staff.

Next, the company training officer, himself a TWI (Training Within Industry) trainer, conducted 'Job Instruction' courses for all those to be involved in induction training. There were four courses of ten hours duration each, made up of five two-hour sessions on consecutive days. Eight persons attended each course. Towards the end of each course, those attending were involved in drawing up instruction schedules for use during induction training in their own departments.

In accordance with the second requirement, the induction training manual was prepared. The words of introduction to the manual state the guiding principles which were followed during its preparation:

> 'A newly engaged employee enters an unfamiliar environment. Everything around him is new: colleagues, supervisor, buildings, plant layout, procedures, product, and inevitably, the job itself. This unfamiliarity tends to create uncertainties and anxieties which are not conducive towards efficient learning. Yet, each new employee has so much to learn.
>
> However, it is a waste of time to overload a new starter with

information provided at a higher rate than he or she can absorb. Thus, by complying with the step-by-step sequence laid down in this manual you can help your new colleagues a great deal. They will become fully experienced and will settle down in their new jobs very much earlier than would otherwise be the case.'

Through the job analysis method the third requirement for good induction training has been met. By this method it has been determined accurately what knowledge employees need so as to become fully effective in their various jobs. In order to construct an efficient step-by-step learning sequence, this knowledge has been grouped under the headings:

1 Company knowledge (conditions of employment, products, layout, location of essential amenities).
2 Departmental knowledge (procedures, paperwork systems, organisation of work, standard practices).
3 Job knowledge (work methods, quality requirements, work-flow, work interfaces, work demands).

The elements contained within each one of the above 'knowledge' areas has been categorised as:

1 Must know
2 Should know
3 May know

By this method, it became possible to construct an outline induction training programme which covers the full period of induction of new employees. It ensures that new knowledge is provided as needed: not too much to overload the learner, not too little to hamper his or her progress in the job. Figure 21:1 shows such an outline training programme. There are separate instruction schedules which cover every training element of this programme.

The program is so arranged that the total time spent in induction training during the first day of employment does not exceed one-and-a-half hours. Thus, 'Must know' company knowledge takes the form of a brief tour of the appropriate part of the premises in order to show the location of the medical department, cloakrooms, canteen

	Training by the Company Training Officer	Training by the Department's Induction Trainer	
	Knowledge of company	Knowledge of department	Knowledge of job
FIRST day of employment	MUST know	MUST know	MUST know
SECOND day of employment	SHOULD know	SHOULD know	SHOULD know
THIRD day of employment	SHOULD know		SHOULD know
FOURTH day of employment			SHOULD know
FIFTH day of employment	MAY know		SHOULD know
Monday of FIFTH WEEK of employment	Follow-up and revision		
First Monday FIFTH MONTH of employment	Follow-up and revision		

FIGURE 21:1 INDUCTION TRAINING PROGRAMME IN OUTLINE

Training under 'Must know' provides only the information which is absolutely essential for a new employee to start work. The main bulk of induction training is provided systematically under the 'Should know' headings. 'May know' is no more than marginally useful information about the company and other necessary facilities. This tour is conducted by the training officer and ends in the department in which the new starter is to work.

The departmental induction trainer now takes over. After being briefly shown round the department, the 'Must know' job knowledge is provided. Only the knowledge which is absolutely essential during the first few hours of employment is included. Thus, in less than two hours from starting, the new employee is effectively able to commence work.

The first one hour of work during the second and third days of employment is spent on 'Should know' company knowledge. This is presented by the training officer and, in effect, covers the company conditions of employment. The presentation is held in a room away from the work-place and its effectiveness is significantly increased by extensive use of suitable visual aids.

Subsequent training sessions are held in accordance with the programme. Each training session commences by revising what has been learned during the previous session. The follow up part of induction training is provided in order to check the accuracy of understanding of the information given previously and to reinforce what has been learned.

This form of induction training is suitable for new employees who join the company with the relevant job experience. Thus, the 'job knowledge' in the case of designers, other professional, managerial and technical employees, secretaries and skilled men, is in fact limited to learning the appropriate procedures, standards, paperwork systems and so on. In the case of semi-skilled manual employees who have to learn how to do the job, the induction training alone is not sufficient. Unless the job is exceedingly simple, operator training is required.

Apprentice training

Companies ensure the supply of skilled and qualified manpower by means of the apprenticeship schemes which they operate. Investment in apprenticeship training is essentially long-term, costly and deserving of close attention.

In the past, an apprentice 'served his time' by on-the-job attachment to a skilled man – a most unsatisfactory and inefficient process.

Especially wasteful was the usual practice during the first year of training, that a young man, while attempting to learn a craft, had to perform all manner of menial and mundane tasks.

Also, even very recently, the quality of apprenticeship training varied a great deal. Large companies have always taken care of their apprenticeship training. At the other extreme, small companies, by and large, have not given proper training; the young man simply spent his five years doing production work of a semi-skilled nature, and afterwards could call himself a skilled man. When, later in life, he applied to different employers, they had no idea what type of training he had in fact received during the apprenticeship.

Nowadays, the most significant development in the 700-year history of apprenticeship in this country – the 'module' system – has been adopted by the engineering industry and other industries follow the principle.

Method

The module training system has been developed by, and is under the control of, the Engineering Industry Training Board. The Board ensure that similar standards of training are provided in all companies which run apprenticeship schemes. The Board provides appropriate training manuals, overall supervision through their system of inspection, and certification.

Each module is a package of learning which contains the skill elements of a craftsman's job. There is a wide choice of modules to suit every company's requirements. They cover practically every skilled job in the engineering industry, for example, turning, milling, grinding, welding, and electrical fitting.

During the last few years, craft apprenticeship has been reduced to four years. It usually follows a sequence as below.

A young man, during his first year, learns the basic skills of his craft in a training workshop. The training is conducted by qualified instructors and the workshops are usually purpose-built and suitably equipped. During the first year, the young man spends four days a week in the workshop on practical training; he spends the fifth day at a technical college following a further education course. The course is one in the City and Guilds of London Institute range and relates to the craft the apprentice is learning.

After completion of the first year, he is awarded the Engineering Industry Training Board Certificate and becomes registered with the Board as a trainee.

During the second year, the apprentice works in the company's workshop. He works on current production under a supervisor who has been trained in the techniques of instruction and the module system of apprenticeship training. During the module training he maintains a log-book in which he describes selected jobs and has to complete satisfactorily the required number of 'phase tests' – normally seven. These are usually production jobs which require particular skills described in the manual. When a module has been completed, a Board's officer examines the log-book and the final phase test. If he is satisfied that the apprentice has attained the necessary standard, he credits him with passing the first module.

It takes about six months to complete a module. Thus, during the second year, the other six months are spent on normal production work. During this year he continues with the further education course on a day- or block-release basis.

During the third year, the apprentice works on his second module, otherwise the arrangements are exactly as during the second year. Completion of two modules is required for the young man to be considered qualified as a craftsman.

The fourth year is the period of consolidation of training and development of full dexterity. By the end of the fourth year, the young man should have gained a City and Guilds Final Certificate and joins the ranks of skilled men.

The difference in effectiveness of informal and systematic learning is illustrated by the improvements achieved in the training of apprentices. Technological advances require more complex skills to build, set up and service the new machines now in use and those which will come into use in the future. Today, an apprentice who has more to learn and needs to acquire more complex skills than did his predecessor of few years ago, does so in four years as against the previous five.

Some companies, in addition to craft apprenticeships, provide training schemes for technician, technologist and commercial apprenticeships. Thus, apprenticeship training has broadened the range and a new field of training has been created to suit the varying needs of different types of apprenticeship scheme.

Non-apprentice training

These are the 'juniors' in companies. They comprise boys and girls in offices, other technical and non-technical departments or in semi-skilled occupations. All are learning their first jobs in life.

In the past, when there was much less concern about efficient use of manpower these boys and girls were left largely to their own resources to learn their jobs. As the cheapest grade of employees in companies, the inefficiency of such learning was acceptable.

Nowadays, a greater concern is taken, and an increasing number of companies have carried out planned juvenile training.

Method

This training, as in other forms of systematic training, requires: the development of training programmes based on a job analysis for which they are to be trained; systematic training procedures, with special attention being paid to young persons' needs as far as induction and safety training are concerned; the company's training officer to have the overall responsibility for training these young people and supervising their progress; at least some of the training to be provided by trained instructors; paid day or half-day release for further education until the age of eighteen years.

Operator training

The term 'operator' is used in industry to denote any person who is employed by a company to perform unskilled or semi-skilled work. Unskilled and semi-skilled occupations are those for which time-served apprenticeship is not required. There are literally thousands of different unskilled and semi-skilled types of jobs in existence. Some may require only a few hours to learn, others may need days, weeks or months, and a few may even need years.

In the past, there was no other way except for charge hands and foremen to train their new employees themselves. However, research indicates that in practice very few supervisors indeed actually instruct new employees. The majority of these employees obtain what instruction they can get from another operator or merely by watching an experienced person doing the work. This method is popularly referred to as learning by 'sitting by Nellie'. It is a trial-and-error method of learning a job.

Nowadays, by systematic training methods it is possible to reduce the time required to learn a job to one half or even to one quarter of what is otherwise required. The true saving to a company is not limited to the fact that the operator becomes fully productive more quickly; it lies also in the reduced cost of scrap, rectification and machines and other people's time. Further, operators trained by systematic methods often achieve and maintain levels of productivity and quality higher than those who were not trained in this way.

Method

Persons who actually train operators are frequently experienced operators who, themselves, have been trained in the techniques of systematic instruction.

In order to achieve the best possible results from an operator training scheme a sequence similar to that given below is usually followed:

Obtain middle managers' and supervisors' support. Before actual training can commence it is necessary to convince middle managers and supervisors that systematic training will bring them tangible benefits. Involvement of production management in planning and controlling the activities of operator training may go a long way towards winning their support.

Inform existing operators. They are likely to take a good deal of helpful interest. Their co-operation will be necessary in the next stage of setting up the scheme; thus, the earlier they know about the plans and understand the methods to be employed the better collaboration is likely to follow.

Analyse the job. Before any training can commence, it is necessary to identify the skills and knowledge needed for an operator to work at EWS (Experienced Worker's Standard). If the job is highly repetitive with short duration cycles of operations, the technique known as skills analysis is likely to be used. For less repetitive and/or longer duration cycles of operation, the simpler TWI job breakdown methods may be adequate.

Establish a standard method. It is usually found through detailed analysis of a job that different experienced operators employ varying methods to achieve satisfactory results. Some of these may or may not be more efficient than others and usually there is no one really best method apparent. Nevertheless, before training can be provided it is desirable to establish a standard method for doing the job.

Prepare the training material. Operator training usually takes place on the shop floor in an area allocated and equipped for the purpose. An experienced instructor devises aids to learning and develops methods for building up the dexterity of his trainees. These make the process of learning more efficient.

Evaluate the effectiveness of training. Regular evaluation of the results is necessary. This helps the instructor to assess his own effectiveness and to prove to middle managers and supervisors that the systematic training actually does bring tangible benefits. Fortunately, operator training is the easiest of all to evaluate and to quantify the results.

Effectiveness

Operator training is a well-developed technique which has been built principally on experience accumulated during the Second World War. Firstly, there was the need to train millions of men and women for the fighting services, leading to detailed study of the skills required for handling and maintaining modern sophisticated equipment. Secondly, the shortage of labour in wartime industry led, in a number of factories, to experiments aimed to training munition workers to achieve higher levels of output more quickly.

Finally, the post-war experiments designed for the investigation of industrial skills and the methods for their acquisition, brought the techniques to their full state of effectiveness. It is now difficult to imagine any type of manual work which cannot be learned much more efficiently by the systematic training method. A typical learning curve for a job which, on average, requires twelve weeks to reach the EWS is shown in Figure 21 : 2.

The same job, when learned through systematic training could well produce a learning curve as shown in Figure 21 : 3.

The shaded area in Figure 21 : 4 represents the gain over the informal type of learning provided by systematic training.

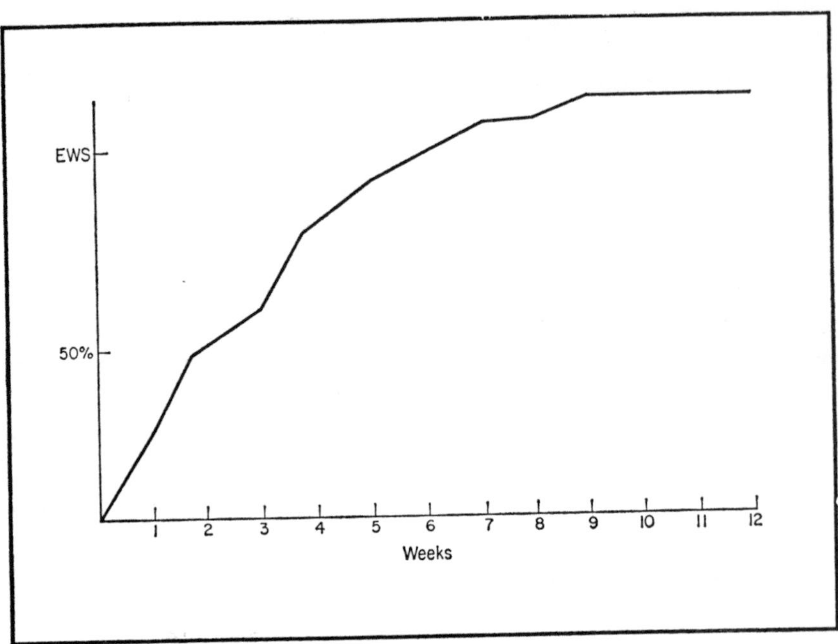

FIGURE 21 : 2 TYPICAL LEARNING CURVE

A representative learning curve for a job which, on average, requires twelve weeks to reach the experienced worker's standard

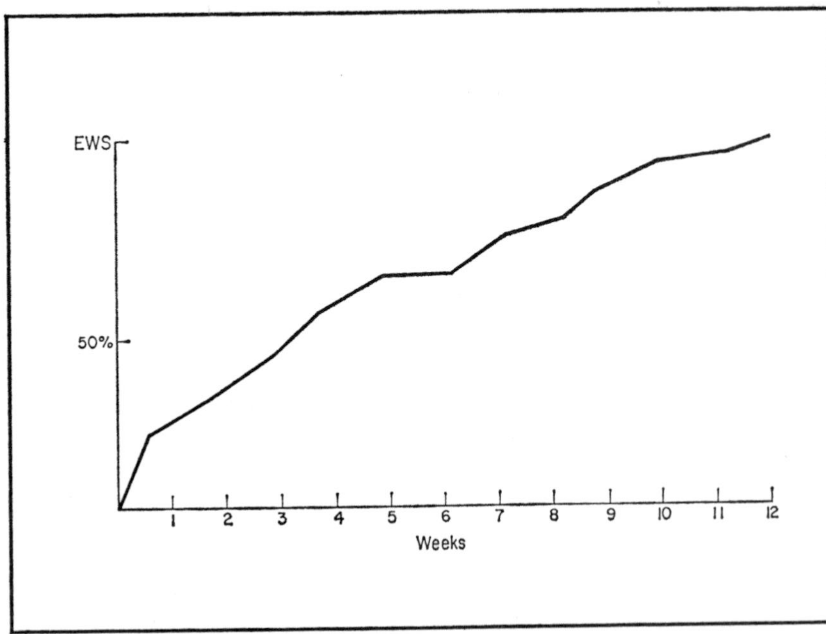

FIGURE 21 : 3 TYPICAL SYSTEMATIC LEARNING CURVE

Representative learning curve for the same job, as that shown in Figure 21 : 2, when learned through systematic training

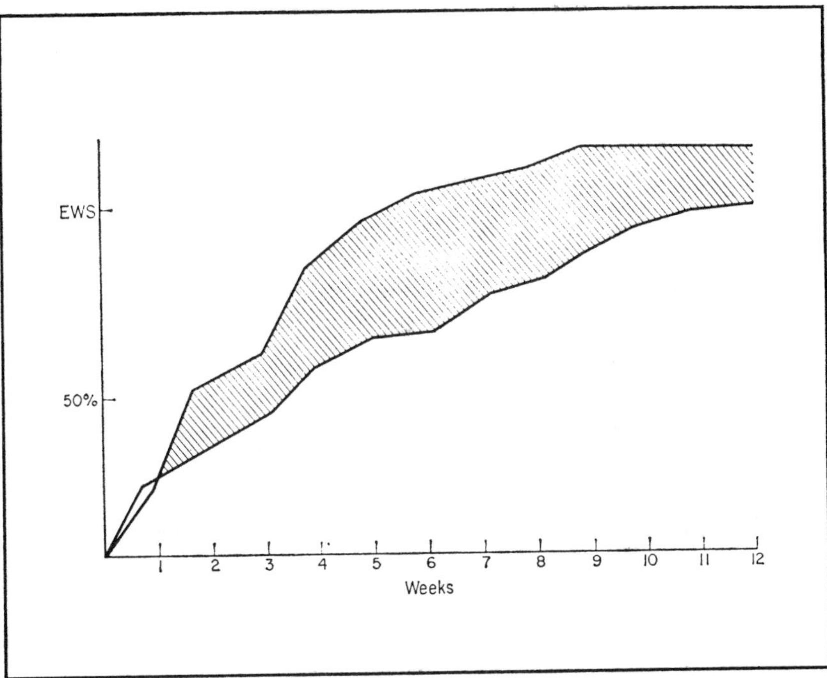

FIGURE 21 : 4 TYPICAL GAIN THROUGH SYSTEMATIC TRAINING

The shaded area represents the superiority of systematic over informal methods of learning the same job

Such an improvement is probably the minimum that systematic training normally produces. For example, W D Seymour in his *Operator Training in Industry* (Institute of Personnel Management, 1959), reports reduction in training time for both male and female capstan-lathe operators from twelve to four weeks, and subsequently to three weeks or even less, with adult male operators. Similarly, systematic training has reduced the period of training two-loom weavers from over twelve months to approximately four months. Girls assembling watch movements reached full proficiency in one week instead of nearly four, and innumerable other examples could be quoted.

Additional benefits of operator training

While preparing for training, an instructor 'refines' the job in order to make it as easy to learn as possible. He establishes the standard method of doing a job by examining critically the way it is being done. This process by itself rarely fails to produce improvements in efficiency.

Instructors know from experience that the best improvements are not produced through inspiration alone. Systematic search for improvements takes the form of considering each one of the following questions in turn:

1 How can any part of the job be eliminated?
2 How can the method of doing the job be simplified?
3 Is the sequence of work as logical as possible?
4 How can the layout of the work station be improved?
5 Are the parts and/or material as accessible as possible?
6 How can the job be made in any way easier to perform?

The following example illustrates improvements which have been achieved by an instructor through refining a job for operator training purposes.

Companies in the automotive industry use a transfer-line type of machinery for mass-producing components for motor-cars. The machines operate at high speeds and the whole line may be a hundred or more feet long. These lines are controlled from control panels which are usually positioned at the end of each section of the line.

Each control panel is normally several feet long and has mounted on it many scores of push-buttons in various colours for controlling the section of the line. An operator, by pushing the appropriate buttons, may set the machines within a section for automatic cycling. Alternatively, he may operate 'manually' by pushing one button at a time so as to obtain single movements of each fixture or machine.

Recently, when one of the motor-car manufacturers accepted a new transfer-line for machining engine blocks, the training officer was asked to organise training in its operation. He, in turn, requested the transfer-line manufacturers to supply him with suitable training information. The manufacturer's own training officer was given the task of preparing this material.

He soon discovered that the task of learning the main sequences of pushing the buttons presented serious problems. The buttons were mounted on the control panels in such a way that they did not appear to form any pattern. For example, the first button to start the line was black, placed third from the right in the second row from the bottom; the next button to be pushed was yellow, fifth from the left in the middle row; the third was the red button seventh from the left in the top row, and so on.

The training officer's examination of the layout led him to the realisation that the need for learning the sequence would disappear if the buttons were arranged in a logical sequence. Furthermore, if the buttons were of one colour for 'manual' operation, a different colour for automatic working and a third colour for emergencies, the line could be more reliably operated and almost no training would be required.

When the instructor reported his ideas to the technical director he was more than surprised by the reaction he received. Of course the buttons could be mounted as suggested. Simply, no one had given any thought to the operator's difficulties in operating the line. Thus, after many years of the old type of layout of push buttons, training was instrumental in bringing about an improvement which has now been adopted by the transfer machinery manufacturer as standard.

Training to maximise yield from changes

Successful companies do not stand still: improvements of all types, progress and innovation are the inevitable ingredients of industrial life. These bring changes and modifications to work methods, products, machines, equipment, materials, standards and even legislation.

In the past, employees affected by such changes had no alternative but to adapt themselves gradually, learn new jobs, develop new skills or acquire new knowledge by any informal means available to them. These informal means reduced the benefits which companies could have obtained by such changes. An additional difficulty is that resistance to change is a human weakness which comes into play in these situations.

Nowadays, systematic training helps companies to obtain the highest yield from changes, whatever they may be. Well-understood and properly-introduced changes bring the intended benefits more quickly. They are less likely to be resisted, thus avoiding the risk of delays and mistakes in their implementation.

Method

Management informs the company's training officer about every significant change which is to be introduced anywhere within the company. It is then his responsibility to ensure that the introduction of the change is as smooth and efficient as possible.

Training maximises yield from changes due to any of the following being installed or introduced:

1 New product or work methods
2 New technology or processes
3 New techniques or standards
4 New procedure or organisation of work
5 New legislation affecting employment
6 New provisions in the conditions of employment

It is the training officer's responsibility to select the most economical training methods. If a number of employees will be affected by the change, he can either provide internal training by using the company's existing resources, or organise internal training by using external trainers.

If only one or very few employees are to be affected by the particular change, an external course may offer a better solution. However, when external courses are to be used, the training officer needs to ensure that they are strictly related to the impending change. External courses are expensive and even the best may be of no value if the content does not provide a good fit to the needs of the learners. For this reason in-company training is usually preferred.

The following is an illustration of methods adopted by a training officer when two changes were to be introduced into his company.

In the first case this was the legislation in the form of the Abrasive Wheels Regulations 1970. It came into operation from 2 April 1971. Regulation 9 says:

> '. . . no person shall mount any abrasive wheels unless he –
> (*a*) has been trained in accordance with the Schedule to these Regulations;
> (*b*) is competent to carry out that duty; and

(*c*) has been appointed by the occupier of the factory to carry out that duty in respect of the class or description of abrasive wheel to which the abrasive wheel belongs; and every such appointment shall be made by a signed and dated entry in, or signed and dated certificate attached to, a register kept for the purpose of this Regulation'.

The company employed sixty men, including three supervisors, who had to be trained. The Employers' Association College, about twenty miles away, conducted the courses. These were of two days' duration, and cost £11 per person. When travelling and meal expenses were added, the total cost approached £20 per person apart from the loss of two days' production per man.

However, the company was in a fortunate position. It employed a young and enthusiastic apprentice supervisor who, previously, had been a skilled grinder. Also, the most experienced supervisor of the company's grinding section was a very competent trainer well versed in systematic training methods.

In order to provide training by using the company's existing resources the following steps were taken. The apprentice supervisor and the grinding section supervisor together attended the two-day course run by the Employers' Association; on returning from the course they formulated a training program and prepared a training manual together with visual aids, and a collection of actual examples and multichoice type of test paper. A copy of the training program and the manual were sent to the Engineering Industry Training Board for approval for the supplementary grant. This was received without any problem. Six courses, each of ten hours' duration split into separate sessions to suit production requirements, were held. Everyone of the sixty who attended attained the required standard.

Instead of expenditure on external training of over £1,000, the cost was about £50. Since the Training Board paid the company a grant of £1.25 per person for providing the course, probably on balance the cost was nil to the company. (The company also received a grant to cover the cost of wages of those attending in the same way as would be the case with this type of external course.) As a bonus, the company has two experts in mounting the grinding wheels who ensure that the provisions of the regulation are complied with and are ready to run further courses when required.

The steps described above can be followed with advantage in many other situations when internal training to maximise yield from changes is required.

The second illustration arises from an occasion when an engineering company asked one of its new suppliers to provide some training. The new supplier was a company manufacturing centralised lubrication systems for automatic lubrication of moving parts of machines. The training was to be provided for the customer company's engineers, designers and draughtsmen.

The training officer of the customer company contacted the supplier, explained what was required and invited those who were to conduct training to visit him beforehand. Of the two men who arrived, one was the sales manager and the second was the senior area sales representative. Understandably, they knew their product exceedingly well. Their intention was merely to show samples and talk generally about the principles of their system, how it worked, how it was installed, and what parts it comprised.

The training officer felt that this could be improved upon, and was able to convince them that a well-prepared presentation with suitable visual aids would be more effective, and worked with them to this end.

They accepted this approach with constructive enthusiasm, and the resulting presentation fully justified the care in preparation. Nearly seventy engineers and designers attended, and the standard of presentation was very high. The trainers were well pleased with their new method of presentation, while the customer company probably saved the equivalent of four engineer-weeks because its employees learned what they needed far more quickly and positively than would have been the case with the usual salesmen's demonstration.

Training to bring about improvements

However efficient a company may be, there is always room for improvement. The ability of companies to identify where these improvements can be made, and effectively to make them, is the key to their continued growth and prosperity.

In the past, management tended to take positive actions to bring about improvements in an aspect of operational efficiency only after it became obvious that something was distinctly unsatisfactory and could not be tolerated any longer. Inevitably, less obvious inefficiencies with potential for improvements usually remained unnoticed, so that avoidable reduction of the company's profitability was allowed to continue.

Nowadays, training is accepted as one of the prime forces in bringing about improvements in the operational efficiency of departments and companies. It operates on the principle that, however well the work is done and organised and however competent are the people doing it, there is always plenty of potential for worthwhile improvements. In practice, training opens a new range of possibilities for realising this potential. Its effectiveness is based on its methods of identifying causes and correcting their effects.

Method

The best way of illustrating this is by way of specific example, and the following may serve as a typical approach.

A heavy engineering company spends thousands of pounds a year on hydraulic cylinders. Each cylinder is ordered to suit the particular design requirements of the machine. They are ordered in a wide range of sizes, lengths of stroke, rod lengths and diameters, piston construction, air bleed positions, accessories and all other features. Many of them are 'specials' not quoted in makers' catalogues and are therefore especially expensive.

Whenever an incorrect cylinder was ordered this did not become apparent until it was being fitted on to the machine. Then the cylinder had to be sent back to the suppliers with the details of required modifications. Each such instance not only attracted additional cost but also adversely affected the company's ability to meet its delivery dates.

For several years, the costs of return and modifications to cylinders amounted to several thousand pounds a year. The usual actions by management to reduce this figure drastically did not produce the desired improvements. Eventually, the company's training officer was called in and asked to organise training to improve the accuracy of completing paperwork for ordering the cylinders.

His method of approach corresponded to that in every other situation where training is to be provided, namely to:

1 Define training objectives
2 Analyse the situation and identify causes
3 Refine the way the job is done
4 Conduct training to meet objectives
5 Evaluate the results actually achieved

In this example, training objectives were precisely defined as follows: 'Training in ordering hydraulic cylinders will have achieved its objectives when the cost of return and modifications during the twelve months from 19.12.1970 has been reduced by sixty per cent of the corresponding costs during the previous twelve months, which amounted to £6,500.'

While 'analysing the situation' the training officer realised that the forms used for ordering cylinders were rather difficult to complete, their layout was lacking any particular logic, and some of the terms used were not clear.

In 'refining the way the job was done' he obtained the assistance of one of the most experienced engineers. With his help, and using a logical sequence of building up the features of a cylinder, a new form was devised. The new form required much less work to complete because the majority of features were listed as a multi-choice and the appropriate ones required only a circle to be drawn round them. Additionally, a very simple but detailed procedure was drawn up, giving step-by-step explanations, a preferred range of features and actual examples.

The phase 'conduct training to meet objectives' consisted of a session where the engineers 'learned by doing'. This meant that small groups of engineers (about eight at a time) were given a number of assembly drawings, blanks of the cylinder sheets which they had not seen before, and the newly drawn-up procedure. Without any teaching by the training officer, they worked individually to complete the first cylinder sheet. When completed, there was a brief discussion, and a correctly-filled sheet was displayed on the overhead projector. This process was repeated several times during each three-hour session. After the sessions had been completed, the new procedure and the cylinder sheets were finally printed and issued.

In no time the improvements in ordering cylinders became apparent and this ceased to be a problem to the company. The results actually achieved during the ensuing twelve months proved that the training objectives had been amply exceeded.

The total costs of getting these improvements were quite insignificant. About one man-week was taken in drawing up the new procedure and cylinder sheets and in preparation for training. A three-hour session per engineer was an insignificant price to pay for an immediate and apparently permanent improvement.

Supervisor training and development

The term 'supervisor' means a member of the first line of management who is responsible for his work group to a higher level of management. Supervisors are employed in offices, manufacturing and other departments.

The Industrial Relations Code of Practice, which has been prepared in accordance with the provisions of the Industrial Relations Act 1971, states in paragraph eight:

> 'The supervisor is in a key position to influence industrial relations. Management should ensure that he: . . . is properly selected and trained . . .'

What is patently true about the supervisor's influence on industrial relations can be extended to other equally vital aspects on which every company's well-being depends. The supervisor is on the spot at the place of action where the company earns its living. He makes an impact on the quality of work which leaves his section, levels of scrap and re-work, and the day-to-day efficiency of his section. Finally, it depends on his effectiveness whether his management policies get through to his work group as intended or in a distorted and even misleading form.

In the past, an experienced employee, on becoming a supervisor, had to learn the requirements of his new job by exposure and through trial and error. The learning process and the necessary adjustment to his new role could extend over years. Though in theory his 'boss' was his guide and mentor in practice he had to be his own teacher.

Nowadays, companies, in their own interest, seek to enhance and accelerate this process by means of training. They provide training for potential supervisors before appointment, newly appointed supervisors, and established supervisors who benefit from the development of understanding and skills which experience alone cannot provide, and whose promotion may have occured before supervisory training was available.

Method

Industry's greatest need at present is to train experienced supervisors. There are two main approaches: the 'common skills' approach and the meeting of specific learning needs.

The Training Within Industry for Supervisors scheme is the best known method of common skills training. The scheme was conceived and implemented under the initiative of the Roosevelt Administration shortly before the United States entered the Second World War. At that time, they were endeavouring to supply their future allies with war materials, and had the resources and the manpower available to expand their armaments industry. However, the problem was how to obtain the required numbers of supervisors to meet the needs of very rapidly expanding industry. In those days it was still thought that it took years to train a supervisor, and there was no time for that.

The TWI scheme went some way towards solving this problem, and during the ensuing war years over two million supervisors in the United States attended the courses. British industrialists who became aware of the results achieved by TWI were instrumental in introducing the scheme to Britain. Since 1945 the Ministry of Labour, as it then was, has provided the TWI training for British supervisors.

TWI for Supervisors is based on a recognition of the essential common needs of supervisors. These are as follows:

1 Knowledge of the work
2 Knowledge of their own responsibilites
3 Skill in instructing, in its broadest sense
4 Skill in leading their work-groups
5 Skill in improving work methods
6 Skill in preventing accidents

Knowledge of the work has been gained by supervisors from their own experience before they were promoted. Knowledge of their own responsibilities is specific to each company, even each department. Thus, the 'knowledge' part of supervisors' needs is not included in the TWI courses, only the skills.

Training in skills is presented in the form of four separate programs, called respectively:

1 Job instruction
2 Job relations
3 Job methods
4 Job safety

Each of these programs is usually completed in ten hours, in five two-hour sessions on successive days. The courses are highly participative, therefore the ideal size of a group is about eight supervisors.

There are two ways of providing TWI training for a supervisor: he may either attend a course run by the Department of Employment's trainers in centres in various parts of the country, or attend a course run within the company. The second alternative is very much more effective.

TWI training in a company is usually organised as follows: a member of the company attends an appropriate nine-day course to become a TWI trainer in the particular programme; on return to his company, he presents the course. It is highly desirable for the trainer to be either a senior supervisor or someone of similar standing and experience in the company.

The number of supervisors employed by a company is the factor which decides whether the external or internal TWI training is provided. Generally, very large companies can have their own full-time trainer, while smaller companies may appoint someone who occasionally runs TWI courses as and when required. In many companies TWI was the starting point from which they developed broader and more sophisticated in-company training schemes for their supervisors.

The disadvantage of externally-run courses is that they necessarily have to deal with those skills and knowledge which are regarded as common to all supervisors throughout industry. This gives them a general and superficial flavour, and the practical benefits to the supervisors of any one company may be no more than marginal.

For supervisory training to yield real benefits it should be run internally in the company, fit the training needs by being accurately job-related, be competently run, and enjoy sympathetic support from the supervisors' immediate and senior managers.

There are numerous reasons why internally-run courses are more effective, including the fact that learning is closely related to real work needs and therefore transfer of knowledge is made easier. Teamwork and team spirit are engendered in a form immediately transferable into the working situation and, therefore, helpful to interface relationships within the company.

For a course to fit the real needs of supervisors, these have first to be correctly ascertained. This takes the form of analysing the jobs of supervisors and compiling job descriptions. Next, the elements of job description are considered in turn so as to identify what the supervisor needs to know and what skills he must use to perform each element really well.

At first sight it might appear fatuous to compile a job description for a supervisor who has been in the same job for many years. Probably only those who have had the experience of drawing up job descriptions in these situations are fully aware of the benefits that this activity alone can provide.

The need for competent running of supervisory courses is obvious. It is a specialist area of industrial training which requires the correct approach if it is to produce the desired results. If a company has no trainer competent to run supervisory courses, there are many organisations who can help to run them within the company.

Training produces improvements, and hence, changes. A trained supervisor will often have a better understanding of the company, of the processes of management, or of some management techniques, than has his own manager who has not been so trained. Understandably, this may cause problems and turn any potential benefit into additional frustrations on both sides. Indeed, if a supervisor is trained in a way which contradicts his own manager's ingrained attitudes, it may be as well for him to forget all the new knowledge as quickly as possible. Thus, a sympathetic interest and encouragement by a supervisor's manager is essential for a company to gain tangible advantages from its supervisory training.

In addition to the formal determination of training needs of supervisors, and the subsequent provision of job-related training, a problem-solving type of approach can sometimes be very effective. For example, in a medium-sized engineering company there were nearly thirty supervisors. During a meeting, the company training officer asked them which aspect of their job they found most difficult. Was there anything which they considered to be the toughest part of their job? The reaction was instantaneous: the company merit-rating scheme was their unanimous selection.

The company employed several hundred skilled men. Its manufacture was non-repetitive, so that the work organisation resembled that of an engineering toolroom. No work measurement of any sort was used – everyone was on day-work. Wages were paid in the form of a salary, the level of which was determined by a man's productivity as assessed by his supervisor. This assessment was considered by the supervisors to be the most difficult part of their job.

This meeting was the starting point for several sessions which the training officer held with various groups of supervisors. First of all, he explained to them the principles and shortcomings of various known methods of merit-rating. Later, he worked with the supervisors, as a catalyst of their accumulated experience, to develop a basis on which more systematic assessments of the productivity of individual employees could be established. Eventually, a new system was devised and worked out in full detail. The system was given the name of 'Performance Evaluation' because in some respects it resembled the principles of the established technique known as job evaluation, and is based on ranking methods.

From then on it was mainly due to insistence by the supervisors that Performance Evaluation replaced the previous methods of assessment. Now it is the established basis for payment by results in the company.

This example well illustrates the prime role of a training officer in a company; it is not to teach, but to ensure that his 'students' learn. The main source of his effectiveness springs from his skill in harnessing the combined capacity of his 'students' for creative thinking in solving problems.

Management training and development

It is generally held – and with good reason – that the profitability of a company is directly related to the combined effectiveness of its managers. All companies strive for profitability – all managers strive to be effective. Management training and development exists only for the purpose of raising the standards of effectiveness of managers.

It has been developed not so much to meet the needs of inadequate managers as to raise the overall standards of all managers. Thus, training most benefits the most successful – and the implication here cannot be ignored.

In the past, the processes involved in management were not properly understood. Managers saw their work as utterly practical, scorning all ideas of theoretical principles and systematic techniques. For their results, managers depended solely on their unaided intuition, innate ability and 'common sense'. Length of experience was regarded as the prime qualification of a manager, as if managerial competence grew in proportion to years spent in the job.

Nowadays, the processes involved in management are fairly well understood. Managers, in addition to their intuition, innate ability and common sense, have at their disposal an extensive range of practical aids. These, in the form of management techniques, raise the effectiveness of work of managers above that which they could otherwise achieve. Management techniques, in general, make the process of management more systematic, more efficient and are the essential tools of professional managers. Management training and development provide the means of transformation from merely intuitive to truly professional management.

Method

Senior managers are sometimes puzzled by the attitude of training officers when asked to book a place on a management training course. Training officers nowadays resist when they are told, for example: 'I have decided to send Mr Jones on a two-week management training course. Will you book a place for him at a good management training college?'

Training officers know that compliance with such instructions, without asking what specifically is Mr Jones to learn, carries a heavy risk that no one, except the college, will derive any benefits from it.

Management is a very broad and complex subject. When management training came into vogue, demands for it grew faster than did the methods for making it effective. There were innumerable courses of varying duration, run by the management training colleges, consultants, small and large industrial companies and public organisations. All displayed an unquenchable desire to improve the effectiveness of managers. The general management courses they ran so enthusiastically were usually excellent in every way, except that they appear to have made little difference to the effectiveness of those who attended.

This spate of well-meant activity missed the pay-off by lacking a true appreciation of the real needs of managers. In consequence the whole field of management training has lost the charisma it once possessed. However, there is much firm ground in this morass if only the area is properly surveyed and prepared.

Management training, because of its very nature, breadth, subjectivity and fragmentation, can be approached in many different ways. Companies may achieve equally good results by different means – there is no one best and universally accepted method in existence. However, the following example of how one engineering company organised its management training may help to clarify some of the underlying principles which are involved.

The company employs just over 1,000 people and there are slightly more than twenty managers and directors. There is a very small training department in the company under a training officer who is also responsible for management training and development.

The term 'training' is used in the company in accordance with the definition given by the Oxford Dictionary which is: 'bringing a person to the desired state or standard of efficiency by instruction and practice'. Thus, training is provided where the 'desired standard' can be specified in terms of new or improved skill in doing something and/or in terms of new or improved knowledge of something.

Activities under the heading of management development follow a plan for a longer-term process of gradual broadening and improvement in professionalism of managers, both as individuals and as a team. The distinction between training and development is made because different methods are employed to meet these different needs of managers.

Figure 21:5 shows the pattern of all management training and development activities in the companies. Inevitably, there is some overlap in these arbitrary groupings, but the pattern helps in deciding on the best method to be used to satisfy each requirement.

The methods for continuing implementation of each part of the outline plan are illustrated by the following:

Individual managers attend external training courses only when

	Management training	Management development
Individual managers	External training courses which meet specific and accurately defined objectives.	General management training courses. Planned job rotation and/or job experience.
Groups of managers	In-company training courses which meet specific and accurately defined objectives.	Group learning activities. Project work. Group studies. "Think tank".

FIGURE 21:5 OUTLINE PLAN OF METHODS FOR MANAGEMENT TRAINING AND DEVELOPMENT

Training—to meet learning objectives in terms of skills and/or knowledge.
Development—a gradual and planned process aimed at individual and team improvements

it is ascertained that the company needs the manager to acquire a specific knowledge or skill. Under this heading some of the courses attended so far were:

1 Value added tax
2 Statistical quality control
3 Training in metrication
4 Systematic selection and interviewing

Specific knowledge and skills which the company needs all managers, or at least a group of them, to acquire are provided by in-company training. Often the training officer conducts the training. Either managers who already have the required expertise or outside specialists are used. Examples of the in-company training provided include:

1 The Industrial Relations Act
2 Communications through briefing groups
3 Critical path method
4 Value engineering
5 Progress appraisals

Development of individual managers takes various forms according to needs. In the case of younger men, the training officer interviewed each one of them and found out their ideas about their own needs. Also, their immediate managers contributed towards identification of their subordinate managers' development needs.

By this process longer-term development plans for each of the younger managers was drawn up. The training officer was given overall reponsibility for ensuring that the plans were implemented and modified as and when required.

It is usual that plans include attendance at external courses which help personal development but only indirectly provide pay-off to the company. Appreciation courses on a wide range of subjects are suitable for this purpose. (In one case a manager was sent on an external four-week general management course. On his return the manager commented that he had been trained in how to be the chairman of the company – in the meantime, nothing useful.)

Finally, there is one example out of the development program of a group of managers. The group consists of five managers, all in their thirties, one from each of the following functions: marketing, customer service, accounts, engineering and manufacturing. The overall objective of the group in this phase of development is to learn about the current concepts in the field of man-management.

The following method is used: a manager studies an allocated topic and prepares a half-hour lecture; the lecture is attended by his four colleagues from the group; also, the company managing director, two other directors and the training officer attend.

Immediately following each lecture, a discussion takes place about the value of the concept to the company and how it could be used and implemented. In this way, the following five topics were covered: management by objectives, concepts of motivation based on findings by behavioural scientists, communications, management styles and job enrichment and enlargement.

Questions of lack of time always arise when management training or development are considered. In this example, the problem has been solved by these lectures taking place forty-five minutes before the normal starting time, thus only fifteen minutes of company's time once in two weeks is involved.

At the end of the cycle of these lectures, a summary presentation was held which was attended by every manager in the company.

The effects on the company's efficiency that these and other in-company training activities have on its overall efficiency have to be experienced to be believed. In-company training brings advantages which external training cannot possibly match, however expertly conducted and however expensive.

There are probably many reasons why management training in-company is so much more effective. Some of these appear to be:

1 It improves vertical and horizontal interface relationships, which are generally thought to be the main source of impediments to the operational efficiency of companies.
2 Training takes the form of learning together, it thus creates an environment in which the resulting ideas and new concepts are better understood and more readily accepted.
3 Learning takes the form of a gradual evolution and development which is more natural than a sudden transformation.
4 Learning and resultant changes are more likely to be implemented then when a single member of management tries to introduce innovation.

Questions

The following seven questions and answers sum up the present-day ideas and beliefs, in very general terms, about in-company training Some of the answers are based on fact and experience, others are more subjective.

WHY train in company?

Companies which are completely satisfied with their level of productivity, the quality of work in every department, meet delivery dates exactly on time, are profitable, easily competitive and do not look for improvements in efficiency obviously do not need any training. And especially if they are not concerned about their future.

All other companies need training because every company has an unrealised potential for improvements of all types. The question is: is there any other way for releasing this potential and converting it nto actual improvement?

WHAT is training?

t is creating learning situations which result in enhanced job ffectiveness of all participants, both individually and collectively.

HOW is training conducted?

By the painstaking process of ensuring that the training which is to e given fits accurately the learning needs of those who will articipate. By selecting the most effective method to suit particular arning needs and situations. Some educationalists believe that the iagram shown in Figure 21:6 is a fairly accurate representation of he way in which people learn, that is, retain information in order make use of when required.

The final stage of every training provided is to evaluate the results. ot on the basis that the 'trainer trained', but that the 'learner arned'.

WHO does the training?

nce training is the antithesis of education, an industrial trainer is e antithesis of a teacher. He does not teach, but ensures that the arners learn.

An illustration may help to make the point. A training officer ggested to a chief engineer that he could help the company by nducting value engineering seminars in order to improve the func- nal effectiveness of future designs. The chief asked the question:

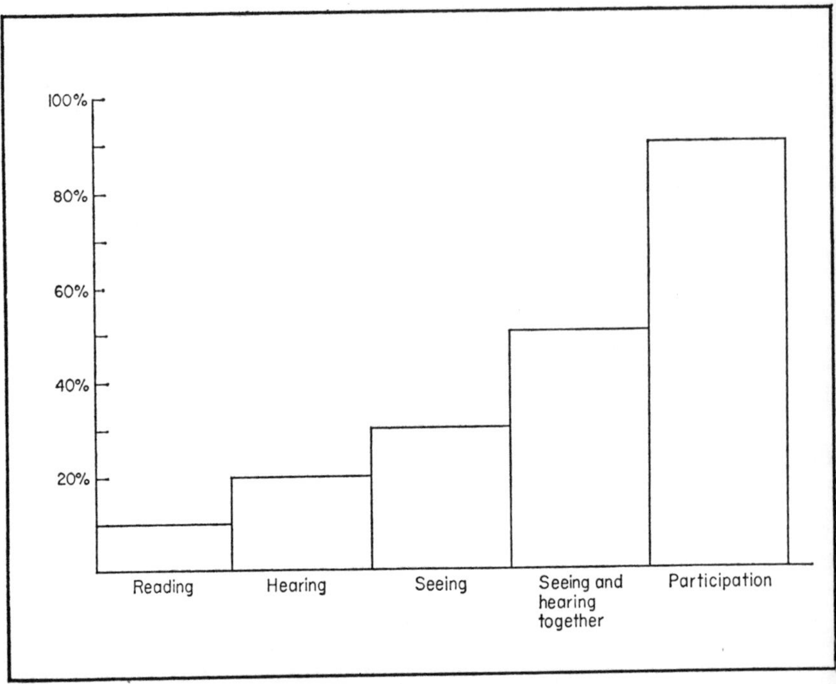

FIGURE 21 : 6 ESTIMATED RELATIVE EFFECTIVENESS OF LEARNING VARIOUS INSTRUCTIONAL TECHNIQUES

This diagram is based on subjective assessments by educationalists. Instructional techniques in each case are:
Reading: instructions, manuals, handouts, books; Hearing: talks, lectures; Seeing: demonstrations without clear explanation; Seeing and hearing together: lectures and talks with clearly understood visual aids; Participation: project work, learning by doing, guided group discussion, role playing, case studies, simulation

how long have you been in this company and what do you know about our products? The training officer replied that he had been there only two years and had only a general appreciation of the product.

The chief engineer did not hide his annoyance with the suggestion and ridiculed the idea of the training officer teaching designers how to design in a company with more than eighty years of experience. The training officer responded that he had a great deal of experience in value engineering. He asked for the opportunity to prove his claim but it was of no avail.

Had it been realised that the training officer had no intention of 'teaching' but rather sought to act as midwife to the designers' potential, a more enlightened response might have prevailed.

WHEN to provide training?

Training in companies is for the companies' sake rather than for that of the employees. It should not be treated as an optional or welfare type of activity. Training should therefore be conducted in the companies' time, not after working hours.

Also, after a day's work it is likely to prove difficult to create an efficient learning situation. Similarly, lecturing immediately after lunch should be avoided. The digestive process is here in competition with the brain for the use of blood, thus learning becomes more difficult.

WHERE should training take place?

Sometimes it can be carried out only on the job; sometimes it can be done off the job; sometimes these two methods can be combined.

Every company needs a room set aside for training, and a means of storing the visual aids and equipment which are so essential if the best training is to be given.

WHICH other persons are involved in training?

Management. Training as a tool at its disposal cannot produce results without its approval, full understanding and sympathetic support.

Management. Only management can implement the changes which are inevitable when training is effective.

Management. It is management who select their training specialist. In the final analysis whether or not the company gains proper benefits from its investment in training depends on the specialist's own experience, competence and status.

Chapter 22

Speaking, Reports and Meetings

Gordon Bell, Senior Partner, Gordon Bell and Partners

Engineers already have most of the qualifications to become able managers. What then is the difficulty? The materials are different, that is all. Instead of selecting, say, a steel to shape, to test and to build with, the manager has to select, develop, test and build a working structure with people. He deals not only with people subordinate to himself but with fellow-managers, directors, customers – people in all directions.

The nub of effective management is Communications. In this chapter we shall discuss three aspects of Communications:

1 Speaking
2 Report writing
3 Meetings

Speaking

'No man is an island unto himself.'

Speaking is for other people. This basic fact about effective speak ing is so obvious and so simple that many men overlook it. An audience always evaluates a speaker subjectively. What did they get from his talk? The answer to this question measures the speaker.

A manager needs to command attention at conferences and other meetings: he must be able to make oral presentations to his board and to professional organisations; to brief his staff, to persuade, to convince. Particularly if he is a technical man, he must be able to clarify technical concepts so that others – not necessarily qualified – can share his thoughts. Even the most brilliant man is useless until his ideas can be shared by others who can use them.

A successful speaker is a man who gives his audience a success.

Many specialists suffer from the delusion that speaking in public is the same as a theatrical performance, or something suitable only for the extrovert and the shiny-surfaced ones. This delusion often serves as a defence. The plain truth is that many specialists fear exposure of their limitations as speakers. This state of affairs is deplorable. If a man has something worth saying, he should not only say it but also learn how to say it with full effect. 'Why should the devil have all the best tunes?' asked General Booth. It is also pertinent to ask, 'Why should the image makers and the tricksters have a monopoly of effective speech?'

Let us examine the fear, sometimes amounting to abject terror, that afflicts otherwise intelligent men when they are asked to speak. What causes this fear? The unpopular but accurate answer is vanity – too great a concern with 'How am I going to do?' and not enough concern with 'How are they – the audience – going to do?' This truth is a hard one to face yet it applies at both ends of the scale. Vanity causes the glib, arrogant, loud-mouthed, no-nerves-at-all-I-can-talk-at-the-drop-of-a-hat chap to subject his audience to a flood of guff and bugaboo: it also causes the timid to worry about themselves at the expense of their hearers.

A successful speaker is a man who gives his audience a success. The speaker's success stems from the audience reaction. If his audience reacts in the desired manner, the speaker has been effective.

Newton's third law of motion roughly translated says 'To every action there is an equal and opposite reaction'. A given stimulus creates the same response if conditions remain constant. Herein lies one of the most important points that a speaker must consider. An audience is never a constant factor. There is no such thing as a production-line human being. Everyone is unique. People in an audience vary in social levels, technical knowledge, prejudices, ages, sexes; even the same people gathered together at different times or under different conditions can change as an audience.

Effective speaking is a human relationship, not something that one person does alone and isolated. A speaker wishing to get the desired reaction must obviously begin with a study of his audience. Unfortunately, many speakers begin with themselves and end in disaster.

So, the first point that a would-be speaker must think about is his attitude to his audience. His thinking must be positive and outward – not so much 'What subject am I going to talk about?' as 'How can I create a powerful relationship with my audience using the subject as both the generator and as the cement which binds that relationship?'

Can you imagine anyone erecting Tower Bridge or building a locomotive who would begin by laying the first brick or polishing the whistle? A rational man starts with a purpose and a plan. So does a professional speaker – and you, whether you realise it or not, are a professional speaker, a professional report- and letter-writer and a professional meeting man. If you analyse your job as a manager you will find that you do little else but talk and write and discuss. Given equal knowledge of his business, a man who knows how to speak, how to write and when to listen always has the advantage over one who does not.

Preparing an effective talk

Many speakers complain that they have no time to prepare properly. If you know your subject you can prepare a talk in one hour. The method we shall discuss now is the one-hour method. There are three stages, roughly twenty minutes each. (When you have ample time, say, three weeks or six, simply extend each stage accordingly.)

Stage 1 : Subject matter

Arm yourself with plenty of large sheets of paper and write down at great speed EVERY idea on your subject that enters your mind. Make no attempt to think these ideas through. Get them down in rapid notes, symbols or any other shorthand form that will enable you to recognise them when you arrive at Stage 2 – the plotting stage. Work at speed. Your aim is quantity, to amass hundreds of facts about your subject, various opinions, prejudices, misunderstandings, possible visual aids, thoughts about the audience, the occasion, anything which in any way might bear on your proposed talk. Note direct facts, oblique, tangential and even remotely relevant facts. Set down page after page of rough notes. During Stage 1 it is most important that you concentrate and work non-stop at great speed. If time allows, do this several times until you have at least ten times more material than your final talk demands. Fix nothing, solidify nothing. Note everything. A thought unnoted often gets lost.

Review the whole subject. This review jogs your memory, gives you flexibility, acts as a solid background for your talk and can prove particularly helpful if you are required to answer questions. Instead of having to excavate facts from the deep recesses of your mind, you have them near the surface, fresh and ready for use.

Quantity. Now you have raw stuff to work on, stacks of it.

Stage 2: Purpose and people

Establish your precise purpose. What reaction do you wish to induce in your hearers? What job has the talk to perform? Write down your purpose; re-write it several times until you can express, exactly, in a few cogent words, the effect you wish to achieve. Know what you are doing, explicitly. Be thorough about this. Do nothing else until you have got your objective clear.

Now that you have ample subject matter and a clear purpose, you must ponder on the real material for your talk – the people who will listen to you. Examine every link they have or might have with your subject because they will be completely uninterested until what you say has something to do with them. Obvious, isn't it? What is their technical level, their social, financial level; what are their needs in connection with you and your subject? Study the people until you can see their view of your subject. You can only put your view across in relation to theirs'. If you do not know anything about your audience, you would be well advised to find out at once. A discussion with the organisers, even a telephone call can prove useful. Get to know your audience and integrate them into your presentation *now*;

it will be too late when you are on your feet talking.

So, purpose and people. These two essential elements for an effective talk rarely receive enough thought or attention.

Purpose. People. Theme. Main points.

After your talk what message will your hearers carry away with them? What big points supported your thesis? No audience will remember everything that you said. Decide at this stage in your preparation what basic theme you wish them to remember. As with your purpose, write down your theme and work on it until it becomes simple, straightforward and crystal clear. Next, separate the one, two or three really important points from the lesser points. Which are the really big points that you want them to have working in their minds? If you do not establish them clearly now, they will not stand out prominently enough in your delivered talk. Your job as a speaker is to clarify the subject for your audience. You cannot do this unless you first clarify it for yourself.

Now build your talk on the foundation of your Purpose, your People, your Theme and your Main points.

A few reminders

A successful speaker knows his subject and is enthusiatic about it.

He makes certain that he is well prepared.

He has considered his audience and believes that the subject is important to them.

Bad speakers are usually people who think about themselves too much.

Pertinent questions to be answered at the end of stage 2

1 What exactly is my subject?
2 Why am I speaking about it to this audience and what do I know about them?
3 What are the most important things I must tell them?
4 Have I picked out the main points which must be highlighted?
5 Have I arranged these points so that this particular audience will fully understand them and be involved in them?
6 Have I made sure that there is a glowing, dominant theme?
7 What will the audience gain from this talk?

Stage 3

The audience must at once be made confident that the speaker knows what he is doing. They must find his first thoughts intensely interesting. This of course rules out the usual dreary openings, for instance, where the speaker talks about himself and his worries as a speaker.

The three-sentence technique can secure a telling impact on opening.

Sentence 1 You make any vivid, unexpected, off-beat, basically interesting remark you like. (Always of course bearing in mind your audience.)
Sentence 2 You link, skilfully, sentence 1 to your subject and make clear exactly what your subject is.
Sentence 3 You INVOLVE the audience in both your opening remark and your subject.

It is essential that you economise and discipline yourself to use only three sentences for this effect. There must be no woolly edges around these three sentences, no hums and hahs, no interpolated oddments, no clutter. You are seeking a clean, crisp, immediate communion, a direct response. Experiment until you have got a really good beginning. Excite. Link. Involve. Do not be satisfied with the first openings you think of: try at least six ways before you decide.

Avoid the word 'I' for at least one minute. Substitute 'you', 'your', or group words describing the audience, such as engineers, Scotsmen, managers. Be as specific as you can. Talk about them and their links with the subject. Get the focus firmly on to them and away from yourself.

As soon as your impact has been achieved and the audience knows what your broad subject is, define your limits so that they will not waste their attention on parts of the subject outside the scope of your talk. Tell them where you intend to take them within your subject, sometimes even which aspects you intend to leave out. From the start concentrate their mental energy on the relevant aspects. Give them clear signposts, briefly.

Now, you have a dynamic purpose in your mind; you and your audience know where you are going. They have been intrigued by your opening remarks and are ready for the statement of your basic theme, ready for the development of your first main point supporting that theme – and they are eager to find out how and where they fit in with what you have to say.

The elements are prepared for you – the catalyst – to do your work.

There are no dull subjects. Everything under the sun teems with interest. From even such beginnings as a dirty ash-tray or the Industrial Training Act a lively mind could create a fascinating talk. How are you going to tell your story, how give your facts their full value as facts plus that life which also gives them interest? The key to power in story telling is to bind everything you say to people and things – the concrete rather than the abstract. You might well be talking about some entirely abstract technical concept. Human beings and concrete, tangible things judiciously woven into your presentation will vitalise even the unlikeliest subject for a potent talk. Also, wherever your can, link your examples directly to your listeners. An earthquake killing thousands in China could leave your audience unmoved: but a gas-explosion in Clay Street, Manchester will engender great interest – especially to those of your audience who live in Clay Street, Manchester.

Facts are sacred and must not be tampered with. Concrete examples emphasise facts and make facts stick in the mind. The closer the examples are to the experience and the environment of the audience the more surely your points will find their target.

Contrary to a common opinion, facts do not always speak for themselves: they need good men to speak for them. No fact of life need be colourless or less interesting than fiction. You must adroitly develop the story of your facts, giving it a good beginning, a vivid motif, substance, excitement, strong examples and a language suitable for your hearers.

Words worry people. They say 'I have plenty of ideas but I haven't the vocabulary to express them'. This assertion is based on a fallacy. Words (or some other set of symbols such as mathematical formulae) are essential to clear thought. If you are fumbling for words, you have not clarified the thought.

Technical language and jargon incur much scorn and contempt; but they have their uses as a shorthand for the initiated. On the other hand, to use such esoteric stuff to show how clever you are or because you lack consideration for your hearers is unpardonable. Use your audience's language or explain your own. Otherwise you will waste your breath and, what is worse, waste their time.

Speaking style

A hypnotist wishing to put someone to sleep employs a subdued, monotonous voice and a single soporific thought repeated and repeated and repeated until the patient gives up and slumbers. To arouse the patient he makes some sharp noise and brings his own voice to life by using a complete change of tone. The patient wakes up.

Human voices possess an immense range of volume, tone, pace, attack. Why be monotonous? Why be dull? Why mutter or why bawl like a bull? Why not work out beforehand how you can give variety and the appropriate vocal values to each part of your talk? Think in terms of main headlines and paragraphs and make sure that each new idea comes to the audience with a change in vocal approach. Particularly when introducing a fresh point, give your voice a lift. Watch sentence-length; see to it that a few crisp short ones intervene between a series of protracted sentences. Watch the ends of sentences: a rising pitch holds more interest than a dying fall.

It is an odd fact of speaking technique that absolute silence for a few seconds – under control – can be the most effective part of a speech. Try to find, perhaps two such moments when you can hold your audience to your thoughts during your calculated pauses.

The human voice is only one of the channels through which ideas can flow. Sound, sight, touch, smell, taste all provide means of conveying thoughts to other people. A good speaker gives his audience a chance to use as many of their senses as the occasion permits. With a little ingenuity you can give their ears a rest and switch channels. One obvious way of doing this is to show them the point, to demonstrate it. The term 'visual aids' does not mean only blackboard – chalk-and-talk stuff – or flipcharts or films or overhead projectors; solid physical, three-dimensional objects have much more effect. If it is practicable, show them the actual thing you are talking about. Let them handle it, smell it, taste it. Use your zest, imagination and enthusiasm to create a worthwhile experience for your audience. You can develop a reputation as a first-class speaker if you work at it and stop worrying about yourself. Few people will understand or appreciate the work you have done. They will say you have a flair for this sort of thing, a gift. You must not mind that. A judicious use of the five senses will help you. However prosaic your subject, give it vigour, colour – life.

Please arm yourself with a pencil and a sheet of paper because we are going to create a graph. I would appreciate your comments on it and your physical cooperation. To begin with, here are the axes (Figure 22:1 facing page). Please read notes and draw the axes exactly.

The shading at the foot of Figure 22:2 represents the grey sludge area at the beginning of so many talks, during what the poor speaker calls 'warming up'. The monologue here tells how unaccustomed the speaker is and what a trying ordeal he is experiencing in facing such a difficult, awesome set of people. In general, the self-centred blockhead isolates himself and destroys the goodwill of the audience by focusing in the wrong direction. No wonder he is nervous. No wonder the audience already begin to doubt whether they should have come.

Eliminate the sludge area altogether. Instead, get some vigour, elevation and impact into your beginning. Hoist the value-and-interest line clean through the sludge up to X, which marks your impact at opening.

Signposts help your hearers to concentrate on the special aspects of the subject that you intend to cover. Define your limits, briefly.

Now drive towards your first main point (a). You have it clear. You have already worked out how to make your facts come to life, how to link your vivid examples both to the facts and to your audience. Follow your line, the theme, and support that theme with facts. Develop your message.

Summaries are a matter for your judgment. At least you must make certain that each main point holds fast in the minds of your audience before you tackle the next point.

Signposting internal to the talk, again, is a matter for you to decide. Will summaries and signposting help the audience? If so, use them.

When you reach the climax of your talk, when you ram home your message you must remind your audience of the main facts which support your theme. Summarise crisply: remind them how the matter of your talk affects them and do have a powerful line at the end. (Make a really sharp, hard, strong point and sit down on it!)

Your comments, please. Yes, the axes are disproportionate: but keep these odd ratios in your mind. Let the horizontal axis represent TIME. Let the vertical axis represent the VALUE AND INTEREST you bring to your hearers in that time. You should never take more of your audience's time than is necessary to do your speaking job properly. The value and interest line should be as high as possible in the time they give to you. Now, please fill in your own graph as shown in Figure 22:2.

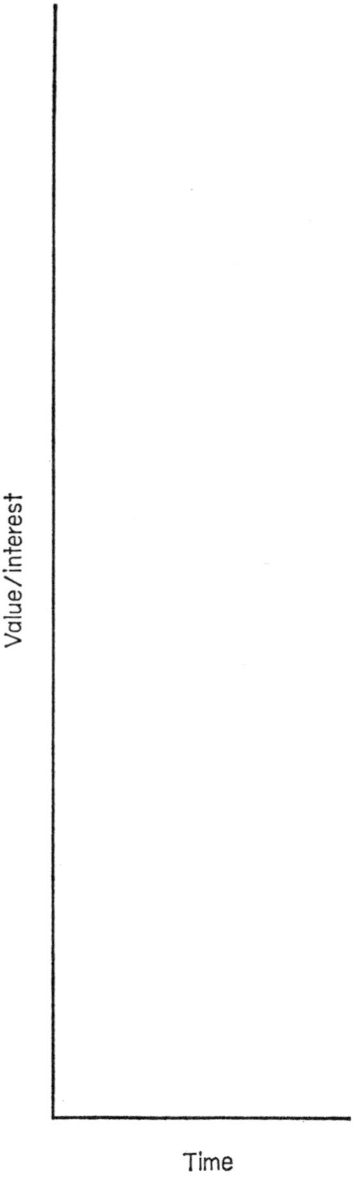

Value/interest

Time

FIGURE 22:1 VALUE/TIME AXES

Use the proportions shown here to prepare the graph in the text

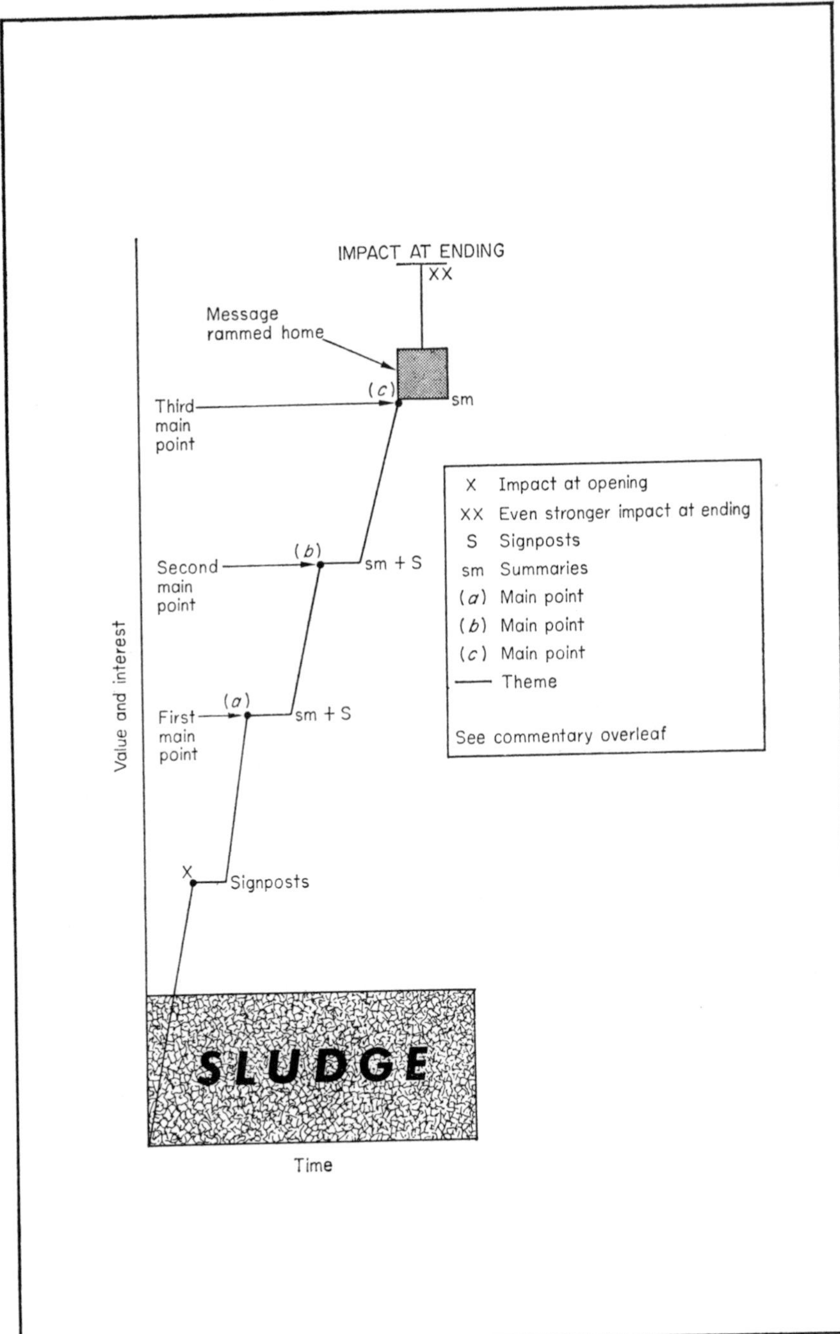

FIGURE 22:2 VALUE AND INTEREST VERSUS TIME

Graphical demonstration of a planned talk programme relating value and interest to time

Speaking for a special occasion

Case presentation

Persuasive speaking, getting people to say 'Yes'.

Please engrave this sentence into your mind: Nothing induces agreement quicker than self-interest – the other fellow's.

Many businessmen have to recommend changes that will cost money. In most companies there is a procedure for this. The proposer has first to prepare a document setting out his proposal in detail. This goes through normal channels and may sometimes be agreed to or rejected as it stands. More frequently the proposer will be asked to appear before some board or committee to explain his proposal and to answer questions about it.

The written part of a proposal is a persuasive report and should be written with that in mind. The oral presentation is part speech, part meeting and part interview.

In preparing such a presentation, the proposer should ask himself these questions:

1 Do you know exactly what you want?
2 Do you really believe in your case?
3 Have you got all the facts that support your case and have you checked them?
4 What are the strongest arguments for your case?
5 What are the benefits for your listeners?
6 Why must the present situation be changed?
7 What is their problem?
8 Who else is affected? (Unions, other divisions, etc.)
9 What are the arguments against your plan?
10 What are the alternatives to your plan?
11 Do your benefits clearly outweigh these arguments and alternatives?
12 To whom are you presenting your plan? Have you done any lobbying? Do you need to?
13 Do you know who your probable allies and opponents are?
14 Have you discussed the finances with the experts?
15 Have you prepared hand-outs of any complicated figures?
16 It was a good idea when you first thought of it. Is it still – from their point of view?

17 Have you prepared a really effective presentation? (Time plus the value and interest ratio are particularly important in case presentation.)
18 How will you sum up and end?
19 Are you ready for questions?
20 Have you emphasised the benefits they (your listeners) will gain? Remember: Nothing induces agreement quicker than self-interest – the other fellow's.

The board is probably only interested in this question: 'Have they a problem and does your proposal solve it for them?'

Social speaking

Social speaking has one simple purpose: to give pleasure. What will make your audience purr? What will cause them to cry 'Hear! Hear!'? What will make them laugh? What will make them proud that they belong to this club, this company, this band of people brought together with a common cause? What sentiment will bring a lump into their throats? What will make them say afterwards 'Oh, I did enjoy that'?

Deliver the answers to these questions and they will be glad that you spoke, especially as you delivered with obvious affection for them, and warm appreciation of their values and you did so without going on and on and on. Work out a good line to end your speech and do not separate it by too long a time from your first-class opening line. Give them pleasure and enjoy the pleasure of their company.

One-to-one talking

An encounter across a desk can often make or break a manager. Failure follows almost inevitably if you present your ideas at the wrong time or if you insist on pushing a proposal from your own point of view. It is said that the only difference between rape and seduction is technique. Only exceptional men remember technique when it comes to a one-to-one discussion. By all means be relaxed but before you go in to win your point, or before the other fellow calls on you, do your homework. Get your purpose clear, have your facts ready. Know his problems in relation to your suggestion and start the discussion of the basis of his problems. Until you have established his problems and have shown that you understand them and are in sympathy with them, you must not try to sell him anything. You want him to react, to say 'Yes'. He will not react in your favour if you spend your time putting yourself across. Try it the other way round. Put him and his problems in the forefront. If what you have to sell solves his problems, he'll agree.

Some thoughts

Make contact with people. Use your eyes. Look at them. Include them in what you say. This is simply good manners. Take the trouble to prepare properly, to ensure that you give them value in exchange for the time they are giving you. Develop a respect, even an affection for your audience. Remember that, however expert you may be, every man and woman there is superior to you in some way and could each you something.

Speaking is probably the oldest form of human communication. It s certainly the most natural to modern man but, unless other minds an process and use what is said, speaking is just a useless shifting f wind.

There are few things more exhilarating than an audience reacting vith interest, excitement and the sheer pleasure of enjoying a first-lass speaker. Deserve such a reaction and your world will be that nuch better for having you around.

Reports

ogie Baird's discovery of the principles of television was useless. instein helped nobody with his thinking on relativity nor did leming with penicillin – until they made their facts and theories nown to other people. Knowledge locked away in the recesses of a ingle mind has little value until other minds receive the key and ain access to it. Many specialists believe that their work stops when hey have uncovered the facts. A question was asked of them. They vorked on it, investigated it thoroughly and found the answer. And hat, they say, is the end of their job. But is it?

Why do industrial concerns employ scientists, engineers and other specialists? The answer to that question is simple. Industrial concerns employ specialists in order to get from them information, and expert guidance towards profitable action. Yet although specialists study and sweat for 5, 10, 15, 20 years, a lifetime, to equip themselves as experts they rarely study the techniques of passing their hard-gained information to other people. And their readers do the sweating.

A report is a working document that helps the other man to do his job. A record may well form the basis for a report but it is not a report. Samuel Pepys's diary recorded his times, brilliantly, but scholars had to delve to extract the meat. Nobody expects to have to delve into a modern technical report; readers expect you to present the meat ready for digestion. A long report is not necessarily better than a short one, if only because fewer people will bother to read it. On the other hand, if you are writing for qualified people who want to know not only the conclusions and recommendations but also the detailed results and the methods used to obtain them, your report must contain such facts in full.

A report is not a detective story. Agatha Christie can take a set of facts and cloak them so skilfully that few readers can get the crucial point until the final page. The facts are all there if only one has the nous to spot them. There should be no mystery about a report. The facts should be clear and the development logical so that the conclusions and recommendations follow them naturally.

There are five main considerations in thinking about reports:

1 Circulation and distribution
2 Physical layout
3 Numerical information
4 Visual aids
5 Language

Circulation and distribution

All communications are a struggle for other people's interest and attention. The furniture in any busy man's office always includes a yawning wastepaper basket. If you have put this busy man on your circulation list for reasons of self-advertisement or because his name happened to be on a routine list, unedited for years, beware!

Before you begin to shape your report, please take the trouble to sort out the people whom it will help in their jobs. Nobody else should have it.

Many a report suffers from a false start. The man who asked for it did not bother to discuss with the writer either the purpose of the report or the intended readership. Or the writer just says 'Yes' and ploughs on blindly into a document which does not meet the real requirements. Such a report will fail or at least have to be rewritten. Both the senior man and the writer contributed to the failure and caused the extra labour, the frustration, perhaps the anger ensuing from a job badly done.

So, before you write a syllable, establish who is going to use your report and what they have a right to expect from you. What is the purpose of the report from their point of view?

In many companies, the circulation is tacked on to the completed report as an afterthought. This deplorable custom should be opposed vigorously. Additions to the circulation list should be exceptional; better still they should have been considered and meshed into the writer's reckoning from the start.

All this does not mean, however, that the facts should be coloured or slanted to affect the truth; no specialist worth his salt would wish to gain a point by distortion or trickery. His credibility would quickly disappear if he did, and rightly so.

Above all, your reader must find your report useful and the facts presented in such a way that he can absorb them easily and accurately. You cannot use suitable language, suitable layout or even select the material properly unless you know whom you are talking to and what he wants from the report. Consider your reader from the beginning. You cannot expect to do this unless you fix the circulation list at the outset. A report looks so forlorn in the wastepaper basket or even put aside – to be read 'later'. Do not plague people with reports they do not require for their own work. People have enough to do. All they want from you is help. Your useful reports will receive a welcome at the right time, at the right place and from the right man.

Physical layout

Your company has probably issued instructions on how its reports should be laid out. Such instructions were not written to while away an idle hour and it is the duty of every report writer to study them. The research department requires for its reports a different approach from the sales or public relations departments. Monsieur Ritz, the hotelier, made a fortune by following the precept 'The customer is always right'. The layout of a report depends almost entirely on how the readers like it. There are no rules, just a few basic principles. Your reader must be able to find his way about the report. If he is accustomed to a summary on the first page, that is where you put it. If he prefers all the graphs, tables, charts and detailed figures in appendices, put them there.

Reports should look as if they expect a welcome and want to be read. The ninety-third copy from a worn-out duplicator lacks inspiration and deserves neglect. The general appearance of a report must be appropriate to the contents and its purpose.

First appearances

The cover should immediately indicate the type of report that is inside: glossy for the chairman's annual report and other such public relations stuff; perhaps blue for research, green for personnel, or whatever the company's standard practice demands. The title and security classification must, obviously, be prominent before a page is turned.

The title page must include the date of the report, the title, the author's name and that of the issuing authority and a reference/file number. Some readers also like the circulation list on the title page – it is often useful to know who else has the report – and a very brief summary.

Any report longer than six pages should have a table of contents, clearly indicating where readers can find the special bits of the report that are all they intend to read. (Do not flatter yourself that everyone will read the whole of your tome.) Even avid readers will want to know where things are. A table of contents, reflecting a logical layout with clear, expressive headings, immediately creates an impression of order, thought and consideration.

The busy man's page

This should tell the busy man the object of the report and the reason why the work was done. It should give him an abbreviated summary of the investigation, the MAIN results, the MAIN conclusions and the MAIN recommendations for action. He should get the guts of the report in fewer than 200 words, if possible.

So, you have already given your reader:

A cover that immediately tells him the style, title and security classification of the report.
A title page that tells who wrote it, when it was written, who authorised it and, sometimes, who else has the information.
A summary – the main elements of the report in a nutshell.
A table of contents that tells him where he can find all the details he wants.

Many of your readers, especially top management and laymen, will go no further into a report. They have all they need – a general appreciation of your work and enough information for discussion or appropriate action at their level. It is advisable to avoid technical language at this stage.

Your fellow specialists will now wish to dig into the report. They will expect an introduction which informs, or reminds, them of the circumstances which prompted your work. They will want to know how you set about your investigation, what methods, what tests, what equipment you used. They will expect a complete validation of your results and figures and to know what standards of accuracy you worked to. They will expect you to separate facts from opinions. The headlines for the main body of the work could read:

Introduction
Experimental details
Results
Discussion
Full summary
Recommendations
Appendices

This format cannot fit all circumstances and must be adjusted to suit the needs of your readers and the purpose of the report.

Please acknowledge the work of other people who have helped you, if only in a bibliography.

Information by numbers

Numbers form the backbone of most reports. Measurements of time, frequencies, distances, etc., are fundamental in presenting facts. Few readers need all the numbers; all readers need the significant numbers and wish them to be displayed significantly. Do not bury them or wall them up behind the background data. When you are planning your report, establish the vital numbers early on so that you can give them due prominence when writing.

Your reader will want to know your tolerances and to what degree of accuracy your figures are presented. Do not bother him with five decimal places if the approximate whole number will suffice for him. The main body of the report will flow more easily if the script is uncluttered by a mass of figures. Many thoughtful writers quote only those figures that make the point and then guide those people who may be interested in greater detail to an appendix which contains more complicated items such as mathematical formulae.

With numbers, significance is all – or nearly all.

Visual aids

If you were the sales director, how would you prefer to have the sales figures from May to October presented – as in (a), (b), (c) or (d) of Figure 22:3?

Sometimes readers would rather see the point than have it related to them. Please consider this.

Language in reports

'The results of a period of ad hoc experimentation supplemented by both statistical analysis and consideration of empirical factors thought

(*a*) The sales figures for May were 20 of type 1, 32 of type 2, 38 of type 3; for June 28 of type 1, 30 of type 2, 36 of type 3; for July, 40 of type 1, 30 of type 2, 28 of type 3; for August, 26 of type 1, 18 of type 2, 28 of type 3: for September, 26 of type 1, 18 of type 2, 30 of type 3: and for October, 44 of type 1, 20 of type 2 and 28 of type 3.

(*b*) Sales figures May–October

	Type 1	Type 2	Type 3
May	20	32	38
June	28	30	36
July	40	30	28
August	26	18	28
September	26	18	30
October	44	20	28

FIGURE 22:3 FOUR WAYS OF PRESENTING NUMERICAL RESULTS

It shows how careful thought can result in a more effective display (improving from *a* to *d*)

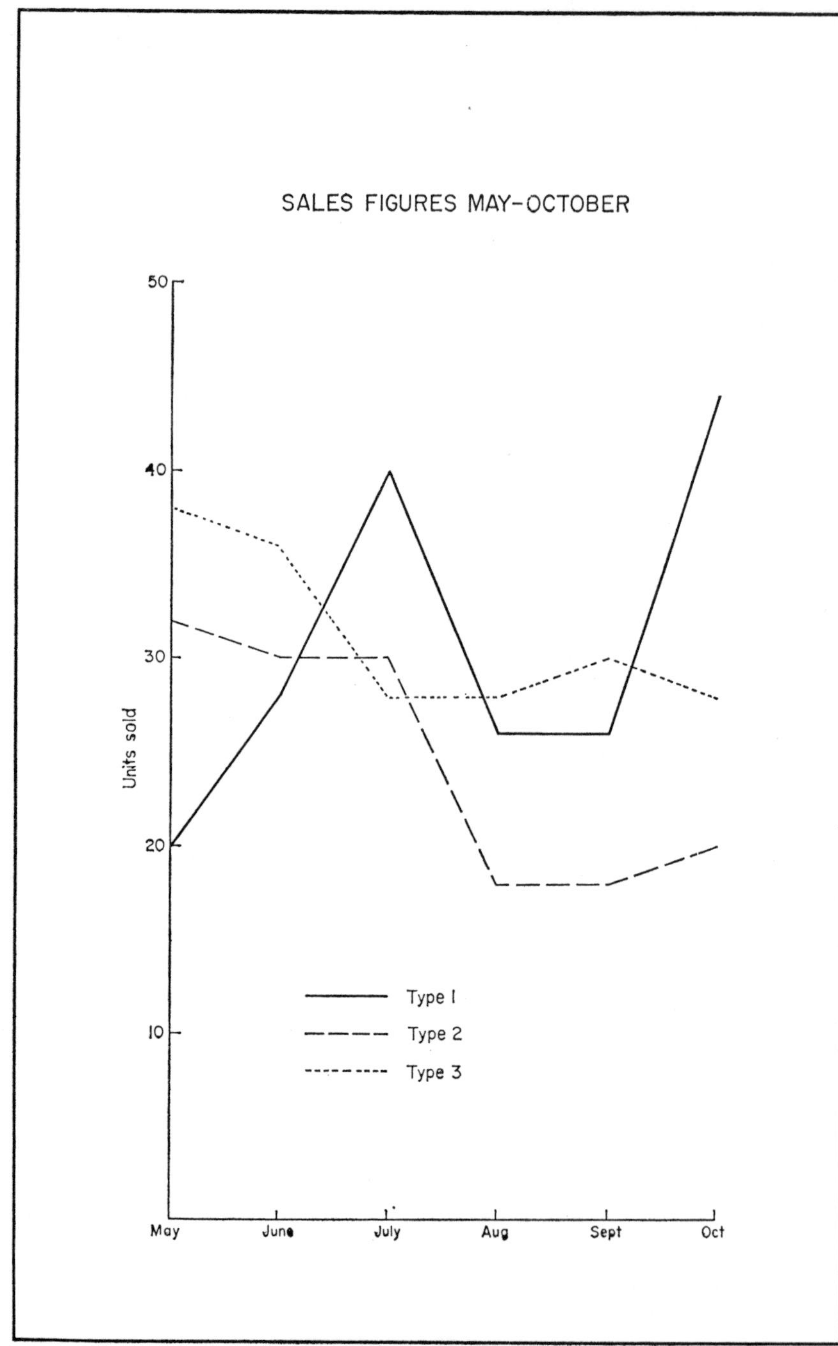
SALES FIGURES MAY–OCTOBER
50
40
30
20
10
Units sold
May
June
July
Aug
Sept
Oct
Type 1
Type 2
Type 3

FIGURE 22:3*c*

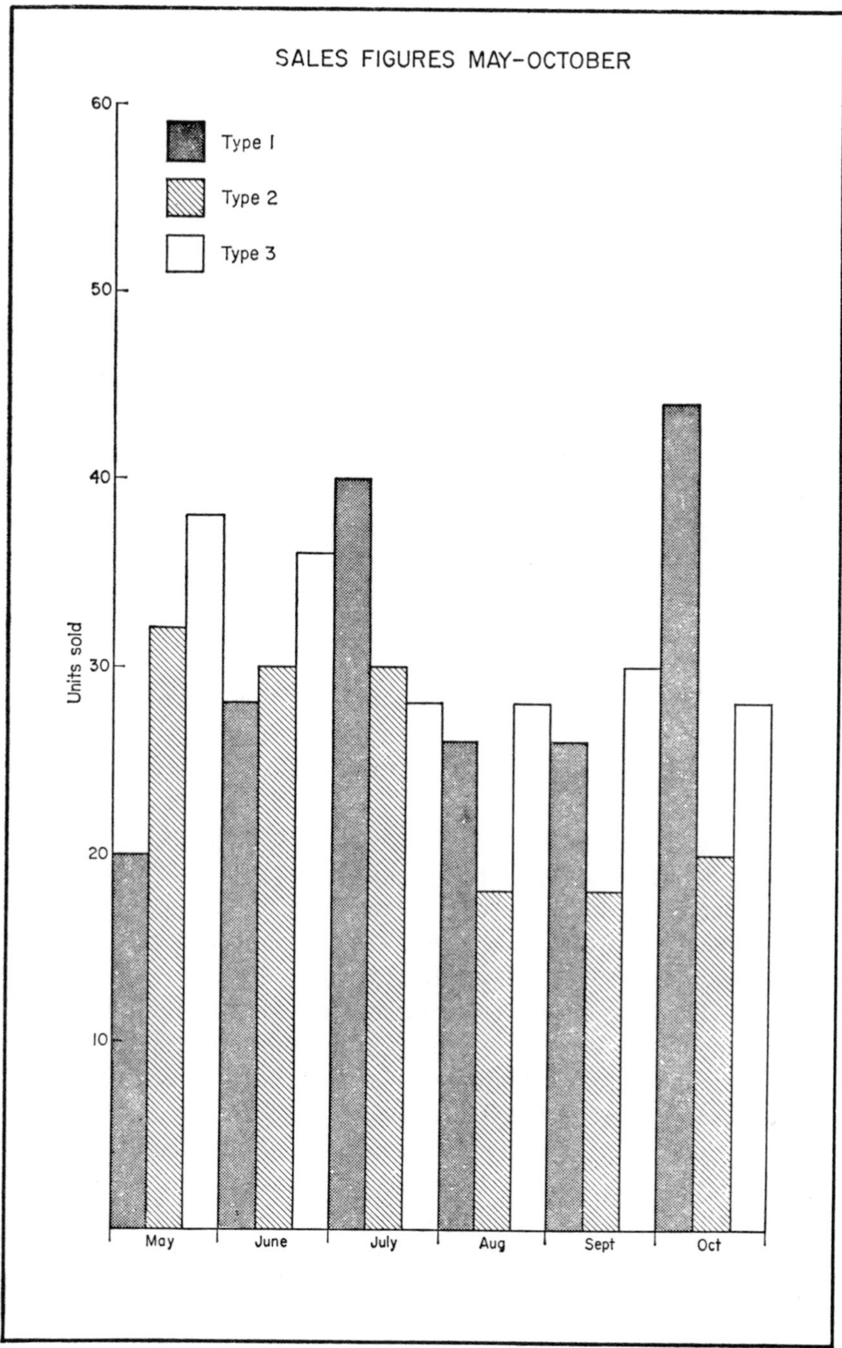
SALES FIGURES MAY–OCTOBER
60
50
40
30
20
10
Units sold
Type 1
Type 2
Type 3
May
June
July
Aug
Sept
Oct

FIGURE 22:3*d*

to be universally viable in the context of the areas in which ultisation could be expected to approach a maximum indicated that the thermal conductivity of that portion of the equipment designed for prehensile digital contact was such as to present a surface whose temperature would markedly exceed the generally accepted threshold of sensory discomfort.' Et cetera, et cetera, et cetera, . . .

Why do so many technicians, trained in logic and precision, write such twaddle? Is it because they are suspicious of the arts, afraid that what they do might lose 'mystique' or is it that they cannot bother to bring logic and precision into their use of language? Many a brilliant young man, on reaching middle age, wonders what went wrong with his career. Let him re-read some of his reports. The answers could be found in them.

We have no space here to discuss grammar and the techniques of clear English, but you should learn a few basic points of control in your writing. You can then leave the rest to your genuine wish to help people to understand you. Please examine these four sentences:

1 Oil lubricates bearings.
2 Bearings are lubricated by oil.
3 The lubrication of bearings is carried out by the use of oil.
4 In so far as the process of lubrication with respect to bearings is concerned, this is carried out by the use of an application of oil.

Exaggerated as it is, sentence 4 shows the beginnings of the decay that attacks so many specialists from about the age of twenty-eight. In any large organisation roughly one-third of the people over the age of twenty-eight are stone dead. They have accumulated sufficient cliché phrases and routine attitudes to lean on until their pensions turn up. There seems to be no reason for them to think any more it is enough just to react according to the rule book and the jargon – 'We are in receipt of your favour of the 19th instant to hand and it must be pointed out that in view of the fact that . . .' 'The conceptual philosophy of commonality and standardisation at this point in time could be said to have, perhaps, groundings in feasibility which, with the basic assumption that . . .' '. . . the viability of these parameters, shiftwise . . .'. all non-think stuff, torture for the reader and highly dangerous for the writer.

Danger? What danger? We live in a sea of words. What is wrong with drifting along in the fashionable waters, swallowing the stuff and regurgitating it into the faces of our fellows? Why not? It's easier than thinking.

What happens to a muscle that gets no exercise? It becomes flabby. What happens to a machine that lies idle for years? It becomes rusty and useless. What happens to a brain that does nothing but gather verbal cobwebs? Adult thinking is impossible without a language or some other set of symbols that label the elements we develop into thoughts. If words, for instance, are the bricks and mortar with which we build the wall of thought does it not follow that the sort of words we habitually use is the sort of thinker we are? Near-enough words, that'll-do words, other people's tired old clichés provide neither keep-fit exercise nor nourishment for an active mind. A factory girl whose eight-hour day consists of fitting component A into component B and endlessly repeating the dreary process to feed some production line would go mad if she thought about it very much. So she works mechanically and dreams of her boyfriend or being a duchess. But this will not do for expensively trained specialists.

Technical language has the advantage of being clearly defined. Used properly, it assists constructive thought and communication among those who understand it. Abused, or flaunted because you want to imply that you are superior to people outside 'the club', it can cause trouble – for you as much as for your victims. The English language provides one of the most precise, subtle, flexible and vigorous aids to clear thought and effective reports. No specialist can claim to be more than half-baked if he does not learn how to control it.

Report writing check-list

Before drafting a report ask yourself:

1 Have I insisted on a thorough briefing from whoever requested the report and discussed with him in detail: (*a*) that there is a need for the report, (*b*) the exact purpose of the report, (*c*) who is going to read the report, (*d*) the exact subject of the report?
2 Have I collected all the information I might need?
3 Have I selected from this the information the readers need?

When drafting a report, ask yourself:

1. Does the layout comply with any company standard and does it make things easy for the reader?
2. Is there a 'busy man's page' and does it contain the right information for him?
3. Does the report look good and can it be reproduced using the equipment available?
4. Is everybody who 'needs to know' on the circulation list?
5. Have I arranged for library copies and spare copies?
6. Is the circulation too wide?
7. Does the report need a security classification?
8. Have I used sufficient active verbs and concrete nouns?
9. Have I used short sentences and simple constructions?
10. Are any technical or scientific words likely to be unknown to the readers?
11. Have I avoided padding?
12. Will the reader easily understand what I have written?
13. Have I avoided slant and bias?
14. Have I clearly stated conclusions and recommendations?
15. Have I used sufficient visual aids?
16. Are the visual aids in the right place, clearly labelled and cross-referenced?
17. Have I shown scales, dimensions and magnifications on my visual aids?
18. Are the tables and charts displayed in the best way?
19. Have I shown the units? Are units consistent and do they comply with British or other accepted standards?
20. Will the visual aids still be clear and easy to follow when reproduced by the available processes?
21. Should I invite someone else to read the draft and discuss it with me?

A report is a working document that helps the other man to do his job. A specialist who learns to write effective reports adds value to himself and his work.

Meetings

Believe it or not, some companies use up more cash at meetings than they spend on the raw materials with which they make their products. Much of this cash goes straight down the drain. Before you dismiss this thought as whimsical, consider the cost of meetings – air and rail fares, cars, hotel bills, salaries and expenses, conference and boardroom rents, rates, cleaning, postage of reports and other documents, typing and more money for many more items. Any large organisation spends millions of pounds each year so that people can discuss, decide and, one hopes, energise some profitable action. The waste is colossal.

Money is important – only a fool would deny that – but much more important is human life. Ineffective meetings not only waste money but they also devalue people's time and shrink the people concerned with them. Human relationships can be soured by bad meetings. A wise man takes the trouble to find out how meetings work and how to make them work for him and his associates.

A definition of business meetings might be 'two or more people getting together for a specific business purpose'.

The meeting itself forms only one link in a chain of events. If the other links lack strength the meeting can become merely the place where the chain breaks. Ninety per cent of an effective meeting happens before the meeting starts. Forging the before-the-meeting link requires thought, horse-sense and skill. If you intend to call a meeting, be completely clear about its intended purpose. What specific business should the meeting achieve? Is it to decide on action, to brief people, to inform, to persuade? What in specific terms – no woolly abstractions – is the business purpose of the meeting? You must then face what might be a deflating question: is a meeting necessary at all? Must you deprive people of their time and put the company to expense? Can the business be done – the decision made, for instance – in some other way – a few telephone calls or half a dozen letters? Why are you proposing to call the meeting? Why?

So you decide that your meeting is a necessity; the business cannot be accomplished without a combination of other minds, interest and experience. Which people can provide you with such a combination? Nobody else should be invited. You want to get some business done. Avoid the hangers-on and the strange creatures who go to meetings just to get out of their own offices for a while. If your business is to get a decision and action, beware of the second-string man who cannot give a firm yes or no. He has to report back to his boss. Then there will have to be another meeting for his boss or even his boss's boss. Invite and accept only the people who can do the job properly. Do not forget, as so often happens, to invite the man who will have to take any action you decide upon. If your meeting decides to change the production line you cannot expect joyous cooperation from the production manager who was elsewhere when you decided how to run his department.

When and where the meeting takes place depends on the urgency of the business and the convenience of the people concerned. Be considerate about this. Just because you operate from Plymouth, does not necessarily mean that your Glasgow and Ipswich colleagues will agree that your office is the perfect location. Must you start your meeting at 09 00, which means an overnight trip for everyone except you? Timing, the date and the hour, can show you to be a thoughtful organiser.

If your colleagues have to examine reports, plans, figures or must equip themselves in other ways in preparation for the meeting, give them a fair chance to do so. Also make clear to them precisely what the business of the meeting will be and that you expect them to come prepared. A meeting which has to be recalled because the relevant facts are missing reflects no credit on the convenor or the members. More meetings fail because the preparation has been neglected or skimped than for any other reason. No one should go to a meeting ill-prepared. Even if the meeting happens to be a quick get-together, and at short notice, a few minutes' thought beforehand will increase your value as a meeting-man. At least one man, you, will be able to talk sense.

The business-like chairman will see to it that he or his secretary arranges a suitable conference room. He will indicate when the meeting is likely to finish; he will arrange breaks for the creature comforts of the conferers, and for telephone messages to be collected, outside the conference room – no interruptions will be allowed except for desperately urgent calls. He will plan an approximate timetable for the agenda so that timeworthy items get their due. Documents and, if required, suitable equipment for presentations must be available. Name cards help people to know who's who; make them bold – and do have them spelled correctly. There are of course a hundred and one other details, any of which might be important. A meeting succeeds in almost direct ratio to its intelligent preparation.

The formal rules for running meetings become more important when the gathering is a large one. For most business meetings, formal rules matter little. It is the spirit in which people attend the meetings that produces a good or bad meeting.

No real progress can be made without agreement. The object of meeings is to produce agreement. Even if, after disagreement, action results because of fear or force of personality, the action will only be half-hearted and possibly poorly performed. The chairman of a meeting must always be striving for agreement, not surrender.

Preparation for the meeting

The chairman

Decide whether the meeting is really necessary. (Especially important with routine meetings which often occur even when there is nothing to be discussed or decided.)

Decide on the purpose of the meeting.

Decide on the subject or subjects.

Decide on the place and time.

Decide who is going to attend the meeting. Only those with something to contribute or who need to know exactly what was said and by whom should be present. Other people can get any necessary information from the minutes. The chairman should ensure that those attending are of sufficient standing, that they really represent their departments, and have the authority to commit them to action.

Decide on the agenda and roughly how much time to allow for each item. It is imperative that items are stated in concrete terms. Abstractions will inevitably result in rambling, woolly discussion that leads nowhere. One or two simple items first will get the meeting off to a good start. Even if the meeting is summoned hurriedly by telephone, members should be told what they are going to discuss. This is the agenda.

Study the subjects. The chairman must be sufficiently familiar with the subjects being discussed to be able to keep the discussion on the right lines.

Study the people attending. He must know the personal alignments that will help or hinder the meeting; who will not talk even though he has valuable contributions to make, and who will talk even though he has not.

The secretary

Responsible for all the mechanics of the meeting.

Must obtain for the chairman any points for the agenda and names of those attending.

Must obtain suitable accommodation, arrange for paper, etc., arrange for refreshments to be available when the chairman wants them, and arrange to disconnect the telephone.

Must circulate the agenda in good time.

Must prepare all the papers the chairman may require.

Members

Must study the subjects to be discussed and, if necessary, departmental opinions and agreements.

Must study the chairman and his idiosyncrasies.

Must study the other members.

Must work out how they are going to sell their ideas.

Conduct of the meeting

The chairman

The meeting must start on time, even if there are absentees. If the chairman is absent the next most suitable person should start it for him. If the speaker on the first point is absent, switch the agenda.

Start briskly, laying down the purpose, the time available, and any other conditions that will help to control the meeting. A chairman cannot demand respect: he can only earn it – usually by giving it to others.

The chairman must watch the time. If he sees that he is getting behind time and wants to extend the meeting he must warn the members early, so that they can make any necessary arrangements or get a move on.

The chairman must keep feeding back to the members the state of the discussion, to ensure that everyone understands the situation. This is particularly important at the end of each item. This will enable the secretary to make an immediate, accurate record of the decisions reached and who is to take action, without any risk of error.

The chairman must try to be impartial and only produce his own opinions late in the discussion, if at all. Otherwise he will inhibit proper discussion.

The chairman may have to keep reminding members of the subject and aim in order to keep them to the point.

The chairman must ensure that everyone has the opportunity to express his opinion, at the same time preventing any individual from taking up an excessive amount of time. A member with very strong views that he is determined to express should be given his head, unopposed, the chairman, at least, giving all his attention to what is being said. The chairman should endeavour to extract the relevant points from what may be a rambling discourse and ensure that they are properly considered by the meeting.

The chairman must summarise, clarify and emphasise the ACTION arising from the meeting, name specifically who is to be responsible for taking ACTION and record who should do what in precise terms.

The meeting should finish at the stated time unless the members have agreed to go on late.

The chairman and the secretary should leave the room immediately after the meeting is over, otherwise another meeting might ensue.

The members

Disagree without being disagreeable. A member must be clear in his mind what points he wants to get across and do it with the aim of convincing the other members that he is right. At the same time, he should have a sufficiently open mind to be able to change his opinion if someone else produces better arguments or ideas.

Avoid distracting personalities.

The secretary

During the meeting the secretary must take copious notes unless he can be sure that the chairman will provide him with the minutes as the meeting goes along. It is therefore impracticable for a member to act as secretary and do both jobs adequately.

Chairmanship—reminders

Before

Ensure that there is a clear, worthwhile purpose.

Check who will be attending.

Check on the points to be discussed.

Ensure the secretary has organised everything.

During

Introduce the meeting and purpose.

Define the limits of the subject and time available.

Control the members. Ensure that all have a fair say and none dominate.

Keep the meeting to the point. Be quick to spot when people are wandering.

Feed back. Ensure that everyone is keeping up with discussions and understands the points that are coming out of the discussions.

Summing-up. Make sure that everyone knows the conclusions reached and especially who is to take action.

Be impartial. EARN RESPECT.

After the meeting

As quickly as possible after the meeting the secretary should write up the minutes, either for rapid circulation or to go on the files. The minutes should be kept as short as is practicable.

The essential parts of the minutes are the decisions, agreed action and who is to take it and when. These must stand out.

At an appropriate time after the meeting someone, probably the secretary, should check that members are getting on with action they undertook or were instructed to take.

THE CHAIRMAN MUST HAVE AT THE FRONT OF HIS MIND ALL THE TIME AND OCCASIONALLY REMIND MEMBERS THAT THE OBJECT OF THE MEETING IS TO BENEFIT THE WHOLE ORGANISATION AND NOT ANY SECTION OR INDIVIDUAL.

Anybody can talk, anybody can write, anybody can hold a meeting, but only he who can also obtain the desired responses ranks as a good communicator. A computer memory and its processing unit contain great quantities of facts; but the computer is simply a speedy automaton, subject to its program. The human memory and its processing unit contain facts, experiences, feelings, prejudices, social attitudes, business needs, expediency, cussedness, warmth, love, hatred and the breath of God.

Programming a computer to obtain a useful print-out the response demands, skill and knowledge. How much more demanding is the need for a manager to acquire the knowledge and the skills for better human relationships. At least you can make a start by speaking more effectively, writing reports that help and by making your meetings successful.

PART FIVE

Production Management

Chapter 23

Value Analysis and Value Engineering

John F A Gibson, Osram (GEC) Ltd and R Dick-Larkam, The British Oxygen Co Ltd

---

A business which does not respond to competition is doomed to failure. In a free enterprise society an unresponding business will, sooner or later, succumb to a more aggressive, dynamic or imaginative competitor. To secure its own economic future a business must produce profit with which to pay for the use of the money it has borrowed from its investors.

Products which carry excessive production costs imply that the business is not obtaining good value from its resources. Products which are too highly priced will lose their value to the customers. Let value be lost for either or both of these causes and the fragile jewel called profit is squeezed between the opposing jaws of price and cost. The company spends its funds on materials, labour and overheads and looks for its money's worth. Customers spend their funds on the company's products (or those of the competitors!) and the purchasing decisions are based on the value of the goods offered. The determining factor is, therefore, neither cost nor quality, considered in isolation, but *value* – the elusive product of the economic reaction between the two.

To keep just one pace ahead of the competition demands an understanding of value and how it can be achieved. The reaction between quality and cost demands a catalyst; this is where value analysis and value engineering come in.

Definition

Value analysis (VA) was developed, as from 1947, by Lawrence D Miles at The General Electric Company of America and was first practised in Britain some ten years later. Its use is now worldwide. In straightforward terms, value analysis is an organised and systematic effort to produce the required function at the lowest cost consistent with the specified performance and reliability.

Use of the value techniques as analysis implies application to a product which is already designed and in production. *Value engineering* is the use of the same techniques in the life history of a product before it reaches actual production.

The first impact of the value concept was in the study of products of the engineering industry, where it rapidly proved itself as a powerful tool for reducing costs. It has since been extended in many directions; to other industries in which designed products are made such as clothing, footwear, foodstuffs, consumer goods, pharmaceuticals; to the more difficult environment of the process industries; to reducing costs in paperwork and to management itself. The field is almost without limit, since the value technique can be applied with success to any instance in which costs are incurred to enable a function to be performed.

Function is the heart of the value technique.

What is value?

The concept of value is something which we all apply in our everyday lives when we part with money to acquire an item of furniture or a washing machine or the weekly supply of groceries. Value is not necessarily represented by the lowest-priced product in its class but rather by the one which, for the purposes for which we want it, gives a better combination of ideas, functions, reliability, etc., for its price than the competition.

Value is not an inherent property of a product. It can only be assessed by comparison with other similar products on offer at the same time and under the same conditions. It can be considered in four types:

1 *Exchange value:* that which enables an article to be offered in exchange for money or for another article.
2 *Cost value:* the sum of the materials, labour and other costs required to produce an article or to perform a service.
3 *Use value:* the sum of the properties and qualities possessed by an article which perform a use or provide a service.
4 *Esteem value:* the sum of the features of the article which, beyond its actual use, prompt the decision to buy.

In industry the principal concern must be with use value, the highest value being obtained where the cost is lowest within the limitation that the product must give a satisfactory performance. However, the VA exercise which tries to ignore esteem value or to eliminate it is very often riding for a fall since it will, more than likely, recommend a product which, although near perfection in respect of its performance, is just not saleable – it has lost those features which attract the buyer.

In certain products it is vital to consider the provision of esteem features as one of the essential functions. A water tank which will be hidden in the roof space of a house needs no features other than those concerned with its use but a cooker to be installed in the kitchen needs many features which have nothing to do with its use or the ladies will never accept it! In summary, good value is the lowest cost reliably to accomplish the essential functions.

Unnecessary cost

Value analysis is an unrelenting search for waste or, put in other words, it is an organised campaign for the elimination of unnecessary cost. Unnecessary cost is defined as any expenditure which can be removed without impairing the quality, reliability, saleability or (if applicable) the maintainability of the subject.

But what allows unnecessary cost to appear? The reasons fall into six main headings which must not be thought to be critical of the design function alone, but are often just as applicable to buying, production, planning and, indeed, to management. They are:

1 *Lack of information.*
Is everbody up-to-date in respect of materials, methods, techniques, etc? And, of prime importance, is accurate, detailed and understandable cost information available outside the enclave of accountancy?

2 *Lack of original ideas.*
What are people doing with their brains? Using them creatively to find and develop new ideas or reducing them to mere memory banks capable only of responding to the dictates of tradition?

3 *Honest wrong beliefs*
Long-established and honestly-held beliefs can be wrong, even on technical matters, and can lead to unnecessary costs.

4 *Temporary or changed circumstances and time pressures.*
A temporary expedient is introduced 'to-get-it-into-production'. 'It's costly but don't worry, old man, it will be put right tomorrow' – and that tomorrow never comes! Or – 'We shall have to do it this way because of the particular conditions of this order – it will be put right later' – or will it?

5 *Habits and attitudes.*
Human beings are creatures of habit and adopt attitudes. The older we get the stronger the habits become and, by consequence, the stronger the built-in resistance to change. To what extent are personal attitudes towards materials, methods, money and, perhaps, of the greatest importance, men, allowed to influence decisions?

6 *Over-designing.*
This should be considered in its broadest sense and not confined to the designer. Does the specification give the customer exactly what he wants? He may want something much more simple. If so, he is getting poor value.

Involvement

Value analysis must be carried out by people who are normally concerned with the various operations involved in the production of the product under scrutiny. It should be guided and coordinated by an engineer trained in the VA approach.

VA is essentially a multi-discipline exercise and one which demands open-mindedness and a willingness to collaborate without any scramble for individual recognition or credit. It thrives when a healthy climate for the giving and sharing of ideas has been properly established and which demands that everyone concerned subscribes to the philosophy that there is always a better way and that there is no future in 'status quo'; that there must be no depreciation of quality or reliability; the aim is to secure good value, not to 'cheapen' the product, that there must be collaboration and not competition between the departments whose work contributes to the ultimate product, and that the exercise is not interested in embarrassing, or taking advantage of, anyone.

Establishment of the healthy climate depends basically on the participants themselves and can be considerably influenced by the personality of the engineer chosen to lead the endeavour. At any stage, but in particular at the outset, it can be positively encouraged or effectively ruined by the attitude and the degree of interest and conviction exhibited by top management.

The team

Value techniques are designed to study cost at the points at which cost is initiated and to coordinate a number of different professional skills towards the objective of achieving equivalent performance and quality but for the lowest cost. This determines two things; firstly, that the exercise must be conducted by a multi-discipline team and, secondly, that the team must include representation from the cost-initiating functions. It will therefore include:

1 *Designers* responsible for what the product is, its specification in detail and the materials from which it is made.
2 *Production engineers* responsible for the control, handling and

processing of materials during manufacture and assembly.

3 *Buyers* responsible for the purchasing of raw materials, part finished components and finished devices.

Add to these representation from those whose business is the actual mathematics of cost, the costing department or the estimating department, and the fundamental team is complete with the exception of its leader.

Depending on the size of the company, the diversity of its products and the extent to which it is intended to utilise value techniques, the leader, the value engineer, the value analyst, the team chairman or whatever title he is given, can be either full-time or part-time. He should, at least, have an office of his own and ready access to secretarial facilities. He must be chosen with care but may come from any of the business disciplines – production, buying, design, accountacy, sales, etc. A sound knowledge of the particular industry involved must be accepted as a first essential but, beyond this, the main consideration will be to select a man who is blessed with tact, the ability to 'get on with people' and, above all, who has a personal enthusiasm for the job.

Two more points in connection with the team demand mention at this stage. Firstly, any value exercise must always keep in touch with the ultimate destination of the product, i.e. the customer, and this must be done through a continuous liaison with those who are in contact with the users. If the product under consideration is offered to the public through the marketing channels of wholesalers, retailers, agents, etc., then marketing and/or distribution representatives should be included as actual members of the team. Secondly, the team must be free to co-opt representatives from other disciplines and departments to assist in its discussions but it must be understood that such co-option is for the particular discussion which has been nominated. Failure to observe this point can result in an increase in the size of the team to unmanageable and, indeed, uneconomic proportions.

The job plan

Value analysis is a method of tackling problems which, by its disciplines, has been shown to achieve results. As a framework within which the disciplines will operate a planned sequence of steps is essential and, allowing for minor variations in details of procedure, the job plan provides the framework for value analysis activity. The job plan comprises the following steps:

1 Information (or definition)
2 Speculation
3 Investigation (and evaluation)
4 Recommendation
5 Implementation (or execution)

These steps (or phases) are considered below.

Information (or definition)

This is work which must be undertaken by the team leader and which must be completed before the team is asked to meet. All the relevant information must be collected and checked as necessary; doubtful, conflicting or ambiguous points must be queried to ensure that the collected information is factual. Much of the essential information in respect of an individual component part can be recorded on a single sheet of paper; it is a useful expedient to devise and reproduce a data sheet for this purpose before the first exercise starts.

If it is practicable, samples of the hardware should be collected; the product itself, the component parts as they are presented for assembly, the materials from which the parts are made, etc. The recent and forecast sales figures are then obtained from marketing together with the probable life of the product and the state of the market. This is not only essential for the exercise but may well determine whether the effort itself is likely to be worthwhile. The specifications and drawings are obtained from design, and details of component manufacture and product assembly are obtained from production.

The full breakdown of costs for each component and each stage of assembly come from costing. These costs are recorded on the data sheet in a tabulated cost summary which shows the material, labour and overhead content of each. The material cost is checked against the prices currently paid by the buying department, not because one doubts the veracity of information given by the costing department but merely to be factual and to avoid falling into the trap of using a standard costing system for a purpose for which it was not intended. The overhead content is split into fixed and variable parts in accordance with the established system, if it exists, or empirically by a percentage agreed with the chief cost accountant if it does not. This is not being unnecessarily pedantic, it is essential if one is to avoid the trap of claiming full overhead savings against a labour cost reduction when, in fact, only the variable portion of the overhead can be claimed.

From *buying*, details of the suppliers of materials, parts and devices bought from outside sources are obtained together with the ordering procedure by which they are purchased.

Definition of function

The information has now been collected and recorded and the team can be called to a planned series of meetings at which the real work of speculation or 'idea getting' and the consequent investigation can be carried out.

Without hesitation the team should come immediately to the heart of the matter – the definition of *function*. Function is the use or uses performed, including the esteem features provided or, in other words, a correct series of answers to the question 'What does it do?'

Any product, sub-assembly, device or component part will have at least one basic function (unless it proves to be unnecessary!) and may have a number of secondary functions. Each function must be defined, the definition agreed by the team and the distinction made between basic and secondary functions.

Definition of each function should be in two words – a verb and a noun. This is an essential rule and is in no sense a gimmick. It places a constraint on the team, which leads to precise thinking. It promotes avoidance of ambiguity and the establishment of a clear understanding of what the functions of the subject really are.

One may take an example as simple as an ordinary lead pencil. It has at least six functions of which the first named is the basic and the other five are secondary:

1 Make marks

2 Protect lead
3 Protect hands
4 Provide grip
5 Provide information
6 Provide esteem

The basic function, in this case 'make marks', is the one which makes the product or component work. The other functions are secondary but this does not mean that they are unnecessary. They can be supplementary in that they enable the basic function to be performed more easily, such as 'protect lead' and 'provide grip' or ancillary in that they provide some additional benefit, such as 'provide information'.

The job of identifying and sorting out the functions is a first demand on the work of the team. It is fundamental, very often highly instructive, and it pays to be really painstaking to ensure that it is properly done.

Function/cost analysis

Consideration of function will be the dominant feature of the whole exercise, but in the initial stages it must play an important part in answering such questions as: 'Where do we start?' and: 'What will be the most rewarding area in which to make the major effort?' Cost analysis, by dividing the product into definable sub-assemblies, may bring to light some high-cost areas, but it can be very misleading because it will not necessarily highlight areas of poor value. These areas must be discovered by cost analysis into functional areas or, in other words, function/cost analysis.

This analysis is a very powerful tool but relatively easy to use. A simple matrix is set out, in which the left-hand column is used to state the name of each component part grouped in the appropriate sub-assemblies. The right-hand column records the cost of each part and the remaining columns are each headed by one of the functions which the team has agreed. The cost of each part is allocated proportionately to the functions to which it contributes. It is not possible to be accurate but one should be 'informed' and take the agreed estimate of the team. Each functional column is added up and converted to a percentage of the total and the result is used to identify areas of high cost and/or poor value. A fundamental chart is illustrated in Figure 23:1. After each group of parts comprising a sub-assembly, a line should be included for the cost of assembling them. If a sub-assembly has to be processed, a line for that is included and at the end another line is used for the cost of final product assembly.

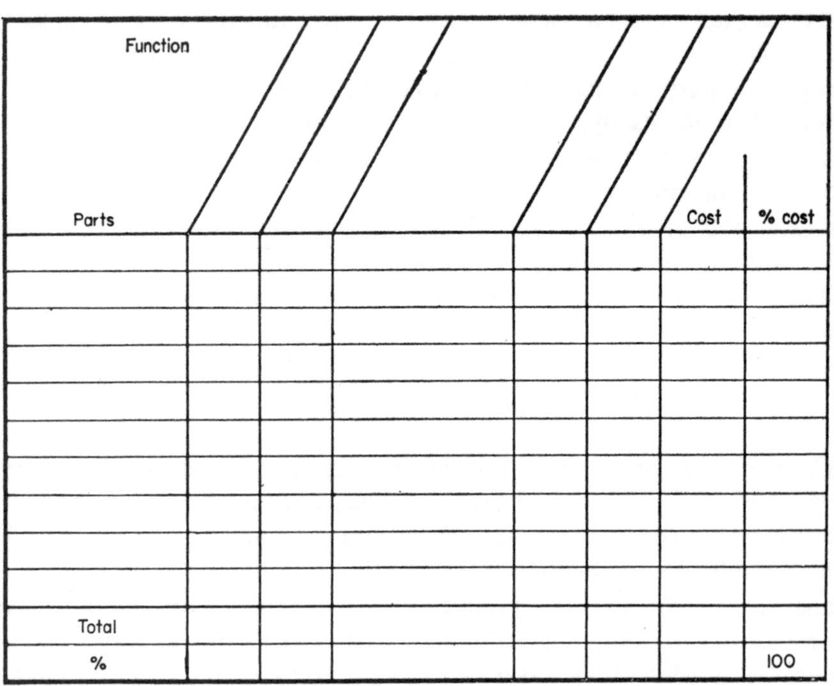

FIGURE 23:1 FUNCTION/COST ANALYSIS CHART

A basic, but simple, chart to establish the relationship between function and cost

Function/cost analysis applied to a product which is an assembly of component parts is a most useful tool in discovering the areas of poor value and in directing the efforts of the team. It plays an even more important part in the application of value techniques to process plants such as those encountered in the chemical industry where the product is a basic substance or mixture of substances. In these cases the product is probably not open to design change and savings must be made either in the method of production or in the operation of the plant.

Methods of production are usually decided when the plant is built and subsequent changes may entail considerable capital expenditure. A value programme will provide a cost and technical analysis which will assist in the design of the next generation of plant but which is unlikely to affect the present plant due to restrictions in respect of capital expense. Value techniques can, however, produce rewarding savings when applied to the operations of the plant and the approach to this is basically through function/cost analysis.

In these cases the subject of the exercise will be an operation taken as a whole. The full range of expenditure is included; the commercial aspects of the supply of raw materials; the transport and handling of materials; the whole operation of processing; the handling, packaging and marketing of the final product. Every function of the composite operation must now be identified and all the costs, of whatever nature, must be recorded and allocated against the functions to build up a matrix of the same type as that already described. This function/cost analysis, painstakingly prepared, will highlight functions which are costing too much as well as functions which are possibly unnecessary and can be eliminated.

Speculation

Having defined and analysed the functions in relation to cost, the team is now in a position to go ahead with the work of speculation – the getting of ideas. The feature, which must run through the whole of this effort, is the continual application of the functional approach which is simply defined as: 'Consider always the cost to perform the function and not the cost to make the present component or to conduct the present operation'. This is an essential feature which distinguishes VA from all other comparable techniques.

The objective now is to find ideas, to discover alternative ways of performing the defined functions. To achieve this one certainly uses all the available *knowledge* but one adds the encouragement of *imagination,* gives full rein to *initiative*. Ideas from *any source* should be accepted; above all, *creativity* should be fostered and developed.

Analytical thinking takes all the available facts and tries to evolve one answer. Creativity, on the other hand, takes the problem as such and tries to produce many solutions. Creativity is like a spark used to ignite a chain reaction. Whatever a person's profession or training may be he becomes creative when he discovers a likeness between things which he did not think to be alike before. The creative mind is one which is always looking for unexpected likenesses. It may well produce some 'off beat' notions but, not to worry, the wild idea is not a sign of mental disturbance; it may contain the clue which leads to the 'value' answer.

Brainstorming, used within the concept of a value exercise, can have most rewarding results. Briefly described, a brainstorming session is a meeting of limited duration (not more than three-quarters of an hour) devoted to idea-getting on one subject, or at most two, and to which the team will invite anyone who may have something to contribute. Such a session can involve twenty or more people drawn from all levels within the organisation. The cost per minute is high – hence the time limitation – and it is essential to ensure that the basic rule is obeyed. The rule is: ideas only – no criticism, no judgment, no argument; leave these to the team at their next meeting.

In value analysis the brainstorm is used as a major weapon to solve a particularly knotty problem. In value engineering a planned series of brainstorming sessions can be organised to cover idea-getting on the whole project, taking each functional area in succession.

Supplier participation

All the material contained in a product is bought in one form or another. It may be in the form of raw material or part finished components or complete devices but, whatever its form, it is handled through the purchasing organisation. The concept of VA started in a purchasing department and the participation of purchasing in all exercises is an essential feature.

But what about the suppliers? In some situations the pursuit of the technique of supplier participation can prove to be most useful. Through the buyer, who will be responsible for ensuring that the ethics of his profession are maintained, technical representatives of reputable suppliers may be invited to come to a team meeting and to add their expertise to the discussion. Alternatively they may be visited. At such a meeting the visitors should be made fully aware of the situation. Do not limit the field to 'Can you make that?' or even 'How would you make that?' but rather describe the function which has to be performed, the components with which this one will be associated and the constraints which will apply. Then ask 'What ideas have you to solve that problem at a cost lower than that which we now envisage?'

Check-list

In conducting value analysis exercises it is often helpful to prepare a check-list of questions under specified headings to which reference can be made to ensure that no aspect of investigation has been overlooked. This is useful but is not, and must never be regarded as, the be-all-and-end-all of the technique. The list may be prepared under these headings:

1 Function: the fundamental heading, which will include the basic questions such as: Are all the functions essential? Can any function be eliminated? What else will perform the same function? Can all or any of the functions be incorporated in another component?
2 Material specification: What material is used and why? What alternative would also do the job?
3 Material content: What has determined the amount of material used?
4 Material waste: How much of the original material has been wasted? What has caused the waste?
5 Standardisation: Is the component standard? Is it made from standard material? If not, why not?
6 Process of manufacture: What is involved in the conversion of the raw material into the finished product?
7 Direct labour costs: a question never to be ignored, but should a case for the use of another technique, such as work study, automation, ergonomics, etc., be prepared?
8 Limits: What tolerances have been specified and why?
9 Surface finish: How does this contribute to function?
10 Direct material costs: the broad hunting ground of the team and the technical buyer. Should the company make or buy? Should there be supplier participation?

Investigation, recommendation and action

Speculation has produced ideas, now they must be investigated. The process of investigation will be conducted partly at the team meetings and partly between meetings. It necessarily takes time and often involves searches in considerable depth. Each member of the fundamental team will have his own contribution to make since any idea will, to a greater or lesser extent, be the concern of design, production, purchasing and costing. It is at this stage that careful and accurate evaluation is demanded so that proper comparison of the cost of one idea against another can be assured.

The conclusion of speculation and investigation will be a proposal. This, when compared with the existing situation, will offer value improvement. The team and its leader have no executive authority of their own and the proposal must go forward to management as a recommendation.

Once management has given its approval the proposal should be put into effect as quickly as possible through the normal routines of the factory. Implementation should, however, remain the concern of the value team and its leader until it has been fully carried out and actual savings have been made, measured and recorded.

Organising a value programme

This chapter would not be complete without some comment on the setting up and organisation of a value programme.

The first essential is that management must not only be convinced that the techniques will produce savings but must demonstrate its confidence to the staff by giving full support to the effort and by being seen to do so. The subsequent steps to be taken are:

1 Appoint a value engineer, or more than one, and ensure that they are properly trained.
2 Establish a training schedule and explain the programme to middle management and staff.
3 Agree the methods of reporting and implementation.
4 Select the first projects and decide priorities.
5 Appoint teams appropriate to the selected projects.

The man chosen to be the leader, the value engineer, should, if possible, be a good practical engineer but his most important attribute must be his ability to work with other people. However good he may be as an engineer and no matter how conversant he may be with the technique, he is unlikely to succeed unless his personality and attitude gain him the respect of those he will involve in the team activity and those from whom he will ask assistance. He must have an open mind, a willingness to try out new ideas and an attitude which will enable him to confront obstacles and to accept frustration without the lost of either temper or enthusiasm.

Training

Value analysis/engineering is a philosophy designed to make everyone, and particularly those who initiate costs, challenge those costs to see if they are giving good value to the company. To accomplish this it is necessary to ensure that proper training is provided. The chosen value engineer should at least attend a five-day course organised by one of the established VA/VE consultants in which actual projects are tackled. Those who are to become team members should attend a two- or three-day programme which will be, in part, practical and certainly above appreciation level. Management should have a good appreciation of the techniques which can be achieved in a one-day course.

Once VA and the value engineer have become established features of the company activity, there is very much to be gained by the continual spread of the value discipline of thought throughout the organisation. The value engineer can do this himself by arranging his own programme of presentations and courses.

Appointing the team

The basic structure of the team has already been stated and it is the experience of practising value engineers that teams of between three and six, in addition to themselves as leaders, produce the best results. Whatever the circumstances the teams should not be allowed to become too large.

A proper balance of skills must be achieved by the inclusion of members from design, production and buying. If development is a separate function in the company, then a development engineer may well be added; if the product is essentially one which demands much from the drawing office, then the addition of a senior draftsman can be advantageous.

The inclusion of a representative from marketing or sales will depend on the manner in which sales of the product are promoted, but in any event a liaison with this function must be established and maintained.

Team meetings should be arranged in accordance with a regular programme – one meeting of two to three hours on the same day and at the same time each week is desirable – and members must regard attendance as a first priority. Substitutes are of little use since they are usually unaware of previous discussions.

Selecting a project

It is not easy to lay down a set of rules by which projects should be selected but a few general guidelines are useful. All the products or product ranges should be listed in descending order of annual sales value. Those at the bottom of the list can probably be ignored, since the potential savings will not be great enough to justify the cost of an exercise.

The expected life of each product and how the marketing position is likely to develop is discovered from marketing. For the exercise to be economic the life of the product must be considerably greater than the sum of the time which will be taken by the exercise and the subsequent time needed for the implementation of changes. These, and other considerations peculiar to the organisation concerned, will produce a priority list, and it is not unlikely that the best selling product will emerge at the top of that list.

When value analysis is being introduced into a company, make certain that the first exercise is conducted on a product which is selling well and making a reasonable profit. The trap of starting with a known loss-maker, however attractive it may seem, should be avoided. This may sound like a paradox, but it is proven wisdom.

Results

What can be expected from the conduct of a value exercise? The tangible results for which the program was set up are to be measured in money saved. A value analysis exercise, properly run, seldom achieves less than five per cent reduction in the cost of the product under study and frequently achieves between ten and twenty per cent. Value engineering programmes, provided that a true comparison of the positions before and after is practicable, have been shown to achieve savings in excess of thirty per cent.

Whilst the tangibles in the form of money saved are doubtless the stated objective and can be most impressive, it is also true that the intangibles can be just as valuable.

Participation in the work of a multi-discipline team results in an increase of cooperation between people and deepens appreciation of the other fellow's job. The discussions will have spread cost consciousness and will have given a desirable emphasis to the importance of the buying function. But, most important of all, it will have provided, for those who participate and those who come into contact with the exercise, an encouragement and an outlet for fresh thinking. Energetically pursued, value programmes generate an attitude of mind, develop a discipline of thought and become a rewarding, perhaps essential catalyst.

Chapter 24

Planning New Production Facilities

Alan J Clarke, Production Engineering and Work Study Manager, Microswitch and Keyboard Group, Honeywell Limited

---

Production is not a commodity which gushes out of a tap and can be turned on and off at will, but a many faceted process which only achieves the desired objectives if suitable groundwork and planning have been first carried out. The process of preparation for making a product may be likened to the nurturing of a tree from seedling to the time when the tree bears fruit. In the beginning suitable ground has to be found and prepared, a healthy seedling planted and fertilised and its growth encouraged, if a tree bearing saleable fruit is to flourish.

The mistaken impression that there is such a thing as 'instant production' is dangerous but common. It is so often linked with the vague knowledge that a 'works' exists for making things, so that a present capability for producing fifty ton presses should equally be capable of turning out alarm clocks. This lack of appreciation of the difference in production requirements results in insufficient time and money being allocated for the production stage of a new product's emergence. It should therefore be remembered that new product introduction is change. Effective change necessitates planning, planning takes time, and implementing the plan takes even longer.

Marketing have decided upon the product, the design has been engineered and the accountants, in conjunction with marketing, have determined a selling price which should yield an acceptable profit. The new product has now to be manufactured but there is no gushing tap. This chapter is devoted to showing how the production manager, using simple techniques, can plan and install the new facility.

Production objectives

The three main objectives of production which should always be paramount are known as the 'three rights':

1 To produce at the *right cost*
2 To produce at the *right quality*
3 To produce at the *right time*

Obviously, the cost objective has to be met if profit is to be made. The quality standard must be attained if sales are to be perpetuated and after-sales problems minimised. Finally, if delivery dates are not achieved, there is always a competitor lurking around the corner ready to take advantage and step in.

To plan and install the new production facility is not the main objective; it is only the means of achieving the objectives stated. If the three rights are achieved, the new production facility is adequate for the task that has been set.

The form of the objectives having been established they may now be quantified and a plan evolved which will enable them to be accomplished. The preparation of such a plan, whether it be a network or simple bar chart, is dealt with elsewhere (see Chapter 25). However, the essential ingredient for the plan, whether it be for the total project or the section devoted to production, is information.

Information

Participation of the production management in the early stages of new product development is always recommended as this ensures awareness of those factors with long lead-times and resultant action which ensures that they are put under way at the earliest opportunity. It would be farcical (but not uncommon) to discover that an essential item of manufacturing equipment cannot be supplied in less than eighteen months although completion of the first production batch has been scheduled for only six months hence.

There is a simple rule, that seldom fails, which states that the higher the cost, the longer the delivery. This rule particularly applies to bought-out parts and any item of a special nature to be incorporated in the final assembly.

The correct questions must be asked and pertinent information must be forthcoming if considered actions and reactions are to take place. The crucial question of whether or not it can be made for the budgeted cost should be answered by production at this stage, not when it has been made and sold for a resounding loss. Only by the initial involvement of the production team can such problems be avoided.

The basic information that must be supplied by marketing and engineering is covered by the questionnaire shown in Figure 24:1. This is typical for a product such as an industrial instrument. For the purpose of clarity some of the detail has been limited in the example, especially in the section relating to standard hours.

This questionnaire should be raised as early as possible, although it is unlikely that all information requested will be immediately forthcoming, as product introduction is not a series operation. Unless the product already exists in its final form, engineers will be working in parallel on its final development. In the event of information not being available, a date by which it will be released must be obtained, considered and only accepted if suitable for the plan of introduction and the time objective.

A detailed sales forecast is essential. The simple form that this can take is shown in Figure 24:2. By breaking down the forecast into monthly increments, seasonal fluctuations and the growth and decay of sales demand is indicated. Stating optimistic demands above the diagonal line in each box and pessimistic figures below widens the picture. It enables an impression to be gained of the degree of flexibility that must be incorporated in the manufacturing facility.

The Gopertz curve (Figure 24:3) illustrates the life-cycle of a product which, in the consumer market, spans approximately three

NEW PRODUCT INFORMATION REQUEST

MODEL NUMBER: ______________________ DATE: ____________

DESCRIPTION: ______________________________________

				Date promised	Date received
ENGINEERING					
Technical/Engineering specification					
Drawings					
Parts lists					
Prototypes					
Test and calibration instructions					
COSTING					
Estimated cost	Raw material	£			
	Bought-out parts	£			
	Labour	£			
	Total	£			
STANDARD-HOURS (Estimated/Synthetics)					
Manufacture	Turning		hrs		
	Milling		hrs		
	Grinding		hrs		
	Drilling		hrs		
	Pressing		hrs		
	Fabricating		hrs		
Assembly	Sub-assembly		hrs		
	Final assembly		hrs		
	Calibration and test		hrs		
ALLOCATED CAPITAL					
	Plant and machinery	£			
	Tooling	£			
	Buildings	£			
	Miscellaneous	£			
SALES					
Sales forecast (Three-year plan)					
Sales models required by:					
Assemblies to stock by:					

FIGURE 24:1 INFORMATION PHASE

To make the right decisions, it is essential that sufficient pertinent information is received in time

SALES FORECAST (UNITS)

PRODUCT: DATE ISSUED:

	JAN	FEB	MAR	APR	MAY	JUN	JUL	AUG	SEP	OCT	NOV	DEC	TOTAL
1971	3 / 3	8 / 6	16 / 14	30 / 25	45 / 40	80 / 50	95 / 80	125 / 100	160 / 130	200 / 170	230 / 210	270 / 230	1262 / 1058
1972	290 / 260	305 / 285	330 / 300	345 / 320	360 / 330	370 / 310	400 / 330	400 / 330	410 / 345	415 / 350	420 / 355	425 / 355	4470 / 3880
1973	430 / 360	435 / 360	440 / 355	440 / 360	440 / 360	445 / 360	445 / 360	440 / 360	440 / 365	435 / 360	440 / 355	430 / 355	5260 / 4310
1974	435 / 355	430 / 360	430 / 355	430 / 350	425 / 350	425 / 345	415 / 345	410 / 345	405 / 340	405 / 335	400 / 330	395 / 325	5005 / 4135
1975	390 / 320	380 / 315	370 / 310	360 / 305	350 / 300	345 / 290	335 / 280	320 / 270	320 / 260	310 / 250	290 / 290	270 / 230	4030 / 3370

FIGURE 24:2 SALES FORECAST
This forecast may be plotted in the form of a curve illustrated in Figure 24 : 3

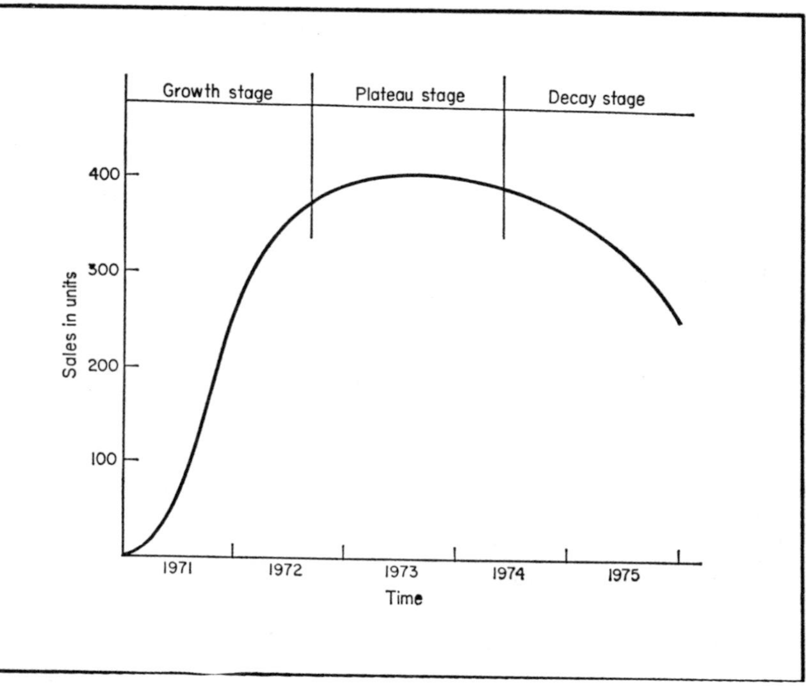

FIGURE 24: 3 GOPERTZ CURVE

The three stages of a product's life have to be accommodated whilst ensuring effective use of capital plant

to five years. After this period it will usually be superseded or subjected to a major change. This curve can be plotted from the sales forecast and should enable the production manager to establish the following stages that the new facility must traverse:

1 The growth stage during which operators are learning, modifications are taking place and the effectiveness of the facility is consolidated.
2 The plateau stage is the period when sales demand is fairly constant, optimum efficiency is obtained and cost reduction and other techniques are most important to minimise costs.
3 The decay stage when sales demand rapidly declines and the assets of the facility must be considered for redeployment to new products.

Resources available and resources required

Information having now been received, stock has to be taken of the resources available and the resources required to satisfy the parameters laid down by the marketing, engineering and costing departments. The first task is to translate standard-hours into terms of machines and men.

The following simple calculation can be carried out for each manufacturing activity, the worked example in this case relating to turning. In this example no attempt is being made to differentiate between the varying types of turning, embracing automatics, capstans, centre-lathes, etc., that would in practice have to be considered.

Standard-hours of turning needed per unit of production	0.29
Number of units to be produced per week	500
Effective capacity of each turning lathe per week (Based on 1 shift working and a 40 hr week)	30 hours
Number of turning lathes required	
$=\dfrac{0.29\times 500}{30}$	=5 machines

The effective capacity is the number of standard hours which may be expected from a machine taking into account the departmental efficiency and absence rate. If there is to be double shift-working or overtime the effective capacity should increase proportionally with the attendance hours.

Similar calculations would need to be carried out in respect of operators for manning the machines and staffing the assembly and calibration areas. Lists of machines and equipment backed by a manpower forecast may now be prepared. The machine lists specifically detail the machines required, whilst the manpower forecast must differentiate between male and female, skilled, semi-skilled and unskilled types of labour needed.

There is a continuous product-cycle in which new products are being introduced and existing products are declining and being phased out. It is unlikely that the new facility will have to be completely equipped with new machinery and staffed by a fresh intake of employees. Many of the machines and a large number of the men can usually be transferred from existing product-lines.

The check-lists of resources required and resources available having been compiled, the balance of resources still needed may now be considered in conjunction with the money or capital available. Production engineering should have determined by this time the tooling to back up the machines and the degree of sophistication and extent of tooling that the quantities involved demand. Economic evaluations must be carried out to justify all expenditure, bearing in mind that a steam-hammer is not necessary to crack a nut.

Whether a component part is to be machined from a block of aluminium or alternatively pressure die-cast in a form requiring no machining is decided by the quantity ordered. This is clearly shown in the table, Figure 24:4. By amortising the tool cost with the production cost, break-even points can be calculated.

Production method	Quantity off	M/C time	Tool cost
Machine from solid	Very low	Very high	Nil
Sand casting	Low	High	Low
Gravity die casting	High	Low	Medium
Pressure die casting	Very high	Nil	High

FIGURE 24:4 PRODUCTION METHOD RELATED TO QUANTITY

As quantities increase, the more sophisticated method of production is used

Today companies are leaning more and more to specialisation and it is not normal to attempt to manufacture everything 'in-house'; a typical example is the motor-car industry. The economic justification of each item of equipment, be it machine-tool or simple drilling-jig, has to be scrutinised. Whenever an adverse return on investment is indicated, the services of outside specialist companies must be sought instead. To make or to buy is a question which has to be continually posed, if capital is to be used wisely.

Sales demand rises to a peak, and then slowly falls away. Provision of men and machines to satisfy maximum demand is not always economically acceptable. Procurement of capital assets which have only a limited period of usefulness is not to be recommended and overtime or sub-contracting should be proposed as the solution to such a problem.

Layout

From the questionnaire and simple calculations carried out, an overall knowledge of the resources required will have been gained. The layout, whether it be for a new factory or a change to an existing machine shop or assembly area has now to be planned.

The specific aim is to obtain optimum relationship between production volume, space occupied and money required, by deploying the resources of men, machines, material and money to best advantage. A good layout will eliminate or reduce bottlenecks, sustain operator effort with comfort and safety, facilitate supervision, whilst maximising the utilisation of machines and equipment for less capital investment.

Types of layout

There are three basic types of layout, although in many factories they may all exist in pure or combined forms as a result of product variety.

Fixed material location is a layout where the material, major component or final product is fixed. Such a system is used for shipbuilding and other high-cost, custom-built equipment for the following reasons:

1 Handling of major assembly is reduced
2 Highly-skilled labour using hand tools and simple machines remains at one work station
3 Product design and manufacturing changes are more easily incorporated

A variety of products with intermittent demand may be readily accommodated
It is flexible and requires the minimum back-up by production service departments

rocess or functional layouts group the same operations and proces-
es together. Machine shops and textile manufacturers use this type of
yout for the following reasons:

Improved machine utilisation
Wide product variety and manufacture changes are readily accepted
It adapts easily to fluctuating demands by production control
Continuity of production is more readily maintained in the event of machine breakdown
Machines do not need to be moved frequently

roduct layout or line production devotes an area to the production
f one product and arranges machines or assembly work stations in a
ries of sequential operations. Motor-car and other mass-produced
nsumer products use this type of layout for the following reasons:

Reduced material handling
Reduced work in progress
More effective use of labour
High quantity and standardised design enable balanced operations with continuity of material flow to be maintained

roup technology layouts. More recently a further method of laying
it production facilities has developed, known as group technology.
his tends to be a result of combining the process- and product-
ientated layouts, enabling a jobbing or small batch-production shop
enjoy the benefits normally attributed to flow production. In group
chnology families of components are manufactured in machine
oups, families being collections of parts related to each other in a
anner based on form, size, material and degree of precision. These
milies may be determined by either using a classification system or
production flow analysis, a technique which groups together parts
ving similar manufacturing operations.

Influencing factors

There are five main factors which will influence the layout to be selected. These are illustrated as follows:

1 What is to be produced, steamship or a tape recorder?
2 How much is to be produced, five a year or five thousand a day?
3 How is it to be produced, by skilled men with standard machines or by specially-designed process plant?
4 What supporting services are required, simple or sophisticated?
5 When is it to be produced, next year only or next year and for the next five years?

Quantity relative to variety is a factor which should always be explored. The relationship between product quantity and the number of product varieties is disproportionate in almost all industries, thirty per cent of the output being spread over seventy per cent of the products. The significance of this product variety/quantity relationship is important. It provides the layout engineer with a basis for determining the production system and layout arrangement, whether it be mass-production using a product layout or batch-production utilising a process layout.

The chart (Figure 24:5) illustrates the product variety/quantity relationship. One end of the curve shows large quantities with relatively few varieties, (essentially mass-production conditions of manufacture) whilst at the other end of the curve, there are many different products with small quantities demanding batch-production or jobbing-type layouts.

It now becomes apparent that the introduction of a new product does not always necessitate a brand new facility, and simple changes to existing layouts are often all that is needed.

Layout planning

The layout plan not only covers the preparation of drawings, it also embraces installation and commissioning. There are four clear steps to be taken.

Determine the location. This is not necessarily a new site problem it is usually a problem of re-layout, as the new layout will be posi-

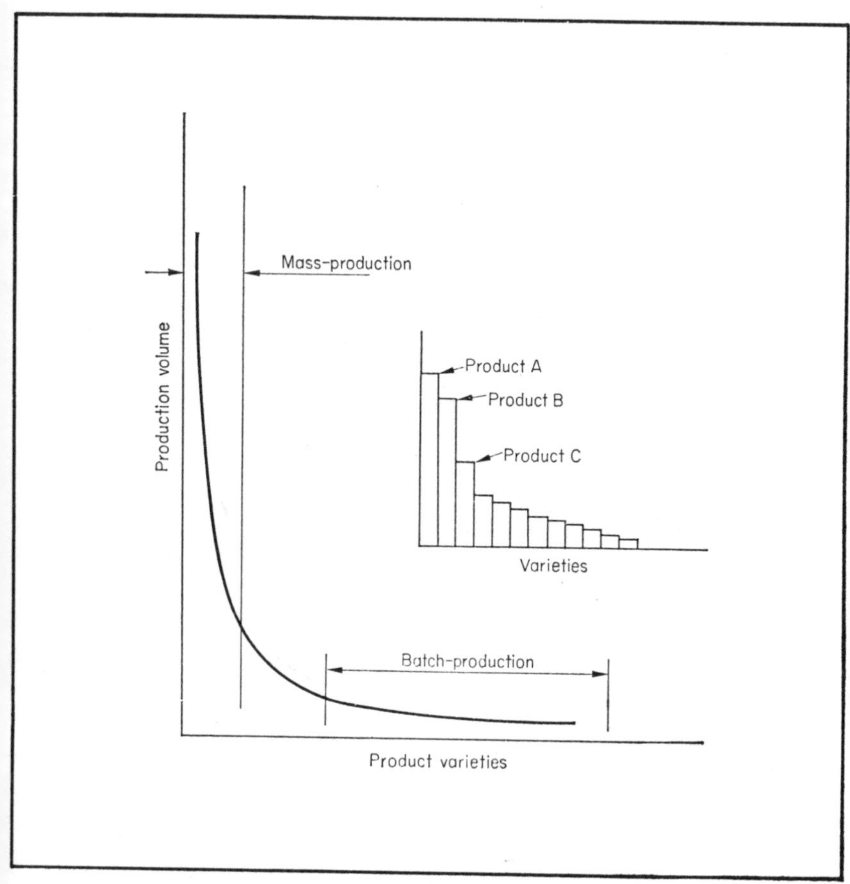

FIGURE 24:5 PRODUCT QUANTITY/VARIETY RELATIONSHIP

The gradient of the curve gives a pointer to the type of layout required

tioned where existing products are being made. The progressive phasing out of one product with the phasing in of the new, is often encountered.

Block layout of facility. This determines the general arrangement of the area. Material and product-flow patterns are laid out so that the general size and relationships of each area are roughly established. A typical block layout is shown in Figure 24:6. The use of flow-process-charts, flow- and string-diagrams greatly assist the preparation of this layout. However, material flow should not be the only

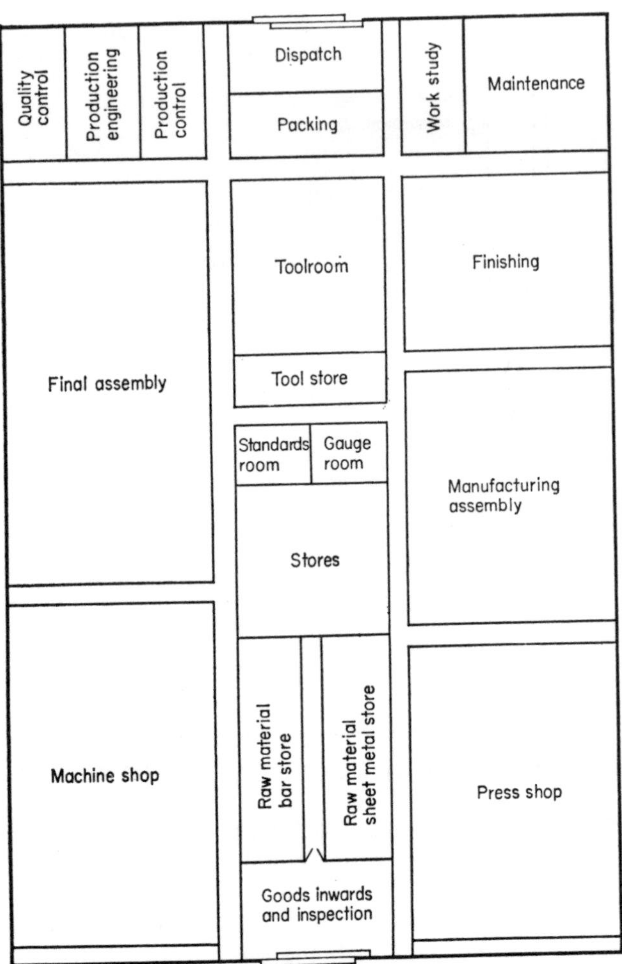

FIGURE 24:6 BLOCK LAYOUT

A typical plan of a facility for small batch-production showing size and relationship of areas

basis for this drawing, as the preparation of activity relationship charts ensures that supporting services integrate in an organised manner.

Detailed floor plan. This enables the expansion of the block layout to show location of each piece of machinery, each work-bench and other items of equipment. The services (air, gas, water and electricity) to machines and benches would also be shown, either on this layout or on an associated plan also derived from the initial drawing.

Installation. The sequence of moves, the arrangement for transfer, is the last stage of the plan, finally culminating in the manufacture of pre-production models.

Layout drawing and models

The preparation of semi-pictorial drawings depicting the layout or a scale model can often sell a system to those who have difficulty in visualising the proposed arrangement. Scale models are expensive and seldom warranted, although there are a number of companies which specialise in this kind of presentation. However, a semi-pictorial drawing may easily be compiled, utilising translucent squared tracing paper and scaled-down standard, transparent symbols of machines and benches, etc. The symbol transparencies are backed with adhesive and, when stuck to the squared paper, can be reproduced. Figure 24:7 illustrates a small jobbing machine-shop. Designing a layout with this technique enables the planner to move the standard symbols about on the squared paper until the best arrangement is obtained.

Drawing office materials for preparing such plans are readily obtainable, the squared paper being available in a square size of quarter of an inch, which enables the popular planning scale of a quarter of an inch to the foot to be used. Initially standard symbols for common machines and items of equipment may be prepared for reproduction on the adhesive transparencies, and, as the need arises, special and new additions to the machinery and equipment range prepared. 'Ozakling', manufactured by the Ozalid company, is one suitable material.

The built-up basic drawing can be used for preparing sub-master tracings and prints for the purpose of showing services, flow-patterns ai ` other more detailed information.

Installation and commissioning

The complexity of this stage of the plan depends upon the type of layout to be installed and the area or building to house the equipment. The re-layout of a jobbing machine-shop, with the introduction of a number of new machines, is a change which can be accomplished over-night, but the installation of a flow-line for manufacturing parts and assembling them into next year's model motor-car is an operation spread over several months. In the first instance, installation and commissioning are as one, whereas the second type of layout has a definite and important commissioning stage.

Installation and pre-production

The movement of existing machines and equipment to their positions in the new layout should be programmed so that the down-time of machines and men is minimised. The supply sources of new machines will usually be outside vendors (although there may be exceptions), and the labour to man the machines may come from existing facilities, new intake or a combination of both.

The existing men and machines provide the greater problem because only a philanthropic company, or one domiciled in a labour-scarce area, will have these resources idle and waiting to be used. A sure indication of the slickness of the operation will be the waiting-time booked by the transient operators during this period.

Machines generally require the primary service of an electrical supply plus compressed air for the ancillary equipment used with the machine. These services should be installed up to the point of connection to the machine prior to the machine being installed, hence ensuring that the time lost by the machine operator is limited to that taken to disconnect his machine from the services, plus the time to move it to its new location and reconnect to the services already installed. Although moves of this sort are more convenient at weekends, tight schedules often preclude this.

Plastic tape or paint can be used to mark the outline of each machine on the floor. Numbering each outline with a number also painted on the machine and specified on the detailed plan helps considerably in speedily locating and positioning machines. Assembly-

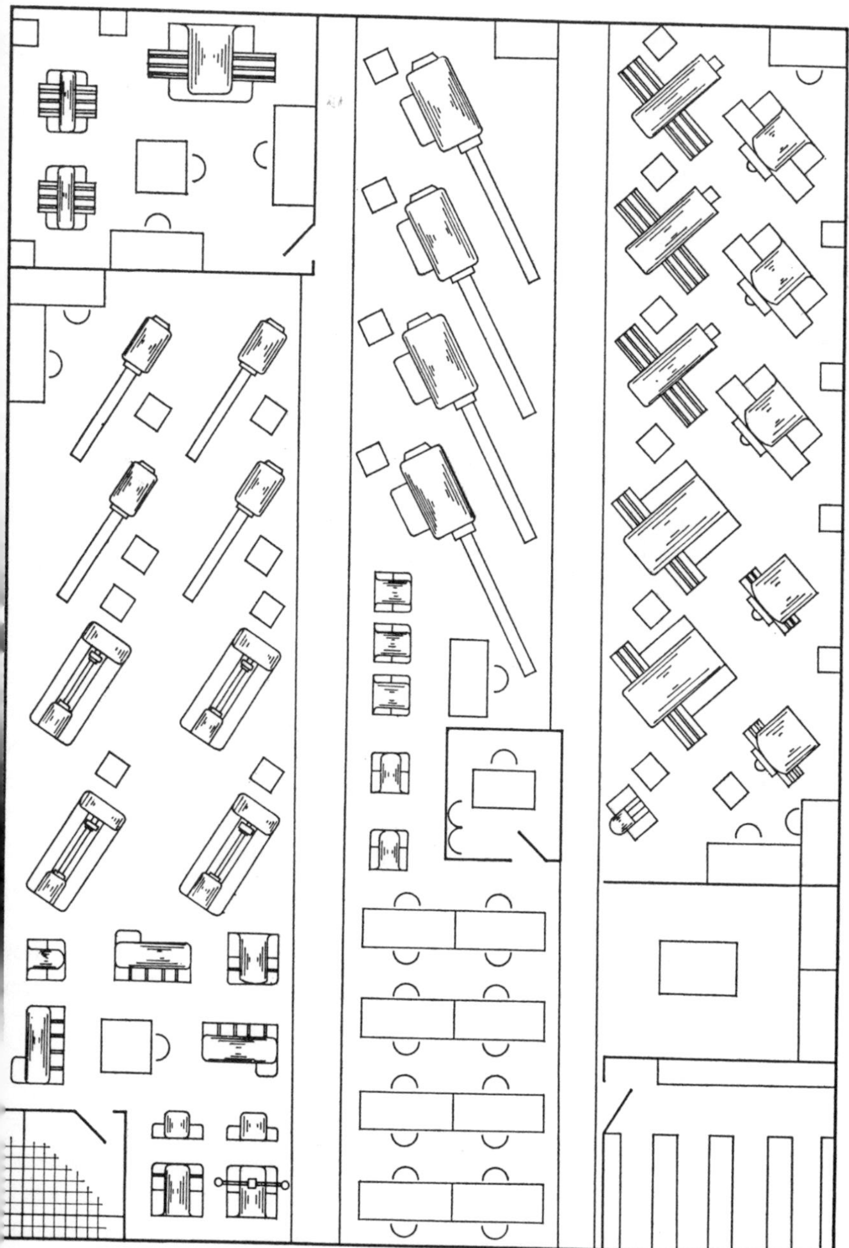

FIGURE 24:7 DETAILED LAYOUT OF JOBBING MACHINE SHOP, USING STANDARD SYMBOLS

The method of preparing this type of drawing can be used for most factory areas, including offices where units of machinery and equipment need to be arranged in the most advantageous positions. It is convenient to make the layout on squared paper

bench runs and other equipment should be moved in a similar way, and stores and supporting services should be moved so that there is no break in service detrimental to the production activity.

With the new arrangement taking shape, a start should now commence on the manufacture and assembly of the pre-production or proving batch which enables a check to be carried out on the correctness and suitability of the following:

1 Component part drawings
2 Parts lists
3 Assembly drawings
4 Process layouts
5 Jigs, tools and fixtures
6 Raw material specifications
7 Test and calibration instructions
8 Machine and test equipment
9 Special finishes and processes

Some companies make a practice of sending out the pre-production batch of piece-parts to outside firms. This approach, they consider, is a surer way of proving drawings and jigs and tools, than can be obtained by using their own machine-shop staff. Company personnel may be so familiar with the manufacture of their company's products that they make corrections to compensate for inadequate information and tooling. The result can be undocumented modifications arbitrarily introduced on the shop floor.

Once mistakes and other problems have been overcome the new product is ready to run, the first pre-production models produced being available for sales and demonstration purposes.

Commissioning a flow-line

When a flow-line goes into production in the consumer industry every-thing has to go according to plan as there is no room for mistakes in what must be a balanced, stringently controlled tool of production. Whereas in small batch-production and jobbing-shop concerns a fault or piece-part error has more nuisance value than serious repercussions a flow-line coming to a standstill in a motor-car plant or similar in dustry for the same reason can cost the company thousands of pounds per hour. The commissioning of a flow-line preparatory to its launching into full production is therefore an exacting and important phase.

The backbone of the commissioning team consists of the try-out engineers. They painstakingly build up the product, systematically prove tools, jigs and fixtures, modify their structure if necessary and feed back and arrange essential design changes for production compatibility. Basically, the try-out engineer is a practical man with an eye for detail and he is completely product-orientated. His ultimate goal is to produce sub-assemblies and main assemblies of the first pre-production models from piece-parts. The line operators and supervisors work closely with the try-out engineers and learn at first hand details of methods and techniques being employed.

Once the try-out engineers have proved that the flow-line is capable of producing the new model to the design specification it is up to the personnel, work study and production control departments to ensure that the line will flow.

During the try-out period everybody concerned with the layout would be following and participating in the proving process, implementing where necessary the changes advocated. Such changes can have an appreciable effect on the manning and balance of the line and if corrections to these factors are not made, bottlenecks and low output will result.

There are three main factors which require consideration. These are:

Manpower. The personnel department, using an analysis of skills, has to provide a pool of labour with the correct skills for introduction into the line as product demand increases.

Balance. Work study has to allow the right balance of work between work stations, avoiding bottlenecks caused by under-manning or material surplus build-up.

Materials. Production control must maintain a balanced supply of parts to the line, from 'in-house' and 'bought-in' sources, in step with product demand.

Evaluating the results

The audit of a new facility cannot take place until some time after it has been in operation and teething troubles have been overcome. Irrespective of how impressive the layout might appear, the proof of the pudding will be in whether the three main objectives (cost, quality and time) are being achieved.

However, in the process of achieving these major objectives there are a number of sub-objectives, which are also relevant and need to be considered and accomplished. When assessing the success of the exercise they should be evaluated using a check-list, which may also be used when selecting the most suitable layout for the job in hand.

The key factors of the following check-list are not set out in order of importance, since their priorities change with the products and processes with which they are associated.

Check-list

1 Expansion. Can the space available be easily increased with the minimum of disruption to cater for higher production rates?
2 Change. Has the arrangement got the flexibility to accept readily changes in design and manufacture?
3 Flow or movement. Are materials and products moved sequentially and directly with the minimum travel-time of men and materials, avoiding possible congestion?
4 Material handling. Can materials be moved smoothly through all areas, avoiding awkward position and excessive manual effort?
5 Storage. Has sufficient space, binnage and racking been made available for carrying and for the desired stocks of material and parts?
6 Production services. Are the supporting services, such as production, control production, engineering and maintenance, suitably housed and positioned?
7 Safety and housekeeping. Have working conditions which ensure cleanliness and adherence to safety codes and regulations been satisfied?
8 Supervision. Can supervisors without difficulty satisfactorily observe and control the operation for which they are responsible?
9 Maintenance. Are machines and equipment laid out in a manner

which enables day-to-day service, repairs and overhauls to be carried out readily and without disrupting adjacent activities?

10 Machine utilisation. Have the machinery and equipment been utilised in the most effective manner?

11 Capital investment. Has the budgeted capital employed given the best return on investment?

Chapter 25

Project Scheduling

Dennis Lock, Chief O & M Officer, Engineering Division, Selection Trust Limited

---

Practically every engineer will become involved in at least one industrial project during his working life. Whilst this is obviously true of those employed in the major contracting companies and other firms specialising in large 'one-off' products, it is also applicable to nearly every other industrial situation. A company which relies on mass-production techniques for its output will have to control projects for the design of new products, the installation of new plant and the provision of new premises. Even institutions and other organisations which carry out no production at all will find that they need to plan new offices at some time or another, and when this time comes they, too, will be associated to some degree with industrial projects.

Project objectives

Every industrial project, whether it is for the provision of an office block or plant and machinery, represents an investment of capital.

This chapter is based on material that was first published in *The Chartered Mechanical Engineer* and is reproduced here by kind permission of the Council of the Institution of Mechanical Engineers.

Any board of directors faced with the decision to authorise expenditure for a new project must first ask themselves how much return can be expected for this investment. In order to make a fully-considered decision they must know not only the expected cost of the new project, but details of operating costs, depreciation, risk factors, and the time that must elapse before the expenditure results in revenue.

When any management team commits money for a new project it must obviously know how the money is to be spent, and it should be in possession of a full description of the project objectives. These objectives can usually be summarised within three categories. These are:

1 The technical performance and quality of the finished work. This could be expressed as a rate of output for a machine, coupled with limits of accuracy for the machined parts. Alternatively, for civil and construction projects, building specifications and various structural strength requirements might constitute the technical objective.
2 The budget within which the total work must be completed. Sometimes this budget will be directly linked to a profit target, but not all projects are undertaken for profit.
3 The time-scale for completion.

It is almost invariably true to say that any project which overruns its programme will also exceed its planned cost. This is explained in terms of the effects of inflation, where the real purchasing power of the money set aside for the project is eroded as time proceeds. Another big factor is the expense of keeping space, men and other facilities and resources tied up in the project for a period longer than that planned, together with the fact that these resources are not released for work on following projects when they are needed.

There is obviously a very close relationship between time and money. Late delivery of a project can lose money, not only for the contracting company, but also for the customer. As competition increases, economic pressures are causing managers to take more and more notice of techniques that can be employed to control the planning and progress of projects. Competition is now truly international, and indeed often political. This influence is seen in defence projects, where the speed with which advanced weapons systems can be developed is regarded as an item of paramount national importance. It is well known that the full-scale exploitation of network analysis techniques was precipitated by the extremely complex and large-scale Polaris submarine project, for the United States Navy.

Properties essential to an effective project schedule

Once the need for project scheduling has been accepted, it is advisable to consider the features most likely to produce effective working plans before embarking upon any detailed methods. The requirements essential to any effective scheduling system can be summarised by a simple check-list. Whenever there exists a choice between two or more techniques, the alternatives should be compared on the basis of their expected performance against this check-list, which is shown in Figure 25:1.

Of course, even when all the conditions specified in the check-list have been satisfied there exist many other possible factors that can determine the ultimate degree of success achieved in controlling a project. If scheduling is seen as a management tool, where engineers provide their expertise in order to give management the best possible working plans that can be devised, it is equally true that management, for its part, must work to provide an environment in which the plans are most likely to succeed. This involves the establishment of a sound project organisation, within which effective lines of communication are set up. It also means that when actual progress falls short of planned achievement, decisions are taken and implemented promptly to reverse adverse trends. Many engineers will be aware of the frustration that can result from attempting to complete a project within an organisation where communications are weak, or where management does not take action to improve poor performance or facilities within departments outside the control of the engineers.

Seven steps for practical scheduling

Although the advent of network analysis has provided management with a powerful project control tool it has not, unfortunately, solved all the problems. Project planning and control will probably always

The most effective schedule will be:	
1	Technically feasible
2	Based upon reliable estimates
3	Matched to available resources
4	Viable with plans for other projects that must share the same resources
5	Flexible to changes in the project specification
6	Sufficiently detailed to provide a basis for measurement and control of progress
7	Capable of highlighting critical tasks

FIGURE 25:1 CHECK-LIST FOR AN EFFECTIVE PROJECT SCHEDULE

Before adopting any new methods for the planning of industrial projects, the planners must consider whether or not the resulting schedules are likely to prove effective as control tools. This check-list can be a useful aid in this respect

present a challenge to those charged with the successful completion of projects. One big difficulty is the diverse range of factors that must be considered each time a plan is prepared. Some of these are illustrated in Figure 25:2.

The existence of so many contributing elements has led, in the past, to the conception of project planning and control as something of an intuitive process. In small-scale situations intuition can sometimes yield practical results, but in projects that involve the management of large amounts of shareholders' capital, or where competition is intense, guesswork must give way to scientific control. The intuitive method for dealing with a large number of factors is to attempt to consider them all at once, in the imagination. The scientific process

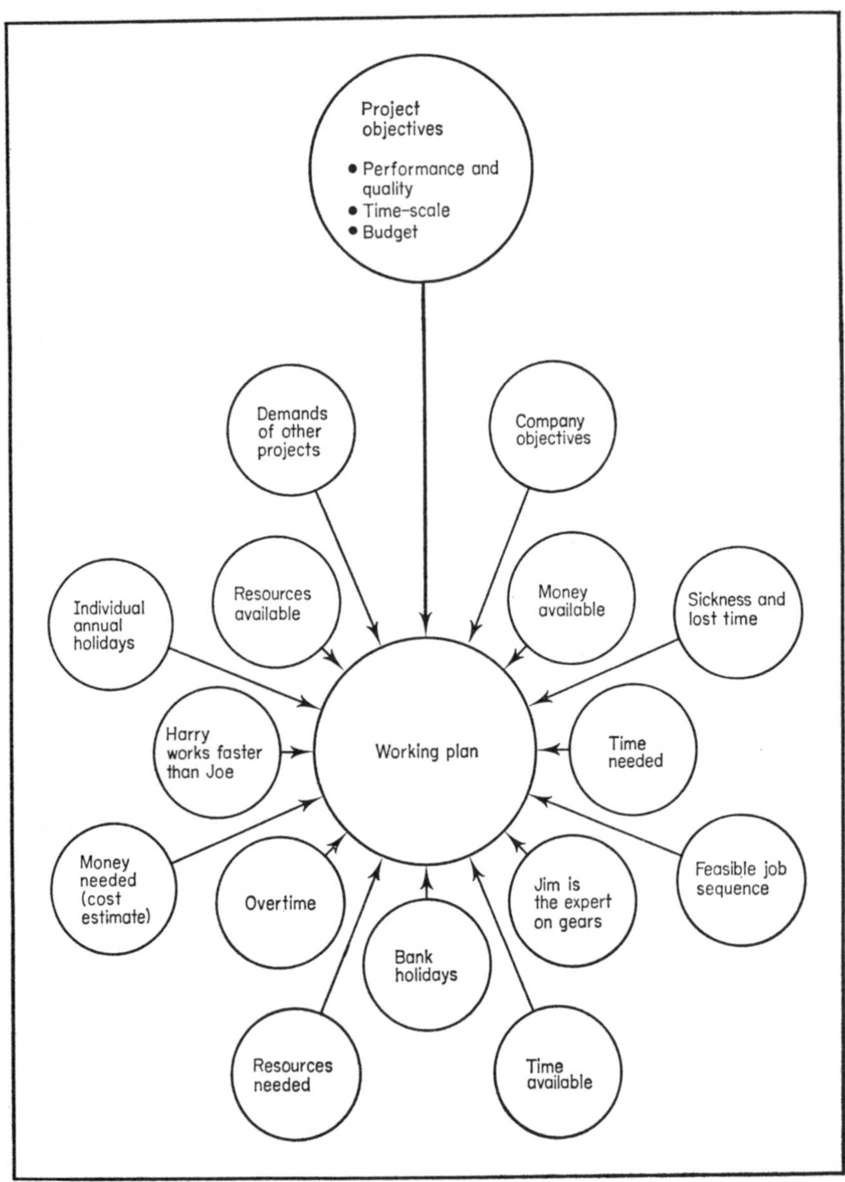

FIGURE 25:2 SOME FACTORS TO BE CONSIDERED IN PROJECT SCHEDULE PREPARATION

The range of items which compete with each other to influence the final choice of a working schedule is usually so extensive that the whole process of planning can be regarded as an intuitive art. The job of the professional planner is to replace intuition with scientific reasoning. He does this by employing a number of different techniques in a logical sequence that is designed to eliminate only one variable at a time actually calls for less individual skill from the manager because he is asked to consider only one variable at a time. In other words, the development of a comprehensive project schedule is undertaken in a series of logical steps. Each of these steps has its own associated problems, and established methods for overcoming them.

Seven separate steps can be identified as necessary for the development of any working plan for a large project. These are introduced in Figure 25:3, together with techniques suitable for their completion. These steps must always be undertaken in the sequence shown, although the amount of attention devoted to each, and the methods employed, must depend upon the size, duration and complexity of the project.

Step 1 : Project definition

Perhaps the biggest handicap of all faced by planners is lack of basic information that adequately defines the scope and objectives of the project. If the project is a commercial venture, for a customer or client, then it is vital for the contracting company to ensure that its commitments are accurately reflected in a commercial and technical specification. The contractor and his client must both agree the objectives. Since nearly all projects involve the preparation of a formal technical proposal, coupled with a quoted price and completion date, it makes good sense to provide the project manager with those same documents as his primary specifications. The engineers responsible for design must know exactly what has been sold. Very often, the design concepts undergo several changes during the proposal stage, with associated price and delivery changes. It is surprising how often projects are authorised where the price and delivery finally agreed relate to the wrong set of technical objectives, with consequent risk of loss to the contractor.

Although sophisticated techniques have been established for the detailed planning and control of major projects, it is seldom possible to introduce them into a new project at the proposal stage. This is a real, if unwelcome, fact of life. When a proposal is being prepared, most emphasis is usually placed upon deciding which technical solution to adopt, and in estimating how much it is likely to cost. These are the main points of discussion with the potential customer, who will often name his own delivery requirements. Knowledge of com-

Step	Method
1 Define the objectives – technical –	Solution, concept or feasibility engineering, with the results documented in a technical specification
– financial –	Cost estimates of the proposed solution, itemised and developed into cost budgets
– programme –	Displayed on a simple chart, with the actual time scale derived from experience of past projects
2 Divide the project into manageable parts	By preparing work breakdown lists that define major areas of work, and those departments or organisations primarily responsible. These areas of work are sometimes called "work packages"
3 Decide, in detail, what has to be done and in what sequence	Bar charts for very simple projects, otherwise by the construction of network diagrams
4 Estimate the duration of each separate activity	Consider the time that will probably elapse between the start of the activity and its completion. Do not take resources into account at this stage
5 Use the activity duration estimates to calculate the estimated project duration, and the relative significance of each activity to time-scale objectives	For very simple projects a small bar chart can be used, but network analysis is usually the better method. For very large projects a computer can be used for the calculations. If results are unacceptable, either the network, the estimates or the time-scale objectives must be changed
6 Reconcile the programme with the resources that can be mustered	For very small projects a bar chart can be used as a loading diagram. For larger projects, and for circumstances where more than one project is making demands on common resources, the computer is used to allocate resources, taking into account the data obtained from network analysis
7 Assign jobs to individuals, by name	This is a supervision skill, outside the normal responsibility of project planners. It demands personal knowledge of each individual, including his degree of technical competence, speed of working, accuracy and special attributes

FIGURE 25:3 THE SEVEN STEPS

There are seven separately identifiable steps necessary to progress from the establishment of project objectives to the formation of a practicable schedule. This table lists those steps, together with some of the more suitable methods for their execution

petition can force a contractor to give an ill-considered delivery promise, only to discover later that the programme agreed is impossible to achieve. There is usually insufficient time, data and money available during the preparation of a proposal to allow detailed planning. However, there is no reason why a company with adequate experience cannot make a reasonably accurate forecast of delivery time based upon its knowledge of previous contracts and its overall capacity situation. Simple planning techniques suffice for this purpose. If a contract is awarded, then the more advanced techniques are used primarily to make certain that the delivery promise is kept, and that budgets are not exceeded.

Step 2: Work breakdown

Consider a project manager, charged with primary responsibility for meeting all project objectives. He knows his budgets, the delivery requirements, and the due completion date. For all but the very smallest projects he must rely heavily upon others to manage and control some work which contributes to his objectives. These others will include departmental managers within his own company, and they may also extend to outside organisations that provide materials and services on a sub-contract basis. If the project manager is able to break his project down into a series of work packages, each can be assigned wholly to one of these other authorities. Every work package can be given its own set of objectives, contrived so that they equate collectively with the total project objectives. Thus the project manager has succeeded in delegating his authority on a specific basis that ensures no duplication of effort between different departments. Each manager in the organisation has an element of work to control that is within his control, well-defined, and sufficiently small to be manageable.

Step 3: Work sequence

It is obvious that any project planning must involve decisions concerning the sequence in which jobs should be carried out, and the priority claims that each job has over its fellows when resources are scarce. Network analysis is the tool which has done most to advance the effectiveness of modern planning in respect of these decisions.

The construction of an arrow diagram can be likened to a production engineering exercise, except that instead of planning the preferred sequence of operations leading to a finished *product* the planner is concerned with the best method for completing a *project*. In the days when bar charts were the only means available it was not possible to indicate complex sequences on the plan, and only very simple interdependencies between different jobs could be taken into account. Network analysis has provided a new notation that allows the planner freedom of expression. He can set down on paper a plan which includes the most complex relationships between activities for very large projects. The resulting schedules are more realistic, and therefore more practicable to achieve.

Even if a project is only planned as far as this stage, and the following steps ignored, provided that the network has been constructed with intelligent reasoning the project will stand a far better chance of smooth progress than if no network had been drawn. It is assumed here that most readers are familiar with the basic concepts of PERT (Project Evaluation and Review Technique) or CPM (Critical Path Method), but a simple comparison between a bar chart and network plan is given in Figure 25:4. Each plan represents the schedule for the same very simple 'project'. A steel cabinet has to be designed and constructed on a castor base. Notice that the bar chart forms a clear display of the time-scale involved, and it can also be used to plan the daily work-load quite easily, simply by adding up the number of engineers or other workers implied by the jobs that appear in each daily column. The network, on the other hand, can demonstrate the inter-relationships between all the jobs far more effectively, but since it is not drawn to scale it cannot by itself be used to plan resource loads. Because bar charts are drawn to a time-scale they cannot be completed until every job has had its duration estimated. When bar charts are used for planning, therefore, steps three and four of the total planning sequence have to be combined.

Step 4: Estimates for activity durations

When the network has been constructed it is necessary to make an estimate of the amount of time that must elapse between the start of every activity and its completion. These estimates are not based directly on the work content in man-hours, but solely upon the time

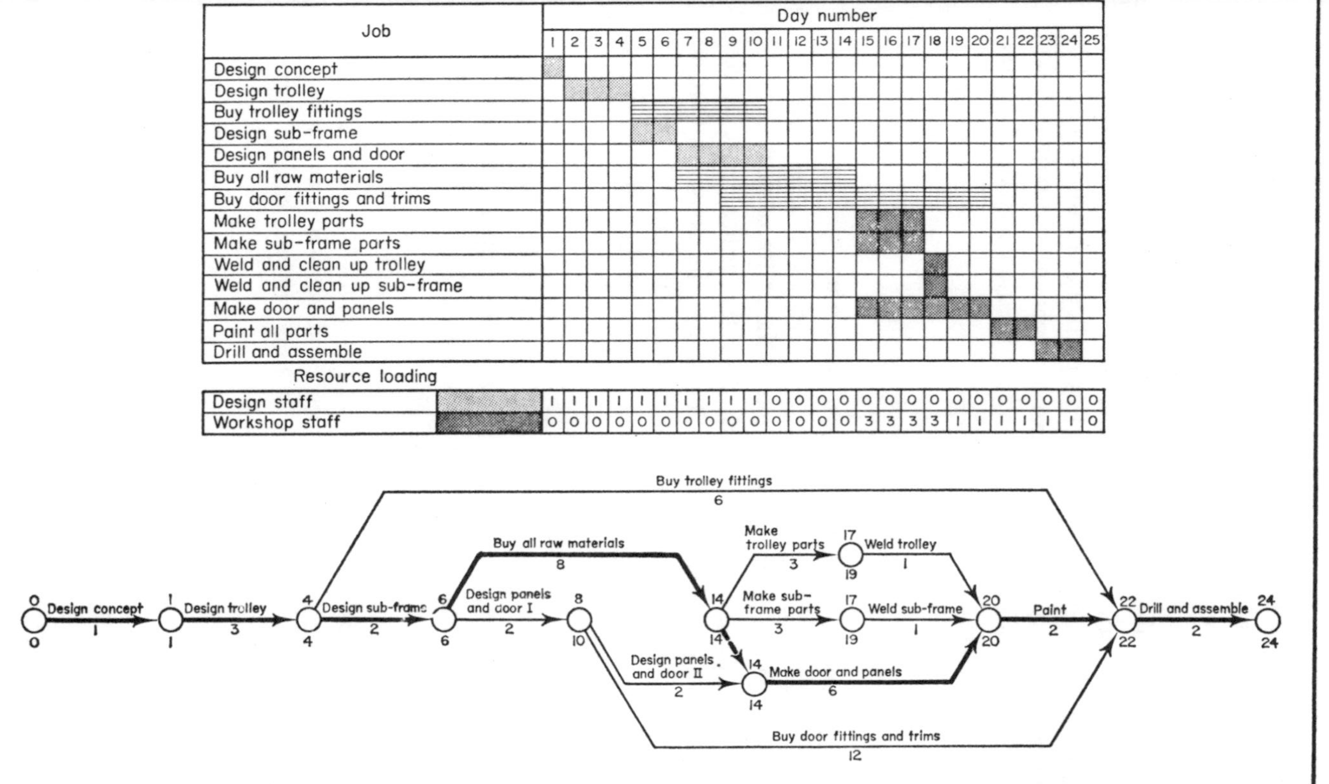

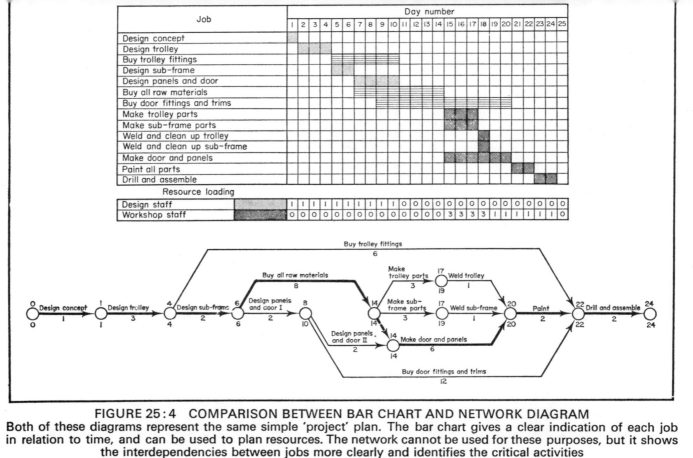

FIGURE 25:4 COMPARISON BETWEEN BAR CHART AND NETWORK DIAGRAM

Both of these diagrams represent the same simple 'project' plan. The bar chart gives a clear indication of each job in relation to time, and can be used to plan resources. The network cannot be used for these purposes, but it shows the interdependencies between jobs more clearly and identifies the critical activities needed, whether this is measured in hours, days or weeks. Resource limitations are not directly considered at this stage. If, for example, an activity needs ten men for an estimated duration of five days, then five days is the figure that must be entered upon the network. No account is taken of the demands made upon the same ten men by other activities in the network, or indeed by activities from other projects. This illustrates the principle of considering the variables one at a time. The only exception in this particular example would be provided by the case where less than ten men of the required skill were *totally* available for work, when the duration would, of course, have to be extended accordingly.

Step 5: Time analysis

Time analysis has three main objectives. These are:

1 To determine the estimated duration of the entire project.
2 To identify those activities which play the critical part in contributing to the overall duration. These are the activities that, together, form the critical path of a network diagram.
3 To quantify the amount of float possessed by all non-critical activities.

The first of these objectives can be achieved by most planning methods. The remaining two objectives depend upon the adoption of some form of network analysis technique. This is highlighted by the fact that the definitions of these objectives contain terms specific to the practice of network analysis. Most networks can be analysed mentally, but it is usually prudent to use a computer for large projects. Computers have the advantage of speed and accuracy, revisions can be made very easily, and the results of time analysis can be printed out in neat, conveniently tabulated reports.

If the results of time analysis predict a project duration longer than that originally wanted by the customer, then the planners must look again at their network and question its contents. It may be possible to reduce some duration estimates, although this must never be done without good reason. A more fruitful approach usually lies in examining the structure of the network itself, and rearranging it so that some activities can be started earlier in relation to others.

Step 6: Resource allocation

If a company happens to be very short of work, with a large reserve of resources waiting to be employed, then it would be theoretically possible to execute a new project without worry about resource loading at all. Each job could simply be started as soon as possible, dependent only upon the type of logical restrictions defined in the network diagram. In other words, if a large number of holes had to be excavated and filled with concrete, they could all be done simultaneously, but the holes must be dug before the cement can be poured in. Time analysis predicts the earliest possible starting and finishing time for each job. If resources are scheduled on this unlimited basis, the load pattern is called a resource aggregation.

Resource aggregation patterns are, characteristically, very uneven. They display sharp peaks and troughs in the day-to-day usage demanded from each type of trade or other resource. This state of affairs is usually undesirable, partly because the peaks are likely to exceed the number of men available and also because uneven usage of men is uneconomic. A company does not want to operate with all its labour working overtime one week only to find that it is on short or idle time the next. Some steps have to be taken to smooth out the working load. This is the process of resource allocation, or, alternatively, resource levelling. It is achieved by delaying the scheduled starting dates for some non-critical activities which would otherwise occur during peak loading periods. The planner endeavours to produce a smooth pattern of resource loading without delaying the completion of the project. In order to produce such a schedule he has to consider both the logical constraints imposed by the sequence of arrows in the network diagram, and the amount of float possessed by each activity. If any activity has to be delayed beyond its calculated float, then the project duration will be extended in consequence.

Now suppose that a project has been estimated to need 20,000 man-hours work from one particular trade skill. This is equivalent to approximately ten man years. Suppose also that the company could assign twenty men of suitable skill to the project. Simple arithmetic reveals that this aspect of the project must take at least six months to complete. Even if time analysis of the network indicates a shortest possible duration of three months, the resource restriction imposed by this trade group must form its own constraint when the working schedules are prepared. When resource allocation is carried out, therefore, it is often found that the completion date for a project has to be delayed beyond that which the network has shown to be possible, simply because there are inadequate resources. A project can sometimes be regarded as an incompressible object, bounded by several constraints that include the prevailing company capacity for work, the demands of the customer, company policies and the technical difficulties of the project itself. Some of these constraints are illustrated in Figure 25:5.

Consider the area within the rectangle formed by the resource limit, the customer's delivery requirement and the two axes of the curve in Figure 25:5. This area can be taken to represent the capacity available, in terms of man-time, which satisfies the limits imposed by resource and time restrictions. Notice that the curve showing planned resource usage cannot take advantage of all the manpower available within the time limits because the build-up of work is not instantaneous, and work must be allowed to tail off gradually as the project nears completion. This curve pattern will depend to some extent upon network diagram restrictions. In geometric terms it cannot be made to fit the rectangle bounded by resource and time-limits. In the example of Figure 25:5, the work content of the project is approximately equal to the resources available, but because of the curve shape the project cannot be contained within the required limits. If the resource limit is imposed, the work must spill over into extra time.

The total process of resource allocation is fairly complex. The planner is asked to arrange a schedule in which the starting and finishing dates of each activity allow the project to be completed on time, but without exceeding available resources, with the sequence and logical restrictions of the network diagram observed, and with a day-to-day rate of working that does not display undue peaks and troughs. In very small projects this kind of comprehensive schedule can be produced by using an adjustable bar chart as a mechanical aid. The activities are simply shuffled around within their permitted float limits until the summation of men needed from day-to-day presents a satisfactory picture. When the totally available resources are insufficient, then either more men must be found or the job must be allowed to run late. Figure 25:6 illustrates these concepts.

Figure 25:6 (a) shows a pattern of resource usage that is typical of

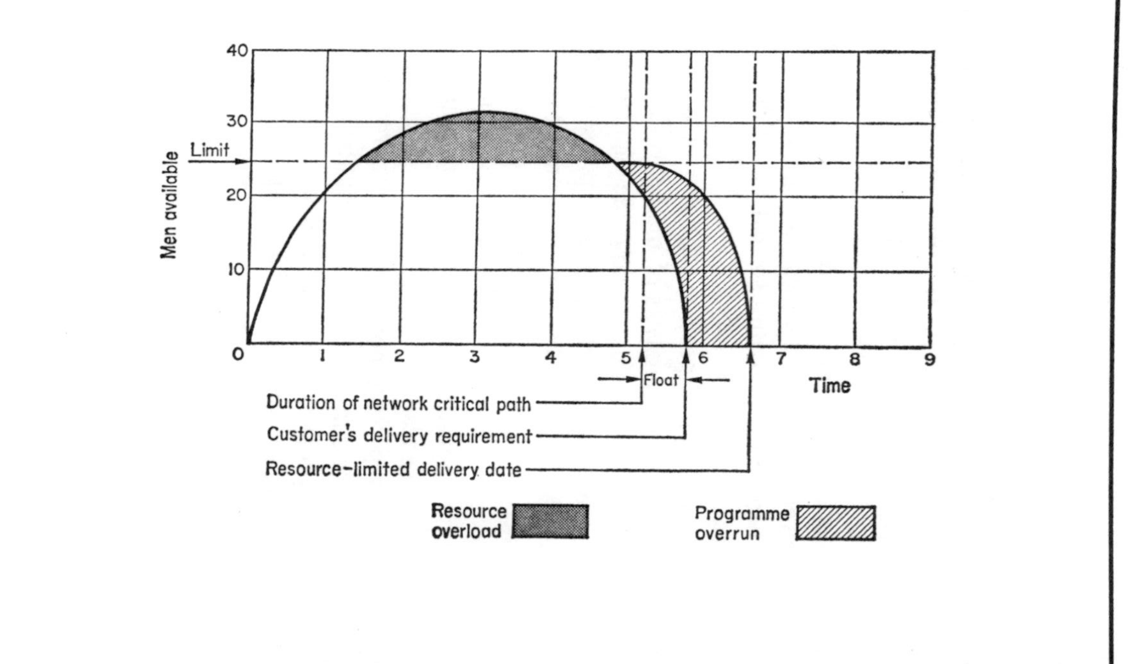

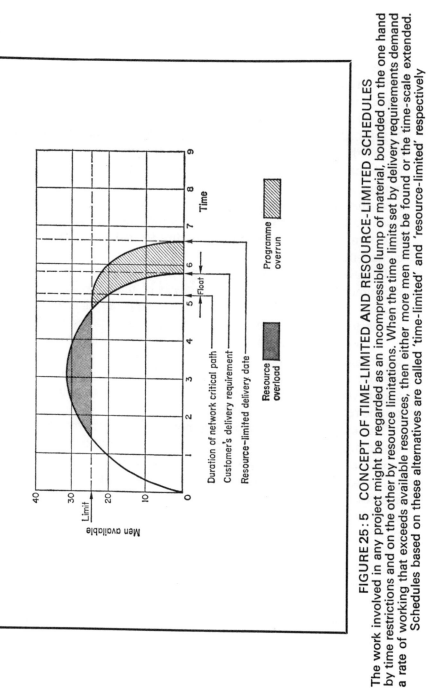

FIGURE 25:5 CONCEPT OF TIME-LIMITED AND RESOURCE-LIMITED SCHEDULES
The work involved in any project might be regarded as an incompressible lump of material, bounded on the one hand by time restrictions and on the other by resource limitations. When the time limits set by delivery requirements demand a rate of working that exceeds available resources, then either more men must be found or the time-scale extended. Schedules based on these alternatives are called 'time-limited' and 'resource-limited' respectively

a resource aggregation schedule, where every activity is started at the earliest possible time predicted by network time analysis. It would prove impracticable to achieve because of the unrealistic demands made on available manpower. If the planner attempted to achieve the same project within the resource limits of his company, he should expect to find that the rearrangement of activity times would correspond to a resource usage pattern similar to that shown in Figure 25:6(b). Notice that in this example the resource restriction has forced the planner to schedule beyond the time-limit. His alternative would have been to produce a time-limited schedule, in which case the pattern should appear like that shown in Figure 25:6(c), where it is seen that the time-limit has been observed at the expense of the resource limit. However, in both examples 25:6(b) and 25:6(c) care has been taken to schedule the activities so that the resource patterns contain no marked peaks or troughs.

For all but the very simplest projects, the use of a computer is recommended to carry out time analysis of the network and the subsequent resource allocation. For this purpose the planner must have access to a computer, equipped with a suitable program. There are many bureaux within the United Kingdom that can provide a service for time analysis of networks, but only a handful are capable of carrying out resource allocation. K and H Business Consultants Limited, and BARIC Computing Services Limited are two companies which can be recommended in this respect.

The use of a computer permits not only the resource allocation of single projects, but also the simultaneous consideration of all activities from the total range of projects being handled within an entire company, so that the computer schedules the company's complete resources. Provided that the networks for all projects have been sensibly constructed, multi-project scheduling by computer tends to produce working schedules that remain valid for the life of each project, and needs little or no revision as week proceeds. Indeed, in one company it was found that the schedules displayed such uncanny precision that progress meetings become unnecessary, and the company was able to predict, with accuracy, when capacity would become available for work on new projects.

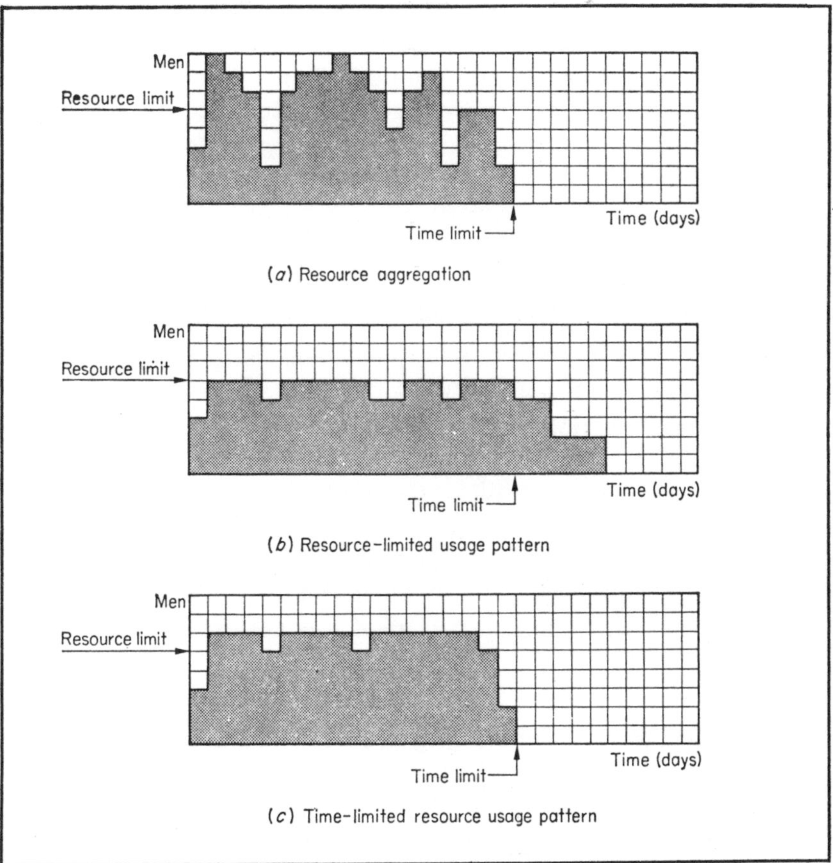

FIGURE 25:6 COMPARISON BETWEEN RESOURCE AGGREGATION, RESOURCE-LIMITED AND TIME-LIMITED SCHEDULES

Diagram (a) shows a typical resource aggregation pattern, corresponding to the usage of resources that would be needed to fulfil a project in which every activity was started at its earliest possible time

In (b), the same amount of work has been scheduled again, but this time efforts have been made to contain all the work within the resource limits available, even though this has meant increasing the overall duration. During the process, care has also been taken to achieve a smoother usage pattern

Diagram (c) is a compromise schedule that does not allow any overrun of time-scale although it does need a higher resource usage than the normally available number of men. Once again, however, care has been taken to keep the day-to-day usage as constant as possible

Step 7: Assignment of jobs to individuals

Project scheduling does not end until every man in the project team has been assigned his own individual tasks. Resource allocation by computer can only be concerned with trade groups or whole departments. It does not take named individuals into account, but is designed to ensure that each department is fed with activities at a rate consistent with the men available and all the other constraints arising from network analysis. Individual assignments demand a detailed knowledge of the personal qualities and skills of each man. This is particularly true of departments employing qualified designers and draughtsmen, and it can also be very true of production departments. Allocation of jobs to men, therefore, must be entrusted to line supervision. Indeed, it is important to stress here that the application of sophisticated project control techniques does not in any way weaken the authority of management. Rather, the service provided by experienced planners can remove many of the administrative chores from foremen, supervisors and other junior managers, leaving them relatively free to concentrate upon the more rewarding aspects of their jobs.

The seven steps of scheduling in relation to project control

Even the most perfect schedule will be utterly wasted if it is not used effectively to control work. Conversely, project control is impossible without some attempt at scheduling. Project management systems have to be established which allow the issue of work instructions, and the recording of the performance achieved against the schedule and other objectives. Figure 25:7 shows how scheduling can be made to fit into such a system, with the relevance of the seven steps highlighted. Each of the steps contributes not only to the realisation of a complete schedule, but also to the establishment of a firm basis for control of both time and money.

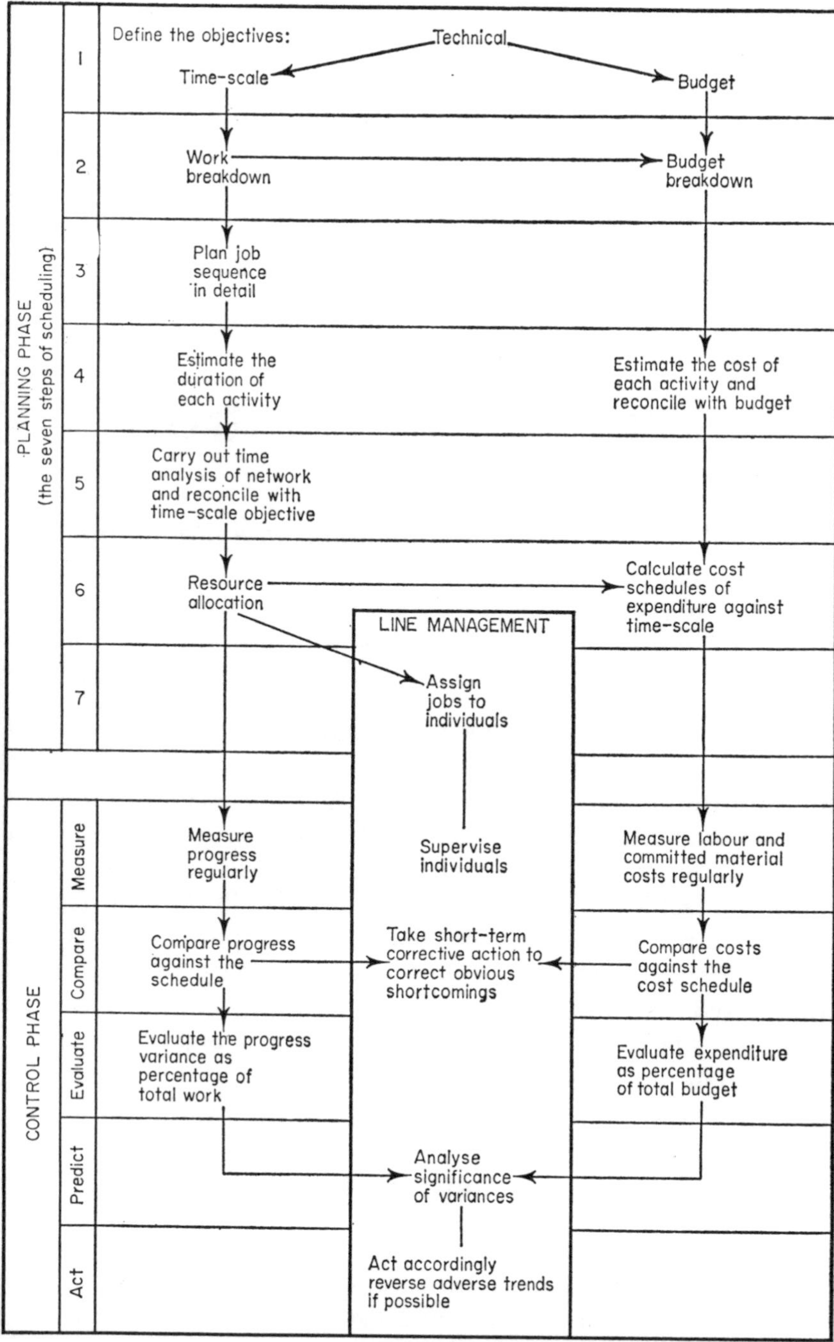

FIGURE 25:7 CONTRIBUTION OF SCHEDULING TO PROJECT CONTROL

Without scheduling, project control would be impossible. This chart shows how each of the seven steps of scheduling fits into the overall pattern of cost and time-scale management

Chapter 26

Production Control

H Beddard, Chairman and Managing Director, A.I.M. Consultants Limited

---

In order for production to be efficient, and for output to be achieved on time, it is necessary to ensure that the *right number* of parts or products are in the *right place* at the *right time* for the *minimum cost*. Optimum use must be made, wherever possible, of all production resources, including plant, equipment, materials and personnel. Usually, a factory or workshop will be engaged in the manufacture of different products at the same time, and each product will consist of a number of components, so that many manufacturing operations are involved. Careful planning and control is necessary to achieve the production objectives stated above. This planning and control is the task of production control.

Definition

The term 'production control' embraces activities which, strictly speaking, are both planning and control activities. The span of work of a production control department and the way in which it should be organised often need to vary from company to company, for they depend on the product and the type and rate of production. However, production control can, in broad terms, usually be considered as consisting of the following activities:

1 Formulating the production program and scheduling
2 Shop loading
3 Dispatching (works manufacturing orders)
4 Progressing
5 Material control

Each of these activities is discussed in some detail below.

The production control department is the nerve-centre of the manufacturing function; it receives information regarding what is to be manufactured and by when this should be done; it processes such information, it issues instructions and advises, it ensures feed-back on the outcome of these instructions and takes appropriate action.

The production control department does not make or sell anything and cannot exist in isolation (see Figure 26:1). Although a vital department, it is a servicing activity and *must* have close liaison with other departments besides the production shops. Examples are:

1 Sales department, where it advises on realistic delivery dates in the light of the load on manufacturing facilities.
2 Purchasing department regarding supplies of material and bought out finished parts and sub-contractors.
3 Design and drawing offices, on introduction of modifications and new designs into production.
4 Production engineering department on bottlenecks which are occurring in production and, hence, possible improvements in the method of manufacture.
5 Costing and wages departments, which need to know how many good parts and products have been produced for costing and wage payment purposes and what material has been received from suppliers who need payment.

Frequent meetings should be held between senior members of staff of the appropriate departments to consider and agree on the necessary action to be taken.

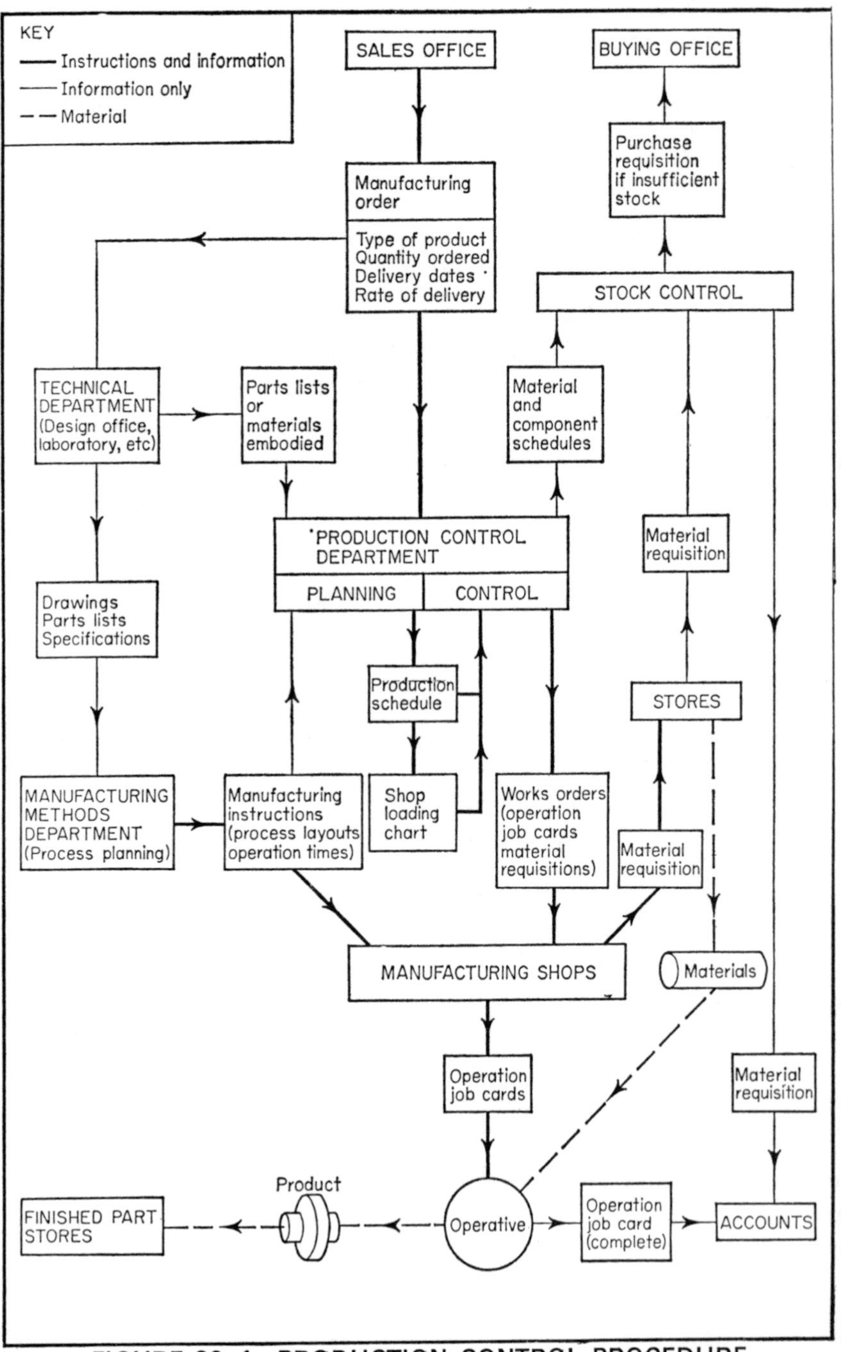

FIGURE 26:1 PRODUCTION CONTROL PROCEDURE

Shows the flow of information to and from a typical production control department (Reproduced by permission of the British Productivity Council

Formulating the production programme

It is very necessary for a company to undertake reliable forecasting of the market requirements. Such forecasts will tell it which products customers are most likely to buy, in what quantity and at what rate. Long-range forecasts will affect allocation of capital and planning, perhaps for product development, additional plant (or even a new factory), further labour and training. Such forecasts should be regularly reviewed in the light of market trends and adjusted to give more accurate short-range forecasts.

The short-range forecast forms the basis of production control activities because it will influence the use of plant and labour as well as the usage of materials. Thus, as already mentioned, close liaison must exist between the sales department and the production control department to ensure that sales are in keeping with what the factory can produce in terms of quantity and delivery dates. Seldom does a factory just make one product and so efficient integration of all products into the manufacturing facilities is essential in formulating the production programme.

Whilst it is generally accepted that forecasting is easier for companies producing repetitive products, it is not impossible to forecast reliably for the one-off product type of firm because an analysis will usually reveal a pattern of requirements.

Scheduling

The base of a schedule is *time*. This is the prime factor in production control. Hence, for any given order for a product or stock manufacture, a master schedule can be drawn up (see Figure 26:2). This shows, against a time-scale, the time needed by the various activities to manufacture a given quantity of the product. The illustration is for a very simple product which consists of two sub-assemblies that contain a total of only five parts. However, the principle remains the same for a much more complicated product.

On studying the master schedule it will be noted that to conserve time some activities (not shown) could be overlapped with other activities. For example, the time needed to supply material could be within the time required to design and manufacture the jigs and tools before production commences.

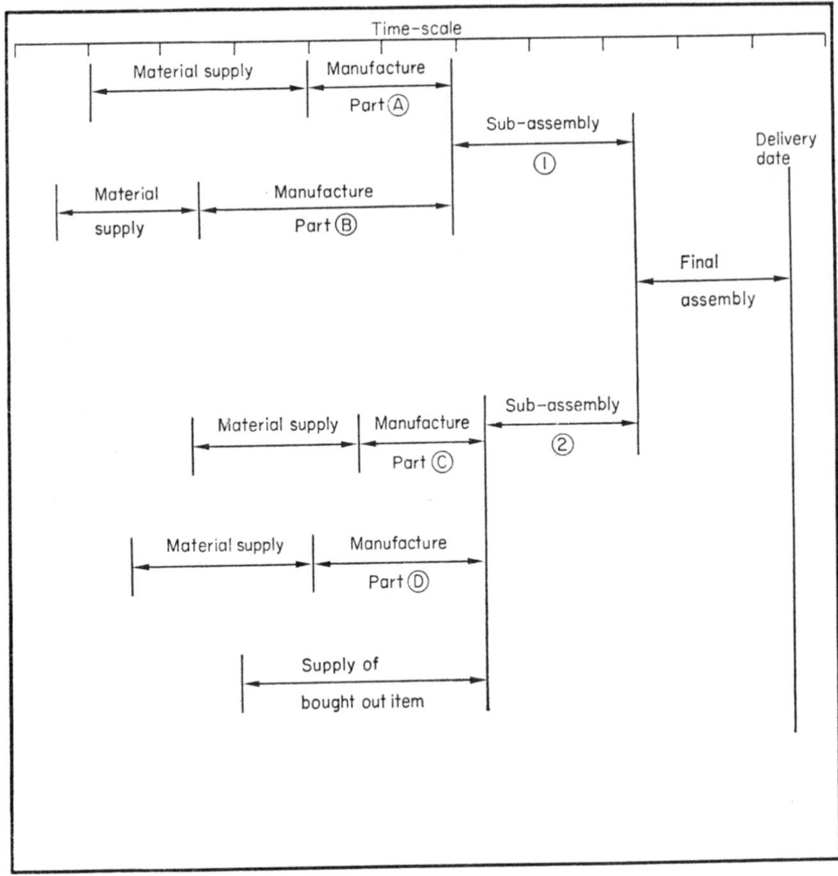

FIGURE 26:2 MASTER SCHEDULE

Showing the time needed by various activities to meet the delivery date for a given quantity of a product

It will also be observed that in terms of time the master schedule shows the ideal plan but in practice this may have to be adjusted. For example, there will probably be different products in process at the same time, and machines and labour may not be available at the precise time demanded by the schedule. Deliveries of material may be late and breakdowns of plant may occur. Thus it is necessary to note from the schedule the *key times* for activities to be completed.

All the parts in a sub assembly must be ready when sub assembly is planned to start. Likewise, sufficient sub assemblies must be ready by the key time when final assembly should start. To meet these key times in the light of breakdowns or late deliveries of materials, overtime working may become necessary, although this should be avoided if possible. On the other hand, earlier starts than those scheduled may become possible through light plant loading and early delivery promises from suppliers. The *major key time* is, of course, the delivery date to the customer and this *must* be adhered to if at all possible. Only in the last resort should this be changed and then, it is hoped, with the approval of the customer. Late deliveries are a rapid way to lose customer goodwill, further sales and profitability.

Those readers who have studied critical path planning will recognise the effectiveness of this method in the development of master schedules. Whilst other methods are more effective for the day-to-day loading of individual manufacturing operations on machines and service departments, the networks are invaluable for determining priorities for material deliveries and for start and finish times for complete manufacturing cycles, in relation to delivery requirements for end-products.

Shop loading

The requirements of the master schedule must be produced for the lowest practicable cost. Many factors, not least design of the product, contribute to costs of production. Obviously, efficient use of men, and of the manufacturing machinery and plant must be achieved. This calls for careful planning in the loading of work to men and machines.

The sequence of operations to be performed on each manufactured part, and the actual disposition of machines and other plant on the shop floor, fall within the area of responsibility of process planners and production engineers. Standard times allowed for each operation will usually be determined by work study engineers. In the case of all batch and jobbing production, however, it is left to the production control department to decide *when* each particular machine or work centre is to undertake each particular operation on every piece-part or batch of parts to be made.

Whether the production control department loads each individual machine, or whether it loads groups of machines and leaves it to the shop floor supervision to distribute to specific machines varies from firm to firm and usually depends on experience.

Such loading has to be arranged in conjunction with all the other work taking place at the particular time, according to predetermined priorities. Thus it is necessary to note the vacant capacity on machines and to endeavour to arrange the various jobs in such an order that the best use is made of available resources in keeping with the scheduled key time for completion of each job.

To assist in loading, estimates or standard times for the total time needed for each manufacturing operation can be used to develop a bar chart. This can be arranged on the Gantt chart principle.[1] A Gantt chart example is provided at Figure 26:3. It shows at a glance the load and vacant capacity for each machine or work centre. A number of planning boards are available commercially which use adhesive tapes, pegs in holes, cards in slots or magnetic strips on steel plates[2].

Dispatching (works manufacturing orders)

The use of the word 'dispatching' here is not to be confused with the dispatch of goods to the customer. In order to commence actual production instruction have to be issued to the works by the production control department in the form of documentation: this is known as dispatching. In addition to working drawings, such documentation will usually include the following:

Route card Figure 26:4. This is a card which stays with the batch of parts or product throughout all its operations. The card lists details of each operation and, as these are shown in sequence, indicates the route the parts (or product) must take in manufacture.

Job card Figure 26:5. Such a card is issued for each operation and is the operator's instruction and authority to carry out the operation. Provision is made for clocking on and off the job and recording good and reject work. From these the operator's earnings on that job may be calculated and cost data can be determined.

Material requisition (Figures 26:6 and 26:7). These documents

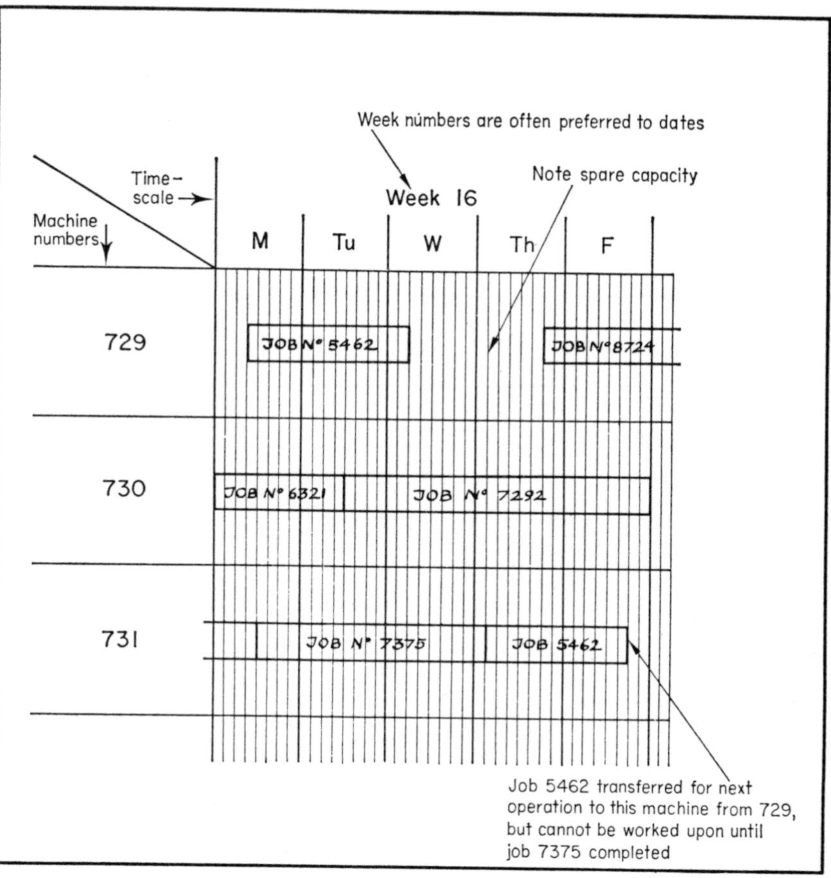

FIGURE 26:3 PART OF SHOP LOADING CHART

Widely used to provide 'at a glance' indication of loads or spare capacity on machines or work centres

authorise the storekeeper to cut off and issue material. They also advise the cost office and stock control department of the amount of material issued.

Finished parts stores receipt (Figure 26:8). This document is evidence that parts or products have been received finished in the stores.

Loading and progress advice (Figure 26:9). Here advice and feed-back is given to the production control department that a particular operation has been carried out. The advice note records the amount of good and scrap work.

<table>
<tr><th colspan="6">ROUTE CARD</th></tr>
<tr><td>Week due to
Start</td><td>Finish</td><td>Type</td><td>Assembled on</td><td>Batch number</td><td>Works order number</td></tr>
<tr><td colspan="2">Quantity required</td><td colspan="3">Part name</td><td>Part number</td></tr>
<tr><td colspan="5">Material specification and unit quantity</td><td>Part number (check)</td></tr>
</table>

Operation number	M/c number or department	Operation description	Jigs, tools and gauges	Set-up time	TA each

FIGURE 26:4 WORKS DOCUMENTATION—ROUTE CARD

Route cards are used to give details of each operation and, as these are listed in sequence, the route that the batch of parts (or product) must follow in manufacture (With acknowledgement to Block and Anderson Ltd)

JOB TIME CARD

Week due to Start / Finish	Type	Assembled on	Batch number	Works order number

Quantity required	Part name	Part number

Operation number	M/c number/ department	Operation	Jigs, tools and gauges	Set-up time	Time allowed each

Number from last operation	Material scrap	Man's scrap	Number for rectification	Number to pay for	Total time allowed	Bonus hours	Bonus earnings

Inspector's signature	Hours brought forward	Hours this week	Time earnings	Total time taken	Rate	Labour cost

FIGURE 26:5 WORKS DOCUMENTATION—JOB CARD

Job cards provide the operator with specific instructions for the batch of parts (or product) being produced, and also allow recording of time and cost information relevant to work actually carried out (With acknowledgement to Block and Anderson Ltd)

<table>
<tr><td colspan="10">MATERIAL REQUISITION (STORES)</td></tr>
<tr><td colspan="2">Week due to
Start | •Finish</td><td>Type</td><td>Assembled on</td><td colspan="3">Batch number</td><td colspan="3">Works order number</td></tr>
<tr><td colspan="2">Quantity required</td><td colspan="5">Part name</td><td colspan="3">Part number</td></tr>
<tr><td colspan="7">Material specification and unit quantity</td><td colspan="3">Part number (check)</td></tr>
<tr><td colspan="4">Actual material issued</td><td>Cwts</td><td>Qrs</td><td>Lbs</td><td>Rate</td><td colspan="2">Value</td></tr>
<tr><td>Received by</td><td>Date</td><td colspan="4">Issued by</td><td colspan="2">Entered stock records by</td><td colspan="2">Entered costs by</td></tr>
</table>

FIGURE 26:6 WORKS DOCUMENTATION—MATERIAL REQUISITION (STORES)
Requisitions authorise storekeepers to release materials for manufacture (With acknowledgement to Block and Anderson Ltd)

MATERIAL REQUISITION (COSTS)

Week due to. Start	Week due to. Finish	Type	Assembled on	Batch number	Works order number

Quantity required	Part name	Part number

Material specification and unit quantity	Part number (check)

Actual material issued	Cwts	Qrs.	Lbs	Rate	Value	

Received by	Date	Issued by	Entered stock records by	Entered costs by

FIGURE 26:7 WORKS DOCUMENTATION—MATERIAL REQUISITION (COSTS)
This document is sent to the cost office in order that materials issued from stores can be costed to each batch of parts (or product) made. Frequently this document is combined with that shown in Figure 26:6 (With acknowledgement to Block and Anderson Ltd)

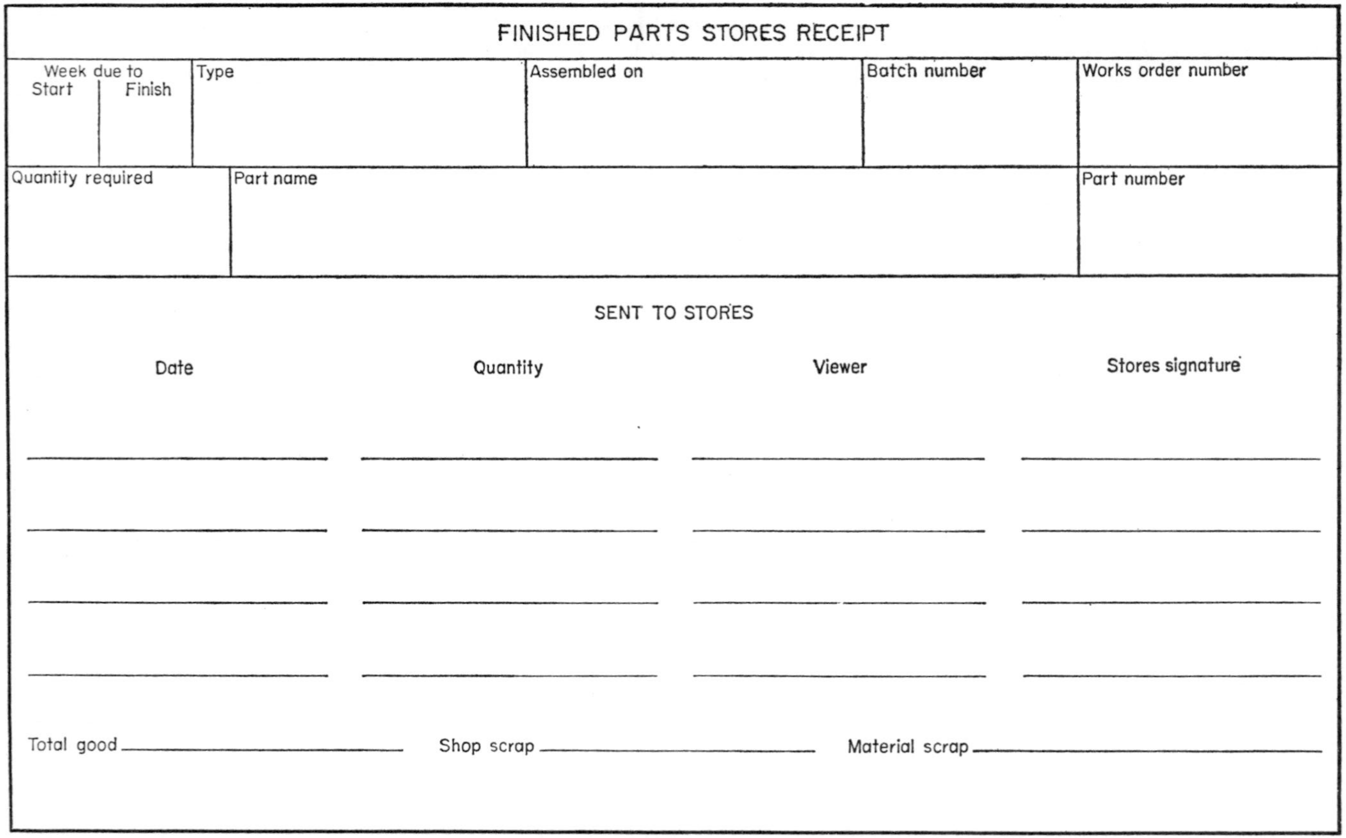

FINISHED PARTS STORES RECEIPT

Week due to Start	Week due to Finish	Type	Assembled on	Batch number	Works order number

Quantity required	Part name	Part number

SENT TO STORES

Date	Quantity	Viewer	Stores signature

Total good ______ Shop scrap ______ Material scrap ______

FIGURE 26:8 WORKS DOCUMENTATION—STORES RECEIPT

The stores receipt note shown here is used to record the addition of finished parts to stocks, in order that stock records can be updated and the company's accounts kept correct (With acknowledgement to Block and Anderson Ltd)

LOADING AND PROGRESS ADVICE				Man's name	Check number

Week due to: Start	Week due to: Finish	Type	Assembled on	Batch number	Works order number

Quantity required	Part name	Part number

	Operation number	M/c number/ department	Operation	Jigs, tools and gauges	Set-up time	Time allowed each
This operation						
Next operation						

Number from last operation	Material scrap	Man's scrap	Number for rectification	Number to pay for	Estimated M/c time	Actual time

Inspector's signature	Date planned	Loader's signature	Date started	M/c used	Reason for delay

FIGURE 26:9 WORKS DOCUMENTATION—LOADING AND PROGRESS ADVICE
Used to report back the status of work to production control from the work centre. This is the feedback function that is important in the maintenance of production control (With acknowledgement to Block and Anderson Ltd)

To expedite preparation of these documents and standardise them, commercially-marketed systems are usually used. The particular details are usually put on the pre-printed forms by a hectographic system (using a special type of carbon). The data for the route card is typed or hand-written on to a master form from which all the other documents can be produced. By using a line-selection spirit duplicator, or by one of several other semi-automatic methods, it is possible to print out selected areas from the master on to job cards and requisitions. Thus re-typing is avoided, and with it the risk of error and the introduction of unnecessary work. Typically, the master card heading would be printed out each time to give the description of the part, its part number, the batch or job number, the quantity in the batch, and other general information. Then, the printing machine would select only one of the operations listed on the master, and print that out to form a document specific for that particular operation. This process would then be repeated for every other operation until a complete set of manufacturing documents had been produced.

Progressing

Once the instructions to manufacture a job have been issued to the work centres it is not sufficient for the production control department to forget about that job. It is necessary to ensure that the job will reach each work station at the scheduled time and that the respective operations are completed on time. This particularly applies to batch-production for here, unlike flow-production, the job does not automatically move on to the next operation. To meet such a requirement 'progress chasers' are employed whose task it is to chase the work on the shop floor and take all the necessary steps. These include liaison with the shop floor supervisors and arranging the necessary transport for work between work stations. They also report back to the production controllers any difficulties encountered so that appropriate action may be taken to safeguard the promised delivery date of the product.

The essence of any control is feed-back. In the case of production control it is necessary to compare the actual production achievements with the schedule. A useful way of noting at a glance adherence or departure from the plan is by a progress chart (see Figure 26:10).

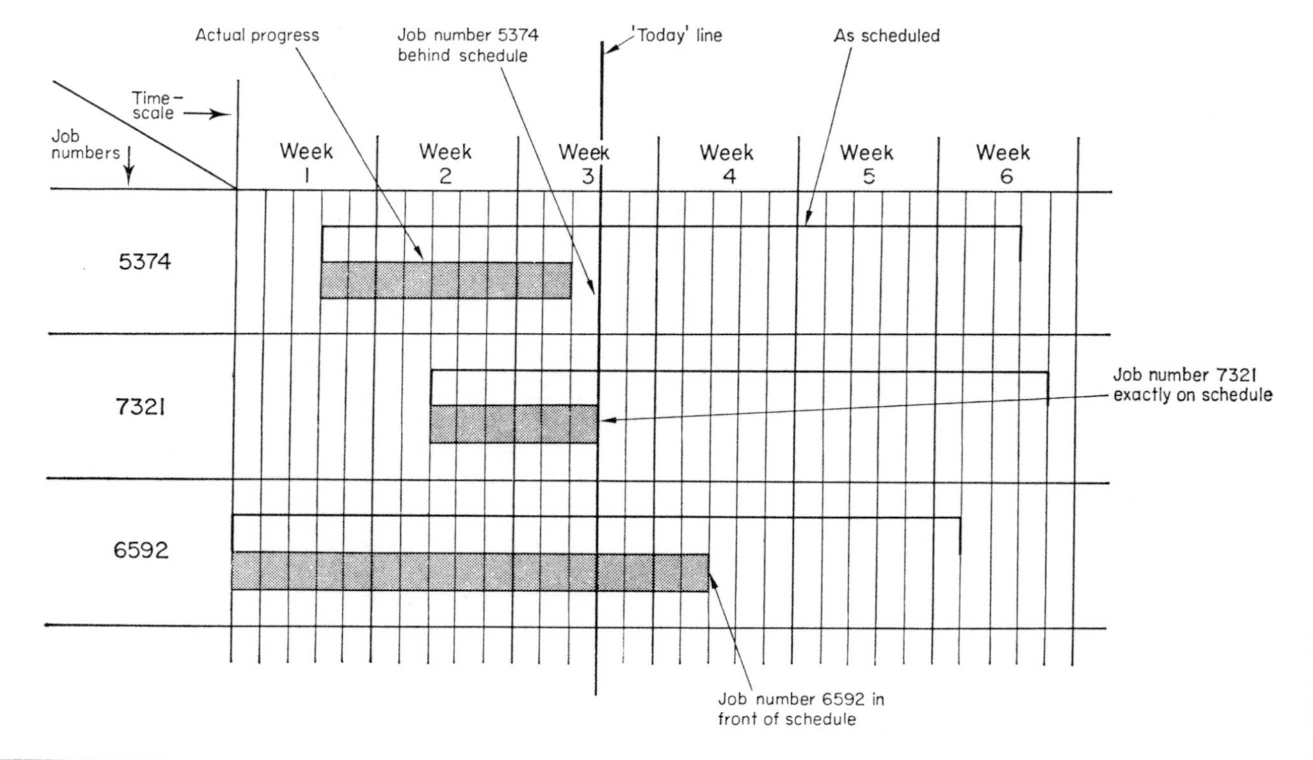

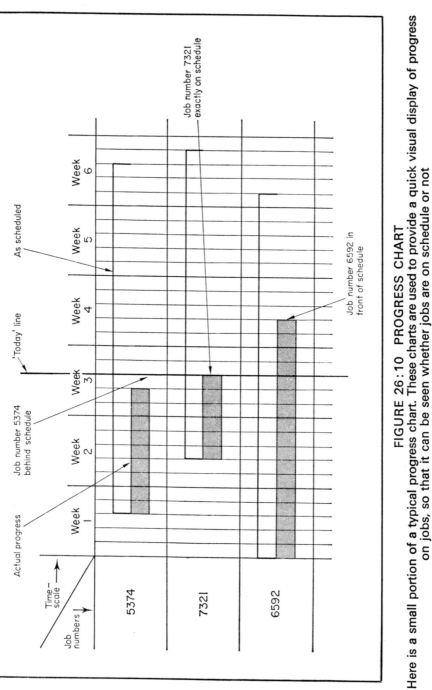

FIGURE 26:10 PROGRESS CHART
Here is a small portion of a typical progress chart. These charts are used to provide a quick visual display of progress on jobs, so that it can be seen whether jobs are on schedule or not

This is again based on the Gantt chart principle, where jobs are displayed against a time-scale which includes the key times.

Material control

An essential part of any manufacturing program is to have the raw material and bought-out parts available when required. This calls for efficient suppliers who will deliver the *right quantity*, at the *right time* in the *right quality* and at the *right price*. Also, a *control on stocks* is necessary so that sufficient time for re-ordering and delivery, known as the 'lead-time', can be given; furthermore the *maximum and minimum stock levels* must be established so that, too much money and space is not tied up in stock, or that the company does not run out of stock. These considerations are discussed in more detail in Chapter 27.

Aids to the quantitative aspects of production control

Much of the information dealt with in production control is of a quantitive nature, such as the number of parts to be made and the rate of production, the load on machines, stocks to be held and to order, etc. Therefore, techniques which will allow such quantitive data to be processed quickly and also optimise results are most useful.

Computers

In the case of complex manufacture, such as a motor-car or aircraft, there are so many parts and operations that to process the production control data manually would be a gigantic task almost beyond human comprehension. However, a computer can easily and quickly process such data and provide a print-out of the results. The large computer manufacturers have now derived package-deal computer programs for production control and these, correctly adapted, save much expense and time in programming of the computer.

It is important that the production controller, who knows what data he wants from a computer, should dictate the format of the print-out. In the past a number of companies have been swamped with piles of unnecessary computer print-outs: in fact, it is mainly the jobs which are going *out of control* that the production controller needs to know about; that is *control by exception.*

Operational research

In production control one is constantly trying to find the optimum solution to a given situation where there are a number of variables such as machine-loading, the size of batches to manufacture, the holding of stocks, etc. Techniques have been developed by operational research specialists to solve such problems through the use of mathematical models of the situation. The techniques are too detailed to describe here, but the reader is referred to the many specialised books on the subject; the British Institute of Management library runs a bibliography covering the area.

Economic order quantity

When products are being produced in batches for stock, the question of how many to make in each batch arises. This same question applies also to the quantity of bought-out materials that should be ordered at any time, and discussed again in Chapter 27. In the production case, the relevant factors are those of the cost of machine-setting versus the holding of produced parts; the larger the batch the fewer the number of machine-settings in a given period of time, but the longer the stock has to be held. Conversely, with small batches the machine-setting cost per unit is relatively high but the stockholding costs are small. These trends are illustrated by the curves in Figure 26:11. If the production cost per unit is plotted as one graph, and the stock-holding cost per unit is plotted as another on the same axis, it is possible to add a third curve which combines both these graphs to show the total works cost for each unit produced, as related to batch-size. The minimum point on this combined curve obviously indicates the lowest theoretical total cost that can be achieved; it corresponds to the most economical batch-size. However, it should be noted that the upper curve is fairly shallow on both sides of its minimum so that the actual batch-size can be adjusted, within limits, without unduly affecting total costs.

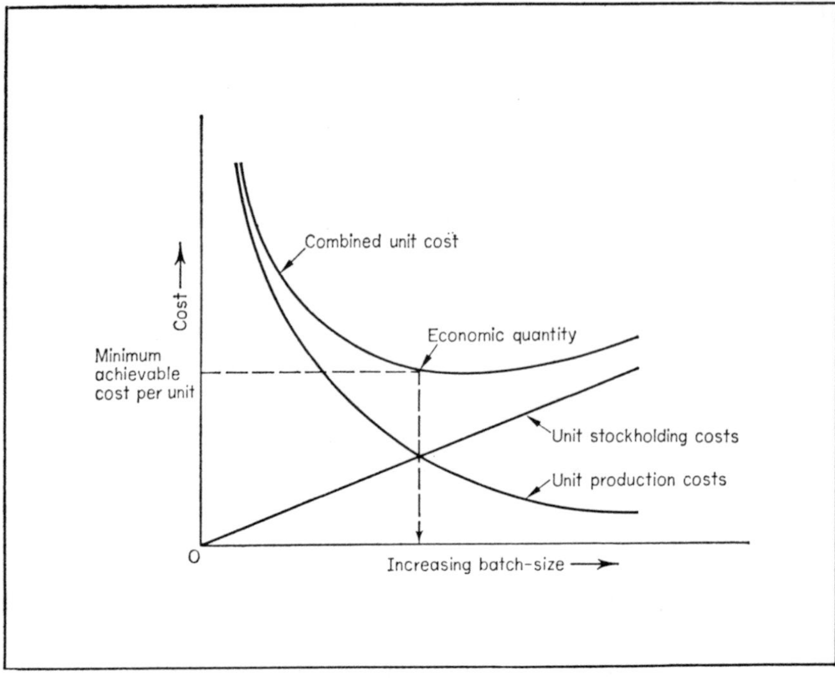

FIGURE 26:11 ECONOMIC BATCH QUANTITY

Graphs can be drawn in order to indicate the economic size of batches for manufacture. Two curves are used to relate the opposing factors of unit stock holding costs (which generally increase with larger batch-size) and unit manufacturing costs (which normally reduce as batch-sizes are increased). The minimum point on the combined unit cost curve indicates the optimum batch size, but in practice a fair degree of latitude can be allowed about this point because the slope of this resultant curve is shallow about this the minimum value

Split batches

In any manufacturing situation the aim should be to get the product from raw material to finished goods stage in the shortest possible time. The longer the work is in progress the longer is money tied up in materials and valuable floor space being used. With many production jobs there is far more waiting than making. This is particularly true with batch production where, if a batch of 100 parts is being made, one part is worked on at a work centre whilst the other 99 parts are either waiting to be worked on or to be moved to the next operation. To overcome this difficulty the proposal of splitting the batch comes to mind; to transfer some of the batch, those which have been completed at, say, the first operation, to the second operation, so that whilst the remainder of the batch is being processed at the first operation the others are undergoing the second operation. This, however, presents more complex control activities with similar parts in different locations and at different stages of manufacture. Most production controllers therefore shun the idea, and look on split batches as nightmares.

However, to treat the situation with a more systematic approach a technique known as *line of balance* has been devised and for those readers who are interested there are publications on the technique which, unfortunately, is too lengthy to describe here[3].

Controlling: batch-production versus flow-production

Much of what has been written in this chapter concerns batch- and jobbing-production for it is here that most problems in production control arise.

With flow-production the rate of manufacture is controlled by, say, a conveyor system, or the machines are laid out in a line and each part passes individually from machine to machine in the course of manufacture, and the production of that part or product is continuous. Then the production control problems of machine-loading and progressing diminish. It is only when the line is first laid out that endeavours are necessary to equalise times of operations but that is more the task of production engineering. Principal control functions to ensure production continuity are centred on maintenance of the plant and materials control.

References

1 See *The Gantt Chart* by Wallace Clark, Pitman.
2 Many are described in *Industrial Scheduling Techniques* by D Lock, Gower Press, 19.
3 See, for example, *Project Management,* D Lock, Gower Press,19.

Chapter 27

Materials Management

Peter Baily, Lecturer in Business Studies, Glamorgan Polytechnic and David Farmer, Principal, David Farmer and Associates

---

The activities involved in managing materials are fast becoming a primary concern of management. Increased manufacturing efficiency reduces the *manufacturing* cost of products and thus increases the proportion of total cost which is due to materials. Improved and novel manufacturing techniques and processes and the development of new alloys and plastics mean that many parts and components which, in former days were made internally, are now purchased from specialist suppliers. Consequently, in many businesses the greatest potential for cost reduction and improved efficiency lies in the area of material procurement and control, rather than in manufacturing.

Tight money conditions, high interest rates, and a sharper interest in regular and prompt deliveries to customers have stimulated interest in the total flow concept as applied to materials. This is an attempt to plan and control for optimal results the *physical supply* flow of parts and materials as well as the commercial and financial aspects of buying and stocking them. It affects personnel who traditionally, at any rate in the larger organisations, have been grouped in different departments: purchasing, stock control, transport, stores, materials handling, and perhaps also production planning and control. This approach tends to produce new organisation structures in which the departments dealing with material activities are grouped together under one head, a materials manager. The total flow approach can, of course, be applied without restructuring the organisation, given the right attitude and the right objectives, and given staff of adequate calibre.

Purchasing and cost reduction

The largest single spending area in most businesses, purchased parts and material, calls for careful attention to the prices paid as well as to the regular supply of acceptable goods at the time required. Looking hard at the price paid is the specific responsibility of the buyer. The designer and the quality controller are particularly concerned with the specification and conformity of quality standards, the production man and the sales people are particularly concerned with on-time delivery; it is the purchasing people who are particularly concerned with price.

Yet no business can survive indefinitely unless it is profitable; the return on assets is becoming a universal yardstick of the efficient use of resources, and the prices paid to suppliers can have a surprisingly large effect on profitability.

This is because most manufacturing businesses spend over half of their total sales revenue on purchases, but earn profits at the rate of only about ten per cent of sales revenue. The purchasing bill is five times as big as the profit account. Consequently a twenty per cent reduction in purchase costs will increase profits by one hundred per cent. A five per cent reduction purchase cost could add as much to profits as increasing sales by twenty-five per cent. Such massive reductions in cost are not impossible, although firms which are already well managed may not have left themselves much elbow room for across-the-board reductions of this order. But that is not really the point: the point is to highlight the profit potential of purchasing.

Many engineers will grudgingly admit that the figures seem to be correct but will doubt their relevance: slash purchase prices by twenty per cent, they feel, and while in theory you have doubled your profit, in practice you have ruined your suppliers. And once your customers realise what a cheap and nasty product you now supply, you have ruined your own business too. But this is a gross oversimplification. *Slashing purchase prices is not the only road to purchase cost reduction.* It is not the price paid which is of prime importance: it is the delivered cost in relation to the specification. Batch-sizes, contractual arrangements, transport costs, stockholding arrangements, all come into the picture.

Manfacturing businesses have made great savings in the payroll area in the last decade or two, by the application of analytical thought-work study, industrial engineering, methods improvement, better layout and group technology – and by better management of the people employed in the business. It is a long time since any business saved money in the payroll area by beating down wage rates. One should not, therefore, fall into the trap of assuming that the only way to save money in the materials area is by beating down purchase prices.

Target selection for cost reduction studies

Most factories place a large number of small orders and a small number of large orders. A simplified picture is shown in Figure 27:1 where eighty per cent of the money spent goes on twenty per cent of the orders placed and the rest of the orders account for only twenty per cent of the expenditure. Actual curves are shown in Figure 27:2.

Until this fact is realised, there is a natural tendency to spend almost as much administrative effort on small orders as on large ones. Adopting one standard form and procedure for every purchase amounts to administrative overkill on cheap routine items, while falling short on the largest non-repeating orders.

These usage value curves (or Pareto curves) are now widely applied in stock control to suit the control procedure to the stock value – ABC analysis, as it is usually called. The same approach is useful in purchasing. Purchases can be classified into three broad groups (with modifications to suit particular requirements in the individual business):

1 Very large non-repeating purchases, and those regular purchases which account for an appreciable portion of the total annual purchase expenditure.

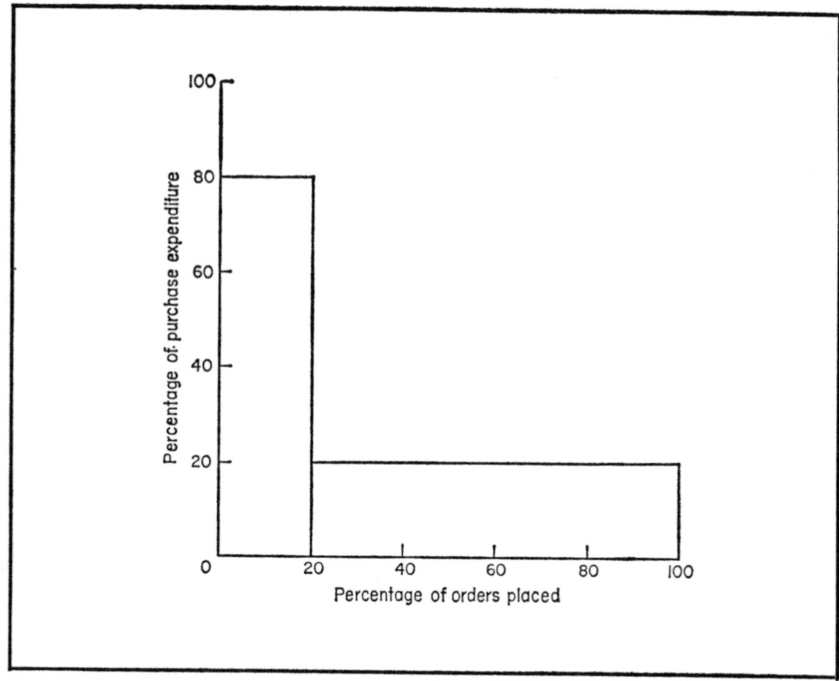

FIGURE 27 : 1 THE 80/20 LAW: SIMPLIFIED PATTERN OF PURCHASE EXPENDITURE

2 Large non-repeating purchases and the intermediate group generally in cost terms.
3 Small usage value items.

The place to look for cost reduction is in group one purchases and some group two purchases. The group three purchases can be a source of useful savings too, both in administrative cost and in prices paid, provided that they are treated collectively in appropriate groups. There is usually nothing to be gained by looking for cost reduction on *individual* small orders – what is saved on price is less than the cost of achieving the saving. But by arranging discounts o nwhole classes of purchases, savings can be made. Group one purchases, which are less than five per cent of the total of items bought, call for individual attention.

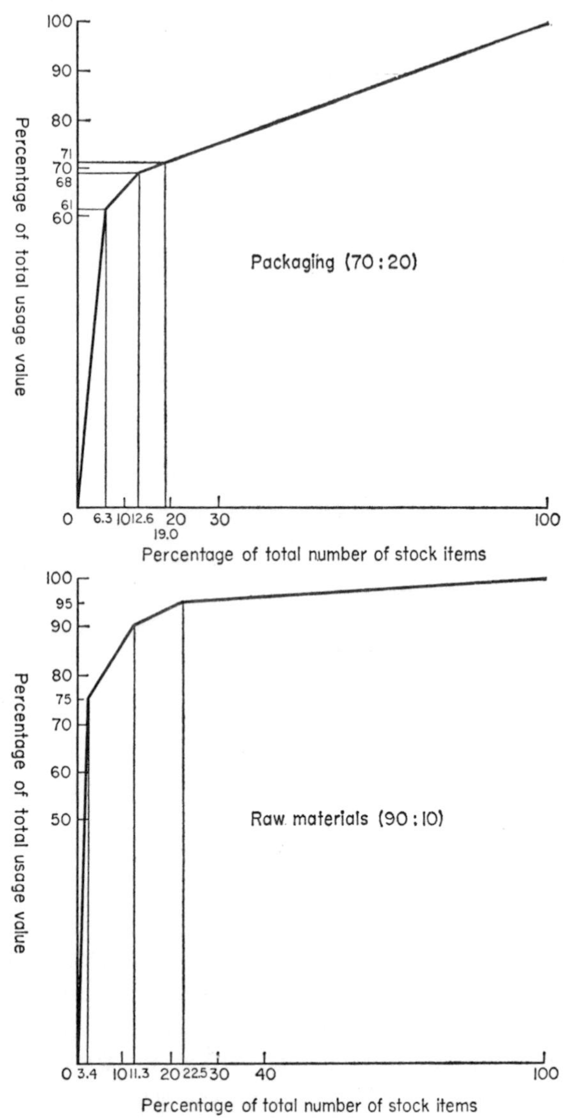

FIGURE 27:2 TYPICAL FOOD INDUSTRY USAGE VALUE CURVES

Value analysis

When analytical thought is applied to purchases the first thing to come under the spotlight is the specification. Purchase department staff should be encouraged to seek out alternative ways to do the job and to supplement their own company's design talent with the often very considerable specialised know-how of suppliers. The savings which can be made by finding a cheaper source for a given specification are often trifling in comparison with those which can be made by finding a better specification.

Design engineers have complicated choices to make in drawing up specifications and having made them they go away and get on with a different design job. Purchasing and production people continue to work with those specifications, perhaps for many years, during which experience or inspiration may suggest better ideas. And apart from that, the options change: relative prices of substitute materials alter, new materials appear on the market. A systematic way to tackle this was first developed in General Electric's corporate purchase department in the United States in the 1940s. L D Miles called it *value analysis*. Essentially this makes use of an inter-departmental task force or team to optimise the specification – and also perhaps the method and the source – in the light of today's options. Very sizeable savings have been made by the value analysis methods which are described in Chapter 23.

Sourcing

Probably the buyer's most important job is to find suppliers who can reliably meet quality requirements and deliver regularly on time, and to agree with them suitable terms, conditions and prices.

Of course, for some purchases there is no choice of supplier, either for technical reasons or because a monopoly situation exists. For other purchases there is a choice but it is not of crucial importance. Which supplier is selected for small tools, stationery, and such incidentals is hardly a life-or-death decision. Buyers try to make arrangements which produce the required goods dependably, with the least fuss, at the lowest cost. Things run more smoothly when they are successful.

This leaves an area in which the buyer's skill can be very important, in shopping round for the best supplier (rather than the best price) and in negotiating suitable supply arrangements with him. Buyers are making much more use of background information than used to be the case. At least one purchase department has added a market research man to its staff, to sift, collate and organise published and other information about some of its supply markets. Economists are sometimes employed to study and collate official statistics and economic trends relevant to major purchases.

Many purchase departments now study balance sheets and annual reports from their main suppliers. These are now publicly available at the Companies Registry for all limited companies, not just public and non-exempt private companies. A very high rate of reported profit on sales would, of course, be a useful negotiating counter when discussing price, but low or non-existent profits are a danger sign indicating a threat to continuity of supply.

The high incidence of strikes is another threat. One large motorcar manufacturer has a group of four people attached to the purchasing director's office, who have personal contact with union officials in supply industries; they also get information from the embassies, have contact with trade secretaries, and read newspapers and magazines. If they think – and this is something based on feeling, not on figures – that an industry is likely to be in trouble, then they contract their operations, try to bring home their safety stock, or at least get it outside the supplier. Smaller purchase departments set up similar early warning systems through their firm's personnel department.

Supplier evaluation

One technique which has been much discussed as a sourcing aid is called *supplier evaluation* in English, and *vendor rating* in American. It consists of the compilation of numerical scores or performance indexes for regular suppliers of certain types of components and material.

In one of the numerous systems which have been tried, four ratings are calculated: one for quality, one for delivery, and two for price. The *delivery* rating is calculated by scoring each delivery on the following scale:

1 Delivered within two weeks of due date: score 100
2 Delivered within three weeks: score 90
and so on, down to eight weeks early or late, score 25; more than eight weeks, score 0.

The *quality* rating is calculated as:

$$\frac{60 \text{ (Number of batches accepted)}}{\text{Number of batches delivered}} + \frac{40 \text{ (number of components accepted)}}{\text{number of components delivered}}$$

One of the two price ratings is price charged as a percentage of the budgeted standard cost; the other is cost predicted one year ahead as a percentage of standard cost.

These figures can be calculated manually but the system seems to be adopted more frequently when the calculations can be done by computer. A typical computer print-out is shown in Figure 27:3.

WEEK 7106	DATE 11 FEB 71		PURCHASING REPORT	
Vendor code	Quality rating %	Delivery rating %	Price rating 1 %	Price rating 2 %
008	100	100	99	0
015	100	57	107	0
020	100	100	83	0
035	100	91	92	100
049	100	41	193	102
068	100	50	100	0

FIGURE 27:3 SUPPLIER EVALUATION

Example of information produced by computer analysis of suppliers' performance

In many supplier evaluation schemes, the separate scores for delivery, quality and price are weighted and combined to give an overall figure: for instance, forty per cent of the delivery rating plus thirty per cent of the quality rating plus thirty per cent of the price rating. This single figure is a kind of measure of supplier worth, which reflects the relative importance attached by the purchasing firm to the factors measured. It is communicated to the buyer concerned and to the supplier concerned. It is claimed that the work involved in compiling these ratings is justified by better motivation, more accurate information readily available, better performance measures and, eventually, better performance by suppliers.

The systems so far reported leave a lot to be desired. Either some better way of compiling the scores than has yet been devised, or else some different way to record and evaluate performance, is needed.

Systems contracting

The terms *systems contracting* and *blanket orders* refer to a number of useful methods of grouping together, either numbers of different item requirements from one source, or else a sequence of requirements of one item over a substantial period of time, say, six months or a year. Instead of treating each order, or requisition, as an independent closed transaction, the idea is to look at the flow of requirements over a time and buy the flow. Instead of taking a bucket to the well every day, a waterpipe is laid on.

For example, a small or intermediate value purchase is carbon paper. Instead of placing a series of orders every month or so for the various sizes and grades required, with this technique once a year there is a review of requirements, alternative specifications and sources. Twelve months' requirements are then covered with just one or two orders which specify so many reams of A4 standard weight, so many reams of lightweight, etc., to be delivered each month. If stocks start to build up or fall short during the year, one or two adjustments may be required. Apart from that, supplies come through autom-matically; and the price, based on a twelve-month contract, is low.

A group one or two production purchase may not seem at first glance amenable to this approach if production programmes are not fixed twelve months in advance. There will usually be a sales forecast going at least a year ahead, and a firm production programme going only one or two months ahead.

The solution then may be to approach management to authorise purchasing to make firm commitments for fifty per cent of the sales estimate for the year, thus getting the benefit of a lower price and also the benefit of a bank stock of finished parts to handle cyclical fluctuations. In one actual case, component X was being bought in lots of 1,000 approximately at a price of 26p a piece. It was built into a product with a current sales estimate of 12,000 a year. Contracting for fifty per cent of this, that is 6,000 pieces, with delivery called off at 1,000 a month, enabled the buyers to bring the price down to 20p, a twenty-three per cent reduction in invoice cost, with further reductions in administrative costs and paperwork. Both cost and availability are improved, and if sales fall short of forecast, it may well take nine or twelve months instead of six months to clear the components but they would still be used up within the year. This is a useful technique for plastic mouldings, castings, electrical and mechanical parts.

Small order procedures

Wherever possible the small orders should be put through a special procedure. If they are repeating or regular requirements they should be bought once a year in one lot, or perhaps twice a year: it is obviously uneconomic to expend £5 worth of man-hours, cheques, stamps and paperwork in procuring an item with a usage value of only £5 a year, but it happens. Non-repeating small orders are often such things as maintenance requirements, design and development prototypes, laboratory requirements. The requisitioner knows exactly what he wants and where to get it and the price is often a listed price. One solution to this problem is the order/requisition/cheque form devised by Kaiser Aluminium in the United States, and adopted by other organisations, including one in the public service. Through clever forms design, the same document which the requisitioner prepares as a requisition serves as an order, and a blank cheque accompanying it (marked 'not valid above £X') cuts out the invoicing/purchase-ledger/payments procedure.

Other approaches to the small order problem include: local cash purchase – a man with a bag of cash goes round in a van picking up requirements and paying for them as he goes; and laundry list – the local stockholder calls once a week and delivers a wide range of sundry materials against a laundry list type of order: invoices come through once a month and prices are negotiated annually.

Negotiation

The most useful aid to better negotiating is thorough preparation. This involves getting the facts, defining the objectives, and planning the discussion. Relevant facts are: what alternatives are there to this material and this supplier?

Make-or-buy studies show the cost and feasibility of one alternative to the outside supplier. Price analysis, a detailed cost-estimating process applied to the outside purchase, shows what it ought to cost on a factual basis. In defining objectives it is advisable to think about the other party's objectives too; the negotiator who is prepared to give something away, preferably some point which is worth more to the other side than it is to him, is well placed to insist on something in return. He is in a much better position than the ill-prepared negotiator whose only objective is to concede nothing and grab all he can. In planning the discussion, a friendly and cooperative opening session is advisable, followed by systematic consideration one-by-one of the points at issue, and finishing with a summary of what has been agreed. To avoid misunderstanding this should be confirmed promptly in writing.

All this is common-sense, yet in practice, because of time pressure, it is often neglected. Another common-sense point is that money should not be wasted by dragging out negotiations and the associated fact-finding exercises to a greater length than is justified by the amount of money at issue.

Stock control and ABC analysis

As stated earlier, Pareto curves can also be applied to stock control. The idea is simple, yet effective, and helps to ensure that management effort is applied in proportion to the importance of the item or group of items.

The curve shown in Figure 27:4 illustrates an application related to stock management. In a typical store ten per cent of the number of items which are stocked will account for about sixty to eighty per cent of the total value of the items held. Conversely, fifty to seventy per cent of the number of items will be worth together only five to ten per cent of the value.

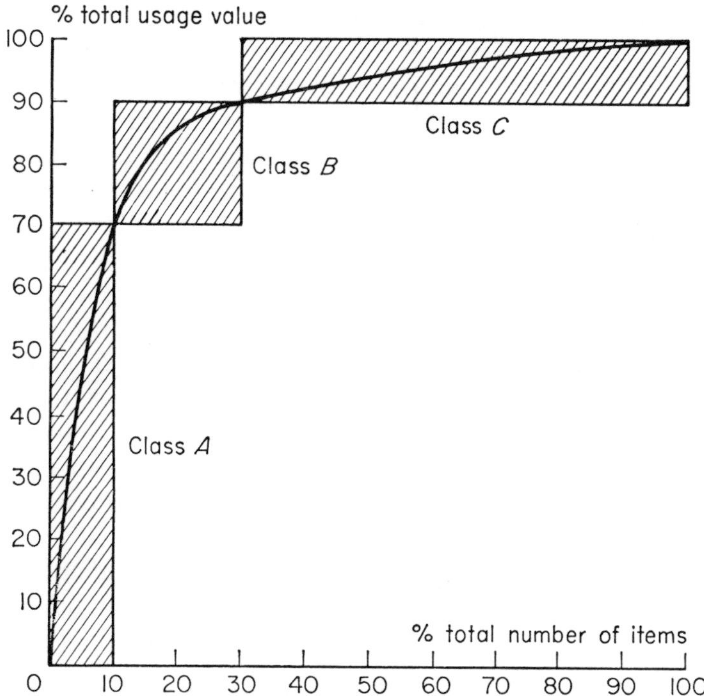

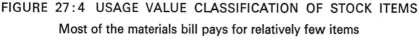

FIGURE 27:4 USAGE VALUE CLASSIFICATION OF STOCK ITEMS

Most of the materials bill pays for relatively few items

By applying this piece of data to particular situations consultants have netted many thousands of pounds for themselves. Yet it is an idea which most managers could themselves use to great effect.

Analysing usage values

Most companies have stock-lists, prepared for a variety of reasons even if only to satisfy the auditors. The long way to find out about specific usage value is to take this list as a starting point. It will show the quantity in stock, the unit price and probably an extension of the total value calculation in the case of each item. For the moment one can forget about the number in stock. What is needed, in addition to the unit price, is the annual usage quantity for each item (this can be estimated from the relevant stock or bin card). Then multiply the item cost by the annual usage to get annual usage value. One then has a list probably giving the part number, annual usage quantity, unit cost and annual usage value. The list should next be shuffled to give the biggest value at the top and the smallest at the bottom.

Instead of re-arranging into a complete list of all items in usage value order, the range can be split into between seven to ten usage bands from which one can establish how many items fall within each band. Finally, the list is summarised to give a short-list of three groups with about one tenth of the items in group A, one fifth in group B and the rest in the C group.

Naturally, this process requires a great many calculations. Where this is not feasible or desirable it is possible to make an approximation of the position by a number of short-cut methods. One useful idea is to take the average usage value and multiply by six to get the boundary between class A and class B. The boundary between class B and C is taken as half the average usage value. (The average usage value can be obtained by dividing the total number of items into the total usage value per annum.) While this quick method is a good approximation in many cases it may be necessary to refine it in the light of subsequent experience, but it would be a good starting point.

Applying the ABC principle

Having got this list it can now be used to achieve improvements in inventory control. Here are some fertile areas:

Stock-turn (and thus return on investment) Concentrate on A items. Examine the possibility of more frequent deliveries. This can reduce the average stock and thus the amount of money tied up.

Service. Since C items represent a small part of the total value, one can afford to keep larger stocks of them. This will reduce the chance of shortages (stock-outs, as the jargon has it); minimise the amount of management effort needed for that group and allow more time to control the A and B items effectively.

Systems. The control systems which one uses can be tailored to emphasise management of the big value items.

Stocktaking. The remarks on control affect stocktaking. Apart from keeping the factory supplied and satisfying the auditors, stocktaking can be a key part of the cost-control system. The C items can be looked after by some simple method like the 'two bin system'. Here the reserve number of items are tied up in a bag, or in a separate bin. While the seal is unbroken one knows how many are there, while the bulk amount can be kept in a bin with 'amount lines' marked on the sides. As and Bs can then be controlled by installing a perpetual inventory system (like painting the Forth Bridge, starting at one end working one's way to the other, then starting again). One can also refine this so that the A items are checked twice as often as the Bs, etc.

Stores layout

Fast moving items nearest the issue points and small value items in 'open store' near the assembly or production units. Issues being made in bulk to the particular section.

The EOQ formula

One needs to decide how much of each item to order at any one time. The EOQ (economic order quantity) formula was devised for this purpose. By using this it is possible to find the optimum value of that order – the one which minimises the total of the various costs involved. The formula is given in various forms of $Q=k\sqrt{A}$ where Q is the value of the order – the order quantity in monetary not physical units, k is the policy variable which takes care of the balance between frequent orders and high stocks and A is the annual usage value – the annual usage quantity in monetary units not physical quantity.

Obviously, it is not efficient to order low usage value items (the Cs) as frequently as those which have high usage value; this formula helps the manager to strike the right balance.

To make this calculation for each stock item would be tedious; thus, where computers or calculating machines are not available, guideline tables such as that illustrated in Figure 27:5 can be used with effect. Where computers are in use, the matter is simplified for the manager. This is particularly true where one of the many packages are in use, most of which are based on some version of this formula.

Expediting

It would never be necessary to progress purchase orders if we always selected the right supplier, if production planning were perfect, if

TABLE OF ECONOMIC ORDERING QUANTITIES

Based on cost of placing an order — £0.30

Cost of holding stock — 15%

	Units	Unit price																				Units	
		2½p	5p	7½p	10p	15p	20p	25p	30p	35p	40p	45p	50p	75p	£1	£1.50	£2	£3	£4	£5	£10	£20		
M	¼	3	3	3	3	3	3	3	3	3	3	3	3	3	3	3	2	2	2	1	1	1	3	A
O	½	6	6	6	6	6	6	6	6	6	6	6	6	6	5	4	3	3	2	2	1	1	6	N
N	¾	9	9	9	9	9	9	9	9	9	9	9	8	7	6	5	4	3	3	3	2	1	9	N
T	1	12	12	12	12	12	12	12	12	12	11	10	10	8	7	6	5	4	3	3	2	1	12	U
H	2	24	24	24	24	24	22	20	18	17	15	15	14	11	10	8	7	6	5	4	3	2	24	A
L	3	36	36	36	36	31	27	24	22	20	19	18	17	14	12	10	8	7	6	5	4	3	36	L
Y	4	48	48	48	44	36	31	28	25	23	22	21	20	16	14	11	10	8	7	6	4	3	48	
	5	60	60	57	49	40	35	31	28	26	24	23	22	18	15	13	11	9	8	7	5	3	60	
	6	72	72	62	54	44	38	34	31	29	27	25	24	20	17	14	12	10	8	8	5	4	72	
C	7	84	82	67	58	47	41	37	33	31	29	27	26	21	18	15	13	11	9	8	6	4	84	C
O	8	96	88	72	62	51	44	39	36	33	31	29	28	23	20	16	14	11	10	9	6	4	96	O
N	9	108	92	76	66	54	46	42	38	35	33	31	29	24	21	17	15	12	10	9	7	5	108	N
S	10	120	98	80	69	57	49	44	40	37	35	33	31	25	22	18	15	13	11	10	7	5	120	S
U	15	170	120	98	85	69	60	54	49	45	42	40	38	31	27	22	19	15	13	12	8	6	180	U
M	20	200	140	110	98	80	69	62	57	52	49	46	44	36	31	25	22	18	15	14	10	7	240	M
P	30	240	170	140	120	98	85	76	69	64	60	57	54	44	38	31	27	22	19	17	12	8	360	P
T	40	280	200	160	140	110	100	88	80	74	69	65	62	51	44	36	31	25	22	20	14	10	480	T
I	50	310	220	180	150	130	110	98	89	83	77	73	69	57	49	40	35	28	24	22	15	12	600	I
O	100	440	310	250	220	180	160	140	130	120	110	100	98	80	69	57	49	40	35	31	25	25	1200	O
N	200	620	440	360	310	250	220	200	180	160	150	150	140	110	98	80	69	57	50	40	50	50	2400	N

Ordering quantity represents over 1 year's consumption (hatched)

Ordering quantity represents under 1 year's consumption (dotted)

FIGURE 27:5 EOQ TABLE

engineering changes were infrequent, or allowed ample time for changeover, if inventory systems of both supplier and buyer were adequate, and full contract information were given to the supplier in time to dovetail with his own production planning.

It is because no system is perfect that controls exist. Apart from one's own deficiencies one has suppliers who are less than perfect. Few readers would find difficulty in naming at least two or three companies whose name they shudder to see on a bill of materials.

Analysis of the performance of various suppliers will show that a relatively small group causes most of the difficulties. Some companies have the idea that orders are 'progressed' by sending printed cards or duplicate letters to all suppliers on a blanket basis. As in all management, effort should be concentrated where it is likely to get the best return.

Perhaps the most difficult expediting situation arises when individual items are bought against the company's own specification. With larger and more complex items it is often not easy to calculate a reliable production date and difficulties result for a variety of reasons. These include mis-communication, mis-management and genuine error, as well as those already listed. Very often the contracts are obtained by the supplier many months after he has quoted for the job. Clearly, prior to accepting the order he ought to ensure that, among other things;

1 He has the necessary materials or components in stock
2 Outside sources can still meet his needs for items which he does not carry himself (including sub-contractors)
3 His own capacity is still available as estimated
4 The production time included in his estimate is reasonable in current conditions
5 He is in possession of full information from the buying company

Some purchasing departments send off their orders to a supplier based upon a quotation they originally received, without checking if any of the circumstances have changed. When delivery is critical to the buying company it is important that this check is made *prior* to placing the order.

Progressing this type of order once it has been placed can then be organised in line with the various stages of production. For example:

1 At the date when tool or jig designs are to be ready
2 When the items from these designs should be available
3 When materials or components should be marshalled for production
4 When the various stages of production can be achieved
5 When final assembly and testing will be completed

Often critical areas may be isolated in this progressing for special attention. For example, special castings with long delivery times could be delivered to suppliers and then be rejected because of their porosity. In consequence, some companies extend their progressing activities in such cases to include secondary suppliers.

Methods which can be applied to help ensure that more general orders are controlled – chased when they ought to be – include:

1 Copy orders filed in date-due order, being actioned, say, one week before that date in general, or as necessary in the particular case.
2 Five divisions made at the top of the copy order numbered one to five (representing weeks in any month). A signal of a different colour is then allocated to each month and one is attached to the relevant square in the particular case. (Thus if January were red and the item were due in week three of that month, a red signal would be placed on square three.) The order copies are then filed in alphabetical order by supplier.
3 A diary system with the serial numbers of orders which are due being entered on the approporiate page of the diary.

Whichever method is used, it is useful to have a record of progressing action. One sound idea is to have a panel printed at the back of the order form in which the date of progressing, reply and subsequent action taken can be entered.

It is worth remembering that expediting can be an important part of management control and care should be taken to select the right man for the job. Good relationships with suppliers can often succeed in this work where the big whip might fail.

Materials handling equipment and techniques

Particularly in mass-production situations, effective materials handling can increase efficiency and reduce cost. Much effort has been given to developing systems and equipment and a large supplying industry exists in this area today where little or nothing was in being before the Second World War.

At the heart of most handling schemes is the *pallet*. This is either a rectangular platform with access slots for the forks of lifting equipment, or a container of some kind built on top of that platform. It allows unit loads of materials or components to be assembled at one point, say, the supplier, and transported intact for off-loading as a unit at the other end. This saves time both at dispatch and receiving ends, minimises manhandling, obviates individual packing in some instances and reduces the risk of damage.

They are frequently delivered direct to the production line and components are taken from the pallet by the operator. They can also be used as storage containers making good use of air space (sometimes stacked five and six high), and facilitate stock control. There are many types, ranging from simple wooden deck varieties to highly complex metal units with specially designed inserts to carry components. They can be two-way entry (the forks can only enter from two sides of the rectangle) or four-way entry.

Pallets are used mainly in conjunction with *fork-lift trucks*. Once again there is a considerable variety of types and sizes available. The basic type has forks mounted at the front which move up and down on a mast formed by two channels. The forks are inserted in the access slots of the pallet and then move up the mast lifting the pallet clear of the deck. The truck is then driven to the point where the loaded pallet is required and the forks are lowered to the level of the receiving deck before being withdrawn to leave the pallet in place.

Specially designed attachments can be fitted to many trucks enabling them to be used for such things as coil and barrel handling. Special designs of truck have also been developed to handle items in confined spaces and at great heights. These are very useful in stores where space is at a premium. Among other special developments is the side-lifter. Here the mast and forks are mounted on the side of the vehicle, often in the centre. These machines, frequently heavy duty and of large dimension, are used for moving such things as timber and heavy pipes.

Among the wide variety of other handling equipment, *tow trucks* and *platform trolleys* are commonly used for distributing materials on large sites. *Tractors* with special attachments, *cranes* with similar equipment and a wide variety of *conveyors* may be seen in many places.

Basically, modern handling equipment is designed to minimise man-handling. This is not only to make the lot of the worker safer and less arduous but, among other things, to save time, reduce man-power, reduce breakage and ease capital tie up.

In certain cases more complex systems involving computerised stores can be used towards this end. Typically, a computer is used to control the assembly of loads made up of specified items. Automatically a robot fork-lift selects the necessary items from racking and assembles the load ready for dispatch. This type of system has been used effectively with such things as paint and groceries.

Other types of handling systems more commonly in use include *dry tankers*. Here a powdered material is pumped into a road or rail container and pumped out again into some form of static container on arrival at the buyer's works. This obviates individual packing in drums and sacks, palletising sheeting, etc., and also speeds loading and unloading while helping to avoid contamination. Liquids are dealt with in a similar way and a variant of the same idea involves the supplier using articulated vehicles or specially designed lorries and leaving one container (mobile or static) with the buyer to be replaced when empty.

As with other areas of materials management which have been touched on in this section, only a brief idea of applications and systems could be given. In closing it is emphasised that, when items are moved or handled, cost is added, but never value. Consequently, one should try to avoid moving items any more than is absolutely necessary; when they have to be moved, the most suitable method to meet the particular need should be used.

Chapter 28

Work Study

B D Speed, Management Consultant, Management Economics Division, PERA

Work study is defined in British Standard 3138 as a generic term for those techniques, particularly method study and work measurement, which are used in the examination of human work in all its contexts, and which lead systematically to the investigation of all factors which affect the efficiency and economy of the situation being reviewed, in order to effect improvement. The terms method study and work measurement in themselves embrace a large number of techniques which are continually being developed and expanded to meet special problems. In all situations their application involves human work and the problem of introducing change. This chapter deals with some of these techniques and their application to engineering production.

Purpose of work study

A prime objective of management is to secure the most effective use of plant, materials and labour. Work study provides the means in both a specific and a general way. By critical examination and the development of an improved method, for example, a production bottleneck may be removed. Move generally, the provision of reliable time standards for manufacturing processes facilitates better production planning and cost control.

One of the main purposes of work study is to establish accurate times for operations and processes. These are used for:

1 Standard costing and budgetary control, based on machine-hour rates and labour-hour rates
2 Production planning, machine loading and scheduling
3 Incentive payment systems which require a relatively high degree of accuracy
4 Manpower budgeting and labour control

Providing the frame-work of control through time is certainly important. The value of work study is also considerable in the sense of organised cost reduction where, by applying method study, value analysis and other techniques based on the general philosophy of critical examination, it can improve material flow, reduce operation times, eliminate waste, improve quality and generally make a useful contribution in the field of production management.

Work study techniques—method study

The scope of work study is wide and as new areas of work are studied, new techniques emerge. In the early days of work study, the techniques fell into two main and related categories; method study and work measurement. The division is still relevant today, though there are techniques which fall into both categories. A third technique is job evaluation but this is not described in this section.

Method study involves the systematic recording and critical examination of existing and proposed methods of doing work and subsequently evolving improvements in these, or sometimes their elimination. This can lead to an improvement in:

1 Plant and work-place layout
2 The use of materials equipment and manpower
3 Product design
4 Working procedures and effectiveness

A number of techniques are used in method investigations but all depend upon the same approach, contained in the following six steps which are the foundation of method study.

Select the problem to be investigated. There is always room for improvement but some problems are uneconomic to solve if, for example, the activity is only temporary, or it is thought that considerable capital investment may be needed at a time when capital is restricted. Often, however, the existence of a problem ensures its selection.

Record all facts relating to the problem (only after critical examination will any irrelevant information be discovered).

Examine the facts critically and systematically at every stage in the operation. For example: What is achieved? Why is it necessary? How is it done? Why is it done that way?

Develop the improved method. It may not be the best but it should be the most practical and economical, having regard to the circumstances.

Install the accepted method and ensure that it is adopted as the standard practice.

Maintain the method by routine checks to see that it remains within the specified standard.

Recording techniques

Depending upon the nature of the work which is going to be studied the technique will either be a chart or a diagram, although, occasionally, a three dimensional model may be used. Charts are used to record the stages in a process, sometimes with the refinement of time and distance for each stage. Diagrams are used to record movement of men, materials or equipment.

The construction and interpretation of charts, collectively called process charts, is simplified by the use of a symbolic short-hand which divides the task into five functions, illustrated in Figure 28:1.

Flow process charts

A typical flow process chart is shown in Figure 28:2, which illustrates the use of the ASME symbols. The work study engineer has used a pre-printed sheet with the symbols, columns for distance, time, etc.

Symbol	Meaning	Example
○	Operation	Dismantle valve
⇨	Transport	Take valve to workshop
□	Inspection	Examine spindle for wear
D	Delay	Awaiting spares
▽	Storage	Finished valve in stock

FIGURE 28:1 PROCESS CHARTING SYMBOLS

The most commonly used symbols are those shown above known as ASME, adopted by the American Society of Mechanical Engineers

It will be noticed that there is space for comments about the various stages of the process to be used during the critical examination. Alternatively the symbols can be drawn, in the sequence which they represent, on plain paper. This is known as an outline process chart, using only the operation and inspection symbols, and is frequently employed to give an overall view of a process, rather than a detailed study.

Two-handed process charts

Where work is confined to one place, such as a machine-tool or work-bench, it may be worth studying the task in detail. The two-handed process chart is used for this purpose with the ASME symbols, except the inspection symbol, and the triangle means hold instead of storage. The chart will show the present method in detail and indicate

FLOW PROCESS CHART

No. 5
Page 1 of 1

SUMMARY

SYMBOLS	Present		Proposed		Difference	
	No.	Time	No.	Time	No.	Time
O OPERATIONS	4					
□ INSPECTIONS	1					
⇨ TRANSPORTATIONS	9					
D DELAYS	4	960				
▽ STORAGES						
DISTANCE TRAVELLED	10 275 Ft.		Ft.		Ft.	

JOB BOILER ANNUAL OVERHAUL

□ MAN OR ☑ MAT'L. HOPKINSON 6" VALVE

CHART BEGINS VALVE ISOLATED IN SITU

CHART ENDS VALVE ON BOILER

CHARTED BY B D S DATE 4. 4. 70

DETAILS OF (Present / ~~Proposed~~) METHOD	SYMBOLS	Distance - Feet	Time - Minutes	ANALYSIS What?	Where?	When?	Who?	How?	NOTES	ACTION Eliminate	Combine	Change Seq.	Simplify
1 Remove valve from boiler	O □ ⇨ D ▽								Block and tackle (190 lb)				
2 To workshop	O □ ⇨ D ▽	90							Sack truck				
3 External clean	O □ ⇨ D ▽												
4 Await lorry	O □ ⇨ D ▽		60										
5 Load on to lorry	O □ ⇨ D ▽	20							3 men				
6 To central workshops	O □ ⇨ D ▽	5000											
7 Unload valve	O □ ⇨ D ▽	15							Crane				
8 Valve to fitter	O □ ⇨ D ▽	15											
9 Overhaul	O □ ⇨ D ▽												
10 Await tester	O □ ⇨ D ▽		145										
11 Test and inspect	O □ ⇨ D ▽												
12 Await lorry	O □ ⇨ D ▽		660						6·30 a.m. next day				
13 Load to lorry	O □ ⇨ D ▽	25							Crane				
14 To Boiler-house	O □ ⇨ D ▽	5000											
15 Unload valve	O □ ⇨ D ▽	20							3 men				
16 Await fitter	O □ ⇨ D ▽		95										
17 Valve to boiler	O □ ⇨ D ▽	90											
18 Refit valve	O □ ⇨ D ▽												
19	O □ ⇨ D ▽												
20	O □ ⇨ D ▽												
21	O □ ⇨ D ▽												
22	O □ ⇨ D ▽												
23	O □ ⇨ D ▽												

FIGURE 28:2 FLOW PROCESS CHART

A typical flow process chart illustrating the use of the ASME symbols

how an improved layout can reduce delays and ineffective time, long movements, and the like.

Flow diagrams

The flow diagram is a type of flow process chart but uses a scale diagram or plan of the area under consideration, and then shows the path of movement of the material or product being studied. The ASME symbols may be used to indicate what happens at each major point, with numbers for reference to a brief description of the activity.

This type of chart is more effective when making a presentation of existing and proposed methods to management or employees, even though several flow process charts may have been compiled during the study.

Multiple activity charts

The multiple activity chart is used where it is necessary to examine the activities of one subject relative to others. By allotting separate bars to represent the activities of, say, different operators against a common time-scale, the chart shows periods of ineffective time on the part of any of the subjects very clearly. The chart can then be studied and the activities rearranged to reduce the ineffective time. An example is given in Figure 28 : 3.

This technique is most useful in organising teams of operators on mass-production, or on maintenance where several trades are involved in a major overhaul of one piece of equipment. It can also be used to determine the number of machines which an operator should look after.

String diagrams

A string diagram is a scale diagram of an area on which is plotted the movement path and distance of the subject under investigation. Thread is used to plot the movement as this has the advantage of giving the distance to scale. A concentration of thread between points indicates several movements, with pins serving the purpose of both locating the thread and identifying the points.

As an example, one may consider the older type of grocer's shop

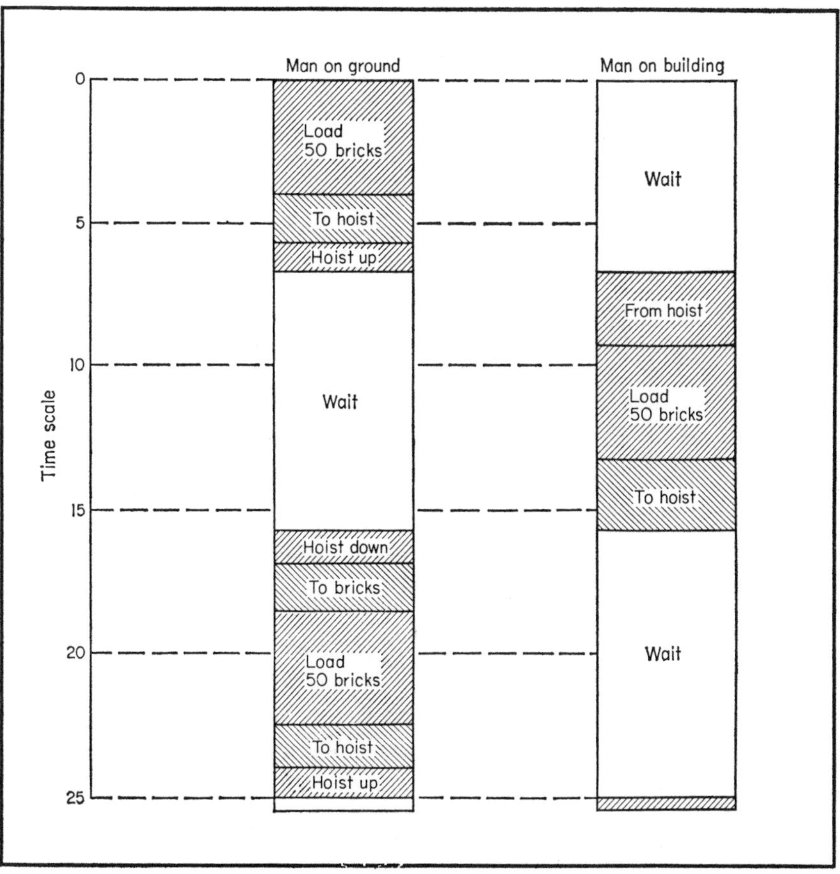

FIGURE 28:3 MULTIPLE ACTIVITY CHART

The chart shows two labourers employed to raise bricks from ground level to the second floor of a building, with one barrow and a manually-operated hoist

with two counters, one down each side, a storeroom at the back and one cash register. If one assistant is studied, a string diagram of movement would look similar to that shown in Figure 28:4. By comparison, in a modern self-service shop, the check-out girl remains stationary at a cash register while the customer does the travelling!

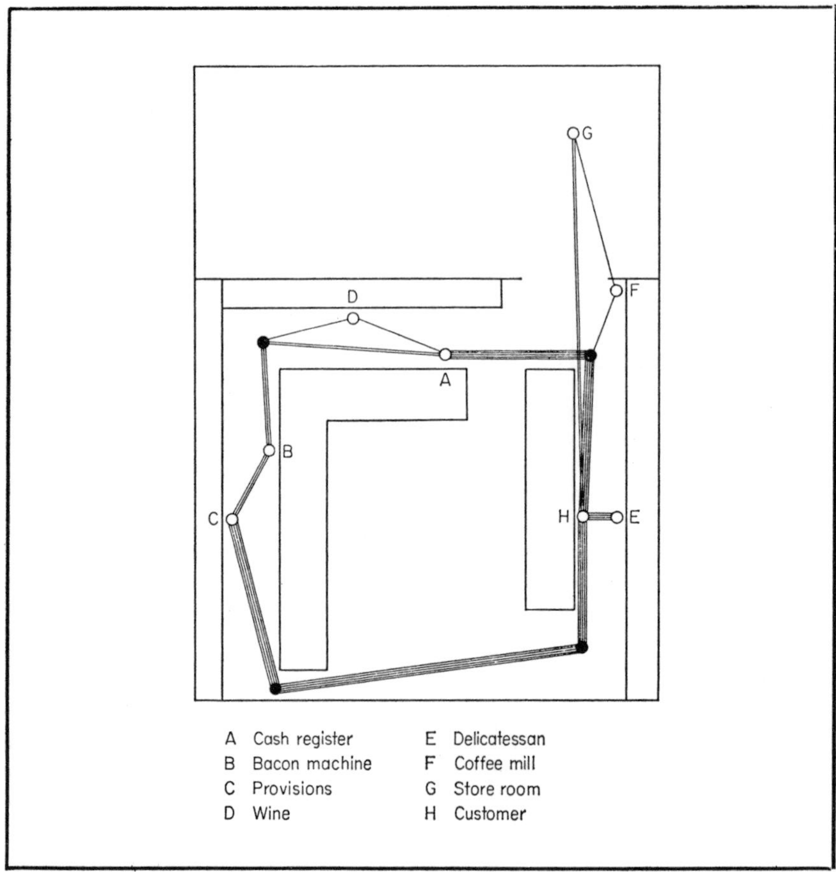

FIGURE 28:4 STRING DIAGRAM

The diagram shows the movement of an assistant in a grocer's shop during one hour

Work study techniques—work measurement

At the beginning of this chapter the importance of reliable time standards was stressed, and the techniques now described represent some of those most commonly used to obtain time standards. The degree of accuracy obtained depends upon the technique used although, by virtue of their disciplines, they are usually more accurate than estimated data. However, absolute accuracy is of less importance than consistency and the techniques outlined below give consistent results in practice.

Two rules should be borne in mind. Firstly, the technique most suitable for the work being measured should be used; this may result in more than one technique being applied to one task. Secondly, the time data collected should be stored in a manner such that maximum use can be gained from it, that is, information common to several jobs needs to be collected only once.

These rules apply whether or not the work is repetitive. *Time study, predetermined motion-time systems* (*PMTS*) and *synthesis* are the techniques most often used to measure repetitive jobs. Non-repetitive work is most often measured by *analytical estimating*, some second order *PMTS*, or *comparative estimating*. This latter class of work is more difficult to measure and, regrettably, it is often left untouched for this reason.

Time study

The most straightforward way to obtain a job time is by direct observation. For this reason time study is the basic measurement technique. It is most commonly used for, and best suited to, the measurement of repetitive work. When properly conducted the disciplines of time study ensure that the results are both accurate and consistent. Good time study practice follows the steps set out below.

A clear record of all facts relevant to the job, the operator and the surrounding conditions is obtained. The time study sheet should be designed to facilitate the recording of these facts, for example:

1 Department
2 Operation
3 Machine number and type
4 Operator's name and clock number
5 Part description and part number
6 Machine feeds and speeds used
7 A sketch of the workplace layout
8 Description of working conditions

By observation of several cycles of the task a concise record of the method used must be set down on the study sheet. It is often

TIME STUDY OBSERVATION SHEET	Date 18.9.70
Occasional elements	Sheet number 016/097

Element reference		1	2	3	4	5	6	7	8	9	10	Total OT	BT	OCC	Sel BT
PU LOAD CLOSE GUARD START	R	100	100	110	100										
	OT	·23	·23	·20	·22							·88			
	BT	·23	·23	·22	·22								·90	4	·222
1ST CUT S.566 F.O.012	R	100	100	100	100										
	OT	·88	·88	·88	·88							3·52			
	BT	·88	·88	·88	·88								3·52	4	·880
ROTATE AND RETURN	R	100	100	100	100										
	OT	·08	·08	·08	·08							·32			
	BT	·08	·08	·08	·08								·32	4	·080
2ND CUT S.566 F.O.012	R	100	100	100	100										
	OT	2·25	2·26	2·26	2·26							9·03			
	BT	2·25	2·26	2·26	2·26								9·03	4	2·257
ROTATE AND RETURN	R	100	100	100	100										
	OT	·10	·10	·10	·10							·40			
	BT	·10	·10	·10	·10								·40	4	·100
3RD CUT S.1450 F.O.012	R	100	100	100	100										
	OT	·80	·80	·80	·80							3·20			
	BT	·80	·80	·80	·80								3·2	4	·800
RETURN TO STOP	R		100	100	100										
	OT		·05	·06	·05							·16			
	BT		·05	·06	·05								·16	3	·052
GUAGE 2 DIA'S	R		100	110	110										
	OT	·47	·30	·18	·18							1·13			
	BT		·30	·20	·20								·70	3	·233
ASIDE SHAFT	R	100	90	110	110										
	OT	·09	·21	·08	·08							·46			
	BT	·09	·18	·09	·09								·45	4	·112

Department MACHINE SHOP	Time check		19·10 4·736
Operation COPY TURN N D E	Time finished 4·36		= lead in 2·75
05 - 043/3 LC 24 C SHAFT	Time started 4·06		= lead out 8·10
Operator J PALMER	Elapsed time	=30·00	= OCC element
Observer A TAYLOR	Total OT = 29·95		
MACHINE : B S A COPY LATHE	Timing error ·05 = ·16 %		

FIGURE 28:5 TYPICAL TIME STUDY OBSERVATION SHEET

appropriate that the method should have been subjected to method study, and improved before timing takes place, but this is not always possible or even desirable. The method record is made in 'elements,' defined as distinct parts of the task selected for convenience of observation, measurement and analysis. As a general principle, the machine controlled parts of the task should be kept separate from the manual parts, a typical task breaking down into seven handling elements and four machine elements, for example (see Figure 28 : 5).

The next step is the measurement. With the method broken down into elements, the time for each element is recorded, normally with a stop-watch, over several cycles of the task. The actual number of cycles required will depend upon:

1 The desired level of accuracy
2 The amount of variation encountered in the elements, caused for example by the variations in raw materials
3 The incidence of occasional elements in the job, such as replenishing a spool of wire or waiting for lifting equipment

All ineffective time, or time unrelated to the task, such as discussing with a supervisor, must be recorded separately for exclusion during analysis.

At the same time as this element time is recorded an assessment of the operator performance is required, termed 'rating'. Throughout the course of the working day the pace and effectiveness of an operator will vary, and similarly between different operators on the same tasks. It is not therefore sufficient to time several cycles of a task and take an average time as the standard. Some factor needs to be applied to that time, to relate it to a norm, thereby eliminating the variable nature of the operators' applied performance. A considerable proportion of time study training is spent learning to recognise this norm or standard rate of working, which is normally designated '100', and corresponds to 60 standard minutes of work in one hour. Thus, if the observed performance appears less than the standard a lower 'rating' is given, say, 90 or 95. Conversely, a higher pace and effort would be rated at, say, 120. The rating is applied to each element and therefore takes account of variations at all times during observation.

When the study is complete, the observed times for all elements and for the task as a whole, must be converted into basic times. The basic time is the time that the task or element would take at standard rating (100), and is calculated as follows:

$$\frac{\text{Observed Time} \times \text{Observed Rating}}{\text{Standard Rating}}$$

For example, an element which took 0.30 minutes and was rated at 90 would have a basic time of:

$$\frac{0.30 \times 90}{100} = 0.27 \text{ minutes.}$$

The basic time is important because it will have the same value irrespective of the operator who was observed, the day on which the study was made, or, indeed, whoever made the study. It will have this value by virtue of the rating applied.

At the start of the time study certain facts were recorded about the job and its conditions, and these will now be used to assess the allowances which need to be added to the basic time. Work causes fatigue, and rest must be taken to recover from it, the amount varying with the kind of job and the effort expended. The most common allowances are:

1 Personal (normally a fixed percentage)
2 Basic fatigue (normally a fixed percentage)
3 Awkward position, for example, kneeling, bending
4 Use of force – lifting, pushing, etc.
5 Heat and humidity
6 Close attention
7 Noise
8 Monotony

It is normal practice to fill in a preprinted assessment sheet to arrive at a percentage allowance to be given. The allowance should be added separately to each element, because the need for allowance will vary. For example, watching a machine cutting will qualify for a minimum allowance, but the loading of a heavy casting into a chuck calls for effort allowance.

It is advisable to have a study summary sheet, on which the basic times for each element can be written against an element description, with a column for allowances. The allowed or standard time of each element can now be calculated. The total allowed times of the element gives the allowed time for the job.

Synthesis

It was stated at the beginning of this section that the data from studies should be stored in such a way that maximum use can be gained from it. There is much that is repetitive in both repetitive and non-repetitive work and studies should be arranged to take advantage of this. For example, the machine elements of an operation are controlled by the feeds and speeds, consequently it is not long before times per inch can be obtained from studies. Furthermore, the handling time of the components is largely common to a particular machine, varying mainly with weight. It is therefore relatively easy to construct a table or tables of data, obtained from time studies, which can be used to obtain the basic times for other components which have not been studied.

The advantage of this procedure, known as synthesis, is twofold. Firstly, new components do not need to be studied if their key dimensions are known; a time value can be synthesised. Secondly, a time can be obtained from a drawing of the part prior to manufacture, thus enabling a cost comparison if required for a new design.

Predetermined motion-time systems (PMTS)

All human work consists of a repetition of similar body motions. Gilbreth realised this in his search for improved methods. In the 1930s in America a number of successful attempts were made to develop Gilbreth's work and establish times for basic motions. All the systems involve a very detailed analysis of the movement of the limbs in carrying out the method. They therefore have the advantage of recording the method in detail facilitating method analysis and improvement. Times for the motions are obtained from a data card and entered on the study sheet beside the motion codes. The values are normally in milliminutes (0.001 of a minute), the total time being a basic time at standard performance (100).

PERA

SIMPLIFIED PMTS—RECORD SHEET

Reposition valve in vice

Op. or Job Ref:
Sheet Ref. 76 Issue 1
Study Ref. Date 2.10.67
Originator G.G.

Description—Left hand	No.	L.H.	Time	R.H.	No.	Description—Right hand
		R–	9·0	SS1		transfer weight
on part and		G5	–	~~R–~~		to handle
hold		R2	–	G5		secure handle
			2·2	R2		
			3·0	G2		loosen off vice
			5·0	AP		
			2·2	M2		
			6·0	M10		
adjust part in		M2	2·2			
vice	2	G2	6·0			
	2	M<1	2·0			
			4·5	M6		secure part in
			5·0	AP		vice
			3·5	M4		
release part		RL1	5·0	AP		nip up
		R–	2·2	M2		
			2·2	R2		release handle
			–	~~RL2~~		
			60·0	milliminutes		

FIGURE 28:6 SIMPLIFIED PMTS

An illustration of a predetermined motion-time system, in this instance Simplified PMTS. Time is given in milliminutes at standard performance. The codes identify the motions; for example, M6 = move 6in

Systems most commonly used are *work factor, methods-time measurement* (*MTM*), and *Simplified PMTS*. An example of a study using Simplified PMTS is shown in Figure 28:6. Apart from the detailed method specification obtained, the need for rating is eliminated because the motion times are at standard performance. Such systems are best used in highly repetitive, short-cycle jobs where the method can remain stable.

Analytical estimating

When work is non-repetitive, such as plant maintenance, or in the small batch and 'one-off' category, establishing the time value of the work content requires a different approach. To begin with, the time-cycle of each job or sub-operation is often quite long and the PMTS described above would be uneconomical to apply. Secondly, the small batch and 'one-off' situation makes it difficult to study sufficient cycles to obtain a reliable method and time. Add to this the fact that product range is often considerable, and the need for a different approach becomes evident.

Analytical estimating is used for measuring non-repetitive work when sufficient data is not available to permit the compilation of synthetic standards from time studies or other sources. The same procedure is used as when conducting a time study, that is, a record of the conditions of the job and an elemental breakdown. The times for each element, instead of being timed are estimated at basic time and allowances for fatigue, etc., added afterwards. Some of the element times may be based on time-studied information. For example painting may have been studied, and times obtained for making ready, travelling to the site, cleaning down per square foot, and painting, per square foot.

Often, because no information on times is available, the estimator must use his experience and judgement. By implication, therefore, the estimator must be a tradesman with sufficient knowledge of the work involved.

Basic work data

A second order PMTS, known as *basic work data* (*BWD*), was devised originally by ICI Limited from simplified PMTS and is suitable for small batch and non-repetitive manual work, especially maintenance. BWD was further developed by British Rail and since the end of 1967 PERA (Production Engineering Research Association) has been responsible for the growth, control and further development of BWD in the United Kingdom. MTM-2 (MTM=Methods-Time Measurement) and some derivations of the original work factor system are also appropriate for this class of work.

BWD recognises the fact that, even in non-repetitive work, many basic motions or elements of work repeat, irrespective of the work being undertaken. For example, a ring spanner has only one function – to do up or undo a threaded fastener (nut or bolt). The variables in using the spanner are thread-size and condition, and the mode of operation – one flat at a time, say, or a circling motion. It is thus possible to construct a synthetic in tabular form which gives the time for various threads and motions of a ring spanner. Similarly, this can be done for other hand tools.

The BWD times were built up from the basic motions involved using SPMTS and are therefore at standard performance in milliminutes. Each SPMTS pattern was given a code – the BWD code – and the times rounded to the nearest five milliminutes to simplfy addition and calculation. All the codes are alpha-numeric. The alpha part identifies the field of data, for example, HA=hammer up to 2 lbs. AK=Allen key. The numeric part both identifies and gives the time in milliminutes. All codes are discrete and provide a precise definition of the activity involved. An example of a BWD synthesis is shown in Figure 28:7. In the example, more descriptive content than is necessary has been included to illustrate the meanings of the codes used.

Comparative estimating

The technique of comparative estimating is gaining wide application for the measurement of non-repetitive work. Its name is self-explanatory – measurement by comparison of one job with another. It is necessary to establish reference tasks or 'bench-mark' jobs to be used for this comparison, and any of the measurement techniques described can be used to obtain an accurate time for each bench-mark task.

Each bench-mark job will cover a range of time, say thirty minutes

PERA—Basic Work Data

BWD Synthesis Record		
Remove injector leak-off pipes, front or rear cylinder head	Op. or Job Ref. LEYLAND	0680
	Sheet Ref.	1 of 1
	Study Ref.	D. 002
	Date	5. 10.70

Description	Frequency		Code	Total	
	Per Part	No. Parts			
Fitter in cab, engine covers					
and accessories removed					
Obtain spanner				OTA	40
Loosen (tow nuts)		4	SP 31		120
Move between		3	MH 5		15
6 threads 60° cant 3/8"	36/6	4	SP 115		2760
1 thread, fingers		4	T 10		40
Aside nuts		4	DL 36		140
Remove leak off pipe			DL 36		35
Moves between points	3		MH 10		30
Obtain rag				OTA	40
Wipe hands				RA	70
Total basic time in milliminutes					3290

FIGURE 28:7 BASIC WORK DATA (BWD)

An example of a BWD synthesis prepared from a written method obtained from a direct observation. A tape-recorder was used to collect the method details

either side of its actual value. For example, one bench-mark job may have a time of three hours, and another, four hours. The first will be given a 'range' value of two-and-a-half to three-and-a-half hours and the second from three-and-a-half to four-and-a-half hours. The number of bench-mark jobs established will depend upon the range of job times existing and the desired span between the bench-marks. As an example, it has been found, in measuring plant maintenance work, that approximately 300 reference jobs per trade is satisfactory.

When the bench-marks are established a job which requires a time estimate is compared with the reference tasks until the most appropriate one is found, when its time is applied to the job in question.

Industrial relations and the introduction of change

Work study is concerned with change; with time and the control of labour by time; and it is concerned with pay. There is a significant effect upon the relationship of the individual with the organisation, whether the application of work study techniques is being introduced for the first time or whether their use is customary. If that relationship is to be maintained or improved, then considerable emphasis must be placed on industrial relations. Good communication is of vital importance.

Wherever work study is to be introduced for the first time careful preparation by the management beforehand will go a long way towards ensuring a successful application. To begin with, senior management must have a clearly-defined objective which it can expound to its managers and supervisors, and must support the work study department throughout.

The objectives must be communicated to all personnel involved before work study commences. This may be difficult. In a small section, all personnel can be told at a specially convened meeting. For a large department or whole factory one must communicate through supervision and union representatives. If there is no union representation, then it is advisable to ask that spokesmen be elected.

It is not sufficient, however, to rely fully on established lines of communication to transmit the message to all employees. Too often a distorted picture may be created, intentionally or otherwise, and it is wise to prepare a written statement and give this to supervisors and union representatives. A copy on each works notice board is also advisable.

After everyone becomes familiar with the objectives some form of appreciation course is essential for as many people as it is practicable to have trained. These should include management and supervision as well as workers and their representatives. In drawing up a course program the emphasis should be placed on practical exercises rather than lectures, and there should be at least one film.

Having established the lines of communication these should be kept open, either by passing on information about a new technique or, more important, giving progress reports. In a large application involving several departments, this should be done as a matter of course.

Communication by itself is not sufficient to ensure good labour relations. To most people, wages earned are most important. The association of work study with incentive schemes means that an unsatisfactory pay structure can generate a labour relations problem for work study and other management functions. Management has two responsibilities in this context: pay structure and management control.

Pay structure

The pay structure must be sound and give the desired results. Any recurring failure in the system brings administrative problems and affects labour relations. Often, payment is based on time which has been derived from work study data. Management must ensure, therefore, that the pay structure is correctly conceived: this implies that:

1 It should be simple to operate and easily understood by those who are paid by it.
2 It should relate closely to the criteria upon which its variable elements depend. A payment system based on individual effort should yield an increase in pay for an increase in effectiveness.
3 If there are factors outside the control of the employees which cannot be eliminated but which affect performances, the pay structure should allow for these factors, by compensators or stabilisers.

4 There should not be any sections of the factory where average payment differs substantially from other sections.
5 Average earnings should be related to skill, with the highest average pay at the top skill grade.
6 The bonus content of gross pay should not be too significant, but in the region of a third of basic rate.

Management control

Once the pay structure has been implemented, it should be monitored to ensure that it remains viable. Payment systems are frequently subject to pressures which stem from the ever changing situation to which they are related. Unless control information supported by a regular audit is available, management will not be aware of the need for modifications. Without controls, dissatisfaction of the labour force will signal the need for change, by which time labour relations have suffered. This may result in expense for a company, because frequently the solution is to 'buy out' and start again.

It has been found in practice that the following statistics represent the minimum requirements for control purposes; first, *weekly*:

1 Individual performance and gross pay, grouped into grades within each section and department
2 Waiting and ineffective time as a percentage of available hours
3 Productive hours as a percentage of available hours
4 Percentage of unmeasured work in the productive hours
5 Percentages of other time such as training, rectification, etc

Second, *monthy*:
6 Department summaries and factory summary of the results from 1 to 5 above
7 Bonus content as a percentage of gross pay
8 Premium content as a percentage of gross pay

If statistics indicate the need for action, this should be taken without delay, even if the solution requires abandonment of the scheme entirely, early in its life.

Conducting work study in an engineering company

To illustrate the practical application of work study, a hypothetical engineering works will be considered, in order to demonstrate the use of some of the techniques described above.

The company has 200 employees engaged in the manufacture of alternators designed to produce 1 kVA – 500 kVA. Some sub-contract machining is undertaken and printed circuit control boards are supplied to a local electrical manufacturer. Work study has not been used in the factory, the production engineer and his assistant have been concentrating on tooling, jig and fixture design and material handling.

A work study manager has been appointed, and two trained and experienced work study engineers recruited. The production director has set the following objective: 'Establish a work study function in the company which will improve productivity by better methods of working and labour control. As a priority, provide more accurate labour cost information relating to all stages of manufacture.'

In many ways the work study manager has an ideal situation from which to develop a good work study function and to make a worthwhile contribution to company profitability. However, a lot of preparation is required before work can begin or results will appear. Communication and education must be given priority by both the work study manager and his senior management colleagues.

The study programme

After the overall policy for work study has been communicated to all levels of management, supervision and employee representatives – union or otherwise – it is advisable to conduct a survey of the factory before embarking on the educational aspects of communication. This will suggest to the work study manager the type of techniques which should be employed and enable the techniques for training to be selected.

The survey mentioned above is important to the formulation of a study programme. It will be necessary to determine:

1 The techniques most appropriate to establish time standards
2 The approximate time-scale for building all the data required

3 The need for additional training of work study staff in new techniques, and the hire of contract work study staff
4 A method study programme
5 The type of incentive scheme

It will then be decided whether method study should be undertaken at this time or later. It is logical to improve methods first and then time the new methods, not *vice versa*. However, method study is a lengthy, time-consuming process and often involves considerable capital expenditure; therefore economic considerations at the time will strongly influence the decision.

From his survey of the manufacturing processes the work study manager identified the main measurement techniques to be used, as shown in Figure 28 : 8.

Implementing the standard times

Productivity is assumed to be low and an incentive scheme is to be introduced using the new standard times. These changes can be considered as a productivity scheme. Two factors must be given considerable thought before implementing the times. Firstly, the type of incentive scheme most appropriate for the company. Secondly, the preparation of an agreement covering the conditions of the scheme.

The success of the scheme will depend upon maintaining the good labour relations established at the introduction of work study. It will founder in the long run if the incentive scheme is not tailored to the conditions. In this hypothetical company a straightforward individual incentive scheme would be suitable for most of the departments. In the assembly departments, however, work measurement is currently less accurate especially on the larger machines, also many jobs are 'one-off' to customer requirements. This can introduce problems in setting time-standards, and variations may occur outside the control of the operators. A system, such as *graded measured day-work*, which minimises the effects of performance variations, is suitable for this situation.

Clear guide-lines for supervision and management are needed to ensure consistent interpretation of the conditions of the incentive scheme. If the company has a wage agreement with a trade union, covering conditions, wages, holidays, etc., then this should be re-

	Section	Process	Technique
1	Machine shop, including bar sawing	Range of lathes, milling machines, drilling and grinding. Some tape-controlled and profile	Time study: to construct synthetics which will accommodate product design changes. Machine set-up times for some of the larger castings to be based on the estimates presently used by the production engineer.
2	Rotor and stator core building	Laminate assembly on keyed shafts. Some arc welding	Time study: establish synthetics to accommodate design changes
3	Press shop		Not to be studied; laminates being bought out within 6 months
4	Coil winding	Mainly hand work, some machines	Time study: classification of coils for study in groups. Develop data tables for ranges of wire sizes
5	Armature winding	Hand work at benches	Time study
6	Stator winding	Hand work	Time study
7	Rotor preparation and winding	Combination of machine and hand work	Time study
8	Electronic components	Bench work, female labour, high volume	PMT system, such as MTM-1, work factor or SPMTS
9	Control gear	Bench work, male and female labour	Combination of time study and PMTS according to the nature of the sub-assembly processes
10	Assembly	Batch-production on smaller m/c's, large m/c's. largely one off to customer	Combination of time study, PMTS, such as MTM-2 or BWD, and analytical estimating on the 400-500 KVA machines
11	Finishing and testing	Performance testing, painting etc.	Time study

FIGURE 28:8 EXAMPLE OF MEASUREMENT TECHNIQUE IDENTIFICATION

written to include all the workings of the incentive scheme, and presented in draft form for negotiation. The agreement should include a grievance procedure to ensure proper channels of communication, and protect the work study department from frequent disputes over standard times. The management must ensure that the proposals are fully documented and presented to the employees in an effective manner.

A lead-in period is needed when the new scheme is introduced because earnings may suffer due to payment being based on individual performance. A period of four to six weeks will allow the employees time to get used to the generally higher pace of working. During this period performance is monitored, every employee is informed of his progress, and supervision assists in raising the tempo. It is during this period that the paperwork involved in the scheme is tested and improved where necessary.

Control

Management will wish to know not only how the scheme progresses, but also what gains in productivity have been achieved. At the survey stage, the work study manager prepared a reference of performance for future comparison. This was obtained by conducting an activity sample study of each department and established the rate of working compared with standard performance and also the amount of ineffective time. Using data showing average wages in a reference period, the cost of a standard hour (one hour at standard performance) can be calculated. This is easily compared with the new cost of a standard hour at the higher performance and incentive pay, for example:

Reference period rate per hour $= £0.500$
Reference period performance $= 70$ BSI

Cost per standard hour $= \dfrac{100 \times 0.50}{70} = £0.714$

New rate per hour $= £0.60$
Current average performance $= 100$ BSI

Cost per standard hour $= \dfrac{100 \times 0.60}{100} = £0.60$

$\therefore$ Cost per standard hour reduced from £0.714 to £0.60

Finally, the control statistics, which are so important in ensuring that the scheme operates successfully, must be set up and maintained. They indicate to management how the incentive scheme is running and point clearly to the need for an audit of the scheme. These will show:

1 When the proportion of waiting time is increasing
2 When the amount of unmeasured work is higher than is considered desirable
3 When performance is drifting upwards, possibly as a result of minor method changes devised by the employees
4 When one department is producing higher performance levels than others

Without control statistics, management will not know what is happening. It is not only difficult to prepare such information when a crisis arises, it may be too late.

Further reading

Work Study, by R M Currie, Pitman, 3rd ed. 1972.
Introduction to Work Study, International Labour Office.
Motion and Time Study, by R M Barnes, Wiley, 1968.
Simplified PMTS, by R M Currie.
Methods-Time Measurement, by Maynard, Stegemerten and Schwab, McGraw-Hill, 1948.
The Social Psychology of Industry, by J A C Brown, Penguin, 1970.
The Industrial Relations Handbook, HMSO, 1961.

Chapter 29

Quality Control

R M McRobb, Management Consultant

Quality is all things to all men. The truth of this statement points to one of the problems which quality assurance faces. No two people have quite the same idea about quality. To one it is the Rolls-Royce car with which nothing ever goes wrong. To another it is a rough, tough item, such as an agricultural implement which gets the worst possible treatment and no attention but still works. These two examples represent differences in quality of design. Each performs its task satisfactorily although one is designed as a precision product and the other is crude. On the other hand, each is of equal standard from the point of view of quality of conformance. The difference between these two 'qualities' must always be remembered. Quality of design may vary widely according to the use to which the product will be put. Quality of conformance, on the other hand, is a single, uniform target. Regardless of the level of design quality, quality of conformance quite simply means that the product conforms to the design specification.

Management attitudes and expectations

The entire success of a quality assurance program depends upon the attitudes of management. The quality manager must have the full confidence and support of the management team. Without this support any quality program will fail. The management team must show by its actions that it believes in the program. This is not always easy to secure. It is often the case that the attitudes of managers to quality assurance are derived from other experiences in their own company and, as a result, their views vary widely. There is one thing, above all others, which will ensure the full support of management for quality assurance programs. It is the ability of the program to save the company direct cost. Quality programs can usually produce savings in indirect cost but these do not carry as much weight with management because they are not seen either readily or quickly. Short-term direct savings are more difficult to produce but are those which create the most impression.

On the other hand, management is usually quite definite and precise about its expectations from quality assurance. For one thing, it is easier to say what one wants than to determine if one is actually getting it. A typical set of management expectations is as follows:

1 Develop operator quality consciousness
2 Produce a quality rating system for operators
3 Produce machine capability data
4 Ensure adequate control of manufacturing processes
5 Prevent defective parts from being produced
6 Provide an adequate system of quality reporting
7 Disseminate quality data
8 Plan for good purchasing/quality assurance/vendor relationships

The economics of quality

In considering the economics of quality one must remember the differences between quality of design and of conformance. The Rolls-Royce will undoubtedly cost more than the agricultural implement in actual cost but if the standards of quality of conformance are not controlled then, in a purely relative sense, the agricultural implement may cost more. Quality has a cost and a value. The cost is the factor of most importance to the producer and the value is usually of more importance to the user. The difficulty is in striking the right balance. Figure 29:1 shows how these two factors together make up the economic picture. It will be seen that the cost of quality rises at an increasing rate whereas the value decreases inversely. The situation is exactly the same when one considers the cost of quality of conformance. There is an optimum value and Figure 29:2 shows how it is made up. The various factors will be referred to in more detail in a later section.

Quality and organisational responsibilities

It is a commonly held fallacy that the quality department is 're-sponsible' for quality. In fact, the only department in a company which has a direct influence on quality is the production department.

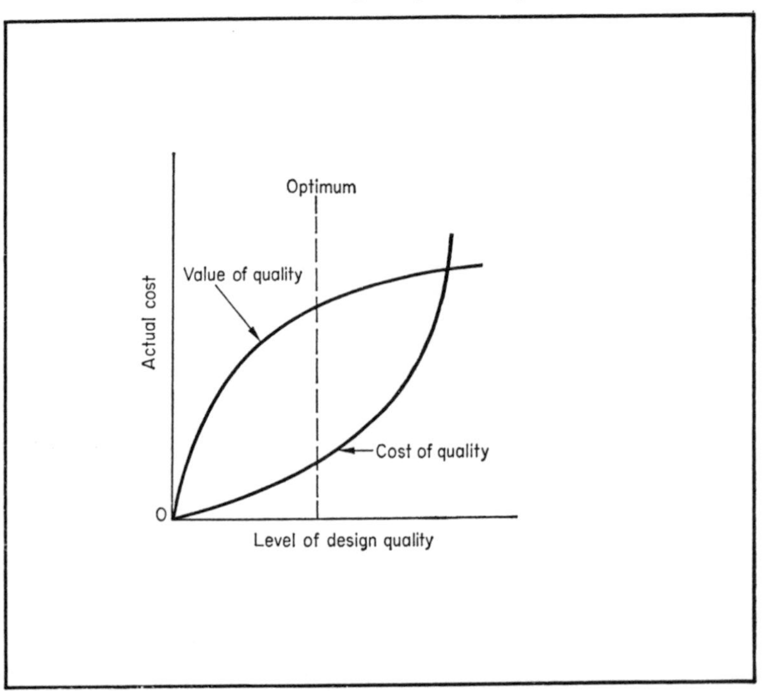

FIGURE 29:1 ECONOMICS OF QUALITY OF DESIGN

An illustration of the way in which the law of diminishing returns operates in the relationships between value and cost of quality and showing that there is an optimum relationship

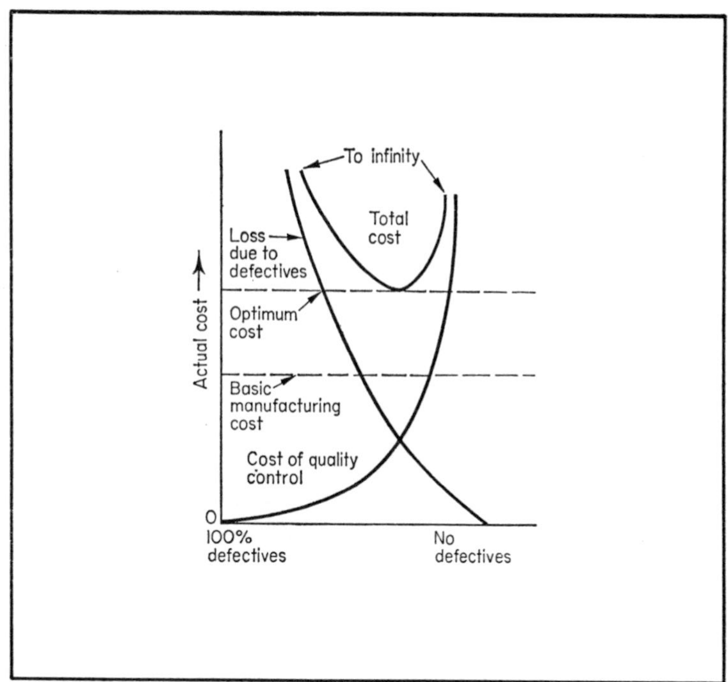

FIGURE 29:2 COSTS OF QUALITY OF CONFORMANCE

It will be seen that as controls are introduced there is a drastic cost reduction but that, eventually, a stage is reached beyond which costs begin to rise again from an optimum value

Its operators make the product and only they can make it right or wrong. Nevertheless, it is true to say that there is not a single part of a company which does not have an influence on the achievement and maintenance of quality. This happens in a variety of ways. The sales department has a responsibility to ensure that misleading claims are not made for the company's product; these could result in a customer claiming that product quality was not as promised. Sales is also responsible for ensuring that customer requirements which are not achievable are not accepted.

The policy of the purchasing department will have an effect. For example, the lowest price regardless can have a profound influence on the ability of the production department to produce the product correctly. The part played by the engineering department in basic design, as well as in tool and equipment design, is a foundation for the producer's achievement of the objective 'right first time'. Less obvious participants in the achievement of quality are the accountants. Quite apart from their hold on the purse strings, the accountants, by prompt and accurate reporting of scrap, re-work and unit cost figures, can greatly aid the production department. With these figures readily available trends can be seen and corrected before an 'out-of-control' situation arises.

For a long time it has been usual for the quality department to control the various inspection activities. These have included process control, final inspection and incoming inspection. Additionally, a variety of other activities have been included. Examples of these are reliability and environmental testing, failure analysis and laboratory staff and quality planning. Although the quality department is completely independent (or should be) reporting to a senior executive not responsible for production, it maintains close relationships with most other company departments. However, changes are taking place in these traditional arrangements which will eventually have a profound effect on quality organisation and responsibilities.

Recognition is gradually being given to the fact that the producer is solely responsible for the quality of his product and that he must, therefore, be provided with all necessary facilities for the verification of quality. For years, in some companies the producer has been provided with these facilities. One result is that direct inspection personnel are being transferred to producer control. In those cases the producer now has all the facilities necessary for the performance of his quality task. He may inspect as much or, indeed, as little as he chooses. His is the responsibility for producing the product to specification. In this situation the role of the quality department has changed and is now precisely that which is implied by the title 'quality assurance'. It is thus the case that in the more advanced companies all departments are considered to have quality responsibilities which are co-ordinated by the quality assurance department. This department also ensures that the desired standards of quality are achieved, and maintained, by the production department. This task is carried out by means of a series of monitoring and audit functions and a comprehensive reporting system. Sanctions are imposed as necessary in those instances where required corrective action is being taken slowly or not at all.

Establishing standards and specifications

Maintenance of basic standards

There are two sets of basic standards with which one is concerned. The first is that which ensures that the fundamental standards of measurement are maintained and is usually the responsibility of a standards laboratory. The laboratory may be for mechanical or electrical standards or for both. One need say no more than that the masters or sub-masters kept should be directly traceable back to the nation's basic standards at the National Physical Laboratory. The second kind of basic standard is that which is laid down in the various specifications controlling the process of manufacture and testing, acceptance of materials and final acceptance of the product prior to delivery to the customer. The chain of which these form some of the links starts with the design department and extends through material procurement, manufacturing, testing and final acceptance specifications. Despite the fact that all are links in one chain it is often forgotten that they are complementary to one another. This is one reason for the specification problems which are so common in industry. It is considered to be essential that companies should have an effective specification control system with responsibility for the co-ordination of the various specification producing activities.

Quality engineering and planning

Preparation of the procedures which control the work of the quality department will normally be the responsibility of its engineering and planning sections. A few of the procedures which one would expect to find in the quality manual and which would have been prepared by the quality engineers are as follows:

1 Manual organisation
2 PPI (purchased parts inspection) procedure
3 Released component traceability
4 Scrap and redundant component cost recovery
5 Specification amendments
6 Control of production operators
7 Control of production inspectors

8 Inspection procedure for fixed capacitors
9 Failure analysis and reporting
10 Final acceptance procedure
11 Returned material procedure
12 Quality audits

The major responsibility of the engineering and planning sections is to ensure that all the functions which are carried out by the department are fully described in procedures. This is to ensure that the functions are carried out as intended and that, despite replacement of individuals, unauthorised changes do not take place. The design of the variety of forms used for recording and displaying information is a further responsibility.

When the introduction of new products is being considered a quality engineer should be assigned to each from the inception of the project. He will be required to become familiar with it and follow it through all stages to full production. He will be an adviser on all features which will, or may, have an effect on quality. Later, the knowledge which he acquires will be the basis for the inspection instructions and procedures which will have to be written. Without them the inspectors and his own quality assurance department will not have the guidelines and instructions which they need.

Another very necessary activity for a quality assurance department, and which deserves more attention than it often gets, is the preparation of an annual plan. This, based upon the company's estimate of its overall position, will be the base-line for measurement of the department's performance against its various targets of personnel, equipment and costs. It is usually the case that the final version will be significantly different from the first attempt. A useful supplement to the plan is a statement of the main tasks which the department intends to undertake during the forthcoming year. The statement should give forecasts of the cost reductions which the department expects to achieve in terms of higher yields of product, fewer personnel, etc. This is a fruitful way to secure the kind of evidence which the department requires to convince management of the value of its function.

Quality audits

In much the same sense that audits are carried out by accountancy auditors, so are audits carried out by the quality assurance department. Indeed, in the light of the current developments in the function of quality departments, auditing is the principal, and sometimes the only, way in which it can carry out its task. It is essential that the audits are carried out in accordance with the prepared procedures which form part of the department's operational manual. See previous section. The engineer carrying out an audit must familiarise himself with the controlling procedure and then with those which govern the process or function being audited. A useful check-list for the engineer is as follows:

1 Verify that process specifications are in order
2 Verify that process control specifications are in order
3 Check process for conformance to specifications
4 List deviations
5 Determine corrective actions
6 Set follow-up time
7 Prepare audit report and distribute
8 Follow up
9 Clear process (or impose sanctions)

It will often be found whilst carrying out an audit that there are many minor deviations from specification, quite apart from any major ones which might be found. Although it may be felt that they are of no great consequence and that no corrective action will be contemplated for them, they should be recorded in the audit report. The report is a source of information for many people in departments other than the quality department and a standardised format should be used. A standard list of section headings for audit reports could be as follows:

1 Statement of purpose
2 Description of process being audited
3 Listing of controlling/relevant specifications
4 Summary of findings, listing deviations
5 Corrective actions required and dates for completion
6 Statement of follow-up date

7 Detailed findings
8 General comments
9 Circulation list

When significant deviations are found and corrective actions are required, the time-scale for their implementation should be fixed in consultation with the engineer who is responsible for the process or function which is being audited. Typical functions for audit are:

1 Design specifications
2 Manufacturing specifications
3 Quality specifications
4 Inspection data
5 Inspection functions
6 Inspection personnel
7 Measuring equipment
8 Customer complaints
9 Feedback systems
10 Follow-up

On the date given for the completion of corrective action the auditor must initiate a follow-up investigation on the relevant deviations in the original report. Normally it will be expected that the deviations have been corrected, or at least that action to correct them is under way, and the follow-up report will make this clear. Once all required corrective actions have been completed, the audit is signed off. Whatever the frequency may be that has been determined for an audit, it is wise, after an unsatisfactory one, to bring forward the date when the next one is due. In the same way, after a series of satisfactory audits, one should consider reducing the frequency. Nevertheless, it must be stressed that a situation should not be allowed to arise in which audits are continually postponed or are not done at all. This will certainly lead to the introduction of unauthorised deviations. It is natural that audit reports should give prominence to deviations; they exist to detect deviations. It is wise, however, to give some prominence to those instances in which a process or function is found to be fully in conformance with the specifications and procedures which govern it. Praise is a wonderful system lubricant.

Development and testing

Product performance targets

Determination of these targets is usually made by the design and sales departments working together and will be based, to some extent, upon market surveys. The quality assurance department is not usually involved at this stage but if, as recommended earlier, a quality engineer has been assigned to the new product, there will be ample opportunity for presentation of the quality viewpoint. A miniature relay is typical of the component type for which product performance targets are important; a number of performance targets which such a relay will have to meet are:

1 2 pole change over contact system
2 5,000,000 operations in any attitude
3 Contacts to break 50V at 120mA
4 No contact chatter at vibration frequencies from 50 to 500Hz at 10G
5 Ambient operating conditions 0°C to 90°C at 95 per cent RH
6 Operating power not to exceed 1.5W at 24V
7 Hold power not to exceed 0.75W at 24V
8 Insulation resistance contact to contact/frame/coil to be not less than 10 megohm

From these requirements the designers will work out the design parameters for a relay which will meet them, and prototypes will be made. The prototypes will be subjected to intensive testing in the design laboratories to prove the design. After any necessary adjustments have been made, pre-production quantities are produced and the quality engineer comes fully into the picture.

Performance testing, planning and reporting

From the requirements in the target list a coordinated series of tests is planned which will verify conformance to the targets individually, and in all combinations of them, which the relay is likely to meet in service. The quantity of relays submitted to these tests is usually arbitrarily chosen and will probably exceed fifty. The units will be numbered serially for test purposes and careful records will be kept at each stage of the test program. Whilst there will have been informal reporting to the design department at all stages of testing it cannot be too strongly emphasised that a detailed and comprehensive report must finally be written. It must include all conclusions that are drawn and any recommendations that may be made for changes in the target requirements or the relay itself. On the report will be based plans for quantity production and marketing.

One of the more important reasons for having a written report upon the results of the test program is because industrial experience has shown that marketing pressures will often push a product into production before it has been confirmed that all the performance targets have been met. One result of this kind of situation is customer dissatisfaction which has to be borne by the quality assurance department directly because of the 'poor quality'. No excuse is made for referring to this situation. It happens, and it is important that engineers should realise that it does and be prepared for it. Preparation of full reports, with conclusions and recommendations, is essential to provide evidence of the degree of test conformance and to prevent future recrimination.

Fault reporting and corrective action

This activity normally falls into two clearly-defined sectors. The first is part of the normal function of quality engineering when monitoring production processes and consists of investigatory action on in-process and final test failures, followed by the appropriate corrective action. In-process and final test failures should be routed automatically to the quality engineer responsible for failure analysis. Equally automatically he will institute standard procedures for examination, testing where possible, and possible stripping down of the unit to determine the cause of failure. Although analysis to determine the cause of failure is often straightforward, it may be very difficult, and the ultimate answer may be hedged with 'ifs' and 'buts'.

Whatever the outcome, a standardised, formal report should be prepared with full details of the investigation. The details should include fault particulars, where in the process the fault arose, details of the tests carried out (such as photo-micrographs), the conclusions that have been drawn and any recommendations for corrective action. Unlike the procedure for audits it is not usual for follow-up checks to be made, although there is no reason why they should not. An example of the corrective action that might be proposed in the case of the relay already mentioned if the fault were that contacts were not always closing, could be as follows: firstly, check the temper of the contact spring material; secondly, institute a closer control on the contact setting operation.

The second sector into which fault reporting and corrective action may fall is in connection with customer complaints. All complaints and defective material received from customers should be examined by a quality engineer. There are a number of steps which have to be taken; a summary of these is as follows:

1 Examine complaint
2 Determine warranty position
3 Examine product as required
4 Determine liability
5 Prepare defect report
6 Inform customer of conclusions and replace product as required

Complications are caused by warranty problems, the need for more details from the customer, the defective material not having been returned and the distinct possibility that responsibility for the failure is the customer's. In the case of the last it is necessary to write very diplomatic letters, but support from a detailed failure investigation report, with photographic evidence where appropriate, usually prevents adverse reaction from the customer.

In the case of both kinds of failure investigation just discussed it is essential that careful records are kept of the faults found and the established causes. From them analyses can be prepared from time to time based upon the class of fault and the type of cause. This information is invaluable in that it will often indicate trends in a process which, if not corrected, could result in the production of defective parts. It has also been known to indicate similar problems being experienced by a number of customers because of inadequate 'use' information from the manufacturer. The corrective action in this case is quite obvious.

Process control and inspection

Establishing process control

Process control is perhaps one of the most important activities within the field of quality control. The processing operations are those within which the product is basically made, right or wrong; corrective action may or may not be possible later on, but these are the stages which matter. In considering the extent to which process control may be applied there are two extremes which limit discussion. The first is that of the manufacturer who exercises no control at all and relies completely upon a final inspection operation to sort the good from the bad. At the other end of the scale is the manufacturer who exercises such a close control over his manufacturing processes that there is no later need for a final inspection as there are no defective products to sort out. Of these two, the first is foolish and the second is, for most industries, generally impracticable. The exceptions to the latter include the petroleum and gas producing industries. In general practice one will find a level of application somewhere between the two extremes. This will have been determined by the producer's desire for a quality product and the economic climate in which he is operating. A reference back to Figure 29:2 will be helpful at this point.

The more progressive companies are undoubtedly diverting more and more of their quality effort towards the task of controlling the processing of the product during manufacture. The additional cost incurred by the extra personnel needed will be recouped many times over in the reduction in the costs of re-work and scrap and in the improvement of customer relationships. Figure 29:3 shows in pictorial form the relationships which have been just discussed and the rich prize which awaits those who are prepared to spend more on the prevention of defectives; that is to say, more process control.

Nine steps to process control

In setting up a process control operation there are three separate control procedures which need to be used and which may be dealt with in parallel. These concern:

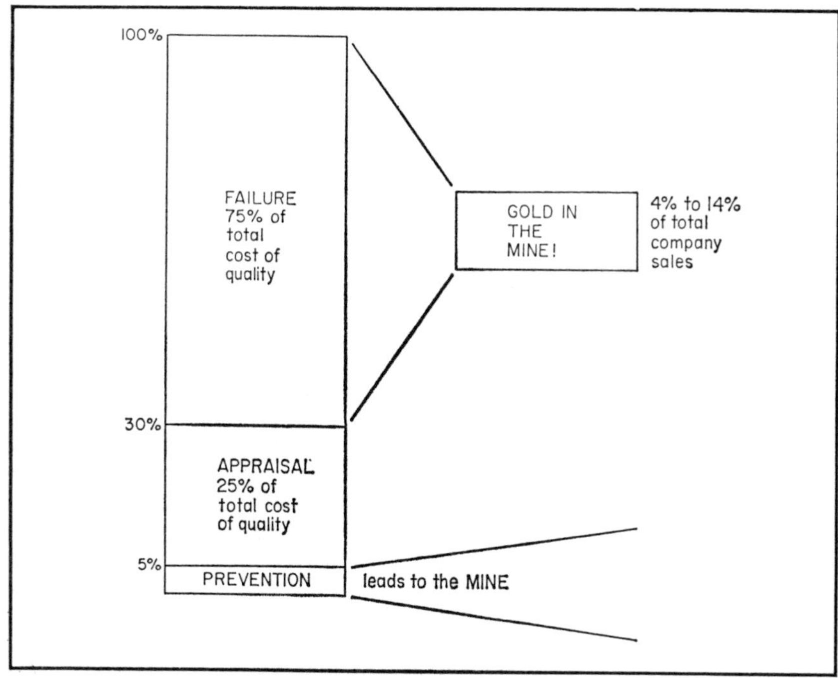

FIGURE 29:3 REAL COST OF QUALITY

It is not generally appreciated just how much quality costs, nor how much money can be saved by comparatively small increase in prevention costs

1 The production operators
2 The production inspectors
3 The process control itself

In each there are a number of steps which have to be taken; for 1 and 2 above these are:

1 Select
2 Train
3 Certify
4 Audit

Steps 1 and 2 are obvious but 3 and 4 require some amplification.

Certification requires that a series of test inspections of the work of the individual is made by an experienced quality technician. These continue until the technician is satisfied that the individual under review fully understands the operation and the various defects which can arise and that his work is of a consistently high standard. Upon certification suitable records are raised which will record, amongst other things, the date of certification and the operations covered. The records also make provision for entering the results of audit checks (step 4) which will be made upon the work of the individual from time to time. An unsatisfactory check will result in the individual being withdrawn from the operation for re-training and subsequent re-certification. A series of unsatisfactory checks will, of course, result in the individual being withdrawn from the operation altogether.

It is desirable to select one production line for the first introduction of process control and this should be one that will give the fewest problems – for obvious reasons! There are nine logical steps to follow and they should be carefully considered on the following basis:

Step 1: Identification of item to be controlled. One needs to be careful in identifying the item of product which is to be controlled to be sure that it is precisely delineated. This will avoid later confusion.

Step 2: Check of manufacturing specifications. The manufacturing process will have to be studied closely to determine if it is being carried out according to the specifications. It is not at all unlikely that one will find that in a variety of ways, some major and some minor, the process does not agree with the specifications which are supposed to control it. In this event one or other will have to be changed to ensure conformity. Without conformity there can be no control.

Step 3: Study of manufacturing specifications. The quality engineer will have to study the process specifications carefully. Without a full understanding he will not be able to carry out step 4 in a satisfactory manner.

Step 4: Preparation of process control specifications. This is the principal step. Writing the process control specifications means writing a series of specifications. One is required for each control point and each must have been agreed in consultation with the production engineer for the process. At each control point consideration has to be given to the immediately preceding and succeeding operations when determining the faults which might occur. The frequency at which checks are to be made has also to be determined and a number of factors are involved. These include the volume of production, the size of sample which will be taken at each check and the allowable number of each defect which can be taken as acceptable. The engineer must also specify the actions which will have to be taken if any check is unsatisfactory.

Step 5: Determination of feedback and sanction system. The type of information recording and feedback system adopted must be concise yet still record all the essential information. It must require and provide for a fast feedback to production supervision of details about unsatisfactory checks. A system of sanctions will have to be decided upon for imposition when corrective actions are not instituted or are unduly delayed. Regular reports will have to be arranged on a weekly or monthly basis. When the factory system uses quality control charts prepared by the production inspectors, endorsements will have to be made to them as necessary.

Step 6: Introduction of controls. The quality control technicians who will be carrying out the control will have to be fully briefed about the process and the control specifications. Nor must it be forgotten that production supervision and operators will also have to receive a briefing about the control and its purpose; this is to enable them to do a better job.

Step 7: Review of operation. After a suitable period of operation it is necessary to review the results. It will be surprising if a need is not found to modify the manufacturing process specifications. Such a need will inevitably result in a need to change the control specifications as well.

Step 8: Change of procedures and specification as required. Arrangements will have to be made for the production engineer to change his specifications and, in parallel, the quality engineer will change his control specifications.

Step 9: Introduction of changes. With the issue of change notices and amendments to the specifications the revised control procedure will be put into effect.

Steps 7, 8 and 9 are then repeated on a regular cyclic basis to ensure that the control system is updated as required to maintain effective operation.

Information feedback and reporting

Reference has been made in the discussion on process control to the importance of feedback and reporting. It must be stressed that the success of a quality department depends to a large degree upon the effectiveness of its information reporting and feedback systems. The extent and depth of reporting and feedback will obviously depend upon the size of the company and its organisation. In all cases the system must be designed in conjunction with the departments for whom the information is intended. It is for their benefit and so must, to the maximum extent possible, conform to their requirements.

Once the system content has been determined a formal procedure will have to be prepared setting it out in detail. This will make it certain that it is carried through according to plan, provided, of course, that regular audits are made. Provision must also be made for a periodic review of the data and reporting requirements. Unless this is done one will assuredly find the all too common situation in which reports continue to be prepared long after their need is ended simply because no one has ever troubled to question their continued existence. This is another 'lost cost'. If the following questions are asked at these periodic reviews it will be found that many reports have no further use.

1 What purpose does it serve?
2 Is it necessary?
3 Is it the minimum to serve the purpose?
4 Can it be informal or must it be formal?
5 How is it to be presented?
6 To whom is it to be presented?
7 How few copies? (*not* how many!)
8 Has its use ended?

In-process and final inspection

It is considered that process inspection and control are among the most important direct methods of ensuring that products are made 'right first time'. The extent of process inspection will clearly depend upon circumstances and local attitudes but attention must be directed towards a current trend which is considered to be a sound one. This has already been mentioned; it is that of placing responsibility for the quality of a product directly in the hands of the producer.

The producer must, of course, be given all the tools necessary to perform the task. One such tool is the inspection function, both process and final. Although advice will be given by the quality department it is entirely the responsibility of the production department to determine just how much inspection is carried out and where. In this situation, however, the quality department will operate a comprehensive system of control audits to ensure adherence to the company-determined standards of quality. The quality department will require that all the inspection operations are planned and written up in procedures which will be used as the basis for quality audits.

Automatic inspection

In high-volume production, and especially in high-technology industry, increasing use is being made on economic grounds of automatic test and inspection equipment which carries out very comprehensive 100 per cent testing. In some cases the equipment is linked to computers for control and sorting purposes and may also provide a continuous data print-out facility. Such equipment is costly (upwards of £50,000 is not uncommon) and its use is helping along the trend towards producer responsibility for quality. Clearly, no company is going to buy two £50,000 pieces of equipment, one for production and another for inspection, if one will suffice. Points to remember when considering the use of equipment of this nature include the following. The skills needed for equipment maintenance are of a very high order and it is difficult to find technicians with them. The engineers who will be controlling and operating them will have to be given special training in computer programming if full advantage is to be taken of the almost unlimited capabilities which these pieces of equipment make available. Very complex analysis of data can be carried out Whilst the data is being gathered and, in the case of electronic components, can provide the groundwork for reliability predictions.

Inspection records

Without recording information the quality department cannot carry out its tasks. Yet it is rare for enough consideration to be given to the tasks of gathering and recording information. Too often one finds that the wrong information is being accumulated and it is wrongly presented to the wrong people. Except that in this case the data is likely to be mostly of an alphanumeric nature, the discussion in the section on information feedback and reporting is relevant here and the questions listed in that section should be referred to again in this context.

These questions should be asked periodically about inspection records, especially with regard to the time that they are kept. Factors of importance in this respect are the length of warranty periods, the requirements of Government quality departments and arrangements which may have been negotiated with particular customers. Neglect of periodic questions results in more 'lost cost'. Apart from the three factors just mentioned the maintenance of full records of inspection will be of great value when reviewing operations before process and procedural changes are made. In incoming goods inspection areas inspection records are of inestimable value for the purposes of vendor rating.

Supplier evaluation

Quality assessment of suppliers

Purchasing staff in most companies usually reckon that they know quite a lot about their suppliers and, in general, they do. So far as the quality-mindedness of suppliers is concerned, however, their knowledge is frequently minimal. This is partly because determination of quality-mindedness requires specialist quality knowledge and partly because, in most cases, little attempt is made to seek the information which is necessary to form a sound judgment. Whether the information which is sought is minimal, as in the case of a small supplier, or considerable, when a large supplier is concerned, it should always be based upon a standard form of questionnaire so that vendor comparisons can be made at a later date. In the case of an existing supplier there will usually be historical evidence upon which to base a decision. If the supplier is a new one there will not be any historical evidence. Recourse must then be made to a survey, small or large, based upon a comprehensive questionnaire which will be the only satisfactory method of reaching a considered judgment. Clearly, the kind of information sought, and its depth, will depend upon the companies concerned and the products involved.

The headings of sections in a questionnaire prepared for use in assessing the quality-mindedness of suppliers are set out below. Not all sections will be used on each occasion because smaller companies will not have all the facilities of larger ones.

1 The company
2 Its departments
3 The quality organisation
4 Incoming inspection
5 Process control
6 Final inspection
7 Quality assurance system
8 Quality engineering and planning
9 Standards facilities
10 Laboratory facilities
11 Other facilities

These surveys may also be used to compare one supplier against another when an order has to be placed if all other factors are similar. Assessment should always be on a formal basis with a standard format for reporting and recording.

Purchased parts inspection

An apt description of this activity would be that it is an evil, albeit a necessary evil. This description stems from the fact that it has to be done at all. A purchaser buys products which should conform to his requirements expressed in a convenient manner, and a supplier ordinarily undertakes to supply to these requirements. That he does not do so on a large scale is the main reason why so many purchasers find it necessary to operate the 'evil' of purchased-parts inspection. This is not the place to go into the reasons for this unhappy state of affairs. It is sufficient to note that the inspection has to be carried out. That being so, it must be organised well, with due regard to its purpose. The progression involved, which is reasonably straightforward, is as follows:

1 Identify incoming material against paperwork
2 Determine quality of conformity

3 Identify material as accepted or rejected
4 Compile necessary records
5 Pass accepted material to stores
6 Pass rejected material to shipping
7 Compile and distribute vendor rating data

Usually there will be a variety of parts to be handled and the inspectors need to be well-experienced and adequately supported by specifications and procedures setting out the acceptance requirements, methods of working and systems to be used, for instance, in dealing with non-conforming parts.

Apart from the usual kinds of standard inspection and measuring equipment it is likely that there will be a substantial need for special gauges and fixtures designed for particular parts. Suitable storage facilities will have to be provided for the various items of equipment and security arrangements will have to be made to ensure that shipments not inspected or passed cannot leave the section. This last requirement is of some importance if the factory uses any method of expediting production. It is worth stressing the point that the inspectors who inspect purchased parts must be 'inspectors' and not 'deciders'. Their job is to determine whether the incoming material conforms to the specification or not. In the case of non-conformity it is *not* the job of the inspector to decide if it may be used; that is the job of the designer or product engineer. This provides another good reason for requiring an effective recording and documentation system when dealing with purchased parts. A more important reason is so that the information gathered may be used for the purposes of vendor rating.

Vendor rating

One of the more difficult decisions which purchasing and quality people have to make concerns the 'goodness' or otherwise of a vendor from the point of view of quality. All too often these decisions are made upon the basis of opinion and hearsay. This is not a satisfactory way in which to reach decisions; it is so often that a wrong decision is made. A sound, factual, approach to this problem is to make use of a system of vendor rating.

It should be pointed out that in this instance only the quality factor is considered, although others, such as price, delivery, product complexity, etc., are often included in a comprehensive system (see Chapter 27). Many vendor rating systems are in use, ranging from simple to very complex ones which require the use of computers.

Here is a description of a very simple system which is capable of being changed at will and of providing a base upon which to build a more comprehensive system after experience of its use. It was developed by the author fifteen years ago and is still regarded as a very effective, albeit simple, plan. It was developed from the following set of simple rules which are self explanatory:

1 Must be simple
2 No difficult calculations
3 Compatible with standard sampling plans
4 Compatible with 100 per cent inspection
5 Recognise the relative importance of faults
6 Show differences in quality levels
7 Easy to modify
8 Minimum of labour requirements

Four classes of fault were selected. Critical, major, minor and incidental. Each was given a weighting of 'demerit' points; 10, 4, 2 and 1 respectively. As samples from shipments of the product were inspected, items found to be defective had demerit scores awarded to them according to the number and class of defects found. These scores were added up and entered upon the record card for each item and supplier, together with the number of pieces in the sample which had been inspected. After a suitable period (which could be monthly or quarterly, but to some extent must depend upon the frequency of receipt of shipments) ratings were worked out. A few simple steps are required. From the record cards the demerit score for the shipments which have been inspected is totalled; also from the record cards, the total number of parts which were actually inspected, good and bad, during the period concerned is obtained (if sample inspection is being used this total will be very much less than the actual shipment quantities); then the total demerit score is divided by the number of hundreds of items actually inspected.

The last step gives a demerit score per hundred of items inspected and *this is the actual rating*. But it now remains to grade the scores so that vendors may be classified. In the system being described a score of less than 100 was considered to be excellent – first division. 101 to 300 was considered to be good – second division. 301 to 600 was labelled as poor – third division. A score of more than 601 was considered to be very bad – non-league.

Depending upon the division in which a vendor was placed, actions were taken on the following basis. Those in the first division were encouraged to improve their performance sufficiently to the stage when their shipments could be received with an agreed certificate of inspection. This certificate would clear them straight through to stock without inspection except for an occasional audit. Those in the second division were generally left alone. Active assistance was given to those in the third division to prevent them from falling to non-league status and also to encourage them to improve their performance so that they could move up to a higher division. Those vendors who found themselves outside the three divisions were regarded as being undesirable and the purchasing department was urged to find replacements for them.

There is ample evidence to show that the use of a vendor rating system is invaluable in enabling a company to determine the worth of its suppliers on a strictly factual basis. Previously this could not be done.

Chapter 30

Planned Maintenance

Adrian F Stedman, Consulting Engineer

Maintenance is not new. It must be practised in every manufacturing, construction and environmental activity. Otherwise, sooner or later, any one of these operations would cease to function. There are two basically different approaches to maintenance. These are *breakdown* and *planned* maintenance.

Breakdown maintenance

When unexpected failure occurs speed is the essential factor, the repairs being carried out during production working hours and probably continuing into an evening- or night-shift, leading to high labour costs with, possibly, little supervision. Some people make the faulty assumption that the cost of the breakdown is the only cost incurred in getting the plant back into service but, in fact, the true cost in considerably higher. To the direct cost of the repair must be added the on-costs of wages paid to idle operatives, the cost of production spoiled and the cost of production lost. It will also follow that the magnitude of the breakdown repair is greater than if the rectification had been carried out under controlled conditions, so preventing premature failure. Furthermore, if spare parts are not immediately available in the event of an unexpected breakdown, one may have to face the extra costs of sub-contracting production if a lengthy period of shutdown is necessary while the spare parts are manufactured and fitted.

When these additional costs are added to the emergency repair cost in terms of material and labour, the cost of a breakdown can be quite serious and, on high-volume productive plant, the rate of loss during a breakdown can reach £100 per hour or more. It can, therefore, be stated that normally, unless an item of equipment is so situated that it will not interrupt the plant production, breakdown maintenance is inherently inefficient on all counts, creating an indeterminate workload on the maintenance staff and there is no justification for its continuance in industry. Even in the case of many of the uncritical units it may be cheaper to bring them under a planned schedule of replacement than to allow them to run to ultimate failure.

Planned maintenance

Planned maintenance is the method of ensuring that maintenance requirements of plant, machinery, tools, buildings, services and utilities are adequately covered. The definition of the verb 'to maintain' is 'to keep working, keep in repair or preserve in a certain state'. This suggests that, ideally, all maintenance should be of a preventive nature and that planned maintenance should meet this requirement.

The process of deterioration is often so slow that it passes unnoticed unless observed by systematic maintenance at stated intervals. Most plant failures commence from minor causes which can be readily eliminated if their presence is known. It is also a well-known fact that plant which requires very little maintenance is more liable to major breakdown, due to complete neglect, than plant in which many minor failures demand continual vigilance. Systematic maintenance on a scheduled basis will, by its regularity, prevent such conditions fully developing and, at the same time, control the expenditure of money on the fixed assets, so that they are maintained at optimum production level for the minimum cost.

So far the necessity for maintenance planning has only been considered from an engineering standpoint, but there are two other major considerations which should be taken into account when evaluating the desirability of introducing planned maintenance. These are the necessity for effective utilisation of manpower and resources, and the possibility of reducing maintenance costs. The recently published Ministry of Technology report on maintenance engineering (HMSO) has emphasised the necessity for increasing productivity in maintenance departments. On financial grounds alone the report states that the annual maintenance cost for British manufacturing industry is in the order of £1,100 million. If all other maintenance activities, apart from those in manufacturing industries, are taken into account, the total maintenance cost for the country will probably be in the region of £3,000 million per annum. By this token it is worthwhile, whatever one's maintenance responsibility, to look at it closely and carry out a review of one's activities to ensure that the maintenance program is adequate, and that labour and resources are effectively utilised. This means planning control of maintenance activity, and it is known that the greatest single reason for failure of any planned maintenance system is the error of not establishing a reliable control method. It should be borne in mind that the system is only as good as its administration.

The maintenance inventory

It is a time-consuming project to establish a good planned maintenance system for, although the underlying principles are similar for all maintenance planning schemes, it does not follow that a system which is satisfactory in one factory will necessarily be so in another, even though the industry for both factories is the same. Any scheme which is introduced must take into account the prevailing local conditions which have a major influence upon the type of maintenance routines and frequencies employed. Unless the scheme is suited to the actual working conditions of the plant concerned there is always a danger that there may be little or no improvement resulting from the introduction of planned maintenance.

In order to relate the maintenance system directly to an individual factory the first essential is to establish a maintenance inventory. This inventory is, in fact, a priority listing, as one may not plan to cover every item of equipment in the plant, but only those pieces of equipment considered important to the continuous operation of the process or activity. Such a priority listing is also important because it may not be economical to cover all units; also, the degree to which planned maintenance can be applied may be restricted by management decision or budgeted funds available. It will therefore be seen that establishing the maintenance inventory is of considerable importance in relating the planned maintenance system to the particular environment, determining the routines and manpower requirements and ensuring that budgeted funds are utilised to maximum effect.

Elements of a planned maintenance system

Having set up the maintenance inventory the design of the planned maintenance system itself can be commenced. At this stage it is desirable to list the basic elements of a sound system. The number of these procedures instituted is directly in proportion to the degree of control required by management. The amount of clerical work involved is also directly related to the extent to which the control is applied. Many works executives have a fear that when planning is applied to maintenance work an excessive amount of clerical procedure is essential, but it will be seen that the amount of clerical procedure can be regulated by the design of the system. A fully comprehensive planned maintenance system will provide for the following:

1 Detailed examination and listing of each section of the plant to determine what has to be done and when it should be done.
2 Work classification by trade.
3 Individual and group man-hour requirements by trade.
4 Organisation of material and labour for individual jobs, job priorities and overall shop loading.
5 Preparation of master overhaul, inspection and lubrication schedules for each item of the maintenance inventory.
6 The integration of the preventive maintenance program with other maintenance work so that it becomes part of the overall planned program.
7 The provision of maintenance records including breakdown reports and cost allocations, from which decisions on plant replacement, service frequency, spares and manning requirements can be made.

Generally the system will be so designed that, having built up a work-load by trade against requirements, these requirements are translated into a shop loading which can be controlled.

Planned preventive maintenance routines

The backbone of any planned maintenance system is the effective utilisation of preventive maintenance routines, the most commonly used routines being the following:

1 Examination at a set frequency with subsequent defect reports and work orders.
2 Examination at a set frequency with immediate rectification of minor defects and a report on major work necessary to be done on work orders.
3 Systematic withdrawal of plant for major overhaul.
4 Replacement of functional parts at prescribed intervals.
5 Scheduled lubrication and cleaning.
6 Spares scheduling and stock control.

Again, it is entirely dependent on the degree of control required by management as to how many of these preventive maintenance techniques are incorporated in the system.

Plant specification

Detailed consideration must be given to the factors influencing the interval between maintenance routines and the serviceability of the plant before any planned maintenance operation can be established. This analysis is carried out by 'specifying' each item of plant called up in the maintenance inventory. When specifying each plant item is reduced to 'maintenance elements' and a detailed note is made of the factors influencing the procedure necessary to maintain serviceability. Upon examination in detail it will be found that these maintenance elements follow a pattern which has a descending order of priority relative to the functional grouping of components. To illustrate this point, in the case of a machine the principal maintenance elements in the descending order of priority relative to function would be: drive and drive unit, location and direction of motion of parts affecting the accuracy of product or operation, type of gearing and bearings, lubrication system, safety provisions, main-frames and foundation blocks. Special note is also taken of operating conditions, lubricant grades required and statutory requirements where applicable.

A similar evaluation is carried out when specifying a building. The maintenance elements in this instance could be as follows: walls, floors, doors, windows, roof and roof trusses, glazing, internal and external drainage system. Each element would be appraised for maintenance relative to the type of process carried on within the building and the local physical conditions.

Electrical equipment is specified in a similar manner, and it will be found that in many instances the maintenance requirement can be resolved into a series of standard specifications which can be varied in frequency to meet local conditions.

When the maintenance specification is complete for an individual plant item, frequencies of attention are allotted to each maintenance element in the specification. Each of these frequencies will be determined by the age of the plant, its operating conditions and performance level required. In order to simplify the specification procedure it is as well to have a suitable standard form. Examples of a suitable layout for this document is shown in Figures 30:1 and 30:2.

Preparation of planned routines

It will be found that, after the specification of any unit of plant has been examined, there will be several items of identical frequency. These items can be segregated and grouped to form a maintenance routine of prescribed time-interval. If desired, maintenance routines of identical frequency can again be grouped on a departmental basis so as to create on overall departmental maintenance routine of set time frequency. The same procedure is followed to produce lubrication tours by synthesising the lubrication data in the plant specification, and taking into account grades and types of lubricant, operating conditions and frequency of servicing. Again, by grouping individual lubrication requirements of similar frequency on a departmental basis, the lubrication tour for that area of the plant is created.

When designing planned maintenance routines it is essential to define clearly the limit to which the servicing operation called for is to apply. For example, a gearbox could be stripped beyond the limits

PLANT MAINTENANCE ANALYSIS SHEET

Plant number 453 / 621 Plant name TRANSFER PUMP

Location CHEMICAL HOUSE Sheet number 1 of 1 date 18 - 5 - 65

Examination analysis	Operating condition		
	Hours/week		
Parts to be examined or serviced	Type of examination /service	Frequency	Specification number
FOR 5-C MOTOR – SEE ELECT SPEC	—	—	—
FLEXIBLE COUPLING	VIS	4	E 392
GLAND SEALS	VIS	1	E 391
AIR COCK AND DRAIN TAPS	VIS	4	E 392
MAIN BEARINGS	VIS	50	E 395
MAIN SHAFT	VIS	50	E 395
IMPELLER AND CASING – INTERNAL	VIS	50	E 395
CASING EXTERNAL	VIS	13	E 393
FLANGED JOINTS AND PIPEWORK	VIS	1	E 391
PRESSURE GAUGE	VIS	1	E 391
ISOLATING VALVES	VIS	1	E 391
BEDPLATE AND FOUNDATION BOLTS	VIS	4	E 392
FOUNDATION BLOCK	VIS	13	E 393
GENERAL CONDITION	VIS	1	E 391
ALIGNMENTS	MRCH	26	E 394
REPLACE SEALS	MRCH	26	E 394

Lubrication analysis

Lubrication details	Lubrication	Quantity	Grade	Frequency		Specification number
				Weeks	Shift	
MAIN BEARINGS						
GREASE PACKED	BRB	PACKED	BRB	26	DAY	L 65
	3		3			
MOTOR 2 GREASE	BRB	1 SHOT	BRB	13	DAY	L 43
NIPPLES	3		3			

FIGURE 30:1 PLANT MAINTENANCE ANALYSIS SHEET—MECHANICAL PLANT

Typical layout and compilation of mechanical plant maintenance analysis sheet

PLANT MAINTENANCE ANALYSIS SHEET

Plant number — Plant name POWDER BLEND HOUSE

Location BLOCK 52 C Sheet number 1 of 1 date 21 - 8 - 64

Examination analysis	Operating condition		
	Hours/week		
Parts to be examined or serviced	Type of examination /service	Frequency	Specification number
VISUALLY EXAMINE EXTERNAL WALLS FOR	VIS	50	B 935
CRACKS AND LOOSE BRICKS			
VISUALLY EXAMINE FLOOR FOR DAMAGE OR	VIS	4	B 934
DEFECT			
ROOF STRUCTURE - CHECK FOR	VIS	4	B 934
GENERAL DAMAGE OR DEFECT			
DOORS - CHECK FOR DAMAGE OR	VIS	4	B934
DEFECT			
WINDOWS - ROOF AND SIDE - CHECK FOR	VIS	4	B934
BROKEN GLAZING			
ROOF - CHECK FOR LEAKS & LOOSE COVERING	V	4	B934

Lubrication analysis

Lubrication details	Lubrication	Quantity	Grade	Frequency		Specification number
				Weeks	Shift	
VENTILATION GEAR	OIL	HAND OIL	VACT.	26	NIGHT	L 25
BOLTON GATE GUIDE PINS	OIL	HAND OIL	VACT.	13	DAY	L24
		1 SHOT EACH				

FIGURE 30:2 PLANT MAINTENANCE ANALYSIS SHEET—BUILDING

Typical maintenance analysis sheet for a building

necessary for an examination requirement if the limits of inspection were not defined. Many planned routines have failed because the instructions contained within the routine were unclear owing to over-simplification of vocabulary.

The completed maintenance routine will clearly specify the task, by whom it has to be done and at what frequency, and an estimate of task-hours. Initially, the period between maintenance routines will be a case of judgment which can subsequently be modified when it is shown that the time-intervals can be lengthened or shortened with advantage.

The effect of frequency upon the cost of plant maintenance is illustrated by the curves plotted in Figure 30:3. From these curves it will be seen that it is possible finally to set the optimum service frequency by statistics provided by the plant itself.

After the planned routines for the equipment to be brought within the planned maintenance system are completed, they can then be pre-printed and filed in trade groups ready for issue. Typical electrical and mechanical routine sheets are shown in Figures 30:4, 30:5 and 30:6. These routine sheets are issued to the appropriate trade section when called for by the control system of the planned maintenance scheme. After completion by the tradesmen the routine sheets are returned to control, so that action can be implemented to effect any repair work required to maintain serviceability.

Control of scheduled maintenance routines

An adequate method of control for scheduled maintenance routines must be provided, otherwise a plant could quickly revert to breakdown maintenance conditions. Various proprietary methods of control suitable for planned maintenance exist, but it is also possible to design a suitable system.

One of the simplest methods to install is the well-known 'tickler' system. The comparative simplicity of this method, together with its low initial cost, will appeal to the smaller concern. All that is required is a control card upon which are entered details of the routine to which the card relates. An example of a typical control card is shown in Figure 30:7. All maintenance routines have individual control cards which cover the total period of time for that item of plant, for

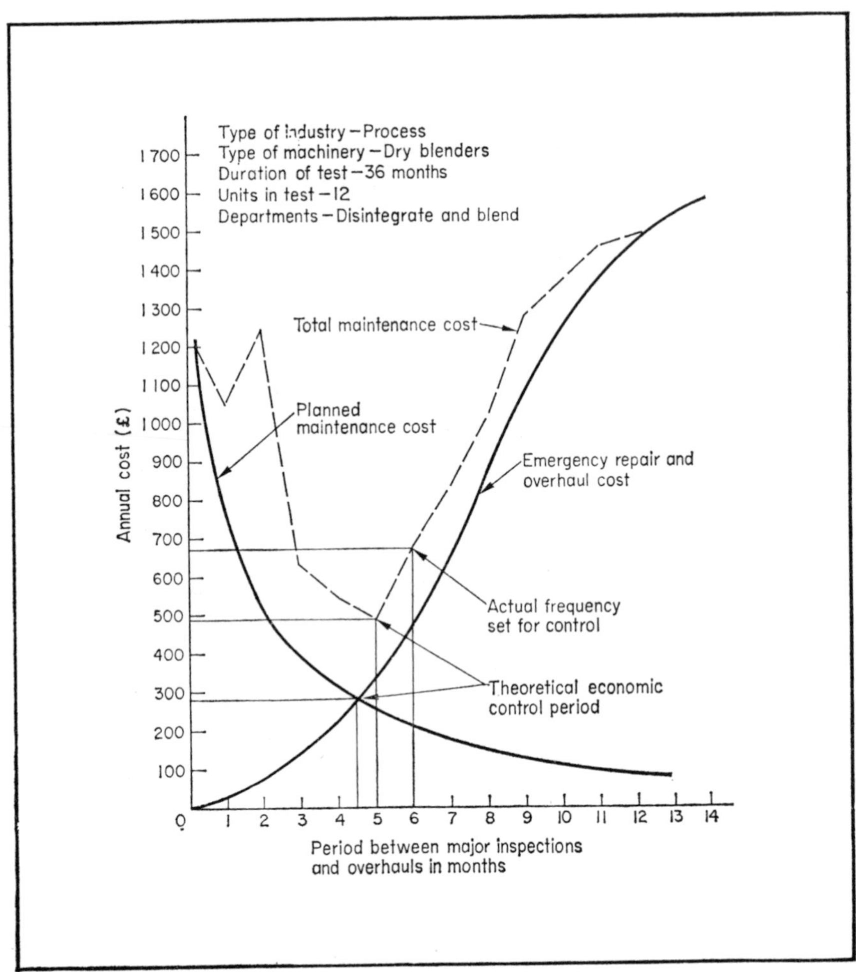

FIGURE 30:3 ECONOMIC PLANNED MAINTENANCE AND FREQUENCY CURVE

Curve showing relationship between planned maintenance cost and frequency of inspection

Location; Wharf; Phosphate Intake Plant Units: Intake Plants 1 and 2 Maintenance Routing: ppm	Freq: 26 Weeks Std. hrs. 18.75 Date Iss. Date Reqd.	Spec No. EG54

GENERAL INSTRUCTIONS

Visually examine for damage or insecurity. Check for oil leaks on resistor tanks where applicable. Open up inspection on panel units, blow out dust accumulation and visually examine for loose components, overheating and general defect. Check selector switches for accurate operation. Check for faulty or damaged push buttons and control handles. Check movement of drum type controller through range. Blow out air cooled resistor bank. Open up and blow out CFS main isolator and check condition of fuses. Check all units where applicable for faulty cable glands, defective hinges and locks on cubicles. Check remote operation units for general defect and wander cable for abrasion, cuts and general defect.

Location	Duty	Maker	Type	Plant 1 Cond.	Plant 2 Cond.
Pump Floor	Main tipper and traversing motor lighting and winch motor control cubicle	Brookhirst	Air break		
	Main pump motor Control cubicle – Inc. Res.	Brookhirst	Air break		
	Traversing drum controller	Brookhirst	Air break		
	Traversing controller Resistor bank	Brookhirst	Air cooled		
	Main isolator	Bill	CFS		
Tipper Floor	Boom control remote unit 1	Allen West	Air break		
	Boom control remote unit 2	Allen West	Air break		
	Boom control remote unit 3 and wander lead	Allen West	Air break		
	Auxiliary control cubicle	Brookhirst	Air break		

FIGURE 30:4 STANDARD ELECTRICAL INSPECTION SHEET LAYOUT

Example of electrical inspection routine

MAINTENANCE ROUTINE: Morton Mixer No. 4. Maintenance Group: Mechanical

PLANNED MAINTENANCE SPECIFICATION AND ROUTINE NUMBER: M/TE5091. Dated 18/8/59.

PLANT No: 9402/36. LOCATION – POWDER BLENDING.
PLANT NAME: Morton Mixer No. 4 – Duplex Pattern.

Frequency 1 month
Std. hours 1.50
Date issued
Date reqd.

Check item	MONTHLY INSPECTION "RUNNING" Inspection details	Morton No. 4 Condition O.K.	 W.R.
Motor	Audibly check for quiet running Check temperature and lubrication satisfactory Check cable entries and terminal boxes secure Check casing Check mounting bolts		
Chain-drives	Audibly check for quiet running to ensure correct meshing and adjustment		
Gear box	Audibly check for quiet running Check temperature and lubrication satisfactory Check through range of operation Check casing for defects and signs of leakage		
Clutch	Check visually for defects Check phosphor bronze thrust pad for wear Check pivot pins and linkage for wear and backlash Check through range of operation		
Beater blade drive gears	Audibly check for quiet running Check casing for defects and leakage		
Beater blade bearings	Check for signs of wear and defects Check temperature while running Check lubrication satisfactory		
Gland packing	Check for signs of mixture leakage Check adjustment of glands		
Boater blades	Visually check for defects and distortion Check for wear between blades and wall of container		
Mix container	Visually check for defect and distortion Check for signs of corrosion Check all bolts for security		
Container elevation mech	Check in operation for defects Check mounting bolts Check linkage		
Lid	Visually check for defects and distortion Check operating linkage		
Safety devices	Check safety plates and linkwork for defects		
General	Visually check all securing bolts – guards and casing Check that machine has been satisfactorily lubricated and is as clean as operation permits		

DEFECT REPORT OVERLEAF

Name	Clock No.	Trade	Hours worked	Date completed

FIGURE 30:5 STANDARD MECHANICAL INSPECTION SHEET LAYOUT

Example of mechanical inspection routine

DATE COMPILED: 4/1/62

LABELLING AND PACKING – 13 WEEKLY INSPECTION – SPEC NO. E 2043

DATE ISSUED: DATE REQUIRED: DATE COMPLETED:

TICK IN APPROPRIATE COLUMN, that is, OK or WR (work required)

PLANT NAME	CHECK ITEM	LINE NUMBER					
		1		2		3	
		OK	WR	OK	WR	OK	WR
DUDLEY CAN UNSCRAMBLER	Check variable speed drive and pulley for wear. Audibly inspect hydraulic pump unit. Visually inspect drive belts from motor. Audibly inspect reduction gearboxes. Check external drive-chains, to separator belts. Visually inspect tipper frame, main bearings and latching arrangements						
CAN UNSCRAMBLER HOIST	Check traverse wheels on trolley unit for wear. Check trolley gear teeth for wear. Inspect traverse chain-wheel. Open hoist inspection covers and check gearing.						
CAN BOOSTERS	Visually inspect spur gear teeth for wear and backlash. Check bearings for lift.						
HIGHSPEED LABELLING MACHINES	Visually inspect main frame and castings for damage, defect and mis-alignment. Check can size changing mechanism for visible defect						
CASE PACKERS	Visually inspect crosshead and slide bars for wear. Check can pushers for damage, wear and distortion						
CASE SEALER HANDY CANS	Check main frame and castings for damage and defect. Audibly inspect reduction gearbox. Check glue rollers and boxes for damage and wear. Check general condition of M/C satisfactory						
COMPRESSION UNIT – HANDY CANS	Visually inspect head tail and tension pulleys for damage or defect. Tension pulley assembly correct. Visually inspect condition of drive-chain. Audibly inspect gearbox						
IMC CASE SEALER	Visually inspect spur gearing in top section for wear. Visually inspect spur gearing in bottom section for wear. Check auxiliary drive-chains. Audibly inspect reduction gearbox						
PANTIN CONVEYORS	Audibly inspect motor gearbox. Visually inspect head, tail jockey and tensioning pulleys. Policeman operating correctly.						
COLLIS CONVEYOR	Remove side panels. Visually inspect gearbox drive. Audibly inspect reduction gearbox. Check conveyor head and tail pulley						

FIGURE 30:6 STANDARD GROUPED INSPECTION SHEET LAYOUT

Example of grouped mechanical inspection routine

example, an air compresser could have four control cards covering weekly, monthly, quarterly and annual maintenance tasks. The yearly maintenance is then divided into a suitable control period (usually weekly) resulting in a series of controlling marker cards numbered from 1 to 52 inclusive.

To operate the 'tickler system' all control cards for the current week are withdrawn from the main file, and the controlling marker card placed to the rear of the file. The relevant task sheets called for by the control cards are then withdrawn from storage and issued to the trade groups responsible for carrying out the maintenance routine. The tickler cards are then placed into a section entitled 'planned work outstanding'. As the completed routines are returned the appropriate control card is withdrawn from the outstanding work-load section and replaced in the main file in the correct position for the next operational cycle. This position is simply calculated by adding the routine frequency in weeks to the current week number, which makes the control system self-progressing. Withdrawals or additions are made to the control cards when plant is either withdrawn from service or new plant is installed.

Other methods which have been successfully employed for the control of planned maintenance operations are Gantt charts, visual planning boards and proprietary forms supplied by the business stationery houses.

Planned rectification and shop loading

Unless the results of scheduled inspection and servicing are followed up the benefits arising from planned maintenance routines are lost. It is therefore an essential part of controlled maintenance to carry out a planned rectification program of defects uncovered by the systematic routine.

When a maintenance or servicing report is returned it will indicate any repairs or adjustments required to maintain serviceability, the time-scale by which such repairs should be completed and the materials required. With such information it is then possible to plan and co-ordinate the whole operation with production departments, arrange formal plant release, manufacture or obtain any spares and allocate the necessary manpower within the trade groups affected. It

MAINTENANCE DEPARTMENT	SHOP LOADING	MAN-HOURS AND TRADE GROUP	SHEET NO. OF
			WEEK ENDING

	BUILDING								MECHANICAL								ELECTRICAL								
Job Cards No. Issued	Bricklayer		Joiners		Painters		Plumbers		Fitters		Welders		M/C shop		Inst Mech		Elect		Wiremen		Mates		Total		Variances
	Est'd	Act	Est'd	Act	Est'd	Act	Est'd	Act	Est'd	Act	Est'd	Act	Est'd	Act	Est'd	Act	Est'd	Act	Est'd	Act	Est'd	Act	Est'd	Act	
TOTALS COMP																									
END LDGS	/		/		/		/		/		/		/		/		/		/		/		/		

NOTE: INCOMPLETE JOBS CARRIED FORWARD FROM THE PREVIOUS WEEK TO BE RECORDED FIRST, THE ESTIMATED MAN-HOURS OF SUCH JOBS BEING THE BALANCE REMAINING AFTER DEDUCTING THE ACTUAL FROM THE ORIGINAL ESTIMATE

FIGURE 30:7 LABOUR CONTROL
Maintenance: weekly shop loading form by trade group

will be seen that the maintenance function is now being controlled because all operational aspects of the job are known. In some cases it will be possible to create a down-time period to carry out essential work by subjecting the plant affected to prior overtime working, which enables sufficient stocks to be built up to cover the estimated shut-down. Maintenance work can also be scheduled for the following periods:

1 Meal breaks for minor repairs
2 Shift changeover periods
3 Week-ends and statutory holidays
4 Periods of low production in seasonal trades

Prior knowledge of maintenance man-hour requirements, which is now created by the planning and estimating operation for any given repair or routine, will enable the shop foreman to summarise his trade labour requirement, and forecast the manning state for the job and amount of overtime required to complete within the down-time for which plant can be released from production. It will also follow that the ordinary day-work load covering shop overhaul of stand-by plant, manufacture of spares and additional facilities, can now be accurately forecast and planned, enabling the maintenance work-force to be fully employed on essential work and planned repairs. Costing of work also becomes more realistic because manpower, material and specialised costs associated with a particular job are now known. Examples of documents that can be used for shop loading and cost control based upon a planned operation are shown in Figures 30:7 and 30:8.

Stabilisation period

It will be found that upon the introduction of maintenance planning there will be an increase in the work-load over the standing work-load as arrears of maintenance are revealed. Over the first three to six months this work-load will attain a peak value, after which there will be a gradual reduction until it is below the original figure. This period is called the 'stabilisation period', and can take anything up to twelve months, according to the size and type of plant. At this juncture the introduction of incentives can be commenced if it is the intention to

MAINTENANCE DEPARTMENT									WEEKLY EXCESS COST ANALYSIS										WEEK ENDING		
NAME	OVERTIME (Cost Day rate)	LOST TIME																		PERIOD TOTALS	
		1		2		3		4		5		6		7		9		10			
		M/hrs	£	M/hrs	£	M/hrs	£	M/hrs	£	M/hrs	£	M/hrs	£	M/hrs	£	M/hrs	£	M/hrs	£	M/hrs	£

FIGURE 30:8 COST CONTROL

Weekly excess cost analysis sheet

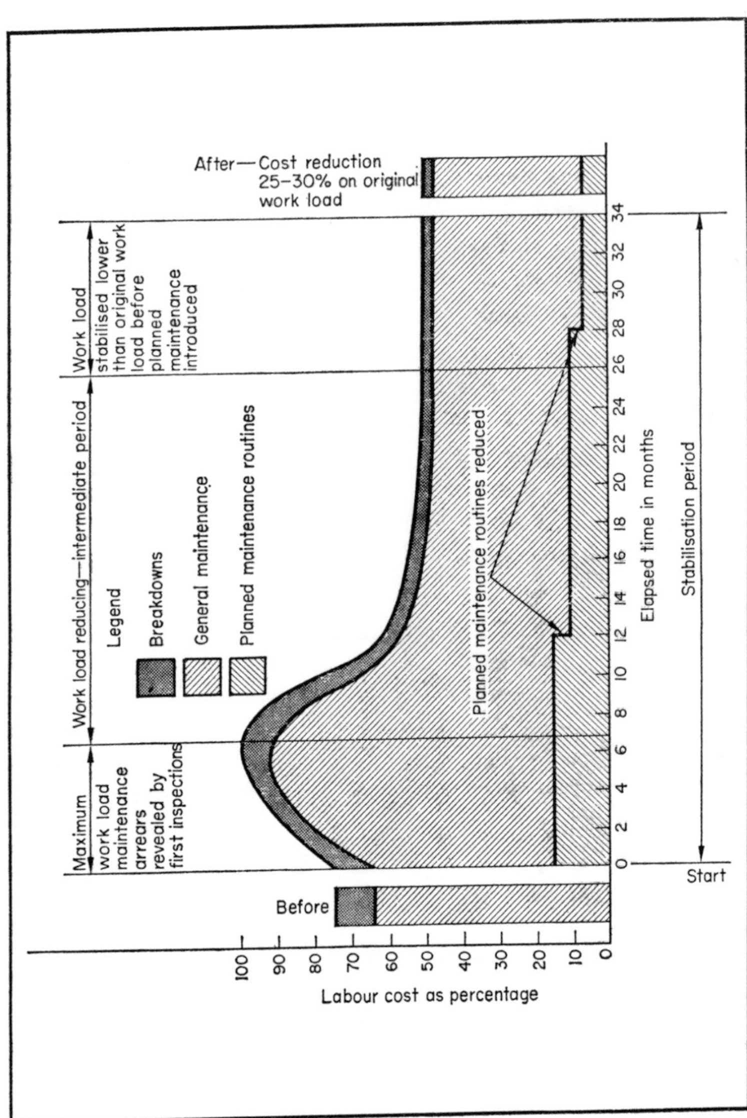

FIGURE 30:9 PLANNED MAINTENANCE STABILISATION CURVE
Relationship between labour cost and elapsed time from introduction of planned maintenance

relate the planned maintenance system to a bonus scheme – see Figure 30:9.

In the long term the benefits achieved by maintenance planning are more tangible than during the stabilisation period. Over a four-year program covering a manufacturing operation, maintenance costs were reduced by thirty-three per cent, man-hours reduced by twenty-five per cent, and the percentage of plant not requiring repairs during examination increased from forty per cent to sixty per cent. An increase in the effective utilisation of skilled maintenance trade manpower from thirty-five per cent to sixty per cent was also attained over the program period. The net gain to the company in financial terms of this increase in productivity in the maintenance department is quite considerable. It indicates the vital role that can be played by planned maintenance in an overall cost reduction policy, but time must be allowed for the full benefit of the system to develop.

Summary

Within the scope of this chapter it has not been possible to cover fully every aspect of planned maintenance. However, the object has been to provide some practical guidance upon the introduction of planned maintenance, and to illustrate that the task is not formidable, and that the scheme must be designed to meet the conditions prevailing at the site. The rewards of a properly designed planned maintenance system are quite considerable and may be summarised as follows:

1 Higher productivity of the maintenance staff.
2 Economy in the use of materials and spares.
3 Minimum down-time due to plant failure.
4 Lower overall maintenance cost per unit of production.
5 Achievement and upkeep of whatever standard and quality of maintenance is determined.
6 The management and engineering staff dictates when and what repairs shall be done, instead of the poor physical conditions of the plant dictating to them when repairs shall be made.
7 It highlights assets which should be replaced due to the uneconomic cost of maintenance and repairs.

8 It allows comparison of the merits and reliability between makes of plant and equipment used on similar work.
9 Budgetary control of maintenance and plant replacement costs can be effected.

Viewed from the broad management angle, planned maintenance is another technique with which to combat rising costs. Maintenance planning is no longer an academic exercise; it is a full-scale component of senior management operation vital to industrial survival in an increasingly competitive world market. To implement a planned program to gain all the benefits may not be initially or economically justifiable in some instances, but it is quite profitable to use even part of a program. If the plan of operation is gradually introduced, progressed and consolidated at a rate which is practical for the individual plant, then the full benefits of planned maintenance will materialise within a reasonable time.

Index

ASME 592, 594
ABC analysis
  materials management 580–8
    applying the principle 582–3
Abrasive Wheels Regulations 1970 442
Absorption
  cost, pricing 134
  overheads 67, 68
Acceptance, contracts between companies 214–17
  keeping offer open for a stipulated time 215
  lapse and revocation of offer 216
  need for special method 216
  postal 216–17
  tenders 217
Acceptances, bills of exchange 15
Acoustics, planning office space 255
Accuracy, overheads 67
Acquisition, of shares 204
Action
  centres 400
  plans
    individual 414–16
    unit 406–10
  request 183–6
Actions, value analysis 508
Activity
  duration, project scheduling 540–2
  sampling, clerical work measurement 238
Actual costs, ascertainment 76–7
Advertising
  employment 312–13
  industrial selling 150–3
  sales engineering enquiries 186–7
  technical journal selection 161
After-sales service 193
Agencies
  advertising and publicity 153
  employment 312–13
Agency shop agreements 372
Agreements, collective 376–8, 386
Allocation
  overheads 67
  resources, assets and capital 22–3
Alternatives, ranking 26
Analysis
  job *see* Job analysis
  manpower planning 295–304
    forecasting future requirements 297–302
    present position and analysis of trends 295–7

Analysis *continued*
manpower planning *continued*
projections 303–4
organisation and methods 233–5
payroll 65–6
product pricing 139–41
time, project scheduling 542
value *see* Value analysis
variance 79–80
Analytical estimating, work measurement 603
Application forms 313
Applications, data processing 273–7
Apportionment, overheads 67
Appraisal *see* Management by objectives
Apprenticeship
contracts of employment 342
training 432–4
Articles of association 200
Assessing candidates, recruitment and selection
final stages 318
interviews 315–17
methods 314–15
use of consultants 319–20
Asset allocation 22–3
Assets
balance sheet 46–9
current 5
in transformation 24–5
Assignment, jobs: project scheduling 548
Attitudes to quality control, management 615–19
Audience
importance of knowledge of, in public speaking 463–4
obtaining attention of 465–7
Auditing, new production facilities 529–30
Audits, quality 621–2
Automatic inspection, process control 631
Averaging performance over time 332–3

Balance sheet 46–9
Bands of performance 332
Bankers 7
Bankruptcy 3
Banks, overdrafts 15
Bargaining
collective *see* Collective bargaining
units 386
Baric Computing Services Ltd 546
Basic work data, work measurement 603–4, 605
Batch
control, clerical work measurement 238
costing 59
production 569
Bench marks
establishing a graded structure 328
work measurement 604–6
Bills of exchange 15–16
contracts 218
Blanket orders, materials management 578–9
Brainstorming, value analysis 506
Breach of contract, damages for 223–6
Breakdown maintenance 637–8
Brech, E.F.L. 85
British Institute of Management 319
British Rail 604
British Standards Institution 331, 337
Budgetary control 81–106
budget preparation 89–97
calculation of direct labour requirements 93–5
calculation of working capital and capital employed 96
determination of manufacturing mix 92–3
determination of sales volume mix 92
budgets 85–9
benefits 85–6
cost centres 87
fixed and flexible 89
period of 88
requirements 86
responsibilities for 86–7
control activity 84
long-term profit planning 105–6
objectives 83
performance reporting 97–101
preparation and use of control information 84
project cost control 102–5
relationship with standard costing 76
Budgetary planning
see also Budgetary control
definition of responsibilities 83
planning period 82–3
objectives 82
Budgeting, computer management 282–3

Budgets
  see also Budgetary control
  capital expenditure 102–3
  cash 9–13
  sales 143–6
Bureaux, computer service 278–9, 282
Buyers, role in value analysis 500, 506

CAPRI 34
CPM *see* Critical path method
Calculations, engineering: computer applications 275
Call report, sales engineering 186
Capacity
  production control 551
  to make contracts 219–20
Capital
  employed 96
  expenditure
    evaluation 19–44
      context 21–5
      need for 20–1
      presentation of results 41–3
      responsibility 21
      risk and return 36–41
      techniques 25–41
    preparation of budgets 102–3
  public limited companies 201–4
  return on 53
  working *see* Working capital
Carrels, planning office space 257
Case presentations 471–2
Cash
  budgets 9–13
  control of 8–9
  balance, technique of evaluation 26–8
  flow, statements 11–13
  unused balances 17–18
Cellular offices 257
Centres, cost 63
Chairmen (of meetings etc.)
  conduct of meetings 488–9
  preparation 487–8
  reminders 490
Charging
  labour costs 66
  materials costs 65
Charts, method study 591–5
Checklists, sales engineering 183, 185
Checking, customer enquiries 159
Cheques, contracts 218
Chief Registrar of Trade Unions and Employers' Associations 366, 368
Circulation, of reports 474–5
City and Guilds of London Institute 433–4
Classification
  costs 60
  functional 62
  performance reporting 97
Cleanliness, Offices Shops and Railway Premises Act 263
Clerical work measurement 237–41
  activity sampling 238
  batch control 238
  estimating 237–8
  group training technique 238–9
  MTM data system 240
  multiple regression analysis (MRA) 240–1
  predetermined standards 239–40
  production study 239
  self recording 237
  time study 239
Closed shop agreements 373
Clothing, storing and drying: legislation on 265
Code of Industrial Relations Practice 378–90
  collective bargaining 385–6
  communication and consultation 383–4
  disciplinary procedure 389–90
  employee representation at place of work 386–8
  employers' associations' responsibilities 382–3
  grievance and disputes procedure 389
  individual employees' responsibilities 383
  management responsibilities 380, 382
  trade unions' responsibilities 382
Collective
  agreements 376–8, 386
  bargaining 376–8, 385–6
  disputes 389
Commission on Industrial Relations 366, 371, 373
Commissioning, new production facilities 526–9
  flow lines 528–9
Commitment, sales engineering 169–72
Common measures 23
Common skills, training 448
Communications 460–91
  meetings 485

Communications *continued*
planning office space 249, 255
report writing 473–84
speaking 460–73
Community, protection of in emergency situations 371–2
Company
financial reports *see* Report and accounts
Company law 197–208
capital and shares 201–4
acquisition and transfer 204
classes of 202–3
debentures 203
membership 201–2
directors 204–7
legal liability 206–7
publicity 205–6
dividends 207–8
formation 198–201
articles of association 200
memorandum of association 199–200
prospectus 200–1
registration 198–9
legal status 197–8
meetings 207
patents 208–13
Comparative estimating, work measurement 604–6
Comparisons, paired: design of payment systems 326–7
Compensation reviews, management by objectives 419
Competition, market research 124, 129
Computers 267–83
applications 273–7
engineering calculations 275
management involvement 277
operational research 275–6
description 267–70
management of 277–83
budgeting and control 282–3
costing computer time 280–1
implementation of systems 281–2
management uses 270–3
data capture 271–2
on-line systems 272–3
production control 566–7
Conditions of employment 347–8
Conducting meetings 488–90
Consideration, contracts between companies 217–18
Consultation, industrial relations 384
Consultants, recruitment and selection 319–20
Context of evaluation 21–5
assets in transformation 24–5
common measure 23
purpose 22
resources, assets and capital 22–3
time value of money 25
Contract costing 59
Contracts, between companies
capacity to make 219–20
consideration 217–18
damages for breach of contract 223–6
form of 218–19
intention to create legal relations 219
misrepresentation 222–3
mistakes in 220–2
offer and acceptance 214–17
specific performance 226
Contracts of employment 342–4
1963 Act 343, 349, 350, 368, 374
compelling employee to fulfil 354–5
employing persons under 18 342
misrepresentation 343
restricting spare-time activities 344
written details 343–4
Control
budgetary *see* Budgetary control
cash 8–9
computer management 282–3
documents, organisation and methods 241–4
management, work study aspects 608, 612–13
of manpower 289–91, 305
production *see* Production control
project *see* Project scheduling
quality *see* Quality control
scheduled maintenance routines 645–50
Conventional pricing 134–8
selling at a loss 137–8
Conveyancing, land 219
Corporate
objectives 289, 396
plans 144
Corrective action, quality control 621–2, 624–5
Cost
accounting 56–80
classification of costs 60
cost units and centres 63
direct and indirect costs 60–2
factory job costing 69–70
functional classification 62

Cost *continued*
  accounting *continued*
    labour costs 65–6
    marginal costing 72–6
    material costs 63–5
    methods and techniques 57–60
      batch 59
      contract 59
      factory job costing 58
      operating 60
      process 60
    overheads 67–9
    process costing 71
    standard costing and variance analysis 76–80
    work in progress 71–2
  analysis, value analysis 503–5
  centres, budgeting 87, 400
  control, project 102–5
  of quality 615–16, 627
  reduction, materials management 571–5
    target selection 572–3
  value 497
Cost-plus pricing 134
Costing
  see also Computers: management of: budgeting and control
  computer time 280–1
Costs
  fixed 73
  implementing new payment systems 335–40
  marginal 72ff
  materials 63–5
    requisitions 561
  of production, new products 514
  planned maintenance 646
  prime 73
  semi-variable 73
  unnecessary, value analysis 497-8
  value analysis 501–2
Creativity, value analysis 506
Credit, trade 14
Critical path analysis, computer applications 276
Critical path method (CPM) 540, 554
Current
  assets 5, 48–9
  liabilities 5
  ratios 7–8
Customer
  inquiries, screening 157–9
    checklist 163–4
    checking 159
    postal inquiries 158

Customer *continued*
  inquiries, screening *continued*
    salesmen's inquiries 158
    telephone inquiries 158
  records, sales engineering 178–86
Customers
  existing, sales engineering 173–4
  industry climate and developments 120–1
  needs 124

DCF *see* Discounted cash flow
Damages
  breach of contract 223–6
    distinction between liquidated and unliquidated 224–5
    distinction between liquidated damages and penalties 225–6
  patent infringement 211–12
  wrongful dismissal 353–5
Data
  base 272
  capture 271–2
  processing applications *see* Computers
Debentures, public limited companies 203
Debt collection 11
Debtors, profit and loss account 49
Declining industries 114–15
Definition
  project 537–9
  in value analysis 501–3
    of function 502–3
Delivery rating, materials management 576–7
Department of Employment 312–13, 319
Depreciation 11–13
Designers, value analysis 499
Desk research 127–9
Detail, performance reporting 97
Development
  management 419–22
  quality control 623–5
  supervisors 447–51
Differentials 337
  payment structures 322–3, 325
Direct
  costs 60–2
  labour, budgeting 93–5
Directors, public limited companies 204–7
  legal liabilities 206–7
  publicity 205–6

Disciplinary procedures, industrial relations 389–90
Disclosure
  of information, Industrial Relations Act 375, 386
  trade secrets 357–9
Discounted cash flow 31, 32–5
Discounts 11
  purchasing 573
Dishonesty, termination of employment 352
Dismissal
  see also Redundancy payments
  see also Termination of employment
  damages for 353–5
  instant, without notice 350
  unfair 373–4
Disobedience, termination of employment 351
Dispatch, works manufacturing orders 556–64
Disputes, individual and collective procedures 389
Distribution, reports 474–5
Docks and Harbours Act 368
Document control, organisation and methods 241–4
Documentation
  computer systems 282
  works manufacturing orders 556–64
Donovan Report 364
Drawings, factory layout 525
Drinking water, Offices, Shops and Railway Premises Act 265
Dry tankers 588

Earnings
  per share 50, 53
  stability of 332–3
Economic order quantity 567–8, 583, 584
Economics
  market 130–42
  of quality 615–16
Efficiency, training as an aid to 444–7
Emergency situations, Industrial Relations Act 371–2
Employees
  representation at place of work 386–8
  responsibilities for industrial relations 383
  rights, Industrial Relations Act 372–5
    agency shop agreements 372
Employees *continued*
  rights, Industrial Relations Act *continued*
    closed shop agreements 373
    disclosure of information 375
    dismissal, unfair 373–4
    membership of trade unions 372–4
    notice 374–5
Employers
  associations
    registration 368–71
    responsibilities for industrial relations 382
  rights, patents 212–13
  unfair industrial practices 375–6
Employment
  agencies 312–13
  contracts of *see* Contracts of employment
Engineering
  calculations, computer applications 275
  quality 619–20
  sales *see* Sales engineering
  value *see* Value engineering
Engineering Industry Training Board 433–4, 443
Engineers
  try-out 529
  value *see* Value engineer
Equal pay 328–9, 346
Equal Pay Act 328–9, 368
Equipment
  planning new production facilities 518–19
  office *see* Office equipment
Equivalent mean, investment period 35–6
Esteem value 497
Estimating
  analytical, work measurement 603
  clerical work measurement 237–8
  comparative, work measurement 604–6
Evaluation
  capital expenditure 19–44
  of manpower 289–91, 305
  suppliers 576–9
  techniques 25–41
Exchange value 497
Exhibitions 150, 152–3
Expediting, materials management 583–6
External cash flows 11

FIFO *see* First in, first out
Factories Act 1961 346
Factoring 11, 16–17
Factors, standard costs 77
Factory
  job costing 58, 69–70
    estimating and price fixing 69
    manufacturing order 69
    preparation of a job cost 69–70
  layout *see* Layout, factories
  orders 69
  overheads 67
Failure analysis, quality control 624–5
Fair wage payments, government contracts 346–7
False
  representations 222
  statements 222
Fault reporting, quality control 624–5
Feedback of information, process control 629–30
Field work, industrial market research 127–9
Files, document control 244
Final inspection, process control 630–1
Finance, short-term sources 13–17
Finished part stores receipts 557, 582
Fire, Offices, Shops and Railway Premises Act 266
First aid, Offices, Shops and Railway Premises Act 266
First in, first out 64, 135–6
Fixed
  budgets 89
  costs 73
  material location 520–1
Flexible budgets 89
Floor plan 525
Flow
  process charts, methods study 591–2
  production 569
Flow-lines, commissioning new production facilities 528–9
Forecasting
  manpower planning 295–304
    forecasting future requirements 297–302
    present position and analysis of trends 295–7
    projections 303–4
  production control 553
Fork lift trucks 587
Form of a contract 218–19
Forms control, organisation and methods 241–4
Frequency of inspection, planned maintenance 644–5
Function layout 521
Functional
  classification, cost accounting 62
  objectives 398–410
Functions, value analysis
  cost analysis 503–5
  definition 502–3

General Electric Corp 575
Gifts, contracts 219
Gopertz curve 514, 517
Government contracts, fair wage payments 346–7
Grades, salary progression 333–5
Grading
  design of payment systems 325
  establishing structures 327–8
Grievances, individual and collective procedure 389
Group
  technology 521
  timing technique, clerical work measurement 238–9
Guarantees, contracts of 218
Guidelines, management by objectives 402–3

Handling *see* Mechanical handling
Heating, Offices, Shops and Railway Premises Act 262
Hire purchase, contracts 218
Human aspects, management by objectives 392

Identification, sales outlets 149
Illness, termination of employment 350–1
Imperial Chemical Industries Ltd 603
Implementation
  computer systems 281–2
  new payment systems 335-40
  organisation and methods 235–7
  planning office space 261
Improvements, training as an aid 444–7
Incentives 321–40
  sales engineering 169–72
  types of scheme 330–3
    amount of payment 331–2

Incentives *continued*
  types of scheme *continued*
    stability of earnings 332–3
  and wage systems 329–30
Incompetence, termination of employment 352
Indirect
  costs 60–2
  labour, budgeting 95
Individual disputes, industrial relations 389
Induction training 428–32
Industrial
  market research *see* Market research, industrial
  products, selling
    see Sales engineering
    see Selling
Industrial Arbitration Board 347, 348, 368
Industrial Relations Act 1971 227, 339, 343, 347, 349, 363–90
  code of industrial relations practice 378–90
  collective bargaining 376–8
  general principles 364–5
  institutions 366–8
  main elements 365–6
  protection for community in emergency situations 371–2
  registration of trade unions and employers' associations 368–71
  rights of employees 372–5
  unfair industrial practices 375–6
Industrial Society 319
Industrial Training Act 368
Information
  control 84
  disclosure of, Industrial Relations Act 375, 386
  feedback in process control 629–30
  planning new product functions 513–17
  planning office space 249–50
  value analysis 501–2
Injury, termination of employment 350–1
In-process inspection, process control 630–1
Inquiries
  checklist 162–3
  screening of customers 157–9
Insolvencies *see* Bankruptcy
Inspection
  frequency of in planned maintenance 644–5
Inspection *continued*
  purchased parts 633–4
  quality control 626–31
    in-process and final inspection 630–1
      automatic 631
      records 631–2
Installation, new production facilities 526–9
  commissioning a flow-line 528–9
  preproduction 526–8
Institute of Personnel Management 319
Interest rates 15
Internal cash flows 11
International convention, patents 209
Interviews, recruitment and selection 315–17
Inventions, patenting 208–13
Inventory
  control, computer applications 276
  maintenance 639–40
Investigation
  organisation and methods 233–5
  value analysis 508
Investment
  analysts 7
  period, equivalent mean 35–6
  short-term 17–18
Invoice discounting 11, 16–17

Job
  analysis
    identification of job requirements 310–12
    management by objectives 410–11
  assignment, project scheduling 548
  cards 69–70
    works documentation 556, 559
  costing, factory 69–70
  descriptions 310–12
  evaluation, design of payment systems 325–6
  planning, value analysis 500–8
    checklist 507
    definition of function 502–3
    function/cost analysis 503–5
    information (or definition) 501–2
    investigation, recommendation & action 508
    specialisation 505–6
  ranking, design of payment systems 326–7

Job *continued*
  requirements, identification through job analysis 310–12
  reviews, management by objectives 415–19
  specification 311–12
Jobbing production 569
Justification, capital expenditure 103

K & H Business Consultants Ltd 546
Kaiser Aluminium 579
Kalamazoo Ltd 178–86
Key areas, management by objectives 399–400
  job analysis 410ff

LIFO *see* Last in first out
Labour
  cost 65–6, 136
    charging labour costs 66
    payroll analysis 65–6
    time recording and analysis 66
  direct, budgeting 93–5
  indirect, budgeting 95
Land, contracts to sell or lease 218
Landscaped offices 254–6, 259–60
Language, report writing 483–6
Lapse of offer, contracts 216
Last in, first out 64, 135–6
Law
  company *see* Company law
  employer/employee relationship 341–62
    contract of employment 342–4
    damages for wrongful dismissal 353–5
    payment of wages and salaries 344–9
    provision of references 355–7
    redundancy payments 359–62
    restraining employees from disclosing trade secrets 357–9
    termination of employment 349–53
Layout
  factories 520–5
    drawings and models 525
    fixed material location 520–1
    group technology 521
    influencing factors 522
    planning 522–5
    product layout or line production 521
    process or function layouts 521
Layout *continued*
  offices *see* Office space, planning of
  reports 481–3
  stores 583
Learning curves 437–8
Ledgers, stores 63
Letters of credit 16
Liabilities, current 5
Liability, directors of public limited companies 205–6
Licensing, patents 212
Life cycles, product 116–17, 160, 509, 512
Lighting, Offices Shops and Railway Premises Act 262
Limitations, manpower planning 292
Limited companies *see* Company law
Limited liability, concept of 199–200
Line of balance 569
Line production 521
Linear programming, computer applications 276
Liquidated damages 224–6
Liquidity
  and operating cycle 5–6
  cash budgets 9–13
  control of 4–5
  control of cash 8–9
  ratios 6–8
  short-term investments 17–18
  sources of short-term finance 13–17
Literature 150, 152
  sales 120
Loading and progress advice, works documentation 557, 563
Loading, shop
  planned maintenance 650–6
  production control 555–6, 557
Long-term profit planning 105–6
Loss
  of profits, damages for 224–6
  selling at 137–8

MTM *see* Methods-time measurement
McCarthy, W.E.J. 323
Machinery, planning new production facilities 518–20
Maintenance
  breakdown 637–8
  of payment structures 339–40
  planned *see* Planned maintenance
Make or buy decisions 519–20
Management
  attitudes to, and expectations of, quality control 615–19

Management *continued*
  communication 460–89
  control, work study 608, 612–13
  development 419–22, 451–6
  information 84
  materials *see* Materials management
  of computers 277–83
    budgeting and control 282–3
    costing computer time 280–1
    implementation of systems 281–2
  of manpower 289
  performance standards 51–4
  responsibilities, industrial relations 322, 380
  sales force 156–7
  training 420, 451–6
Management by objectives (MBO) 391–426
  business strategies and plans 394–8
  characteristics of successful MBO 424–7
  definition 392–3
  individual managers' contributions 410–19
    action plans 414–16
    job analysis 410–11
    job and potential reviews 415–19
    results guides 411–14
  management development 419–22
  setting unit and functional objectives 398–410
    critical search and analysis 400–402
    definition of purpose 398–9
    identification of key areas 399–400
    policy constraints and guidelines 402–3
    setting unit objectives 403–6
    unit action plans 406–10
  the system 393–4
Managers, contribution to MBO 410-19
Manpower
  planning 287–307
    analysis and forecasting 295–304
    checklists 293
    control and evaluation 289–91, 305
    limitations 292
    procedure for 290
    role and context 288–91
    time scale 291–2
  recruitment and selection *see* Recruitment and selection
Manufacturing
  order 69
  specification, quality control 628
  volume/mix 92–3
Marginal costs 72–6
  assessment of cost variability 73
  definitions 72–3
  practice 74–6
  pricing 134
  theory 72
Margins 51
Market
  economies 130–42
    conventional pricing 134–8
    finding market price 138–41
    market price 132–4
    price, quality and volume relationships 132
    standard and non-standard products 131–2
  price 132–4
    finding 138–41
  research, industrial
    competition 123–4
    essentials of 125–7
    market size and share 124
    presentation of survey 129
    reputation 123–4
    trends and developments 125
  share 124
  size 124
  structure, industrial selling 147
Marketing
  basic problem 113–16
  engineering industry 111–13
  improving profits 120–3
  improving sales 119–20
  new products 117–19
Marketing for engineering industry 111–13
  basic problems 114–16
  general problems 124–5
  improving profits 120–3
  improving sales 119–20
  new products 117–19
Material
  control 566
  costs 63–5, 135–6
    charging 65
    pricing stores issues 64
    stores ledgers 63
Material requisitions, works documentation 556–7
  costs 561
  stores 560
Materials management 570–88

Materials management *continued*
  handling equipment and techniques 587–8
  purchasing and cost reduction 571–5
    target selection 572–3
  sourcing 575–80
    negotiation 580
    small-order procedures 579–80
    supplier evaluation 576–8
    systems contracting 578–9
  stock control and ABC analysis 580–6
    analysing usage values 581–2
    applying the ABC principle 582–3
    economic order quantity formula 583
    expediting 583–6
    stores layout 583
  value analysis 575
Materials, standard costs 77–8
Measured daywork 332
  graded 609
Measures common 23
Mechanical Engineering Economic Development Committee 129
Mechanical handling, materials management 587–8
  dry tankers 588
  fork lift trucks 587
  pallets 587
  platform trolleys 588
Meetings 485–91
  chairmanship 490–1
  conduct 488–90
  of public limited companies 207
  preparation 487–8
  salesmen 156
Membership, public limited companies 201–2
Memorandum of association 199–200
Method study 590–5
  flow diagrams 594
  flow process charts 591–2, 593
  multiple activity charts 594–5
  recording techniques 591
  string diagrams 594–6
  two-handed process charts 592–3
Methods-time measurement (MTM) 240, 603
Metra 34
Miles, L.D. 575
Minors, contracts of employment 342
Misbehaviour, termination of employment 352–3

Misbehaviour, termination of employment *continued*
  outside working hours 353
Misrepresentation
  contracts between companies 22–3
  contracts of employment 343
Mistakes, contracts 220–2
Models, of factories 525
Module training system 433–4
Money 23
  time value 25
Monopoly rights, compulsory licensing of patents 212
Motivation
  pay and performance 324
  sales engineering 169–72
Multi-processing 273
Multiple
  activity charts, method study 594–5
  regression analysis, clerical work measurement 240–1

National Board for Prices and Incomes 323, 325–6
National Cash Register Co. Ltd 182
National Economic Development Office 129
National Industrial Conference Board 392
National Industrial Relations Court 366–7, 370, 371, 373, 377
National Physical Laboratory 619
National Research Development Corporation 35
Negligence, termination of employment 352
Negotiable instruments, bills of exchange 15–16
Negotiation, materials management 580
Net current assets 48–9
Network analysis 534, 540
New
  business, sales engineering 174–7
  products 116–19
  planning facilities 512–31
Non-standard products
  market economics 131–2
  pricing 134–42
  sales engineering 183–5
Notice
  dismissal, without 350
  minimum period of 374–5
  statutory period of 349–50

Notice *continued*
  termination by employee without notice 353
Nottingham University 35
Numbers, use of in report writing 478

Objectives
  budgetary control 83
  budgetary planning 82
  industrial market research 127
  management by *see* Management by objectives
  manpower 289
  organisation and methods 229
  production 513
  project 532–4
  unit and functional 398–410
    action plans 406–10, 414–16
    setting 403–6
Objects clause
  contracts 219–20
  limited companies 199
Offer, contracts between companies 214–17
  keeping offer open for a stipulated time 215
  lapse and revocation 216
  need for special method of acceptance 216
  postal acceptance 216–17
  tenders 217
Office equipment, selection 245–6
Office space, planning of 248–66
  analysis 250–8
  government legislation 261–6
  implementation 261
  information 249–50
  layout types 251–8
    carrels 257–8
    cellular 257
    half height partitions 257
    open-space or landscaped 254–6, 259–60
  relationship patterns 251
  solutions 258–60
  space standards 250–1
Offices, Shops and Railway Premises Act 1963 248, 261–6
On-line systems, computers 272–3
Open space offices 254–6, 259–60
Operating cycle, liquidity and 5–6
Operation costing 60
Operational research
  computer applications 275–6
Operational research *continued*
  production control 567–9
Operators, training 435–41
Opinions, industrial market research 126–7
Optical character recognition 271
Order processing, sales engineering 192
Orders
  economic quantities 567–8, 583, 584
  small, materials management 579–80
Ordinary shares 202–3
Organisation and methods 228–47
  approach to 229–30
  clerical work measurement 237–41
  conduct of 230–7
    formulation of proposals 235
    implementation 235–7
    investigation and analysis 233–5
    preliminary survey 230–1
    selecting starting point 231
  contribution of 228–30
  document control 241–4
  establishing objectives 229
  selection of office equipment 245–6
Organisational responsibilities, for quality 616–19
Outlets, selling 146–9
  identification 149
  market structure 147
  product characteristics 147
  purchasing influences 148–9
  sales planning 148
Overcrowding, Offices, Shops and Railway Premises Act 262–3
Overdrafts, bank 15
Overheads
  accuracy 67
  allocation, apportionment and absorption 67
  calculation of 95–6
  conventional pricing 135
  factory 67
  over- and under-absorbed 68–9
  standard variable costs 78
  standard fixed costs 78
  standard other costs 79
Ozalid Company 525

PERT *see* Project evaluation review technique
Packages, computer programs 282
Paired comparisons, design of payment systems 326–7

Pallets, mechanical handling 587
Pareto curves 572, 580
Parts, purchased: inspection 633–4
Patents 208–13
  application procedure 209
  compulsory licences 212
  employers' rights 212–13
  grant of 211
  international convention 209
  opposition to a grant 210
  reasons for refusing 209
  revocation 210–11
  rights of patentee 211–12
Pay, equal 328–9
Payback period, techniques of project evaluation 28–9
Payment
  by results 323
  of Wages Act 1960 346
  redundancy *see* Redundancy payments
  structures 321–40
    design of system 325–9
      establishing a graded structure 327–7
      job evaluation 325–6
      paired comparisons 326–7
    equal pay 328–9
    implementing new system 335–40
      maintenance of 339–40
    principles 322–4
      differentials 322–3
      pay and performance 323–4
    relating salaries and performance 333–5
      devising system of progression 333–4
      progression procedure 334–5
    relating wages and performance 329–33
      incentives and wages systems 329–30
      types of incentive scheme 330–3
    work study aspects 607–8
  wages and salaries, legal aspects 344–9
    equal pay 346
    fair wage payments in government contracts 346–7
    methods of 345
    statutory regulation 348–9
    Terms and Conditions of Employment Act 1959 347–8
Payroll analysis 65–6
Penalty, distinction between liquidated damages and 225–6
Performance
  see also Management by objectives
  pay and 323–5
    averaging 332–3
    bands 332
  relating salaries and 333–5
    devising system 333–4
    progression procedure 334–5
  reporting, budgetary control 97–102
    for subordinate manager 102
    for top management 98
    form of 98
    requirements 97–8
  sales engineers 176–7
  standards
    management 51–4
    standard costs 77
  targets, quality control 623
  testing, planning and reporting 623–5
Physical layout, reports 476–8
Piecework 323, 332
Plan
  corporate 144
  sheet, sales engineering 182
Planned maintenance 637–56
  control of scheduled maintenance routines 645–6
  elements 640–1
  inventory 639–40
  plant specification 641–2
  preparation of routines 642–5
  preventive routines 641
  rectification and shop loading 650–6
  stabilisation period 652–6
Planning
  budgetary *see* Budgetary planning
  corporate, management by objectives 394–8
  layout 522–5
  manpower, *see* Manpower planning
  new production facilities 512–31
  office space 248–66
  performance 623–5
  profit
    long-term 105–6
    short-term *see* Budgetary control
  quality control 625–4
  sales 148
  sales engineering 172–8
Plant specification, planned maintenance 641–2

Platform trolleys 588
Policy
  constraints and guidelines, MBO 402–3
  sales 143–6
Postal
  acceptance, contracts 216–17
  inquiries, screening 158
Potential reviews, management by objectives 415–19
Predetermined motion-time systems (PMTS) 601–3
  see also Basic work data
Predetermined standards, clerical work measurement 239–40
Preference shares/holders 50, 202–3
Preliminary survey, organisation and methods 230–1
Preparations, meetings 487–8
Preproduction, new production facilities 526–8
Present value, techniques of project evaluation 29–32
Presentation, results of project evaluation 41–3
Press relations 153
Preventive maintenance, planned routines 641
Price
  incentives 11
  market 132–4
Prices
  sales policy and budget 143–6
  standard 64
Pricing 130–42
  conventional 134–8
  policy 120
  price-quality and price-volume relationship 132
  product analysis 139–41
  sales proposals and quotations 160–1
  stores issues 64
Prime costs 73
Priority date, patents 209
Probability 38–41
Procedures
  disciplinary 389–90
  grievances and disputes 389
Process
  charts, method study 591–3
  control
    computer applications 276
    quality control 626–32
      establishing 626
Process *continued*
  control *continued*
    quality control *continued*
      in-process and final inspection 630–1
      information feedback and reporting 629–30
      nine steps 626–9
  costing 60, 71
  layouts 521
Processing orders, sales engineering 192
Product
  analysis, pricing 139–41
  characteristics, industrial selling 147
  function *see* Functions, value analysis
  layout 521
  life-cycle 160, 509, 517
  performance targets, quality control 623
Production
  control 550–69
    batch versus flow-production 569
    definition 550–1
    dispatching (works manufacturing orders) 556–64
    formulating the programme 553
    materials control 566
    progressing 564–6
    quantitative aids 566–9
      computers 566–7
      economic order quantity 567–8
      operational research 567–9
      split batches 568–9
    scheduling 553–5
    shop loading 555–6, 557
  engineers, value analysis 499–500
  flow analysis 521
  planning new facilities 512–31
    evaluating results 530–1
    information 513–17
    installation and commissioning 526–9
    layout 520–5
      influencing factors 522
      planning 522
      types 520–1
    objectives 513
    resources available and required 518–20
Productivity 340
  studies 300
Products
  life cycles 116–17, 160, 514, 517

Product *continued*
standard and non-standard, market economics 131–2
Professional and Executive Register 312–13
Profit
and loss account 49–51
planning, long term 105–6
trading, maximisation 130
Profitability 6
Profits
damages for loss of 224–6
distribution as dividends 207–8
improvement with market research 120–3
developments in user industries 121
dynamics of user industries 120–1
production 121, 122
pre-interest 50
trading 50
Progress
advice, works documentation 557, 563
chasers 564
Progressing 564–6
see also Expediting
progress chart 565
Progression, salaries 333–5
Project
completion, reports 103, 105
cost control 102–5
preparation of capital expenditure budgets 102–3
progress status reports 103–5
evaluation review technique (PERT) 540
scheduling 532–49
essential properties 534
project objectives 532–4
seven steps for practical scheduling 534–48
assignment of jobs to individuals 548
estimates for activity duration 540–2
project definition 537–9
resource allocation 543–7
time analysis 542
work breakdown 539
work sequence 539–40
selection, value analysis 510
status reports 103–4
Projections, manpower planning 303–4
Promissory notes, contracts 218
Properties, product pricing 139–40
Property valuations 48
Proposals
organisation and methods 235
sales engineering 175–7, 188–92
checklist 162–3
format 189
processing the order 189–92
sales, preparation 160–1
Prospectus, public limited companies 200–1
Protection of community in emergency situations 371–2
Public limited companies *see* Company law
Public relations 150
Publicity
directors of public limited companies 205–6
industrial selling 150–3
Purchased parts, inspection 633–4
Purchasing
see also Materials management
cost reductions 571–5
target selection 572–3
department, responsibility for quality 617
influences, industrial selling 148–9
Purpose, project evaluation 21–2

Quality
price-quality and price-volume relationships 132
rating, materials management 577
Quality assurance *see* Quality control
Quality control 614–36
development and testing 623–5
fault reporting and corrective action 624–5
performance testing, planning and recording 623–4
product performance targets 623
establishing standards and specifications 619–22
quality audits 621–2
quality engineering and planning 619–20
management attitudes and expectations 615–18
economics of quality 615–16
organisational responsibilities 616–19
process control and inspection 626–32
automatic inspection 631

Quality control *continued*
process control and inspection *continued*
establishment 626
in-process and process inspection 630–1
information feedback and reporting 629–30
inspection records 631–2
nine steps 626–9
supplier evaluation 632–6
purchased parts inspection 633–4
quality assessment 632–3
vendor rating 634–6
Questionnaires, industrial market research 128
Quotations
checklist 162–3
sales engineering 188–92
format 189
presentation 160–1
processing the order 189–92

Random access 273
Ranking
alternatives, evaluation 26
job, design of payment systems 326–7
Rating
time study 599
vendors, quality control 634–6
Ratios
company performance 51–3
current 7–8
liquidity 6–8
Recognition, trade unions 385–6
Recommendations, value analysis 508
Recording
customer inquiries 159
techniques, method study 591–5
time 66
Records
customer, sales engineering 178–86
inspection, process control 631–2
Recruitment and selection
assessing candidates 313–19
final stages 318
identifying job requirements through job analysis 310–12
seven point plan 311
interviews 315–17
main steps 308–10
methods 314–15
reaching candidates, employment agencies 312–13
Recruitment and selection *continued*
salesmen 154–5
targets, manpower planning 391
use of consultants 319–20
Rectification, planned maintenance 650–6
Redundancy payments 359–62
1965 Act 359–62, 368
calculating payment due 361–2
lack of entitlement 362
meaning of 359–60
means of dismissal 360
when payment must be made 360–1
References
provision of 355–7
defences 356
liability for a false reference 356–7
recruitment and selection 314
Registration
public limited companies 198–9
trade unions and employers' associations 368–71
Repeat business, sales engineering 172–4
Report and accounts 45–55
coverage 45–54
balance sheet 46–9
management performance standards 51–4
profit and loss account 49–51
window dressing 6
Report writing 473–82
checklists 481–2
circulation and distribution 474–5
information by numbers 478
language 478–81
physical layout 476–8
Reports
performance 97–101
for subordinate managers 102
for top management 98
form of 98
requirements 97–8
project completion 103–5
project status 103–4
quality control 623–5
sales engineering 178–86
Representation
employees at place of work 386–8
false 222
Reputation of company 123–4
Research, industrial market *see* Market research, industrial
Resource allocation 22–3
project scheduling 543–7

Resources, planning new production facilities 518–20
Responsibilities
budgetary planning 82–3
for budget 86–7
of engineer for evaluation 21
organisational, for quality 616–19
Restraint, disclosure of trade secrets 357–9
Results guides, management by objectives 411–14
Return on capital 53
Reviews
compensation 419
job and potential, management by objectives 415–19
Revision, sales policy and budget 145–6
Revocation
of offer, contracts 216
patents 210–11
Rights of employees: Industrial Relations Act 372–5
Risk 24
and return 36–41
Route cards, works documentation 556

Safety, Offices, Shops and Railway Premises Act 265
Salary structures *see* Payment structures
Sales
see also Selling
budget 92, 143–6
department, responsibilities for quality 617
engineering
after-sales service 192–3
inquiries from advertising 186–7
personnel factors 167–72
commitment to responsibilities 169–72
engineering ability 168
salesmanship 168–9
training 169
planning activities 172–8
existing customers 173–4
individual targets 172–3
individual territory 177–8
new business 174–7
quotations and proposals 188–92
format 189
processing the order 189–92
reports and customer records 178–86
Sales *continued*
reports and customer records *continued*
action request 183–6
call report 186
customer record card 182
plan sheet 182
weekly report form 182–3
force, organising and managing 154–7
management 156–7
meetings 156
recruitment 154–5
remuneration 156
sales office 157
training 155–6
forecasts, planning new production facilities 514, 516
improvement with market research 119–20
inquiries 157–9, 162–3
literature 120
planning, industrial selling 148
policy 143–6
proposals, sales engineering 100–1, 175–7
checklist 162–3
quotations 160–1
checklist 162–3
Salesmanship, sales engineering 168–9
Salesmen's inquiries, screening 157–9
Sanitation, Offices, Shops and Railway Premises Act 263–5
Scheduling
production control 553–5
project *see* Project scheduling
Screening, customer inquiries 157–9
Seasonal variations, effects on cash flows 9–10
Seat reservation systems, computer applications 276
conduct of meetings 490
preparation for 488
Selection, manpower *see* Recruitment and selection
Selective Employment Payments Act 368
Self recording, clerical work measurement 237, 239
Selling
see also Sales
at a loss 137–8
industrial products 143–64
checklists 161–4
establishing sales policy and budget 143–6

Selling *continued*
organising and managing technical sales force 154–7
outlets 146–9
preparation of proposals and quotations 160–1
publicity and advertising 150–3
screening customer inquiries 157–9
Semi-variable costs 74
Sensitivity, management by objectives 424
Sequence, work: project scheduling 539–40
Service
after sales 192–3
bureaux, computer *see* Bureaux, computer service
Servicing *see* Planned maintenance
Seymour, W. D. 439
Share/s
in public limited companies 199–204
acquisition and transfer 204
classes of 202–3
debentures 203
membership 201–2
of market 124
of prosperity, payment structures 339–40
price 50–1
transfer of, contracts 218
Shop loading
planned maintenance 650–6
production control 555–6, 557
Shop stewards 387–8
Short-term
finance, sources 13–17
bank overdrafts 15
bills of exchange 15–16
factoring and invoice discounting 16–17
trade credit 14
investments 17–18
profit planning *see* Budgetary control
Signatures, mistakes: contracts 222
Simplified predetermined motion-time systems 602–3
Simulation techniques, computer applications 276
Size of market 124
Small orders, materials management 579–80
Social speaking 472
Source and application of funds 11
Sourcing, materials management 575–6
Spare-time activities, restricting employees' 344
Spares, after sales service 192–3
Speaking 460–89
case presentation 471–2
one-to-one talking 472–3
preparation 462–7
obtaining audience's attention 465–7
purpose and people 463–4
subject matter 462–3
Specification
plant, planned maintenance 641–2
quality control 619–22, 626–9
Speculation, value analysis 505–6
Split batches, production control 568–9
Stabilisation period, planned maintenance 652–6
Stability of earnings 332–3
Standard
costing 76–80
cards 79
compared with actual cost ascertainment 76–7
factors 77
performance standards 77
relationship with budgetary control 76
setting standard costs for other overheads 79
setting standard fixed overhead costs 78
setting standard material costs 77–8
setting standard wages costs 78
price 64
products
market economics 131–2
price-quality and price-volume relationships 132
times 555, 610–12
Standardisation, document control 244
Standards
management performance 51–4
performance, standard costs 77
predetermined, clerical work measurement 239–40
quality control 619–22
space, office planning 250–1
Statements, false 222
Statistics, control of work study schemes 613
Statutory regulation of wages 348–9
Stock control
efficiency in 11

Stock control *continued*
materials management 580–6
analysing usage values 581–2
applying the ABC principle 582–3
economic order quantity formula 583, 584
expediting 583–6
stores layout 583
Stock Exchange 204
Stores
issues, pricing 64
layout 583
ledgers 63
materials requisitions 560
receipts, finished parts: works documentation 557, 562
String diagrams, method study 594–6
Summary, report writing 477
Supervisors, training 477-51
advantages of in-company 449–50
Suppliers
evaluation 632–6
materials management 576–8
purchased parts inspection 633–4
quality assessment 632–3
vendor rating 634–6
participation in value analysis 506–7
payment of 11
Supply, manpower 302–3
Surveys, market *see* Market research
Synthesis, work measurement 601
Systems contracting, materials management 578–9

Targets
management by objectives 396
product performance 623
sales engineering 170
planning 172–3
Taxation
effects on capital evaluation 27–8
profit and loss account 50
Technical journal selection, advertising 161
Techniques of project evaluation 25–41
cash balance, capital and expense 26–8
discounted cash flow 31, 32–5
equivalent mean investment period 35–6
present value 29–32
payback period 28–9
ranking of alternatives 26
Telephone inquiries, screening 158
Temperature control, Offices, Shops and Railway Premises Act 262
Tenders, offer and acceptance of contracts 217
Terminals, computer 272–3
Termination of employment 349–53
see also Redundancy payments
by employee without notice 353
dishonesty 352
disobedience 351
illness and injury 350–1
incompetence and negligence 352
instant dismissal without notice 350
misbehaviour 352–3
statutory period of notice 349–50
Terms and Conditions of Employment Act 1959 347–8
Territories, sales engineering 177–8
Testing, quality control 623–5
performance 623–4
Tests, recruitment and selection 314
Third party sales 49–50
Time
analysis, project scheduling 542, 546
recording 66
study
clerical work measurement 239
work measurement 597–601
Time-scale, manpower planning 291–2
Time value, money 25
Timing
capital budget expenditure 103
performance reporting 97–8
Top management
involvement in management by objectives 423–5
involvement in value analysis 498
Total investment, maximisation 130
Trade credit 14
Trade secrets, restraining employees from disclosing 357–9
and trade connections 358
area and duration 358–9
test of reasonableness 357–8
Trade unions
1871–1964 Acts 368
and office workers 227
employees' representation at place of work 386–8
membership of 372–4

Trade unions *continued*
recognition 385–6
registration 368–71
responsibilities of 382
unfair industrial practice 376
Trading profit 50
maximisation 130
Training
management by objectives 421
sales engineering 169
salesmen 155–6
shop stewards 388
value analysis/engineering 509
within companies 427–59
apprentices 432–4
induction 428–32
location 459
management 451–6
maximising yield from changes 441–4
methods of conducting 457
non-apprentice 435
objectives 427–8, 457
operator 435–41
reasons for 457
supervisors 447–51
timing 459
to bring about improvements 444–7
training officer 457–9
Transfer
cash 18
shares 204
Transformation, assets 24–5
Treasury bills 18
Trends
manpower planning 295–304
market research 125
Truck Acts 345
Try-out engineers 529
Two-handed process charts, method study 592–3

Ultra vires, contracts 219–20
Unfair industrial practices 375–6
Uniformity, performance reporting 97
Unit
bargaining 385
costs 63, 135
objectives 398–410
action plans 406–10, 414–15
setting 403–6
Unliquidated damages 224–5

Usage values, materials management 581–2
Use value 497
Users
industry climate 120–1
industry developments 121
needs 124

Value
analysis 160, 495–511
definition 496
involvement 499
job plan 500–8
checklist 507
definition of function 502–3
function/cost analysis 503–5
information (or definition) 501–2
investigation, recommendation and action 508
speculation 505–6
supplier participation 506–7
materials management 575
organising a programme 508–10
appointing the team 509–10
project selection 510
selection of value engineer 509
training 509
representation 499–500
results 511
unnecessary costs 497–8
value, definition 496–7
engineer, selection 509
engineering 495–511
see also Value analysis
definition 496
of quality 615–16
present, techniques of project evaluation 29–32
Variability, assessment of cost variability 73
Variance analysis 79–80
Ventilation, Offices, Shops and Railway Premises Act 262
Visual aids
public speaking 467
report writing 478
Voice, use of in public speaking 467
Volume, price-quality and price-volume relationships 132

Wage structures *see* Payment structures

Wages, standard costs 77–8
Wages Councils 348
Washing facilities, Offices, Shops and Railway Premises Act 263–5
Waste, value analysis 497
Water, drinking: Offices, Shops and Railway Premises Act 265
Weekly report form, sales engineering 182–3
Weighted average 64
Window dressing, report and accounts 6
Women, equal pay 346
Work
  breakdown, project scheduling 539
  factor, work measurement 603
  in progress 71–2
  measurement 596–606
    analytical estimating 603
    basic work data 603–4, 605
    clerical *see* Clerical work measurement
    comparative estimating 604–6
    predetermined motion-time systems (PMTS) 601–3
    synthesis 601
    time study 597–601
  sequence, project scheduling 539–40

Work *continued*
  study 555, 589–614
    conduct in an engineering company 609–13
      control 612–13
      implementing standard times 610–12
      study programme 609–10
    industrial relations 606–8
    method study 590–5
    purpose 589–90
    standard costing 76, 78
    work measurement 596–606
Working capital
  calculation of 96
  management of 3–18
    and operating cycle 5–6
    cash budgets 9–13
    control of cash 8–9
    control of liquidity 4–5
    liquidity ratios 6–8
    short-term investments 17–18
    sources of short-term finance 13–17
Works order 69
Wrongful dismissal, damages 353–5

Youth Employment Service 312–13